THE POWER OF
POSITIVE PARENTING

THE POWER OF POSITIVE PARENTING

Transforming the Lives of Children, Parents, and Communities Using the Triple P System

Edited by

Matthew R. Sanders

AND

Trevor G. Mazzucchelli

OXFORD
UNIVERSITY PRESS

OXFORD

UNIVERSITY PRESS

Oxford University Press is a department of the University of Oxford. It furthers
the University's objective of excellence in research, scholarship, and education
by publishing worldwide. Oxford is a registered trade mark of Oxford University
Press in the UK and certain other countries.

Published in the United States of America by Oxford University Press
198 Madison Avenue, New York, NY 10016, United States of America.

Library of Congress Cataloging-in-Publication Data
Names: Sanders, Matthew R., editor. | Mazzucchelli, Trevor G., editor.
Title: The power of positive parenting : transforming the lives of children, parents,
and communities using the triple P system / edited by Matthew R. Sanders,
Trevor G. Mazzucchelli. Description: 1 Edition. | New York : Oxford University Press, 2018. |
Includes bibliographical references and index. Identifiers: LCCN 2017040494 (print) |
LCCN 2017042251 (ebook) | ISBN 9780190629076 (updf) | ISBN 9780190669492 (epub) |
ISBN 9780190629069 (paperback : alk. paper) Subjects: LCSH: Child rearing. | Parenting. |
Problem children—Behavior modification. | Child psychology. |
BISAC: PSYCHOLOGY / Clinical Psychology. | PSYCHOLOGY / Developmental /
Child. | PSYCHOLOGY / Developmental / Adolescent. Classification:
LCC HQ769 (ebook) | LCC HQ769 .P8284 2017 (print) |
DDC 649/.1—dc23 LC record available at https://lccn.loc.gov/2017040494

DISCLOSURE STATEMENT

The Parenting and Family Support Centre is partly funded by royalties stemming from published resources of the Triple P—Positive Parenting Program, which is developed and owned by The University of Queensland (UQ). Royalties from the program are also distributed to the Faculty of Health and Behavioural Sciences at UQ and contributory authors of Triple P programs. Triple P International (TPI) Proprietary Limited is a private company licensed by Uniquest Proprietary Limited, a commercialization company of UQ, to publish and disseminate Triple P worldwide. The editors and contributing authors of this volume have no share or ownership of TPI. Ms. Forster, Dr. McWilliam, Dr. Ralph, Dr. Studman, and Ms. Wilkinson are employees of TPI. Dr. Baker, Dr. Bartlett, Dr. Burke, Dr. Cobham, Dr. Day, Dr. Dittman, Dr. Haslam, Dr. Healy, Dr. Hodge, Dr. Hodges, Dr. Kirby, Dr. Mazzucchelli, Dr. Metzler, Ms. McIlduff, Dr. Morawska, Dr. Prinz, Dr. Ralph, Dr. Sanders, Dr. Sofronoff, Dr. Stallman, and Dr. Turner are employees of, or hold honorary positions at UQ. Ms. Brown, Dr. Cobham, Dr. Dittman, Dr. Haslam, Dr. Healy, Dr. Hodges, Dr. Kirby, Ms. Lee, Dr. Mazzucchelli, Dr. McDermott, Dr. Morawska, Dr. Prinz, Dr. Ralph, Dr. Rusby, Dr. Sanders, Dr. Shapiro, Dr. Sofronoff, Dr. Stallman, Dr. Studman, and Dr. Turner have received, receive, or may in the future receive royalties and/or consultancy fees from TPI. Dr. Calam, Dr. Doyle, Dr. Einfeld, Dr. El-Khani, Mr. Farrell, Dr. Gray, Ms. Hegarty, Ms. Heavey, Dr. Keown, Dr. McPherson, Dr. Mejia, Dr. Ohan, Mr. Owens, Dr. Schroeter, Dr. Shepherd, Dr. Tonge, and Dr. Wittkowski have no conflicts to declare.

CONTENTS

SECTION 3 APPLICATIONS OF POSITIVE PARENTING WITH DIFFERENT TYPES OF FAMILIES AND FAMILY MEMBERS

SECTION 4 USING POSITIVE PARENTING PROGRAMS IN DIFFERENT DELIVERY SYSTEMS

SECTION 5 RESPONDING TO CULTURAL DIVERSITY IN FAMILIES

PREFACE

The single most important thing we can do as a society to positively transform the lives of children and prevent social, emotional, and behavioral problems and child maltreatment is to increase the knowledge, skills, and confidence of parents in the task of raising children at a whole-of-population level. Good parenting can be thought of as the "clean water" of children's mental health and well-being and must be a public policy priority. As it turns out, good parenting is also very good for adults in a parenting or caring role and for entire communities because people relate to each other in more positive and healthy ways.

For more than four decades, a group of clinical researchers at The University of Queensland's Parenting and Family Support Centre in the School of Psychology have been pioneering an approach to supporting parents by developing and testing a sophisticated multilevel system of parenting and family support known as the Triple P—Positive Parenting Program. This is a unique system of parenting support that combines universal, indicated, and targeted prevention programs to make evidence-based parenting support more widely available for all parents in the community.

This book brings together for the first time the key learnings and cumulative wisdom from hundreds of studies and applications of Triple P from around the world. We aim to show how a comprehensive, multilevel, evidence-based system of parenting and family support can be deployed to promote the development, well-being, and mental health of children, adolescents, and parents across the community.

All contributors to this volume have been actively involved in various aspects of Triple P's evolution by researching, disseminating, or practicing Triple P. They bring a wealth of cumulative knowledge and experience to the task of considering how we best support families and communities in the challenging task of raising their children.

The book is structured in eight sections. Section 1 begins with an exploration of the basic theoretical foundations of parenting informed by the science of human development and the critical importance of children's families, and parenting in particular, throughout children's lives (Sanders & Mazzucchelli, Chapter 2). We then provide a rationale for the adoption of a population approach to parenting support and contrast this approach with traditional clinical treatment models of parent training (Sanders & Prinz, Chapter 3) in terms of its capacity to reach many more parents who may require assistance with parenting. We then move to a brief description of the core positive parenting principles based primarily on the integration of social learning theory, applied behavior analysis, cognitive-behavioral principles, and developmental theory (Sanders & Mazzucchelli, Chapter 4). This foundational material sets the stage for examining more closely the different specific applications of Triple P within a variety of different problems and delivery settings.

Section 2 highlights the incredibly diverse applications of Triple P programs employing these principles and techniques to a wide range of child social, emotional, and behavioral problems; targeted audiences include parents of children with externalizing behavior problems (Mazzucchelli & Sanders, Chapter 6); peer relationship difficulties (Healy, Chapter 7); anxiety problems (Cobham, Chapter 8); children with a developmental disability (Mazzucchelli & Studman, Chapter 9); children with serious mental health problems (Burke, Chapter 10); children and adolescents with chronic health conditions (Morawska, Chapter 11); children who are overweight and obese (Bartlett & Sanders, Chapter 12); and adolescents and young adults with psychosocial difficulties (Ralph, Chapter 13). This section documents how improving the quality of parent–child interaction relates to both the prevention and the treatment of problems of children at different developmental periods, including babies, toddlers, preschool-aged children, elementary or primary school-aged children, and preadolescents and adolescents. In some areas, the strength and magnitude of evidence is greater than others, with most studies focusing on the early years of toddlers, preschoolers, and school-aged children and somewhat fewer studies focusing on adolescents.

In Section 3, the focus extends beyond child problems to examine the theoretical and practical issues involved in working successfully with different types of parents and caregivers. Fathers are less likely than mothers to participate in most health and well-being services, including parenting support and education. Keown's Chapter 15 is an important reminder that a parenting program such as Triple P can do a lot to ensure parenting programs are relevant, interesting, and effective with fathers. Her chapter highlights the important role of fathers in promoting positive developmental outcomes for children. Kirby (Chapter 16) explores a similar theme relating to the neglected role of grandparents in parenting programs and outlines new research showing how involvement of grandparents in parenting programs can result in a three-generational benefit for grandparents, parents, and grandchildren. This section also highlights the critical importance of parenting programs for parents who themselves experience serious personal adjustment problems (Calam & Wittkowski, Chapter 17). Adult mental health services are typically not sufficiently attuned to the needs of children living with a parent with a mental illness and the extra stress adults have to deal with through their parenting and family responsibilities. Exciting new work documenting the value of providing access to online parenting programs to complement adult's mental health treatments is also highlighted in this section. Parents who experience family breakdown undergo a major life transition that can affect the entire family, including parents, children, carers, and extended families (such as grandparents). This is a time when everyday parenting practices can be seriously disrupted. Stallman and Ohan (Chapter 18) address the issue of parenting in the context of separation or divorce and show how Triple P has been successfully adapted to this context.

Section 4 examines why a successful population approach needs to be multidisciplinary or, in other words, why parenting support grounded in a prevention agenda has to be delivered by practitioners from a range of human service providers. Each delivery context has unique advantages and opportunities to increase parental engagement, participation, and therefore reach of programs. But, each delivery context also has significant limitations and barriers. We explore all major service delivery contexts that might be used to positively influence the lives of children and families, including the primary health care system (Turner & Metzler, Chapter 20); the early childhood development and child care setting (Turner, Dittman, Rusby, & Lee, Chapter 21); the school system (Hodges & Healy, Chapter 22); and the workplace (Haslam & Penman, Chapter 23). Section 4 also discusses the challenge of supporting parents in the context of natural disaster when multiple environments are disrupted (Cobham, McDermott, & Sanders, Chapter 24). Metzler and Rusby (Chapter 25) explore the important role of media in promoting positive parenting through the creative use of broadcast media such as television, radio, and other forms of modern communication. This theme is developed further to describe how Triple P has embraced advances in technology and the explosion of often-conflicting, non–evidence-based information parents now have access to globally. The field of child and adolescent mental health and family intervention services is now in the process of determining how best to work with technology-based solutions to parenting problems. Turner, Baker, and Day (Chapter 26) document the development, evaluation, and subsequent dissemination of Triple P Online, an interactive online platform for parents of children aged 2 to 12 years. Triple P research has explored the value of several web platforms, including the use of social media, to improve access to parenting support as, clearly, the Internet is the preferred and most convenient delivery system for many parents seeking to access information about parenting.

Section 5 explores how evidence-based parenting can best respond to and embrace the cultural diversity of families everywhere. The advocacy of parenting support for every family means programs such as Triple P need to be comprehensive and inclusive. Concepts concerning parenting from the cultures of some of the most vulnerable and disadvantaged families, particularly First Nations and Indigenous people, have been so adversely disrupted by colonization, we must acknowledge the past and the associated disruption to lives and culture and provide respectful ways to engage with these communities. Turner, Sanders, Keown, and Shepherd (Chapter 28) describe how a collaborative cultural engagement model can be used as a guide to the provision of culturally responsive adaptations of evidence-based programs. This section also examines processes that have been employed in Triple P research and practice to successfully engage Indigenous families (Turner, Hodge, Forster, & McIlduff, Chapter 29), ways of accommodating race and ethnicity (Haslam & Mejia, Chapter 30), and parental values and religious beliefs in positive parenting interventions (El-Khani & Calam, Chapter 31).

Section 6 turns to the strategies needed to make large-scale, population-level implementations of the multilevel Triple P system succeed. The experience of disseminating and implementing Triple P around the world has led to the development of a comprehensive, theoretically informed, and empirically derived implementation framework for the delivery of the Triple P system. McWilliam and Brown (Chapter 33) describe the Triple P Implementation Framework, which draws on advances in implementation science to support successful delivery of the Triple P system. The Triple P Implementation Framework provides a way to address organizational issues so that evidence-based programs can be sustained outside research or demonstration trials.

This section also describes issues concerning training a multidisciplinary workforce in evidence-based parenting programs using standardized competency-based training methods (Ralph & Dittman, Chapter 34). Parents must be engaged in large numbers if a population approach is going to work in a sustainable way. Social marketing strategies and rolling campaigns are an important part of all successful public health interventions, and successful implementation of a population-level system of parenting support is no different. Public health campaign strategies encourage participation as well as destigmatize the idea of doing something active and specific to promote personal health and well-being, such as quitting smoking, eating healthfully, and becoming active. A sophisticated communication strategy to enhance program reach called Stay Positive was developed. Wilkinson (Chapter 35) describes the development of this universal outreach program and how it is deployed in population rollouts of Triple P across communities. Parenting programs need to be evaluated to ensure they are meeting the needs of parents in local contexts. Morawska and Sanders (Chapter 36) discuss issues involved in selecting and deploying suitable outcome and process measures to track child, parent, family, and community outcomes at both an individual and a population level. Finally, the effectiveness of Triple P depends on the program being implemented with fidelity. A peer-assisted supervision and support or PASS model of supervision is discussed by McPherson and Schroeter in Chapter 37. This system of support blends peer mentoring and self-regulation and can be used by agencies to support the implementation of Triple P.

In Section 7, the emphasis shifts to consideration of real-world examples where coordinated efforts have been made to implement a full multilevel approach to parenting support at a population level. This section seeks to "join the dots" by describing some key learnings derived from large-scale, population-level implementations of the Triple P system in Australia, the United States, and Ireland. These best practice exemplars demonstrate how population health principles can be successfully employed and how population outcomes can be achieved for every parent, including parents of children with a disability. We begin with a description of a place-based population trial conducted in the United States that successfully reduced the level of child maltreatment at a population level (Prinz & Shapiro, Chapter 39). Chapter 40 by Owens, Doyle, Hegarty, Heavey, and Farrell describes a partnership model that was employed in the Midland counties in the Republic of Ireland to implement a population-level intervention. The final example involves the delivery of Triple P as a multilevel system across three states of Australia to support all parents of children with a disability (Sofronoff, Gray, Einfeld, & Tonge, Chapter 41).

The final section of the book, Section 8, highlights our learnings about the conditions that need to be met to ensure evidence-based programs thrive and continuously learn, adapt, and evolve. Evidence-based programs can easily peak, then become "yesterday's" program, seen as out of touch, outdated, and needing to be reinvigorated to survive. A system of parenting support must be "a living, breathing," constantly evolving program that adapts and learns and is constantly replenished by ongoing research and development. This development process is informed by both developer-led research and independent evaluation with minimal or no developer involvement. Sanders and Kirby (Chapter 43) begin by discussing how to design quality assurance procedures from the outset and describe the processes that promote ongoing program development and innovation. How a quality assurance process relates to a broader translational research agenda that supports program development and successful dissemination of programs is also discussed.

The discussion then turns to how systems and procedures within research groups can be designed to sustain ongoing innovation in parenting programs (Sanders, Turner, & Mazzucchelli, Chapter 45). Finally, in exploring possible future directions for research, development, and dissemination of the Triple P system, the broader range of contextual and logistical issues about how the science of parenting and child development can better inform policy decisions, the professional community, and members of the wider public is discussed (Sanders, Chapter 46).

As editors of this work, it has been a pleasure and an honor to draw together this volume that captures an innovation stemming from the application of theory and evidence from the behavioral and social sciences spanning almost four decades. It has been an amazing journey to be part of. From tiny beginnings in a doctoral thesis completed at The University of Queensland in 1981 to the evolution of a program we now call Triple P, a comprehensive system of parenting support that has benefited millions of families and children worldwide has been the collective effort of many people. This volume demonstrates the important contributions of various researchers, collaborators, and stakeholders whose scholarship and professional work is represented throughout. Their efforts ensure Triple P continues to evolve and learn and remains firmly committed to ensuring every aspect of the program is evaluated and informed by ongoing development in theory and research.

ACKNOWLEDGMENTS

Alarge number of people have contributed to this volume. We wish to thank our colleagues and former students in the Parenting and Family Support Centre, School of Psychology, at The University of Queensland and to our international collaborators who have contributed the development and evaluation of the Triple P system of intervention and to its dissemination around the world. We particularly thank all our contributing authors, who have made distinctive contributions to extending our understanding of how to successfully apply every aspect of the Triple P system as a multilevel approach to parenting and family support. Thanks to Jessica Bartlett, Paddy Hintz, and Kirsten Young for their fantastic assistance with editing and proofreading the various chapters. We also wish to thank our successive heads of the School of Psychology, Executive Dean of Health and Behavioural Sciences, and the senior executive at The University of Queensland, who have strongly supported Triple P through strategic funding support. We also acknowledge and thank Uniquest Proprietary Limited, The University of Queensland's main technology transfer company, for their ongoing assistance in dissemination of the program. Special thanks to Triple P International for its tireless and outstanding work in disseminating Triple P globally.

Special thanks go to the thousands of families who have participated in studies around the world evaluating various aspects of Triple P and whose views have helped shape the program. Special thanks also go to the many practitioners who have delivered one or more versions of Triple P in foundation clinical trials that have established the program's efficacy.

We also wish to thank key individuals whose research work inspired the evolution of Triple P as a multilevel population-based system of intervention. These include Professors Ted Glynn, Todd Risley (deceased), Gerald Patterson (deceased), Albert Bandura, Barr Taylor, and Mark Dadds, whose work has informed various aspects of the model.

We also acknowledge the following organizations that have provided financial support to the Parenting and Family Support Centre to support our research work into parenting, including the National Health and Medical Research Council, Australian Research Council, US Centers for Disease Control and Prevention, US National Institute on Drug Abuse, US National Institute of Mental Health, the Robert Wood Johnson Foundation, the Australian Government, the Victorian Government, Queensland Government, Western Australian Government,

New Zealand Government (Ministry of Health), Sylvia and Charles Viertel Charitable Foundation, Australian Rotary Health Research Fund, Beyond Blue, Telstra Foundation, Kids Helpline, Asthma Australia, Edmund Rice Foundation and Sidney Myer Fund and Triple P International.

Finally and importantly, we thank the ongoing support of our parents, partners, children, and grandchildren for their love, emotional support, and practical assistance in completing this work.

ACKNOWLEDGMENT OF COUNTRY

The editors and contributing authors of this volume acknowledge Indigenous families of all nations, including Aboriginal and Torres Strait Islander peoples of Australia; First Nations peoples of Canada; American Indian/Alaska Native families of the United States of America; and Māori families (whānau) of New Zealand. We pay our respects to ancestors and Elders, past and present. We are committed to honoring Indigenous peoples' unique cultural and spiritual relationships to the land, waters, and seas and their rich contribution to society.

ABOUT THE EDITORS

Dr. Matthew Sanders is a professor of clinical psychology, founder of the Triple P—Positive Parenting Program, and director of the Parenting and Family Support Centre at The University of Queensland. He is considered a world leader in the development, evaluation, and global dissemination of evidence-based parenting programs. He has held visiting appointments at multiple universities, including the University of Auckland, University of Manchester, Glasgow Caledonian University, and the University of South Carolina. He has conducted a large number of high-quality projects on the role of parenting in influencing developmental outcomes in children and adolescents. He has developed or codeveloped a range of specific parenting programs. His work has been recognized with a number of international awards.

He is a Fellow of the Australian Psychological Association, and the New Zealand Psychological Association and is former honorary president of the Canadian Psychological Association. He has received a Trailblazer Award from the Association for the Advancement of Behavior Therapy Special Interest Group on Parenting and Families and a Distinguished Career Award from the Australian Psychological Association, and the New Zealand Psychological Society; and is an Inaugural Honorary Fellow of the Australian Association for Cognitive Behavior Therapy. He is a Fellow of the Academy of Social Science in Australia and the Academy of Experimental Criminology. He has received an International Collaborative Prevention Research Award from the Society for Prevention Science. He has received a Top Innovator Award and an Innovation Champion Award from Uniquest, The University of Queensland's main technology transfer company. He is a former Queenslander of the Year. He is married to his wife, Trish, and has two children (Emma and Ben) and four grandchildren (Charlotte, Sam, Alex and Lucy).

Dr. Trevor Mazzucchelli is a senior lecturer of clinical psychology at Curtin University's School of Psychology and Speech Pathology and an honorary senior lecturer at the Parenting and Family Support Centre at The University of Queensland. Over the past 20 years, Trevor has held several clinical positions, conducted research in the area of parenting children with disability, and written many articles on this and related topics for scientific journals and publications. He is a coauthor of Stepping Stones Triple P, has developed programs to help parents of children with disability prevent and manage commonly encountered behavioral and emotional problems, and trained practitioners in more than 10 countries to support parents in using these

programs. His doctoral research focused on behavioral interventions for adults with mood disorders and the promotion of well-being. He is a member of the Australian Psychological Society
and a Foreign Affiliate of the American Psychological Association. He is a past president of the
Western Australian branch of the Australian Association for Cognitive and Behaviour Therapy
and was awarded life membership for his services to this association in 2002. He is married to
his wife, Jodie, and has three children, Indigo, Xavier, and April.

CONTRIBUTORS

Sabine Baker
Research Fellow,
Parenting and Family Support Centre,
School of Psychology,
The University of Queensland,
Brisbane, Australia

Jessica A. Bartlett
Head of Lifestyle Triple P Research,
Parenting and Family Support Centre,
School of Psychology,
The University of Queensland,
Brisbane, Australia

Jacquie Brown
Executive Director,
Families Foundation,
Hilversum, The Netherlands;
Head of International Development,
Triple P International,
Brisbane, Australia;
Principal Implementation Specialist,
Jacquie Brown and Associates,
Toronto, Canada

Kylie Burke
Senior Research Fellow,
Parenting and Family Support Centre,
School of Psychology,
The University of Queensland,
Brisbane, Australia

Rachel Calam
Professor of Child and Family
Psychology,
Division of Psychology and Mental
Health,
The University of Manchester,
Manchester, England

Vanessa E. Cobham
Head of Research on Families and
Anxiety,
Parenting and Family Support Centre,
School of Psychology,
The University of Queensland,
Brisbane, Australia

Jamin J. Day
Research Fellow,
Parenting and Family Support Centre,
School of Psychology,
The University of Queensland,
Brisbane, Australia

Cassandra K. Dittman
Head of Curriculum Development,
Parenting and Family Support Centre,
School of Psychology,
The University of Queensland,
Brisbane, Australia

Orla Doyle
Associate Professor,
School of Economics,
University College Dublin,
Dublin, Ireland;
Research Fellow,
Geary Institute for Public Policy,
University College Dublin,
Dublin, Ireland

Stewart L. Einfeld
Professor,
Brain and Mind Centre,
The University of Sydney,
Sydney, Australia

Aala El-Khani
Research Associate,
Division of Psychology and Mental
Health,
The University of Manchester,
Manchester, England

Eamonn Farrell
Family Support Services/Prevention
Partnership and Family Support
Manager,
Tusla Child and Family Agency,
Athlone Health Centre,
Athlone, Ireland

Michell Forster
Indigenous Implementation Consultant,
Triple P International,
Brisbane, Australia

Kylie M. Gray
Associate Professor and Director (Acting),
Centre for Developmental Psychiatry and
Psychology,
Department of Psychiatry, School of
Clinical Sciences at Monash University,
Monash University,
Melbourne, Australia

Divna M. Haslam
Head of International Research
Development,
Parenting and Family Support Centre,
School of Psychology,
The University of Queensland,
Brisbane, Australia

Karyn L. Healy
Research Fellow,
Parenting and Family Support Centre,
School of Psychology,
The University of Queensland,
Brisbane, Australia

Karen Heavey
Community Health Promotion Officer,
Health Promotion and Improvement,
Health Service Executive,
Athlone, Ireland

Mary Hegarty
Senior Researcher,
Department of Public Health—Midlands,
Health and Wellbeing Division,
Health Service Executive,
Athlone, Ireland

Lauren M. Hodge
Advisor, Implementation,
Centre for Evidence and Implementation,
Melbourne, Australia

Julie Hodges
Research Fellow,
School of Psychology,
The University of Queensland,
Brisbane, Australia

Louise J. Keown
Senior Lecturer,
School of Learning, Development,
and Professional Practice, Faculty of
Education and Social Work,
University of Auckland,
Auckland, New Zealand

James N. Kirby
Clinical Psychologist and Lecturer,
Compassionate Mind Research Group,
School of Psychology,
The University of Queensland,
Brisbane, Australia

Shawna Lee
Professor,
School of Early Childhood Education,
Seneca College of Applied Arts and
Technology,
Toronto, Canada;
Doctoral Student in Psychology,
Applied Educational Psychology,
University of Western Ontario,
London, Canada

Trevor G. Mazzucchelli
Senior Lecturer of Clinical Psychology,
School of Psychology and Speech
Pathology,
Curtin University,
Perth, Australia;
Honorary Senior Lecturer,
Parenting and Family Support Centre,
School of Psychology,
The University of Queensland,
Brisbane, Australia

Brett McDermott
Professor of Psychiatry,
College of Medicine and Dentistry,
James Cook University,
Townsville, Australia

Cari D. McIlduff
Doctoral Student in Clinical Psychology
and Research Assistant,
Parenting and Family Support Centre,
School of Psychology,
The University of Queensland,
Brisbane, Australia

Kerri E. McPherson
Reader,
Department of Psychology, Social Work
and Allied Health Sciences,
Glasgow Caledonian University,
Glasgow, Scotland

Jenna McWilliam
Head of Organisational Development,
Triple P International,
Brisbane, Australia

Anilena Mejia
Researcher,
Instituto de Investigaciones Científicas y
Servicios de Alta Tecnología (Institute for
Scientific Research and High Technology
Services),
Panama City, Panama

Carol W. Metzler
Senior Scientist and Science Director,
Oregon Research Institute,
Eugene, Oregon, USA;
Honorary Research Fellow,
Parenting and Family Support Centre,
School of Psychology,
The University of Queensland,
Brisbane, Australia

Alina Morawska
Associate Professor and Deputy Director
(Research),
Parenting and Family Support Centre,
School of Psychology,
The University of Queensland,
Brisbane, Australia

Jeneva L. Ohan
Senior Lecturer,
School of Psychology,
The University of Western Australia,
Perth, Australia

Conor Owens
Senior Psychologist, Primary Care,
Health Service Executive,
Athlone, Ireland

Nicole Penman
Research Assistant,
Parenting and Family Support Centre,
School of Psychology,
The University of Queensland,
Brisbane, Australia;
Doctoral Student in Chemical
Engineering,
Energy and Poverty Research Group,
The University of Queensland,
Brisbane, Australia

Ronald J. Prinz
Carolina Distinguished Professor and
Director,
Parenting and Family Research Center,
Department of Psychology,
University of South Carolina,
Columbia, South Carolina, USA;
Honorary Professor,
School of Psychology,
The University of Queensland,
Brisbane, Australia

Alan Ralph
Honorary Associate Professor,
Parenting and Family Support Centre,
School of Psychology,
The University of Queensland,
Brisbane, Australia;
Head of Training,
Triple P International,
Brisbane, Australia

Julie C. Rusby
Senior Research Scientist,
Oregon Research Institute,
Eugene, Oregon, USA

Matthew R. Sanders
Founder of Triple P, Professor of Clinical
Psychology and Director,
Parenting and Family Support Centre,
School of Psychology,
The University of Queensland,
Brisbane, Australia

Birgit Schroeter
Lecturer in Psychology,
School of Health and Life Sciences,
Glasgow Caledonian University,
Glasgow, Scotland

Cheri J. Shapiro
Research Associate Professor,
Institute for Families in Society, College
of Social Work,
University of South Carolina,
Columbia, South Carolina, USA;
Adjunct Associate Professor,
Department of Psychology,
University of South Carolina,
Columbia, South Carolina, USA

Matthew Shepherd
Senior Lecturer in Social Work,
School of Counselling, Human Services
and Social Work, Faculty of Education
and Social Work,
University of Auckland,
Auckland, New Zealand;
Senior Lecturer in Psychological
Medicine,
School of Medicine, Faculty of Medical
and Health Sciences,
University of Auckland,
Auckland, New Zealand

Kate Sofronoff
Associate Professor in Clinical
Psychology,
School of Psychology, and
Head of Disability Research,
Parenting and Family Support Centre,
The University of Queensland,
Brisbane, Australia

Helen M. Stallman
Senior Lecturer,
School of Psychology, Social Work and
Social Policy,
University of South Australia,
Adelaide, Australia;
Honorary Senior Research Fellow,
Parenting and Family Support Centre,
School of Psychology,
The University of Queensland,
Brisbane, Australia

Lisa J. Studman
Senior Training and Implementation
Consultant and Clinical and
Developmental Psychologist,
Triple P International,
Perth, Australia

Bruce J. Tonge
Emeritus Professor,
Centre for Developmental Psychiatry and
Psychology, Department of Psychiatry,
School of Clinical Sciences,
Monash University,
Melbourne, Australia

Karen M. T. Turner
Associate Professor and Deputy Director
(Programs and Innovation),
Parenting and Family Support Centre,
School of Psychology,
The University of Queensland,
Brisbane, Australia

Leanne Wilkinson
Global Communications Strategist,
Triple P International,
Brisbane, Australia

Anja Wittkowski
Senior Lecturer in Clinical Psychology
and Clinical Psychologist,
School of Health Sciences,
The University of Manchester,
Manchester, England

FOUNDATIONS AND OVERVIEW OF THE TRIPLE P SYSTEM

*A Population
Approach to Parenting Support*

A POPULATION APPROACH TO EVIDENCE-BASED PARENTING SUPPORT

An Introduction

MATTHEW R. SANDERS

Public health promotion is focused on optimizing well-being and healthy functioning (Patel, Flisher, Hetrick, & McGorry, 2007). Prevention is intended to avert unnecessary suffering and distress. Treatment seeks to effectively resolve identified problems as early as possible before problems become severe and entrenched. The integration of all three domains—promotion, prevention, and treatment—into a cohesive, integrated, theoretically consistent system of evidence-based parenting support can transform the way communities support families. This introductory section of the book makes the case for the importance of parenting programs that tackle all three domains if children's developmental and mental health outcomes are to be substantially improved.

Many theoretical models have informed the ongoing development, evaluation, and dissemination of the Triple P—Positive Parenting Program as a multilevel system of parenting support. These include enhanced knowledge about the determinants of human development and developmental psychopathology. There is now much greater knowledge about how genetic, biological, and environmental relationships influence development, health, and lifetime well-being and the critical role that parenting plays in influencing diverse developmental outcomes in children (Collins, Maccoby, Steinberg, Hetherington, & Bornstein, 2000; Shonkoff, Radner, & Foote, 2017). This research shows the bidirectional and reciprocal nature of parent–child interactions and how both children and parents are affected for the better and worse by the quality of their family relationships.

As shown in Chapter 2, the quality of parent–child relationships concurrently influences multiple developmental processes associated with children's healthy brain development, attachment, language, emotional and behavior self-regulation, social skills, peer relationships, academic attainment, and mental and physical health. The implications of this research on human development are highlighted to identify possible content areas that need to be part of a comprehensive parenting strategy to enable both children and parents to relate well to each other in ways that promote prosociality and the capacity to self-regulate and be resilient.

Chapter 3 by Sanders and Prinz explores behavioral family interventions (BFIs), which include both behavioral and cognitive-behavioral approaches to change interactional processes in the family. However, a population-based approach that seeks to blend universal prevention and early intervention approaches is better served by a more generic term, such as *evidence-based parenting support* (EBPS). This term more succinctly describes the full breadth of empirically supported means of helping parents raise their children. These means of support include communication messaging as part of a social marketing campaign and the use of low and higher intensity parenting interventions using the Internet. Each of these delivery modalities has become an integral part of a population-based approach to the provision of parenting support. Sanders and Prinz define EBPS as a generic term used to describe a process of change that aims to positively influence the prosocial development (including social, emotional, and behavioral adjustment) of children and young people through corresponding changes in those aspects of the family environment that are implicated in the development, maintenance, and modification of a child's or young person's behavior and development. It involves the application of evidenced-based social learning principles and relevant behavioral, affective, and cognitive change techniques with an emphasis on reciprocity of change among family members.

The final chapter in Section 1 then moves to a description of the core principles of positive parenting employed in various Triple P programs. These principles and techniques integrate social learning theory, applied behavior analysis, cognitive-behavioral therapy principles, and developmental theory (Chapter 4).

This foundational theoretical material sets the stage for readers to examine more closely the different specific applications of Triple P programs to a wide variety of different age groups, problems, and delivery settings.

REFERENCES

Collins, W. A., Maccoby, E. E., Steinberg, L., Hetherington, E. M., & Bornstein, M. H. (2000). Contemporary research on parenting: The case for nature and nurture. *American Psychologist, 55,* 218–232. doi:10.1037/0003-066X.55.2.218

Patel, V., Flisher, A. J., Hetrick, S., & McGorry, P. (2007). Mental health of young people: A global public-health challenge. *The Lancet, 369,* 1302–1313. doi:10.1016/S0140-6736(07)60368-7

Shonkoff, J. P., Radner, J. M., & Foote, N. (2017). Expanding the evidence base to drive more productive early childhood investment. *The Lancet, 389,* 14–16. doi:10.1016/S0140-6736(16)31702-0

HOW PARENTING INFLUENCES THE LIVES OF CHILDREN

MATTHEW R. SANDERS AND TREVOR G. MAZZUCCHELLI

INTRODUCTION

The provision of parenting programs that seek to support parents in raising healthy, well-adjusted children is based on a fundamental assumption that the quality of parenting a child experiences meaningfully influences the course of child development (Bronfenbrenner, 1986). It assumes that the quality of the parent–child relationship is not predestined by genes and biology, but that parents can actively learn to parent their children and can change their current parenting practices (including behaviors, cognitions, and emotions) in ways that enhance positive developmental outcomes for children and simultaneously positively influence their own (adult) development. Parenting influences the lives of children, particularly during the first 3 years of life, but also at every stage of development from conception to adolescence and beyond (Black et al., 2017; Luthar, 2006). Parental influence is pervasive and affects many aspects of a child's development, including the child's language, cognition, emotion regulation, social skills and peer relationships, academic attainment, personal values, physical and mental health, and overall well-being (Center on the Developing Child at Harvard University, 2016). It is important to note that throughout this volume, the term *parent* is used to encompass the broad range of parents and caregivers responsible for raising children.

The ubiquitous nature of parental influence can be positive, life enhancing, and opportunity creating. It can also be negative, diminishing, and restricting of children's life chances. Learning how to parent children competently is one of life's great challenges, and it can be extremely rewarding and fulfilling. It can also be stressful, exhausting, and, at times, overwhelming. All parents learn many aspects of the parent role "on the job" through trial-and-error learning.

However, of all the potentially modifiable environmental risk and protective factors that can change the course of children's development, none is more important than the quality of parenting children receive. Good parenting can be thought of as the "clean water" of children's mental health and well-being. Given the importance of parenting in determining life course outcomes, the increased attention that is being devoted to assisting parents in the task of raising children is justified (Prinz, 2012).

This book makes the case for the adoption of a population perspective in delivering parenting programs for all families. The current chapter examines the reasons why parenting is so important. We present an ecological model for understanding the specific ways that parenting can influence children's development. The quality of parenting children receive is influenced by the broader ecological and sociopolitical context within which a family lives. Understanding this context is crucial in the design of effective population-based strategies to improve parenting practices and thereby create a nurturing environment in which to raise children (Biglan, 2015).

THE FUNCTIONS OF PARENTING AND WHY PARENTING IS IMPORTANT

Parenting involves a set of purposeful activities designed to ensure the survival, care, development, and well-being of children (Hoghughi & Long, 2004). Parents engage in multiple caring activities, in varying contexts, throughout a child's life to promote the well-being of their children. These activities include providing physical care and nurturance that meets their survival needs (i.e., food, warmth, shelter, clothing, love, affection). It involves ensuring that children are safe, and that harm or risk is prevented or minimized. Social care involves helping children develop the social competencies they need to relate well to others, including parents, siblings, grandparents, and other extended family members; peers; teachers; and eventually employers. The development of children's social and emotional capabilities helps children become well integrated, accepted by their peers, and part of a social network and broader community. Emotional care focuses on the emotional well-being of children. It involves creating a caring, nurturing environment that ensures children and adolescents feel loved and accepted and helps children learn to self-regulate their emotions. Emotional care includes the development of a secure parent–child attachment. Secure attachment, when combined with positive parenting practices, helps children become self-regulated and more resilient in the face of adversity (Waters et al., 2010).

Parenting also involves developing expectations for children's conduct and includes providing role models as well as setting limits and boundaries in a developmentally and culturally appropriate manner so that children learn acceptable patterns of behavior. Parental expectations are informed by culture, values, and beliefs that are influenced by family-of-origin socialization experiences, peers, and the media, including social media. Consequently, parents have a crucial role in children's socialization by establishing expectations. This socialization process includes monitoring and supervising children, actively teaching children the social, emotional, and problem-solving skills they need to become independent in skills of daily living (e.g., toilet training, dressing, and table manners) and by providing sanctions and consequences to help children learn acceptable, age-appropriate behavior (e.g., sharing, turn-taking, and helping others). It includes learning to control impulses and to refrain from unacceptable behavior (e.g., hitting, bullying, temper tantrums, and disobedience) and how to behave appropriately in specific situations (e.g., visiting relatives). It also involves disciplining children when they behave improperly both at home and in the community and requires parents to have clear expectations, rules, and planned consequences that they are prepared to use as needed to back up an instruction (e.g., removal of troublesome toy, planned ignoring, quiet time, or time-out). Backup consequences used will vary as a function of the child's age and level of development.

EFFECTS OF PARENTING ON CHILDREN'S DEVELOPMENT

Research from the behavioral and social sciences combined with advances in neuroscience, molecular biology, and epigenetics have created a clear picture of what is needed to promote the healthy development of children (Beach, Brody, Barton, & Philibert, 2016; Shonkoff et al., 2012). Growing up in a caring, responsive environment where children experience positive stimulating activities promotes healthy brain development. Conversely, when children are exposed to toxic early family experiences, including chronic poverty, exposure to family violence, or child maltreatment, normal development is disrupted, and children are at greater risk for learning and behavioral problems and poorer physical and mental health (Moffitt & the Klaus-Grawe Think Tank, 2013).

Parenting affects many different aspects of a child's development. It is clear that parenting is also the common pathway through which any number of interrelated developmental goals pertaining to children's safety, physical and mental health, language, capacity for self-regulation, relationships with significant siblings and peers, cognitive functioning, academic success, and overall well-being can be supported.

GROWING UP IN A SAFE, ENGAGING, AND NURTURING ENVIRONMENT

Children's very survival depends on having a carer who ensures that their basic physical and emotional needs are met, that they are kept safe and at low risk of injury by ensuring their physical environment is "safety proofed," and that close supervision of the children is provided. This environment needs to provide children with stimulating and engaging activities (toys and materials) so there are plenty of opportunities to explore, discover, experiment, and learn to talk. Not only should the environment be made physically safe for a child, but also the child's emotional safety is paramount to the child's development (Biglan, 2015). A caring, nurturing environment where parents are attuned to children's needs, responsive to their requests for assistance, and provide plenty of positive attention and physical nurturance helps children become securely attached to their caregiver (Wolff & van Ijzendoorn, 1997).

Implication for Parenting: Parenting programs should encourage parents to create safe, interesting, and nurturing environments for children.

BRAIN ARCHITECTURE AND FUNCTION

Belsky and de Haan (2011) argued that children's brain development is affected by three different types of neural processes. These include gene-driven processes, which are viewed as being sensitive to experience. Brain formation is also influenced by experience-expectant processes, which is when the brain is primed to receive particular classes of information from the environment and therefore is expectant. In this process, neurons that are inactive are eliminated, whereas "those that are actively stimulated by experience are strengthened and maintained" (p. 143). Finally, they described experience-dependent synapse formation, which is how an individual's unique experience can influence both the formation of new synapses and modify existing ones across the life course. These varied experiences can include recurring social experiences and interactions, study or training, and therapy or counseling. Child maltreatment is the most commonly cited way in which parenting can affect brain structure and function. Shonkoff (2011) argued that early stress-induced changes in the architecture of different regions of the brain (e.g., amygdala, hippocampus, and prefrontal cortex) can have permanent negative effects on important functions, such as the child's capacity to regulate stress physiology, learn new skills and behavior, and adapt to adversities.

Implication for Parenting: To promote healthy brain development, parenting programs should seek to reduce or eliminate toxic stress in the lives of children and their parents.

LANGUAGE, COMMUNICATION, AND COGNITION

Parent–child interactions influence children's capacity to learn language, to communicate with others, and to develop their intellect. The first 3 years are particularly important for the development of language. Hart and Risley (1995) conducted a classic observational study of children's language experiences and demonstrated that the type and amount of daily language interaction between a parent and a child influences the rate at which new words are added to a child's vocabulary between the ages of 12 and 36 months. Substantial individual differences along socioeconomic lines emerged in children's exposure to language and consequently their language proficiency (vocabulary) by age 3 years. The rate of vocabulary growth, in turn, was related to IQ and academic attainments at age 9 years. Parents from disadvantaged homes (i.e., families from low socioeconomic groups and those on welfare) speak to their children less frequently than parents of children from middle-class homes (Hoff, 2006).

Implication for Parenting: Parenting programs should encourage parents to talk and read frequently to their children to foster language, literacy, and positive communication in the family.

PARENTING AND CHILD EXTERNALIZING PROBLEMS

A wealth of evidence has shown that everyday interactions between parents and children influence oppositional behaviors and conduct problems (Charach et al., 2013; Patterson, 1982). Commonly observed parent behaviors, such as the use of harsh disciplinary techniques (Global

Initiative to End All Corporal Punishment of Children, 2017), low levels of positive attention to desirable behavior, and high rates of conflictual interactions between parents leading to inconsistent parenting, are related to the frequency and intensity of child conduct problems (Patterson, Reid, Jones, & Conger, 1975). Several large-scale meta-analyses of parenting programs based on social learning principles showed that when parents learn to respond positively and contingently to children's appropriate behavior, children have lower levels of disruptive behavior (Epstein, Fonnesbeck, Potter, Rizzone, & McPheeters, 2015; Piquero et al., 2016; Sanders, Kirby, Tellegen, & Day, 2014).

Implication for Parenting: Parenting programs need to equip parents with specific parenting skills to manage oppositional and other conduct problems.

PARENTING AND CHILDREN'S SELF-REGULATION CAPACITY

A great deal of emphasis has been placed on the critical importance of children learning to self-regulate their emotions and behavior (Moffitt & the Klaus-Grawe 2012 Think Tank, 2013; Moffitt, Poulton, & Caspi, 2013; Shanker, 2012). Self-regulation refers to children's capacity to modulate their emotions, delay impulses and gratification, and develop executive functions such as paying attention, planning, anticipating, organizing, reasoning, and problem-solving. Executive functions help the brain organize and act on information. These skills enable people to plan, organize, remember things, prioritize, pay attention, and get started on tasks. They also help people use information and experiences from the past to solve current problems.

Many children experience some problems with self-regulation (e.g., children with attention deficit hyperactivity disorder [ADHD], conduct disorders, autism spectrum disorders), particularly in the areas of impulsivity, sustained attention, lack of organization, memory, task completion, and problem-solving. Research has shown that problems with self-regulation can have long-term impacts. For example, Moffitt et al. (2011), in a birth cohort longitudinal study of children, found that the level of self-control children displayed at age 3 predicted their health, wealth, and level of antisocial behavior as adults 30 years later, after controlling for the education level of the parent when the child was at age 3 and the level of family socioeconomic disadvantage.

To avoid the long-term consequences that children can experience as a result of having poor self-regulation and impulse control, parenting programs can play an important role in helping parents teach their child better self-control over behavior and emotions. Parenting has been hypothesized to positively influence children's capacity for emotion and behavior self-regulation through a number of related mechanisms (Brumariu, 2015; Sanders & Mazzucchelli, 2013). These include assisting in the development of healthy, secure attachment; helping children learn language, social, emotional, and problem-solving skills; and through providing contingency management strategies to help children deal with dysregulated emotions (such as aggression, anger, frustration, and disappointment).

Implication for Parenting: Parenting programs can play an important role in helping parents facilitate children's self-regulatory capability while concurrently developing parents' self-regulatory capacity.

PARENTING AND CHILDREN'S MENTAL HEALTH PROBLEMS

Deficits in emotion and behavior self-regulation can also be related to the development, mainte-nance, and treatment of a variety of serious mental health problems in children and adolescents (including anxiety, depression, eating disorders, recurrent pain syndromes, obsessive-compulsive disorders) and response to traumatic events such as natural disasters (Chapters 8 and 10, this volume).

In the case of child anxiety, Cobham (Chapter 8) argues that parenting may affect child anxiety through a number of different mechanisms. Parent anxiety creates a family environment that predisposes children to develop anxiety through vicarious learning (Askew & Field, 2008). Parents' own anxiety may lead to parenting behaviors (such as overprotectiveness, limited auton-omy granting, and reinforcement of avoidance) that may inadvertently encourage the develop-ment of anxiety in children. The relationship between parent and child anxiety is considered to be reciprocal. Children's anxiety elicits a pattern of parenting that then helps to maintain the child's anxiety. Other potentially modifiable family factors that have also been shown to contrib-ute to anxiety include lower family cohesion, expressiveness, and support; higher interparental conflict; and stressful negative family environments (see Rapee, Schniering, & Hudson, 2009).

However, there is some evidence that changing parenting practices can decrease children's anxiety. A small number of intervention studies with parents of children with anxiety problems have shown that parenting groups that incorporate principles of positive parenting can reduce levels of anxiety and distress in children (Cobham, Chapter 8, this volume; Özyurt, Gencer, Öztürk, & Özbek, 2015). For example, Cobham, Filus, and Sanders (2017) conducted the first randomized controlled trial (RCT) of Fear-less Triple P (Cobham & Sanders, 2009), a parent-only, six-session group variant of Triple P that specifically targets parental knowledge of anxiety and parenting practices implicated in the development and maintenance of anxiety. Following the intervention, fewer children met criteria for an anxiety disorder. These positive effects on anxiety were maintained 12 months postintervention, providing preliminary evidence of the potential value of Fear-less Triple P.

Implication for Parenting: Prevention or treatment programs targeting serious mental health prob-lems in children should consider routinely including in the intervention mix specific skill training for parents in positive parenting that includes how to respond constructively to children's anxiety, avoidance, and other forms of emotional distress.

SCHOOLING AND ACADEMIC ATTAINMENT

Success in schooling has important long-term impacts on children's well-being and life oppor-tunities, and parenting has an important role to play in education (Sanders, Healy, Grice, & Del Vecchio, 2017). By the time children enter formal schooling at age 5 or 6, the family environment has typically already had a major influence on children's preparedness to start school (Chazan-Cohen et al., 2009). Differences in readiness to handle formal schooling can be related to whether parents have promoted children's use of language through frequent language interactions; have regularly read to children; have taught children basic social skills, such as cooperating with instructions, following rules, sharing, and turn taking; have promoted the development of self-care skills, such as dressing, toileting independently, tidying away toys, handling temporary separations from parents; and have facilitated peer interactions. Once children start school, parental involvement with the child's school continues to be important to children's academic attainment (Chapter 22, this volume). The quality of home–school communication influences children's academic accomplishments, school attendance, and classroom behavior (Galindo & Sheldon, 2011). Powell, Son, File, and San Juan (2010) found that parental school involvement positively predicted children's social skills and mathematics skills and negatively predicted problem behaviors. Perceived teacher responsiveness to the child/parent was positively related to children's early reading and social skills and negatively related to problem behaviors. A meta-synthesis by Wilder (2014) found that there was a positive relationship between parental involvement and child success at school, including higher academic achievement, higher rates of graduation and tertiary education, self-efficacy for learning, attendance, peer relationships, behavior at school, and general school connectedness.

Implication for Parenting: Schools have an important role in the delivery of parenting programs, particularly at points of transition (such as starting school). Parenting programs should be adapted to teach parents effective communication skills to engage with teachers and schools about children's learning so that parents can support their children's education and be meaningful partners with the child's school.

CHILDREN'S RELATIONSHIPS WITH PEERS

Children's social relationships with their peers are influenced by the kind of parenting they receive. McDowell and Parke (2009) described three distinct paths through which parents influence children's social competence and peer acceptance: parent–child interaction, direct instruction, and provision of opportunities. The concept of facilitative parenting (FP) was defined by Healy, Sanders, and Iyer (2015) as parenting that enables the development of children's social competence and peer relationships. FP is characterized by warm and responsive parent–child relating, enabling appropriate child independence (as opposed to being overly directive or protective), effective management of parent–child conflict, active coaching of social and emotional skills, provision of opportunities for the child to socialize with peers, and effective communication with school staff. Healy and Sanders (2014) conducted an RCT to evaluate the efficacy of training parents in FP through a program variant (Resilience Triple P) developed specifically for parents of children who had been bullied at school by peers. More information about this program is reported by Healy in Chapter 7.

Implication for Parenting: Parenting programs, through the promotion of prosocial behavior, friendship making, and teaching children skills to stand up for themselves, have an important role in protecting children from bullying.

CHILDREN'S RELATIONSHIPS WITH SIBLINGS

Sibling relationships have an important effect on children (Pickering & Sanders, 2017). Positive prosocial sibling interactions and conflict management equip children with important life skills, including negotiating, perspective taking, patience, and acceptance (Bedford,

Volling, & Avioli, 2000). Conversely, sibling conflict and low sibling warmth increase the risk of externalizing and internalizing problems (Buist, Deković, & Prinzie, 2013). The way parents interact with their children significantly predicts the quality of the sibling interactions, and management of conflict helps children learn life skills, such as negotiating, reasoning, perspective taking, and acceptance (Ross & Lazinski, 2014). Parents' interactions with their children can shape the quality of sibling relationships and therefore the outcomes of the sibling relationship.

There is preliminary evidence that brief parenting programs can improve some aspects of sibling relationships. Pickering, Crane, Hong, Nickel, and Sanders (2017) conducted an RCT that evaluated the effects on sibling relationships of a brief, one-session parenting intervention (Triple P Discussion Group) that focused specifically on managing sibling fighting and aggression. Parents in the intervention group reported a significantly greater improvement in sibling warmth and in the emotional behavior of the sibling compared to the wait-list group.

Implication for Parenting: Parenting programs can assist parents develop strategies to improve sibling relationships and promote long-term harmonious family relationships.

PARENTING AND CHILDREN'S PHYSICAL HEALTH

Parenting has a major influence on children's physical health and well-being (Chapter 11, this volume; Wood et al., 2008). It is a parental responsibility to ensure that children grow up in living conditions that provide the children with basic necessities of life to remain healthy. These include providing adequate nutrition, clean water, and sanitation; avoidance of exposure to toxic fumes; immunizations; sufficient sleep; and access to appropriate health care when needed. Parents also have a role in ensuring that children have plenty of physical activity and limiting access to screens of phones, computers, and the like.

Sick-role behaviors that involve children learning how to behave when they feel unwell (e.g., complaining, grimacing, lying down) are learned in part through parental modeling and family experiences (Walker & Zeman, 1992). Recurrent pain syndromes, such as headache and recurrent abdominal pain, are influenced by family context. Solicitous responding through parental attention can reinforce pain complaints and avoidance of nonpreferred activities. Children's compliance with medical treatments for chronic health conditions, such as asthma, diabetes, eczema, and obesity, are all influenced by parenting.

Parenting programs for parents of children with a chronic health condition have been clearly articulated (Morawska, Calam, & Fraser, 2015), and research is increasingly focused on developing and evaluating brief, low-intensity parenting interventions for this population (Mackey et al., 2016; Morawska, Mitchell, Burgess, & Fraser, 2016). Several recent trials showed that brief, low-intensity parenting interventions can reduce levels of noncompliance with medical treatments.

Implication for Parenting: Parenting programs can play an important role in helping parents promote children's long-term physical health and well-being.

DETERMINANTS OF PARENTING: IMPLICATIONS

Recognition that multiple factors interact and combine to influence parenting is important in planning a population approach to parenting support. For all parents, learning to parent well takes time and requires continuous adaptation through each successive phase of life as both children and parents change and mature. Individual differences in parenting capability arise from multiple sources, some of which are amenable to parenting intervention. Children do not come with an instruction manual, and being a parent involves the mastery of a complex set of skills that gradually develop through experience. Parenting is influenced by a complex mix of genetic and biological factors, experience, opportunity, motivation, and relationships and a range of social, cultural, and economic factors. Gaining an understanding of how these multiple interacting determinants affect parenting capability has important implications for the design and delivery of a comprehensive, need-responsive, and population-based system of parenting support. The implications of each determinant are discussed next.

BIOLOGICAL AND GENETIC INFLUENCES ON PARENTING

Parents differ, as children do from each other, as a result of the interaction between a parent's unique genetic makeup, biological factors, and life experience. These interacting determinants of individuality together shape how parents undertake their parenting responsibilities as well as their physical and mental health, capacity to deal with stress, and their child's temperament. *Temperament* is defined as "constitutionally based individual differences in reactivity and self-regulation in the domains of affect, activity and attention" (Rothbart & Bates, 2006, p. 100). Individual differences in response to a parent's own family-of-origin life experiences contribute to how parents approach the task of raising their own children.

A recent meta-analysis by Slagt, Dubas, Deković, and van Aken (2016) involving 6,153 children from 84 studies explored the relationship between parenting and child temperament. As a test of a differential susceptibility hypothesis, children with more difficult temperaments (compared to those with an easy temperament) not only were more vulnerable to the effects of negative parenting, but also benefited more from positive parenting.

Research also supports a biological underpinning of healthy parenting (Gordon, Zagoory-Sharon, Leckman, & Feldman, 2010; Saphire-Bernstein, Way, Kim, Sherman, & Taylor, 2011). The neuropeptide oxytocin has been implicated as one of the key hormones involved in parent–infant bonding, with higher levels of oxytocin associated with increased frequency of affectionate parenting behaviors, such as the expression of positive affect and affectionate touch (Gordon et al., 2010). It is likely that genetic and biological influences affecting parents themselves interact with experience and environmental factors (including influences of education and partners) to influence how parents interact with their children.

Implication for Practice: Practitioners should encourage parents to recognize that the personal resources they have to parent children are partly determined by factors beyond their control, such as their genetic and family backgrounds. However, there are many other factors within their control that can influence how they choose to raise their children.

FAMILY-OF-ORIGIN EXPERIENCES

Prior to becoming parents themselves, parents have a range of life experiences in their family of origin that influences the personal resources that each parent brings to the parenting role. If both parents were raised in stable, loving, low-conflict environments by competent and stable parents, first-time mothers and fathers are more likely to be confident in their personal capacity to cope with the demands of parenthood and are more likely to look forward to becoming parents with eager anticipation (Rholes, Simpson, Blakely, Lanigan, & Allen, 1997). However, if one or more parents were raised in households characterized by dysfunctional family experiences, parents can find the transition to parenthood stressful, and their parental efficacy can be low.

The specific parenting practices used by parents are influenced by the family-of-origin socialization experiences (e.g., when mothers should return to work after childbirth; distribution of household tasks; working hours for mothers; whether children should have a religious education, attend a public or private school, participate in a particular sport, learn a musical instrument, learn additional languages, and so on).

Many parents have been exposed to one or more adverse childhood experiences. Being exposed to harsh or coercive parenting practices; chaotic, unpredictable, or neglectful parenting; or other forms of child maltreatment (e.g., sexual abuse) can increase children's risk for poor developmental outcomes, including increased risk of developing serious behavioral or emotional problems (Prinz, 2016). Other family experiences, such as parental divorce, repeated breakdown of parental relationships, or living in a household characterized by intimate partner violence (IPV), parental mental illness or substance abuse, homelessness, parental absence, and poverty, can cumulatively have an adverse effect on the well-being of parents, their mental and physical health, and personal resources to take care of children (Felitti et al., 1998). Family dysfunction in childhood is a form of toxic stress that can have lifelong adverse consequences for physical and mental health and overall well-being (Shonkoff et al., 2012).

Implication for Practice: Practitioners must adjust their delivery of parenting programs to accommodate differences between parents in terms of their past experiences and learning and the coping skills and personal resources they possess when they first become parents. Every parent, regardless of personal past history and motivation, has the potential to become more effective in his or her parenting practices.

INTERACTIONAL PROCESSES

The immediate context of parent–child interaction can have a major effect on children. The day-to-day, moment-to-moment interactions between parents and children are important determinants of both children's and parents' behavior. When parents interact with children, their behavior is often in response to immediate situational cues from the child (smiling, cooing, laughing, or fussing, grimacing, crying, and complaining) that signal to the parent that a change in parental action is required. An observant, attuned, responsive parent is likely to respond to these child cues and change or adjust their actions to reduce the child's distress or upset (e.g., feed their child, change their child's diapers, and introduce stimulation or a distraction). These parental actions may result in a change in the child's behavior (e.g., the child may settle, become calm, sleep, or escalate behavior). Parents tend to repeat behaviors that lead to positive consequences and avoid behavior that leads to negative responses.

Patterson's coercion theory (Patterson et al., 1975) provided a clear example of how family interactional processes lead to the development of aggressive and disruptive behavior in children. For example, a parent may request that a child who is watching television come to the dinner table. If the child refuses and complains, a parent may initially repeat the direction but now with a raised voice. If the child continues noncompliance, the parent may escalate his or her reaction, raise the voice further, and perhaps threaten (in an angry voice) a negative consequence (e.g., banning the television or threatening to spank the child). If the child cooperates after the parent escalates, the child may inadvertently reinforce the parent for yelling. Conversely, children are learning that cooperation is not needed when parents ask civilly and only when parents escalate and threaten a negative consequence or punishment. These coercive patterns of escalation followed by parental or child compliance or withdrawal of demands/requests are common in the families of children with conduct problems, and as such, they are a primary target of parenting interventions to reduce aggression.

Implication for Practice: Parenting programs need to help parents become self-regulated so they can identify how their own and their child's behavior is reciprocally influenced by the consequences of their actions during daily interactions. This requires parents to be observant and become aware of their own behavior, to reflect, to generate hypotheses, and to experiment with different ways of responding.

CHARACTERISTICS OF CHILDREN

Parents often claim that children in the same family raised in the "same way" can be very different from each other. Parents attribute these individual differences to intrinsic heritable qualities of children. There is little doubt that parents can be influenced by the characteristics and behavior of children. Children vary in terms of their physical health (as a result of preterm birth, low birth weight, disability, physical appearance, illnesses); their temperament (how outgoing, sociable, fussy, timid, and shy they are); and their patterns of behavior (reacting with crying, sleep, responses to attempts to settle, cooperativeness, aggression, tantrums). Some children, due to constitutional differences that emerge very early in life, appear to be easier to care for (soothe, calm, settle, feed) than others.

Children also shape the responses of caregivers by differentially reinforcing parents for both prosocial and problem behavior (Slagt et al., 2016). For example, when a child laughs and smiles in response to parents making a funny face, a parent or other carer is likely to repeat the actions that led children to laughter in the future. Conversely, a child who eventually cooperates in a compliance situation only after being threatened with a negative consequence may inadvertently reinforce (through cooperation) a parent for escalating quickly because threatening produces child cooperation (termination of child's noncompliance and associated parental stress). When children are cooperative, polite, and engage in acts of caring, kindness, or compassion toward others, parents experience positive emotions (being proud, showing caring) toward their children. Conversely, when children engage in difficult, disruptive, or challenging behavior parents experience increased levels of arousal and stress and may think negative thoughts ("What's wrong with this child?") and feel negative emotions (anger, frustration, anxiety, sadness) toward their children.

Clinical Implication: Practitioners need to acknowledge that children's characteristics will influence parent's behavior and that parents must be responsive to the needs of their individual child—A "one-size-fits-all" approach to raising children in the same family is unlikely to work.

IMPORTANCE OF PARENTAL SELF-EFFICACY

Self-efficacy is an important part of self-regulation. Self-efficacy refers to parents' beliefs about their capacity to successfully complete necessary tasks or responsibilities. When parents have low self-efficacy they are more likely to feel discouraged, anxious, or depressed about the parenting role (T. L. Jones & Prinz, 2005). Task-specific self-efficacy refers to being able to successfully complete the basic tasks of parenthood, such as feeding, dressing, getting children to bed, supervising homework, assisting with project work, and monitoring screen time or accessing and using electronic devices. Sanders and Woolley (2005) distinguished between behavior-specific (management of specific child behaviors such as tantrums, aggression) or setting-specific task self-efficacy (management of children's behavior in specific situations, such as shopping trips, car travel, bedtime). Parents of children with conduct problems tend to have lower levels of both task- and setting-specific self-efficacy prior to participating in a parenting program.

Parental self-efficacy typically increases following participating in parenting programs such as Triple P (e.g., Sanders et al., 2014). Participation in parenting programs can enhance self-efficacy by helping parents set realistic but attainable goals for themselves; by encouraging parents to try something new, challenging, or difficult that is achievable; by encouraging parents to be self-reflective and review their accomplishments; and by scheduling within- and between-session tasks that provide an opportunity for skills development.

Implication for Practice: Parenting programs should arrange incrementally challenging activities that enhance parents' task and setting self-efficacy.

COGNITIVE FACTORS

Azar and colleagues' work on social information processing (SIP; Azar, 2002; Azar, Barnes, & Twentyman, 1988) of parents at risk of harming their children has highlighted the critical importance of cognitive processes in parenting, particularly in understanding parents at risk of harming their children (e.g., Azar, Okado, Stevenson, & Robinson, 2013). The SIP model argues that caregivers who have unrealistic expectations of children show poorer problem-solving in childrearing situations and who make more negative intent attributions to children's behavior are at greater risk for inadequate and inappropriate parenting, including child maltreatment. Parental expectations of children and of themselves are influenced by the kinds of role models that parents were exposed to in their own families and through exposure to prevailing social and community cultural, ethnic, and religious norms. In a society where parents are exposed to multiple ethnic, racial, religious, and community influences (through social media), the socialization contexts influencing parental beliefs and expectations are more diverse than ever.

Another important cognitive factor relates to parents' attributional style. An attribution refers to a person's belief about the causes of a behavior or action. Parents develop an explanatory framework to make sense of the world and to explain both their child's and their own behavior. When parents attribute a child's behavior (e.g., accidentally spilling a glass of milk on the kitchen floor) to a cause that is internal to the child, is stable, and is negative ("He is just a clumsy, careless boy," "He's always been like that and always will be," "She's so careless," "He's just like his father"), the parent is more likely to become angry or annoyed with the child and feel that the child's behavior is deliberate. Under these circumstances, the parent may feel he or she is the victim and that retribution is justified ("I'll show her who is boss around here"). Consequently, training parents to change dysfunctional blaming attributions is important so that parents can identify alternative mitigating reasons for a child's actions ("She's only three. Three-year-olds sometime have accidents") that prevent anger escalation.

Population-based efforts to influence parenting knowledge, beliefs, and expectations need to be attuned to the different ways in which parents acquire information and knowledge about parenting. Immediate family members such as partners, grandparents, and siblings with children, but also extended family members remain the primary source of information about parenting. However, many parents seek parenting advice from teachers and family doctors, mass media, and the Internet. Attending a positive parenting program is another source from which parents are more likely to learn skills; increase their intentions to implement them; and actually implement and maintain them. This occurs when targeted parenting skills are modeled and demonstrated, when dysfunctional attributions or beliefs about the reasons for children's behavior are changed, and when positive expectancies and parenting self-efficacy are increased.

Implication for Practice: Parenting programs need to address parental cognitions, particularly dysfunctional attributions that increase the risk that parents become angry, overreact, and harm children.

PARENTAL EMOTIONAL REGULATION

A parent's own mental health and well-being can have a substantial effect on how parents raise their children. Parents who manage their own emotions well are advantaged in raising children. Parents who can remain reasonably calm or at least avoid becoming agitated, highly anxious, angry, or highly distressed when faced with a parenting challenge are less vulnerable to actions that can inadvertently worsen a situation. For example, not becoming personally distressed when toddlers have tantrums in a public place means that parents are more likely to maintain their resolve in the face of threat or challenge (including disapproval from others). Conversely, when parents have difficulty regulating their emotions, they are more inclined to succumb to social disapproval pressure from others (e.g., giving in to a child's demands). Parents with severe mental health problems, such as major depression, bipolar disorder, or psychosis, often experience disruptions to their parenting of offspring.

Parents suffering from bipolar disorder have patterns of communication, impulse control, and motivation that can make parenting particularly challenging (S. Jones et al., 2014). Children of bipolar parents also have a significantly elevated risk for a wide range of psychiatric conditions, including ADHD, anxiety, depression, substance use, and sleep disorders, in addition to experiencing rates of bipolar disorder higher than those seen in the general population (Duffy, Alda, Crawford, Milin, & Grof, 2007; S. Jones & Bentall, 2008).

Children of parents with mental illness are at increased risk of abuse and neglect and are likely to need support in coping with their parent's often confusing and distressing mental illness (Barnett, Miller-Perrin, & Perrin, 2005). When parents seek treatment for their own mental health problems, their parenting needs should not be ignored. Recent RCT evidence has shown that providing an online positive parenting intervention (Triple P Online) when combined with an online cognitive-behavioral therapy (CBT) program for bipolar patients reduces the risk of offspring behavioral and emotional problems (S. Jones et al., 2014). Parents in the intervention group reported improvements in child behavior problems compared to controls.

Clinical Implication: Adult treatment services should make parenting programs available to enhance parents' emotion regulation skills so that they can better respond, even during periods of increased stress, to parenting challenges they face.

RELATIONSHIPS WITH PARTNERS

A couple's relationship influences how each parent undertakes his or her parenting responsibility, the degree to which the parent feels supported in the parenting role, and the level of stress the parent experiences (Sanders & Keown, 2017). When parents have supportive relationships and communicate well with their partner about roles, responsibilities, and the sharing of parenting tasks, there is less conflict in parenting, better teamwork, and greater interparental consistency. Children benefit by being exposed to a loving and predictable home environment. Fewer arguments about parenting and an absence of Intimate Partner Violence (IPV) translate into children having better role models for harmonious family lives. Parental disagreements can escalate into conflict that may include use of verbal or physical threats and actual IPV. Parents who are victims of IPV are more likely to be depressed, stressed, and less confident in parenting. If a parent feels unsafe, his or her parenting of children is frequently disrupted.

Grasso et al. (2016) found that mothers reporting a greater occurrence of psychologically aggressive IPV (e.g., yelling, name-calling) more often engage in psychological and physical aggression toward their children. Mothers reporting a greater occurrence of IPV in the form of physical assault more often engage in mild to more severe forms of physical punishment with potential harm to the child. Psychological and physical forms of IPV and harsh parenting are all significantly correlated with maternal reports of child disruptive behavior. These findings highlight the importance of parenting programs for both victims and perpetrators of IPV to reduce the risk that children will develop serious mental health concerns.

Clinical Implication: Parenting programs should be delivered in a way that enables both parents in two-parent families to participate to ensure greater interparental consistency and teamwork.

RELATIONSHIPS WITH GRANDPARENTS AND EXTENDED FAMILY

Grandparents play an important role in childrearing in many societies. The involvement of grandparents in childrearing ranges from virtually no involvement at all to adoption of a full-time custodial grandparenting role. Grandparents provide a substantial amount of regular child care in the United States, with approximately 24% of all children under five receiving child care from their grandparents (Laughlin, 2013). A similar trend occurs in Australia, with approximately 25% of children 12 years or younger receiving regular child care from their grandparents (Australian Bureau of Statistics, 2012). Across Europe, it is estimated that 40% of children receive regular child care from their grandparents (Glaser, Price, Di Gessa, Montserrat, & Tinker, 2013). Kirby (2015) argued that it is important that the field of parenting and family psychology examine the impact that grandparents can have on family functioning.

The nature of a parent's relationship with their own parent or parent-in-law can influence a parent's capacity to parent children both positively and negatively. Positive influences include being a source of practical help (child care, financial support) and advice around parenting and child care issues (e.g., feeding, caring for, and disciplining children). When parents actively seek and receive useful advice and support from grandparents, the burden of parenthood can be shared and is a social support buffer against stress. However, if a parent has an acrimonious relationship with a grandparent who is viewed as intrusive, critical, or interfering, a parent may feel judged and become avoidant of the grandparent. Such a relationship can adversely affect a parent's relationship with his or her partner, particularly if the couple is living with a partner's parents. When there are shared child care responsibilities, the active involvement of grandparents in a parenting program can improve the grandparents' relationship with the parent and the grandchildren (Kirby & Sanders, 2014).

Clinical Implication: Because many children are raised by multiple carers, not just biological parents, parenting programs should actively seek to engage all relevant carers involved in child care responsibilities, including grandparents, nannies, and kinship carers.

ECONOMIC FACTORS

Living in poverty is one form of chronic stress that affects both parents and children and has a pervasive adverse impact on the family and parents' capacity to undertake their parenting responsibilities. It has been well documented that poverty adversely affects child well-being (Bornstein & Bradley, 2014). Brooks-Gunn and Duncan (1997) summarized the effects of poverty on children by noting that poorer children have higher incidences of adverse health, developmental, and other outcomes than nonpoor children, including (a) poorer physical health (low birth weight, growth stunting, and lead poisoning); (b) lower cognitive ability (e.g., intelligence, verbal ability, and academic achievement); (c) poorer school achievement (e.g., years of schooling, high school completion); (d) greater emotional and behavioral problems; and (e) teenage out-of-wedlock childbearing. According to a policy statement from the American Academy of Pediatrics (2016), it is estimated that half of young children in the United States live in poverty or near poverty.

Some of the effects of poverty on children are linked to the reduced capacity of adults to care for their children. Parents living in poverty have many more stressors in their lives than other families. Poorer parents are more likely to have problems, such as mental illness and substance abuse; chronic unemployment; poorer physical health; greater exposure to family and neighborhood violence; greater likelihood of discrimination; food and housing insecurity; limited access to good schools; and limited access to quality health, dental, and family support services.

The adverse effects of poverty on child development can be mitigated to some degree by strengthening parenting. There has been considerable emphasis in the parenting field to ensure that parenting programs target vulnerable families from low socioeconomic areas. Within a whole-of-population–based approach, special efforts over and above efforts to engage all families in a community are often needed to reach out to and engage more vulnerable low-income parents with multiple risk factors from ethnic minority groups, including indigenous, migrant, and refugee families living in low-resource settings.

Clinical Implication: Professionals should advocate for government policies and services that will improve access and engagement of families in low-resource settings to reduce social and economic inequity between families. Parenting programs potentially can mitigate some, but not all, of the adverse effects of raising children in poverty.

SOCIAL SUPPORT, NEIGHBORHOOD, AND COMMUNITY FACTORS

Poor families are more likely to live in poorer neighborhoods. Poorer neighborhoods expose parents to other stressors, such as higher rates of crime; substance abuse; more unemployment; greater social isolation; lower levels of social connectedness to other parents; less monitoring and supervision of children and adolescents; greater social disorganization; and fewer community resources (e.g., safe play spaces for children, parks, child care centers, libraries, health care, and afterschool programs).

Participating in a parenting program is one way for parents in low-resource settings to become less socially isolated and increase social support for the parenting role. Parents can be strong advocates about the value of parenting programs for other parents in a neighborhood. Some evidence shows that parents completing parenting programs share their learnings with people they know who have not participated (Fives, Purcell, Heary, NicGabhainn, & Canavan, 2014).

Clinical Implication: Parenting programs have the potential to mitigate the adverse effects of living in low-resource settings by increasing social support and enhancing community connectedness of these parents.

CULTURAL BACKGROUND

Parenting practices are markedly influenced by cultural context. Every country tends to be characterized by a certain amount of cultural diversity where the dominant culture (comprising the largest number of residents) lives with and shares the environment with parents from other cultural groups or different ethnic and language backgrounds. Within any given country, parents vary with respect to their connection to and active involvement with the dominant culture's values, norms, language, and traditions. For example, Muslim families often closely observe religious traditions from their country of origin, and others have little engagement with those traditions.

The challenge for parenting programs is to ensure that programs are broadly culturally relevant and acceptable to a diverse range of parents before scaling of programs (see Chapter 28, this volume). There is growing evidence from cultural acceptability studies of Triple P (Morawska et al., 2011, 2012), controlled evaluations with particular ethnic groups in both individualistic and collectivistic cultures (Chapter 30, this volume), and studies examining the transportability of findings of parenting programs from one culture to another that show that the basic principles and techniques of positive parenting are seen as relevant and acceptable to parents from diverse cultural backgrounds. Evidence-based parenting programs generally transport well from countries of development to countries of adoption (Gardner, Montgomery, & Kerr, 2015).

However, parenting programs must be adapted to ensure that principles of positive parenting and the cultural values and traditions can work in harmony. Turner et al. (Chapter 28, this volume) provided an example of how this can be done using a collaborative partnership adaptation model with indigenous Māori elders whānau (families) in New Zealand.

Clinical Implication: It is important that parenting programs develop convincing evidence pertaining to a program's cultural relevance, acceptability, and effectiveness.

PARENTAL MENTAL HEALTH

Parents with major mental health problems, such as depression, anxiety, bipolar disorders, substance abuse disorders, and personality disorders, are more likely to raise children with mental health and behavioral problems themselves (see Chapter 17, this volume). In addition, millions of people worldwide have experienced tremendous emotional distress as a consequence of the traumatic experiences of war, including dislocation, flight, imprisonment, resettlement in other countries, and chronic poverty. In a context of ongoing trauma, parents find it difficult to care for their children.

Implication for Practice: Special efforts should be made to ensure that adults with mental health and substance abuse problems or living with the mental health consequences of exposure to traumatic events are able to access parenting support both to improve their own mental health and to reduce the risk that their children will develop serious mental health problems.

PARENTING DISRUPTED BY SEPARATION

Parents whose family lives are disrupted because their partners or they themselves experience periods of separation from their children are at greater risk of psychological distress and having disrupted parenting practices (Dittman, Henriquez, & Roxburgh, 2016). These disruptions can arise in multiple separation contexts, such as living in a family where at least one parent is a "fly-in, fly-out" worker in mines or is deployed by the military or where families are experiencing separation due to divorce, incarceration, or hospitalization due to poor parental health. When children experience prolonged separation, they are at greater risk of a variety of adverse developmental outcomes. For example, Murray, Bijleveld, Farrington, and Loeber (2014) documented the effects of imprisonment on families. Parental arrest can leave children feeling shocked, bewildered, and scared (Richards et al., 1994). Some children experience post-traumatic stress disorder with flashbacks about their parent's arrest. The experience of having a parent in jail is stigmatizing, disrupts the development of the parent–child relationship, results in less parental supervision and effective discipline of children, and increases the risk that children will become involved in antisocial behavior and crime themselves (Murray et al., 2014).

Implication for Practice: Specific parenting programs are needed to assist families who experience unavoidable parental separations.

SOCIOPOLITICAL FACTORS

Parenting takes place in a broader sociopolitical environment that includes the provision of basic primary health care, education, and welfare services and laws related to the rights and treatment of children. The UN Convention on the Rights of the Child (United Nations, 1989) and other international and regional human rights treaties require states to prohibit corporal punishment of children in all settings of their lives. The banning of corporal punishment in parenting across 51 countries from around the world (Global Initiative to End All Corporal Punishment of Children, 2017) is an example of how international policy advocacy can put pressure on governments to change the law. However, although legally sanctioned codes of conduct help regulate parental actions to some degree, banning parental use of corporal punishment practices does not necessarily mean that parents will adopt effective alternative practices or prevent children from developing behavioral and emotional problems. Parents clearly need replacement strategies that are effective.

Implication for Practice: Professional advocacy to ban corporal punishment should only occur alongside advocacy for the provision of evidence-based parenting programs to teach parents alternative noncoercive means of disciplining children.

OTHER FACTORS INFLUENCING PARENTING

Parental capacity occurs in, and is influenced by, broader social and economic factors affecting the population. Although these factors are not easily influenced by parents, how they cope with the demands and stress of daily life can nevertheless affect their psychological availability to children and their parenting practices. Such factors include the state of the global economy; level of unemployment; level of pollution; availability of affordable housing, good schools, quality child care; food security; availability of welfare payments to support needy families; amount of personal debt, interest rates, and level of inflation; and access to extended family financial and emotional support. These broader social and economic factors can influence the level of personal stress parents experience and test their coping resources in managing stress. High levels of parental stress are often associated with children having more behavioral and emotional problems (Anthony et al., 2005).

Implication for Practice: Practitioners delivering parenting programs should determine the presence of external stressors that parents are dealing with and seek to enhance parent strategies for dealing with everyday stress.

PARENTING ACROSS THE LIFE SPAN

Each phase of human development is associated with new challenges and demands for parents. Parental knowledge and skills in dealing with responsibilities and tasks relating to their child's current phase of development are cumulative and always interact with previously learned knowledge, tasks, and responsibilities from previous phases of development. From the moment of conception, parents have primary responsibility to ensure that they create the conditions that enable their children to develop in a safe, healthy, and responsive environment so they can acquire the social, emotional, cognitive, academic, and physical competencies they need to flourish and reach their potential (Black et al., 2017).

Although there is considerable emphasis on the importance of the parent–child relationship in the first 3 years of life (e.g., Heckman, 2012), parenting as a social role continues to evolve, and the current parenting practices that children and adolescents experience exert an influence throughout the life of both a parent and the child. An adult can be highly distressed if he or she has experienced destructive interpersonal conflict with their own parents, parents-in-law, or adult siblings. Conversely, good relationships with their own parents when children are young can be an enormous support to parents. Table 2.1 summarizes the changing nature of parental tasks and responsibilities at different stages of development from infancy to early adulthood.

IMPLICATIONS FOR POLICY AND PRACTICE

The important role that parents play in influencing developmental outcomes for children has been highlighted by many scientific and professional groups (e.g., National Academies of Science Engineering and Medicine, 2016). These groups include professional organizations, such as those for psychologists, social workers, pediatricians, psychiatrists, and educators (American Academy of Pediatrics, 2016). There is now clear recognition that enhancing parents' access to evidence-based parenting programs is important so that parents are better prepared to undertake their responsibilities. Three emerging themes are influencing the provision of parenting programs.

INCREASING ADOPTION OF POPULATION-BASED APPROACH TO PARENTING PROGRAMS

Despite the importance of parenting, most of the major investments in improving access to evidence-based parenting programs in the United States, United Kingdom, Australia, and many other countries are focused on the most vulnerable or disadvantaged families. This process of

Table 2.1: Parental Tasks and Responsibilities Across the Life Span

Phase of Life	Major Parental Tasks and Responsibilities
Antenatal (from conception to birth)	• Create healthy environment for growth of fetus. • Ensure healthy nutrition of mother. • Restrict use of alcohol, tobacco, or other drugs. • Create a "nest" for the care of baby. • Ensure family has sufficient financial resources to support a family. • Ensure safe, affordable housing. • Reach agreement with partner about parental roles and responsibilities.
Infancy (0–1.5 years)	• Promote safe, secure attachment. • Be caring and nurturing. • Provide adequate stimulation to infants. • Be observant and responsive to infants' cues. • Ensure that engaging activities are available. • Establish predictable routines. • Establish sleep patterns. • Find suitable child care as needed. • Read often to children. • Restrict exposure to screens (smartphones, tablets, computers, TV).
Toddlerhood (1.5–3 years)	• Use praise and positive attention to encourage desirable behavior. • Use incidental teaching to promote children's language and communication. • Encourage children to do things for themselves. • Promote positive sibling interaction. • Foster cooperation with adult instructions and age-appropriate rules. • Establish consistent, predictable discipline routines for inappropriate behavior.
Preschool (4–6 years)	• Encourage a love of learning through books. • Facilitate successful sibling and peer interactions. • Prepare children for making a successful transition to school. • Communicate well with children's teachers.
Middle childhood (7–12 years)	• Show an interest in children's learning and communicate well with children's teacher. • Help children learn self-management skills. • Encourage participation in physical activity and out-of-school activities. • Assist children in managing their emotions (anxiety, disappointment). • Assist children in becoming comfortable with gender identity and sexuality.
Teen (13–17 years)	• Encourage independence skills (e.g., transport, study, cooking, washing). • Support teenagers to solve their own problems, including practical and social problems. • Teach skills to help teenagers manage peer pressure and temptations that may lead to undesirable consequences. • Support teenagers to develop and pursue recreational interests. • Teach teenagers how to discuss opinions calmly and how to listen to others' views with respect. • Encourage teenagers to contribute to the family's chores.
Young adult (18–25 years)	• Provide guidance to promote financial independence. • Provide advice and support regarding life decisions (e.g., study, employment, housing). • Provide advice and practical support regarding childrearing.

targeting "needy" or "high-risk" families, while laudable, can inadvertently create some stigma for parents who are identified as requiring parenting support. An alternative, less stigmatizing approach involves the development of a comprehensive, multilevel system of parenting support that enables a much wider range of parents to participate. To be successful, such an approach needs a blend of universal and targeted programs so that differences in the needs of parents can be accommodated. Furthermore, this approach needs to avoid an inoculation approach that targets a single developmental stage to provide parenting support (e.g., infancy), to recognize that parenting challenges are not confined to the first 1,000 days of life, and that good and poor parenting influence the well-being of children throughout childhood, adolescence, early adulthood, and indeed through a person's adult life. Parents need to access parenting advice that is relevant to the current ages and developmental levels of their children (from infancy to young adulthood). Parents also need to access advice that addresses the unique circumstances that may arise from having a child with special needs (parents of preterm children; parents of children with a disability, autism, chronic health condition, ADHD, conduct problems, anxiety, depression) or challenging parenting context (families experiencing separation or divorce, parental absence due to military deployment, parental incarceration, parental ill health), or parental mental illness or substance abuse. Because of the diverse needs of families and variations in the level of support parents require to resolve difficulties they experience, an integrated, population-based parent and family support system is needed.

CONSUMER ENGAGEMENT AND CREATING "PULL" DEMAND FOR PARENTING PROGRAMS

Lack of parental engagement and high dropout rates of parents from existing parenting programs have highlighted the need to enhance parental engagement in parenting programs (Sanders & Kirby, 2012). Parents are more likely to be motivated to participate in a program when it has become socially normative and provides an opportunity for parents to achieve their own valued outcomes in a destigmatized context. When parents themselves, as consumers, are consulted about the kinds of supports and information they are seeking about parenting and programs are planned accordingly to address these needs, parents are more likely to become involved and to advocate for others to also participate.

MOVING FROM INDIVIDUAL- TO COMMUNITY- LEVEL SUPPORT FOR PARENTING

The adoption of a population-based approach to parenting support can facilitate the creation of caring, nurturing communities that are "family-friendly" places to live and raise children. A community engagement strategy around parenting can create a broad coalition of stakeholders interested in building a community's capacity to support parents with evidence-based programs. Stakeholders can include local government, agencies serving families (including state and not-for-profit organizations), schools, child care centers, local libraries, law enforcement agencies, local businesses, the media, and parent consumers. The ultimate goal is increasing a sense of collective efficacy—a belief that a community has the capacity and resources to solve problems and promote a positive and nurturing community and neighborhood environment for raising children and youth.

TAKE-HOME MESSAGES

- Parenting has a pervasive influence on children's development and life opportunities.
- Parents' capacity to raise their children well is influenced by a range of potentially modifiable social, emotional, relational, and contextual factors.
- Parenting programs provide a common pathway to influence many diverse child and parent outcomes.
- A blending of universal and targeted programs drawing on a common theoretical framework is needed to ensure local partnerships can effectively collaborate in delivery programs that work across the community.

REFERENCES

American Academy of Pediatrics. (2016). Poverty and child health in the United States. *Pediatrics, 137,* 1–14. doi:10.1542/peds.2016-0339

Anthony, L. G., Anthony, B. J., Glanville, D. N., Naiman, D. Q., Waanders, C., & Shaffer, S. (2005). The relationship between parenting stress, parenting behavior and preschoolers' social competence and behavior problems in the classroom. *Infant and Child Development, 14,* 133–154. doi:10.1002/icd.385

Askew, C., & Field, A. P. (2008). The vicarious learning pathway to fear 40 years on. *Clinical Psychology Review, 28,* 1249–1265. doi:10.1016/j.cpr.2008.05.003

Australian Bureau of Statistics. (2012). *Childhood education and care, Australia, June 2011* (Catalogue No. 4402.0). Canberra, Australia: Australian Bureau of Statistics.

Azar, S. T. (2002). Child abuse. In M. Bornstein (Ed.), *Handbook of Parenting* (Vol. 4, pp. 361–388). New York, NY: Erlbaum.

Azar, S. T., Barnes, K., & Twentyman, C. T. (1988). Developmental outcomes in physically abused children: Consequences of parental abuse or the effects of a more general breakdown in caregiving behaviors? *The Behavior Therapist, 11,* 27–32.

Azar, S. T., Okado, Y., Stevenson, M. T., & Robinson, L. R. (2013). A preliminary test of a social information processing model of parenting risk in adolescent males at risk for later physical child abuse in adulthood. *Child Abuse Review, 22,* 268–286. doi:10.1002/car.2244

Barnett, O., Miller-Perrin, C. L., & Perrin, R. D. (2005). *Family violence across the lifespan: An introduction.* Thousand Oaks, CA: Sage.

Beach, S. R., Brody, G. H., Barton, A. W., & Philibert, R. A. (2016). Exploring genetic moderators and epigenetic mediators of contextual and family effects: From gene x environment to epigenetics. *Development and Psychopathology, 28,* 1333–1346. doi:10.1017/S0954579416000882

Bedford, V. H., Volling, B. L., & Avioli, P. S. (2000). Positive consequences of sibling conflict in childhood and adulthood. *International Journal of Aging and Human Development, 51,* 53–69. doi:10.2190/G6PR-CN8Q-5PVC-5GTV

Belsky, J., & de Haan, M. (2011). Annual research review: Parenting and children's brain development: The end of the beginning. *Journal of Child Psychology and Psychiatry, 52,* 409–428. doi:10.1111/j.1469-7610.2010.02281.x

Biglan, A. (2015). *The nurture effect: How the science of human behavior can improve our lives and our world*. Oakland, CA: New Harbinger.

Black, M. M., Walker, S. P., Fernald, L. C. H., Andersen, C. T., Digirolamo, A. M., Lu, C., . . . Grantham-Mcgregor, S. (2017). Early childhood development coming of age: Science through the life course. *The Lancet, 389*, 77–90. doi:10.1016/S0140-6736(16)31389-7

Bornstein, M. H., & Bradley, R. H. (2014). *Socioeconomic status, parenting, and child development*. New York, NY: Routledge.

Bronfenbrenner, U. (1986). Ecology of the family as a context for human development: Research perspectives. *Developmental Psychology, 22*, 723–742. doi:10.1037/0012-1649.22.6.723

Brooks-Gunn, J., & Duncan, G. J. (1997). The effects of poverty on children. *The Future of Children, 7*, 55–71. doi:10.2307/1602387

Brumariu, L. E. (2015). Parent-child attachment and emotion regulation. *New Directions for Child and Adolescent Development, 148*, 31–45. doi:10.1002/cad.20098

Buist, K. L., Deković, M., & Prinzie, P. (2013). Sibling relationship quality and psychopathology of children and adolescents: A meta-analysis. *Clinical Psychology Review, 33*, 97–106. doi:10.1016/j.cpr.2012.10.007

Center on the Developing Child at Harvard University. (2016). *From best practices to breakthrough impacts: A science-based approach to building a more promising future for young children and families*. Boston, MA: Author.

Charach, A., Carson, P., Fox, S., Ali, M. U., Beckett, J., & Lim, C. G. (2013). Interventions for preschool children at high risk for ADHD: A comparative effectiveness review. *Pediatrics, 131*, e1584–e1604. doi:10.1542/peds.2012-0974

Chazan-Cohen, R., Raikes, H., Brooks-Gunn, J., Ayoub, C., Pan, B. A., Kisker, E. E., . . . Fulignis, A. S. (2009). Low-income children's school readiness: Parent contributions over the first five years. *Early Education and Development, 20*, 958–977. doi:10.1080/10409280903362402

Cobham, V. E., Filus, A., & Sanders, M. R. (2017). Working with parents to treat anxiety-disordered children: A proof of concept RCT evaluating Fear-less Triple P. *Behaviour Research and Therapy, 95*, 128–138. doi:org/10.1016/j.brat.2017.06.004

Cobham, V. E., & Sanders, M. R. (2009). *Fear-less Triple P group program for parents of anxiety-disordered children*. Brisbane, Australia: Triple P International.

Dittman, C. K., Henriquez, A., & Roxburgh, N. (2016). When a non-resident worker is a non-resident parent: Investigating the family impact of fly-in, fly-out work practices in Australia. *Journal of Child and Family Studies, 25*, 2778–2796. doi:10.1007/s10826-016-0437-2

Duffy, A., Alda, M., Crawford, L., Milin, R., & Grof, P. (2007). The early manifestations of bipolar disorder: A longitudinal prospective study of the offspring of bipolar parents. *Bipolar Disorders, 9*, 828–838. doi:10.1111/j.1399-5618.2007.00421.x

Epstein, R. A., Fonnesbeck, C., Potter, S., Rizzone, K. H., & McPheeters, M. (2015). Psychosocial interventions for child disruptive behaviors: A meta-analysis. *Pediatrics, 136*, 947–960. doi:10.1542/peds.2015-2577

Felitti, V. J., Anda, R. F., Nordenberg, D., Williamson, D. F., Spitz, A. M., Edwards, V., . . . Marks, J. S. (1998). Relationship of childhood abuse and household dysfunction to many of the leading causes of death in adults. The Adverse Childhood Experiences (ACE) Study. *American Journal of Preventive Medicine, 14*, 245–258. doi:10.1016/S0749-3797(98)00017-8

Fives, A., Purcell, L., Heary, C., NicGabhainn, S., & Canavan, J. (2014). *Parenting support for every parent: A population-level evaluation of Triple P in Longford Westmeath. Final Report*. Athlone, Ireland: Longford Westmeath Parenting Partnership. Retrieved from http://www.atlanticphilanthropies.org/app/uploads/2015/09/Report-Parenting-Support-for-Every-Parent.pdf

Galindo, C., & Sheldon, S. B. (2011). School and home connections and children's kindergarten achievement gains: The mediating role of family involvement. *Early Childhood Research Quarterly*. doi:10.1016/j.ecresq.2011.05.004

Gardner, F., Montgomery, P., & Kerr, W. (2015). Transporting evidence-based parenting programs for child problem behavior (age 3–10) between countries: Systematic review and meta-analysis. *Journal of Clinical Child & Adolescent Psychology*, 45, 749–762. doi:10.1080/15374416.2015.1015134

Glaser, K., Price, D., Di Gessa, G., Montserrat, E., & Tinker, A. (2013). *Grandparenting in Europe: Family policy and grand-parents' role in providing child care.* London, England: Grandparent Plus.

Global Initiative to End All Corporal Punishment of Children. (2017). *States which have prohibited all corporal punishment.* Retrieved January 27, 2017, from http://www.endcorporalpunishment.org/progress/prohibiting-states/

Gordon, I., Zagoory-Sharon, O., Leckman, J. F., & Feldman, R. (2010). Oxytocin and the development of parenting in humans. *Biological Psychiatry*, 68, 377–382. doi:10.1016/j.biopsych.2010.02.005

Grasso, D. J., Henry, D., Kestler, J., Nieto, R., Wakschlag, L. S., & Briggs-Gowan, M. J. (2016). Harsh parenting as a potential mediator of the association between intimate partner violence and child disruptive behavior in families with young children. *Journal of Interpersonal Violence*, 31, 2102–2126. doi:10.1177/0886260515572472

Hart, B., & Risley, R. T. (1995). *Meaningful differences in the everyday experience of young American children.* Baltimore, MD: Brookes.

Healy, K. L., & Sanders, M. R. (2014). Randomized controlled trial of a family intervention for children bullied by peers. *Behavior Therapy*, 45, 760–777. doi:10.1016/j.beth.2014.06.001

Healy, K. L., Sanders, M. R., & Iyer, A. (2015). Parenting practices, children's peer relationships and being bullied at school. *Journal of Child and Family Studies*, 24, 127–140. doi:10.1007/s10826-013-9820-4

Heckman, J. J. (2012). *The Heckman equation.* Retrieved January 27, 2017, from http://heckmanequation.org/content/resource/invest-early-childhood-development-reduce-deficits-strengthen-economy

Hoff, E. (2006). How social contexts support and shape language development. *Developmental Review*, 26, 55–88. doi:10.1016/j.dr.2005.11.002.

Hoghughi, M. S., & Long, N. (2004). *Handbook of parenting: Theory and research for practice.* London, England: Sage.

Jones, S., & Bentall, R. P. (2008). A review of potential cognitive and environmental risk markers in children of bipolar parents. *Clinical Psychology Review*, 28, 1083–1095. doi:10.1016/j.cpr.2008.03.002

Jones, S., Calam, R., Sanders, M. R., Diggle, P. J., Dempsey, R., & Sadhnani, V. (2014). A pilot web based positive parenting intervention to help bipolar parents to improve perceived parenting skills and child outcomes. *Behavioural and Cognitive Psychotherapy*, 42, 283–296. doi:10.1017/S135246581300009X

Jones, T. L., & Prinz, R. (2005). Potential roles of parental self-efficacy in parent and child adjustment: A review. *Clinical Psychology Review*, 25, 341–363. doi:10.1016/j.cpr.2004.12.004

Kirby, J. N. (2015). The potential benefits of parenting programs for grandparents: Recommendations and clinical implications. *Journal of Child and Family Studies*, 24, Advance Online Publication. doi:10.1007/s10826-015-0123-9

Kirby, J. N., & Sanders, M. R. (2014). A randomized controlled trial evaluating a parenting program designed specifically for grandparents. *Behaviour Research and Therapy*, 52, 35–44. doi:10.1016/j.brat.2013.11.002

Laughlin, L. (2013). *Who's minding the kids? Child care arrangements: Spring 2011. Current Population Reports* (pp. 70–135). Washington, DC: US Census Bureau.

Luthar, S. (2006). Resilience in development: A synthesis of research across five decades. In D. Cicchetti & S. Cohen (Eds.), *Developmental psychopathology: Risk disorder and adaptation* (Vol. 3, pp. 739–795). New York, NY: Wiley.

Mackey, E. R., Herbert, L., Monaghan, M., Cogen, F., Wang, J., & Streisand, R. (2016). The feasibility of a pilot intervention for parents of young children newly diagnosed with type 1 diabetes. *Clinical Practice in Pediatric Psychology, 4*, 35–50. doi:10.1037/cpp0000123

McDowell, D. J., & Parke, R. D. (2009). Parental correlates of children's peer relations: An empirical test of a tripartite model. *Developmental Psychology, 45*, 224–235. doi:210.1037/a0014305

Moffitt, T. E. (2013). Childhood exposure to violence and lifelong health: Clinical intervention science and stress-biology research join forces. *Development and Psychopathology, 25*, 1619–1634. doi:10.1017/S0954579413000801

Moffitt, T. E., Arseneault, L., Belsky, D., Dickson, N., Hancox, R. J., Harrington, H., . . . Caspi, A. (2011). A gradient of childhood self-control predicts health, wealth, and public safety. *Proceedings of the National Academy of Sciences of the United States of America, 108*, 2693–2698. doi:10.1073/pnas.1010076108

Moffitt, T. E., & the Klaus-Grawe 2012 Think Tank. (2013). Childhood exposure to violence and life-long health: Clinical intervention science and stress-biology research join forces. *Development & Psychopathology, 25*, 1619–1634. doi:10.1017/S0954579413000801

Moffitt, T. E., Poulton, R., & Caspi, A. (2013). Lifelong impact of early self-control: Childhood self-discipline predicts adult quality of life. *American Scientist, 101*, 352–359.

Morawska, A., Calam, R., & Fraser, J. (2015). Parenting interventions for childhood chronic illness: A review and recommendations for intervention design and delivery. *Journal of Child Health Care, 19*, 5–17. doi:10.1177/1367493513496664

Morawska, A., Mitchell, A., Burgess, S., & Fraser, J. (2016). Effects of Triple P parenting intervention on child health outcomes for childhood asthma and eczema: Randomised controlled trial. *Behaviour Research and Therapy, 83*, 35–44. doi:10.1016/j.brat.2016.06.001

Morawska, A., Sanders, M. R., Goadby, E., Headley, C., Hodge, L., McAuliffe, C., . . . Anderson, E. (2011). Is the Triple P-Positive Parenting Program acceptable to parents from culturally diverse backgrounds? *Journal of Child and Family Studies, 20*, 614–622. doi:10.1007/s10826-010-9436-x

Morawska, A., Sanders, M. R., O'Brien, J., McAuliffe, C., Pope, S., & Anderson, E. (2012). Practitioner perceptions of the use of the Triple P—Positive Parenting Program with families from culturally diverse backgrounds. *Australian Journal of Primary Health, 18*, 313–320. doi:10.1071/PY11106

Murray, J., Bijleveld, C. C. J. H., Farrington, D. P., & Loeber, R. (2014). *Effects of parental incarceration on children: Cross-national comparative studies*. Washington, DC: American Psychological Association.

National Academies of Science Engineering and Medicine. (2016). *Parenting matters: Supporting parents of children ages 0–8*. Washington, DC: The National Academies Press.

Özyurt, G., Gencer, Ö., Öztürk, Y., & Özbek, A. (2015). Is Triple P Positive Parenting Program effective on anxious children and their parents? Fourth month follow up results. *Journal of Child and Family Studies*, 1–10. doi:10.1007/s10826-015-0343-z

Patterson, G. R. (1982). *Coercive family process*. Eugene, OR: Castalia.

Patterson, G. R., Reid, J. B., Jones, R. R., & Conger, R. E. (1975). *A social learning approach to family intervention: Families with aggressive children* (Vol. 1, p. 526). Eugene, OR: Castalia.

Pickering, J. A., Crane, M. E., Hong, J., Nickel, A., & Sanders, M. A. (2017). *A randomized controlled trial of a parenting program to improve sibling relationships*. Manuscript submitted for publication.

Pickering, J. A., & Sanders, M. R. (2017). Integrating parents' views on sibling relationships to tailor an evidence-based parenting intervention for sibling conflict. *Family Process, 56*, 105–125. doi:10.1111/famp.12173

Piquero, A., Jennings, W., Diamond, B., Farrington, D., Tremblay, R., Welsh, B., & Gonzalez, J. (2016). A meta-analysis update on the effects of early family/parent training programs on anti-social behavior and delinquency. *Journal of Experimental Criminology, 12*, 229–248. doi:10.1007/s11292-016-9256-0

Powell, D. R., Son, S.-H., File, N., & San Juan, R. R. (2010). Parent–school relationships and children's academic and social outcomes in public school pre-kindergarten. *Journal of School Psychology, 48*, 269–292. doi:10.1016/j.jsp.2010.03.002

Prinz, R. J. (2012). Effective parenting to prevent adverse outcomes and promote child well-being at a population level. In D. G. Mick, S. Pettigrew, C. Pechmann, & J. L. Ozanne (Eds.), *Transformative consumer research for personal and collective well-being.* New York, NY: Routledge/Taylor & Francis Group.

Prinz, R. J. (2016). Parenting and family support within a broad child abuse prevention strategy: Child maltreatment prevention can benefit from public health strategies. *Child Abuse & Neglect, 51*, 400–406. doi:10.1016/j.chiabu.2015.10.015

Rapee, R. M., Schniering, C. A., & Hudson, J. L. (2009). Anxiety disorders during childhood and adolescence: Origins and treatment. *Annual Review of Clinical Psychology, 5*, 311–341. doi:10.1146/annurev.clinpsy.032408.153628

Rholes, W., Simpson, J. A., Blakely, B. S., Lanigan, L., & Allen, E. A. (1997). Adult attachment styles, the desire to have children, and working models of parenthood. *Journal of Personality, 65*, 357–385. doi:10.1111/j.1467-6494.1997.tb00958.x

Richards, M., McWilliams, B., Allcock, L., Enterkin, J., Owens, P., & Woodrow, J. (1994). *The family ties of English prisoners: The results of the Cambridge project on imprisonment and family ties.* Cambridge, UK: Centre for Family Research, University of Cambridge.

Ross, H. S., & Lazinski, M. J. (2014). Parent mediation empowers sibling conflict resolution. *Early Education and Development, 25*, 259–275. doi:10.1080/10409289.2013.788425

Rothbart, M. K., & Bates, J. E. (2006). Temperament. In N. Eisenberg, W. Damon, & R. M. Lerner (Eds.), *Handbook of child psychology: Vol. 3, Social, emotional, and personality development* (6th ed., pp. 99–166). Hoboken, NJ: Wiley.

Sanders, M. R., Healy, K. L., Grice, C., & Del Vecchio, T. (2017). Evidence-based parenting programs: Integrating science into school-based practice. In M. Thielsking & M. D. Terjesen (Eds.), *Handbook of Australian school psychology: Bridging the gaps in international research, practice, and policy* (pp. 537–551). New York, NY: Springer.

Sanders, M. R., & Keown, L. J. (2017). Parenting in couple relationships. In J. Fitzgerald (Ed.), *Foundations for couples' therapy: Research for the real world* (pp. 302–309). New York, NY: Routledge.

Sanders, M. R., & Kirby J. (2012). Consumer engagement and the development, evaluation and dissementation of evidence-based parenting progarms. *Behavior Family, 43*, 236–250. doi:10.1016/j.beth.2011.01.005

Sanders, M. R., Kirby, J. N., Tellegen, C. L., & Day, J. J. (2014). The Triple P-Positive Parenting Program: A systematic review and meta-analysis of a multi-level system of parenting support. *Clinical Psychology Review, 34*, 337–357. doi:10.1016/j.cpr.2014.04.003

Sanders, M. R., & Mazzucchelli, T. G. (2013). The promotion of self-regulation through parenting interventions. *Clinical Child and Family Psychology Review, 16*, 1–17. doi:10.1007/s10567-013-0129-z

Sanders, M. R., & Woolley, M. L. (2005). The relationship between maternal self-efficacy and parenting practices: Implications for parent training. *Child: Care, Health and Development, 31*, 65–73. doi:10.1111/j.1365-2214.2005.00487.x

Saphire-Bernstein, S., Way, B. M., Kim, H. S., Sherman, D. K., & Taylor, S. E. (2011). Oxytocin receptor gene (OXTR) is related to psychological resources. *Proceedings of the National Academy of Sciences of the United States of America, 108*, 15118–15122. doi:10.1073/pnas.1113137108

Shanker, S. (2012). *Calm, alert, and learning: Classroom strategies for self-regulation.* Toronto, ON, Canada: Pearson.

Shonkoff, J. P. (2011). Protecting brains, not simply stimulating minds. *Science, 333*, 982. doi:10.1126/science.1206014

Shonkoff, J. P., Siegel, B. S., Garner, A. S., Dobbins, M. I., Earls, M. F., Mcguinn, L., . . . Wood, D. L. (2012). The lifelong effects of early childhood adversity and toxic stress. *Pediatrics, 129*, e232–e246. doi:10.1542/peds.2011-2663

Slagt, M., Dubas, J. S., Deković, M., & van Aken, M. A. G. (2016). Differences in sensitivity to parenting depending on child temperament: A meta-analysis. *Psychological Bulletin, 142*, 1068–1110. doi:10.1037/bul0000061

United Nations. (1989). Convention on the Rights of the Child. *Treaty Series, 1577*, 3.

Walker, L. S., & Zeman, J. L. (1992). Parental response to child illness behavior. *Journal of Pediatric Psychology, 17*, 49–71. doi:10.1093/jpep-sy/17.1.49

Waters, S. F., Virmani, E. A., Thompson, R. A., Meyer, S., Raikes, H. A., & Jochem, R. (2010). Emotion regulation and attachment: Unpacking two constructs and their association. *Journal of Psychopathology and Behavioral Assessment, 32*, 37–47. doi:10.1007/s10862-009-9163-z

Wilder, S. (2014). Effects of parental involvement on academic achievement: a meta-synthesis. *Educational Review, 66*, 377–397. doi:10.1080/00131911.2013.780009

Wolff, M. S., & van Ijzendoorn, M. H. (1997). Sensitivity and attachment: A meta-analysis on parental antecedents of infant attachment. *Child Development, 68*, 571–591. doi:10.1111/j.1467-8624.1997.tb04218.x

Wood, B. L., Lim, J., Miller, B. F., Cheah, P., Zwetsch, T., Ramesh, S., & Simmens, S. (2008). Testing the biobehavioral family model in pediatric asthma: Pathways of effect. *Family Process, 47*, 21–40. doi:10.1111/j.1545-5300.2008.00237.x

EMERGENCE OF A POPULATION APPROACH TO EVIDENCE-BASED PARENTING SUPPORT

MATTHEW R. SANDERS AND RONALD J. PRINZ

INTRODUCTION

The emergence of an evidence-based population approach to the provision of parenting and family support services represented a major change in how parenting programs have been deployed (Prinz & Sanders, 2007; Sanders, 1999). Traditionally, empirically supported parenting programs based on social learning theory, applied behavior analysis, cognitive-behavioral principles, and developmental theory were delivered as individual or group treatments and primarily offered to parents of children with clinical-level behavior problems (McMahon, 1999). This approach was, and remains, an outstanding success in providing effective family intervention to assist parents of children with conduct problems.

Despite the clear value of the approach variously known as behavioral parent training (McMahon & Forehand, 2005), parent management training (Kazdin, 2008), and behavioral family intervention (Sanders & Dadds, 1982), these parenting programs have not been used widely enough by practitioners or mental health and family support agencies. Intervention provided active "coaching" to parents in how to apply positive parenting strategies and included strategies for both rearranging antecedents (e.g., providing engaging activities and giving clear, calm, instructions) and the application of contingent consequences to change children's prosocial behavior (e.g., descriptive praise and positive attention) and problem behavior (e.g., planned ignoring, a logical consequence such as removing a toy, nonexclusionary and exclusionary time-out). The interventions were primarily applied to disruptive behavior and conduct disorders. Over time, it became clear that problematic or dysfunctional parenting practices were implicated in the origins and maintenance of a wider range of child problems (including internalizing behavior), and that the techniques of behavior change, when used appropriately, could also be successfully applied by parents to prevent or manage many of these problems.

We begin this chapter with a brief overview of the historical context that led to the emergence of population-based strategies. We then describe the Triple P system as an exemplar of a population-based approach to providing parenting support that involves using an integrated multilevel system of parenting interventions. We discuss the essential criteria that need to be met for a population approach to work in practice and some of the distinguishing features of the Triple P system as a model. Finally, we discuss implications for policy, research, and practice derived from large-scale dissemination of the Triple P system.

HISTORICAL FOUNDATIONS OF THE POPULATION APPROACH TO PARENTING SUPPORT

Behavioral parent training has its roots in the early 1960s (Hanf & Kling, 1973; Patterson, 1976; Tharp & Wetzel, 1969; Wahler, 1969), when major changes were beginning to take place in the field of mental health. The prevailing paradigm of psychoanalytic and other intrapsychic assumptions about the origins of mental health disorders was beginning to give way to a new paradigm focused on the role of the environment. Child mental health witnessed this shift more quickly than the adult area, perhaps because it was easier to recognize the impact of the family environment on children. Accordingly, mental health professionals began to call on parents as active "therapists" to alter the social-environmental conditions and contingencies operating at home and elsewhere in their children's lives. This approach to treatment, namely behavioral parent training, emerged from social learning theory and applied behavior analysis, eventually becoming the cornerstone of clinical child psychology (O'Dell, 1974).

By the 1990s, behavioral parent training specifically, and evidence-based treatments more generally, had become mainstream. The benefits to children and families with social, emotional, and behavioral problems were well documented, but a strong interest in prevention began to emerge. There are several compelling reasons to pursue prevention as it applies to children, youth, and their families. Intervening early in a developmental trajectory before children's problems rise to a dysfunctional level is less costly in both economic and human terms (Arruabarrena & De Paúl, 2012). Furthermore, letting problems continue without intervention until adolescence can make the intervention task more difficult because family processes might have significantly deteriorated and youth problems become more serious and intransigent.

In the child maltreatment area, prevention is essential because (a) many parents engage in problematic parenting that does not usually trigger official involvement of the child welfare system; (b) waiting until child protective services become involved before intervening often results in the accumulation of adverse consequences for children, families, and society; and (c) the cost of child maltreatment is high, and the return on investment in prevention not only offsets this cost but also yields other economic and societal benefits (e.g., associated with gains in child development productivity and reduction in child protection and juvenile justice involvement; Christian & Schwarz, 2011). Finally, in comparison with treatment, prevention strategies have a greater potential to reach large numbers of families (Altafim & Linhares, 2016).

The result of research and application over several decades is a broad and cogent approach to parenting and family intervention. A generic term to describe this approach is *evidence-based parenting support* (EBPS), which denotes a process of change that aims to positively influence the prosocial development, including social, emotional, and physical well-being, of children and youth through corresponding changes in those aspects of the family environment implicated in the development, maintenance, and alteration of children's behavior and capabilities. EBPS involves the systematic application of data-based principles and techniques derived from social learning theory, public health, and relevant behavioral, affective, and cognitive change strategies, with an emphasis on reciprocity of change and relationship building among family members.

WHAT IS THE TRIPLE P SYSTEM?

The Triple P—Positive Parenting Program (Sanders, 2008, 2012) is a unique, multilevel system of parenting support derived from social learning theory, applied behavior analysis, cognitive-behavioral principles, developmental theory, and population health principles discussed previously. It extends traditional population health models through a unique blending of universal and targeted parenting programs and covers the full spectrum of interventions, including universal, selected, and indicated prevention; early intervention; and treatment. The specific parenting and behavior change principles and strategies employed in the Triple P system are outlined by Sanders and Mazzucchelli in Chapter 4 of this volume.

GOALS OF THE TRIPLE P SYSTEM

The overarching aim of the Triple P system is to reduce the prevalence rates of serious social, emotional, and behavioral problems in children and the level of child maltreatment in the community. It seeks to achieve these outcomes by making high-quality EBPS programs widely available to all parents. The specific parent and child outcomes that the population approach to parenting support seeks to accomplish are as follows:

1. To increase the number of parents who have the necessary knowledge, skills, and confidence to parent their children and adolescents well by increasing the number of parents who complete an evidence-based, culturally appropriate parenting program.
2. To increase the number of children and adolescents who are thriving socially, emotionally, and academically.
3. To decrease the number of children and adolescents who develop serious social, emotional, and behavioral problems.
4. To decrease the number of children and adolescents who are maltreated or at risk of being maltreated by their parents.

DEFINING A POPULATION APPROACH
TO PARENTING SUPPORT

The Triple P system builds on the principles of population health articulated by Rose (2008). There are two separate, but related, aspects to the population approach used in Triple P. The first relates to targeting prevalence rates of child and parent problems and using population indicators to judge impact. The second aspect involves conceptualizing the intervention needed in terms of how larger segments of the community are engaged (in contrast to a typical clinical intervention that is conceptualized in terms of action with one family at a time). The goals are to move the population distribution curve of a targeted child outcome (e.g., social, emotional, and behavioral problems or child maltreatment), a risk factor (e.g., coercive parenting), or a protective factor (e.g., positive parenting) toward healthier levels of functioning and to decrease the distribution of the targeted problem, enabling a higher proportion of the eligible population to be within healthy limits. In the population approach, if the population mean for a target problem and its standard deviation can be shifted toward healthier positive functioning by a defined amount (e.g., one half to one third of a standard deviation on a reliable population measure), many more children and families will benefit as a result compared to an approach that exclusively targets only the most disadvantaged (e.g., children in the bottom quintile of the income distribution). The study of distribution curves to identify, on measures at a population level, the proportion of a population above and below the clinical diagnosis threshold before and after an intervention differentiates the population approach from a clinical treatment approach (Sarkadi, Sampaio, Kelly, & Feldman, 2014).

PRINCIPLES OF POSITIVE PARENTING

Triple P has five basic principles of positive parenting designed to promote children's development by teaching them the social and emotional skills they need to thrive: (a) ensuring a safe, engaging, and healthy environment for children; (b) having a positive learning environment; (c) using assertive, consistent, and nonviolent discipline; (d) having reasonable expectations of children and oneself as a parent; and (e) taking care of oneself. These principles are applied through a range of specific techniques to change behavioral and emotional problems and promote child development (e.g., brief quality time, incidental teaching, descriptive praise, quiet time). The specific techniques applied vary depending on the developmental level of the child and the type of problem or parenting focus (see Chapter 4, this volume, for a description of these principles and how they are operationalized into parenting skills).

THE MULTILEVEL SYSTEM EXPLAINED

Triple P uses a multilevel system of parenting support rather than a single "one-size-fits-all" program as parents differ in terms of their needs, the type of problems they experience, and the type of help they require and prefer. The system includes programs of varying intensity, ranging from very "light-touch" single-session programs through to more intensive multiweek group or individual programs. Different resources are available for all developmental periods, from infants, toddlers, preschool, elementary, or primary school–aged children to adolescents. Different delivery modalities have also been developed for some levels to enhance population reach, including individual, group, self-directed, telephone-based, and web-based delivery formats. Figure 3.1 summarizes the multilevel system of intervention and identifies different modes of delivery available at each level.

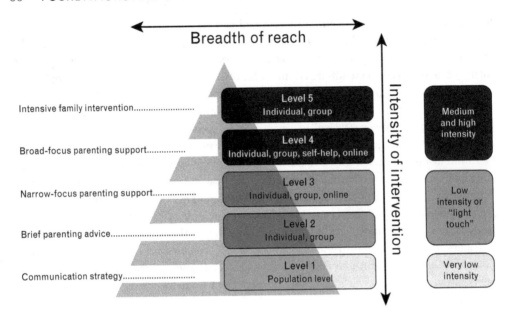

FIGURE 3.1: The multilevel Triple P system.

When the system is delivered at a population level, it is expected that the majority of parents with mild-to-moderate problems will participate in brief, low-intensity parenting support programs. These light-touch programs include accessing information (simple tips and parenting advice) through a communications campaign known as Stay Positive (Level 1; Chapter 35, this volume). Parents can also access parenting tip sheets through one to four brief consultations with a primary care provider (Levels 2–3). They can attend one or more large-group parenting seminars (Level 2), one or more smaller group topic-specific discussion group (Level 3). Families who have children with more serious problems or if parenting is complicated by other family problems are more likely to need a more intensive multisession program. At Level 4, more intensive programs include Group Triple P or Group Teen Triple P (8 sessions), Standard Triple P (10 sessions), Triple P Online (8 modules), Group Stepping Stones Triple P for families with a child with a disability (8 sessions), or Group Lifestyle Triple P for families of children with obesity or health issues (14 sessions). At Level 5, additional program modules can be added to address broader family issues, as in Enhanced Triple P for families with parental adjustment or relationship difficulties (up to 12 sessions), Pathways Triple P for families at risk of child maltreatment (up to 9 sessions), or Family Transitions Triple P for parents going through separation or divorce (up to 12 sessions). Table 3.1 provides a summary of Triple P intervention levels and formats.

Parents enter the system of parenting support at the level most appropriate to their needs, preferences, and capacity to engage in the requirements of the specific program. The system is not linear. Parents do not need to start at the least intensive level of intervention and move progressively toward the more intensive levels. The system is designed so that parents participate in as little or as much as they require to address their current parenting concerns. The model is based on the assumption that most parents (with some professional guidance when necessary) can choose between the level of support and mode of delivery they need. Providing flexibility for parents to select a program appropriate to their needs avoids expensive population screening to identify families considered at risk or providing only intensive programs.

Table 3.1: Triple P System Programs, Contexts, and Delivery Modes

Level of Intervention	Target Population	Intervention Methods	Facilitators
Level 1 Communications strategy • *Universal Triple P*	All parents interested in information about parenting and promoting their child's development.	Coordinated communications strategy raising awareness of parent issues and encouraging participation in parenting programs. May involve electronic and print media (e.g., brochures, posters, websites, television, talk-back radio, newspaper and magazine editorials).	Typically coordinated by communications, health or welfare staff.
Level 2 Health promotion strategy/brief selective intervention • *Selected Triple P:* *Triple P Seminars* *Brief Primary Care Triple P* • *Selected Teen Triple P:* *Teen Triple P Seminars* *Brief Primary Care Teen Triple P*	Parents interested in parenting education or with specific concerns about their child's development or behavior.	Health promotion information or specific advice for a discrete developmental issue or a child's minor behavior problem. May involve a group seminar format or brief (up to 20 minutes) telephone or face-to-face clinician contact.	Practitioners who provide parent support during routine well-child health care (e.g., health, education, allied health, and child care staff).
• *Selected Stepping Stones Triple P:* *Stepping Stones Triple P Seminars*	Parents of children with disabilities, with concerns as above.	A parallel program with a focus on disabilities.	Same as above.
Level 3 Narrow-focus parent training • *Primary Care Triple P* • *Triple P Discussion Groups* • *Triple P Online Brief* • *Primary Care Teen Triple P* • *Teen Triple P Discussion Groups*	Parents with specific concerns as above who require consultations or active-skills training.	Brief program (about 80 minutes over four sessions or 2-hour discussion groups) combining advice, rehearsal, and self-evaluation to teach parents to manage a discrete child problem behavior. May involve telephone contact.	Same as for Level 2.
• *Primary Care Stepping Stones Triple P*	Parents of children with disabilities, with concerns as above.	A parallel program with a focus on disabilities.	Same as above.

(continued)

Table 3.1: Continued

Level of Intervention	Target Population	Intervention Methods	Facilitators
Level 4 Broad focus parent training • *Standard Triple P* • *Group Triple P* • *Self-Directed Triple P* • *Triple P Online Standard* • *Standard Teen Triple P* • *Group Teen Triple P* • *Self-Directed Teen Triple P* • *Standard Stepping Stones Triple P* • *Group Stepping Stones Triple P* • *Self-Directed Stepping Stones Triple P*	Parents wanting intensive training in positive parenting skills. Typically parents of children with behavior problems such as aggressive or oppositional behavior. Parents of children with disabilities who have or are at risk of developing behavioral or emotional disorders.	Broad focus program (about 10 hours over 8–10 sessions) focusing on parent–child interaction and the application of parenting skills to a broad range of target behaviors. Includes generalization-enhancement strategies. May be self-directed; online; involve telephone or face-to-face clinician contact; group sessions. A parallel series of tailored programs with a focus on disabilities.	Intensive parenting intervention workers (e.g., mental health and welfare staff and other allied health and education professionals who regularly consult with parents about child behavior). Same as above.
Level 5 Intensive family intervention • *Enhanced Triple P*	Parents of children with behavior problems and concurrent family dysfunction, such as parental depression or stress or conflict between partners.	Intensive individually tailored program with modules (60- to 90-minute sessions), including practice sessions to enhance parenting skills, mood management and stress coping skills, and partner support skills.	Intensive family intervention workers (e.g., mental health and welfare staff).
• *Pathways Triple P*	Parents at risk of child maltreatment. Targets anger management problems and other factors associated with abuse.	Intensive individually tailored or group program with modules (60- to 120-minute sessions depending on delivery model), including attribution retraining and anger management.	Same as above.
• *Group Lifestyle Triple P*	Parents of overweight or obese children. Targets healthy eating and increasing activity levels as well as general child behavior.	Intensive 14-session group program (including telephone consultations) focusing on nutrition, healthy lifestyle, and general parenting strategies. Includes generalization enhancement strategies.	As above plus dieticians/ nutritionists with experience in delivering parenting interventions.
• *Family Transitions Triple P*	Parents going through separation or divorce.	Intensive 12-session group program (including telephone consultations) focusing on coping skills, conflict management, general parenting strategies, and developing a healthy coparenting relationship.	Intensive family intervention workers (e.g., counselors, mental health and welfare staff).

The system of support is designed so that parents can enter, exit, and reenter the system on multiple occasions depending on the family's needs and current circumstances (Figure 3.2 and 3.3). For example, a parent of a toddler or preschooler might complete the eight-session Group Triple P, then participate in a brief program on a specific issue, such as a 2-hour Triple P Discussion Group (e.g., Managing Fighting and Aggression) when the child is in elementary or primary school and then, if needed, a Teen Triple P program for any concerns in adolescence. Figure 3.2 illustrates an example of a family engaging in tailored Triple P interventions at two separate developmental stages. The approach assumes that parenting support needs to be continuously accessible throughout childhood and adolescence as new problems can emerge or old ones reemerge at any time in a child's development. It is expected that a lower proportion of parents who have had an effective early intervention will need intensive later intervention, but they may wish to access lighter touch programs relating to later phases of development.

To effect change on population-level indicators of child functioning or well-being, a significant proportion of the population of eligible parents with children in a target age group must be reached. Participation in parenting programs is not socially normative in most countries (after almost-universal engagement in birthing or antenatal classes in Western countries). In many communities, relatively few parents complete an EBPS program (Sanders, Markie-Dadds, Rinaldis, Firman, & Baig, 2007; Sanders et al., 2008). To achieve a meaningful reduction in the prevalence rates of children who develop serious problems, specific outreach and engagement strategies are needed to ensure that a sufficient number of parents complete evidence-based prevention and intervention programs.

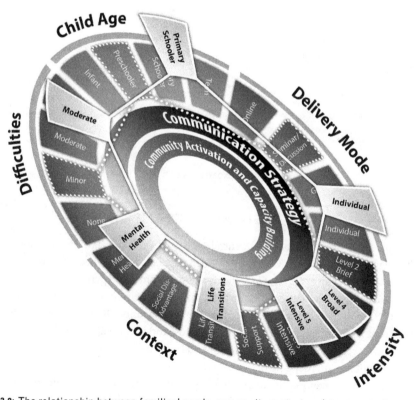

FIGURE 3.2: The relationship between families' needs, community context, and program options.

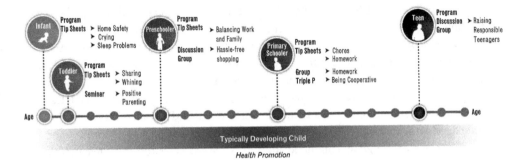

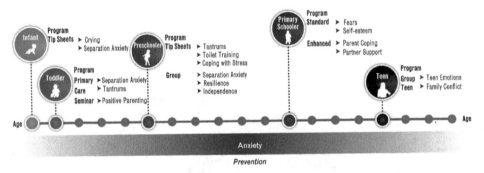

FIGURE 3.3: Individual differences in parents' experience of Triple P over time.

SELF-REGULATION FRAMEWORK

The principle of self-regulation was a central construct in the design of the Triple P system from the beginning (Sanders & Glynn, 1981). Self-regulation is a process whereby individuals are taught skills to change their own behavior and become independent problem-solvers in a broader social environment that supports parenting and family relationships (Karoly, 1993; Sanders, 2008; Sanders & Mazzucchelli, 2013). The approach to self-regulation used in Triple P is derived from social cognitive theory. According to Bandura (1986, 2000), the development of self-regulation is related to personal, environmental, and behavioral factors; these factors operate separately but are interdependent.

Self-regulation is a central skill in building parental competence and confidence. In the context of Triple P, this involves teaching parents strategies to modify their own ways of thinking and behaving that enable them to become independent problem-solvers (Karoly, 1993). The aim is for parents to become self-sufficient (parent effectively, trust their judgment, seek support if they need it); have self-efficacy (believe they can effectively deal with parenting situations); self-manage (set goals, choose strategies to try, and self-evaluate their success); have a sense of personal agency (attribute positive changes to their own or their child's efforts); and be able to problem-solve (define a problem, identify potential solutions, develop a tailored parenting plan, try it out, review, and refine as necessary). The success of a parenting intervention is not only parents' ability to resolve current issues but also their capacity to address a diverse range of family challenges over time with relative autonomy (Sanders & Mazzucchelli, 2013).

To further operationalize the concept of self-regulation as it applies to parenting, consider the characteristics of a parent who has strong self-regulatory capability. Such a parent (e.g., a mother) would have a clear sense of the sorts of behaviors, skills, and values she wishes to manifest in herself as a parent and adult, instill in her child, and foster in her home and broader community. She would have realistic expectations of herself, of others in a caring role for her child, and knowledge regarding what she could reasonably expect of her child at different points of his or her development. Monitoring her performance against these standards would be automatic, rather than conscious or deliberate (Papies & Aarts, 2011). On detecting a discrepancy between a personal standard and current performance (be it performance of herself, her child, or a significant other), goal-relevant habitual behavior would be brought under her volitional control. Deliberately attending to these behaviors would provide information from which she develops hypotheses about why the discrepancy has come about and clarity with regard to her objectives.

The parent would have a rich repertoire of knowledge and skills from which to draw when formulating options and developing a plan or new way of responding. These would include not only parenting and interpersonal skills (such as clear instructions, descriptive praise, and planned ignoring), but also personal management skills (such as verbal self-cueing, attentional control, and ideas on how to arrange her environment to prompt and reinforce her own behavior). The parent would proceed to execute the plan and evaluate the outcome, revising the plan as required until a desirable outcome has been achieved. At this point, the parent would allow the new behavior(s) to come under the control of new environmental stimuli—that is, her behavior would again become automatic.

The self-regulating parent would have positive expectations that she could successfully enact her plan and bring about future positive outcomes. She would be self-reflective, open to and capable of identifying personal strengths and weaknesses, successes and failures, without being unhelpfully critical. Her self-evaluations and attributions would be constructive and serve to increase her competence and confidence for addressing future challenges. As parents attempt to achieve their goals, they are frequently confronted with potentially emotion-arousing situations.

Affect is naturally linked to goal-directed behavior. Diverse feeling states arise as a result of success, failure, frustration, slowing, or delay in the pursuit of goals (Carver & Scheier, 2011). But, feelings can also be elicited by stimuli as a result of respondent conditioning. The self-regulating parent would be capable of accepting, ignoring, or downregulating emotions that might otherwise interfere with successful goal pursuit (Koole, van Dillen, & Sheppes, 2011). However, and importantly, rather than ploughing through life with a stony grimness, the parent would mostly enjoy the process. Having genuinely high self-regulatory capacity, the parent would have the ability to deploy conscious self-regulation skills when required and suspend them when they are not required. On occasion, the parent would let go of end-state cognitions to enjoy the moment and experience contentment (Csikszentmihalyi, 1990).

LOGIC MODEL FOR THE TRIPLE P SYSTEM

Figure 3.4 presents Triple P's logic model as it has been applied to reducing the prevalence of child maltreatment (Chapter 39, this volume). To produce sustained improvements in child outcomes, changes are predicted to occur at the child, parent, and family levels and wider community and policy levels.

WHAT IS REQUIRED FOR A POPULATION APPROACH TO WORK?

A number of criteria need to be met for a population approach to be successful.

CONSISTENT THEORETICAL FRAMEWORK

The content and structure of the program components need to be theoretically based and consistent and make sense at all levels of the intervention. Characterizing the theoretical base of a system of parenting support is not straightforward. Triple P is not easy to pigeonhole into a simplistic grouping, such as a behavioral, cognitive-behavioral, attachment-based, or public health group. While the theoretical foundations of Triple P evolved from a broad body of basic and applied research on principles of learning, cognitive, and behavior change, over time the model has evolved to become a population approach to parenting support. This shift from individuals to populations demanded a different and expanded theoretical base. As a consequence, Triple P is best characterized as a transtheoretical model that integrates empirically supported principles of behavioral, cognitive, and affect change at a population level.

This integrative approach allowed new knowledge, principles, and understandings from different areas of research in experimental and applied psychology and, more broadly, the social and behavioral sciences that are relevant to enhancing human potential over the life span to be incorporated. For example, recent advances in cognitive neuroscience, epigenetic, and developmental research highlighting the importance of early brain development, developmental plasticity, and the quality of early parent–child relationships provides further theoretical justification for Triple P's historically strong emphasis on the importance of self-regulation in both parents and children. Developmental research on the importance of early learning, in particular language, has informed Triple P's emphasis on the important role of communication interactions to promote school readiness (Hart & Risley, 1995). Marmot's (2010) important work on the social determinants of health and the concept of "proportionate universalism" provides theoretical justification for adopting a whole-of-population approach, and research on the adverse long-term effects of poverty and social disadvantage continues to inform Triple P's research and development work on how to better serve vulnerable, marginalized, socially disadvantaged, and socially excluded groups. Organizational theories and advances in implementation science have informed how Triple P is disseminated to organizations.

Triple P System Logic Model

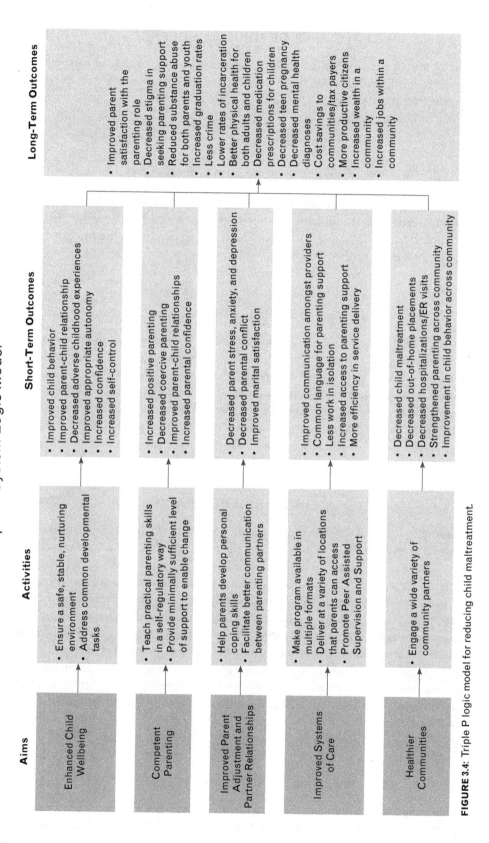

FIGURE 3.4: Triple P logic model for reducing child maltreatment.

PRINCIPLE OF MINIMAL SUFFICIENCY

An integrated population health approach that draws on the principle of *minimal sufficiency* refers to the process whereby parents receive the minimally sufficient or "just enough" level of intervention support needed to resolve the problem and to enable the parents to parent their children confidently, competently, and independently.

EVIDENCE-BASED APPROACH

With an evidence-based system of intervention, it almost goes without saying that each of the program components should have well-established efficacy and effectiveness. The system for professional training and supervision also needs to be empirically validated and able to produce a well-trained and supported workforce (Chapter 34, this volume).

WIDE APPEAL

To be in a position to achieve population-level change, EBPS programs need broad appeal for a variety of parents, taking into account their needs and preferences. There are many needs that EBPS can serve, including, but not limited to, improvement of school readiness, early intervention for children's problems, prevention of child maltreatment, and reduction of risk for subsequent adverse outcomes (such as substance abuse, academic difficulties or school dropout, teen parenthood, and delinquency). Similarly, parental preference for different modes of program delivery can be met by providing a variety of options, such as individual, group, telephone, online, and brief formats.

ACCESS AND REACH

Quality and breadth of programming are necessary but not sufficient for a population approach to work. Access and reach are also important. Access can be optimized by involving many delivery venues and settings across a broad range of service sectors (e.g., health, education, mental health, and community nongovernmental organizations); drawing on program personnel from several professional disciplines, and utilizing a range of delivery formats couched in destigmatized contexts. Reach is critical as well. A cogent population approach needs to ensure that enough parents participate to reduce the prevalence rates associated with parenting difficulties and child problems while increasing parental confidence and efficacy. Having a system that engages large numbers of eligible parents is key to prevalence reduction. Strategies that destigmatize parental participation in a parenting and family program help to eliminate barriers to broad community reach. Normalizing such participation via various strategies (e.g., framing, media messages, modeling) can help take the stigma out of seeking parenting support.

UNIVERSAL PROVISION

Another important consideration pertains to universal preventive intervention. Sometimes, the field intimates that universal versus targeted prevention is a forced choice, and that the two intervention approaches are mutually exclusive. An alternative is blended prevention, by which universal and targeted interventions are integrated into a combined approach. The universal representations of the program are less intensive and more appealing to a broader parental audience, while targeted programming can include more intensive intervention and can serve the specialized needs associated with narrower segments of the parent and child population (e.g., parents with mental health problems, parents of children with a disability). The notion of "proportionate universalism" is apropos here, which emphasizes the resourcing and delivering of universal programming at a scale and intensity proportionate to the degree of need. Proportionate universalism speaks to the criticism by social justice advocates, who worry that universal interventions might leave those with the greatest need without adequate support.

FAVORABLE POLICY ENVIRONMENT

Finally, a supportive policy and funding environment is critical to the sustainability of a population approach to EBPS (Kirp, 2012). Without policy support, programs that have been introduced in the context of a funded trial cannot be sustained without securing additional funding to continue.

DISTINGUISHING FEATURES OF TRIPLE P

In addition to taking a population approach to providing EBPS, Triple P differentiates itself from other evidence-based parenting programs because it is a comprehensive tiered system of parenting support covering a wider range of ages than most other evidence-based programs. Some of its key characteristics that collectively define its uniqueness are outlined next.

LIFE-SPAN PERSPECTIVE

Although Triple P began as a home-delivered intervention with parents of preschool-aged children with disruptive behavior problems (Sanders & Glynn, 1981), the approach gradually evolved to include interventions covering infancy through to adolescence. A life-span perspective emphasizes both continuities (love, care, attention, time, age-appropriate activities, consistency, monitoring) and discontinuities (increasing importance of peers, independence, conflict management, negotiation and problem-solving skills) at different phases of the life cycle. It also emphasizes the importance of the parent–child relationship and the need for parenting support at every stage of parenting, including for grandparents.

MULTIPLE LEVELS AND DIFFERENT DELIVERY MODALITIES

As noted, the multilevel system of Triple P is based on an assumption that the type of support parents need varies as a function of the severity and complexity of a child's or parent's problems. For example, more intensive support, such as Standard Stepping Stones Triple P (10 individual sessions), may be initially needed for a parent of a preschool child with severe challenging behavior in the context of a developmental disability. This allows for one-on-one support and skill development tailored to the family's unique needs. If the intervention is successful, the same parents might later benefit from a briefer (2-hour) Triple P Discussion Group to address peer relationship difficulties once their child is at school. In this model, as the same child may face new or additional challenges at a later stage of development, parents may require a "booster" to refine their strategies for a new developmental phase, which can be achieved using a brief intervention format. This brief contact avoids burden on the family and reinforces parenting skills, and the group format provides a supportive environment for parents to share concerns, ideas, and successes.

EXTENSIVE CONSUMER AND END-USER FEEDBACK TO ENSURE CONTEXTUAL RELEVANCE

Sanders and Kirby (2014) argued that programs are more likely to be adopted, implemented, and sustained if there is meaningful engagement with consumers (parents) and end users (practitioners). Consumer and end-user engagement can occur through focus groups or participation in consumer advisory groups to help program implementers tackle issues such as how best to engage parents, particularly in vulnerable, hard-to-reach, marginalized, or high-risk groups. This engagement process can include conducting online surveys and focus groups with target parents to determine the cultural relevance and acceptability of Triple P with ethnically diverse populations (Chapter 28, this volume).

DEMONSTRATED EFFECTIVENESS ACROSS DIFFERENT CULTURAL GROUPS

The population approach seeks to share basic positive parenting principles and strategies with the entire population of parents. For the approach to work, it has to be culturally relevant and acceptable to all parents to enable engagement in the program in large numbers. Over time, a wealth of quantitative and qualitative evidence has shown that Triple P's core principles and parenting techniques are considered culturally acceptable to a wide range of parents both with individual countries and across continents (Chapter 30, this volume). For example, a range of parents from different cultural and language backgrounds have rated Triple P strategies favorably (Morawska et al., 2011). Cultural acceptability studies have been conducted in Australasia (Australia, New Zealand); in the United Kingdom and Ireland; in Europe (Germany, the Netherlands, Belgium, Switzerland, Sweden, Turkey); in North America (United States, Canada), Central America (Panama), and South America (Chile); in the Caribbean (Curaçao); and in Africa (South Africa, Kenya); South East Asia (Singapore, Indonesia); North Asia (Japan, China); and the Middle East (Iran). These countries range from individualist cultures in Western Europe, North America, and Australasia to more collectivistic cultures in Asia, Latin America, Africa, and the Middle East. Taken together, these studies showed a remarkable consistency across cultures and language groups in the acceptability of the basic positive parenting methods used in Triple P. However, for specific programs to work in a local context, practitioners need to ensure that the examples used to illustrate principles and strategies are locally relevant.

CULTURALLY INFORMED DELIVERY

Within any culture, there are individual differences across the community in views relating to raising children (e.g., use of corporal punishment in disciplining children), and based on cultural and religious beliefs, individual parents and practitioners may have strongly held views on practices and expectations across the developmental spectrum (e.g., the benefits of co-sleeping with young children or the acceptability and timing of adolescent behaviors associated with dating and relationships). The use of a self-regulation framework greatly facilitates cultural acceptability as parents are encouraged to formulate their own goals informed by their culture, history, traditions, and priorities.

The Triple P model embraces cultural diversity and has made numerous efforts over the past two decades to facilitate the participation of parents from different cultural and ethnic groups. For example, Turner et al. (Chapter 28, this volume) have developed and tested a collaborative partnership adaptation model (CPAM) as a cultural adaptation process that can be applied to determine the relevance and cultural acceptability of existing Triple P resources and delivery formats. CPAM is a multistage process that involves working collaboratively with communities (elders, professionals, parents) to gain knowledge and a clear understanding of the specific local context. Focus groups with parents and with practitioners have been used effectively to explore the perceived usefulness, relevance, and cultural acceptability of the program; these groups have included specific parenting techniques, types of group activities, and audiovisual and written material used in the program. Changes are not made to the existing program if there is little evidence suggesting that the program is culturally unacceptable. Core Triple P program resources (e.g., parent workbooks, slide presentations, video resources) have been translated into and successfully used in approximately 20 languages across 27 countries (at time of writing), but have required little alteration other than language. It is important to note that not all English resources are available in every language.

The CPAM process aims to identify possible changes that need to be made (if any) to core program materials to increase consumer acceptability where there may be a significant barrier to participation, executing these changes through revisions of program materials, then testing the modified or adapted program in a robust evaluation, such as conducting a randomized controlled trial (RCT) (Frank, Keown, Dittman, & Sanders, 2015). Finally, if trial outcomes are successful using culturally adapted materials, the recommended changes can be made to program resources, materials, and the delivery of professional training. Such changes are not undertaken lightly as they need to be funded and can be expensive (e.g., reshooting material for a DVD). Tailored resources and delivery have been successfully developed for Australian indigenous communities, and additional cultural resources have been developed for Māori communities in New Zealand.

INCLUSIVENESS

The model of intervention seeks to involve all parents and parental figures in a caring role with children. This includes mothers, fathers, step-parents, grandparents, and other relevant extended family members and caregivers who have a caring responsibility for a child. True inclusiveness requires practitioners to be able to tailor program delivery sensitively for the unique needs of diverse community groups (e.g., parents with mental health or substance abuse problems; parents with low literacy; migrant and refugee families).

Research on parenting shows that mothers are far more likely to participate in a parenting program than fathers. There is less evidence available relating to the effects of Triple P and other parenting programs with fathers than mothers (Chapter 16, this volume). Although the meta-analysis by Sanders, Kirby, Tellegen, and Day (2014) found positive outcome effects for fathers, the effect sizes were larger for mothers than fathers. In the past 5 years, a concerted effort to increase father participation in Triple P has taken place. For example, Frank et al. (2015) conducted focus groups and a web survey with fathers to identify parenting topics and issues that were particularly relevant to fathers and to identify barriers and enablers to their participation. These father-relevant topics were then systematically introduced into the delivery of Group Triple P for a mixed group of mothers and fathers. Both mothers and fathers reported positive outcomes on child behavior, parenting, and conflict over parenting and a high level of consumer satisfaction. Other efforts to increase father engagement have been the offering of Triple P Online and delivering versions of Triple P in the workplace (see Haslam, Sanders, & Sofronoff, 2013).

There have also been several trials showing grandparents benefit from participating in Triple P (Kirby & Sanders, 2014), and a new variant of Triple P for Early Child Educators (Chapter 21, this volume) is currently being evaluated.

PRINCIPLE OF PROPORTIONATE UNIVERSALISM TO REDUCE SOCIAL DISPARITIES

Universal programs have been criticized on the basis that parents who function well or are socioeconomically advantaged will consume scarce resources that are desperately needed to assist more vulnerable or disadvantaged families. Rather than decreasing inequality, universal interventions are seen as increasing social disparities. It should be noted that parenting difficulties and child social, emotional, and behavioral problems exist across all socioeconomic groups; however, the risk of disproportionate assistance can be mitigated by applying the principle of proportionate universalism (Marmot, 2010) in population rollouts. When this principle is applied correctly, special efforts are made to engage the most vulnerable parents. Having tailored programs for specific types of children and families (e.g., Family Transitions Triple P for families going through separation or divorce, Indigenous Triple P, and Pathways Triple P for families at risk of maltreatment) and having outreach and engagement strategies that specifically target vulnerable and hard-to-reach families helps ensure the neediest families have the opportunity to participate. Successful examples of this include offering Triple P to incarcerated parents, through organizations that support parents with mental illnesses, and through services for immigrant and refugee families.

MEASUREMENT AND PROMOTION OF FIDELITY

Like all EBPS programs, positive outcomes are unlikely if a program at any level is not implemented with fidelity by competent, well-trained practitioners, as has been evident in a small number of studies that have failed to achieve positive outcomes with Triple P (e.g., Little et al., 2012). In an effort to promote program fidelity, each program has a detailed practitioner manual that outlines session-by-session procedures for monitoring a practitioner's adherence to core intervention protocols and for measuring client outcomes (e.g., Sanders, Markie-Dadds, & Turner, 2001). Sanders and Kirby (2015) developed an observational tool for assessing both session content (material covered) and process fidelity (quality of the delivery).

FLEXIBLE TAILORING OF CONTENT AND PROCESS

To ensure that practitioners tailor interventions to the specific needs of individual families, Mazzucchelli and Sanders (2010) developed guidelines to encourage practitioners to vary the content and process of their delivery in certain circumstances. Low-risk variations to content included changing examples to make them more salient (e.g., for fathers or for parents from a specific cultural background), whereas high-risk variations included leaving out a core procedure or skill altogether (e.g., how to use time-out effectively). Low-risk variations to process included extending or shortening the length of sessions based on the observed skill of the parent. Other variations to process were considered high risk (e.g., not practicing a core skill such as descriptive praise or preparation for and use of time-out). Practitioners are encouraged to use their judgment, experience, and knowledge of the client population to tailor program delivery to the needs of participating parents while ensuring the core content and session activities are delivered.

PROGRAM COORDINATION AND MANAGEMENT

Achieving population-level change requires interagency collaboration, local alliances, and partnerships to support the promotion and implementation of the program and to ensure trained practitioners deliver agreed intervention targets. A program director or manager appointed from a lead agency is needed to manage and coordinate the logistics associated with the entire rollout, including the organization of training and supervision of the multidisciplinary, multisector, or agency workforce. The best examples of the successful implementation of the Triple P system have all paid close attention to the importance of forming effective partnerships and alliances (e.g., Chapter 40, this volume; Prinz, Sanders, Shapiro, Whitaker, & Lutzker, 2009; Sanders et al., 2008).

ROUTINE EVALUATION OF OUTCOMES

Each Triple P variant includes a set of recommended measures that can be used to evaluate the outcomes achieved by parents. We recommend the use of measures that are in the public domain and can be used free of charge by agencies. Outcomes are generally assessed at four levels—child outcomes, parenting outcomes, family adjustment outcomes, and consumer satisfaction (Chapter 36 in this volume for details). In some programs, behavioral diaries and behavior-monitoring forms are also recommended to track child or parent progress through the intervention (Level 3–5 programs). The Triple P Provider Network includes an Automated Client Scoring and Reporting Application (ASRA) to enable practitioners to track and monitor client outcomes using a selection of child, parent, and family outcome measures. ASRA is available to all accredited Triple P practitioners to enable individual client data to be entered and scored and to produce a profile of the assessment results. When data collection procedures become routinized and embedded in the way programs are delivered, higher rates of assessment form completion by parents are more likely.

CHILD WELL-BEING INDICATORS TRACKED AT A POPULATION LEVEL

Beyond the clinical assessment of outcomes for individual families, the hallmark of a population approach is having suitable population-level indicators of child outcomes to track changes in prevalence rates over time. Different kinds of population-level data can be used for this purpose. Prinz and colleagues (2009) used routinely collected state government administrative data to evaluate the effects of the Triple P system on aggregate county-level rates of child maltreatment, emergency room visits due to child maltreatment–related injuries and out-of-home placements. Fives, Purcell, Heary, NicGabhainn, and Canavan (2014) used in-person household surveys to assess the prevalence of child social and emotional problems, whereas Sanders and colleagues (2008) used a random digit dialing telephone survey to assess behavioral problems and parenting practices at a population level.

Each data source has its own advantages and limitations. The International Parenting Survey (Lee et al., 2014) is a web-based population survey instrument used to gain information on child behavior, parenting practices, parent participation on parenting programs, and parent preferences concerning how they wish to access parenting information. This survey can be used to measure population-level outcomes relating to parenting. However, it should be noted that currently there is no widely accepted or used measure of parenting that is routinely collected at the population level. Such an instrument would be extremely valuable but would need to be validated in multiple countries to facilitate cross-cultural comparisons.

IMPLEMENTATION FRAMEWORK

Developments in implementation science and practical learnings from large-scale rollouts of Triple P have highlighted the critical importance of adequate preparation of organizations involved in the implementation of Triple P before, during, and after staff have been trained to implement new evidence-based practices (McWilliam, Brown, Sanders, & Jones, 2016). Purveyor organizations responsible for the dissemination of interventions have increasingly incorporated principles of implementation science and organizational change (Fixsen, Naoom, Blase, Friedman, & Wallace, 2005) in working with organizations interested in adopting a population approach. The Triple P Implementation Framework, developed by Triple P International, provides a framework of support for communities and organizations through five phases of implementation: engagement, commitment and contracting, implementation planning, training and accreditation, and implementation and maintenance.

DELIVERY AND PARTICIPATION TARGETS

A major challenge for all population-based rollouts is to ensure trained practitioners and the agencies employing them honor their commitments to deliver programs to an agreed number of parents over a defined period (e.g., a 3-year plan). The targets negotiated with agencies need to be realistic given competing commitments and demands. Targets are more likely to be achieved when the programs that staff are being trained in are organized and advertised in advance of practitioners undertaking training so that practitioners can begin delivery as soon as possible after training is completed. Having too great a delay between training and starting program implementation can erode practitioners' confidence and decrease the likelihood of implementation.

SUSTAINED INVESTMENT IN RESEARCH AND DEVELOPMENT

There has been a sustained commitment over almost four decades of ongoing research and development to improve Triple P. The commitment to building a strong scientific foundation for each component in the system has ensured that Triple P has kept evolving (informed by evidence of outcomes) in an effort to remain relevant to the contemporary needs of parents. This ongoing search for innovation has led to the development and evaluation of new program variants following the development of the core five-level system. These additional programs included programs for parents of adolescents (Teen Triple P), parents of a child who has a disability (Stepping Stones Triple P), parents at risk of child maltreatment (Pathways Triple P), parents experiencing separation and divorce (Family Transitions Triple P), parents of overweight and obese children (Lifestyle Triple P), a suite of online programs (Triple P Online and Triple P Online Brief), and two programs under development for parents of children with chronic health problems (Positive Parenting for Healthy Living Triple P) and parents of infants (Baby Triple P). Each of these variants is discussed in Parts 2 and 3 of the current volume.

HOW EFFECTIVE IS TRIPLE P?

Evaluating a multilevel system of parenting support is complex. Each level can be evaluated as well as the system as a whole. The traditional effectiveness question needs to be reworked for a multilevel system to ask, What intervention is effective with which child problems at what age, delivered by which delivery modality, at what level of intensity, to which type of parent and family, in what community context, and how does the intervention effect come about? The evidence base supporting different aspects of the Triple P system has evolved gradually over almost decades and is now quite extensive, but never complete. Space precludes a thorough overview of the evidence supporting Triple P, and readers are referred to various meta-analyses that have been conducted on Triple P (e.g., Nowak & Heinrichs, 2008; Sanders et al., 2014). A comprehensive database of Triple P studies is maintained by the Parenting and Family Support Centre (https://www.pfsc.uq.edu.au/research/evidence).

Evidence relating to the effectiveness of Triple P should also be considered in the wider context of the substantial evidence relating to the effectiveness of social learning approaches to parent intervention (e.g., Dretzke et al., 2009; Lundahl, Tollefson, Risser, & Lovejoy, 2008). At the time of writing, 137 RCTs and 261 total evaluations of Triple P have been conducted around the world, with a further 20 trials in progress that we know of, making it the most extensively studied parenting program yet developed.

A search of the Triple P evidence base conducted in February 2017 revealed that a total of 773 papers have been written on Triple P. Of those, 499 were theoretical or conceptual papers, and 274 were evaluation papers (comprising 137 RCTs). The vast majority of evaluation studies showed positive findings for Triple P (95%). There were 13 papers with null findings for Triple P (5%). A total of 134 papers (49%) had no developer involvement. This research is truly international and has involved researchers from 30 different countries, 1,187 individual researchers from 358 academic or research institutions across multiple cultures and 20 languages. The Triple P evidence base involves a mix of developer-involved and independent studies. Approximately 49% of all Triple P evaluation studies have been independent of developers, with positive effects obtained for both independent and developer-involved studies (Sanders et al., 2014). Of the few papers (13) with null findings, 63% involved the developer. A more detailed discussion of the importance of both developer-led and independent-of-developer studies are discussed in more detail by Sanders and Kirby (Chapter 43, this volume).

The evaluation philosophy adopted has been to critically evaluate every element of the Triple P system. Only programs that have sufficient evidence of effectiveness are included in the system. Programs that have failed to reach this evidence threshold are not disseminated. The strength of evidence required for a program to be included since 2000 is the successful completion and publication of the results of a randomized clinical trial, robust quasiexperimental evaluation, or a series of well-conducted single-subject experiments (Sanders, 2012).

The first outcome studies were published in the early 1980s as single-subject experiments for an individually administered intervention now known as Standard Triple P, a Level 4 intervention (Sanders & Dadds, 1982; Sanders & Glynn, 1981). A number of different approaches to evaluation have been employed, including single-subject experiments, RCTs, meta-analyses, quasiexperimental evaluations, uncontrolled service-based evaluations, economic analyses, and qualitative studies using focus group and survey methodology (Sanders, 2012). Several studies have use mixed methods combining RCTs and qualitative evaluation. The most recent and comprehensive meta-analysis of Triple P involving 101 studies and over 16,000 parents (Sanders et al., 2014) showed that each level of the intervention was associated with significant positive intervention effects for child social, emotional, and behavioral problems; parental self-efficacy and satisfaction; positive parenting; family conflict; and parental distress.

In addition, three large-scale population-level evaluations have been conducted of the implementation of the multilevel system. The most comprehensive of these deployed a place-based randomized design (Prinz et al., 2009; Prinz, Sanders, Shapiro, Whitaker, & Lutzker, 2016) and found implementation of the Triple P system produced meaningful reductions in founded cases of child maltreatment, hospital-treated child maltreatment–related injuries, and out-of-home placements, with statistically significant and large Cohen d effect sizes ranging from 1.01 to 1.61.

A more recent evaluation of the population-level effects of the Triple P system in Midland counties in Ireland (Fives et al., 2014) showed, based on an epidemiological household survey of parents with children aged 3–8 years, that counties implementing the Triple P system, compared to a county receiving services as usual, experienced a 37% reduction in the number of borderline and clinically elevated cases of children with social and emotional problems. This finding was consistent with findings showing population effects on a measure of child adjustment from an earlier large-scale population trial in Australia that used a similar approach (Sanders et al., 2008).

Several other large-scale replication studies are in progress that will add further important information about outcomes achieved with a population approach. There have been insufficient numbers of studies to conduct systematic review or meta-analysis of the population effects of implementing the Triple P system. All population trials have targeted young children, aged 3–9 years, and no population trials have been conducted with very young children (under 3 years) or with adolescents. Ways of further strengthening the evidence base are discussed in chapters 45 and 46 in this volume.

CHALLENGES IN MAKING A POPULATION APPROACH WORK

As a population approach to parenting support is still novel, only a few population trials have been published to date. However, much has been learned about how to best deploy the Triple P system to achieve outcomes at a population-level change. This section discusses these challenges and ways of addressing them.

IMPLEMENTATION WITH FIDELITY

Population-level change is unlikely if programs are not implemented with fidelity. It is important that staff who deliver Triple P are competent. Unskilled, inadequately trained, and poorly supervised staff are unlikely to produce satisfactory outcomes with families. Indeed, a poorly delivered parenting program can have adverse effects on children and parents (Scott, Carby, & Rendu, 2008). It is therefore essential that funds are allocated to ensure necessary technical assistance and support are available to the implementation team and supervision is provided to practitioners delivering programs. The routine use of the peer-assisted supervision and support (PASS) model of supervision offers opportunities for practitioners to improve their consultation skills in working with parents and should be extensively used in population rollouts of any program (McPherson, Sanders, Schroeter, Troy, & Wiseman, 2016; Sanders & Murphy-Brennan, 2013). Access to supervision is particularly important in low-resource settings (Chapter 29, this volume), where the available workforce is unlikely to have graduate-level professional training. This situation characterizes many low- and middle-income countries; many indigenous communities, particularly in regional and remote areas; and parents living in impoverished neighborhoods in large cities.

FAMILY DIVERSITY

Critics of EBPS have expressed concern that programs that apply social learning and cognitive-behavioral principles are trying to eliminate diversity in parenting, fearing that everyone will start to parent their children in the same way and that children will become too similar. This is an understandable but unfounded concern. The adoption of a self-regulation framework where parents choose their own personal goals, and the parenting strategies they wish to apply in achieving those goals, means that different parents completing the same program have a unique experience. Parents are encouraged to acknowledge individual temperament-based differences in children and to focus on teaching children the social and emotional skills they need to achieve success in education, relationships, and life goals.

A "HOME" FOR THE DELIVERY OF
EVIDENCE-BASED PARENTING PROGRAMS

The population model underpinning Triple P is based on an assumption that there is no single service delivery context for the provision of EBPS. The task of supporting good parenting is a shared community responsibility that is inherently multidisciplinary and must involve multiple agencies and settings. There are considerable advantages of having parenting services and programs better coordinated and having a shared community vision focused on prevalence rate reduction of problems through competent parenting. Better coordination and planning between services about delivery of Triple P ensure greater efficiency and better access for parents, avoid unnecessary duplication or overservicing, and ensure more cost-effective utilization of scarce resources. The American Academy of Pediatrics (2016) has argued that pediatric practices can function as a "medical home" for the provision of coordinated parenting advice and education. Similar arguments can be made for use of the early childhood education settings and schools as a point of wide (if not universal) access to parents in a destigmatized context.

ROLE OF PARENTING PROGRAMS IN ADDRESSING
ADVERSE CHILDHOOD EXPERIENCES

A great deal of focus is currently being placed on the importance of services being trauma sensitive. This emphasis stems from the findings by Felitti et al. (1998) and others, who have documented the links between exposure to adverse and potentially traumatic experiences in childhood (e.g., child verbal, physical, emotional or sexual abuse or neglect or a household involving substance abuse, mental illness, incarceration, domestic violence, or family breakup) and adverse physical and mental health in adulthood. Having four or more categories of childhood exposure has been linked to a 4- to 12-fold increase in health risks such as alcoholism, drug abuse, depression, and attempted suicide; a 2- to 4-fold increase in smoking, poor self-rated health, 50 sexual partners or more, and sexually transmitted disease; and a 1.4- to 1.6-fold increase in physical inactivity and severe obesity.

Triple P has developed programs that can be used to minimize children's exposure to adverse family experiences and to assist parents with significant adjustment difficulties. Of the 10 categories of adverse experiences in the Adverse Childhood Experiences (ACEs) Index (Felitti et al., 1998), five relate to child maltreatment. The implementation of the Triple P system has been shown to reduce the level of maltreatment in the community (Prinz et al., 2009), and Pathways Triple P directly addresses anger management and attribution retraining for parents at risk of maltreatment. In relation to the other categories, Family Transitions Triple P seeks to minimize the adverse effects of separation and divorce; Group Triple P, Enhanced Triple P, and Triple P Online have been shown to reduce adult parental mental health and substance abuse problems. Group Triple P and Pathways Triple P have also been successfully implemented in prisons for both men and women, although there are no controlled outcome data available at this time.

IMPLEMENTING PARENTING PROGRAMS
IN LOW-RESOURCE SETTINGS

Fewer parents raising children in low-resource environments compared to high-resource environments have access to evidence-based parenting programs. Most research on parenting programs has been conducted in a handful of the richest countries in North America, Western Europe, and Australasia. Fortunately, there is growing evidence that existing evidence-based programs can transport well to other cultures with relatively little adaptation.

There are numerous challenges to be addressed before evidence-based programs can be implemented in low- and middle-income countries, including lack of funds, a trained workforce to deliver parenting programs, and basic health, mental health, and family support services. A major challenge is to ensure that relevant programs that do work can be delivered and scaled effectively in low-resource settings. This is likely to require alternative, lower cost ways of providing professional training, program delivery, and technical and consultation support in these settings to enable programs to be implemented in a sustainable way (Ward, Sanders, Gardner, Mikton, & Dawes, 2016).

IMPLICATIONS FOR POLICY, RESEARCH, AND PRACTICE

INFLUENCING POLICY AND SECURING FUNDING

Despite clear evidence that the quality of parenting that children receive affects many important life course outcomes and that EBPS can positively influence children's development and is highly cost-effective, investments in parenting typically target the most vulnerable and disadvantaged parents with significant preexisting problems. Agencies and organizations that might deliver preventively focused parenting programs require additional funding to undertake this work. Securing necessary funds to implement a population-based program properly is a major challenge in many countries. The wheels of government can move slowly, and it is common for advocates and champions of the population approach to take years to secure the necessary resources to commence implementation. Some organizations use a "bootstrapping" approach to secure funds to deliver one or two levels of the Triple P system (often the more intensive levels), then gradually work to secure additional braided funding to extend the program to other levels to eventually become a multilevel system.

A mix of strategies is often needed to influence policy decisions. Strategies that have been employed include submitting programs for review to influential evidence-based lists of empirically supported interventions, such as Blueprints for Heathy Youth Development (Mihalic & Elliott, 2015); policy statements by professional groups (e.g., American Academy of Pediatrics, 2016; National Academies of Science Engineering and Medicine, 2016); direct lobbying of politicians and policy advisors; advocacy from consumers and end users of programs; media coverage of important new research findings; and responding in a timely and helpful manner to requests for information from government, community organizations, and media. Undertaking a careful analysis of policy statements that links specific program outcomes to publicly stated policy aspirations or commitments is a useful approach when engaging with government.

AN INTEGRATED SYSTEM OR A PATCHWORK OF MULTIPLE PROGRAMS?

The model of parenting support that Triple P employs is designed as a fully integrated, internally consistent, multilevel suite of related programs using a common theoretical framework. Having a named program or a "brand" that has a clear public identity raises issues relating to restriction of consumer choice and concerns that home-grown or preexisting programs sometimes based on different theoretical models will be threatened and their funding cut. However, the introduction of the Triple P system often fills gaps not covered by local services, and it can complement and work comfortably alongside any other evidence-based parenting program. The main advantage of adopting an integrated multilevel system is that it facilitates agencies working together in partnership with a shared vision, common language and approach to parenting, and a commitment to achieving population-level change.

FUNDING OF PARENTING SERVICES AND PROGRAMS

Funding models for supporting the implementation of EBPS programs are extremely varied, and a number of different mechanisms are used. Typically, there is a lack of a funding model that is consistently applied even within the same country. Funding can include specific allocation of funds by governments to provide parenting programs through government-funded services in health, mental health, education, and welfare services. Many not-for-profit organizations delivering parenting programs use braided funding models from multiple sources (e.g., grants, donations, service contracts). Medical or health insurance schemes sometimes allow EBPS programs if a child or parent has a specific clinical diagnosis, but rarely to support preventive work. Some provider groups deliver Triple P as part of workplace employee assistance programs or through block grants to schools for mental health programs. Others deliver Triple P as part of a clinical practice in psychology, social work, nursing, or pediatrics. The lack of a consistent funding mechanism or pathway to support parenting programs is a fundamental limitation on the growth of EBPS programs.

NEED FOR ADDITIONAL POPULATION TRIALS

The few large-scale population trials of the full Triple P system conducted to date have been promising. These trials have identified a range of practical and logistical programming, organizational, and implementation issues that must be addressed to ensure that an integrated system of EBPS works in practice and reaches families most in need of parenting support. Further large-scale place-randomized trials are needed to specifically clarify the population effects of the Triple P system on subgroups of disadvantaged and vulnerable families.

The current *Every Family* population trial targeting parents of 3- to 8-year-olds is using Australian federal and state administrative data on child development outcomes to specifically examine intervention effects in 33 low-socioeconomic areas in the state of Queensland, with matched comparison areas in other states that are not receiving the Triple P System. This trial will help to determine whether existing programming efforts to activate community change processes to support competent parenting across an entire community will be successful in engaging the most vulnerable families living in socioeconomically disadvantaged circumstances.

MEDIATORS AND MODERATORS
OF POPULATION-LEVEL EFFECTS

Little is known about how to explain population-level effects. In a complex multilevel system like Triple P that has many moving parts, it is unclear how best to explain intervention effects. The mechanisms used to explain improvements in child behavior in RCTs such as changes in positive parenting or parental efficacy, reduced harsh or negative parenting, more consistent discipline, and reduced interparental conflict are likely to be inadequate in explaining population-level effects. Possible additional candidates include activation of a "parent-to-parent" social contagion by which participating parents become champions and influence other parents to participate; increased parental awareness and participation; changing social norms and expectations; reduced stigma about participation in parenting programs; increased access to and completion of evidence-based programs; and policy-based changes that could affect how parenting programs are funded.

DIFFERENTIAL SUSCEPTIBILITY
TO ENVIRONMENTAL INFLUENCE

An evolutionary biology perspective underpins the contention that children vary in their developmental plasticity and susceptibility to environmental influence. The Pluess and Belsky (2010) differential susceptibility hypothesis states that children have varying biological sensitivity to differences in social context. Specifically, they contended that children who are most adversely affected by adversity and stressors are the same children who respond most positively to environmental support and enrichment (including positive parenting). Biologically based individual differences in plasticity mean positive parenting may be especially valuable for those children with difficult temperaments, who are impulsive, and who have poor self-regulation over behavior and emotions compared to other less temperamentally difficult children. A twin study that measured both increases in positive prosocial behavior and reductions in problem behavior in relation to varying dosages of positive parenting programs (low vs. high intensity) would be particularly valuable to determine how active manipulation of the strength of environmental influence through parenting interacts with genetic or biological vulnerability.

DETERMINING FISCAL VALUE

The key economic question is whether the benefits of the intervention are worth the implementation costs. To answer this, we need to know how much it costs to implement parenting programs, what benefits can be expected, and any effects the intervention might have on other costs (e.g., leading to increased or reduced use of other services). EBPS programs, including Triple P, are widely considered to have good fiscal value, as reflected in the economic analyses reported by the independent Washington State Institute for Public Policy (WSIPP; 2017) and underscored by the Institute of Medicine and National Research Council (2014). In their most recent report, the WSIPP (2017) indicated that the Triple P system has shown a return of $8.14 for each dollar of investment, and Level 4 Individual Triple P showed a return of $3.36 for each invested dollar.

PROMOTING COLLABORATIVE INTERAGENCY PARTNERSHIPS

The successful implementation of a population approach requires coordinated multiagency involvement and ongoing collaboration (Fives et al., 2014; Chapter 40, this volume). Owens et al. (Chapter 40) describe a successful approach to partnership formation and maintenance that supported the implementation of the Triple P system in Ireland.

TRAINING THE RIGHT PEOPLE TO DELIVER PROGRAMS

To achieve sufficient population reach, an intervention needs to train a sufficient number of practitioners who can deliver the intervention with fidelity. It has become increasingly clear that not all trained practitioners have the capacity to become sustained implementers of a program. To increase the likelihood of sustained implementations, practitioners should be selected who meet the following criteria: (a) They have roles that enable them to devote a certain percentage of allocated time to actually deliver Triple P, so they have the capacity to deliver on participation targets; (b) they have line management support for program delivery and allocated work time to implement programs with families; (c) they are able to attend peer support supervision sessions; (d) they are fully accredited; (e) they are required to collect assessment data for all participating families so that an outcome is known for all cases; and (f) their agencies allocate resources to promote and socially market the program to ensure participation targets are reached.

ACHIEVING IMPLEMENTATION TARGETS

When agencies enter into an agreement to deliver Triple P to a defined number of families per year, it should mean a major organizational undertaking to commit the necessary resources to ensure targets are reached. Service managers need to make staff available to deliver programs, to promote the availability of the programs to parents, and then to deliver programs in a manner required to ensure adequate fidelity of program delivery. If participation targets are not reached or trained practitioners simply do not deliver at all, the implementation team needs to address the issue with line managers. It is helpful for implementation consultants to work with trained staff as well to identify the source of the problem and to initiate a remedial plan to get practitioners active.

CONCLUSIONS

The development of the Triple P system as a comprehensive population-based approach and its subsequent dissemination, adoption, implementation, scaling up, and ongoing evaluation have been a major undertaking involving the sustained efforts of many people for almost four decades. As the population approach to parenting support is relatively new, Triple P remains a work in progress as new findings help refine the way the system is best implemented in different communities. From small beginnings as an in-home "coaching" model, using a self-management framework, single-subject experimental designs, and careful observation procedures to track child and parent behavior, Triple P has evolved into a suite of interrelated programs. EBPS as a population approach is an extremely promising strategy to achieve change on a large scale in parenting practices and child outcomes associated with inadequate or dysfunctional parenting.

KEY MESSAGES

- Problems of parenting are a major public health issue that is best tackled at a whole-of-population level.
- A self-regulation approach to positive parenting helps promote parenting independence in problem-solving and reduces dependency on others.
- A multilevel system of intervention such as Triple P has the greatest potential to ensure adequate population reach to achieve change in target problems at a population level.
- Adoption of the principle of "proportionate universalism" helps ensure that social equalities are addressed in any implementation plan.
- The field of implementation science is still in its infancy in relation to the establishment, evaluation, and long-term sustainment of universal population-level EBPS strategies, and Triple P is an early exemplar on which to build the knowledge base.

REFERENCES

Altafim, E. R. P., & Linhares, M. B. M. (2016). Universal violence and child maltreatment prevention programs for parents: A systematic review. *Psychosocial Intervention*, *25*, 27–38. doi:10.1016/j.psi.2015.10.003

American Academy of Pediatrics. (2016). Poverty and child health in the United States. *Pediatrics*, *137*, 1–14. doi:10.1542/peds.2016-0339

Arruabarrena, I., & De Paúl, J. (2012). Early intervention programs for children and families: Theoretical and empirical bases supporting their social and economic efficiency. *Psychosocial Intervention*, *21*, 117–127. doi:10.5093/in2012a18

Bandura, A. (1986). *Social foundations of thought and action: a social cognitive theory/Albert Bandura*. Englewood Cliffs, NJ: Prentice-Hall.

Bandura, A. (2000). Exercise of human agency through collective efficacy. *Current Directions in Psychological Science*, *9*, 75–78.

Carver, C. S., & Scheier, M. F. (2011). Self-regulation of action and affect. In K. D. Vohs & R. F. Baumeister (Eds.), *Handbook of self-regulation: Research, theory, and applications* (2nd ed., pp. 3–21). New York, NY: Guilford Press.

Christian, C. W., & Schwarz, D. F. (2011). Child maltreatment and the transition to adult-based medical and mental health care. *Pediatrics*, *127*, 139–145. doi:10.1542/peds.2010-2297

Csikszentmihalyi, M. (1990). *Flow: The psychology of optimal experience*. New York, NY: Harper Perennial.

Dretzke, J., Davenport, C., Frew, E., Barlow, J., Stewart-Brown, S., Bayliss, S., … Hyde, C. (2009). The clinical effectiveness of different parenting programmes for children with conduct problems: A systematic review of randomised controlled trials. *Child and Adolescent Psychiatry and Mental Health, 3*, 7. doi:10.1186/1753-2000-3-7

Felitti, V. J., Anda, R. F., Nordenberg, D., Williamson, D. F., Spitz, A. M., Edwards, V., . . . Marks, J. S. (1998). Relationship of childhood abuse and household dysfunction to many of the leading causes of death in adults. The Adverse Childhood Experiences (ACE) Study. *American Journal of Preventive Medicine, 14*, 245–258. doi:10.1016/S0749-3797(98)00017-8

Fives, A., Purcell, L., Heary, C., NicGabhainn, S., & Canavan, J. (2014). *Parenting support for every parent: A population-level evaluation of Triple P in Longford Westmeath. Final Report.* Athlone, Ireland: Longford Westmeath Parenting Partnership.

Fixsen, D. L., Naoom, S. F., Blase, K. A., Friedman, R. M., & Wallace, F. (2005). *Implementation research: A synthesis of the literature.* Tampa, FL: University of South Florida, Louis de la Parte Florida Mental Health Institute, the National Implementation Research Network (FMHI Publication #231).

Frank, T. J., Keown, L. J., Dittman, C., & Sanders, M. R. (2015). Using father preference data to increase father engagement in evidence-based parenting programs. *Journal of Child and Family Studies, 24*, 937–947. doi:10.1007/s10826-014-9904-9

Hanf, C., & Kling, J. (1973). *Facilitating parent-child interaction: A two-stage training model.* Unpublished manuscript, University of Oregon Medical School, University of Oregon, OR.

Hart, B., & Risley, R. T. (1995). *Meaningful differences in the everyday experience of young American children.* Baltimore, MD: Brookes.

Haslam, D. M., Sanders, M. R., & Sofronoff, K. (2013). Reducing work and family conflict in teachers: A randomised controlled trial of Workplace Triple P. *School Mental Health, 5*, 70–82. doi:10.1007/s12310-012-9091-z

Institute of Medicine and National Research Council. (2014). *Considerations in applying benefit-cost analysis to preventive interventions for children, youth, and families (workshop summary).* Washington, DC: National Academy of Sciences. Retrieved from https://www.nap.edu/catalog/18708/considerations-in-applying-benefit-cost-analysis-to-preventive-interventions-for-children-youth-and-families

Karoly, P. (1993). Mechanisms of self-regulation: A systems view. *Annual Review of Psychology, 44*, 23–52. doi:10.1146/annurev.ps.44.020193.000323

Kazdin, A. E. (2008). *Parent management training: Treatment for oppositional, aggressive, and antisocial behavior in children and adolescents.* New York, NY: Oxford University Press.

Kirby, J. N., & Sanders, M. R. (2014). A randomized controlled trial evaluating a parenting program designed specifically for grandparents. *Behavior Research and Therapy, 52*, 35–44. doi:10.1016/j.brat.2013.11.002

Kirp, D. L. (2012). *Kids first: Five big ideas for transforming children's lives and America's future.* New York, NY: Public Affairs.

Koole, S. L., van Dillen, L. F., & Sheppes, G. (2011). The self-regulation of emotion. In K. D. Vohs & R. F. Baumeister (Eds.), *Handbook of self-regulation: Research, theory, and applications* (2nd ed., pp. 22–40). New York, NY: Guilford Press.

Lee, C. M., Smith, P. B., Stern, S. B., Piche, G., Feldgaier, S., Ateah, C., . . . Chan, K. (2014). The international parenting survey–Canada: Exploring access to parenting services. *Canadian Psychology/Psychologie Canadienne, 55*, 110–116. doi:10.1037/a0036297

Little, M., Berry, V., Morpeth, L., Blower, S., Axford, N., Taylor, R., . . . Tobin, K. (2012). The impact of three evidence-based programmes delivered in public systems in Birmingham, UK. *International Journal of Conflict and Violence, 6*, 260–272. doi:0070-ijcv-2012293

Lundahl, B. W., Tollefson, D., Risser, H., & Lovejoy, M. C. (2008). A meta-analysis of father involvement in parent training. *Research on Social Work Practice, 18*, 97–106. doi:10.1177/1049731507309828

Marmot, M. (2010). *Fair society, healthy lives: The Mamort Review; Strategic review of health inequalities in England post-2010*. London, England: Marmot Review.

Mazzucchelli, T. G., & Sanders, M. R. (2010). Facilitating practitioner flexibility within an empirically supported intervention: Lessons from a system of parenting support. *Clinical Psychology: Science and Practice, 17*, 238–252. doi:10.1111/j.1468-2850.2010.01215.x

McMahon, R. J. (1999). Parent training. In S. W. Russ & T. H. Ollendick (Eds.), *Handbook of psychotherapies with children and families* (pp. 153–180). Boston, MA: Springer US.

McMahon, R. J., & Forehand, R. (2005). *Helping the noncompliant child: Family-based treatment for oppositional behavior* (2nd ed.). New York, NY: Guilford Press.

McPherson, K. E., Sanders, M. R., Schroeter, B., Troy, V., & Wiseman, K. (2016). Acceptability and feasibility of peer assisted supervision and support for intervention practitioners: A Q-methodology evaluation. *Journal of Child and Family Studies, 25*, 720–732. doi:10.1007/s10826-015-0281-9

McWilliam, J., Brown, J., Sanders, M. R., & Jones, L. (2016). The Triple P implementation framework: The role of purveyors in the implementation and sustainability of evidence-based programs. *Prevention Science, 17*, 636–645. doi:10.1007/s11121-016-0661-4

Mihalic, S. F., & Elliott, D. S. (2015). Evidence-based programs registry: Blueprints for Healthy Youth Development. *Evaluation and Program Planning, 48*, 124–131. doi:10.1016/j.evalprogplan.2014.08.004

Morawska, A., Sanders, M. R., Goadby, E., Headley, C., Hodge, L., McAuliffe, C., . . . Anderson, E. (2011). Is the Triple P-Positive Parenting Program acceptable to parents from culturally diverse backgrounds? *Journal of Child and Family Studies, 20*, 614–622. doi:10.1007/s10826-010-9436-x

National Academies of Sciences, Engineering, and Medicine. (2016). *Parenting matters: Supporting parents of children Ages 0–8*. Washington, DC: Academies Press. Retrieved from https://www.nap.edu/catalog/21868/parenting-matters-supporting-parents-of-children-ages-0-8

Nowak, C., & Heinrichs, N. (2008). A comprehensive meta-analysis of Triple P-Positive Parenting Program using hierarchical linear modeling: Effectiveness and moderating variables. *Clinical Child and Family Psychology Review, 11*, 114–144. doi:10.1007/s10567-008-0033-0

O'Dell, S. (1974). Training parents in behavior modification: A review. *Psychological Bulletin, 81*, 418–433. doi:10.1037/h0036545

Papies, E. K., & Aarts, H. (2011). Nonconscious self-regulation, or the automatic pilot of human behavior. In K. Vohs & R. Baumeister (Eds.), *Handbook of self-regulation: Research, theory, and applications* (2nd ed., pp. 125–142). New York, NY: Guilford Press.

Patterson, G. R. (1976). The aggressive child: Victim and architect of a coercive system *Behavior Modification and Families, 1*, 267–316.

Pluess, M., & Belsky, J. (2010). Children's differential susceptibility to effects of parenting. *Family Science, 1*, 14–25. doi:10.1080/19424620903388554

Prinz, R. J., & Sanders, M. R. (2007). Adopting a population-level approach to parenting and family support interventions. *Clinical Psychology Review, 27*, 739–749. doi:10.1016/j.cpr.2007.01.005

Prinz, R. J., Sanders, M. R., Shapiro, C. J., Whitaker, D. J., & Lutzker, J. R. (2009). Population-based prevention of child maltreatment: The US Triple P system population trial. *Prevention Science, 10*, 1–12. doi:10.1007/s11121-009-0123-3

Prinz, R. J., Sanders, M. R., Shapiro, C. J., Whitaker, D. J., & Lutzker, J. R. (2016). Addendum to "Population-based prevention of child maltreatment: The US Triple P system population trial." *Prevention Science, 17*, 410–416. doi:10.1007/s11121-016-0631-x

Rose, G. (2008). *Rose's strategy of preventive medicine*. New York, NY: Oxford University Press.

Sanders, M. R. (1999). Triple P-Positive Parenting Program: Towards an empirically validated multilevel parenting and family support strategy for the prevention of behavior and emotional problems in children. *Clinical Child and Family Psychology Review, 2*, 71–90. doi:10.1023/A:1021843613840

Sanders, M. R. (2008). Triple P-Positive Parenting Program as a public health approach to strengthening parenting. *Journal of Family Psychology, 22,* 506–517. doi:10.1037/0893-3200.22.3.506

Sanders, M. R. (2012). Development, evaluation, and multinational dissemination of the Triple P-Positive Parenting Program. *Annual Review of Clinical Psychology, 8,* 1–35. doi:10.1146/annurev-clinpsy-032511-143104

Sanders, M. R., & Dadds, M. R. (1982). The effects of planned activities and child management procedures in parent training: An analysis of setting generality. *Behavior Therapy, 13,* 452–461. doi:10.1016/S0005-7894(82)80007-5

Sanders, M. R., & Glynn, T. (1981). Training parents in behavioral self-management: An analysis of generalization and maintenance. *Journal of Applied Behavior Analysis, 14,* 223–237. doi:10.1901/jaba.1981.14-223

Sanders, M. R., & Kirby, J. N. (2014). A public-health approach to improving parenting and promoting children's well-being. *Child Development Perspectives, 8,* 250–257. doi:10.1111/cdep.12086

Sanders, M. R., & Kirby, J. N. (2015). Surviving or thriving: Quality assurance mechanisms to promote innovation in the development of evidence-based parenting interventions. *Prevention Science, 16,* 421–431. doi:10.1007/s11121-014-0475-1

Sanders, M. R., Kirby, J. N., Tellegen, C. L., & Day, J. J. (2014). The Triple P-Positive Parenting Program: A systematic review and meta-analysis of a multi-level system of parenting support. *Clinical Psychology Review, 34,* 337–357. doi:10.1016/j.cpr.2014.04.003

Sanders, M. R., Markie-Dadds, C., Rinaldis, M., Firman, D., & Baig, N. (2007). Using household survey data to inform policy decisions regarding the delivery of evidence-based parenting interventions. *Child: Care, Health and Development, 33,* 768–783. doi:10.1111/j.1365-2214.2006.00725.x

Sanders, M. R., Markie-Dadds, C., & Turner, K. M. T. (2001). *Practitioner's manual for Standard Triple P* (Revised ed.). Brisbane, Australia: Triple P International.

Sanders, M. R., & Mazzucchelli, T. G. (2013). The promotion of self-regulation through parenting interventions. *Clinical Child and Family Psychology Review, 16,* 1–17. doi:10.1007/s10567-013-0129-z

Sanders, M. R., & Murphy-Brennan, M. (2013). *Triple P in action: Peer-assisted supervision and support manual.* Milton, Australia: Triple P International.

Sanders, M. R., Ralph, A., Sofronoff, K., Gardiner, P., Thompson, R., Dwyer, S. B., & Bidwell, K. (2008). Every family: A population approach to reducing behavioral and emotional problems in children making the transition to school. *Journal of Primary Prevention, 29,* 197–222. doi:10.1007/s10935-008-0139-7

Sarkadi, A., Sampaio, F., Kelly, M. P., & Feldman, I. (2014). A novel approach used outcome distribution curves to estimate the population-level impact of a public health intervention. *Journal of Clinical Epidemiology, 67,* 785–792. doi:10.1016/j.jclinepi.2013.12.012

Scott, S., Carby, A., & Rendu, A. (2008). *Impact of therapists' skill on effectiveness of parenting groups for child antisocial behavior.* London, England: Kings College London, Institute of Psychiatry.

Tharp, R. G., & Wetzel, R. J. (1969). *Behavior modification in the natural environment.* New York, NY: Academic Press.

Wahler, R. G. (1969). Oppositional children: A quest for parental reinforcement control 1. *Journal of Applied Behavior Analysis, 2,* 159–170. doi:10.1901/jaba.1969.2-159

Ward, C., Sanders, M. R., Gardner, F., Mikton, C., & Dawes, A. (2016). Preventing child maltreatment in low- and middle-income countries: Parent support programs have the potential to buffer the effects of poverty. *Child Abuse and Neglect, 54,* 97–107. doi:10.1016/j.chiabu.2015.11.002

Washington State Institute for Public Policy. (2017). *Benefit-cost results.* Seattle, WA: Author. Retrieved from http://www.wsipp.wa.gov/BenefitCost

CORE PRINCIPLES AND TECHNIQUES OF POSITIVE PARENTING

MATTHEW R. SANDERS AND TREVOR G. MAZZUCCHELLI

Positive parenting is an approach to raising children that aims to promote children's optimal development. It concerns the activities of parenting that create a nurturing environment that will allow children to grow up healthy and well adjusted. This includes establishing a warm and responsive relationship that creates the interactional context for children to learn the skills and competencies they will need to relate well to others, to benefit from their experiences during their schooling years, and to successfully participate as part of the broader community. At its core, the approach is constructive; it aims to build the essential social, emotional, and self-regulatory capabilities that children will need throughout their lives (Chapter 2, this volume).

Parents' capacity to raise their children well is influenced by a range of potentially modifiable social, emotional, relational, and contextual factors (Chapter 2, this volume). Triple P recognizes these influences and seeks to help parents to increase their confidence, skills, and knowledge about raising children; to be less coercive, depressed, stressed, or anxious; to improve communication with partners over parenting issues; and to have lower levels of stress and conflict in managing work and family responsibilities (Sanders, 2008). These outcomes can be achieved by creating a supportive context in which parents can reflect on their parenting and receive practical information about parenting skills that they can incorporate into everyday interactions with their children. The goal is to support parents to create an environment for their children in which prosocial behaviors and related skills and competencies are taught, encouraged, and richly reinforced.

CORE PRINCIPLES OF POSITIVE PARENTING

Five core principles of positive parenting form the basis of Triple P: safe and engaging environment, positive learning environment, assertive discipline, realistic expectations, and parental self-care. These principles were selected from the developmental literature to address specific modifiable risk and protective factors known to predict positive developmental and mental health outcomes in children.

SAFE AND ENGAGING ENVIRONMENT

Children of all ages need a safe, supervised, and therefore protective environment that provides opportunities for them to explore, experiment, and play. This principle is essential to promote healthy development and prevent accidents and injuries in the home (Cole, Koulouglioti, Kitzman, Sidora-Arcoleo, & Anson, 2009; Kendrick, Barlow, Hampshire, Stewart-Brown, & Polnay, 2008). Older children and adolescents need adequate supervision and monitoring in an appropriate developmental context (Dishion & McMahon, 1998; Smetana, 2008). Adequate supervision means knowing where a child is, who they are with, and what they are doing at all times. Triple P also draws on the work of Todd Risley and his colleagues, who have articulated how the design of living environments can promote engagement and skill development across the life span (Risley, Clark, & Caltaldo, 1976). An environment that is full of interesting things to do stimulates children's curiosity as well as their language and intellectual development. It also keeps children engaged and active and reduces the likelihood of misbehavior.

POSITIVE LEARNING ENVIRONMENT

A positive learning environment involves educating parents in their role as their child's first teacher. The program specifically targets how parents can respond positively and constructively to child-initiated interactions in naturally occurring situations (e.g., requests for help, information, advice, and attention). Parents are encouraged to provide brief moments of uninterrupted attention to children, to have brief conversations with children about a current interest, to be an information resource that children can access when they need assistance, and to use incidental teaching. Incidental teaching involves parents being receptive to child-initiated interactions when children attempt to communicate with their parents. This procedure has been used extensively in the teaching of language, social skills, and social problem-solving (e.g., Hart & Risley, 1975, 1995, 1999).

A positive learning environment is a critical protective factor in the face of other adversities in children's lives that promotes healthy development. Focusing on the positive includes attending to children's prosocial skills and behaviors. This is achieved through the use of contingent positive attention, such as the use of praise and physical contact, the use of behavior charts to encourage appropriate behavior or new skills, and the use of modeling and verbal, gestural, and manual guidance prompts to teach children new skills.

ASSERTIVE DISCIPLINE

Specific child management and behavior change strategies are presented as alternatives to coercive, ineffective, and inconsistent discipline practices (such as shouting, threatening, or using physical punishment). When parents use assertive discipline, children learn to accept responsibility for their behavior, to become aware of the needs of others, and to develop self-control. Children are also less likely to develop behavioral or emotional problems when parents are consistent and predictable from one day to the next. A parent can value their child's individuality and still expect reasonable behavior. Assertive discipline involves being consistent, responding quickly and decisively when children misbehave, and teaching children to behave in an acceptable way. The range of behavior change procedures demonstrated to parents include selecting and discussing ground rules for specific situations; using directed discussion and planned ignoring; giving clear, calm, age-appropriate instructions; and backing up instructions with logical consequences, quiet time (nonexclusionary time-out), and time-out. Parents are taught to use these skills in the home as well as in community settings (e.g., going visiting or shopping) to promote the generalization of parenting skills to diverse parenting situations.

REALISTIC EXPECTATIONS

The principle of realistic expectations involves exploring with parents their expectations, assumptions, and beliefs about the causes of children's behavior and choosing goals that are developmentally appropriate for the child and realistic for the parent. Parents who are at risk of abusing their child are more likely to have unrealistic expectations of children's capabilities (Azar & Weinzierl, 2005). Problems may arise when parents expect too much too soon or expect their children to be perfect. For example, parents who expect their child will always be polite, happy, and cooperative or always tidy and helpful are setting themselves up for disappointment and conflict with their children. Developmentally appropriate expectations are taught in the context of parents' specific expectations concerning difficult and prosocial behaviors rather than through a more traditional "ages-and-stages" approach to child development. It is also important for parents to have realistic expectations of themselves. Parents who strive to be perfect often feel frustrated, ashamed, and inadequate when things do not go as planned.

PARENTAL SELF-CARE

Parenting is influenced by a range of factors that affect a parent's personal adjustment and sense of well-being. All levels of Triple P specifically address this issue by encouraging parents to view parenting as part of a larger context of personal self-care, resourcefulness, and well-being and by teaching practical parenting skills. It is much easier for parents to be patient, consistent, and available to children when their own needs are being met. In more intensive levels of intervention (Level 5), couples are explicitly taught effective communication skills and are encouraged to explore how their own irrational assumptions and negative self-talk affect their parenting and consequently their child's behavior. Parents also develop specific coping strategies for managing difficult emotions, such as such as those related to depression, anger, anxiety, and high levels of parenting stress at high-risk times.

The application of these principles and associated techniques through daily parent–child interactions helps children learn the prosocial and relationship skills they need with parents, siblings, peers, teachers, grandparents, and others in their lives to deal with the everyday issues they have to manage (such as influencing decisions that will affect the whole family, dealing with bullying, or negotiating an extension on a school assignment). The approach to positive parents is constructive in the sense that it aims to build children's social, emotional, and self-regulating capabilities. The approach is not about controlling and suppressing behaviors that simply irritate parents; rather, it is primarily an approach that builds relational competencies children need to get on well with others and to acquire other important developmental competencies (e.g., language and communication, dealing with difficult emotions, managing conflict) so that children have the skills to lead heathy, happy, and productive lives.

SPECIFIC TECHNIQUES USED

Application of Triple P's principles teaches parents to encourage their child's social and language skills, emotional self-regulation, independence, and problem-solving ability. It is hypothesized that attainment of these skills promotes family harmony, reduces parent–child conflict, fosters successful peer relationships, and prepares children to be successful at school and through their adulthood. To achieve these child outcomes, the principles are operationalized into a range of specific parenting skills that are presented to parents as options they might use (see Table 4.1).

Each skill a parent acquires and implements creates a context for children to learn and to practice a reciprocal skill. All parenting skills introduced in Triple P can be justified because of the developmental value that is attached to the child's reciprocal skill. For example, when a parent uses descriptive praise to encourage a desirable behavior, an opportunity is created for children to practice receiving a compliment appropriately (without embarrassment, showing off, or bragging). Similarly, when parents learn to give clear, calm instructions and to back up their instructions, an opportunity is created for children to learn how to receive instructions by listening and paying attention to what is required of them. When parents give a brief time-out to children for persistent misbehavior, such as aggression or temper tantrums, children have an opportunity to practice self-regulation of difficult emotions (anger) by calming down without relying on an adult's presence to do so.

TECHNIQUES FOR YOUNGER CHILDREN

Table 4.2 summarizes the core parenting skills introduced in the Triple P program. These techniques fall into four main categories: (a) skills to strengthen the parent–child relationship; (b) skills to encourage desirable behavior; (c) skills for teaching children new behaviors and skills; and (d) skills for managing misbehavior and teaching self-regulation skills.

TECHNIQUES FOR ADOLESCENTS

Teen Triple P extends the core program to parents of adolescents by providing guidance regarding how the skills introduced for younger children can be tailored for this developmental period. This tailoring acknowledges teenagers' impending transition into adulthood by placing an increased emphasis on negotiation, compromise, and shared decision-making. Also, the attention to antecedent or preemptive parenting strategies for younger children shifts to a focus on preparing teenagers to safely negotiate events or activities that pose a potential risk to

Table 4.1: Core Parenting Principles and Skills Promoted in Triple P for Children Aged 0–12 Years

Safe and Engaging Environment	Positive Learning Environment	Assertive Discipline	Realistic Expectations	Parental Self-Care
Spending brief quality time	Giving nonverbal attention	Establishing ground rules	Monitoring children's behavior	Catching unhelpful thoughts
Talking with children	Giving descriptive praise	Using directed discussion	Setting developmentally appropriate goals	Using relaxation and stress management
Showing affection	Setting a good example	Using planned ignoring	Setting practice tasks	Developing personal coping statements
Providing engaging activities	Using incidental teaching	Giving clear, calm instructions	Self-evaluating strengths and weaknesses	Challenging unhelpful thoughts
	Using "ask-say-do"	Using logical consequences	Setting personal goals for change	Developing coping plans for high-risk situations
	Using behavior charts	Using brief interruption		Improving personal communication habits
		Using quiet time		Giving and receiving constructive feedback
		Using time-out		Having casual conversations
				Supporting each other when problem behavior occurs
				Problem-solving
				Improving relationship happiness

their health or well-being. As such, the parenting skills that form the foundation of Triple P are adapted or in some cases replaced by more age-appropriate ones. Unique strategies introduced to address developmental tasks and common issues that arise during adolescence include coaching problem-solving, holding a family meeting, dealing with emotional behavior, and using skills to manage risky behavior (see Chapter 13, this volume).

Table 4.2: Description and Applications of Core Parenting Skills Promoted Through Triple P

Skill	Description	Applications
DEVELOPING GOOD RELATIONSHIPS WITH CHILDREN		
Spending quality time with children	Spending frequent, brief amounts of time (as little as 1 or 2 minutes) involved in child-preferred activities	Encouraging exploration and providing opportunities to build children's knowledge and for children to self-disclose and practice conversational skills
Talking with children	Having brief conversations with children about an activity or interest of the child	Promoting vocabulary, conversational and social skills
Showing affection	Providing physical affection (e.g., hugging, touching, tickling, patting)	Providing opportunities for children to become comfortable with intimacy and physical affection
ENCOURAGING DESIRABLE BEHAVIOR		
Using descriptive praise	Providing encouragement and approval by describing the behavior that is appreciated	Encouraging appropriate behavior (e.g., speaking in a pleasant voice, playing cooperatively, sharing, drawing pictures, reading, cooperating)
Giving attention	Providing positive nonverbal attention (e.g., a smile, wink, pat on the back, watching)	As above
Having interesting activities	Arranging a child's physical and social environment to provide interesting and engaging activities, materials, and age-appropriate toys (e.g., board games, pencils and paper, CDs, books, construction toys)	Encouraging independent play and promoting appropriate behavior when in the community (e.g., shopping, traveling)
TEACHING NEW SKILLS AND BEHAVIORS		
Setting a good example	Demonstrating desirable behavior through parental modeling	Showing children how to behave appropriately (e.g., speak calmly, wash hands, tidy up, solve problems)
Using incidental teaching	Using a series of questions and prompts to respond to child-initiated interactions and promote learning	Promoting language, problem-solving, cognitive ability, and independent play
Using ask-say-do	Using verbal, gestural, and manual prompts to teach new skills	Teaching self-care skills (e.g., brushing teeth, making bed) and other new skills (e.g., cooking, using tools)

Using behavior charts	Setting up a chart and providing social attention and backup rewards contingent on the absence of a problem or the presence of an appropriate behavior	Encouraging children for appropriate behavior (e.g., doing homework, playing cooperatively, asking nicely) and for the absence of problem behavior (e.g., swearing, lying, stealing, tantrums)

MANAGING MISBEHAVIOR

Setting clear ground rules	Negotiating in advance a set of fair, specific, and enforceable rules	Clarifying expectations (e.g., for watching TV, shopping trips, visiting relatives, going out in the car)
Using directed discussion for rule breaking	Identifying and rehearsing the correct behavior following rule breaking	Correcting occasional rule breaking (e.g., leaving school bag on the kitchen floor, running through the house)
Using planned ignoring for minor problems	Withdrawing attention while the problem behavior continues	Ignoring attention-seeking behavior (e.g., answering back, protesting after a consequence, whining, pulling faces)
Giving clear, calm instructions	Giving a specific instruction to start a new task or to stop a problem behavior and start an appropriate alternative behavior	Initiating an activity (e.g., getting ready to go out, coming to the dinner table) or terminating a problem behavior (e.g., fighting over toys, pulling hair) and saying what to do instead (e.g., share, keep your hands to yourself)
Backing up instructions with logical consequences	Using a specific consequence that involves removing an activity or privilege from a child or the child from an activity for a set time	Dealing with disobedience and mild problem behaviors that do not occur often (e.g., not taking turns)
Using quiet time for misbehavior	Removing a child from an activity in which a problem has occurred and having the child sit on the edge of the activity for a set time	Dealing with disobedience and children repeating a problem behavior after a logical consequence
Using time-out for serious misbehavior	Taking a child to an area away from others for a set time when problem behavior occurs	Dealing with temper outbursts, serious misbehavior (e.g., hurting others), and children not sitting quietly in quiet time

TECHNIQUES FOR CHILDREN WITH A DISABILITY

Stepping Stones Triple P provides guidance and examples regarding how the core principles and skills may be applied by parents of children with a developmental disability. This parallel system of parenting support acknowledges the importance of parents and family members adapting to the additional stressors that often come with having a child with a disability as well as participating in community life. Stepping Stones also introduces a number of additional parenting skills to accommodate the diverse support needs of this population. These skills include the use of other rewards, activity schedules, physical guidance, teaching backward, diversion to an appropriate activity, teaching children to communicate what they want, and brief interruption (see Chapter 9, this volume).

TECHNIQUES FOR OTHER CHILDREN

Additional techniques mainly derived from principles of cognitive-behavioral therapy are used in programs for specific populations; these techniques include Group Pathways Triple P for parents involved in the child protection system (e.g., attributional retaining and anger management; Sanders & Pidgeon, 2011); Group Lifestyle Triple P for parents of overweight or obese children (information on healthy eating and physical activity; West, Sanders, Cleghorn, & Davies, 2010); Family Transitions Triple P for parents following separation and divorce (e.g., psychoeducation on effects of divorce on children and training in conflict management; Stallman & Sanders, 2007); and Fear-less Triple P for parents of anxious children (e.g., psychoeducation about anxiety and the role of parenting and exposure principles; Chapter 8, this volume). In each instance, specific additional skills are included in the parenting solution of the specific problem on the basis of theory and empirical evidence showing the techniques are relevant and effective with the target population.

Additional detailed information about how individual techniques are used appear in a range of training resources, such as practitioner kits developed for specific populations. Some resources are only accessible through official professional training courses run by Triple P International (see http://www.triplep.net/glo-en/home/).

PARENTAL SELF-REGULATION

Self-regulation provides a central framework for conceptualizing the provision of positive parental support. Triple P recognizes parents' fundamental right to make decisions about how they raise their children. Instead of dictating to parents what they must do, parents are offered empirically supported information and strategies so that they can make more informed choices about how to tackle their concerns about parenting. Parents' capacity to manage their own behavior is viewed as a key factor that will the influence the quality of the environment in which children will be raised. As such, an important role of parenting support is to impart skills that strengthen parents' ability to change their own behavior and become independent problem-solvers (Karoly, 1993; Sanders & Mazzucchelli, 2013). The approach to self-regulation used in Triple P is derived from social cognitive theory. According to Bandura (1986, 1999), the development of self-regulation is related to personal, environmental, and behavioral factors; these factors operate separately but are interdependent. The self-regulatory framework from which Triple P operates is operationalized to include the following: self-sufficiency, self-efficacy, self-management, personal agency, and problem-solving.

SELF-SUFFICIENCY

As a parenting program is time limited, parents need to become independent problem-solvers so they trust their own judgment and become less reliant on others in carrying out basic parenting responsibilities. Self-sufficient parents have the resilience, resourcefulness, knowledge, and skills to parent with confidence. When confronted with a new problem, they use their knowledge, skills, and personal resources to resolve the problem. Encouraging parents to become self-sufficient means that parents become more connected to social support networks (e.g., partners, extended family and friends, social and recreational groups). It is hypothesized that the more self-sufficient parents become, the more likely they are to seek appropriate support when they need it, advocate for their children, remain involved in their children's schooling, and help protect them from harm (e.g., by effectively managing conflict with partners and creating a secure, low-conflict environment).

SELF-EFFICACY

Self-efficacy refers to a parent's belief that he or she can overcome or solve a parenting or behavior management problem. Parents with high self-efficacy have more confidence and have positive expectations about the possibility of change. Parenting programs can build parent's self-efficacy by conveying optimism that change is possible. For example, in Universal Triple P, media strategies are used that involve the realistic depiction of possible solutions to commonly encountered parenting situations (e.g., bedtime problems). These potential solutions can be illustrated through various media, including television programs, community service announcements, "talkback" radio, newspaper columns, and advertising. The messages are optimistic and promote the idea that even the most difficult parenting problems are solvable or preventable. In more intensive programs, parents are guided to select realistic goals for which they are provided the support necessary to accomplish.

SELF-MANAGEMENT

The tools or skills that parents can use to become more self-sufficient include self-monitoring, self-determination of goals and performance standards, self-evaluation of their own performance against a performance criterion, and self-selection of change strategies. As each parent is responsible for the way he or she chooses to raise his or her children, parents select those aspects of their own and their child's behavior they wish to work on, set goals, choose specific parenting and child management techniques they wish to implement, and self-evaluate their success with their chosen goals against self-determined criteria. Triple P aims to help parents make informed decisions by sharing knowledge and skills derived from contemporary research into effective childrearing practices. The active skills training processes incorporated into Triple P interventions enable skills to be modeled and practiced. Parents receive feedback regarding their implementation of skills learned in a supportive context using a self-regulatory framework (see Sanders, Mazzucchelli, & Ralph, 2012). Self-determination of personal goals enables parents to take into consideration their values and cultural traditions and to check whether the goals and methods they plan to use are consistent. An example of how this can be done is described by Turner, Sanders, Keown, and Shepherd in Chapter 28.

PERSONAL AGENCY

For personal agency, the parent increasingly attributes changes or improvements in their situation or their child's behavior to their own or their child's efforts rather than to chance, age, maturational factors, or other uncontrollable events (e.g., genetic makeup). This outcome is achieved by prompting parents to realistically identify causes or explanations for their child's or their own behavior; doing so increases parents' self-efficacy.

PROBLEM-SOLVING

A final aspect of self-regulation is parents' ability to apply the skills and knowledge they have acquired to issues beyond the presenting concern. It refers to parents' ability to flexibly adapt or generalize what they have learned to new problems, at later developmental phases, with different children, and for a variety of child behavior problems and family concerns. This means the test of whether a parenting intervention is truly successful is not only parents' ability to resolve current issues but also their capacity to address a diverse range of family challenges over time with relative autonomy.

This model is robust; it applies equally to all participants of positive parenting programs, including parents and children, service providers, disseminators, program developers, and researchers (Sanders & Mazzucchelli, 2013). The components of self-regulation outlined previously can be taught to children by parents in developmentally appropriate ways. For instance, attending and responding to child-initiated interactions and prompting, modeling, and reinforcing children's problem-solving efforts promote emotional self-regulation, independence, and problem-solving in children. Self-regulated parents are more likely to raise children who develop self-regulatory skills. Self-regulation principles can also be applied by service providers to be responsive to the needs of parents, by disseminators to support practitioners to refine their consultation skills (Chapter 34, this volume), by developers to be innovative (Chapter 45, this volume), and by researchers to manage evaluation challenges (Chapter 39, this volume).

PRINCIPLES OF DELIVERING POSITIVE PARENTING SUPPORT

Triple P interventions combine quality parenting information with particular principles for imparting this information and upskilling parents. These methods are designed to maximize efficiency, ensure that the program is relevant and responsive to each family's particular needs, and enhance parents' ability to independently manage novel parenting challenges that arise in the future. Some of the guiding principles for accomplishing these objectives are discussed next.

ACTIVE PARTICIPATION

Triple P incorporates active skills training methods (modeling, rehearsal, practice, feedback, and homework) to teach new parenting skills in all its programs. For practitioner-supported parenting programs, Triple P draws on a guided participation model. This model articulates a framework and microskills that are used in every interaction to support parents' involvement and active participation in the important tasks of the behavior change process, such as building a collaborative relationship, facilitating parent receptivity to new ideas or skills, and managing within-session resistance. These skills maximize the likelihood that parents will engage with the program, that sessions will run smoothly, and that skill acquisition will be optimized (Sanders & Burke, 2013; Sanders & Mazzucchelli, 2013).

SUFFICIENCY

Parents differ according to the strength of intervention they may require to enable them to independently manage a problem. Triple P aims to provide the "minimally sufficient" amount of support each parent requires. This guiding principle led to the development of the multilevel intervention strategy by which the intensity of intervention can be tailored to the needs and desires of individual families (see Chapter 3, this volume). But, the principle also extends to practitioners providing support to individual families. The goal is to tailor the level of support offered to parents over the course of the intervention. As the parent becomes more proficient at managing the change process themselves, practitioners fade their support. The principle of minimal sufficiency not only maximizes efficiency but also promotes parent independence, autonomy, and self-efficacy.

FLEXIBLE TAILORING AND RESPONSIVE PROGRAM DELIVERY

There are high- and low-risk variations in the content and the consultation processes of evidence-based parenting support (EBPS) that can influence clinical outcomes. Practitioners work collaboratively with parents and are responsive to their needs and situational context while preserving the key or essential elements of the program. The needs of specific client populations can be met by adapting examples used to illustrate key teaching points, through customized homework, and by adjusting the number of sessions and level of prompts and feedback provided. This type of tailoring preserves core concepts and procedures while it meets the idiosyncratic needs of a particular parent (e.g., a parent who has an intellectual disability, a parent of twins or triplets, a parent of a gifted child; Mazzucchelli & Sanders, 2010; Morawska & Sanders, 2009).

SUPPORTING THE GENERALIZATION OF PARENTING SKILLS

Triple P interventions emphasize the generalization of parenting skills across child care settings, siblings, and different parenting challenges and over time. Several strategies are used to achieve this, including those outlined next.

Instruction in Social Learning Principles

Parents are introduced to social learning explanations for children's behavior. They are then supported and provided opportunities to experiment in ways that allow them to recognize how this social learning framework applies to their child. The social learning model empowers parents to make sense of and to support their child's positive behavior and development.

Sufficient Exemplars

A sufficient exemplar approach is used in the consultation process with parents. This involves selecting one parenting situation or behavior target (e.g., mealtime behaviors) with which parents are supported to step through the behavior change process. Parents are then supported to apply their skills to new situations or behavior targets (e.g., going shopping, being a good sport in team games). The goal is for parents to have worked through a sufficient number of examples to facilitate the generalization of this behavior change process.

Training Loosely

Training loosely involves varying nonessential aspects of stimuli during parent consultation, such as providing parents with examples of how the parenting skills can be applied to different child behaviors and parenting situations. In this way, parents learn to apply the skills to varied and novel situations rather than learning to apply specific skills to a child's single behavior.

MYTHS ABOUT POSITIVE PARENTING PROGRAMS

In discussing EBPS, it is important to address a number of myths, which are often based on misunderstandings of how underlying theories and research literatures have informed these approaches (Mazzucchelli & Sanders, 2014).

MYTH: PARENTING PROGRAMS ARE ABOUT PARENTS CONTROLLING THEIR CHILDREN

While it is true that EBPS typically views cooperation with requests as a legitimate and important prosocial skill for children to develop, it is misleading to suggest that this is what parenting programs emphasize. EBPS targets a range of modifiable family risk and protective factors known to predict positive developmental and mental health outcomes in children. In particular,

EBPS aims to equip parents with the information and skills needed for parents to foster a safe, stable, nurturing relationship with their children and to help their children develop the social and language, emotional competence, independence, and problem-solving skills they need to get along with others and feel good about themselves. Of course, it is up to parents to select the values and behaviors they wish to impart to their children, but in our experience, most parents value and encourage their children's creativity and independence while expecting them to behave in socially appropriate ways.

MYTH: PARENTING PROGRAMS EMPHASIZE PUNISHMENT

Again, while it is true that EBPS includes information on effective discipline strategies that parents may use as alternatives to coercive acts such as yelling or physical punishment, these approaches provide coaching in many more strategies to promote a positive relationship between parents and their children, to encourage desirable behavior, and to teach new prosocial skills and competencies. Further, Triple P, along with other EBPS programs, explicitly teaches parents how to combine these strategies into anticipatory or preemptive routines that minimize the likelihood that problem behavior will occur and parents will use discipline strategies (e.g., Harrold, Lutzker, Campbell, & Touchette, 1992; Sanders & Dadds, 1982). It is also important to note that permissive parenting, devoid of any discipline, is associated with greater rates of child noncompliant and antisocial behavior (Querido, Warner, & Eyberg, 2002).

MYTH: PARENTING PROGRAMS IGNORE PARENT–CHILD RELATIONSHIPS

Contrary to this myth, EBPS considers warm and responsive caregiver–child relationships to be essential for children's healthy development. It is largely through the day-to-day interactions or relationship with attentive and attuned caregivers that children learn the core social, emotional, and behavioral competencies they will need to be accepted by their peers, get along with others, and participate in the larger community. Research has found that "attachment" behaviors (including infant crying and smiling and proximity-establishing and -maintaining behaviors) can be understood according to the same behavioral principles that have informed EBPS (e.g., Dunst & Kassow, 2008; Schlinger, 1995). This research has practical implications for how parents can improve the quality of their relationship with their child. And indeed, participating in EBPSs has been associated with significant improvements in the quality of parent–child attachment (e.g., O'Connor, Matias, Futh, Tantam, & Scott, 2013; Wiggins, Sofronoff, & Sanders, 2009).

SUMMARY

This chapter has described the five core principles of positive parenting that form the basis of Triple P as well as how these principles are operationalized into a range of specific parenting skills suitable for different developmental periods. The model self-regulation that acts as a central organizing framework for the provision of parenting support was reviewed along with guiding principles of program delivery, such as ensuring parents' active participation, sufficiency, flexible tailoring and responsive delivery, and methods for supporting the generalization of skills. Finally, a number of myths about behaviorally informed parenting support programs were dispelled. In Section 6, Chapter 34 by Ralph and Dittman on the Triple P approach to workforce training and accreditation and Chapter 33 by McWilliam and Brown introduce the model of implementation that supports practitioners and organizations after training.

KEY MESSAGES

- Positive parenting is an approach to raising children that aims to promote children's optimal development. It concerns the activities of parenting that create a nurturing environment that will allow children to grow up healthy, happy, and responsible participants of a broader community.
- Evidence-based parenting support, such as Triple P, aims to positively influence a range of social, emotional, relational, and contextual factors that affect parents' capacity to raise their children well.
- Five core principles of positive parenting form the basis of Triple P. These principles address specific modifiable risk and protective factors known to predict positive developmental and mental health outcomes in children. These include ensuring a safe, interesting environment; creating a positive learning environment, using assertive discipline; having realistic expectations; and taking care of oneself as a parent.
- Parents can enact Triple P's principles by incorporating a range of parenting skills into their everyday interactions with their children.
- Triple P draws on a model of self-regulation as an organizing framework for the provision of parenting support. This model applies equally to parents, practitioners, disseminators, program developers, and researchers.
- Triple P interventions combine quality parenting information with particular principles for imparting this information and upskilling parents. These methods are designed to maximize efficiency, ensure that the program is relevant and responsive to each family's particular needs, and enhance parents' ability to independently manage novel parenting challenges that arise in the future.

REFERENCES

Azar, S. T., & Weinzierl, K. M. (2005). Child maltreatment and childhood injury research: A cognitive behavioral approach. *Journal of Pediatric Psychology, 30*, 598–614. doi:10.1093/jpepsy/jsi046

Bandura, A. (1986). *Social foundations of thought and action: A social cognitive theory*. Englewood Cliffs, NJ: Prentice Hall.

Bandura, A. (1999). Social cognitive theory: An agentic perspective. *Asian Journal of Social Psychology, 2*, 21–41.

Cole, R., Koulouglioti, C., Kitzman, H., Sidora-Arcoleo, K., & Anson, E. (2009). Maternal rules, compliance, and injuries to preschool children. *Family & Community Health: The Journal of Health Promotion & Maintenance, 32*, 136–146. doi:10.1097/FCH.0b013e318199477f

Dishion, T. J., & McMahon, R. J. (1998). Parental monitoring and the prevention of child and adolescent problem behavior: A conceptual and empirical formulation. *Clinical Child and Family Psychological Review, 1*, 61–75. doi:10.1023/A:1021800432380

Dunst, C. J., & Kassow, D. Z. (2008). Caregiver sensitivity, contingent social responsiveness, and secure infant attachment. *Journal of Early and Behavioral Intervention, 5*, 40–56.

Harrold, M., Lutzker, J. R., Campbell, R. V., & Touchette, P. E. (1992). Improving parent-child interactions for families of children with developmental disabilities. *Journal of Behavior Therapy and Experimental Psychiatry, 23*, 89–100. doi:10.1016/0005-7916(92)90006-5

Hart, B., & Risley, T. R. (1975). Incidental teaching of language in the preschool. *Journal of Applied Behavior Analysis, 8*, 411–420. doi:10.1901/jaba.1975.8-411

Hart, B., & Risley, T. R. (1995). *Meaningful differences in the everyday experience of young American children*. Baltimore, MD: Brookes.

Hart, B., & Risley, T. R. (1999). *The social world of children learning to talk*. Baltimore, MD: Brookes.

Karoly, P. (1993). Mechanisms of self-regulation: A systems view. *Annual Review of Psychology, 44*, 23–52. doi:10.1146/annurev.ps.44.020193.000323

Kendrick, D., Barlow, J., Hampshire, A., Stewart-Brown, S., & Polnay, L. (2008). Parenting interventions and the prevention of unintentional injuries in childhood: Systematic review and meta-analysis. *Child: Care, Health and Development, 34*, 682–695. doi:10.1111/j.1365-2214.2008.00849.x

Mazzucchelli, T. G., & Sanders, M. R. (2010). Facilitating practitioner flexibility within an empirically supported intervention: Lessons from a system of parenting support. *Clinical Psychology: Science and Practice, 17*, 238–252. doi:10.1111/j.1468-2850.2010.01215.x

Mazzucchelli, T. G., & Sanders, M. R. (2014). Parenting from the outside-in: A paradigm shift in parent training? *Behaviour Change, 31*, 102–109. doi:10.1017/bec.2014.4

Morawska, A., & Sanders, M. (2009). An evaluation of a behavioral parenting intervention for parents of gifted children. *Behavior Research and Therapy, 47*, 463–470. doi:10.1016/j.brat.2009.02.008

O'Connor, T. G., Matias, C., Futh, A., Tantam, G., & Scott, S. (2013). Social learning theory parenting intervention promotes attachment-based caregiving in young children: Randomized clinical trial. *Journal of Clinical Child and Adolescent Psychology, 42*, 358–370. doi:10.1080/15374416.2012.723262

Querido, J. G., Warner, T. D., & Eyberg, S. M. (2002). Parenting styles and child behavior in African American families of preschool children. *Journal of Clinical Child and Adolescent Psychology, 31*, 272–277. doi:10.1207/153744202753604548

Risley, T. R., Clark, H. B., & Caltaldo, M. F. (1976). Behavior technology for the normal, middle-class family. In E. J. Mash, L. A. Hamerlynck, & L. C. Handy (Eds.), *Behavior modification and families* (pp. 34–60). New York, NY: Brunner/Mazel.

Sanders, M. R. (2008). Triple P-Positive Parenting Program as a public health approach to strengthening parenting. *Journal of Family Psychology, 22*, 506–517. doi:10.1037/0893-3200.22.3.506

Sanders, M. R., & Burke, K. (2013). The "hidden" technology of effective parent consultation: A guided participation model for promoting change in families. *Journal of Child and Family Studies, 23*, 1289–1297. doi:10.1007/s10826-013-9827-x

Sanders, M. R., & Dadds, M. R. (1982). The effects of planned activities and child management procedures in parent training: An analysis of setting generality. *Behavior Therapy, 13*, 452–461. doi:10.1007/BF00918375

Sanders, M. R., & Mazzucchelli, T. G. (2013). The promotion of self-regulation through parenting interventions. *Clinical Child and Family Psychology Review, 16*, 1–17. doi:10.1007/s10567-013-0129-z

Sanders, M. R., Mazzucchelli, T. G., & Ralph, A. (2012). Promoting parenting competence through a self-regulation approach to feedback. In R. M. Sutton, M. J. Hornsey, & K. M. Douglas (Eds.),

Feedback: The communication of praise criticism, and advice (Vol. 11, pp. 305–321). New York, NY: Lang.

Sanders, M., & Pidgeon, A. (2011). The role of parenting programmes in the prevention of child maltreatment. *Australian Psychologist, 46*, 199–209. doi:10.1111/j.1742-9544.2010.00012.x

Schlinger, H. D. (1995). *A behavior analytic view of child development.* New York, NY: Plenum Press.

Smetana, J. G. (2008). "It's 10 o'clock: Do you know where your children are?" Recent advances in understanding parental monitoring and adolescents' information management. *Child Development Perspectives, 2*, 19–25. doi:10.1111/j.1750-8606.2008.00036.x

Stallman, H. M., & Sanders, M. R. (2007). "Family Transitions Triple P": The theoretical basis and development of a program for parents going through divorce. *Journal of Divorce and Remarriage, 47*, 133–153. doi:10.1300/J087v47n03_07

West, F., Sanders, M. R., Cleghorn, G. J., & Davies, P. S. W. (2010). Randomised clinical trial of a family-based lifestyle intervention for childhood obesity involving parents as the exclusive agents of change. *Behavior Research and Therapy, 48*, 1170–1179. doi:10.1016/j.brat.2010.08.008

Wiggins, T., Sofronoff, K., & Sanders, M. R. (2009). Pathways Triple P-Positive Parenting Program: Effects on parent-child relationships and child behavior problems. *Family Process, 48*, 517–530. doi:10.1111/j.1545-5300.2009.01299.x

APPLICATIONS OF POSITIVE PARENTING TO SOCIAL, EMOTIONAL, AND HEALTH PROBLEMS

APPLICATIONS OF POSITIVE PARENTING

An Introduction

TREVOR G. MAZZUCCHELLI

Since its inception, Triple P has been concerned with generalization of positive parenting and how learning in one context can be applied to another context or to new situations. The intervention that evolved into Triple P began as a home-delivered program for preschool children with disruptive behavior (Sanders & Glynn, 1981). The focus of this foundational research concerned the effectiveness of methods to enhance parents' ability to generalize parenting skills from one setting (the home) to a variety of other settings (such as the playground or school) and the benefits of doing so. Triple P continues to be concerned with generalization, transfer of learning, and psychological flexibility; however, since Triple P has evolved into a multilevel system of intervention, developers and researchers are now concerned with the extent to which the system can be applied to address a range of problems and support a variety of different populations.

Externalizing behavior problems are the leading reason for psychiatric referral of young children and place children at increased risk for a range of other developmental problems (National Institute for Health and Care Excellence, 2013). In Chapter 6, Mazzucchelli and Sanders summarize the costs of these problems and the relevance of parenting interventions. They note that applications of Triple P to the prevention and treatment of externalizing behavior problems go back to the very origin of Triple P, and that interventions at each level of the Triple P system have been found to have a positive impact on parenting practices and disruptive behavior. Although the available evidence clearly supports Triple P as an effective approach for the prevention and treatment of externalizing behavior problems, there are many areas that require further exploration. Two of the most pressing (and related) issues are how to increase the reach of evidence-based parenting support and how to increase the engagement of vulnerable, disadvantaged, parents.

Peer relationships play a vital role in children's development and well-being (Rubin, Bukowski, & Parker, 2006). Because children learn social skills through patterns of interactions in the home, parenting has the potential to have a major impact on the development of child social competence and emotional control. These competences, in turn, have been found to affect children's peer relationships. In Chapter 7, Healy introduces the concept of facilitative parenting and describes how Resilience Triple P, a new variant, combines facilitative parenting and child peer relationship training to reduce victimization and aggression towards peers and promote positive peer relationships.

Anxiety disorders are the most common form of psychopathology reported by children and adolescents; these disorders can have debilitating consequences and, in many cases, follow a chronic and persistent course (Rapee, Schniering, & Hudson, 2009). Although child-focused psychotherapy is considered the gold standard approach for these issues, in Chapter 8, Cobham describes the compelling reasons for working with parents when treating child anxiety. In this chapter, the conceptual and empirical support for Triple P in the prevention and treatment of childhood anxiety is reviewed.

Children with a developmental disability are at a substantially greater risk, when compared to their typically developing peers, of showing a variety of emotional and behavioral problems (Einfeld, Ellis, & Emerson, 2011). These problems, along with a family's adjustment to the disability, can have a profound impact on the child's and family's life course. In Chapter 9, Mazzucchelli and Studman provide an overview of Stepping Stones Triple P and how this parallel system of parenting support has been applied to improve child and family outcomes for families who have a child with a disability.

Triple P aims to equip carers with the skills to raise well-adjusted, healthy, children. However, a significant number of children and adolescents experience serious mental illness that adversely affects all family members and complicates parents' role in the care of their child (Lawrence et al., 2016). Parents are a critical protective factor in children's lives. The challenge is to capitalize on this and complement mental health treatment with parenting support to maximize symptom reduction and encourage well-being. In Chapter 10, Burke reviews the significance of this issue and the important role that parenting can have in promoting the development of children experiencing mental health problems. Examples of how Triple P has and could be used to promote evidence-based parent consultation in child and adolescent mental health services are described.

Childhood chronic illness, such as asthma and diabetes, are common and threaten the health and development of children and the well-being of families (Australian Institute of Health and Welfare, 2012). Morawska (Chapter 11, this volume), in the sixth chapter of this section, examines the relationship between chronic childhood illness, parenting, and child and family adjustment, as well as how Triple P has been applied to assist families manage and adjust to these conditions. Evidence is presented suggesting that parenting interventions have the potential to improve not only children's and families' quality of life but also children's physical health. Parenting and family interventions have a critical role in the care of children with chronic health conditions, and this is clearly an area requiring further research and practical attention.

The rising prevalence of childhood obesity may be considered a global health challenge (Ng et al., 2014). The public health costs associated with the physical consequences of obesity alone are estimated to be enormous (e.g., Cawley & Meyerhoefer, 2012). In Chapter 12, Bartlett and Sanders explore the potential of parenting support to address this challenge. They present the rationale for parents being recruited as agents of lifestyle change, as well as the obstacles that have been encountered when adopting this approach. They go on to describe Lifestyle Triple P—a system of interventions developed specifically to prevent and treat childhood obesity—and how this variant of Triple P may overcome these obstacles. They report evidence supporting Lifestyle Triple P in addition to considering how evidence-based parenting support could be implemented to be a major part of the solution to this serious public health dilemma.

Problem behaviors in adolescence range from everyday issues such as fighting with siblings, talking back to parents, and not doing to schoolwork, to high-risk behaviors, such as the use of alcohol, tobacco, and other drugs, through to very serious problems such as suicide, delinquency, and unintended pregnancy (Chu, Farruggia, Sanders, & Ralph, 2012). All these problems are potentially preventable. In the final chapter of this section, Ralph (Chapter 13, this volume) explores the role that parenting factors have in the emergence, maintenance, and exacerbation of these problem behaviors in adolescence. Ralph then reviews how an upward extension of the core Triple P suite of programs, Teen Triple P, has been applied to manage and prevent serious adolescent behavior problems. The argument is that parenting support for the carers of adolescents should not be considered to be an "optional extra" but rather an essential component of a population-wide system of parenting support to promote the healthy development of children and adolescents.

In summary, the series of eight chapters that comprise the remainder of this section illustrate that the Triple P system is robust in addressing a diverse range of child behavioral, emotional, and health problems and for a variety of different groups of high-risk or vulnerable parents and children. From Sanders and Glynn's (1981) nascent study investigating transfer of learning and parents' generalization of parenting skills, there is evidence that the Triple P system is widely applicable and has enormous potential to improve the lives of children and families.

REFERENCES

Australian Institute of Health and Welfare. (2012). *A picture of Australia's children 2012* (Cat. no. PHE 167). Canberra, Australia: Author. Retrieved from http://www.aihw.gov.au/WorkArea/DownloadAsset.aspx?id=10737423340

Cawley, J., & Meyerhoefer, C. (2012). The medical care costs of obesity: An instrumental variables approach. *Journal of Health Economics, 31,* 219–230. doi:10.1016/j.jhealeco.2011.10.003

Chu, J. T., Farruggia, S. P., Sanders, M. R., & Ralph, A. (2012). Towards a public health approach to parenting programmes for parents of adolescents. *Journal of Public Health, 34,* i41–i47. doi:10.1093/pubmed/fdr123

Einfeld, S. L., Ellis, L. A., & Emerson, E. (2011). Comorbidity of intellectual disability and mental disorder in children and adolescents: a systematic review. *Journal of Intellectual and Developmental Disabilities, 36,* 137–143. doi:10.1080/13668250.2011.572548

Lawrence, D., Hafekost, J., Johnson, S. E., Saw, S., Buckingham, W. J., Sawyer, M. G., . . . Zubrick, S. R. (2016). Key findings from the second Australian Child and Adolescent Survey of Mental Health and Wellbeing. *Australian and New Zealand Journal of Psychiatry, 50,* 876–886. doi:10.1177/0004867415617836

National Institute for Health and Care Excellence. (2013). *Antisocial behaviour and conduct disorders in children and young people: Recognition, intervention and management* (National Clinical Guideline Number 158). London, England: British Psychological Society and Royal College of Psychiatrists.

Ng, M., Fleming, T., Robinson, M., Thomson, B., Graetz, N., Margono, C., . . . Gakidou, E. (2014). Global, regional, and national prevalence of overweight and obesity in children and adults during 1980–2013: A systematic analysis for the Global Burden of Disease Study 2013. *Lancet, 384,* 766–781. doi:10.1016/S0140-6736(14)60460-8

Rapee, R. M., Schniering, C. A., & Hudson, J. L. (2009). Anxiety disorders during childhood and adolescence: Origins and treatment. *Annual Review of Clinical Psychology, 5,* 311–341. doi:10.1146/annurev.clinpsy.032408.153628

Rubin, K. H., Bukowski, W., & Parker, J. (2006). Peer interactions, relationships, and groups. In N. Eisenberg (Ed.), *Handbook of child psychology: Social, emotional, and personality development* (pp. 571–645). New York, NY: Wiley.

Sanders, M. R., & Glynn, T. (1981). Training parents in behavioral self-management: An analysis of generalization and maintenance. *Journal of Applied Behavior Analysis, 14,* 223–237. doi:10.1901/jaba.1981.14-223

CHAPTER 6

CHILDREN WITH EXTERNALIZING BEHAVIOR PROBLEMS

TREVOR G. MAZZUCCHELLI AND MATTHEW R. SANDERS

A well-known distinction in the field of child psychology and psychiatry is that between externalizing and internalizing behavior problems. While internalizing behaviors, such as anxious and depressed behaviors, refer to problems that primarily affect the child's *internal* psychological state, externalizing behaviors refer to the child acting negatively on the *external* environment. The term *externalizing behavior* refers to behaviors ranging from complaining, refusal to comply with rules and requests, to lying, aggression, destroying property, and stealing. Dimensional and categorical systems are used in efforts to classify externalizing behavior problems, and these problems include the diagnostic categories of oppositional defiant disorder (ODD) and conduct disorder (CD; American Psychiatric Association, 2013).

Externalizing behavior problems are among the most common of all childhood adjustment problems and are the main reason for referral to child and adolescent mental health services (Kazdin, 2008). The worldwide prevalence rates of ODD and CD are estimated to be 3.6% and 2.1%, respectively (Polanczyk, Salum, Sugaya, Caye, & Rohde, 2015). Disruptive behavior disorders in childhood are associated with a range of serious short- and long-term problems and are the most reliable predictor of adult mental health problems (Copeland, Shanahan, Costello, & Angold, 2009). Children with externalizing behavior disorders often experience learning problems (Moilanen, Shaw, & Maxwell, 2010); poor social skills and interpersonal relationships (Olweus, 2013); depression (Burke, Hipwell, & Loeber, 2010); substance abuse (Fergusson, Horwood, & Ridder, 2007); violent criminal behavior (Piquero, Jennings, & Barnes, 2012); and suicide (Nock et al., 2008).

In addition to the costs to the individual, long-term disruptive behavior represents a large cost to the community. For instance, the cost of additional public services provided to children with conduct problems have been estimated to be US$10,000 a year (Foster, Jones, & the Conduct Problems Prevention Research Group, 2005). The lifetime cost of crime imposed on society by a child with conduct problems is estimated to be in the millions of dollars (Cohen & Piquero, 2009). Furthermore, there are many victims of arson, burglary, murder, rape, spouse or child abuse, and vandalism, crimes that are carried out to a much greater extent by people with a history of externalizing behavior problems than by others (Mordre, Groholt, Kjelsberg, Sandstad, & Myhre, 2011).

DEVELOPMENT AND COURSE OF EXTERNALIZING BEHAVIOR PROBLEMS

At least two pathways have been identified for the development of externalizing behavior problems in children, a life-course-persistent (LCP) path and an adolescent-limited (AL) path (Moffitt, 2006; Piquero et al., 2012). The LCP pathway refers to a developmental progression of conduct problems that have been evident from an early age. The LCP pathway often begins before preschool and is characterized by a more persistent life course and more severe and pervasive problems. Children following the AL pathway do not show oppositional behavior as young children but show conduct-disordered behaviors such as deceitfulness, skipping school, taking drugs, and other delinquent activities as teenagers. These adolescents exhibit less impairment than the LCP pathway children and are more likely to remit their problem behaviors before adulthood (Moffitt, 2006).

The principal settings for the development of externalizing behavior problems may differ for the LCP and AL pathways. Moffitt (2006) suggested that children on the LCP path have neuropsychological impairments, such as poor attention and hyperactivity, that interact with an adverse home environment and set the stage for problem behavior persisting throughout the child's life. In contrast, for the AL pathway, externalizing behavior is believed to take place with same-age peers during the teenage years. AL externalizing problems may be precipitated or exacerbated by family stressors such as parental conflict or job loss that disrupts parenting practices (Conger et al., 2002; Dishion & Patterson, 2006). This disruption provides youth with the opportunity to spend time with deviant peer groups (e.g., youth on the LC path), where they are exposed to antisocial acts. There is evidence that AL youth then mimic the antisocial behavior of others to obtain peer approval and escape the aversive behaviour of peers (Piehler & Dishion, 2014; Van Ryzin & Dishion, 2013).

PARENTING AND FAMILY FACTORS AS DETERMINANTS OF DEVELOPMENTAL OUTCOMES

The expression and causes of externalizing behavior problems vary according to developmental stage. Predisposing child factors include genetic risk (Bornovalova, Hicks, Iacono, & McGue, 2010); male gender (at least for early-onset disruptive behavior; Eme, 2007); neurobiological deficits such as low arousal and reactivity (van Goozen, Fairchild, & Harold, 2008); temperamental difficulties (De Pauw, & Mervielde, 2010); and some social information-processing biases and deficits (Mize & Pettit, 2008). A variety of environmental and interactional factors appear to increase or decrease the risk of those children who are already vulnerable. Some child characteristics, such as emotional reactivity, appear to make children differentially susceptible to certain environmental conditions, including parenting practices—exhibiting worse functioning when exposed to adverse parenting practices and better functioning when exposed to sensitive parenting (e.g., Bakermans-Kranenburg, & van Ijzendoorn, 2011; Scott & O'Connor, 2012). For young children, interactions between family members appear to be the most important factor in shaping the development of externalizing behavior problems.

Parental Coerciveness

Parents of children with externalizing behavior problems tend to be more coercive and use more severe forms of discipline than parents of children without such problems (Lansford et al., 2011). Parents of children with externalizing behavior problems are also more likely to respond negatively to children's behavior and to prolong conflict than parents of nonproblem children (Gardner, Ward, Burton, & Wilson, 2003). Children with behavior problems show a similar pattern when interacting with their parents, being more likely to initiate, continue, and escalate conflict compared to their nonproblem peers (Scaramella & Leve, 2004).

Parents may model disruptive behavior; however, the quality of parent–child interactions cultivates the development of externalizing behavior problems beyond the effects of modeling alone. The mechanisms for this have been described by Patterson and colleagues in their coercive family process model (Patterson, 1982, 2016). According to this process, children of coercive parents learn to use a range of defiant and disruptive behaviors to terminate parents' aversive behaviors. In this way, coercive behaviors are maintained for both children and parents by patterns of mutual negative reinforcement. Over time, the rate and intensity of these behaviors can escalate, sometimes leading to physical aggression. Both parent and child become sensitized to each other's aversive behavior, differentially responding to these behaviors compared to nonaversive behavior (Scaramella & Leve, 2004).

Parental Responsiveness

Another parenting factor related to child outcomes concerns the quality of the parent–child relationship. This relationship may be described in terms of parents' ability to be attentive to, nurturant, and responsive to their children. Responsiveness consists of being physically and emotionally available, indicated by behaviors such as showing interest in the child's activities, providing supervision and help, and recognizing the child's achievements. Parental responsiveness also concerns the setting and enforcement of developmentally appropriate limits, with the use of fair and nonphysical methods of discipline (Sanders, Gooley, & Nicholson, 2000). This style of parenting has been referred to as authoritative parenting (Baumrind, 2013). There is a wealth of evidence that supports the relationship between authoritative or responsive parenting and positive developmental outcomes in children (e.g., Larzelere, Morris, Sheffield, & Harrist, 2013; Wille, Bettge, & Ravens-Sieberer, 2008).

THE ROLE OF FAMILY INTERVENTIONS

The rationale for family intervention is that particular aspects of family functioning are related to the etiology, maintenance, or exacerbation of child externalizing behavior problems. Family interventions aim to change these aspects of family functioning by alleviating behavioral or emotional problems of individual family members, improving the quality of relationships between family members (parental dyad relationships, parent–child relationships, sibling relationships), or improving the relationships between the family and the broader community. Practitioners seek to accomplish these goals via parenting programs that aim to improve parent–child relationships, and broader family interventions that aim to improve parental adjustment by influencing family and marital communication and problem-solving skills, stress management skills, and social support.

Numerous meta-analyses have found that evidence-based parenting support (EBPS) programs are effective in reducing child disruptive behavior (e.g., R. A. Epstein, Fonnesbeck, Potter, Rizzone, & McPheeters, 2015; Piquero et al., 2016; van Aar, Leijten, Orobio de Castro, & Overbeek, 2017). Further, reviews of psychosocial and pharmacological treatments have found that EBPS is the most critical intervention component for the prevention and treatment of child disruptive behavior disorders (e.g., R. Epstein, Fonnesbeck, Williamson, et al., 2015).

APPLICATIONS OF TRIPLE P TO EXTERNALIZING BEHAVIOR PROBLEMS

INDIVIDUAL FACE-TO-FACE INTERVENTIONS

Applications of Triple P to the prevention and treatment of externalizing behavior problems go back to the origins of Triple P. The first application of Triple P was as a home-delivered program targeting parents of children with externalizing behavior problems (Sanders & Glynn, 1981). This foundational study demonstrated not only the efficacy of the program on independently observed measures of child disruptive behavior and parenting but also that teaching parents self-regulation skills in addition to contingency management skills increased parents' ability to apply these skills to different child care settings.

Sanders and Dadds (1982) tested the effects of adding planned activities training (PAT) to Triple P's contingency management procedures. PAT emphasizes antecedent or preemptive parenting strategies rather than contingency management. They found that the addition of PAT resulted in greater reductions in externalizing behavior from that achieved by contingency management alone and an enhancement in parents' generalization of parenting strategies to other home and community settings.

These foundational studies led to the development of Standard Triple P, a 10-session program in which parents are taught 17 parenting strategies and a routine for planning activities using active skills training methods through face-to-face support from a practitioner (see Box 6.1 for an example of this approach). The first randomized controlled trial (RCT) of this program involving a wait-list comparison condition included 87 preschoolers with co-occurring disruptive behavior and attentional/hyperactive difficulties (Bor, Sanders, & Markie-Dadds, 2002). Parents who participated in Standard Triple P reported lower levels of child behavior problems, lower levels of dysfunctional parenting, and greater parental competence. These changes were sustained through to 1-year follow-up, at which time 80% of the children also showed clinically reliable improvement in observed negative behavior.

To widen the reach and normalize the provision of parenting support, a brief face-to-face version of Triple P was developed for delivery in primary health care settings. Primary Care

BOX 6.1: The Delivery of Standard Triple P to Support a Family With Child Disruptive Behavior

Hugo, aged 6, was frequently angry and aggressive at home and at school. At home, Hugo argued with his parents, started fights with his siblings, and smashed toys and furniture if he didn't get his own way. At school, Hugo frequently fought with peers but denied any wrongdoing. When Hugo required stitches to his foot after kicking a window, the family's general practitioner referred the family to a psychologist. The initial assessment—involving an interview, the completion of questionnaires, and an observation of a family problem-solving discussion—revealed discrepant parenting practices between Hugo's parents. Hugo's father had a tendency to be quite lax, although at times overreacted and resorted to spanking. In contrast, his mother tended to use a lot of talking and reasoning when Hugo misbehaved. Hugo's parents reported many disagreements about how they should manage Hugo's behavior. They also reported financial stress and significant personal adjustment problems. Hugo's father had sustained a neck injury after a car accident and had been in work only intermittently over the previous 2 years. He spent much of his time at home sleeping or watching TV. Hugo's mother worked full time in a dry cleaning shop. She had a history of anxiety and depression.

After a session in which assessment findings were shared with the parents and possible influences on Hugo's behavior were explored, the parents agreed to put aside their differences and work together as a team in managing Hugo's behavior. The parents found that setting up interesting activities for Hugo and his siblings, talking calmly, and praising calm and cooperative behavior had the immediate effect of reducing the frequency of Hugo's emotional outbursts. The greatest challenge for the parents were finding ways to manage their own frustration and responding calmly when misbehavior did occur. The psychologist problem-solved with the parents how they could effectively implement strategies for managing misbehavior. Fortunately, the parents reported that Hugo was becoming more compliant, and many of his problem behaviors could be prevented or managed with calm instructions. Corresponding to an improvement in Hugo's behavior at home and at school, Hugo's parents reported feeling happier and more confident. The parents also showed evidence of being more proactive and future oriented themselves. At the end of the intervention, Hugo's father indicated that he was actively looking for part-time work to supplement the family's income, and that they intended taking a family holiday at the end of the year. Twelve sessions were provided over a 4-month of period.

Triple P can be delivered either as a three- to four-session program with skill rehearsal for parents of children with mild-to-moderate specific emotional, behavioral, or developmental concerns or as a brief one- to two-session intervention providing early anticipatory guidance for mild issues. Trials of Primary Care Triple P have found benefits for families, including lower levels of child behavior problems, dysfunctional parenting, and parental anxiety and stress (see Chapter 20, this volume, for a review).

GROUP INTERVENTIONS

Group Triple P, consisting of four 2-hour group sessions and four brief telephone consultations, was developed to increase the reach of Triple P. The first trial of Group Triple P employed a quasi-experimental design involving 1,610 parents from two low-income catchment areas in Perth, Western Australia. Parents who participated in Group Triple P reported significantly less child disruptive behavior and dysfunctional parenting and lower levels of parent mental health problems and relationship distress than parents in comparison communities who received their usual services. These intervention effects were sustained at 1- and 2-year follow-up (Zubrick et al., 2005). The beneficial effects of Group Triple P for children and parents have been replicated in many RCTs with families from a diverse range of cultures and countries (see Sanders, Kirby, Tellegen, & Day, 2014).

Two other group variants of Triple P have also shown promise for the prevention and treatment of disruptive behavior disorders. A three-session, large-group seminar series was developed as a transition-to-school program (Sanders et al., 2008). Large-scale rollouts of Triple P incorporating this seminar series have been shown to result in reductions in the number of children with emotional and behavioral problems (e.g., Sanders et al., 2008). In addition, stand-alone topic-specific discussion groups have been developed. Two RCTs have shown medium-to-large effects on disruptive behavior for groups devoted to disobedience and addressing problem behavior during shopping. These intervention effects were sustained through to 6-month follow-up in both trials (Joachim, Sanders, & Turner, 2010; Morawska, Haslam, Milne, & Sanders, 2011).

SELF-HELP INTERVENTIONS

To improve the access of parents living in rural and remote settings to parenting support, a self-directed version of Triple P was developed (Connell, Sanders, & Markie-Dadds, 1997). An RCT demonstrated that this parenting program could be successfully provided either via a workbook alone or in combination with a brief (10- to 30-minute) weekly telephone consultation to parents living in remote areas (Connell et al., 1997). Subsequent RCTs have demonstrated that this self-help plus telephone-assisted intervention is effective when delivered by a regular telephone counseling service for parents of toddlers (Morawska & Sanders 2006) and parents of preschoolers displaying externalizing behavior problems (Markie-Dadds & Sanders 2006).

In response to consumer preference studies indicating a desire to access parenting advice through the Internet (e.g., Sanders, Haslam, Calam, Southwell, & Stallman, 2011), a web-based self-help version of Triple P was developed. Known as Triple P Online (TPOL), this program consists of eight educational modules with interactive exercises and brief instructional videos. The foundational trial found that TPOL is associated with reductions in child problem behavior, dysfunctional parenting, and parental anger and with improvements in parenting confidence, with delayed effects also found for observed child behavior, parental stress, and partner conflict (Sanders, Baker, & Turner, 2012). Importantly, the magnitude of these effects was similar to those for in-person group delivery, and satisfaction with the program was high. Since this original RCT, several other trials have replicated the effectiveness of TPOL (see Chapter 26, this volume).

MULTILEVEL SYSTEMS APPROACHES

More recently, studies have begun investigating the potential of simultaneously implementing evidence-based parenting programs of the Triple P system at all levels of intensity. The assumption is that this approach allows synergies to develop, permitting effects to be detectable at a population level. Examples of this approach in creating population-level change in parenting practices, child externalizing behavior problems, as well as other child mental health outcomes are described in this volume by Owens, Doyle, Hegarty, Heavey, and Farrell (Chapter 40), Prinz and Shapiro (Chapter 39), and Sofronoff, Gray, Einfeld, and Tonge (Chapter 41).

UPWARD EXTENSION TO ADOLESCENTS

The physical, emotional, behavioral, and environmental changes that occur at the time of puberty can challenge parents' ability to support their child's healthy development. Parents must make adjustments in how they interact with their children as they transition into adulthood. In response to these challenges, an upward extension of Triple P known as Teen Triple P was developed that includes parallel versions of each of the intervention variants outlined previously. Efficacy and effectiveness studies indicate that participation in these interventions result in decreases in teen disruptive behaviors and parent–teen conflict, as well as reductions in ineffective parenting strategies and conflict between parents over childrearing issues (see Chapter 13, this volume, for a review).

SUMMARY OF EVIDENCE

Triple P has accumulated a large evidence base for the prevention and treatment of externalizing behavior problems in children, including independent replications of various Triple P interventions across several countries and cultures. Several meta-analyses and reviews have been conducted describing this evidence, with all concluding that Triple P has a positive effect on children's behavior and adjustment. Most recently, Sanders et al. (2014) synthesized the data from 101 studies involving 16,000 families. When data from all levels of Triple P were combined, there were significant short-term medium effect sizes for child social, emotional, and behavioral outcomes and parenting practices. Significant small-to-medium effects were also found for parental adjustment and parental relationship satisfaction. These effects sustained through to follow-up. These results indicate that Triple P can both improve child social, emotional, and behavioral outcomes and improve other family factors implicated in the development of externalizing behavior problems. While targeted and treatment studies were associated with larger effect sizes than universal studies, all three types of study produced significant effect sizes. This indicates that the Triple P system has value as a preventive intervention and as a treatment for disruptive behavior disorders.

IMPLICATIONS FOR PRACTICE, POLICY, OR RESEARCH

The quality of parenting that children receive has a major impact on the onset, maintenance, and exacerbation of child externalizing behavior problems. Importantly, every intervention of the

Triple P system has been demonstrated to be effective in modifying implicated parenting and family variables as well as improving child emotional and behavioral outcomes. This provides practitioners with a range of options to provide effective parenting support in a manner that meets consumers' preferences and needs.

Despite the effectiveness of Triple P, the uptake of parenting support is likely to be affected by the prevailing sociopolitical climate. Parenting programs work best when they are provided in a sociopolitical context that values children, recognizes the importance of parenting, and is prepared to commit to the provision of high-quality parenting support (Sanders, 2012). It is thus incumbent on social policy advocates and policymakers to ensure child- and family-friendly policies and practices that promote the well-being of children and families (e.g., extended paid parental leave, housing subsidies, universal parenting education).

The available evidence clearly supports Triple P as an effective approach for the prevention and treatment of externalizing behavior problems in children; however, there are a number of areas that require further exploration. First, there is a need to examine potential mediators of Triple P intervention effects. To date, few studies have explored the mechanisms that may account for the observed changes in various child and parent outcomes. For instance, are changes in child behaviors due to increased responsiveness and less coerciveness in interactions? Are other potential mechanisms also implicated in intervention effects? For example, these changes include changes in parental emotion (anger), cognitions (dysfunctional attributions), as well as behavior. While Triple P has been demonstrated to be an effective program when compared to no treatment and wait-list control conditions, more research is needed to compare Triple P to active alternative intervention conditions to determine whether it can produce outcomes beyond other services. The evidence base for Teen Triple P is not yet as comprehensive as it is for the Triple P programs targeting 2- to 12-year-old children, and more effectiveness trials are needed for parenting programs involving adolescents. Finally, despite evidence suggesting that family interventions are efficacious and cost-effective approaches to child externalizing behavior problems, when given the opportunity, the majority of families who might benefit often do not participate. More work is needed regarding how to engage vulnerable, disadvantaged parents to participate in effective parenting support.

CONCLUSION

The present chapter has summarized the costs and influences of child externalizing behavior problems and reviewed the applications of Triple P to these problems. Interventions at each level of the Triple P system have been demonstrated to have a positive impact on parenting practices and externalizing behavior problems (ranging from self-directed interventions to intensive individual face-to-face interventions). With increasing recognition of the importance of parenting and the benefits of delivering all levels of Triple P in an integrated manner, there is the prospect that a considerably greater number of children will grow up in responsive family environments and be spared the pernicious consequences of externalizing behavior problems.

KEY MESSAGES

- Externalizing behavior problems are common, can have an early age of onset, are relatively stable, and bring enormous costs to the child, family, and broader community.
- Two primary pathways for the development of externalizing behavior problems have been identified, the LCP path and the AL path.
- Parenting and other family factors have been implicated in both the LCP and the AL pathways.
- Evidence-based parenting support can play an important role in the prevention and treatment of externalizing behavior problems.
- All intensities and delivery modes of Triple P have been found to be effective in reducing externalizing behavior problems, reducing associated family risk factors, and enhancing family protective factors.
- A multilevel system population approach in which evidence-based parenting programs are incorporated into existing services has the potential to achieve a population-level decrease in rates of externalizing behavior problems.

REFERENCES

American Psychiatric Association. (2013). *Diagnostic and statistical manual of mental disorders* (5th ed.). Washington, DC: Author.

Bakermans-Kranenburg, M. J., & van Ijzendoorn, M. H. (2011). Differential susceptibility to rearing environment depending on dopamine-related genes: new evidence and a meta-analysis. *Developmental Psychopathology, 23,* 39–52. doi:10.1017/S0954579410000635

Baumrind, D. (2013). Authoritative parenting revisited: History and current status. In R. E. Larzelere, A. S. Morris, & A. W. Harrist (Eds.), *Authoritative parenting: Synthesizing nurturance and discipline for optimal child development* (pp. 11–34). Washington, DC: American Psychological Association.

Bor, W., Sanders, M. R., & Markie-Dadds, C. (2002). The effects of the Triple P—Positive Parenting Program on preschool children with co-occurring disruptive behavior and attentional/hyperactive difficulties. *Journal of Abnormal Child Psychology, 30,* 571–587. doi:10.1023/A:1020807613155

Bornovalova, M. A., Hicks, B. M., Iacono, W. G., & McGue, M. (2010). Familial transmission and heritability of childhood disruptive disorders. *The American Journal of Psychiatry, 167,* 1066–1074. doi:10.1176/appi.ajp.2010.09091272

Burke, J. D., Hipwell, A. E., & Loeber, R. (2010). Dimensions of oppositional defiant disorder as predictors of depression and conduct disorder in preadolescent girls. *Journal of the American Academy of Child and Adolescent Psychiatry, 49,* 484–492. doi:10.1016/j.jaac.2010.01.016

Cohen, M. A., & Piquero, A. R. (2009). New evidence on the monetary value of saving a high risk youth. *Journal of Quantitative Criminology, 25,* 25–49. doi:10.1007/s10940-008-9057-3

Conger, R. D., Wallace, L. E., Sun, Y., Simons, R. L., McLoyd, V. C., & Brody, G. H. (2002). Economic pressure in African American families: A replication and extension of the family stress model. *Developmental Psychology, 38,* 179–193. doi:10.1037/0012-1649.38.2.179

Connell, S., Sanders, M. R., & Markie-Dadds, C. (1997). Self-directed behavioral family intervention for parents of oppositional children in rural and remote areas. *Behavior Modification, 21,* 379–408. doi:10.1177/01454455970214001

Copeland, W. E., Shanahan, L., Costello, J., & Angold, A. (2009). Childhood and adolescent psychiatric disorders as predictors of young adult disorders. *Archives of General Psychiatry, 66,* 764–772. doi:10.1001/archgenpsychiatry.2009.85

De Pauw, S. S. W., & Mervielde, I. (2010). Temperament, personality and developmental psychopathology: A review based on the conceptual dimensions underlying childhood traits. *Child Psychiatry and Human Development, 41,* 313–329. doi:10.1007/s10578-009-0171-8

Dishion, T. J., & Patterson, G. R. (2006). The development and ecology of antisocial behavior in children and adolescents. In D. Cicchetti & D. J. Cohen (Eds.), *Developmental psychopathology, Vol. 3: Risk, disorder, and adaptation* (2nd ed., pp. 503–541). Hoboken, NJ: Wiley.

Eme, R. F. (2007). Sex differences in child-onset, life-course persistent conduct disorder. A review of biological influences. *Clinical Psychology Review, 27,* 607–627. doi:10.1016/j.cpr.2007.02.001

Epstein, R., Fonnesbeck, C., Williamson, E., Kuhn, T., Lindegren, M. L., Rizzone, K., . . . McPheeters, M. (2015). *Psychosocial and pharmacologic interventions for disruptive behavior in children and adolescents* (Comparative Effectiveness Review No. 154). Rockville, MD: Agency for Healthcare Research and Quality. Retrieved from https://www.ncbi.nlm.nih.gov/pubmedhealth/n/cer154/pdf/

Epstein, R. A., Fonnesbeck, C., Potter, S., Rizzone, K. H., & McPheeters, M. (2015). Psychosocial interventions for child disruptive behaviors: A meta-analysis. *Pediatrics, 136.* doi:10.1542/peds.2015-2577

Fergusson, D. M., Horwood, L. J., & Ridder, E. M. (2007). Conduct and attentional problems in childhood and adolescence and later substance use, abuse and dependence: Results of a 25-year longitudinal study. *Drug and Alcohol Dependence, 88,* S14–S26. doi:10.1016/j.drugalcdep.2006.12.011

Foster, E. M., Jones, D. E., & the Conduct Problems Prevention Research Group. (2005). The high costs of aggression: Public expenditures resulting from conduct disorder. *American Journal of Public Health, 95,* 1767–1772. doi:10.2105/AJPH.2004.061424

Gardner, F., Ward, S., Burton, J., & Wilson, C. (2003). The role of mother-child joint play in the early development of children's conduct problems: A longitudinal observational study. *Social Development, 12,* 361–378. doi:10.1111/1467-9507.00238

Joachim, S., Sanders, M. R., & Turner, K. M. T. (2010). Reducing preschoolers' disruptive behavior in public with a brief parent discussion group. *Child Psychiatry and Human Development, 41,* 47–60. doi:10.1007/s10578-009-0151-z

Kazdin, A. (2008). Evidence-based treatments and delivery of psychological services: Shifting our emphases to increase impact. *Psychological Services, 5,* 201–215. doi:10.1037/a0012573

Lansford, J. E., Criss, M. M., Laird, R. D., Shaw, D. S., Pettit, G. S., Bates, J. E., & Dodge, K. A. (2011). Reciprocal relations between parents' physical discipline and children's externalizing behavior during middle childhood and adolescence. *Development and Psychopathology, 23,* 225–238. doi:10.1017/S0954579410000751

Larzelere, R. E., Morris, A. Sheffield, & Harrist, A. W. (Eds.). (2013). *Authoritative parenting: Synthesizing nurturance and discipline for optimal child development.* Washington, DC: American Psychological Association.

Markie-Dadds, C., & Sanders, M. R. (2006). Self-Directed Triple P (Positive Parenting Program) for mothers with children at-risk of developing conduct problems. *Behavioral and Cognitive Psychotherapy, 34,* 259–275. doi:10.1017/S1352465806002797

Mize, J., & Pettit, G. S. (2008). Social information processing and the development of conduct problems in children and adolescents: Looking beneath the surface. In C. Sharp, P. Fonagy, & I. Goodyer (Eds.), *Social cognition and developmental psychopathology* (Chapter 6). New York, NY: Oxford University Press.

Moffitt, T. E. (2006). Life-course-persistent versus adolescence-limited antisocial behavior. In D. Cicchetti & D. J. Cohen (Eds.), *Developmental psychopathology, Vol. 3: Risk, disorder, and adaptation* (2nd ed., pp. 570–598). Hoboken, NJ: Wiley.

Moilanen, K. L., Shaw, D. S., & Maxwell, K. L. (2010). Developmental cascades: Externalizing, internalizing, and academic competence from middle childhood to early adolescence. *Developmental Psychopathology*, *22*, 635–653. doi:10.1017/S0954579410000337

Morawska, A., Haslam, D., Milne, D., & Sanders, M. R. (2011). Evaluation of a brief parenting discussion group for parents of young children. *Journal of Developmental and Behavioral Pediatrics*, *32*, 136–145. doi:10.1097/DBP.0b013e3181f17a28

Morawska, A., & Sanders, M. R. (2006). Self-administered behavioral family intervention for parents of toddlers: Part I. Efficacy. *Journal of Consulting and Clinical Psychology*, *74*, 10–19. doi:10.1037/0022-006X.74.1.10

Mordre, M., Groholt, B., Kjelsberg, E., Sandstad, B., & Myhre, A. M. (2011). The impact of ADHD and conduct disorder in childhood on adult delinquency: A 30 years follow-up study using official crime records. *BMC Psychiatry*, *11*, 57. doi:10.1186/1471-244x-11-57

Nock, M. K., Borges, G., Bromet, E. J., Alonso, J., Angermeyer, M., Beautrais, A., . . . Williams, D. (2008). Cross-national prevalence and risk factors for suicidal ideation, plans and attempts. *The British Journal of Psychiatry*, *192*, 98–105. doi:10.1192/bjp.bp.107.040113

Olweus, D. (2013). School bullying: Development and some important challenges. *Annual Review of Clinical Psychology*, *9*, 751–780. doi:10.1146/annurev-clinpsy-050212-185516

Patterson, G. R. (1982). *Coercive family process: A social learning approach* (Vol. 3). Eugene, OR: Castalia.

Patterson, G. R. (2016). Coercion theory: The study of change. In T. J. Dishion & J. J. Snyder (Eds.), *The Oxford Handbook of Coercive Relationship Dynamics* (pp. 7–22). New York, NY: Oxford University Press.

Piehler, T. F., & Dishion, T. J. (2014). Dyadic coregulation and deviant talk in adolescent friendships: Interaction patterns associated with problematic substance use in early adulthood. *Developmental Psychology*, *50*, 1160–1169. doi:10.1037/a0034698

Piquero, A. R., Jennings, W. G., & Barnes, J. (2012). Violence in criminal careers: A review of the literature from a developmental life-course perspective. *Aggression and Violent Behavior*, *17*, 171–179. doi:10.1016/j.avb.2012.02.008

Piquero, A. R., Jennings, W. G., Diamond, B., Farrington, D. P., Tremblay, R. E., Welsh, B. C., & Reingle Gonzalez, J. M. (2016). A meta-analysis update on the effects of early family/parent training programs on antisocial behavior and delinquency. *Journal of Experimental Criminology*, *12*, 229–248. doi:10.1007/s11292-016-9256-0

Polanczyk, G. V., Salum, G. A., Sugaya, L. S., Caye, A., & Rohde, L. A. (2015). Annual research review: A meta-analysis of the worldwide prevalence of mental disorders in children and adolescents. *Journal of Child Psychology and Psychiatry*, *56*, 345–365. doi:10.1111/jcpp.12381

Sanders, M. R. (2012). Development, evaluation, and multinational dissemination of the Triple P—Positive Parenting Program. *Annual Review of Clinical Psychology*, *8*, 345–379. doi:10.1146/annurev-clinpsy-032511-143104

Sanders, M. R., Baker, S., & Turner, K. M. T. (2012). A randomized controlled trial evaluating the efficacy of Triple P Online with parents of children with early-onset conduct problems. *Behaviour Research and Therapy*, *50*, 675–684. doi:10.1016/j.brat.2012.07.004

Sanders, M. R., & Dadds, M. R. (1982). The effects of planned activities and child management procedures in parent training: An analysis of setting generality. *Behavior Therapy*, *13*, 452–461. doi:10.1007/BF00918375

Sanders, M. R., & Glynn, T. (1981). Training parents in behavioral self-management: An analysis of generalization and maintenance. *Journal of Applied Behavior Analysis*, *14*, 223–237. doi:10.1901/jaba.1981.14-223

Sanders, M. R., Gooley, S., & Nicholson, J. (2000). *Early intervention in conduct problems in children* (Vol. 3). Adelaide, Australia: Australian Early Intervention Network for Mental Health in Young People.

Sanders, M. R., Haslam, D. M., Calam, R., Southwell, C., & Stallman, H. M. (2011). Designing effective interventions for working parents: a web-based survey of parents in the UK workforce. *Journal of Children's Services, 6,* 186–200. doi:10.1108/17466661111176042

Sanders, M. R., Kirby, J. N., Tellegen, C. L., & Day, J. J. (2014). The Triple P—Positive Parenting Program: A systematic review and meta-analysis of a multi-level system of parenting support. *Clinical Psychology Review, 34,* 337–357. doi:10.1016/j.cpr.2014.04.003

Sanders, M. R., Ralph, A., Sofronoff, K., Gardiner, P., Thompson, R., Dwyer, S., & Bidwell, K. (2008). Every family: A population approach to reducing behavioral and emotional problems in children making the transition to school. *The Journal of Primary Prevention, 29,* 197–222. doi:10.1007/s10935-008-0139-7

Scaramella, L. V., & Leve, L. D. (2004). Clarifying parent-child reciprocities during early childhood: The early childhood coercion model. *Clinical Child and Family Psychology Review, 7,* 89–107. doi:10.1023/B:CCFP.0000030287.13160.a3

Scott, S., & O'Connor, T. G. (2012). An experimental test of differential susceptibility to parenting among emotionally-dysregulated children in a randomized controlled trial for oppositional behavior. *Journal of Child Psychology and Psychiatry, 53,* 1184–1193. doi:10.1111/j.1469-7610.2012.02586.x

van Aar, J., Leijten, P., Orobio de Castro, B., & Overbeek, G. (2017). Sustained, fade-out or sleeper effects? A systematic review and meta-analysis of parenting interventions for disruptive child behavior. *Clinical Psychology Review, 51,* 153–163. doi:10.1016/j.cpr.2016.11.006

van Goozen, S. H. M., Fairchild, G., & Harold, G. T. (2008). The role of neurobiological deficits in childhood antisocial behavior. *Current Directions in Psychological Science, 17,* 24–228. doi:10.1111/j.1467-8721.2008.00579.x

Van Ryzin, M. J., & Dishion, T. J. (2013). From antisocial behavior to violence: A model for the amplifying role of coercive joining in adolescent friendships. *Journal of Child Psychology and Psychiatry, 54,* 661–669. doi:10.1111/jcpp.12017

Wille, N., Bettge, S., & Ravens-Sieberer, U. (2008). Risk and protective factors for children's and adolescents' mental health: Results of the BELLA study. *European Child and Adolescent Psychiatry, 17,* 133–147. doi:10.1007/s00787-008-1015-y

Zubrick, S. R., Ward, K., Silburn, S. R., Lawrence, D., Williams, A. A., Blair, E., . . . Sanders, M. R. (2005). Prevention of child behavior problems through universal implementation of a group behavioral family intervention. *Prevention Science, 6,* 287–304. doi:10.1007/s11121-005-0013-2

C H A P T E R   7

CHILDREN WITH PEER RELATIONSHIP DIFFICULTIES

KARYN L. HEALY

No road is long with good company.

Turkish proverb

THE NATURE OF THE PEER RELATIONSHIP PROBLEMS

Peer relationships play a vital role in children's well-being. Positive peer relationships protect children and teenagers against the mental health consequences of bullying (Denny, Clark, Fleming, & Wall, 2004; Hodges, Boivin, Vitaro, & Bukowski, 1999) and predict better emotional adjustment, school retention (Jimerson, Egeland, Sroufe, & Carlson, 2000), and academic achievement (DeRosier, Kupersmidt, & Patterson, 1994) over time. A range of peer relationship problems have been described, including bullying, aggression, rejection and neglect, shyness and social withdrawal, conflict, lack of friendships, and parental concerns about peer pressure (Malik & Furman, 1993). This chapter focuses primarily on bullying, as arguably the most serious peer problem given its associations with major psychosocial problems such as conduct disorders and depression (LeBlanc, Sautter, & Dore, 2006).

Bullying is intentional and repeated behavior that causes hurt, or harm, to someone who feels powerless to protect themselves (National Centre Against Bullying, 2016). It can include actions that are verbal, physical, or social (such as exclusion) and can be carried out in person or through technology (cyberbullying). Being bullied by peers has been described as the single most important modifiable risk factor for mental illness in children and adolescents (Scott, Moore, Sly, & Norman, 2014). Well-controlled, longitudinal studies have shown that it leads to increased ongoing risk of depression, anxiety, psychosis, and self-harm (Arseneault et al., 2008; Fisher et al., 2012; Schreier et al., 2009). Ramifications continue into adult life, with victims at increased risk of poor health, psychiatric, and social problems well into adulthood, leading to a loss of income and employment and to poorer quality of life (Copeland, Wolke, Angold, & Costello, 2013; Wolke, Copeland, Angold, & Costello, 2013). Perpetrators of bullying are also at risk; children who bully in primary school have a higher risk of ongoing conduct problems, criminality, impaired mental health, and substance abuse problems in adolescence (Kumpulainen & Räsänen, 2000) and early adulthood (Copeland et al., 2013).

Most international efforts to reduce bullying have focused on school interventions, which, according to recent meta-analyses, make modest improvements in bullying and victimization (Merrell, Gueldner, Ross, & Isava, 2008; Ttofi & Farrington, 2011). A critical factor that discriminates effective from ineffective whole-school programs is the involvement of parents (Ttofi & Farrington, 2011). Recent research has examined the potential of parenting interventions to assist with children's peer problems through influencing peer relationships.

HOW PARENTING AFFECTS CHILDREN'S PEER RELATIONSHIPS AND RELATIONSHIP PROBLEMS

McDowell and Parke (2009) identified three distinct paths through which parenting influences children's social competence and peer relationships over time: (a) the quality of the parent–child relationship, (b) support of children to manage peer issues, and (c) provision of opportunities for peer interaction. The relationship between children's sibling relationships and peer relationships has been studied through separate research and is introduced as a fourth path of potential parental influence. All four paths are discussed in turn.

THE QUALITY OF THE PARENT–CHILD RELATIONSHIP

The parent–child relationship has been described as the template for all other relationships in a child's life. According to Parke and Ladd (1992), children learn how to relate to others through interacting with their parents and then transferring these patterns of behavior into other relationships, including peer relationships. The importance of warm, responsive parent–child relating is emphasized in both attachment theory and social learning theory. Warm, responsive parenting has been associated with better peer skills and relationships over time (McDowell & Parke, 2009) and was found, in a recent meta-analysis, to protect children against being bullied by peers (Lereya, Samara, & Wolke, 2013). On the other hand, low levels of warm parenting are associated with peer relationship problems: both being bullied (Ladd & Ladd, 1998) and bullying other children (Bowes et al., 2009).

SUPPORTING CHILDREN TO MANAGE PEER ISSUES

The second path through which parents influence good peer relationships is supporting children to manage peer issues (McDowell & Parke, 2009). This means supporting children to make decisions, rather than just telling them what to do. McDowell, Parke, and Wang (2003) found that parenting that was warm and responsive, but not overly controlling, predicted better peer relationships. A recent 14-year study found that greater parental support for child autonomy prior to starting school predicted reduced bullying at school (Rajendran, Kruszewski, & Halperin, 2016). On the other hand, overly intrusive or directive parenting has been associated with increased risk of victimization by peers (Ladd & Ladd, 1998).

PARENTS AS GATEKEEPERS OF PEER OPPORTUNITIES

Parents make many decisions that influence children's opportunities to develop relationships with peers, including choice of neighborhood, school, leisure activities, and opportunities to socialize (e.g., through play dates). McDowell and Parke (2009) found that this gatekeeper role predicts children's development of peer relationships. Parents of children who are bullied tend to be more overprotective than other parents (Bowers, Smith, & Binney, 1994), so in protecting children, may inadvertently deny children access to peers to develop friendships.

PARENTAL INFLUENCE THROUGH SIBLING RELATIONSHIPS

Parke and Ladd (1992) theorized that sibling relationships are an intermediate step through which children transfer relating skills from parent–child to peer relationships. Accordingly, victimization by peers is predicted by prior sibling victimization in both preschool and secondary school (Pellegrini & Roseth, 2006; Wolke & Samara, 2004).

THE ROLE OF PARENTING AND FAMILY INTERVENTIONS FOR CHILDREN'S PEER PROBLEMS

WHY PARENTING SUPPORT IS IMPORTANT IN RESOLVING THE PROBLEM

We have discussed several paths through which parents influence children's peer relationships. It therefore follows that interventions involving parents may help address peer relationship problems. Children are more likely to tell parents about peer problems than they are to tell teachers (Fekkes, Pijpers, & Verloove-Vanhorick, 2005), which places parents in a good position to coach the child. Unlike teachers, parents can assist away from the view of peers, thus reducing risk to the child's social reputation. Parents can also teach children to manage peer problems through issues with siblings. We first examine the role of parenting in addressing victimization and then in addressing perpetration of bullying.

THE ROLE OF PARENTING INTERVENTIONS FOR CHILDREN VICTIMIZED BY PEERS

Children who are bullied demonstrate distinctive patterns of peer interaction that are potentially modifiable. They have poorer social skills than other children (Cook, Williams, Guerra,

Kim, & Sadek, 2010). Quality of friendships is an important protective factor against bullying (Hodges et al., 1999). Most children who are bulled are "passive victims" who do little to provoke the perpetrator and tend to be submissive, depressed, and anxious (Perry, Hodges, & Egan, 2001). A significant minority of children who are bullied are "provocative victims" (Olweus, 1993), who tend to bully as well as be bullied (Schwartz, Dodge, Pettit, & Bates, 1997) and react angrily with unskilled aggression (Perry, Perry, & Kennedy, 1992). For both passive and provocative victims, the inability to regulate strong emotional reactions is a key determinant for ongoing victimization, forming a recursive pattern of worsening victimization and emotional reactivity over time (Reijntjes et al., 2011; Reijntjes, Kamphuis, Prinzie, & Telch, 2010). Interestingly, the same kind of parenting that positively influences children's peer relationships (McDowell & Parke, 2009) also influences children's skills in regulating emotions.

Both warm supportive parenting and overly directive parenting predict children's ability to regulate negative emotions. Warm, responsive parenting is associated with lower levels of child anger and better regulation of negative emotions (Robinson et al., 2009) and can also buffer children against adverse emotional consequences of bullying by peers (Bowes, Maughan, Caspi, Moffitt, & Arseneault, 2010). Graziano, Keane, and Calkins (2010) found that earlier parental overcontrol predicted poorer ability of children to cope with frustration on entering preschool. So, consistent parenting practices appear to support children's development of peer social skills and emotional regulation, and deficits in these skills are associated with peer problems. Healy, Sanders, and Iyer (2015) described these parenting practices together under the term *facilitative parenting*.

Facilitative parenting combines warm relating, enabling of child independence, coaching, support of friendships, and effective communication with the school. Healy et al. (2015) found that facilitative parenting and children's social and emotional behavior discriminated children reported by teachers to be bullied by peers from those who were not bullied. Facilitative parenting is the basis of Resilience Triple P, a program for the families of children bullied by peers described in the following section. Before discussing Resilience Triple P, we consider the relevance of parenting to children who bully.

THE ROLE OF PARENTING INTERVENTIONS FOR CHILDREN WHO BULLY PEERS

Bullying of peers is associated with conduct problems, antisocial behavior, and callous-unemotional traits characterized by low empathy (Golmaryami et al., 2016). Parents of children who bully tend to display high levels of harsh, hostile parenting; lower levels of warmth; and laxness in supervision (Atik & Güneri, 2013; Demaray & Malecki, 2003; Loeber & Dishion, 1984). These same parenting styles are linked with conduct problems (Gardner, Ward, Burton, & Wilson, 2003; Patterson, 1982) and children's callous-unemotional traits (Waller, Gardner, et al., 2015). Parents' use of coercive parenting can lead to an escalating pattern of coercion and conflict between parents and children (Patterson, 1982). Lack of supervision allows these children to use the same coercion and aggression to assert their will over peers (Olweus, 1980). Moreover, a lack of parental warmth predicts poorer development of empathy in children (Waller, Shaw, Forbes, & Hyde, 2015), which allows these children to overlook the impact of their behavior on others.

There is substantial evidence that cognitive-behavioral parenting programs can reduce harsh, hostile, or lax parenting and conduct and behavior problems (Sanders, Kirby, Tellegen, & Day, 2014). There is also recent evidence that cognitive-behavioral parenting interventions that increase warmth and decrease harsh parenting can reduce callous-unemotional traits (Pasalich, Witkiewitz, McMahon, Pinderhughes, & Conduct Problems Prevention Research Group, 2016). Although it has not yet been investigated, it seems likely then that these same parenting interventions may also help reduce bullying.

HOW TRIPLE P HAS BEEN APPLIED TO CHILDREN'S PEER RELATIONSHIP PROBLEMS

INTERVENING WITH CHILDREN BULLIED BY PEERS

Resilience Triple P (Healy & Sanders, in press) is a cognitive-behavioral family intervention designed to reduce victimization and child distress, thus interrupting the downward spiral of emotional reactivity and victimization. It includes four sessions for parents and four sessions for children with parents present. Table 7.1 summarizes the content.

Healy and Sanders (2014) conducted an RCT of Resilience Triple P involving 111 families of children aged between 6 and 12 years who had been bullied at school. Compared with control families, intervention children had greater reductions in distress and depression, and teachers reported greater reductions in overt victimization, aggression toward peers, and better acceptance by peers. Box 7.1 provides a typical example of a child and family's experience with Resilience Triple P.

IMPLICATIONS FOR PRACTICE, POLICY, OR RESEARCH

The outcomes of the first trial of Resilience Triple P raises questions about the potential applicability of facilitative parenting to other peer problems. Resilience Triple P is an intensive Level 4 program. Future research may investigate if lower intensity interventions can prevent peer

Table 7.1: Description and Applications of Core Parenting Skills Promoted Through Resilience Triple P

Child Skills	Parent Skills
• Play and friendship skills	• Providing warm support
• Everyday body language	• Coaching social and emotional skills
• Interpreting peer behavior	• Encouraging independence
• Responding to problems with peers	• Supporting child friendships
• Resolving conflict	• Communicating with the school

BOX 7.1: Case Example of a Child Bullied by Peers

When Mara was 10 years old, her parents noticed she was increasingly moody and resisted going to school. Mara confided to her mother that she was upset about problems with other girls at school. It all began when Mara's best friend started spending time with another girl, who made derogatory comments about Mara's appearance and made Mara feel unwelcome by whispering and turning her back to Mara. Mara also received a mean picture on her desk and had her bag rifled. Mara would end up spending her lunch hours helping in the library or doing schoolwork. She felt depressed and alone at school.

Through participation in Resilience Triple P, Mara developed friendships with other children; she enjoyed becoming involved in activities like handball and started enjoying school again. She learned to address problems directly with other children rather withdrawing or telling the teacher. Mara's mother and father helped Mara practice standing up for herself. They encouraged Mara to play an active role in decisions that affected her, such as her choice of clothing. They also agreed to Mara's choice of high school, where Mara had friends attending.

---

relationship problems or assist with transient concerns such as dealing with peer pressure. Further research could investigate whether Resilience Triple P is sufficient for children with disabilities, such as autism spectrum disorder, that increase risk for victimization (Schroeder, Cappadocia, Bebko, Pepler, & Weiss, 2014). Children who are provocative victims have very poor long-term prognoses (Dulmus, Sowers, & Theriot, 2006), so research might examine the impact of Resilience Triple P on both bullying and victimization for these children.

Most work on intervening in bullying has focused on whole-school interventions with modest outcomes (Merrell et al., 2008). Recent research showed that parenting interventions can reduce both victimization (Healy et al., 2015) and callous-unemotional traits relevant to bullying behavior (Pasalich et al., 2016). Future research could explore the combination of parenting and school interventions in addressing children's peer problems.

KEY MESSAGES

- Children's peer relationships are vitally important for children's well-being.
- Involvement in school bullying (as victim or perpetrator) has serious consequences.
- Children learn skills to relate to peers through patterns of interaction from the family.
- Specific parenting practices predict children's involvement in bullying.
- Parents can play an important role in assisting children with peer problems.
- Facilitative parenting is parenting that is supportive of children's peer relationships.
- Resilience Triple P combines facilitative parenting and child peer relationship training; it has been shown to reduce victimization at school.
- Parenting interventions such as Triple P are also likely to reduce bullying.

REFERENCES

Arseneault, L., Milne, B. L., Taylor, A., Adams, F., Delgado, K., Caspi, A., & Moffitt, T. E. (2008). Being bullied as an environmentally mediated contributing factor to children's internalizing problems: A study of twins discordant for victimization. *Archives of Pediatric and Adolescent Medicine*, *162*, 145–150. doi:10.1001/archpediatrics.2007.53

Atik, G., & Güneri, O. Y. (2013). Bullying and victimization: Predictive role of individual, parental, and academic factors. *School Psychology International*, *34*, 658–673. doi:10.1037/0022-006X.64.2.333

Bowers, L., Smith, P. K., & Binney, V. (1994). Perceived family relationships of bullies, victims and bully/victims in middle childhood. *Journal of Social and Personal Relationships*, *11*, 215–232. doi:10.1177/0265407594112004

Bowes, L., Arseneault, L., Maughan, B., Taylor, A., Caspi, A., & Moffitt, T. E. (2009). School, neighborhood, and family factors are associated with children's bullying involvement: A nationally representative longitudinal study. *Journal of the American Academy of Child & Adolescent Psychiatry*, *48*, 545–553. doi:10.1097/CHI.0b013e31819cb017

Bowes, L., Maughan, B., Caspi, A., Moffitt, T. E., & Arseneault, L. (2010). Families promote emotional and behavioural resilience to bullying: Evidence of an environmental effect. *Journal of Child Psychology and Psychiatry*, *51*, 809–817. doi:810.1111/j.1469-7610.2010.02216.x

Cook, C. R., Williams, K. R., Guerra, N. G., Kim, T. E., & Sadek, S. (2010). Predictors of bullying and victimization in childhood and adolescence: A meta-analytic investigation. *School Psychology Quarterly*, *25*, 65–83. doi:10.1037/a0020149

Copeland, W. E., Wolke, D., Angold, A., & Costello, E. J. (2013). Adult psychiatric outcomes of bullying and being bullied by peers in childhood and adolescence. *JAMA Psychiatry*, *70*, 419–426. doi:10.1001/jamapsychiatry.2013.504

Demaray, M. K., & Malecki, C. K. (2003). Perceptions of the frequency and importance of social support by students classified as victims, bullies, and bully/victims in an urban middle school. *School Psychology Review*, *32*, 471–489.

Denny, S., Clark, T. C., Fleming, T., & Wall, M. (2004). Emotional resilience: Risk and protective factors for depression among alternative education students in New Zealand. *American Journal of Orthopsychiatry*, *74*, 137–149. doi:110.1037/0002-9432.1074.1032.1137.

DeRosier, M. E., Kupersmidt, J. B., & Patterson, C. J. (1994). Children's academic and behavioral adjustment as a function of the chronicity and proximity of peer rejection. *Child Development*, *65*, 1799–1813. doi:10.2307/1131295

Dulmus, C. N., Sowers, K. M., & Theriot, M. T. (2006). Prevalence and bullying experiences of victims and victims who become bullies (bully-victims) at rural schools. *Victims and Offenders*, *1*, 15–31. doi:10.1080/15564880500498945

Fekkes, M., Pijpers, F. I. M., & Verloove-Vanhorick, S. P. (2005). Bullying: who does what, when and where? Involvement of children, teachers and parents in bullying behavior. *Health Education Research*, *20*, 81–91. doi:10.1093/her/cyg1100

Fisher, H. L., Moffitt, T. E., Houts, R. M., Belsky, D. W., Arseneault, L., & Caspi, A. (2012). Bullying victimization and risk of self harm in early adolescence: Longitudinal cohort study. *British Medical Journal*, *344*, 1–9.

Gardner, F., Ward, S., Burton, J., & Wilson, C. (2003). The role of mother–child joint play in the early development of children's conduct problems: A longitudinal observational study. *Social Development*, *12*, 361–378. doi: 10.1111/1467-9507.00238

Golmaryami, F. N., Frick, P. J., Hemphill, S. A., Kahn, R. E., Crapanzano, A. M., & Terranova, A. M. (2016). The social, behavioral, and emotional correlates of bullying and victimization in a school-based sample. *Journal of Abnormal Child Psychology*, *44*, 381–391. doi:10.1007/s10802-015-9994-x

Graziano, P. A., Keane, S. P., & Calkins, S. D. (2010). Maternal behaviour and children's early emotion regulation skills differentially predict development of children's reactive control and later effortful control. *Infant and Child Development*, 19, 333–353. doi:10.1002/icd.670

Healy, K. L., & Sanders, M. R. (2014). Randomized controlled trial of a family intervention for children bullied by peers. *Behavior Therapy*, 45, 760–777. doi:10.1016/j.beth.2014.06.001

Healy, K. L. & Sanders, M. R. (in press). *Facilitator's manual for Resilience Triple P.* Brisbane, Australia: Triple P International.

Healy, K. L., Sanders, M. R., & Iyer, A. (2015). Parenting practices, children's peer relationships and being bullied at school. *Journal of Child and Family Studies*, 24, 127–140. doi:10.1007/s10826-10013-19820-10824

Hodges, E. V. E., Boivin, M., Vitaro, F., & Bukowski, W. M. (1999). The power of friendship: Protection against an escalating cycle of peer victimization. *Developmental Psychology*, 35, 94–101. doi:10.1037/0012-1649.35.1.94

Jimerson, S. R., Egeland, B., Sroufe, L. A., & Carlson, B. (2000). A prospective longitudinal study of high school dropouts: Examining multiple predictors across development. *Journal of School Psychology*, 38, 525–549.

Kumpulainen, K., & Räsänen, E. (2000). Children involved in bullying at elementary school age: Their psychiatric symptoms and deviance in adolescence: An epidemiological sample. *Child Abuse and Neglect*, 24, 1567–1577. doi:10.1016/S0145-2134(00)00210-6

Ladd, G. W., & Ladd, B. K. (1998). Parenting behaviors and parent-child relationships: Correlates of peer victimization in kindergarten? *Developmental Psychology*, 34, 1450–1458. doi:10.1037/0012-1649.34.6.1450

LeBlanc, L. A., Sautter, R. A., & Dore, D. J. (2006). Peer relationship problems. In M. Hersen (Ed.), *Clinician's handbook of child behavioral assessment* (pp. 377–399). San Diego, CA: Elsevier Academic Press. doi:10.1016/B978-012343014-4/50016-2

Lereya, S. T., Samara, M., & Wolke, D. (2013). Parenting behavior and the risk of becoming a victim and a bully/victim: A meta-analysis study. *Child Abuse and Neglect*, 37, 1091–1108. doi:1010.1016/j.chiabu.2013.1003.1001

Loeber, R., & Dishion, T. J. (1984). Boys who fight at home and school: Family conditions influencing cross-setting consistency. *Journal of Consulting and Clinical Psychology*, 52, 759–768. doi:10.1037/0022-006X.52.5.759

McDowell, D. J., & Parke, R. D. (2009). Parental correlates of children's peer relations: An empirical test of a tripartite model. *Developmental Psychology*, 45, 224–235. doi:210.1037/a0014305

McDowell, D. J., Parke, R. D., & Wang, S. J. (2003). Differences between mothers' and fathers' advice-giving style and content: Relations with social competence and psychological functioning in middle childhood. *Merrill-Palmer Quarterly*, 49, 55–76. doi:10.1353/mpq.2003.0004

Malik, N. M., & Furman, W. (1993). Practitioner review: Problems in children's peer relations: What can the clinician do? *Journal of Child Psychology and Psychiatry*, 34, 1303–1326. doi:10.1111/j.1469-7610.1993.tb02093.x

Merrell, K. W., Gueldner, B. A., Ross, S. W., & Isava, D. M. (2008). How effective are school bullying intervention programs? A meta-analysis of intervention research. *School Psychology Quarterly*, 23, 26–42. doi:10.1037/1045-3830.1023.1031.1026

National Centre Against Bullying (Alannah and Madeline Foundation). (2016, October 1). *Definition of bullying*. Retrieved from https://www.ncab.org.au/bullying-advice/bullying-for-parents/definition-of-bullying/

Olweus, D. (1980). Familial and temperamental determinants of aggressive behavior in adolescent boys: A causal analysis. *Developmental Psychology*, 16, 644–660. doi:10.1037/0012-1649.16.6.644

Olweus, D. (1993). *Bullying at school: What we know and what we can do. Understanding children's worlds.* Malden, MA: Blackwell.

Parke, R. D., & Ladd, G. W. (Eds.). (1992). *Family-peer relationships: Modes of linkage.* Hillsdale, NJ: Erlbaum.

Pasalich, D. S., Witkiewitz, K., McMahon, R. J., Pinderhughes, E. E., & Conduct Problems Prevention Research Group. (2016). Indirect effects of the fast track intervention on conduct disorder symptoms and callous-unemotional traits: Distinct pathways involving discipline and warmth. *Journal of Abnormal Child Psychology, 44,* 587–597. doi:10.1007/s10802-015-0059-y

Patterson, G. R. (1982). *Coercive family process.* Eugene, OR: Castelia.

Pellegrini, A. D., & Roseth, C. J. (2006). Relational aggression and relationships in preschoolers: A discussion of methods, gender differences, and function. *Journal of Applied Developmental Psychology, 27,* 269–276. doi:10.1016/j.appdev.2006.02.007

Perry, D. G., Hodges, E. V. E., & Egan, S. K. (2001). Determinants of chronic victimization by peers: A review and new model of family influence. In J. Juvonen & S. Graham (Eds.), *Peer harassment in school: The plight of the vulnerable and victimized* (pp. 73–104). New York, NY: Guilford.

Perry, D. G., Perry, L. C., & Kennedy, E. (1992). Conflict and the development of antisocial behavior. In C. U. Shantz & W. W. Hartup (Eds.), *Conflict in child and adolescent development. Cambridge studies in social and emotional development* (pp. 301–329). New York, NY: Cambridge University Press.

Rajendran, K., Kruszewski, E., & Halperin, J. M. (2016). Parenting style influences bullying: a longitudinal study comparing children with and without behavioral problems. *Journal of Child Psychology and Psychiatry, 57,* 188–195. doi:10.1111/jcpp.12433

Reijntjes, A., Kamphuis, J. H., Prinzie, P., Boelen, P. A., Van der Schoot, M., & Telch, M. J. (2011). Prospective linkages between peer victimization and externalizing problems in children: A meta-analysis. *Aggressive Behavior, 37,* 215–222. doi:10.1002/ab.20374

Reijntjes, A., Kamphuis, J. H., Prinzie, P., & Telch, M. J. (2010). Peer victimization and internalizing problems in children: A meta-analysis of longitudinal studies. *Child Abuse and Neglect, 34,* 244–252. doi:210.1016/j.chiabu.2009.1007.1009

Robinson, L. R., Morris, A. S., Heller, S. S., Scheeringa, M. S., Boris, N. W., & Smyke, A. T. (2009). Relations between emotion regulation, parenting, and psychopathology in young maltreated children in out of home care. *Journal of Child and Family Studies, 18,* 421–434. doi:10.1007/s10826-008-9246-6

Sanders, M. R., Kirby, J. N., Tellegen, C. L., & Day, J. J. (2014). The Triple P—Positive Parenting Program: A systematic review and meta-analysis of a multi-level system of parenting support. *Clinical Psychology Review, 34,* 337–357. doi:10.1016/j.cpr.2014.04.003

Schreier, A., Wolke, D., Thomas, K., Horwood, J., Hollis, C., Gunnell, D., . . . & Harrison, G. (2009). Prospective study of peer victimization in childhood and psychotic symptoms in a nonclinical population at age 12 years. *Archives of General Psychiatry, 66,* 527–536. doi:10.1001/archgenpsychiatry.2009.23

Schroeder, J. H., Cappadocia, M. C., Bebko, J. M., Pepler, D. J., & Weiss, J. A. (2014). Shedding light on a pervasive problem: A review of research on bullying experiences among children with autism spectrum disorders. *Journal of Autism and Developmental Disorders, 44,* 1520–1534. doi:10.1007/s10803-013-2011-8

Schwartz, D., Dodge, K. A., Pettit, G. S., & Bates, J. E. (1997). The early socialization of aggressive victims of bullying. *Child Development, 68,* 665–675. doi:10.1111/j.1467-8624.1997.tb04228.x

Scott, J. G., Moore, S. E., Sly, P. D., & Norman, R. E. (2014). Bullying in children and adolescents: A modifiable risk factor for mental illness. *Australian and New Zealand Journal of Psychiatry, 48,* 209–212. doi:10.1177/0004867413508456

Ttofi, M. M., & Farrington, D. P. (2011). Effectiveness of school-based programs to reduce bullying: A systematic and meta-analytic review. *Journal of Experimental Criminology, 7,* 27–56. doi:10.1007/s11292-11010-19109-11291

Waller, R., Gardner, F., Shaw, D. S., Dishion, T. J., Wilson, M. N., & Hyde, L. W. (2015). Callous-unemotional behavior and early-childhood onset of behavior problems: The role of parental harshness and warmth. *Journal of Clinical Child and Adolescent Psychology, 44*, 655–667. doi:10.1080/15374416.2014.886252

Waller, R., Shaw, D. S., Forbes, E. E., & Hyde, L. W. (2015). Understanding early contextual and parental risk factors for the development of limited prosocial emotions. *Journal of Abnormal Child Psychology, 43*, 1025–1039. doi:10.1007/s10802-014-9965-7

Wolke, D., Copeland, W. E., Angold, A., & Costello, E. J. (2013). Impact of bullying in childhood on adult health, wealth, crime, and social outcomes. *Psychological Science, 24*, 1958–1970. doi:10.1177/0956797613481608

Wolke, D., & Samara, M. M. (2004). Bullied by siblings: Association with peer victimisation and behaviour problems in Israeli lower secondary school children. *Journal of Child Psychology and Psychiatry, 45*, 1015–1029. doi:1010.1111/j.1469-7610.2004.t1001-1011-00293.x

CHAPTER 8

CHILDREN WITH ANXIETY PROBLEMS

VANESSA E. COBHAM

UNDERSTANDING FEAR AND ANXIETY

Marks (1969) described fear as "a normal response to active or imagined threat . . . [comprising] an outer behavioural expression, an inner feeling, and accompanying physiological changes" (p. 1). Anxiety is a closely related construct and has been defined as an aversive feeling that is related to the expectation of threat or danger, which may be either internal or external. Although distinctions are made between the two constructs, they are conceptualized as having similar physiological, cognitive, and affective manifestations. The experience of anxiety or fear is common, typically transitory, and entirely normal. Indeed, the patterns of fears and anxieties in children follow a predictable developmental progression. Anxiety and fears are typically regarded as existing on a continuum; with the degree of distress, impairment in functioning, or interference with daily life caused, discriminating between what is viewed as falling within the "normal" range of anxiety, compared to clinically significant anxiety. At the clinically significant end of the continuum can be found the anxiety disorders, where significant distress or interference as a consequence of the anxiety experienced is a criterion for diagnosis. Within the most recent version of the *Diagnostic and Statistical Manual of Mental Disorders* (American Psychiatric Association, 2013), the following anxiety disorders (any of which a child may be diagnosed with) are listed: separation anxiety disorder, selective mutism, specific phobia, social anxiety disorder (social phobia), panic disorder, agoraphobia, generalized anxiety disorder, substance-/ medication-induced anxiety disorder, anxiety disorder due to another medical condition, other specified anxiety disorder, and unspecified anxiety disorder.

THE SIGNIFICANCE OF CHILDHOOD ANXIETY

Childhood anxiety is of immense significance. Anxiety disorders are among the most common mental health disorders experienced by children, with 6.5% of youth worldwide meeting criteria for at least one anxiety diagnosis (Polanczyk, Salum, Sugaya, Caye, & Rohde, 2015). These disorders negatively affect academic and social performance and are commonly associated with social isolation and physical health problems (Wood, Piacentini, Southam-Gerow, Chu, & Sigman, 2006). Untreated, childhood anxiety has a poor prognosis, often persisting into adulthood (Cummings, Caporino, & Kendall, 2014). Anxiety disorders in children also predict the presence of other forms of psychopathology (e.g., depression and substance abuse) in adolescence and adulthood (Bittner et al., 2007). Finally, anxiety disorders pose a significant societal cost, with the public expenses associated with an anxious child 20 times those associated with a nonanxious child (Bodden, Dirksen, & Bögels, 2008).

Unsurprisingly, clinically significant anxiety also has an impact on the child's family. Compared with parents of nonanxious children, parents of anxiety-disordered children report significantly worse family functioning (Hughes, Hedtke, & Kendall, 2008). In terms of siblings, Dia and Harrington (2006) reported that 12% of siblings of children being treated for an anxiety disorder met criteria for a previously undiagnosed anxiety disorder themselves. Finally, Fox, Barrett, and Shortt (2002) found that, compared with control children, the sibling interactions of anxious children were characterized by more conflict and control and less warmth. In summary, the anxious child may be the identified patient or client, but it is clear that the entire family is experiencing distress. It is suggested that there is enormous clinical benefit (for both the identified anxious child and the child's whole family) in a treatment approach that has the potential to directly help the entire family of the anxiety-disordered child, not just the child.

Finally, although efficacious interventions exist, most anxiety-disordered children do not receive any kind of treatment—evidence based or otherwise (Essau, Conradt, & Petermann, 2002). Essau (2005) reported that, of a representative school sample of 1,035 German adolescents aged 12 to 17 years, only 18% of youth meeting criteria for an anxiety disorder received mental health treatment of any kind. This is consistent with an Australian child and adolescent population sample (Johnson et al., 2016; Sawyer et al., 2001). The most likely reasons for this include the financial cost and the amount of time required to access treatment and the social stigma associated with attending therapy (Jorm & Wright, 2007). Kazdin (2008) clearly articulated the challenge, noting that "the salient issue before us is that we do not reach the vast majority of youth in need with *any* treatment" (p. 202). Kazdin suggested that the way forward involves a broad suite of nontraditional models of intervention with a potentially large reach, including brief, minimal, and low-cost treatments.

PARENTING AND FAMILY FACTORS
AS DETERMINANTS OF DEVELOPMENTAL OUTCOMES

Anxiety is transmitted within families (Weissman, Leckman, Merikangas, Gammon, & Prusoff, 1984), with twin studies indicating that heritability accounts for upward of 30%–40% of the variance (Hettema, Neale, & Kendler, 2001). In relation to anxiety in children, both top-down and bottom-up studies (that is, studies focusing on the children of anxiety-disordered parents and the parents of anxiety-disordered children, respectively) have consistently demonstrated a strong relationship between anxiety in parents and in their biological offspring, with over 60% of children of anxious parents meeting criteria for an anxiety disorder and roughly 80% of parents of anxious children also experiencing clinically significant anxiety (Ginsburg & Schlossberg, 2002).

The data relating to the nature of this relationship appear less clear, however, with a number of studies finding that shared environmental factors contribute significantly to the variance (Eley et al., 2003; Feigon, Waldman, Levy, & Hay, 2001). There has thus been a recognition that, while a genetic contribution to the development of childhood anxiety seems likely, the interaction between genetic predisposition and a child's environment is key (Farmer, Eley, & McGuffin, 2005; Murray, Creswell, & Cooper, 2009).

Most recently, a children-of-twins study provided important support "for the direct, environmentally mediated transmission of anxiety from parents to their adolescent offspring over and above any genetic confounding of this association" (Eley et al., 2015, p. 634). The authors noted that there are three possible interpretations of their conclusion that the relationship between parent and offspring anxiety is environmentally mediated:

1. Parent anxiety creates a family environment that predisposes children to develop anxiety. Thus, children may learn anxiety from their parents—for instance, through vicarious learning (Askew & Field, 2008).
2. Parent anxiety results in rearing or parenting behaviors that encourage the development of anxiety in children.
3. There is a reciprocal relationship between parent and child anxiety: Children's anxiety elicits a pattern of parenting that then contributes to the maintenance of their anxiety.

The existing literature examining the role of parenting and family factors in the development and maintenance of child anxiety provides some support for each of the three potential interpretations, with the prevailing consensus being that a reciprocal relationship is the best way of understanding the role of parenting and family factors in the development of childhood anxiety (for a review, see Rapee, 2012). Thus, there is evidence to support the role of vicarious learning in the development of childhood anxiety, specifically that parents' verbal and behavioral expression of anxiety increases children's anxiety (de Rosnay, Cooper, Tsigaras, & Murray, 2006; Muris & Field, 2010). Although some research has examined the role of the family environment more generally—in terms of level of conflict, for instance—the evidence that a particular type of family environment makes either a significant or a specific contribution to the development of childhood anxiety is inconclusive.

The strongest support has been found for parenting variables—in particular, overprotective or overinvolved parenting. While most of the empirical research in this area has employed cross-sectional designs, some longitudinal research (mainly conducted with families of preschool-aged children) has supported the importance of overprotective parenting, with results generally indicating either that parental overprotection at baseline predicts child anxiety at a later time point or the reverse. In a longitudinal study involving the parents of over 600 children who were 4 years old, maternal reports of overprotection predicted symptoms of child anxiety 1 year later, and child anxiety symptoms predicted maternal overprotection 1 year later, supporting the idea of a reciprocal relationship between parent and child behaviors (Edwards, Rapee, & Kennedy, 2010).

Some of the key mechanisms through which parenting is thought to contribute to the development of childhood anxiety include modeling of a threat-biased cognitive style (Field & Cartwright-Hatton, 2008); protecting children from situations in which they feel anxiety and depriving them of opportunities to face their fears and cope; and reinforcing anxious, avoidant, behaviors. Two meta-analyses have found small-to-medium effects between parenting and child anxiety, with medium effects found when overcontrolling or overprotective parenting alone was examined (McLeod, Wood, & Weisz, 2007; van der Bruggen, Stams, & Bögels, 2008).

The most recent meta-analysis examined studies involving children up to the age of 5 years only and found only small associations between parenting and anxiety and its precursors (Möller, Nikolić, Majdandžić, & Bögels, 2016). However, when post hoc meta-analyses were conducted, a stronger association was found between both maternal and paternal parenting and child anxiety symptoms (as opposed to precursors such as temperament style). In addition, the authors recalculated the effect sizes for the earlier meta-analyses using only those studies that involved children under the age of 6 years. In both cases, smaller effect sizes were found, lending support to the idea that parenting appears to make a relatively small contribution to anxiety symptoms in young children, but that the effects of parenting may be cumulative and become more pronounced as children get older. This of course is related to the idea of a reciprocal influence between parents and children—as children get older, their anxiety is more likely (compared to younger children) to elicit "anxiety-maintaining" parenting (including more overprotection and less granting of autonomy).

WHY PARENTING SUPPORT IS IMPORTANT IN RESOLVING THIS PROBLEM

In the past, treatment outcome research has focused on child-focused cognitive-behavioral therapy (CBT). However, as the role of parental and family factors in the etiology of child anxiety has become clearer, attention has moved toward the development and evaluation of parent-plus child CBT protocols. A much smaller body of work has examined parent-focused interventions in their own right.

CHILD-FOCUSED COGNITIVE-BEHAVIORAL THERAPY

There is a growing consensus that child-focused CBT is an evidence-based treatment for anxiety in children (A. James, Soler, & Weatherall, 2005; A. C. James, James, Cowdrey, Soler, & Choke, 2013; Seligman & Ollendick, 2011; Walkup et al., 2008). A systematic review of child-focused CBT interventions noted that, at the post-treatment assessment point, the average remission rate was 56% (Cartwright-Hatton, Roberts, Chitsabesan, Fothergill, & Harrington, 2004). Child-focused CBT (with 10–16 sessions the most common duration) is regarded as the international "gold standard" in the treatment of childhood anxiety disorders.

Importantly, although child-focused CBT protocols inevitably do include some parental involvement (e.g., reviewing progress at the beginning of sessions, setting homework tasks at the end of sessions), they do not specifically target family members other than the identified child. This is proposed to be an important limitation in light of (a) the impact one child's anxiety has on the entire family and (b) the likely reciprocal pattern of influence between anxious children and their parents in terms of the maintenance of the anxiety. The significant proportion of children who do not respond to child-focused CBT is also worth noting.

CHILD-FOCUSED CBT VERSUS PARENT-PLUS-CHILD CBT

Several studies have evaluated CBT protocols incorporating parental involvement and reported positive outcomes. Few studies, however, have directly compared a child-focused intervention with an intervention focused on parent plus child (Cobham, Dadds, & Spence, 1998; Cobham, Dadds, Spence, & McDermott, 2010). Those studies that have examined this comparison have yielded inconsistent findings (Barmish & Kendall, 2005), with two meta-analyses finding inadequate evidence for the superiority of family-focused interventions compared to the more traditional child-focused CBT interventions (In-Albon & Schneider, 2007; Reynolds, Wilson, Austin, & Hooper, 2012). However, a number of suggestions have been put forward to explain the variation in results for family-focused treatments—including methodological differences across studies, failure to adequately address those parenting targets associated with child anxiety (e.g., overinvolvement), failure to measure change in parenting targets where these were addressed by the evaluated intervention, and failure to ask which anxious children might benefit from family-focused interventions (Breinholst, Esbjørn, Reinholdt-Dunne, & Stallard, 2012).

Given that published family-focused interventions can involve up to 24 sessions, there is a clear burden for families associated with these treatments (in relation to both time and financial cost) in the absence of clear evidence that the addition of a family focus enhances outcomes.

PARENT-FOCUSED PROGRAMS

Parent-focused programs would seem to offer a useful alternative—they are often briefer and, potentially, offer the opportunity to address crucial parent-related etiological and maintaining factors. Some of the parenting behaviors hypothesized to be theoretically important include modeling of anxious behaviors, modeling of anxious cognitions and information-processing biases, promotion of avoidance, overinvolvement or overprotection, and negativity.

To date, a small number of studies have indicated that well-supported parents can be effective "lay therapists" in the treatment of their children's anxiety disorders (Cobham, 2012; Lyneham & Rapee, 2006; Thirlwall et al., 2013). Another, equally small, number of studies (all with significant methodological problems, disparate interventions, and a predominant focus on younger children) have examined parent-only, clinic-based interventions in the treatment of child anxiety. Each of these studies is briefly reviewed next.

Mendlowitz and colleagues found that family-focused, child-focused, and parent-focused interventions produced comparable outcomes in anxious children aged 7–12 years (Mendlowitz et al., 1999). However, the small sample size ($n = 62$) relative to the number of conditions and lack of follow-up beyond post-treatment make it difficult to draw firm conclusions from this study.

Cartwright-Hatton and her colleagues (Cartwright-Hatton, McNally, & White, 2005; Cartwright-Hatton, McNally, White, & Verduyn, 2005) reported substantial reductions in parents' reports of their children's internalizing scores on the Child Behavior Checklist (CBCL) following a parenting skills program. Children in these two studies were aged 4–9 years and 2–5 years, respectively. Noteworthy limitations in both Cartwright-Hatton studies include the small sample sizes ($n = 11$ and 43, respectively) and the lack of control groups. It is also important to note that inclusion in these studies was based on elevated internalizing scores on the CBCL, not clinical diagnosis.

Thienemann, Moore, and Tompkins (2006) reported significant reductions in the number of anxiety diagnoses met by 24 children aged 7–16 years following a parent-only intervention. Again, the small sample size and lack of any control group are important limitations.

Waters, Ford, Wharton, and Cobham compared a parent-plus-child condition with a parent-only condition in the treatment of 49 anxiety-disordered children aged 4–8 years (Waters, Ford, Wharton, & Cobham, 2009). No differences were reported between the two active treatments, both of which were superior to the wait-list control group. However, as with the other research in this area, the small sample size means this study was underpowered to detect differences between the active conditions.

Lebowitz and colleagues conducted an open trial of a parent-focused intervention (10–12 sessions) with the parents of 10 anxiety-disordered children aged 9 to 13 years who had refused individual child-focused therapy (Lebowitz, Omer, Hermes, & Scahill, 2014). These authors reported significant post-treatment reductions in children's anxiety symptoms as rated by parents; however, small sample size, lack of follow-up data, and lack of diagnostic data are important limitations.

Smith and colleagues compared a parent-focused intervention (10 modules) with a wait-list condition with parents of 31 anxiety-disordered 7- to 13-year-olds (Smith, Flannery-Schroeder, Gorman, & Cook, 2014). Children whose parents received the parent intervention had fewer anxiety diagnoses, reduced parent ratings of impairment, and reduced clinician ratings of anxiety severity at post-treatment relative to children in the wait-list condition, with these gains being maintained at the 3-month follow-up point. While promising, this study is limited by its small sample.

Most recently, a parent–child intervention was compared with a parent-only intervention (11 sessions) with parents of 77 anxiety-disordered 5- to 7-year-olds, with results indicating that substantially greater improvements were found up to 12-month follow-up for children in the combined parent–child condition (Monga, Rosenbloom, Tanha, Owens, & Young, 2015). More work is needed in this area—with larger samples, designs that include diagnostic outcomes at multiple follow-up points, and a focus on children of primary school age.

HOW TRIPLE P HAS BEEN APPLIED TO THE PROBLEM

The effect of Triple P interventions on child anxiety disorders has only recently been examined. Ozyurt, Gencer, Ozturk, and Ozbek (2016) randomized the families of 50 anxiety-disordered children aged 8 to 12 years to either Group Triple P ($n = 26$) or a wait-list control group ($n = 24$). Group Triple P covered the following content: examining causes of child behavior problems, setting specific goals, and using strategies to promote child development, manage misbehavior, and plan for high-risk situations.

Children and parents completed the Screen for Anxiety Related Emotional Disorders (SCARED; Birmaher et al., 1997) questionnaire. Parents also completed the Strengths and Difficulties Questionnaire (SDQ; Goodman, 1997); the General Health Questionnaire (GHQ; Goldberg, 1986); and the State Trait Anxiety Inventory (STAI; Spielberger, Gorsuch, Lushene, Vagg, & Jacobs, 1983). Clinicians completed the Children's Global Assessment Scale (CGAS; Shaffer et al., 1983) and the Clinical Global Impression—Severity (CGI-S; Guy, 1976). Children's anxiety caseness was determined using composite ratings from the parent and child versions of the Schedule for Affective Disorders and Schizophrenia for School Age Children Present and Lifetime (KIDDIE-SADS-PL; Birmaher et al., 2009). All children met criteria for at least one anxiety disorder. However, no information was provided about the severity of primary diagnoses, the number of anxiety diagnoses met, or other diagnostic comorbidity.

Parents in the active intervention group received five 2-hour group sessions and three (15- to 30-minute) individual telephone consultations spread across an 8-week period. All participants were assessed prior to treatment commencing and approximately 6 months later (that is, 4 months after completion of Group Triple P). At time 1 (pretreatment), there were no differences between the two groups on any of the questionnaire measures. However, at time 2 (4 months after participants had either completed Group Triple P or a 6-month wait), significant reductions on the SDQ, the CGI-S, and the SCARED (both parent and child versions) were reported for the Group Triple P families compared to the wait-list families. In addition, parents who completed Group Triple P reported significant reductions on the GHQ and the STAI compared to wait-list parents.

Importantly, this is the first study to have evaluated Triple P with anxiety-disordered children, with both parent and child reports of children's anxiety symptomatology having reduced significantly over time compared to the wait-list group. Without knowing whether the children were also experiencing other difficulties (e.g., behavioral problems) in addition to anxiety, it is difficult to know to what extent measures such as the SDQ and the CGI-S reflected changes in anxiety symptoms. In addition, the lack of diagnostic data following treatment and the limited follow-up are significant limitations. However, this study provides preliminary evidence for the utility of Group Triple P in the treatment of childhood anxiety disorders.

Fear-less Triple P was developed and subsequently revised by Cobham and Sanders (2009, 2015) as a specialized Level 4 intervention for parents of anxiety-disordered children. The intervention consists of six weekly sessions that can be conducted in either a group or an individual format. In addition, a half-day workshop version of the program is currently being trialed at the University of Queensland. The content of the program is presented in Table 8.1.

Cobham, Filus, and Sanders (2017) conducted the first RCT of the intervention—comparing Fear-less Triple P with a wait-list control group. Participants were 61 children aged 7 to 14 years and their parents. To be included in the trial, children had to meet criteria for at least one clinically significant anxiety disorder on the Anxiety Disorders Interview Schedule for Children (ADIS-IV-C/P, Anxiety Disorders Interview Schedule Child/Parent Version; Silverman & Albano, 1996). Families were randomly assigned to either Fear-less Triple P or wait list. At posttreatment (postwait for the wait-list families), significantly more children whose parents had participated in the Fear-less intervention were free of any anxiety diagnosis compared to children in the wait-list condition. Maternal and child questionnaire data showed the same pattern, with significant reductions from pre- to post-treatment demonstrated for participants in the Fear-less condition but not the wait-list condition. For children in the Fear-less condition, the number who were free of any anxiety diagnosis continued to rise over time, with over 80% of

Table 8.1: Contents of Fear-less Triple P

Session Number	Session Title	Contents
1	Anxiety: What is it and how does it develop?	Psychoeducation: What is anxiety? The three systems of anxiety; What does anxiety look like? The impact on your family. Why children become anxious. Goals for change. Homework.
2	Promoting resilience in children	What is emotional resilience, and why does it matter? Recognizing and accepting feelings. Encouraging children to express emotions appropriately. Helping children develop an optimistic outlook. Celebrating the "bounce-back" moments. Homework.
3	Modeling and the way children think	Setting a good example of coping with anxiety. Communicating a sense of threat or danger. The way you think—The ABC model. Changing the way you think: Two common traps. Learning to think more realistically and flexibly: Why bother? Homework.
4	The way you behave: Avoidance and exposure	The way you behave: A focus on avoidance. Why is avoidance so important? Parents of anxious children and avoidance. Exposure: Just do it! An exposure hierarchy. Steps in developing an exposure hierarchy. Modeling brave, nonanxious behavior. Developing an exposure hierarchy for and with your child. Developing a reward system. Homework.
5	Parental strategies for responding to children's anxiety	Strategies for dealing with anxiety in children: What helps your child and what doesn't? Some examples. Homework.
6	Constructive coping—How to promote it; and maintaining gains	Some suggestions: A step-by-step guide to promoting constructive coping in your children. Strategies in action. Planning ahead and troubleshooting. Reviewing progress. Obstacles. Guidelines for maintaining change. Future goals.

children anxiety diagnosis free at the final assessment at 12 months—an outcome that is comparable to any reported in the child anxiety literature. Box 8.1 provides an example of a child and family's experience with Fear-less Triple P.

IMPLICATIONS FOR PRACTICE, POLICY, OR RESEARCH

The research reviewed has important implications for clinical practice and research. Parent-focused interventions have been found to be efficacious in treating both anxiety symptoms in preschool-aged children and anxiety disorders in primary school–aged children. Fear-less

---

BOX 8.1: Case Example of a Child With Anxiety

Max was a 9-year-old boy with idiopathic generalized epilepsy who was referred by his neurologist for treatment of anxiety. Max lived within an intact family (parents Ruby and Chris; half-sister Jess, 22 years; and brother Liam, 12 years). At the time of presentation, Max's epilepsy had been well controlled with medication for the past 12 months. Prior to this, however, Max's parents reported that Max's seizures (generalized tonic-clonic) had been frequent and poorly controlled, and they described these as "terrifyingly unpredictable." Max met diagnostic criteria for social anxiety disorder and generalized anxiety disorder and was within the clinical range for each of these subscales, as well as the total score on the Spence Children's Anxiety Scale. He found it difficult to attend school (with Ruby describing each morning as a battle) and had few friends. Academically, Max was doing well, despite having missed a significant amount of school in the previous year. Following assessment, the parents elected to receive the Fear-less Triple P program (delivered weekly and individually). During therapy, Ruby and Chris were able to articulate and reflect on their own anxiety (both Ruby's trait anxiety and the anxiety they shared about Max's epilepsy). It was hypothesized that, in relation to managing Max's anxiety, many of the decisions being made by Ruby and Chris were heavily influenced by their perception of their son as medically unwell and their own anxiety about this. For example, Max was allowed to avoid a number of anxiety-provoking situations (such as invitations to peers' houses) because Ruby and Chris were concerned that he might have a seizure (despite the neurologist having advised that this was highly unlikely given the success of Max's antiepileptic medication). As they learned about anxiety management strategies (such as mental flexibility and graduated exposure) and discussed different ways of responding to Max's anxiety, Ruby and Chris were encouraged to think about how they would manage Max's anxiety if he did not have epilepsy. Max's epilepsy was certainly not the only factor involved in a parenting pattern that was hypothesized to be contributing to his anxiety. However, "permission" from the therapist and the neurologist to worry less about the epilepsy (and still be "good" parents) allowed Ruby and Chris what they described as a "do-over" in terms of thinking about how they responded to Max's anxiety. Over the course of therapy, parental attention gradually switched to instances of courage and resilience, as opposed to anxiety. A graduated exposure hierarchy (with accompanying reward system) was used to great effect to overcome Max's avoidance of getting together with peers—culminating in a sleepover at a classmate's house. Three months after the six-session program of therapy had finished, Max was free of any clinically significant anxiety diagnosis and had just attended his first school camp, with Ruby and Chris noting that they had used the strategies they had learned to manage their own anxiety about this.

Triple P, with its compelling diagnostic outcomes, offers many important advantages when compared with the more traditional, child-focused CBT interventions in the treatment of child anxiety. The brevity of the program means that it is both more cost-effective and more easily accessible for families. The program also takes a "whole-of-family" approach that is lacking in child-focused interventions. Future research is required to examine questions such as the following: Is Fear-less Triple P suitable for all families of anxiety-disordered children? What are the key mechanisms of change? And, how does the intervention affect family-related outcomes, such as sibling relationships, sibling anxiety, family functioning, and parent anxiety?

KEY MESSAGES

- Globally, 6.5% of children meet criteria for at least one anxiety disorder. Without intervention, anxiety disorders in children tend to persist—causing psychosocial impairment and predicting the onset of depressive disorders, substance use, and suicidal ideation. Unfortunately, less than 20% of anxiety-disordered children access any kind of intervention.
- Although underresearched, children's anxiety appears (unsurprisingly) to have a significant impact on the whole-family system.
- Anxiety is transmitted within families, with the interaction between genetic predisposition and a child's environment being key. Environmentally mediated transmission from parent to child has been found to contribute significantly over and above genetic transmission.
- Although child-focused CBT interventions are regarded as the gold standard in this field, for many reasons (e.g., increased reach, the role of parents in the development of their children's anxiety) it makes sense to treat child anxiety by working with parents.
- Recent research has suggested that Fear-less Triple P (designed for parents of anxiety-disordered children) is highly efficacious over a 12-month follow-up period in reducing children's anxiety symptoms.

REFERENCES

American Psychiatric Association. (2013). *Diagnostic and statistical manual of mental disorders* (5th ed.). Washington, DC: Author.

Askew, C., & Field, A. P. (2008). The vicarious learning pathway to fear 40 years on. *Clinical Psycholology Review, 28*, 1249–1265. doi:10.1016/j.cpr.2008.05.003

Barmish, A. J., & Kendall, P. C. (2005). Should parents be co-clients in cognitive-behavioral therapy for anxious youth? *Journal of Clinical Child and Adolescent Psychology, 34*, 569–581. doi:10.1207/s15374424jccp3403_12

Birmaher, B., Ehmann, M., Axelson, D. A., Goldstein, B. L., Monk, K., Kalas, C., ... Brent, D. A. (2009). Schedule for Affective Disorders and Schizophrenia for School-Age Children (K-SADS-PL) for the assessment of preschool children—A preliminary psychometric study. *Journal of Psychiatric Research, 43*, 680–686. doi:10.1016/j.jpsychires.2008.10.003

Birmaher, B., Khetarpal, S., Brent, D., Cully, M., Balach, L., Kaufman, J., & Neer, S. M. (1997). The Screen for Child Anxiety Related Emotional Disorders (SCARED): Scale construction and psychometric characteristics. *Journal of the American Academy of Child and Adolescent Psychiatry, 36*, 545–553. doi:10.1097/00004583-199704000-00018

Bittner, A., Egger, H. L., Erkanli, A., Jane Costello, E., Foley, D. L., & Angold, A. (2007). What do childhood anxiety disorders predict? *Journal of Child Psychology and Psychiatry, 48,* 1174–1183. doi:10.1111/j.1469-7610.2007.01812.x

Bodden, D. H. M., Dirksen, C. D., & Bögels, S. M. (2008). Societal burden of clinically anxious youth referred for treatment: A cost-of-illness study. *Journal of Abnormal Child Psychology, 36,* 487–497. doi:10.1007/s10802-007-9194-4

Breinholst, S., Esbjørn, B. H., Reinholdt-Dunne, M. L., & Stallard, P. (2012). CBT for the treatment of child anxiety disorders: A review of why parental involvement has not enhanced outcomes. *Journal of Anxiety Disorders, 26,* 416–424. doi:10.1016/j.janxdis.2011.12.014

Cartwright-Hatton, S., McNally, D., & White, C. (2005). A new cognitive behavioural parenting intervention for families of young anxious children: A pilot study. *Behavioural and Cognitive Psychotherapy, 33,* 243–247. doi:10.1017/S1352465804002036

Cartwright-Hatton, S., McNally, D., White, C., & Verduyn, C. (2005). Parenting skills training: An effective intervention for internalizing symptoms in younger children? *Journal of Child and Adolescent Psychiatric Nursing, 18,* 45–52. doi:10.1111/j.1744-6171.2005.00014.x

Cartwright-Hatton, S., Roberts, C., Chitsabesan, P., Fothergill, C., & Harrington, R. (2004). Systematic review of the efficacy of cognitive behaviour therapies for childhood and adolescent anxiety disorders. *British Journal of Clinical Psychology, 43,* 421–436. doi:10.1348/0144665042388928

Cobham, V. E. (2012). Do anxiety-disordered children need to come into the clinic for efficacious treatment? *Journal of Consulting and Clinical Psychology, 80,* 465–476. doi:10.1037/a0028205

Cobham, V. E., & Sanders, M. R. (2009). *Fear-less Triple P. Group workbook for parents of anxious children.* Brisbane, Australia: The University of Queensland.

Cobham, V. E., & Sanders, M. R. (2015). Fear-less Triple P revised{Silverman, 1996, The Anxiety Disorders Interview Schedule for DSM-IV - Child and Parent versions.}. Group workbook for parents of anxious children. Brisbane, Australia: The University of Queensland.

Cobham, V. E., Dadds, M. R., & Spence, S. H. (1998). The role of parental anxiety in the treatment of childhood anxiety. *Journal of Consulting and Clinical Psychology, 66,* 893–905. doi:10.1037/0022-006X.66.6.893

Cobham, V. E., Dadds, M. R., Spence, S. H., & McDermott, B. (2010). Parental anxiety in the treatment of childhood anxiety: A different story three years later. *Journal of Clinical Child and Adolescent Psychology, 39,* 410–420. doi:10.1080/15374411003691719

Cobham, V. E., Filus, A., & Sanders, M. R. (2017). Working with parents to treat anxiety-disordered children: A proof of concept RCT evaluating Fear-less Triple P. *Behaviour Research and Therapy, 95,* 128–138. doi:10.1016/j.brat.2017.06.004

Cummings, C. M., Caporino, N. E., & Kendall, P. C. (2014). Comorbidity of anxiety and depression in children and adolescents: 20 years after. *Psychological Bulletin, 140,* 816–845. doi:10.1037/a0034733

de Rosnay, M., Cooper, P. J., Tsigaras, N., & Murray, L. (2006). Transmission of social anxiety from mother to infant: An experimental study using a social referencing paradigm. *Behaviour Research and Therapy, 44,* 1165–1175. doi:10.1016/j.brat.2005.09.003

Dia, D. A., & Harrington, D. (2006). What about me? Siblings of children with an anxiety disorder. *Social Work Research, 30,* 183–188.

Edwards, S. L., Rapee, R. M., & Kennedy, S. (2010). Prediction of anxiety symptoms in preschool-aged children: Examination of maternal and paternal perspectives. *Journal of Child Psychology and Psychiatry, 51,* 313–321. doi:10.1111/j.1469-7610.2009.02160.x

Eley, T. C., Bolton, D., O'Connor, T. G., Perrin, S., Smith, P., & Plomin, R. (2003). A twin study of anxiety-related behaviours in pre-school children. *Journal of Child Psychology and Psychiatry, 44,* 945–960.

Eley, T. C., McAdams, T. A., Rijsdijk, F. V., Lichtenstein, P., Narusyte, J., Reiss, D., . . . Neiderhiser, J. M. (2015). The intergenerational transmission of anxiety: A children-of-twins study. *The American Journal of Psychiatry, 172*, 630–637. doi:10.1176/appi.ajp.2015.14070818

Essau, C. A. (2005). Frequency and patterns of mental health services utilization among adolescents with anxiety and depressive disorders. *Depression and Anxiety, 22*, 130–137. doi:10.1002/da.20115

Essau, C. A., Conradt, J., & Petermann, F. (2002). Course and outcome of anxiety disorders in adolescents. *Journal of Anxiety Disorders, 16*, 67–81. doi:10.1016/S0887-6185(01)00091-3

Farmer, A., Eley, T. C., & McGuffin, P. (2005). Current strategies for investigating the genetic and environmental risk factors for affective disorders. *British Journal of Psychiatry, 186*, 179–181. doi:10.1192/bjp.186.3.179

Feigon, S. A., Waldman, I. D., Levy, F., & Hay, D. A. (2001). Genetic and environmental influences on separation anxiety disorder symptoms and their moderation by age and sex. *Behavior Genetics, 31*, 403–411. doi:10.1023/A:1012738304233

Field, A. P., & Cartwright-Hatton, S. (2008). Shared and unique cognitive factors in social anxiety. *International Journal of Cognitive Therapy, 1*, 206–222. doi:10.1680/ijct.2008.1.3.206

Fox, T. L., Barrett, P. M., & Shortt, A. L. (2002). Sibling relationships of anxious children: A preliminary investigation. *Journal of Clinical Child and Adolescent Psychology, 31*, 375–383. doi:10.1207/153744202760082630

Ginsburg, G. S., & Schlossberg, M. C. (2002). Family-based treatment of childhood anxiety disorders. *International Review of Psychiatry, 14*, 143–154. doi:10.1080/09540260220132662

Goldberg, D. (1986). Use of the General Health Questionnaire in clinical-work. *British Medical Journal, 293*, 1188–1189.

Goodman, R. (1997). The strengths and difficulties questionnaire: A research note. *Journal of Child Psychology and Psychiatry and Allied Disciplines, 38*, 581–586. doi:10.1111/j.1469-7610.1997.tb01545.x

Guy, W. (1976). *ECDEU assessment manual for psychopharmacology*. Rockville, MD: US Department of Health, Education, and Welfare, Public Health Service, Alcohol, Drug Abuse, and Mental Health Administration, National Institute of Mental Health, Psychopharmacology Research Branch, Division of Extramural Research Programs. Retrieved from https://archive.org/details/ecdeuassessmentm1933guyw

Hettema, J. M., Neale, M. C., & Kendler, K. S. (2001). A review and meta-analysis of the genetic epidemiology of anxiety disorders. *American Journal of Psychiatry, 158*, 1568–1578. doi:10.1176/appi.ajp.158.10.1568

Hughes, A. A., Hedtke, K. A., & Kendall, P. C. (2008). Family functioning in families of children with anxiety disorders. *Journal of Family Psychology, 22*, 325–328. doi:10.1037/0893-3200.22.2.325

In-Albon, T., & Schneider, S. (2007). Psychotherapy of childhood anxiety disorders: A meta-analysis. *Psychotherapy and Psychosomatics, 76*, 15–24.

James, A., Soler, A., & Weatherall, R. (2005). Cognitive behavioural therapy for anxiety disorders in children and adolescents. *Cochrane Database of Systematic Reviews, (4)*, CD004690.

James, A. C., James, G., Cowdrey, F. A., Soler, A., & Choke, A. (2013). Cognitive behavioural therapy for anxiety disorders in children and adolescents. *Cochrane Database of Systematic Reviews, (6)*, CD004690. doi:10.1002/14651858.CD004690.pub3

Johnson, S. E., Lawrence, D., Hafekost, J., Saw, S., Buckingham, W. J., Sawyer, M., . . . Zubrick, S. R. (2016). Service use by Australian children for emotional and behavioural problems: Findings from the second Australian Child and Adolescent Survey of Mental Health and Wellbeing. *Australian and New Zealand Journal of Psychiatry, 50*, 887–898. doi:10.1177/0004867415622562

Jorm, A. F., & Wright, A. (2007). Beliefs of young people and their parents about the effectiveness of interventions for mental disorders. *Australian and New Zealand Journal of Psychiatry, 41*, 656–666. doi:10.1080/00048670701449179

Kazdin, A. E. (2008). Evidence-based treatments and delivery of psychological services: Shifting our emphases to increase impact. *Psychological Services, 5*, 201–215. doi:10.1037/a0012573

Lebowitz, E. R., Omer, H., Hermes, H., & Scahill, L. (2014). Parent training for childhood anxiety disorders: The SPACE Program. *Cognitive and Behavioral Practice, 21*, 456–469. doi:10.1016/j.cbpra.2013.10.004

Lyneham, H. J., & Rapee, R. M. (2006). Evaluation of therapist-supported parent-implemented CBT for anxiety disorders in rural children. *Behaviour Research and Therapy, 44*, 1287–1300. doi:10.1016/j.brat.2005.09.009

Marks, I. M. (1969). *Fears and phobias*. Oxford, England: Academic Press.

McLeod, B. D., Wood, J. J., & Weisz, J. R. (2007). Examining the association between parenting and childhood anxiety: A meta-analysis. *Clinical Psychology Review, 27*, 155–172. doi:10.1016/j.cpr.2006.09.002

Mendlowitz, S., Manassis, K., Bradley, S., Scapillato, D., Miezitis, S., & Shaw, B. E. (1999). Cognitive-behavioral group treatments in childhood anxiety disorders: The role of parental involvement. *Journal of the American Academy of Child and Adolescent Psychiatry, 38*, 1223–1229. doi:10.1097/00004583-199910000-00010

Monga, S., Rosenbloom, B. N., Tanha, A., Owens, M., & Young, A. (2015). Comparison of child–parent and parent-only cognitive-behavioral therapy programs for anxious children aged 5 to 7 years: Short- and long-term outcomes. *Journal of the American Academy of Child & Adolescent Psychiatry, 54*, 138–146. doi:10.1016/j.jaac.2014.10.008

Muris, P., & Field, A. P. (2010). The role of verbal threat information in the development of childhood fear. "Beware the Jabberwock!" *Clinical Child and Family Psychology Review, 13*, 129–150. doi:10.1007/s10567-010-0064-1

Murray, L., Creswell, C., & Cooper, P. J. (2009). The development of anxiety disorders in childhood: An integrative review. *Psychological Medicine, 39*, 1413–1423. doi:10.1017/S0033291709005157

Möller, E. L., Nikolić, M., Majdandžić, M., & Bögels, S. M. (2016). Associations between maternal and paternal parenting behaviors, anxiety and its precursors in early childhood: A meta-analysis. *Clinical Psychology Review, 45*, 17–33. doi:10.1016/j.cpr.2016.03.002

Ozyurt, G., Gencer, O., Ozturk, Y., & Ozbek, A. (2016). Triple P positive parenting program effective on anxious children and their parents? 4th Month follow up results. *Journal of Child and Family Studies, 25*, 1646–1655. doi:10.1007/s10826-015-0343-z

Polanczyk, G. V., Salum, G. A., Sugaya, L. S., Caye, A., & Rohde, L. A. (2015). Annual research review: A meta-analysis of the worldwide prevalence of mental disorders in children and adolescents. *Journal of Child Psychology and Psychiatry, 56*, 345–365. doi:10.1111/jcpp.12381

Rapee, R. M. (2012). Family factors in the development and management of anxiety disorders. *Clinical Child and Family Psychology Review, 15*, 69–80. doi:10.1007/s10567-011-0106-3

Reynolds, S., Wilson, C., Austin, J., & Hooper, L. (2012). Effects of psychotherapy for anxiety in children and adolescents: A meta-analytic review. *Clinical Psychology Review, 32*, 251–262. doi:10.1016/j.cpr.2012.01.005

Sawyer, M. G., Arney, F. M., Baghurst, P. A., Clark, J. J., Graetz, B. W., Kosky, R. J., . . . Zubrick, S. R. (2001). The mental health of young people in Australia: key findings from the child and adolescent component of the national survey of mental health and well-being. *Australian and New Zealand Journal of Psychiatry, 35*, 806–814. doi:10.1046/j.1440-1614.2001.00964.x

Seligman, L. D., & Ollendick, T. H. (2011). Cognitive-behavioral therapy for anxiety disorders in youth. *Child and Adolescent Psychiatric Clinics of North America, 20,* 217–238. doi:10.1016/j.chc.2011.01.003

Shaffer, D., Gould, M. S., Brasic, J., Ambrosini, P., Fisher, P., Bird, H., & Aluwahlia, S. (1983). A Childrens Global Assessment Scale (CGAS). *Archives of General Psychiatry, 40,* 1228–1231. doi:10.1001/archpsyc.1983.01790100074010

Silverman, W. K., & Albano, A. (1996). *The Anxiety Disorders Interview Schedule for DSM-IV: Parent and Child Versions.* Psychological Corporation.

Smith, A. M., Flannery-Schroeder, E. C., Gorman, K. S., & Cook, N. (2014). Parent cognitive-behavioral intervention for the treatment of childhood anxiety disorders: A pilot study. *Behaviour Research and Therapy, 61,* 156–161. doi:10.1016/j.brat.2014.08.010

Spielberger, C. D., Gorsuch, R. L., Lushene, R., Vagg, P. R., & Jacobs, G. A. (1983). *Manual for the State-Trait Anxiety Inventory.* Palo Alto, CA: Consulting Psychologists Press.

Thienemann, M., Moore, P., & Tompkins, K. (2006). A parent-only group intervention for children with anxiety disorders: Pilot study. *Journal of the American Academy of Child and Adolescent Psychiatry, 45,* 37–46. doi:10.1097/01.chi.0000186404.90217.02

Thirlwall, K., Cooper, P. J., Karalus, J., Voysey, M., Willetts, L., & Creswell, C. (2013). Treatment of child anxiety disorders via guided parent-delivered cognitive–behavioural therapy: Randomised controlled trial. *The British Journal of Psychiatry, 203,* 436–444. doi:10.1192/bjp.bp.113.126698

van der Bruggen, C. O., Stams, G. J., & Bögels, S. M. (2008). Research review: The relation between child and parent anxiety and parental control: A meta-analytic review. *Journal of Child Psychology and Psychiatry, 49,* 1257–1269. doi:10.1111/j.1469-7610.2008.01898.x

Walkup, J. T., Albano, A. M., Piacentini, J., Birmaher, B., Compton, S. N., Sherrill, J. T., . . . Kendall, P. C. (2008). Cognitive behavioral therapy, sertraline, or a combination in childhood anxiety. *The New England Journal of Medicine, 359,* 2753–2766. doi:10.1056/NEJMoa0804633

Waters, A. M., Ford, L. A., Wharton, T. A., & Cobham, V. E. (2009). Cognitive-behavioural therapy for young children with anxiety disorders: Comparison of a child + parent condition versus a parent only condition. *Behaviour Research and Therapy, 47,* 654–662. doi:10.1016/j.brat.2009.04.008

Weissman, M. M., Leckman, J. F., Merikangas, K. R., Gammon, G. D., & Prusoff, B. A. (1984). Depression and anxiety disorders in parents and children. Results from the Yale family study. *Archives of General Psychiatry, 41,* 845–852.

Wood, J. J., Piacentini, J. C., Southam-Gerow, M., Chu, B. C., & Sigman, M. (2006). Family cognitive behavioral therapy for child anxiety disorders. *Journal of the American Academy of Child and Adolescent Psychiatry, 45,* 314–321. doi:10.1097/01.chi.0000196425.88341.b0

CHAPTER 9

PARENTING SUPPORT FOR CHILDREN WITH DEVELOPMENTAL DISABILITY

TREVOR G. MAZZUCCHELLI AND LISA J. STUDMAN

*D*evelopmental disability is a term that covers a range of conditions that have an adverse impact on physical or intellectual development. It includes intellectual, cognitive, neurological, sensory, and physical impairments that first occur during developmental years and result in reduced capacity in areas of life, including self-care, communication, learning, mobility, decision-making, living independently, and economic self-sufficiency (Schalock et al., 2010; United States of America Developmental Disabilities Act of 1984, 1984). Children with a developmental disability are at a substantially greater risk, when compared to their typically developing peers, of showing a variety of emotional and behavioral problems (Einfeld, Ellis, & Emerson, 2011). These problems, along with a family's adaptation to having a child with a disability, can have a profound impact on the child's and family's life course. This chapter describes how Triple P has been applied to improve child and family outcomes for families who have a child with a disability.

FAMILY ISSUES AND CHILD BEHAVIOR

Parents report both benefits and burdens associated with raising a child who has a developmental disability. For example, parents report personal benefits such as an increased ability to cope with hardships and a greater sense of optimism; positive sibling adjustment; a sense of accomplishment in having done one's best for the child; becoming a better person (e.g., more compassionate, less selfish, more tolerant); and making the most of each day or living life at a slower pace (Hastings & Taunt, 2002). On the other hand, parents also report additional burdens from raising a child with a disability that can be related to practical demands (e.g., daily hassles around additional caregiving tasks and managing difficult behavior and financial strain from additional costs and loss of employment); psychological and health burdens (e.g., grief, emotional stress, and personal adjustment); and burdens on the family unit (e.g., more conflict, decreased marital happiness; Edwards, Higgins, Gray, Zmijewski, & Kingston, 2008). How a family adapts to the impact of having a child with a disability is influenced by the extent of burden and stress the family experiences, the level of resources and support the family has or acquires, and parent cognitive coping styles (Studman, 2014).

Significant predictors of caregiver burden and stress are child behavior problems and daily hassles related to providing care (Mazzucchelli & Moran, 2017; Plant & Sanders, 2007; Whittingham, Wee, Sanders, & Boyd, 2012). These child behavior problems (e.g., aggressive/destructive behavior, self-injurious behavior, generalized noncompliance) also have serious developmental repercussions for children themselves. They can threaten the physical health of children, lead to inappropriate treatment such as physical or psychopharmacological restraint or abuse, exclusion from community-based services such as educational and recreational programs (Emerson & Einfeld, 2011), and reduced occupational opportunities in the postschool period (Anderson, Lakin, Hill, & Chen, 1992). Parents of children with disabilities are more likely than others to need to use public respite services (Chan & Sigafoos, 2000) and to relinquish the care of their child due to the burden of care (Nankervis, Rosewarne, & Vassos, 2011). Because of the seriousness of child behavioral and emotional problems and their sequelae, there is widespread recognition of the importance of prevention and early intervention. In addressing these issues, childrearing practices, parental adjustment, and family relationships are obvious foci for supporting parents and families.

PARENTING AND FAMILY FACTORS AS DETERMINANTS OF DEVELOPMENTAL OUTCOMES

A range of child, parenting, and family factors can contribute to the development and maintenance of behavioral and emotional problems in children with a developmental disability. Child factors include certain behavioral phenotypes, patterns of behavior that are likely to present in syndromes caused by chromosomal or genetic abnormalities (see Chapter 41, this volume, for examples). The type and severity of child disability and level of adaptive behavior are also risk factors. The more debilitating the impairment, the greater the distress experienced by parents (Plant & Sanders, 2007). Children who require greater levels of support for activities of daily living and who have more severe communication impairments also typically show more severe behavior problems (Emerson & Einfeld, 2011), as do those with health and medical issues (Wallander, Decker, & Koot, 2006).

While certain biological and psychological factors may place children with a disability at increased risk for developing behavioral and emotional problems, there is strong evidence that these child-related factors interact with social and environmental factors to precipitate and perpetuate problem behavior. In particular, coercive parenting practices, emotional adjustment difficulties of carers, and relationship conflict between caregivers have been implicated in the development and maintenance of these problems (Hartley, Seltzer, Barker, & Greenberg, 2011; Sigafoos, Arthur, & O'Reilly, 2003; Woodman, Mawdsley, & Hauser-Cram, 2015).

Studies have indicated that children with developmental disabilities are more likely to be exposed to such risk factors than their nondisabled peers. For instance, there is evidence suggesting maternal expressed emotion toward children with an intellectual disability is more negative than expressed emotion toward children without intellectual disability (Beck, Daley, Hastings, & Stevenson, 2004). In developing countries, caregivers of children with a disability are more likely to believe that using corporal punishment is necessary as a form of discipline; children with a disability are treated more harshly than children without a disability and are more likely to be subjected to severe physical violence (Hendrinks, Lansford, Deater-Deckard, & Bornstein, 2014). There is also considerable evidence that children with disabilities are more likely to be abused than those without a disability (see Stalker & McArthur, 2012, for a review).

Parent beliefs and expectations about their child's condition, behavior, and the effectiveness of intervention also play an important role in child outcomes. If parents attribute their child's problem behavior to biological factors or if they have unrealistically low expectations for their child to learn new skills, the parents may relax and remove rules, make fewer demands, or overuse physical guidance, causing prompt dependence and fewer opportunities for the child to learn adaptive behavior. In doing so, a "nurturance trap" can emerge whereby dependent, helpless, or inappropriate behaviors are reinforced instead of desired adaptive behaviors (Mazzucchelli & Sanders, 2012). Parent beliefs about the effectiveness of interventions have also been found to predict parent expectations and beliefs about the likelihood of child behavior change (Hastings & Johnson, 2001).

In terms of parents' personal adjustment, parental stress and self-efficacy affect quality of parenting and child behavioral outcomes. Mothers of children with a disability are reported to have higher levels of stress and poorer psychological well-being than other mothers (Eisenhower, Baker, & Blacher, 2009; Hayes & Watson, 2013). Significantly, a bidirectional relationship has been found between parenting stress and child behavior problems: High parenting stress contributes to a worsening in child behavior problems over time, and child behavior problems exacerbate parental stress (Neece, Green, & Baker, 2012; Woodman et al., 2015).

Increased parental self-efficacy is related to active coping and problem-solving styles that influence positive outcomes for parents and children more than passive, emotion-focused coping styles. Self-efficacy has been shown to improve parent coping, maternal warmth, sensitivity, and consistent parenting in families (Lloyd & Hastings, 2008; Paczkowski & Baker, 2007). In a study by Sanders and Woolley (2005), lower levels of self-efficacy significantly predicted both parental overreactivity (harsh discipline) and laxness (permissive and inconsistent discipline). It was concluded that parent support should incorporate a focus on increasing self-efficacy through teaching parents effective strategies to manage a wide range of behavior problems and to promote child development.

Marital quality is another family factor that has a significant effect on parenting stress, child behavior (Bradley, Rock, Whiteside, Caldwell, & Brisby, 1991), and parent well-being (Kersh, Hedvat, Hauser-Cram, & Warfield, 2006). Families of children with disabilities have a slightly higher rate of separation and divorce compared to those with children who are developing typically (Risdal & Singer, 2004); however, child behavior problems show a greater association to marital satisfaction than child disability status (Baker, Blacher, Crnic, & Edelbrock, 2002). There is some support for a bidirectional relationship between marital satisfaction and behavior problems in children with a disability and that marital satisfaction affects child behavior through exposure to conflict between parents. The effect of low marital satisfaction on child behavior problems may also be mediated by harsh parenting and parenting lacking in involvement, warmth, and emotional support (Floyd & Zmich, 1991; Hartley et al., 2011).

THE ROLE OF PARENTING AND FAMILY INTERVENTIONS FOR CHILDREN WITH DISABILITIES

Improving parenting practices can lead to a reduction in child problem behavior and improvements in child adaptive skills and have a positive impact on parental adjustment and relationship quality (Roberts, Mazzucchelli, Studman, & Sanders, 2006; Sanders, Kirby, Tellegen, & Day, 2014; Tellegen & Sanders, 2013). Parenting interventions with these targets should occur in the context of promoting positive family environments and facilitating family adaptation. Interventions should also account for the various factors that influence a particular family's parent–child interactions, such as the child's level and mode of communication, behavioral phenotype and parental attributions, and identified functions of behavior problems (e.g., escape/avoidance). Interventions for children with a disability should also be flexibly tailored to address identified risk and protective factors; focus on antecedent/environmental manipulations to prevent problem behavior; support methodical and structured teaching of adaptive skills; use the least restrictive strategies; promote the use of socially acceptable parenting strategies; and provide minimally sufficient parent support with a focus on generalization enhancement.

Supporting parents to generalize newly learned parenting skills to novel problems, different situations, and children other than the child who is the primary focus of the program is efficient; it also consolidates learning and reduces the risk of relapse. It can be achieved by promoting parents' confidence and problem-solving skills; adopting a sufficient exemplar approach to teaching new skills; training "loosely" by supporting parents to apply parenting skills in a diverse range of situations; and supporting parents with other adversity factors, such as poor coping skills, lack of partner support, or family dysfunction that may affect parenting (Sanders, Mazzucchelli, & Studman, 2004).

STEPPING STONES TRIPLE P FOR FAMILIES OF CHILDREN WITH DEVELOPMENTAL DISABILITIES

Stepping Stones Triple P (SSTP) is a parallel system of Triple P parenting and family support for families of children with a developmental disability; the system evolved from a program of clinical research (see Mazzucchelli & Sanders, 2012; Tellegen, & Sanders, 2013). The aim of SSTP is to increase parental competence and confidence in raising children with a disability by (a) increasing parents' confidence and competence in helping children develop and in managing common behavioral and emotional problems and developmental issues; (b) reducing parents' use of coercive and punitive methods of disciplining children; (c) improving parents' communication about parenting issues; and (d) reducing parenting and family stress associated with raising their child.

Stepping Stones Triple P is consistent with many of the defining features of positive behavior support (Carr et al., 2002; O'Neill, Albin, Storey, Horner, & Sprague, 2015). It is a family-centered program in which parents set their own goals and play an active role in the assessment and intervention process. It has a prevention focus and aims to enhance parenting skills, a central protective factor for children's development. Parenting plans are based on an understanding of the child's interactions within the family environment, acquired through an individualized process of assessment. Parents are supported to develop, implement, and monitor plans that are focused on teaching their child functional skills, rather than suppressing unwanted behavior. These plans typically have multiple components, including enriching environments, as well as rearranging antecedents and the consequences of behavior. SSTP has been demonstrated to be acceptable and effective for children who have a variety of developmental disabilities, including intellectual, physical, and sensory disabilities, as well as autism spectrum disorders (for a review, see Tellegen & Sanders, 2013).

Stepping Stones Triple P incorporates five levels of intervention on a tiered continuum of increasing strength for parents of preadolescent children from birth to 12 years of age. Level 1, a universal parent information strategy, provides parents with access to useful information about parenting through a coordinated media and promotional campaign. Level 2 involves a series of parent education seminars focusing on positive parenting and the promotion of children's healthy development. Seminar topics include the following:

- *Positive Parenting for Children With a Disability.* The focus of this seminar is on incorporating seven core principles of positive parenting into everyday interactions.
- *Helping Your Child Reach Their Potential.* This seminar provides a step-by-step guide to teaching and supporting children to acquire functional adaptive skills.
- *Changing Problem Behavior Into Positive Behavior.* The focus of this seminar is on understanding the function of challenging behavior and replacing it with more appropriate, functionally equivalent, adaptive skills.

Level 3 Primary Care SSTP, a four-session individually delivered intervention incorporating active skills training, targets parents of children with mild-to-moderate behavioral difficulties. After a brief assessment session, parents are introduced to relevant behavior support plans that are individualized to suit their particular needs. These plans are resources that are available in booklets grouped by theme (Figure 9.1).

Level 4 is an intensive, 10-session individual or 9-session group parent training program for parents of children with more severe behavioral difficulties or parents wanting to learn a range of positive parenting skills. This program can also be undertaken in a self-directed fashion. A case study from a Level 4 group SSTP intervention is provided in Box 9.1. Level 5 comprises enhanced behavioral family intervention that targets family factors associated with the persistence of child behavior problems (e.g., relationship conflict, parental depression or high levels of stress).

CORE PRINCIPLES

There are seven core principles of positive parenting in SSTP. These were selected to address specific risk and protective factors known to predict positive developmental and

A guide to positive parenting	**A guide to early learning skills**	**A guide to promoting communication skills**
• What is positive parenting • Developmental disability • Causes of behavior problems • Getting started on making a change • Promoting children's development • Managing misbehavior • Family survival tips	• Attending skills–making eye contact • Imitating–following simple instructions • Teaching independent play skills	• Promoting communication before words • Promoting communication with words • Using augmentative and alternative communication • Repetitive questioning • Echolalia–copying words and sounds
A guide to self-care skills	**A guide to social skills**	**A guide to fears and anxiety**
• Dressing • Washing • Teeth brushing • Bedtime problems	• Play • Sharing • Having friends around to visit • Repetitive behavior	• Fears • Separation anxiety • Medical procedures • Tactile defensiveness • Nightmares and night terrors • Self-injurious behavior
A guide to toileting	**A guide to mealtimes**	**A guide to being part of the community**
• Toilet training • Bedwetting • Smearing	• Independent eating • Mealtime problems • Selective eating • Oral hypersensitivity • Pica–eating nonfood	• Shopping • Wandering • Traveling in the car • Haircuts

A guide to disruptive behavior	**A guide to family adaptation**
• Whining and tantrums • Disobedience • Hurting and aggression • Interrupting • Swearing	• Adapting to having a child with a disability • Coping with stress • Parent coping • Supporting your partner • Helping siblings to adjust • Dealing with health professionals

FIGURE 9.1: Stepping Stones Triple P Primary Care booklet series topics.

mental health outcomes in children. In addition to the five core positive parenting principles described by Sanders and Mazzucchelli in Chapter 4 of this book, SSTP includes two additional principles—adapting to having a child with a disability and being part of the community.

Family Adaptation to Having a Child With a Disability

The principle of family adaptation to having a child with a disability involves parents coming to terms with their child's disability, finding a balance between the demands and stresses of parenting and the resources they have to cope, and developing optimism and adaptive coping styles (Studman, 2014). SSTP resources that focus on family adaptation provide ideas about creating a balance between demands and resources, increasing personal coping, supporting partners, helping siblings' adjustment, and developing good working relationships with health professionals involved in children's care.

Being Part of the Community

The principle of being part of the community emphasizes valuing people with disabilities, the acceptance of impairments, and the importance of providing the necessary supports to ensure

> **BOX 9.1: A Case Example From Group Stepping Stones Triple P**
>
> Sarah (6 years) was born 4 months prematurely and became severely hearing impaired after a life-saving drug treatment for infection. As she developed, she began to display a range of increasingly challenging behaviors, such as severe tantrums, noncompliance, and volitional vomiting in response to not getting her own way. Her parents felt responsible for her difficulties and had always tried to provide her with everything she wanted, not expecting her to learn to wait or to follow instructions. They were exhausted and demoralized and, given the aversive nature of time spent together, had begun to avoid contact with her. Despite this, misbehavior was a reminder to them that she had a disability, and in response to their feelings of guilt, they would respond by trying to soothe and comfort her. Inadvertently, the parents had fallen into a nurturance trap that contributed to Sarah developing and continuing to display challenging behaviors. Despite attempts to teach her sign language, she used little functional communication.
>
> The family participated in Group Stepping Stones Triple P over eight weekly sessions. Initial group sessions focused on challenging parents' beliefs about the cause of Sarah's behavior and helping them to recognize that her behavior was an effective way for her to gain attention, tangible rewards, access to stimulating environments, and avoid disliked or effortful tasks. Her parents deliberately worked on building and strengthening a warm and loving relationship with her by responding to her when she approached, spending time playing with her, providing physical affection, and using incidental teaching to encourage her to communicate using key signs. They learned how to teach Sarah to make eye contact, imitate, and follow instructions—early learning skills that provided avenues to teach her functional communication and sign language, how to engage in play and social interaction, and positive adaptive behaviors. Her parents also learned ways to structure her environment to prevent distress and overstimulation and strategies to encourage her development of self-control and emotional regulation so she was able to calmly wait for what she wanted. After eight sessions, Sarah's parents reported enjoying being with her more and feeling confident in managing her behavior. Their parenting styles had shifted from clinical levels of laxness and overreactivity to being in the normal range. Sarah was enjoying a warm, reciprocal, relationship with them. She was able to communicate using some signs and was developing new skills and competencies expected for her age and capacity. Her level of disruptive behavior was reduced from clinical to normal levels.

that children with a disability participate successfully in the same social contexts as their typically developing peers (Carr et al., 2002; Perrin & Nirje, 1985).

ADDITIONAL SSTP STRATEGIES

In addition to the core Triple P techniques described by Sanders and Mazzucchelli (Chapter 4, this volume), SSTP includes seven parenting strategies drawn from the disability literature (Table 9.1).

Table 9.1: Description and Applications of Additional Parenting Skills Promoted Through Stepping Stones Triple P

Skill	Description	Applications
ENCOURAGING DESIRABLE BEHAVIOR		
Providing other rewards	Providing tangible rewards desired by the child (e.g., a toy, mirror, article of clothing, food) with praise and attention.	Encouraging positive adaptive behavior (e.g., speaking, playing, sharing, self-care skills).
Setting up activity schedules	Arranging a series of photos, pictures, or words representing a routine of activities.	Prompting participation in activities of daily living.
TEACHING NEW SKILLS AND BEHAVIOR		
Using physical guidance	Providing just enough pressure to gently move a child's arms or legs through the motions of a task.	Teaching early learning and self-care skills (e.g., imitation, following simple instructions, brushing teeth).
Teaching backward	Using verbal, gestural, or manual prompts to teach new skills beginning with the last step of the task.	Teaching skills for which the most rewarding step is at the end (e.g., making toast, tying shoelaces, feeding self with a spoon).
MANAGING MISBEHAVIOR		
Using diversion to another activity	Using instructions, questions, and prompts to divert or redirect a child who is about to misbehave.	Preventing problem behaviors (e.g., self-injurious behavior, property damage, running away).
Teaching children to communicate what they want	Teaching a functionally equivalent way of making needs known or met.	Providing an alternative to mild-severe problem behavior (e.g., temper outbursts, self-injurious behavior, pica).
Using blocking for dangerous behavior	Catching or blocking hands or legs to prevent the completion of a behavior.	Dealing with dangerous behavior (e.g., reaching for something hot, running into the road, banging own head) or terminating a problem behavior (e.g., hitting someone).
Using brief interruption for disruptive or repetitive behavior	Having a child sit quietly, when a problem has occurred, for a set time.	Dealing with sensory or escape/avoidance maintained behavior (e.g., some self-injurious behavior; struggling during physical guidance).

IMPLICATIONS FOR PRACTICE

Trained practitioners should deliver SSTP in conjunction with early childhood development services within an inter-/transdisciplinary team model (Bell, Corfield, Davies, & Richardson, 2010). Health professionals such as early educators, medical officers, pediatric physiotherapists, psychologists, occupational therapists, social workers, and speech pathologists who use this family-centered approach inform the development of individual support and education plans that are implemented primarily through one practitioner within the home or clinic situation. The benefit of this model is the reduced of number of practitioners working directly with the child and family and therefore the reduction of parent stress associated with working with multiple providers. Practitioners should apply a principle of minimal sufficiency such that families receive the minimal level of support required to affect the changes and improvements they wish to see and to meet the goals they want to achieve. This forms part of the self-regulatory model employed within the Triple P system (see Sanders & Mazzucchelli, 2013).

Low-intensity variants of SSTP can be used to induct or orient families into early childhood programs. For example, Selected Seminar SSTP introduces the principles of positive parenting that promote adaptive skill development and may prevent the onset of behavioral problems. Low-intensity variants such as Primary Care SSTP can also be incorporated into child-/family-centered therapy programs and home-visiting services provided by all disability support workers. Ideally, practitioners would take advantage of opportunities to implement these programs rather than waiting for issues to develop and result in referrals requiring more intensive interventions. For example, if in the course of therapy a speech pathologist notices early signs of toileting readiness, the therapist could suggest that parents consider toilet training and offer to provide some guidance using the *SSTP: A Guide to Toileting* booklet. Alternatively, if they were to notice fine-motor control developing, then using the *SSTP: A Guide to Mealtimes* could offer parents ideas on how to teach independent eating skills or using *SSTP: A Guide to Self-Care Skills* could encourage parents to consider teaching their child to dress him- or herself in the morning in their natural home environment. Level 2 and 3 SSTP can be provided in a preventive manner before problems become entrenched or as a wait-list management strategy while families wait for more intensive interventions, such as Level 4 and Level 5 programs, to become available.

IMPLICATIONS FOR POLICY AND RESEARCH

Efficacy and effectiveness trials have demonstrated that each of the SSTP variants results in desirable outcomes, such as reduced child problems, improved parenting practices, enhanced parental satisfaction and efficacy with parenting, and improved parental adjustment and relationship satisfaction (for a review of this evidence, see Tellegen & Sanders, 2013). The multilevel nature of the SSTP system, characterized by interventions of varying strengths and modes of delivery, was designed to appeal to and serve all families who have a child with a disability. As such, SSTP has the potential to improve the lives of the entire population of children with a developmental disability and their families.

The most cost-effective way to reduce the prevalence of emotional and behavioral problems is to apply a population health approach (Prinz, Sanders, Shapiro, Whitaker, & Lutzker, 2009). By applying the principle of proportionate universalism (Strategic Review of Health Inequalities in England, 2010), actions to target social, health, and well-being inequities in a population must be delivered universally but with scale and intensity that are proportionate to the level of disadvantage and need. This means providing access to supports to prevent the development of problems, to target emerging issues, and to intervene in established child and family interactional problems. Mechanisms by which to provide a population health approach to implementing SSTP were reviewed by Mazzucchelli and Sanders (2011). An application of this approach for families with children with a disability is described by Sofronoff et al. (Chapter 41, this volume).

A potential facilitator for this population health approach is the implementation of individual funding packages (e.g., the National Disability Insurance Scheme in Australia) that allow for the development of individually tailored and community-integrated supports for adults and children with disabilities. Such packages should be inclusive of all services that the general community can access, including evidence-based preventive supports and inter-/transdisciplinary team-based programs. This means that individual funding packages should provide access to evidence-based parenting support programs such as SSTP whether delivered as an individual, group, seminar, online, or self-directed program. Evidence-based outcomes from SSTP align with identified Insurance Scheme services that target both Early Childhood Early Intervention and family support (see https://www.ndis.gov.au/families-carers.html for examples).

A possible barrier to the provision of evidence-based parenting supports are government and agency policies concerning the use of restrictive practices. These generally apply to adults with disabilities and aim to protect them from the use of interventions and practices that have the effect of restricting the rights and freedom of a person with a disability. These include chemical, mechanical, social, or physical restraints and seclusion as a response to challenging behavior in settings such as supported accommodation and group homes, mental health facilities, hospitals, prisons, and schools (Australian Government: Australian Law and Reform Commission, 2014). Such policies are important and necessary to protect vulnerable adults with disabilities but should not disadvantage parents of children with disabilities by precluding them from using common, evidence-based, parenting techniques contained within SSTP such as "physical guidance," "planned ignoring," "brief interruption," "quiet time," and "time-out" (Mazzucchelli & Sanders, 2012).

In terms of future research directions for SSTP, there is a need to evaluate the delivery of the program's content through novel modalities that may provide more accessible ways for parents to access effective parenting support. To this end, an evaluation of Triple P Online with SSTP provider support and enhancement is currently under way (Hinton, 2016). An initial trial of presentations in a small-group format on specific topics for parents of children with a disability (Discussion Group SSTP) has also been conducted, with promising results (Mazzucchelli, 2016). There is also demand from both professionals and families for a tailored parenting intervention for teenagers with a disability (Hamilton, Mazzucchelli, & Sanders, 2015; Mazzucchelli & Moran, 2017).

KEY MESSAGES

- Raising a child with a disability brings many benefits and burdens to families. Children with developmental disabilities are at significantly higher risk than others to develop behavioral and emotional problems. These behavior problems have a major negative impact on children's development and adversely impact child and family quality of life.

- There is a reciprocal relationship between child behavior problems, parental adjustment, and parenting practices.
- Parenting interventions should account for specific conditions that influence parent–child interactions, such as behavioral phenotypes and related parental attributions, the child's level and mode of communication, and the function of behavior. Interventions should also focus on antecedent/environmental manipulations to prevent problems, structured teaching of functionally equivalent adaptive skills, the use of least restrictive reactive strategies, and the use of socially acceptable parenting strategies.
- Stepping Stones Triple P is a parallel version of the core Triple P multilevel system of parent support that has been adapted for families of children with developmental disabilities.
- Stepping Stones Triple P has been demonstrated to be both efficacious and effective.
- Stepping Stones Triple P can be integrated into existing services and made available with a population health approach.
- Current research efforts are exploring alternative modes of service delivery and the effectiveness of population-based implementation.

REFERENCES

Anderson, D. J., Lakin, K. C., Hill, B. K., & Chen, T. H. (1992). Social integration of older persons with mental retardation in residential facilities. *American Journal on Mental Retardation, 96*, 488–501.

Australian Government: Australian Law and Reform Commission (2014). *Equality, capacity, and disability in commonwealth laws* (DP 81). Retrieved from https://www.alrc.gov.au/publications/disability-dp81

Baker, B. L., Blacher, J., Crnic, K. A., & Edelbrock, C. (2002). Behavior problems and parenting stress of three-year-old children with and without developmental delays. *American Journal on Mental Retardation, 107*, 433–444. doi:10.1352/0895-8017(2002)107<0433:BPAPSI>2.0.CO;2

Beck, A., Daley, D., Hastings, R. P., & Stevenson, J. (2004). Mothers' expressed emotion towards children with and without intellectual disabilities. *Journal of Intellectual Disability Research, 48*, 628–635. doi:10.1111/j.1365-2788.2003.00564.x

Bell, A., Corfield, M., Davies, J., & Richardson, N. (2010). Collaborative transdisciplinary intervention in early years-Putting theory into practice. *Child: Care, Health and Development, 36*, 142–148. doi:10.1111/j.1365-2214.2009.01027.x

Bradley, R. H., Rock, S. L., Whiteside, L., Caldwell, B. M., & Brisby, J. (1991). Dimensions of parenting in families having children with disabilities. *Exceptionality, 2*, 41–61. doi:10.1080/09362839109524765

Carr, E. G., Dunlap, G., Horner, R. H., Koegel, R. L., Turnbull, A. P., Sailor, W., . . . Fox, L. (2002). Positive behavior support: Evolution of an applied science. *Journal of Positive Behavior Interventions, 4*, 4–16.

Chan, J. B., & Sigafoos, J. (2000). A review of child and family characteristics related to the use of respite care in developmental disability services. *Child and Youth Care Forum, 29*, 27–37. doi:10.1023/A:1009420206722

Edwards, B., Higgins, D. J., Gray, M., Zmijewski, N., & Kingston, M. (2008). *The nature and impact of caring for family members with a disability in Australia* (AIFS Research Report No. 16). Melbourne, Australia: Australian Institute of Family Studies. Retrieved from https://aifs.gov.au/publications/nature-and-impact-caring-family-members-di

Einfeld, S. L., Ellis, L. A., & Emerson, E. (2011). Comorbidity of intellectual disability and mental disorder in children and adolescents: A systematic review. *Journal of Intellectual and Developmental Disabilities, 36*, 137–143. doi:10.1080/13668250.2011.572548

Eisenhower, A. S., Baker, B. L., & Blacher, J. (2009). Children's delayed development and behavior problems: Impact on mothers' perceived physical health across early childhood. *Social Science and Medicine, 68*, 89–99. doi:0.1016/j.socscimed.2008.09.033

Emerson, E., & Einfeld, S. L. (2011). *Challenging behaviour* (3rd ed.). Cambridge, England: Cambridge University Press.

Floyd, F. J., & Zmich, D. E. (1991). Marriage and the parenting partnership: Perceptions and interactions of parents with mentally retarded and typically developing children. *Child Development, 62*, 1434–1448.

Hamilton, A., Mazzucchelli, T. G., & Sanders, M. R. (2015). Parental and practitioner perspectives on raising an adolescent with a disability: A focus group study. *Disability and Rehabilitation, 37*, 1664–1673. doi:10.3109/09638288.2014.973969

Hartley, S. L., Seltzer, M. M., Barker, E. T., & Greenberg, J. S. (2011). Marital quality and families of children with developmental disabilities. *International Review of Research in Developmental Disabilities, 41*, 1–29. doi:10.1016/B978-0-12-386495-6.00001-1

Hastings, R. P., & Johnson, E. (2001). Stress in UK families conducting intensive home-based behavioral intervention for their young child with autism. *Journal of Autism and Developmental Disorders, 31*, 327–336. doi:10.1023/A:1010799320795

Hastings, R. P., & Taunt, H. M. (2002). Positive perceptions in families of children with developmental disabilities. *American Journal on Mental Retardation, 107*, 116–127. doi:10.1352/0895-8017(2002)107<0116:PPIFOC>2.0.CO;2

Hayes, S. A., & Watson, S. L. (2013). The impact of parenting stress: A meta-analysis of studies comparing the experience of parenting stress in parents of children with and without autism spectrum disorder. *Journal of Autism and Developmental Disorders, 43*, 629–642. doi:10.1007/s10803-012-1604-y.

Hendrinks, C., Lansford, J. E., Deater-Deckard, K., & Bornstein, M. H. (2014). Associations between child disabilities and caregive discipline and violence in low- and middle-income countries. *Child Development, 85*, 513–531. doi:10.1111/cdev.12132

Hinton, S. (2016, June). *Engaging online: A randomised controlled trial to assess the efficacy of using "technology-assisted guided self-help" to deliver parenting support to parents of children with a disability*. Paper presented at 8th World Congress of Behavioral and Cognitive Therapies, Melbourne, Australia.

Kersh, J., Hedvat, T. T., Hauser-Cram, P., & Warfield, M. E. (2006). The contribution of marital quality to the well-being of parents of children with developmental disabilities. *Journal of Intellectual Disability Research, 50*, 883–893. doi:10.1111/j.1365-2788.2006.00906.x

Lloyd, T., & Hastings, R. P. (2008). Psychological variables as correlates of adjustment in mothers of children with intellectual disabilities: cross-sectional and longitudinal relationships. *Journal of Intellectual Disability Research, 52*, 37–48. doi:10.1111/j.1365-2788.2007.00974x

Mazzucchelli, T. (2016, June). *Stepping Stones Triple P Discussion Group: Evaluation of a single session parenting group to address child disobedience*. Paper presented at 8th World Congress of Behavioral and Cognitive Therapies, Melbourne, Australia.

Mazzucchelli, T. G., & Moran, L. C. (2017). *Predictors of stress in parenting adolescents with a disability*. Manuscript in preparation.

Mazzucchelli, T. G., & Sanders, M. R. (2011). Preventing behavioral and emotional problems in children who have a developmental disability: A public health approach. *Research in Developmental Disabilities, 32*, 2148–2156. doi:10.1016/j.ridd.2011.07.022

Mazzucchelli, T. G., & Sanders, M. R. (2012). *Stepping Stones Triple P: A population approach to the promotion of competent parenting of children with disability* (Vol. 2). Brisbane, Australia: University of Queensland. Available from https://www.researchgate.net/publication/233757423_Stepping_Stones_Triple_P_A_population_approach_to_the_promotion_of_competent_parenting_of_children_with_disability

Nankervis, K. L., Rosewarne, A., & Vassos, M. V. (2011). Why do families relinquish care? An investigation of the factors that lead to relinquishment in out-of-home respite care. *Journal of Intellectual Disability Research, 55*, 422–433. doi: 10.1111/j.1365-2788.2011.01389.x.

Neece, C. L., Green, S. A., & Baker, B. L. (2012). Parenting stress and child behavior problems: A transactional relationship across time. *American Journal of Intellectual and Developmental Disability, 117*, 48–66. doi:10.1352/1944-7558-117.1.48.

O'Neill, R. E., Albin, R. W., Storey, K., Horner, R. H., & Sprague, J. R. (2015). *Functional assessment and program development for program behavior: A practical handbook* (3rd ed.). Stamford, CT: Cengage Learning.

Paczkowski, E., & Baker, B. L. (2007). Parenting children with and without developmental delay: The role of self mastery. *Journal of Intellectual Disability Research, 51*, 435–446. doi:10.1111/j.1365-2788.2006.00894.x

Perrin, B., & Nirje, B. (1985). Setting the record straight: A critique of some frequent misconceptions of the normalization principle. *Australia and New Zealand Journal of Developmental Disabilities, 11*, 69–74. doi:10.3109/13668258509008748

Plant, K. M., & Sanders, M. R. (2007). Predictors of care-giver stress in families of preschool-aged children with developmental disabilities. *Journal of Intellectual Disability Research, 51*, 109–124. doi:10.1111/j.1365-2788.2006.00829.x

Prinz, R. J., Sanders, M. R., Shapiro, C. J., Whitaker, D. J., & Lutzker, J. R. (2009). Population-based prevention of child maltreatment: The US Triple P system population trial. *Prevention Science, 10*, 1–12. doi:10.1007/s11121-009-0123-3

Risdal, D., & Singer, G. H. S. (2004). Marital adjustment in parents of children with disabilities: A historical review and meta-analysis. *Research and Practice for Persons With Severe Disabilities, 29*, 95–103. doi:10.2511/rpsd.29.2.95

Roberts, C., Mazzucchelli, T., Studman, L., & Sanders, M. R. (2006). Behavioral family intervention for children with developmental disabilities and behavioral problems. *Journal of Clinical and Adolescent Psychology, 35*, 180–193. doi:10.1207/s15374424jccp3502_2

Sanders, M. R., Kirby, J. N., Tellegen, C. L., & Day, J. J. (2014). The Triple P Positive Parenting Program: A systematic review and meta-analysis of a multi-level system of parenting support. *Clinical Psychology, 34*, 337–357. doi:10.1016/j.cpr.2014.04.003

Sanders, M. R., & Mazzucchelli, T. G. (2013). The promotion of self-regulation through parenting interventions. *Clinical Child and Family Psychology Review, 16*, 1–17. doi:10.1007/s10567-013-0129-z

Sanders, M. R., Mazzucchelli, T. G., & Studman, L. J. (2004). Stepping Stones Triple P: The theoretical basis and development of an evidence-based positive parenting program for families of a child who has a disability. *Journal of Intellectual and Developmental Disability, 29*, 265–283. doi:10.1080/13668250412331285127

Sanders, M. R., & Woolley, M. L. (2005). The relationship between maternal self-efficacy and parenting practices: Implications for parent training. *Child: Care, Health and Development, 31*, 65–73. doi:10.1111/j.1365-2214.2005.00487.x

Schalock, R. L., Borthwick-Duffy, S. A., Bradley, V. J., Buntinx, W. H. E., Coulter, D. L., Craig, E. M., . . . Yeager, M. H. (2010). *Intellectual disability: Definition, classification, and systems of supports* (11th ed.). Washington, DC: AAIDD.

Sigafoos, J., Arthur, M., & O'Reilly, M. (2003). *Challenging behavior and developmental disability.* London, England: Whurr.

Stalker, K., & McArthur, K. (2012). Child abuse, child protection and disabled children: A review of recent research. *Child Abuse Review, 21*, 24–40. doi:10.1002/car.1154

Strategic Review of Health Inequalities in England. (2010). *Fair society, healthy lives: The Marmot Review.* London, England: Marmot Review. Retrieved from http://www.instituteofhealthequity.org/projects/fair-society-healthy-lives-the-marmot-review

Studman, L. (2014). *Family adaptation and developmental disability.* (Doctoral thesis, Curtin University of Technology, Perth, Australia). Retrieved from http://espace.library.curtin.edu

Tellegen, C. L., & Sanders, M. R. (2013). Stepping Stones Triple P—Positive Parenting Program for children with disability: A systematic review and meta-analysis. *Research in Developmental Disabilities, 34,* 1556–1571. doi:10.1016/j.ridd.2013.01.022

United States of America Developmental Disabilities Act of 1984, S. 2662, 98th Cong. § 102 (1984). Retrieved from https://www.aucd.org/docs/urc/DD%20Act%20of%201984.pdf

Wallander, J. L., Decker, M. C., & Koot, H. M. (2006). Risk factors for psychopathology in children with intellectual disability: A prospective longitudinal population-based study. *Journal of Intellectual Disability Research, 50,* 259–268. doi:10.1111/j.1365-2788.2005.00792.x

Whittingham, K., Wee, D., Sanders, M., & Boyd, R. (2012). Predictors of psychological adjustment, experienced parenting burden and chronic sorrow symptoms in parents of children with cerebral palsy. *Child: Care, Health and Development, 39,* 366–373. doi:10.1111/j.1365-2214.2012.01396x

Woodman, A. C., Mawdsley, H. P., & Hauser-Cram, P. (2015). Parenting stress and child behaviour problems within families of children with developmental disabilities: Transactional relations across 15 years. *Research in Developmental Disabilities, 36,* 264–276. doi:10.1016/j.ridd.2014.10.011

CHAPTER 10

SUPPORTING PARENTS OF CHILDREN WITH SERIOUS MENTAL HEALTH PROBLEMS

KYLIE BURKE

INTRODUCTION

Serious mental illness affects between 10% and 20% of children and adolescents (Kieling et al., 2011; Lawrence et al., 2016; Merikangas et al., 2011), thus representing a significant number of the world's children and adolescents. Clearly, the prevention and treatment of mental health problems in children is a major challenge worldwide. Preventive approaches are necessary if we are to reduce the number of children who are vulnerable to mental health problems. However, for the substantial number of children who are experiencing or will experience mental illness, we require more effective and evidence-based, contextually driven, approaches to reducing symptoms and promoting factors associated with well-being. This chapter describes the complementary role of parenting programs in supporting parents of children with serious mental health problems.

CHILD AND ADOLESCENT MENTAL HEALTH PROBLEMS: IMPACT AND SIGNIFICANCE

As already noted, a significant number of children experience serious mental health issues. The most common disorders are reported to be externalizing behaviors, followed by anxiety disorders (Lawrence et al., 2016; Polanczyk, Salum, Sugaya, Caye, & Rohde, 2015). With rates increasing worldwide, estimates suggest that between 5% and 10% of children and adolescents (aged 5–19 years) are diagnosed with an externalizing behavior disorder (e.g., disruptive behavior, attention deficit hyperactivity disorder [ADHD]), and similar numbers are diagnosed with an internalizing disorder (e.g., anxiety or depression; Lawrence et al., 2016; Polanczyk et al., 2015). These issues are also the most common reason for referral to child and adolescent mental health services, placing significant personal and economic burden on adolescents, families, society, and the mental health system (National Institute for Health and Care Excellence [NICE], 2013). However, issues such as high-risk self-harm or suicidal behaviors, eating disorders, and psychosis also predominate child and adolescent mental health services (Gowers & Rowlands, 2005). Children and adolescents who experience mental illness are at risk of a range of significant and costly health and social problems—including the persistence of mental illness into adulthood, unintentional injury requiring hospital admission, substance abuse, criminal behavior, academic failure or dropout, unemployment, and family breakdown—that frequently persist well into adulthood (NICE, 2013; Patel, Flisher, Hetrick, & McGorry, 2007).

The impacts of serious mental health problems in children not only affect the child but also extend to their parents and caregivers (Taylor-Richardson, Heflinger, & Brown, 2006). Caring for a child with a disability is an additional stressor for which many parents and other caregivers are often not prepared. Studies exploring the impact of childhood mental illness have shown that the associated behavioral and emotional problems that children experience alongside the primary symptoms of their illness are the most powerful predictors of caregiver strain. Further, high levels of parent stress and ineffective parenting are a significant predictor of treatment outcome, including readmission to the hospital (Blader, 2004; Fite, Stoppelbein, & Greening, 2009). For example, Blader (2004), in a study of 109 children followed for 1 year postdischarge from inpatient care, found that harsh parental discipline and poorer parent–child relationships were significant predictors for readmission, and that this was even more predictive when coupled with high levels of parenting stress.

In addition to the impact on the child and immediate family, there is evidence that child mental health problems are transmitted across generations (e.g., Raudino, Fergusson, Woodward, & Horwood, 2013). For example, behavioral genetic research indicates significant heritability of conduct disorder, with between 41% and 61% of variance in antisocial behavior linked to genetic factors. The intergenerational continuity of child behavioral and emotional problems is also likely linked to the social and contextual variables that influence and persist across generations. For example, the experience of social disadvantage (low socioeconomic status, living standards); family conflict, violence, and breakdown; parental adjustment (mental illness, substance misuse); and exposure to childhood physical and sexual abuse by parents are all factors that have been associated with conduct problems, substance use disorders, anxiety, depression, and suicidal behaviors in children and adolescents and are environmental variables that are known to persist across generations (Fergusson, Horwood, & Lynskey, 1996; Fergusson, Horwood, & Woodward, 2000; Flaherty et al., 2013).

Given the significance of the problem, it is important to reduce the burdens and stressors on parents associated with childhood mental illness so that parents can maintain their own mental health/well-being and so they can adequately care for and support their child (Taylor-Richardson et al., 2006), thus reducing the likelihood that these problems will transfer from one generation to the next.

PARENTING AND FAMILY FACTORS AS DETERMINANTS OF DEVELOPMENTAL OUTCOMES FOR CHILDREN AND ADOLESCENTS EXPERIENCING SERIOUS MENTAL ILLNESS

Family background and the family environment play a central role in the development of serious mental health problems and subsequently for determining the adult outcomes of children and young people. Factors such as living in an unstable family environment that features high levels of family or marital conflict and divorce, parental alcohol or substance addictions, and parental mental illness all contribute to vulnerability for the development of serious mental illness.

Parenting also has long been shown to be critical to the development and well-being of children. There is considerable evidence to suggest that ineffective parenting or poor-quality relationships between parents and children are important precursors for behavioral and emotional difficulties in children and adolescents (Odgers et al., 2008), including conduct disorder, antisocial behavior, anxiety, depression, and suicide (Repetti, Taylor, & Seeman, 2002). Difficulties experienced during childhood and adolescence then frequently translate into more serious difficulties in adulthood. Harsh and coercive parenting practices have been linked to a range of poor outcomes for children as they mature through adolescence and into adulthood, including higher incidences of mental health or substance addictions, school failure and unemployment, and relationship problems.

A range of protective factors that aid resilience and lower levels of risk for the development of mental health problems have also been noted. Many of these factors relate to the characteristics of the individual child (e.g., behavior, values, attitudes, and beliefs); to their relationship with their peers (e.g., friends who do not engage in risk-taking activities such as alcohol or drug consumption); and to their relationship with their school and community (e.g., strong social support and connectedness through friendship groups, positive role models, positive relationships with teachers, and engagement in social activities and the community; Patel et al., 2007). Effective parenting, characterized by a warm, loving relationship combined with clear expectations and rules, discipline practices, and effective supervision, have been linked to positive health and developmental outcomes for children (Wille, Bettge, & Ravens-Sieberer, 2008).

Parenting practices are also highly likely to transfer from one generation of parents to the next (Capaldi, Pears, Kerr, & Owen, 2008; Chung et al., 2009), thus adding to the intergenerational transmission of child behavioral and emotional difficulties. For example, in Capaldi et al.'s (2008) study of harsh discipline practices in at-risk men, childhood experience of harsh discipline was related to their own use of harsh discipline with their 2- to 3-year-old children. Similarly, Chung and colleagues (2009), in their study of infant spanking, found that parents who had been exposed to physical or verbal abuse during childhood were more likely to spank than mothers without this history of abuse.

Addressing the needs of a child experiencing mental illness is challenging. Parents require the knowledge and skills to adequately support their child and to maintain a family environment that promotes their children's development and well-being. When the family includes a child with a mental illness, the parent must also balance the needs of their child with the needs of the rest of the family, as well as their own. Challenges faced by families include financial burden, sibling issues, stigma, self-doubt and blame, relationship/marital stress, and service access issues. On top of this are the challenges of dealing with the child's symptoms and associated externalizing behaviors (Fite, Stoppelbein, & Greening, 2008). Despite the considerable impact of parenting and parental well-being on the treatment outcomes of children, many child and adolescent mental health therapeutic approaches do not adequately recognize or address the needs of parents (Mount & Mendenhall, 2011).

THE ROLE OF PARENTING INTERVENTIONS IN THE CHILD AND ADOLESCENT MENTAL HEALTH CONTEXT

Parents are tasked with the ongoing responsibility of assisting their child to manage his or her symptoms and to promote activities and behaviors that are associated with well-being. A recent Australian study revealed that parents reported a lack of information about their child's illness or treatment, frequently do not feel supported or included by their child's mental health team, and feel excluded and even blamed for their child's difficulties, despite their expressed interest in wanting more information and to be more involved in their child's admission and treatment (Geraghty, McCann, King, & Eichmann, 2011). Further, in their longitudinal study of family empowerment and child psychosocial functioning outcomes for 2,301 children involved with mental health services, Resendez, Quist, and Matshazi (2000) found that caregivers who perceive themselves to be more competent, knowledgeable, efficacious, and advocates for their child within the service system were more satisfied with their child's treatment outcomes and had children who were functioning better at the end of treatment.

In the mental health setting, the family environment is critical to maintenance of post-admission gains and ongoing symptom management. If parents do not have the skills or confidence to implement their child's treatment plan at home (or to support their child to do so), are not emotionally available to their child, or have a home environment characterized by high levels of stress and inconsistent and ineffective parenting practices, such as harsh discipline, then the child's risk for readmission or dropout from treatment is increased (Fite et al., 2008).

Despite the demonstrated importance of parents and parenting in the protection and risk for the development of mental health problems in children and adolescents (e.g., Wang, Dishion, Stormshak, & Willett, 2011) as well as the large evidence base for parenting interventions as effective preventive and treatment approaches for a range of child and family difficulties, there has been little or no systematic approach to the inclusion or evaluation of parenting interventions in child and adolescent mental health services. A recent meta-analysis evaluating the effectiveness of child and adolescent psychotherapies identified only 13 studies in which parent- or family-focused interventions were evaluated (Weisz et al., 2013).

There is some evidence to suggest that incorporating parenting interventions within child and adolescent mental health practice is beneficial to children. The most successful of these take a behavioral family intervention (BFI) approach, which is based on social learning theory and functional analysis and incorporates principles from cognitive-behavioral therapy (CBT) and is delivered either as stand-alone interventions or incorporated within other evidence-based interventions, such as multisystemic family therapy (Henggeler & Schaeffer, 2010). BFI has consistently been shown to be effective in reducing child behavioral difficulties, including ADHD (van Den Hoofdakker et al., 2007) and oppositional defiant disorder (Costin & Chambers, 2007). The evidence for parenting programs targeting internalizing disorders such as anxiety have been mixed, with some research indicating that combining child-focused CBT with family or parenting components produces superior outcomes and follow-up effects compared to CBT-only approaches (e.g., Bögels & Siqueland, 2006), while other studies have not shown superior outcomes for interventions incorporating parenting components (e.g., Barrett, Duffy, Dadds, & Rapee, 2001). Despite these contradictory findings, on balance it would appear that parental involvement in treatment for both externalizing and internalizing mental health issues is warranted.

THE ROLE OF TRIPLE P IN CHILD AND ADOLESCENT MENTAL HEALTH SETTINGS

Increasing parental effectiveness by incorporating evidence-based parent consultation into child and adolescent mental health services as part of care as usual has the potential to enhance parents' skills and confidence in supporting their child to manage the symptoms of the child's illness and to engage in health-promoting behaviors (e.g., eating, sleep, exercise) and activities (e.g., study, connecting to friends) both during the admission period and once the child has been discharged. Further, it offers the potential to affect one of the strongest predictors for referral and treatment outcome: parental stress (Fite et al., 2008). Along with the impact the program has on reducing a range of child social, behavioral, and emotional problems, Triple P has repeatedly been shown to reduce symptoms of stress and depression associated with the parenting role (Sanders, Kirby, Tellegen, & Day, 2014), a critical factor, in providing a nurturing and supportive environment both during and beyond the child's treatment. Parents who feel more effective and able to self-regulate their emotions and behavior may be more able to adhere to their child's treatment demands, maintain effective parenting practices, and foster a warm, involved relationship with their child.

Triple P has demonstrated efficacy for use with parents of children with a range of mental health problems, including conduct disorder (see Chapter 6, this volume); ADHD (Bor, Sanders, & Markie-Dadds, 2002); anxiety (see Chapter 8, this volume); and recurrent pain (Sanders Shepherd, Cleghorn, Woolford, 1994), and with children who have experienced or are at risk for maltreatment or abuse (Prinz, Sanders, Shapiro, Whitaker, & Lutzker, 2009).

More recently, the potential to support parents of children experiencing mental health problems by incorporating the Triple P program within inpatient child and adolescent mental health services has received attention from both researchers and mental health service providers. For example, Glazemakers (2012) evaluated the delivery of the Triple P program within an inpatient unit in Belgium. A randomized controlled trial was conducted with 50 mothers of children (aged < 12 years) admitted to the unit for treatment. Mothers were randomized to participate in either the Group Triple P program or a wait-list control (W-L) group. The W-L group received routine care as usual. Parents completed pre- and postassessments; a 6-month follow-up focused on child externalizing and internalizing behavior difficulties, parenting practices, and parent stress. Findings indicated that the Triple P program has potential to enhance the effects of routine inpatient treatment, with parents in the Triple P group reporting decreases in child externalizing behavior problems, parental stress, and ineffective parenting, with results maintained at 6-month follow-up.

In a second example, a child inpatient unit that provides intensive assessment and treatment to children (up to 13 years 11 months) with serious mental illness and their families within a pediatric children's hospital in Australia has explicitly adopted Triple P as part of routine treatment since 2010. The primary mental health diagnoses treated within the unit include eating disorders, obsessive-compulsive disorder, conduct disorders, attachment disorders, depression and anxiety, acute risk associated with self-harm and suicide, as well as aggression and antisocial behavior. A number of contextual factors associated with family and parenting difficulties; difficulties within social and educational systems; as well as exposure to significant stressors are also frequently noted as areas that require formal intervention. All parents are expected to participate in a modified Group Triple P program during their child's admission, and parents provide consent for the principles of Triple P to be applied with their child while they are on the unit. The format of Group Triple P has been modified to fit within an average 2-week admission period. All content is delivered with fidelity. A formal evaluation of the outcomes from the inclusion of Triple P within the unit is under way; however, the example described in Box 10.1 demonstrates that it is possible to sustainably include evidence-based parenting within a child and adolescent mental health setting.

BOX 10.1: Perspective of a Health Practitioner on the Benefits of Triple P in an Acute Pediatric Hospital

"We offer the group program to all of our families. We basically send out, in pre-admission, information about the Triple P program, the dates it is on, we ask the families to commit to participate in the program as part of their admission here. By having all staff trained in Primary Care and Group Triple P, it allows the nursing staff to role model, I suppose, and have some of those corridor conversations with parents. Before Triple P, there was often disagreement amongst staff about how to manage a child's behavior. So, the program has been able to offer some consistency in how we manage, it provides a common language. I think it gives staff a great deal of satisfaction in seeing a change in some of the children, in that they arrive with really a lot of externalising behavior, and gradually there's a reduction in the amount of restrictive interventions that are used, so there's a great deal of satisfaction in seeing that and seeing how families engage in that process. I think the benefit is that we are able to offer an intensive for parents where they have the role-modelling as well as a theoretical component. I think that's quite unique."—Senior Psychologist, Child Inpatient Unit, Acute Pediatric Hospital

IMPLICATIONS FOR PRACTICE, POLICY, AND RESEARCH

Child and adolescent mental health is a significant problem worldwide, with prevalence rates rising. Population-based preventive approaches are critical for reducing these issues over time. However, for the 10% to 20% of children and adolescents who do experience mental illnesses such as disruptive behavior disorders, anxiety, and depression and the myriad other childhood illnesses, treatment and support from tertiary services remain essential. Many interventions have been developed that target the child and the child's symptoms with good effects. However, not all children recover, and many are vulnerable to symptom recidivism and the need for readmission or engagement with mental health services.

Parents are a key risk and protective factor in the lives of their children. They are the agent most responsible for seeking assistance for their child, and they provide the daily context in which children must manage their symptoms and adhere to any treatment requirements. Therefore, to effectively address the significant challenges and impacts associated with child and adolescent mental health problems, policymakers and service providers not only need to consider the therapeutic approaches directed toward the child to reduce symptoms and promote recovery but also must take into account the context in which the child lives, that is, parenting and the family environment. Therapeutic approaches are required not only that target the child but also that work to provide parents with the education, support, and skill building required to decrease strain on parents and assist them to better support their child through the child's illness while creating a healthier environment for their family.

The paucity of high-quality research examining the specific and combined contributions of parenting interventions within child and adolescent mental health services also warrants attention by researchers, policymakers, and service providers. To better understand the contribution that parent-focused interventions such as Triple P can make to short-term and longer term treatment and recovery from child and adolescent mental health services, better processes for evaluating outcomes are required, including effective methods for tracking therapies children and families receive and standardized processes and measures for assessing both child and parent outcomes from involvement with services.

The Triple P program contains a number of features that make it amenable for integration at the service level and within system-based research studies, including that the program can be flexibly tailored to individual children with diverse and complex needs; has clearly articulated and theoretically coherent principles that can be applied to address a range of clinical symptoms; consists of a set of strategies and processes that are accessible and feasible for deployment across outpatient and inpatient child and adolescent mental health service contexts; and has a training model that can be deployed in a sustainable way that can accommodate overtime shifts in staffing.

KEY MESSAGES

- Parenting a child or adolescent with serious mental illness places significant strain and burden on the caregiver.

- Children respond better to treatment when parents feel involved and effective within their child's treatment.
- Parents are a critical protective factor in their child's life—they are needed for supporting the child during treatment, managing symptom reduction, maintaining treatment gains, and promoting their child's development and well-being.
- Better incorporation of evidence-based parenting interventions within routine care of a child's serious mental health services is needed.
- Triple P has the potential to be flexibly and sustainably incorporated into treatment as usual within services providing treatment for children and adolescents with serious mental health problems.

REFERENCES

Barrett, P. M., Duffy, A. L., Dadds, M. R., & Rapee, R. M. (2001). Cognitive-behavioral treatment of anxiety disorders in children: Long-term (6-year) follow-up. *Journal of Consulting and Clinical Psychology, 69*, 135–141. doi:10.1037//0022-006X.69.1.135

Blader, J. C. (2004). Symptom, family, and service predictors of children's psychiatric rehospitalization within one year of discharge. *Journal of the American Academy of Child and Adolescent Psychiatry, 43*, 440–451. doi:10.1097/00004583-200404000-00010

Bögels, S. M., & Siqueland, L. (2006). Family cognitive behavioral therapy for children and adolescents with clinical anxiety disorders. *Journal of the American Academy of Child and Adolescent Psychiatry, 45*, 134–141. doi:10.1097/01.chi.0000190467.01072.ee

Bor, W., Sanders, M. R., & Markie-Dadds, C. (2002). The effects of the Triple P—Positive Parenting Program on preschool children with co-occurring disruptive behavior and attentional/hyperactive difficulties. *Journal of Abnormal Child Psychology, 30*, 571–587. doi:10.1023/A:1020807613155

Capaldi, D. M., Pears, K. C., Kerr, D. C., & Owen, L. D. (2008). Intergenerational and partner influences on fathers' negative discipline. *Journal of Abnormal Child Psychology, 36*, 347–358. doi:10.1007/s10802-007-9182-8

Chung, E. K., Mathew, L., Rothkopf, A. C., Elo, I. T., Coyne, J. C., & Culhane, J. F. (2009). Parenting attitudes and infant spanking: The influence of childhood experiences. *Pediatrics, 124*, e278. doi:10.1542/peds.2008-3247

Costin, J., & Chambers, S. M. (2007). Parent management training as a treatment for children with oppositional defiant disorder referred to a mental health clinic. *Clinical Child Psychology and Psychiatry, 12*, 511–524. doi:10.1177/1359104507080979

Fergusson, D. M., Horwood, L. J., & Lynskey, M. T. (1996). Childhood sexual abuse and psychiatric disorder in young adulthood: II. Psychiatric outcomes of childhood sexual abuse. *Journal of the American Academy of Child and Adolescent Psychiatry, 35*, 1365–1374.

Fergusson, D. M., Horwood, L. J., & Woodward, L. J. (2000). The stability of child abuse reports: A longitudinal study of the reporting behaviour of young adults. *Psychological Medicine, 30*, 529–544.

Fite, P., Stoppelbein, L., & Greening, L. (2008). Parenting stress as a predictor of age upon admission to a child psychiatric inpatient facility. *Child Psychiatry and Human Development, 39*, 171–183. doi:10.1007/s10578-007-0080-7

Fite, P., Stoppelbein, L., & Greening, L. (2009). Predicting readmission to a child psychiatric inpatient unit: The impact of parenting styles. *Journal of Child and Family Studies, 18*, 621–629. doi:10.1007/s10826-009-9284-8

Flaherty, E. G., Thompson, R., Dubowitz, H., Harvey, E. M., English, D. J., Proctor, L. J., & Runyan, D. K. (2013). Adverse childhood experiences and child health in early adolescence. *JAMA Pediatrics, 167*, 622–629. doi:10.1001/jamapediatrics.2013.22

Geraghty, K., McCann, K., King, R., & Eichmann, K. (2011). Sharing the load: Parents and carers talk to consumer consultants at a child and youth mental health inpatient unit. *International Journal of Mental Health Nursing, 20*, 253–262. doi:10.1111/j.1447-0349.2011.00730.x

Glazemakers, I. (2012). *A population health approach to parenting support: Disseminating the Triple P—positive parenting program in the Province of Antwerp* (Unpublished doctoral dissertation). University of Antwerpen, Antwerp, Belgium.

Gowers, S. G., & Rowlands, L. (2005). Inpatient services. *Current Opinion in Psychiatry, 18*, 445–448. doi:10.1097/01.yco.0000172066.24391.be

Henggeler, S. W., & Schaeffer, C. M. (2010). Treating serious emotional and behavioural problems using multisystemic therapy. *Australian and New Zealand Journal of Family Therapy, 31*, 149–164. doi:10.1375/anft.31.2.149

Kieling, C., Baker-Henningham, H., Belfer, M., Conti, G., Ertem, I., Omigbodun, O., . . . Rahman, A. (2011). Global Mental Health 2: Child and adolescent mental health worldwide: Evidence for action. *The Lancet, 378*, 1515–1525. doi:10.1016/S0140-6736(11)60827-1

Lawrence, D., Hafekost, J., Johnson, S. E., Saw, S., Buckingham, W. J., Sawyer, M. G., . . . Zubrick, S. R. (2016). Key findings from the second Australian Child and Adolescent Survey of Mental Health and Wellbeing. *Australian and New Zealand Journal of Psychiatry, 50*, 876–886. doi:10.1177/0004867415617836

Merikangas, K. R., He, J.-P., Burstein, M., Swendsen, J., Avenevoli, S., Case, B., . . . Olfson, M. (2011). Service utilization for lifetime mental disorders in US adolescents: results of the National Comorbidity Survey–Adolescent Supplement (NCS-A). *Journal of the American Academy of Child & Adolescent Psychiatry, 50*, 32–45. doi:10.1016/j.jaac.2010.10.006

Mount, K., & Mendenhall, A. N. (2011). Parents of children with mental Iilness: exploring the caregiver experience and caregiver-focused interventions (Report). *Families in Society: The Journal of Contemporary Social Services, 92*, 183–190.

National Institute for Health and Care Excellence (NICE). (2013). *Antisocial behaviour and conduct disorders in children and young people: Recognition, intervention and management*. London, England: British Psychological Society and Royal College of Psychiatrists.

Odgers, C. L., Moffitt, T. E., Broadbent, J. M., Dickson, N., Hancox, R. J., Harrington, H., . . . Caspi, A. (2008). Female and male antisocial trajectories: From childhood origins to adult outcomes. *Development and Psychopathology, 20*, 673–716. doi:10.1017/S0954579408000333

Patel, V., Flisher, A. J., Hetrick, S., & McGorry, P. (2007). Adolescent Health 3: Mental health of young people: A global public-health challenge. *The Lancet, 369*, 1302–1313. doi:10.1016/S0140-6736(07)60368-7

Polanczyk, G. V., Salum, G. A., Sugaya, L. S., Caye, A., & Rohde, L. A. (2015). Annual Research Review: A meta-analysis of the worldwide prevalence of mental disorders in children and adolescents. *Journal of Child Psychology and Psychiatry, 56*, 345–365. doi:10.1111/jcpp.12381

Prinz, R., Sanders, M., Shapiro, C., Whitaker, D., & Lutzker, J. (2009). Population-based prevention of child maltreatment: The US Triple P system population trial. *Prevention Science, 10*, 1–12. doi:10.1007/s11121-009-0123-3

Raudino, A., Fergusson, D., Woodward, L., & Horwood, L. J. (2013). The intergenerational transmission of conduct problems. *Social Psychiatry and Psychiatric Epidemiology, 48*, 465–476. doi:10.1007/s00127-012-0547-0

Repetti, R. L., Taylor, S. E., & Seeman, T. E. (2002). Risky families: Family social environments and the mental and physical health of offspring. *Psychological Bulletin, 128*, 330–366. doi:10.1037/0033-2909.128.2.330

Resendez, M., Quist, R., & Matshazi, D. (2000). A longitudinal analysis of family empowerment and client outcomes. *Journal of Child and Family Studies, 9,* 449–460. doi:10.1023/A:1009483425999

Sanders, M. R., Kirby, J. N., Tellegen, C. L., & Day, J. J. (2014). The Triple P—Positive Parenting Program: A systematic review and meta-analysis of a multi-level system of parenting support. *Clinical Psychology Review, 34,* 337–357. doi:10.1016/j.cpr.2014.04.003

Sanders, M. R., Shepherd, R. W., Cleghorn, G., & Woolford, H. (1994). The treatment of recurrent abdominal pain in children: A controlled comparison of cognitive-behavioral family intervention and standard pediatric care. *Journal of Consulting and Clinical Psychology, 62,* 306–314. doi:10.1037/0022-006X.62.2.306

Taylor-Richardson, K. D., Heflinger, C. A., & Brown, T. N. (2006). Experience of strain among types of caregivers responsible for children with serious emotional and behavioral disorders. *Journal of Emotional and Behavioral Disorders, 14,* 157–168. doi:10.1177/10634266060140030301

van Den Hoofdakker, B. J., van Der Veen-Mulders, L., Sytema, S., Emmelkamp, P. M. G., Minderaa, R. B., & Nauta, M. H. (2007). Effectiveness of behavioral parent training for children with ADHD in routine clinical practice: A randomized controlled study. *Journal of the American Academy of Child and Adolescent Psychiatry, 46,* 1263–1271. doi:10.1097/chi.0b013e3181354bc2

Wang, M.-T., Dishion, T. J., Stormshak, E. A., & Willett, J. B. (2011). Trajectories of family management practices and early adolescent behavioral outcomes. *Developmental Psychology, 47,* 1324–1341. doi:10.1037/a0024026

Weisz, J. R., Kuppens, S., Eckshtain, D., Ugueto, A. M., Hawley, K. M., & Jensen-Doss, A. (2013). Performance of evidence-based youth psychotherapies compared with usual clinical care: A multi-level meta-analysis. *JAMA Psychiatry, 70,* 750–761. doi:10.1001/jamapsychiatry.2013.1176

Wille, N., Bettge, S., & Ravens-Sieberer, U. (2008). Risk and protective factors for children's and adolescents' mental health: results of the BELLA study. *European Child & Adolescent Psychiatry, 17,* 133–147. doi:10.1007/s00787-008-1015-y

CHILDREN AND ADOLESCENTS WITH CHRONIC HEALTH CONDITIONS

ALINA MORAWSKA

THE NATURE OF THE PROBLEM

Chronic childhood health conditions are common, and rates are on the rise (Van Cleave, Gortmaker, & Perrin, 2010). For example, more than a third of Australian children live with one or more chronic health conditions, such as asthma, eczema, or diabetes (Australian Institute of Health and Welfare [AIHW], 2012). The burden of illness tends to be greatest in childhood (AIHW, 2005) and significantly affects the child and family in a number of ways (Halterman et al., 2004; Moore et al., 2006). The impact on children and families depends on a number of factors, such as the family environment, illness severity, and chronicity (e.g., Bennett, 1994; Svavarsdottir & Arlygsdattir, 2006). For example, eczema is often not considered as serious as other health conditions and is rarely fatal, but it causes indescribable misery for affected children and families (Lewis-Jones, 2006). The stress, anxiety, sleeplessness, and impact on everyday activities experienced by children with a chronic health condition and their parents are constant, time consuming, and demanding:

> [On] a bad day it would take 2 hours in the morning just to cream her up and to get the routine done. . . . I was so exhausted and you've still got to do everything else. (Santer et al., 2013, p. 2496)

There is consistent and extensive evidence that a child's chronic illness significantly contributes to parental and family stress, and the burden of caring for a child with a chronic health condition is well recognized (e.g., Dewey & Crawford, 2007; Holm, Patterson, Rueter, & Wamboldt, 2008). Parents of chronically ill children experience more stress than parents of healthy children (Cousino & Hazen, 2013), and this appears to be unrelated to illness duration or severity.

Importantly, higher levels of parenting stress are associated with more difficulties in psychological adjustment in both parents and their children (Helgeson, Becker, Escobar, & Siminerio, 2012; Verkleij et al., 2015).

Childhood health conditions affect child behavior, emotional adjustment, and quality of life (e.g., Boling, 2005; Svavarsdottir & Arlygsdattir, 2006). There is some evidence that children with chronic health conditions have a greater likelihood of experiencing emotional and behavioral problems (e.g., Hysing, Elgen, Gillberg, Lie, & Lundervold, 2007; Hysing, Elgen, Gillberg, & Lundervold, 2009). For example, studies have shown higher levels of depression and anxiety (LeBovidge, Lavigne, Donenberg, & Miller, 2003; Vila, Nollet-Clemencon, de Blic, Mouren-Simeoni, & Scheinmann, 2000) and lower self-esteem (Sultana, Oommen, & Shanmugham, 2007), as well as social difficulties (Meijer, Sinnema, Bijstra, Mellenbergh, & Wolters, 2000) among children with a chronic health condition. Aggression (Borge, Wefring, Lie, & Nordhagen, 2004), using the illness as a way of getting their own way or avoiding school (Eksi, Molzan, Savasir, & Guler, 1995), or behavior problems associated with illness management have also been documented.

The majority of chronic health conditions require some form of prescribed medical regimen, including monitoring, medication, lifestyle interventions, and physical therapies. At least half of children do not adhere to their prescribed treatment (Morton, Everard, & Elphick, 2014), and suboptimal adherence results in poor disease control (Bender & Zhang, 2008) and increased risk of hospital admission (Rohan et al., 2010) and is a major cause of treatment failure (Bass, Anderson, & Feldman, 2015).

THE ROLE OF PARENTS AND THE FAMILY IN UNDERSTANDING CHILDREN'S HEALTH OUTCOMES

The theoretical and empirical literatures provide compelling evidence that parenting plays a central role in children's health outcomes (Wood et al., 2008) and parent characteristics contribute to disease course and onset (Tibosch, Verhaak, & Merkus, 2011). Parenting factors have been shown to affect illness onset (Mrazek et al., 1999) and disease course (Rohan et al., 2014). Positive parenting (e.g., warmth, low restrictiveness) is associated with better illness management (Davis et al., 2001), illness control and regimen adherence, and better child adjustment (e.g., Jaser & Grey, 2010; Sullivan-Bolyai, Knafl, Deatrick, & Grey, 2003), as well as greater levels of health-related behaviors (Park & Walton-Moss, 2012). Likewise, low parental self-efficacy (e.g., Streisand, Swift, Wickmark, Chen, & Holmes, 2005) and use of less effective parenting strategies, such as overprotection (e.g., Gustafsson, Kjellman, & Bjorksten, 2002), ineffective parental problem-solving strategies (e.g., Wade, Holden, Lynn, Mitchell, & Ewart, 2000), and criticism and rejection (e.g., Wamboldt, Wamboldt, Gavin, Roesler, & Brugman, 1995), have been associated with poorer health and more emotional and behavior problems. Yet, parents of chronically ill children are reluctant to discipline their child (Holmbeck et al., 2002), discipline more inconsistently (Walker, Garber, & Van Slyke, 1995; Wilson et al., 1993), have different expectations for behavior (Walker et al., 1995), have communication that is more hostile (Murphy, Murray, & Compas, 2017), and have parent–child relationships that are more negative (Pinquart, 2013).

Responsibility for illness management, medication administration, and ensuring adherence rests with parents. Children do not have a mature understanding of disease prevention or understand the long-term benefits of treatment, but do experience adverse treatment effects. Therefore, treatment requires the parent to have the child do something the child does not want to do. Parents identify their child's resistance to medication as a significant obstacle to adherence (e.g., Burgess, Sly, Morawska, Cooper, & Devadason, 2008; Santer et al., 2013). In fact, children themselves recognize that simply not wanting to take their medication is a major barrier to adherence (Penza-Clyve, Mansell, & McQuaid, 2004). To compound this problem, as noted previously, parents of children with chronic health conditions often lack the confidence and effective parenting skills to manage child behavior (Chiang, Huang, & Lu, 2003; Mitchell, Fraser, Ramsbotham, Morawska, & Yates, 2015).

THE ROLE OF PARENTING INTERVENTIONS

Existing approaches to childhood chronic health care largely focus on a medical education model targeted at improving adherence. However, meta-analyses of interventions to improve adherence generally show small effects (e.g., Dean, Walters, & Hall, 2010; Kahana, Drotar, & Frazier, 2008; Pai & McGrady, 2014), which often do not last (Kahana et al., 2008). Combinations of behavioral and educational interventions tend to have the highest effect sizes, but there is significant variability in outcomes (e.g., Graves, Roberts, Rapoff, & Boyer, 2010; Kahana et al., 2008). Similarly, recent meta-analyses showed limited effects of parenting and family interventions on outcomes, including parent mental health and child symptoms (Eccleston, Palermo Tonya, Fisher, & Law, 2012; Law, Fisher, Fales, Noel, & Eccleston, 2014; Lohan, Morawska, & Mitchell, 2015). The available psychosocial interventions to improve adherence and to support families have largely focused on education and social support and rarely targeted parenting specifically (e.g., Lohan et al., 2015).

The need for parenting programs for parents of children with a chronic health condition has been articulated (Morawska, Calam, & Fraser, 2015), and research is increasingly focused on developing and evaluating parenting interventions for this population (e.g., Mackey et al., 2016; Morawska, Mitchell, Burgess, & Fraser, 2016), yet much remains to be done.

TRIPLE P AND CHILDHOOD CHRONIC HEALTH CONDITIONS

The Triple P—Positive Parenting Program has an extensive evidence base across multiple populations and problems (Sanders, Kirby, Tellegen, & Day, 2014), but until recently children's health conditions have received limited attention. Older research found positive effects for reductions in children's abdominal pain symptoms (Sanders, Shepherd, Cleghorn, & Woolford, 1994), and more recent studies have found positive, albeit mixed, effects of Triple P in the context of childhood asthma (Clarke, Calam, Morawska, & Sanders, 2014) and diabetes (Doherty, Calam, & Sanders, 2013; Westrupp, Northam, Lee, Scratch, & Cameron, 2015). Most recently, a format based on a brief discussion group, Positive Parenting for Healthy Living, has shown considerable promise in the context of childhood asthma and eczema (Morawska et al., 2016; Morawska, Mitchell, Burgess, & Fraser, 2017b) and diabetes (Lohan, Mitchell, Sofronoff, & Morawska, 2016).

Doherty et al. (2013) evaluated the effects of Self-Directed Teen Triple P for parents of adolescents (aged 11–17 years) with type 1 diabetes. Intervention effects included improved diabetes-related family conflict problems after participating in Triple P compared to those in usual care. Westrupp et al. (2015) evaluated Standard Triple P for parents of children (4–12 years) with type 1 diabetes. Parents in Triple P reported improved parent mental health, parenting skills, and family functioning at postintervention, but no effects were seen on child mental health, child behavior, and glycemic control at either 3- or 12-month follow-up. In neither of these evaluations was Triple P content adapted or tailored specifically for parents of children with type 1 diabetes, and both interventions were lengthy (10 sessions), which presents implementation challenges considering that the day-to-day management of diabetes and many other health conditions is in itself challenging and time consuming and engagement of parents has often proved to be a challenge (Clarke et al., 2014; Herbert, Gillespie, Monaghan, Holmes, & Streisand, 2016).

A number of factors drove the development of Positive Parenting for Healthy Living for parents of children with a chronic health condition (Morawska et al., 2015). It was apparent that children with a chronic health condition are vulnerable to the development of behavioral and emotional problems. The research evidence with child behavioral and emotional problems clearly points to the role of parents in providing a safe, supportive environment for their child's development and for implementing behavior change techniques to alter children's behavior. Parents of children with a chronic health condition report a range of specific concerns and issues that are unique to this population and are not specifically targeted in regular parenting programs. Anecdotally, parents of children with chronic health conditions also report that they do not feel that the available parenting programs cater to their needs.

Positive Parenting for Healthy Living (Morawska & Sanders, 2011) is a brief, tailored group program with two 2-hour sessions. Parents of children with a chronic health condition often report feelings of isolation and lack of social support (e.g., Gannoni & Shute, 2010). Thus, a group program was thought to provide an opportunity to connect with other parents experiencing similar issues. Likewise, the program is brief to take into account the already-demanding and stressful illness management regimens required for many health conditions. Positive Parenting for Healthy Living aims to increase positive parenting practices; reduce ineffective, coercive, and inconsistent strategies; empower parents to develop better daily routines; reduce child and family stress; encourage children to carry out health-related activities that they might otherwise resist; reduce child behavior problems and improve child adjustment; improve medical adherence and child health; and improve the quality of life for the child and family. The model shown in Figure 11.1 describes the cascading effects anticipated as a result of this intervention.

Positive Parenting for Healthy Living incorporates a number of elements, including a brief psychoeducation component (e.g., information to assist parents to understand the link between illness and behavioral and emotional adjustment and the impact of the family environment); strategies for effective illness management (e.g., maintaining regular routines); strategies to prevent emotional and behavioral problems (e.g., helping children learn coping skills, helping siblings cope); and strategies to manage child behavioral difficulties (e.g., using assertive discipline).

The evidence to date suggests that Positive Parenting for Healthy Living has effects on parenting confidence, parent behavior, and child behavior, although these may depend on illness type and severity. The mechanisms of the effects are yet to be elucidated, but as illustrated in Box 11.1, they may partially work though parenting cognitions and beliefs about illness management and

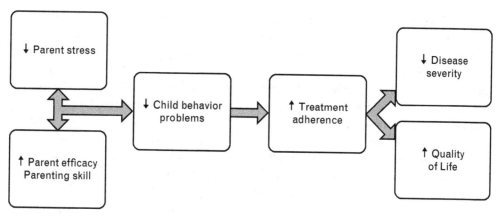

FIGURE 11.1: Effects of parenting intervention on child health outcomes.

their role as a parent. In addition, effects have extended to improvements in quality of life and child symptoms (Mitchell et al., 2016; Morawska et al., 2016, 2017b), and both mothers and fathers report positive outcomes (Morawska, Mitchell, Burgess, & Fraser, 2017a).

IMPLICATIONS FOR PRACTICE, POLICY, AND RESEARCH

Childhood chronic health conditions have a considerable impact on children, their families, and the broader community. There is no doubt that parenting and family interventions have

---

BOX 11.1: Focusing on Day-to-Day Parenting Is Important

Parents of children with a chronic health condition often struggle to make the connection between their child's health condition and their own parenting. When a child is unwell, most parents will make allowances for the child's behavior; however, when a child has a chronic health condition, making allowances can become a routine part of parenting. Parents taking part in Healthy Living Triple P have often experienced a light bulb moment, when they realized that they have been so focused on illness management that they had overlooked day-to-day parenting. For example, one parent said, "I think it actually made me become more aware of the way I deal with it and the way I deal with him and my way of parenting as well. . . . It actually made me stop and think . . . what kind of effects is my parenting having on my child too." Many parents also described that what really helped them was to focus on day-to-day parenting rather than trying to find a better medication or a cure for the health condition. This increased awareness or acceptance that the health condition was chronic and was not going to resolve helped parents to focus on the here and now of parenting.

a critical place in the care of these children; however, we still know relatively little about how best to support parents, how to integrate new interventions into existing medically oriented ones, and how these interventions interact with other treatments to result in better child health outcomes. From a research perspective, while parenting interventions have shown promise, future research needs to examine the extent to which the positive psychosocial outcomes can translate into better adherence and improved health outcomes for children. Likewise, from a practice perspective, consideration needs to be made of how to engage not only parents but also health practitioners. Many parents of children with a chronic health condition already attend a multitude of health and allied health interventions, and it is critical to examine which practitioners, in which contexts are best placed to deliver parenting interventions to these families. In the United States, recent calls suggest that primary care health settings may create the best context for the delivery of parenting intervention (Perrin, Leslie, & Boat, 2016), and this would certainly be a natural fit for children with chronic health conditions who are likely to see their primary health clinician regularly. Finally, we must not neglect the broader context of the family environment, where the child's health condition affect all members of the family. Further research into how to best to support parents, children, and siblings is important to ensure the best care.

KEY MESSAGES

- Chronic childhood health conditions are common and significantly affect children, parents, and families.
- Parents play a critical role in illness management and need to integrate regular parenting and child development tasks with specific treatment needs of the child.
- Parenting interventions have been identified as an important element of treatment services.
- Evidence is beginning to emerge of the efficacy of parenting interventions in helping to improve the life of children with chronic health conditions.
- This is an emerging area of research and much remains to be done to understand the links between parenting and children's physical health.

REFERENCES

AIHW. (2005). *Chronic respiratory diseases in Australia: their prevalence, consequences and prevention.* Canberra: Australian Institute of Health and Welfare.

Australian Institute of Health and Welfare (AIHW). (2012). *A picture of Australia's children 2012* (Cat. no. PHE 167). Canberra, Australia: Author.

Bass, A., Anderson, K., & Feldman, S. (2015). Interventions to increase treatment adherence in pediatric atopic dermatitis: A systematic review. *Journal of Clinical Medicine, 4,* 231–242. doi:10.3390/jcm4020231

Bender, B., & Zhang, L. (2008). Negative affect, medication adherence, and asthma control in children. *Journal of Allergy and Clinical Immunology, 122,* 490–495. doi:10.1016/j.jaci.2008.05.041

Bennett, D. S. (1994). Depression among children with chronic medical problems: A meta-analysis. *Journal of Pediatric Psychology. Special Issue: Chronic illness, 19*, 149–169. doi:10.1093/jpepsy/19.2.149

Boling, W. (2005). The health of chronically ill children: Lessons learned from assessing family caregiver quality of life. *Family and Community Health, 28*, 176–183.

Borge, A. I. H., Wefring, K. W., Lie, K. K., & Nordhagen, R. (2004). Chronic illness and aggressive behaviour: A population-based study of 4-year-olds. *European Journal of Developmental Psychology, 1*, 19–29. doi:10.1080/17405620344000004

Burgess, S. W., Sly, P. D., Morawska, A., Cooper, D. M., & Devadason, S. G. (2008). Assessing adherence and factors associated with adherence in young children with asthma. *Respirology, 13*, 559–563. doi:10.1111/j.1440-1843.2008.01292.x

Chiang, L. C., Huang, J. L., & Lu, C. M. (2003). Educational diagnosis of self-management behaviors of parents with asthmatic children by triangulation based on PRECEDE-PROCEED model in Taiwan. *Patient Education and Counseling, 49*, 19–25. doi:10.1016/s0738-3991(02)00037-x

Clarke, S. A., Calam, R., Morawska, A., & Sanders, M. (2014). Developing web-based Triple P "Positive Parenting Programme" for families of children with asthma. *Child: Care, Health and Development, 40*, 492–497. doi:10.1111/cch.12073

Cousino, M. K., & Hazen, R. A. (2013). Parenting stress among caregivers of children with chronic illness: A systematic review. *Journal of Pediatric Psychology, 38*, 809–828. doi:10.1093/jpepsy/jst049

Davis, C. L., Delamater, A. M., Shaw, K. H., La Greca, A. M., Eidson, M. S., Perez-Rodriguez, J. E., & Nemery, R. (2001). Brief report: Parenting styles, regimen adherence, and glycemic control in 4- to 10-year-old children with diabetes. *Journal of Pediatric Psychology, 26*, 123–129. doi:10.1093/jpepsy/26.2.123

Dean, A. J., Walters, J., & Hall, A. (2010). A systematic review of interventions to enhance medication adherence in children and adolescents with chronic illness. *Archives of Disease in Childhood, 95*, 717–723. doi:10.1016/S0140-6736(96)01073-2

Dewey, D., & Crawford, S. G. (2007). Correlates of maternal and paternal adjustment to chronic childhood disease. *Journal of Clinical Psychology in Medical Settings, 14*, 219–226. doi:10.1007/s10880-007-9069-4

Doherty, F. M., Calam, R., & Sanders, M. R. (2013). Positive Parenting Program (Triple P) for families of adolescents with type 1 diabetes: A randomized controlled trial of Self-Directed Teen Triple P. *Journal of Pediatric Psychology, 38*, 846–858. doi:10.1093/jpepsy/jst046

Eccleston, C., Palermo Tonya, M., Fisher, E., & Law, E. (2012). Psychological interventions for parents of children and adolescents with chronic illness. *Cochrane Database of Systematic Reviews*, (8). doi:10.1002/14651858.CD009660.pub2

Eksi, A., Molzan, J., Savasir, I., & Guler, N. (1995). Psychological adjustment of children with mild and moderately severe asthma. *European Child and Adolescent Psychiatry, 4*, 77–84. doi:10.1007/BF01977735

Gannoni, A. F., & Shute, R. H. (2010). Parental and child perspectives on adaptation to childhood chronic illness: a qualitative study. *Clinical Child Psychology and Psychiatry, 15*, 39–53. doi:10.1177/1359104509338432

Graves, M. M., Roberts, M. C., Rapoff, M., & Boyer, A. (2010). The efficacy of adherence interventions for chronically ill children: A meta-analytic review. *Journal of Pediatric Psychology, 35*, 368–382. doi:10.1093/jpepsy/jsp072

Gustafsson, P., Kjellman, N.-I., & Bjorksten, B. (2002). Family interaction and a supportive social network as salutogenic factors in childhood atopic illness. *Pediatric Allergy and Immunology, 13*, 51–57. doi:10.1034/j.1399-3038.2002.00086.x

Halterman, J. S., Yoos, H. L., Conn, K. M., Callahan, P. M., Montes, G., Neely, T. L., & Szilagyi, P. G. (2004). The impact of childhood asthma on parental quality of life. *Journal of Asthma, 41*, 645–653.

Helgeson, V. S., Becker, D., Escobar, O., & Siminerio, L. (2012). Families with children with diabetes: Implications of parent stress for parent and child health. *Journal of Pediatric Psychology, 37*, 467–478. doi:10.1093/jpepsy/jsr110

Herbert, L. J., Gillespie, C., Monaghan, M., Holmes, C., & Streisand, R. (2016). Factors associated with recruitment and retention in randomized controlled trials of behavioral interventions for patients with pediatric type 1 diabetes. *Journal of Clinical Psychology in Medical Settings, 23*, 112–125. doi:10.1007/s10880-015-9448-1

Holm, K. E., Patterson, J. M., Rueter, M. A., & Wamboldt, F. (2008). Impact of uncertainty associated with a child's chronic health condition on parents' health. *Families, Systems, and Health, 26*, 282–295. doi:10.1037/a0012912

Holmbeck, G. N., Johnson, S. Z., Wills, K. E., McKernon, W., Rose, B., Erklin, S., & Kemper, T. (2002). Observed and perceived parental overprotection in relation to psychosocial adjustment in preadolescents with a physical disability: The mediational role of behavioral autonomy. *Journal of Consulting and Clinical Psychology, 70*, 96–110. doi:10.1037/0022-006X.70.1.96

Hysing, M., Elgen, I., Gillberg, C., Lie, S. A., & Lundervold, A. J. (2007). Chronic physical illness and mental health in children. Results from a large-scale population study. *Journal of Child Psychology and Psychiatry, 48*, 785–792. doi:10.1111/j.1469-7610.2007.01755.x

Hysing, M., Elgen, I., Gillberg, C., & Lundervold, A. J. (2009). Emotional and behavioural problems in subgroups of children with chronic illness: Results from a large-scale population study. *Child: Care, Health and Development, 35*, 527–533. doi:10.1111/j.1365-2214.2009.00967.x

Jaser, S. S., & Grey, M. (2010). A pilot study of observed parenting and adjustment in adolescents with type 1 diabetes and their mothers. *Journal of Pediatric Psychology, 35*, 738–747. doi:10.1093/jpepsy/jsp098

Kahana, S., Drotar, D., & Frazier, T. (2008). Meta-analysis of psychological interventions to promote adherence to treatment in pediatric chronic health conditions. *Journal of Pediatric Psychology, 33*, 590–611. doi:10.1093/jpepsy/jsm128

Law, E. F., Fisher, E., Fales, J., Noel, M., & Eccleston, C. (2014). Systematic review and meta-analysis of parent and family-based interventions for children and adolescents with chronic medical conditions. *Journal of Pediatric Psychology, 39*, 866–886. doi:10.1093/jpepsy/jsu032

LeBovidge, J. S., Lavigne, J. V., Donenberg, G. R., & Miller, M. L. (2003). Psychological adjustment of children and adolescents with chronic arthritis: A meta-analytic review. *Journal of Pediatric Psychology, 28*, 29–39. doi:10.1093/jpepsy/28.1.29

Lewis-Jones, S. (2006). Quality of life and childhood atopic dermatitis: The misery of living with childhood eczema. *International Journal of Clinical Practice, 60*, 984–992. doi:10.1111/j.1742-1241.2006.01047.x

Lohan, A., Mitchell, A., Sofronoff, K., & Morawska, A. (2016). Positive Parenting for Healthy Living (Triple P) for parents of children with type 1 diabetes: Protocol of a randomised controlled trial. *BMC Pediatrics, 16.* doi:10.1186/s12887-016-0697-4

Lohan, A., Morawska, A., & Mitchell, A. (2015). A systematic review of parenting interventions for parents of children with type 1 diabetes. *Child: Care, Health and Development, 41*, 803–817. doi:10.1111/cch.12278

Mackey, E. R., Herbert, L., Monaghan, M., Cogen, F., Wang, J., & Streisand, R. (2016). The feasibility of a pilot intervention for parents of young children newly diagnosed with type 1 diabetes. *Clinical Practice in Pediatric Psychology, 4*, 35–50. doi:10.1037/cpp0000123

Meijer, S. A., Sinnema, G., Bijstra, J. O., Mellenbergh, G. J., & Wolters, W. H. G. (2000). Social functioning in children with a chronic illness. *Journal of Child Psychology and Psychiatry, 41*, 309–317. doi:10.1111/1469-7610.00615

Mitchell, A., Fraser, J., Ramsbotham, J., Morawska, A., & Yates, P. (2015). Childhood atopic dermatitis: A cross-sectional study of relationships between child and parent factors, atopic dermatitis management, and disease severity. *International Journal of Nursing Studies, 52*, 216–228. doi:10.1016/j.ijnurstu.2014.09.008

Mitchell, A., Morawska, A., Lohan, A., Filus, A., Sofronoff, K., & Batch, J. (2016, June). *Randomised controlled trial of Positive Parenting for Healthy Living (Triple P) for parents of children with type 1 diabetes.* Paper presented at the 8th World Congress of Behavioural and Cognitive Therapies, Melbourne, Australia.

Moore, K., David, T. J., Murray, C. S., Child, F., & Arkwright, P. D. (2006). Effect of childhood eczema and asthma on parental sleep and wellbeing: a prospective comparative study. *British Journal of Dermatology, 154*, 514–518.

Morawska, A., Calam, R., & Fraser, J. (2015). Parenting interventions for childhood chronic illness: A review and recommendations for intervention design and delivery. *Journal of Child Health Care 19*, 5–17. doi:10.1177/1367493513496664

Morawska, A., Mitchell, A., Burgess, S., & Fraser, J. (2017a). Fathers' perceptions of change following parenting intervention: Randomised controlled trial of Triple P for parents of children with asthma or eczema. *Journal of Pediatric Psychology, 42*, 792–803. doi:10.1093/jpepsy/jsw106

Morawska, A., Mitchell, A., Burgess, S., & Fraser, J. (2017b). Randomised controlled trial of Triple P for parents of children with asthma or eczema: Effects on parenting and child behaviour. *Journal of Consulting and Clinical Psychology, 85*, 283–296.

Morawska, A., Mitchell, A., Burgess, S., & Fraser, J. (2016). Effects of Triple P parenting intervention on child health outcomes for childhood asthma and eczema: Randomised controlled trial. *Behaviour Research and Therapy, 83*, 35–44. doi:10.1016/j.brat.2016.06.001

Morawska, A., & Sanders, M. R. (2011). *Positive Parenting for Healthy Living parent discussion group.* Brisbane, Australia: Parenting and Family Support Centre, University of Queensland.

Morton, R. W., Everard, M. L., & Elphick, H. E. (2014). Adherence in childhood asthma: The elephant in the room. *Archives of Disease in Childhood, 99*, 949–953. doi:10.1136/archdischild-2014-306243

Mrazek, D., Klinnert, M., Mrazek, P., Ikle, D., Brower, A., & McCormick, D. (1999). Prediction of early onset asthma in genetically at risk children. *Pediatric Pulmonology, 27*, 85–94. doi:10.1002/(SICI)1099-0496(199902)27:2<85::AID-PPUL4>3.0.CO;2-B

Murphy, L. K., Murray, C. B., & Compas, B. E. (2017). Topical review: Integrating findings on direct observation of family communication in studies comparing pediatric chronic illness and typically developing samples. *Journal of Pediatric Psychology, 42*, 85–94. doi:10.1093/jpepsy/jsw051

Pai, A. L. H., & McGrady, M. (2014). Systematic review and meta-analysis of psychological interventions to promote treatment adherence in children, adolescents, and young adults with chronic illness. *Journal of Pediatric Psychology, 39*, 918–931. doi:10.1093/jpepsy/jsu038

Park, H., & Walton-Moss, B. (2012). Parenting style, parenting stress, and children's health-related behaviors. *Journal of Developmental and Behavioral Pediatrics, 33*, 495–503. doi:10.1097/DBP.0b013e318258bdb8

Penza-Clyve, S. M., Mansell, C., & McQuaid, E. L. (2004). Why don't children take their asthma medications? A qualitative analysis of children's perspectives on adherence. *Journal of Asthma, 41*, 189–197. doi:10.1081/JAS-120026076

Perrin, E. C., Leslie, L. K., & Boat, T. (2016). Parenting as primary prevention. *JAMA Pediatrics, 170*, 637–638. doi:10.1001/jamapediatrics.2016.0225

Pinquart, M. (2013). Do the parent–child relationship and parenting behaviors differ between families with a child with and without chronic illness? A meta-analysis. *Journal of Pediatric Psychology, 38*, 708–721. doi:10.1093/jpepsy/jst020

Rohan, J., Drotar, D., McNally, K., Schluchter, M., Riekert, K., Vavrek, P., . . . Kercsmar, C. (2010). Adherence to pediatric asthma treatment in economically disadvantaged African-American children and adolescents: An application of growth curve analysis. *Journal of Pediatric Psychology, 35*, 394–404. doi:10.1093/jpepsy/jsp074

Rohan, J. M., Rausch, J. R., Pendley, J. S., Delamater, A. M., Dolan, L., Reeves, G., & Drotar, D. (2014). Identification and prediction of group-based glycemic control trajectories during the transition to adolescence. *Health Psychology, 33*, 1143–1152. doi:10.1037/hea0000025

Sanders, M. R., Kirby, J. N., Tellegen, C. L., & Day, J. J. (2014). The Triple P-Positive Parenting Program: A systematic review and meta-analysis of a multi-level system of parenting support. *Clinical Psychology Review, 34*, 337–357. doi:10.1016/j.cpr.2014.04.003

Sanders, M. R., Shepherd, R. W., Cleghorn, G., & Woolford, H. (1994). The treatment of recurrent abdominal pain in children: A controlled comparison of cognitive-behavioral family intervention and standard pediatric care. *Journal of Consulting and Clinical Psychology, 62*, 306–314.

Santer, M., Burgess, H., Yardley, L., Ersser, S. J., Lewis-Jones, S., Muller, I., . . . Little, P. (2013). Managing childhood eczema: qualitative study exploring carers' experiences of barriers and facilitators to treatment adherence. *Journal of Advanced Nursing, 69*, 2493–2501. doi:10.1111/jan.12133

Streisand, R., Swift, E., Wickmark, T., Chen, R., & Holmes, C. S. (2005). Pediatric parenting stress among parents of children with type 1 diabetes: The role of self efficacy, responsibility, and fear. *Journal of Pediatric Psychology, 30*, 513–521. doi:10.1093/jpepsy/jsi076

Sullivan-Bolyai, S., Knafl, K., Deatrick, J., & Grey, M. (2003). Maternal management behaviors for young children with type 1 diabetes. *American Journal of Maternal Child Nursing 28*, 160–166.

Sultana, S., Oommen, A., & Shanmugham, V. (2007). Psychological adjustment in juvenile diabetics. *Journal of the Indian Academy of Applied Psychology, 33*, 39–46.

Svavarsdottir, E. K., & Arlygsdattir, B. (2006). Comparison of health-related quality of life among 10- to 12-year-old children with chronic illnesses and healthy children: The parents' perspective. *Journal of School Nursing, 22*, 178–185.

Tibosch, M. M., Verhaak, C. M., & Merkus, P. J. F. M. (2011). Psychological characteristics associated with the onset and course of asthma in children and adolescents: A systematic review of longitudinal effects. *Patient Education and Counseling, 82*, 11–19. doi:10.1016/j.pec.2010.03.011

Van Cleave, J., Gortmaker, S. L., & Perrin, J. M. (2010). Dynamics of obesity and chronic health conditions among children and youth. *Journal of the American Medical Association, 303*, 623–630. doi:10.1001/jama.2010.104

Verkleij, M., van de Griendt, E. J., Colland, V., van Loey, N., Beelen, A., & Geenen, R. (2015). Parenting stress related to behavioral problems and disease severity in children with problematic severe asthma. *Journal of Clinical Psychology in Medical Settings, 22*, 179–193. doi:10.1007/s10880-015-9423-x

Vila, G., Nollet-Clemencon, C., de Blic, J., Mouren-Simeoni, M. C., & Scheinmann, P. (2000). Prevalence of DSM IV anxiety and affective disorders in a pediatric population of asthmatic children and adolescents. *Journal of Affective Disorders, 58*, 223–231. doi:10.1016/j.jadohealth.2007.05.023

Wade, S. L., Holden, G., Lynn, H., Mitchell, H., & Ewart, C. (2000). Cognitive-behavioral predictors of asthma morbidity in inner-city children. *Journal of Developmental & Behavioral Pediatrics, 21*, 340–346.

Walker, L. S., Garber, J., & Van Slyke, D. A. (1995). Do parents excuse the misbehavior of children with physical or emotional symptoms? An investigation of the pediatric sick role. *Journal of Pediatric Psychology, 20*, 329–345. doi:10.1093/jpepsy/20.3.329?

Wamboldt, F. S., Wamboldt, M. Z., Gavin, L. A., Roesler, T. A., & Brugman, S. M. (1995). Parental criticism and treatment outcome in adolescents hospitalized for severe, chronic asthma. *Journal of Psychosomatic Research, 39*, 995–1005. doi:10.1016/0022-3999(95)00507-2

Westrupp, E. M., Northam, E., Lee, K. J., Scratch, S. E., & Cameron, F. (2015). Reducing and preventing internalizing and externalizing behavior problems in children with type 1 diabetes: a randomized controlled trial of the Triple P-Positive Parenting Program. *Pediatric Diabetes, 16*, 554–563. doi:10.1111/pedi.12205

Wilson, S. R., Mitchell, J. H., Rolnick, S., & Fish, L. (1993). Effective and ineffective management behaviors of parents of infants and young children with asthma. *Journal of Pediatric Psychology, 18*, 63–81.

Wood, B. L., Lim, J., Miller, B. F., Cheah, P., Zwetsch, T., Ramesh, S., & Simmens, S. (2008). Testing the biobehavioral family model in pediatric asthma: Pathways of effect. *Family Process, 47*, 21–40. doi:10.1111/j.1545-5300.2008.00237.x

CHAPTER 12

A POPULATION APPROACH TO PARENTING SUPPORT FOR CHILDHOOD OBESITY

JESSICA A. BARTLETT AND MATTHEW R. SANDERS

INTRODUCTION

Childhood obesity presents a major public health dilemma. The dramatic increase in the prevalence of overweight and obesity among children has created concern among government agencies, policymakers, and health professionals. Obesity leads to considerable physical and psychological comorbidities, and estimates of the public health costs are staggering. Evidence-based, parent-centered interventions are a recommended pathway to prevent and treat childhood obesity (World Health Organization [WHO], 2012); however, recruitment remains a challenge. No parenting interventions to date have utilized a population health framework to reduce obesity at a population level. Emphasis must be placed on addressing this public health dilemma from both a preventive and a treatment perspective if improvements in obesity rates are to be achieved.

This chapter presents the argument for a population health model to prevent and treat childhood obesity. The increased prevalence rates and significant health risks associated with obesity are presented, along with the evidence supporting a parent-centered approach. The Lifestyle Triple P multilevel parenting and family support strategy is outlined. The existing research evidence for components of this suite are presented, along with the clinical and research-related needs associated with applying a public health framework.

THE RATIONALE FOR A POPULATION APPROACH TO PARENTING SUPPORT FOR OBESITY

THE GLOBAL EPIDEMIC OF OBESITY

The WHO (2012) defines obesity as an excess of body fat that may significantly impair health. Obesity is commonly defined using body mass index (BMI), which is weight (in kilograms) divided by height (in meters) squared. In the pediatric population, large variations in BMI due to pubertal status, age, and gender mean that age- and sex-specific BMI centile charts based on a large set of reference data are used. Height and weight can be plotted on a growth chart, and the corresponding centile can be used to classify weight, such as WHO Child Growth Standards (WHO, 2006) or the US Centers for Disease Control and Prevention (CDC) 2000 growth charts (Kuczmarski et al., 2000).

Childhood obesity has reached epidemic proportions worldwide, with 24% of males and 23% of females classified as overweight or obese in 2013 (Ng et al., 2014). The highest prevalence rates are in the upper-middle-income countries; however, there is also a rising trend in developing regions (Kelishadi, 2007). Although prevalence remains high, emerging evidence suggests that the rapid rise in obesity prevalence may be plateauing in some countries (e.g., Australia and the United States; Olds et al., 2011). Obesity rates in the adolescent population and the proportion of severely obese children are still worsening at a dramatic rate (Garnett, Baur, Jones, & Hardy, 2016; Kelly et al., 2013). The risk of obesity is higher for children from socioeconomically disadvantaged groups, with around 30% of children in these groups overweight or obese, compared with around 20% in those with higher socioeconomic status (Hardy, King, Espinel, Cosgrove, & Bauman, 2011).

A MAJOR PUBLIC HEALTH BURDEN

Excess body fat has serious health consequences. Obese children have higher risks of cardiovascular disease (Park, Falconer, Viner, & Kinra, 2012); type 2 diabetes mellitus and fatty liver disease (Cruz et al., 2005); sleep apnea (Narang & Mathew, 2012); and bone and joint problems (Napolitano, Walsh, Mahoney, & McCrea, 2000). Emerging evidence suggests that even very young children who are overweight exhibit signs of adverse health effects, including elevated blood pressure and impaired blood glucose metabolism (Gardner et al., 2009). Children with excess body fat are exposed to psychosocial comorbidity, emotional and physical bullying, and social exclusion (Griffiths, Wolke, Page, Horwood, & ALSPAC Study Team, 2006).

Overweight and obese children are more likely to carry their excess weight into adulthood, with 75% of obese children remaining obese as adults (James, 2004). The adverse effects of adult obesity have been well substantiated, including higher rates of type 2 diabetes mellitus, cardiovascular disease, hypertension, osteoarthritis, gout, cancers, and polycystic ovarian syndrome (Guh et al., 2009). Obesity is one of the leading factors contributing to premature mortality (Prospective Studies Collaboration, 2007). It is likely that the public health problems associated with obesity will be amplified as the current generation of overweight children grows into adulthood.

The public health burden of obesity is enormous. In 2008, the total cost of death and disability arising from obesity in Australia was estimated to be $58.2 billion per year, representing a three-fold increase from 2005 (Crowle & Turner, 2010). A recent meta-analysis estimated that medical spending attributable to obesity in the United States was $149 billion in 2014 US dollars at the national level (Kim & Basu, 2016). These data suggest that obesity has progressed from being a problem of the individual to a worldwide challenge, which must be addressed at a population level. Policymakers are becoming increasingly aware of the statistics, and many are calling for evidence-based interventions.

PARENTS AS THE AGENTS OF LIFESTYLE CHANGE

Parents can have a large impact on their children's health and well-being, particularly in relation to eating behaviors and physical activity levels. Parents who are active and eat well tend to have children who adopt similar habits (Cullen et al., 2003). There is a strong association between the dietary intake of children and that of their parents. Parental intake of fruit and vegetables and high-fat foods has been positively associated with child intake (van der Horst et al., 2007). A similar association has also been found between parent and child activity levels. Active parents tend to raise active children, with children of active parents up to five times more active than those with inactive parents (Moore et al., 1991).

Parents are in a prime position to promote a healthy home environment. When healthy foods, such as fruits and vegetables, are available and accessible to children in the home, child intake of these foods subsequently increases (Rasmussen et al., 2006). Children exhibit increased activity levels when their parents engage in active games with them (Sallis et al., 1992), support physical activity behaviors (Gustafson & Rhodes, 2006), and provide transportation to locations where physical activity is held (Sallis, Alcaraz, McKenzie, & Hovell, 1999).

Parenting style has also been associated with children's lifestyle patterns and obesity risk (Gerards, Dagnelie, Jansen, De Vries, & Kremers, 2012). An authoritative parenting style is associated with a lower risk of obesity in children (Sleddens, Gerards, Thijs, De Vries, & Kremers, 2011). Inadequate monitoring of the child's food intake can result in decreased vegetable intake and increased consumption of unhealthy foods and beverages (De Bourdeaudhuij et al., 2006). Failure to set reasonable screen time limits can result in more television viewing and lower physical activity levels (Arredondo et al., 2006; Gentile & Walsh, 2002). Conversely, stringent controls of food intake can compromise the child's ability to learn how to self-regulate eating and may lead to overeating (Faith, Scanlon, Birch, Francis, & Sherry, 2004). The child's preference for and consumption of palatable foods has been found to increase when parents restrict access to these foods (Clark, Goyder, Bissell, Blank, & Peters, 2007). Poor family functioning (characterized by poor communication and high levels of conflict) is also correlated with an increased risk of excess body fat (Halliday, Palma, Mellor, Green, & Renzaho, 2014).

Parents influence their child's early lifestyle behaviors and health habits carried into adulthood (Mamun, Lawlor, O'Callaghan, Williams, & Najman, 2005). Maternal food preferences, timing of eating, and where food is consumed in the home is correlated with children's eating behaviors when they are adults (Benton, 2004). The benefits of an active child who eats healthily include an enhanced health status, better academic performance, and improved social and emotional outcomes (Bauman, 2004; Rampersaud, Pereira, Girard, Adams, & Metzi, 2005).

Parenting interventions delivered at a young age before lifestyle habits have become established are likely to be an effective and sustainable approach.

Evidence of Effectiveness of Parent-Centered Obesity Programs

There is general consensus that obesity initiatives should target parents (Golan, 2006). Systematic reviews highlight the importance of targeting parents as agents for change in the treatment and prevention of obesity (e.g., Loveman et al., 2015; Waters et al., 2011). Greater body size reductions are associated with interventions that combine parenting, nutrition and physical activity elements, as opposed to programs that focus on diet or physical activity alone (Reinehr, 2013). Furthermore, parent-only interventions have shown maintenance of treatment gains 7 years post-intervention (Golan & Crow, 2004). A family-based approach shifts the focus from child weight control to promoting parenting skills and confidence in establishing a home environment conducive to healthy living. This approach reduces the likelihood that the child feels targeted, which is likely to reduce the risk of inappropriate dietary restriction, weight preoccupation, and distorted body image in children (Davison & Birch, 2001).

Limitations of Current Parent-Centered Obesity Programs

Although parenting interventions are an important tool for obesity management and prevention, there continue to be significant barriers with implementation and engagement. Many programs suffer from recruitment and retention issues and have little or no emphasis on improving parenting skills (Lindsay, Sussner, Kim, & Gortmaker, 2006). The length of existing obesity-specific parenting interventions may be another barrier to attendance, with an average of 10 sessions per intervention ranging from 9 weeks to 6 months (Gerards, Sleddens, Dagnelie, De Vries, & Kremers, 2011). Parents have identified program length as one of the major barriers to attendance (Nguyen et al., 2012).

Parents may fail to identify the relevance of obesity-specific interventions to their child. There is a clear disconnect in parental perceptions of child weight status and the child's actual weight, with only 17% of parents correctly identifying their child as overweight (Carnell, Edwards, Croker, Boniface, & Wardle, 2005). Furthermore, when parents are able to correctly identify their child's weight status as a problem, they may fail to identify weight as a significant health issue for the child (Jones et al., 2011). Obesity stigma may further hinder parents from self-selecting into interventions where weight is the target for change (Puhl & Heuer, 2010). Research suggests that parents resist attendance for fear of creating an adverse emotional impact on their child's self-esteem (Haynos & O'Donohue, 2012). Currently, there is little information in the literature identifying effective ways to engage parents in lifestyle interventions.

THE CASE FOR A POPULATION APPROACH
TO CHILDHOOD OBESITY

In the past, reactive management of childhood obesity has shaped management programs, resulting in delivery to families in which the child is already overweight or obese. According to WHO (2012), the key platform in the management of the obesity epidemic should be a population health approach. Such an approach may achieve population-level behavior change through a blend of universal and targeted parenting interventions, with differing levels of intervention intensity and breadth of reach. A universally accessible program that promotes the health of all children, whether at risk of obesity or not, is more likely to engage parents and enhance parental recruitment. It could potentially serve as a platform for referrals into more targeted programs for children with significant weight issues. A media campaign designed to raise public awareness in relation to lifestyle choices and destigmatize parenting support would complement prevention and treatment initiatives.

LIFESTYLE TRIPLE P—PARENTING AS A POPULATION HEALTH PRIORITY

THE LIFESTYLE TRIPLE P MULTILEVEL SYSTEM

Lifestyle Triple P is a variant of the Triple P—Positive Parenting Program developed specifically to prevent and treat childhood obesity through empowering parents with strategies and confidence to manage both lifestyle-specific and general child behavior. To our knowledge, it is currently the only evidence-based parenting program designed specifically as a comprehensive population health model for childhood obesity. There are currently three levels of the model: (a) a universal media campaign for all parents (Level 1); (b) a low-intensity, seminar series for all parents regardless of child weight status (Level 2); and (c) a targeted intensive program for children who are already overweight or obese (Level 5). Table 12.1 provides a description of each intervention.

THE LIFESTYLE TRIPLE P EVIDENCE BASE

The Triple P system has a strong evidence base (Sanders, Kirby, Tellegen, & Day, 2014) and is one of the only parenting interventions to demonstrate reductions in population-level indices of child maltreatment and behavioral problems (Chapter 44, this volume). The Lifestyle Triple P system has not yet been evaluated at a population level. Three randomized controlled trials (RCTs) and a number of pilot studies have evaluated the efficacy of the intensive Group Lifestyle Triple P (Level 5) intervention. More recently, the brief Lifestyle Triple P Seminar Series (Level 2) has also been evaluated in an RCT.

Group Lifestyle Triple P Research

West, Sanders, Cleghorn, and Davies (2010) evaluated Group Lifestyle Triple P with 101 parents of overweight or obese children aged 4 to 11 years in Brisbane, Australia. Parents were randomly allocated to the intervention or wait-list control groups. Results demonstrated a significant decrease in child BMI z scores following the intervention, with additional BMI improvements at 12-month follow-up. A significant decrease was also observed for child weight-related problem behavior and dysfunctional parenting styles, and parental confidence in managing child behavior improved. These intervention effects were medium to large and were maintained at

Table 12.1: The Lifestyle Triple P Multilevel System of Parenting and Family Support for Childhood Obesity

Program	Intensity	Target Population	Duration	Content
Stay Positive and Healthy Media and Communication Strategy (Level 1)	Very low intensity	All parents and community members interested in healthy lifestyle information	—	Aimed at improving awareness of healthy options and normalizing parenting support. The campaign may involve school newsletters, newspaper advertisements, radio spots, and a website.
Lifestyle Triple P Seminar Series (Level 2)	Low intensity	Parents of children from all weight status categories	3-session seminar series delivered over 3 weeks	Aimed at improving practical parenting skills to encourage healthy living. Topics include positive parenting, fussy eating, reading food labels, modifying recipes, and nutrition and activity guidelines.
Group Lifestyle Triple P (Level 5)	High intensity	Parents of overweight or obese children	14-session group program (including 10 group sessions and 4 telephone consultations) delivered over 17 weeks	Content includes understanding nutrition, understanding physical activity, modifying recipes, limiting sedentary activity and playing active games, reading food labels, managing problem behavior, and planning ahead.

12-month follow-up. These results support the efficacy of this intervention as a treatment tool for children who are already overweight or obese.

Data from two pilot trials conducted in community health settings in Western Australia further supported the efficacy of the intervention (Child & Adolescent Community Health Service, 2011a, 2011b). Both trials found a significant reduction in child BMI z score, child lifestyle problem behavior, child emotional difficulties, and dysfunctional parenting. Improvements in parental functioning and confidence were also observed. Although the trials had small sample sizes and no control group comparison, the findings support the results from larger RCTs advocating the effectiveness of the program.

Further support for Group Lifestyle Triple P comes from research investigating its efficacy when combined with adjunct care. Bartlett, Desha, and colleagues (2017) evaluated Group Lifestyle Triple P combined with three overnight family camps and dietetic consultations in an RCT with a group of 97 parents of overweight and obese children aged 5 to 12 years. Parents were assessed on a range of child and parent outcomes at baseline and 6- and 12-month follow-ups. Significant improvements in child body size were found at 6 months, including significant reductions in BMI z scores and weight z scores. Dysfunctional parenting styles also improved following the intervention. Weight z-score improvements were maintained at 12-month follow-up. While these findings suggest that the intervention plus conventional care intervention was superior to conventional care alone at 6-month follow-up, future research should focus on evaluating the individual treatment components and their relative contribution to intervention effects.

A further promising finding for the efficacy and cross-cultural applicability of Group Lifestyle Triple P comes from an RCT conducted in the Netherlands with 86 parents of overweight and obese children aged 4 to 8 years (Gerards et al., 2015). Positive short-term intervention effects were found for children's soft-drink consumption, parental responsibility regarding physical activity, encouragement to eat, psychological control, and parental confidence and satisfaction with parenting. At 12 months postintervention, effects were found on sedentary behavior, time spent playing outside, parental monitoring of food intake, and responsibility regarding nutrition. No significant intervention effects were found on child body size. This finding may be due to the degree of child adiposity in the sample. Children had a mean baseline BMI z score of 1.85, with only 63% classified as obese. Conversely, the Australian trial children had a mean baseline BMI z score of 2.11 (i.e., more overweight; West et al., 2010). Therefore, it may be that there was insufficient power to detect a statistically significant change in BMI z score. Another explanation for the lack of findings on child BMI could be due to baseline differences in parent weight. Parents in the intervention group had a higher BMI than the control parents. It may be that parents with weight issues may find it more difficult to make lifestyle changes in their family. It is recommended that future research should statistically control for differences in parental weight status at baseline to see if significant BMI z scores result.

Lifestyle Triple P Seminar Series Research

The first trial of the Lifestyle Triple P Seminar Series was conducted in Brisbane, Australia (Bartlett, Sanders, & Leong, 2017). One hundred and sixty parents were randomly allocated to either the intervention or the control condition and were assessed at preintervention, postintervention, and 6- and 12-month follow-up. Results revealed significant improvements on lifestyle-specific and general parental confidence, parenting styles, and child lifestyle problem behavior

---

BOX 12.1: Feedback From Parents Who Completed a Lifestyle Triple P Seminar Series

- Dinnertime was horrid—it was like a battleground. I would spend my whole time pressuring Chloe to eat her vegetables and making empty threats. After Lifestyle Triple P, we can have meals together in peace. We don't focus on her eating (or lack of eating) and can actually spend quality time together as a family.
- I now serve all children the same foods, and we have a rule of no television on during dinner. Dinner is much better! One meal for all the family saves me time.
- We make more time as a family as a whole engaging in active games, like going to parks more frequently, taking nature walks around the neighborhood. We have made physical activity a normal part of the family routine.
- It was great to actually look at our own activity levels and be realistic about how this affected/reflected on our children. We have set limits and rules around screen time.
- Before the seminar I had never stopped to think about how much time my kids spend in front of a screen. The guide time allowance of 1 hour per weekday was very helpful.
- It has definitely helped us achieve a healthier household—not just through how we eat and how active we are, but it has also brought us closer together as a family, and my husband and I are now on the same page, which has brought us closer together as well.
- We were so overwhelmed by how easy it was to modify little things on the home front which led to big results.
- I *actually* read nutritional labels when doing shopping now.

---

at the 12-month follow-up. Parents in the control condition showed an increase in the total time the child spent watching television over the 12 months, with no such worsening of screen time in the intervention condition. Child BMI z scores and weight z scores showed a trend in the intended direction, with a reduction in the intervention condition; however, this difference was not statistically significant. The positive benefits for families participating in a Lifestyle Triple P seminar are provided in Box 12.1.

The potential benefits of this program are substantial. No RCT to date has demonstrated that a brief lifestyle-specific parenting intervention produces success at 12-month follow-up (Reinehr, 2013). Evidence for maintenance of treatment change at 12 months following the intervention is important given the long-term health benefits associated with such changes. A successful short program delivered to all children at a young age could have meaningful implications for public health. Participation can be seen as being universal and health oriented. It has the capacity to effect a long-term change in attitudes toward healthy living in both child and parent. There is potential for this program to produce additional effects for public health problems beyond obesity, such as prevention of disordered eating. The health burden of obesity, diabetes, and other chronic lifestyle-related diseases could be significantly reduced.

PARAMETERS FOR SERVICE DELIVERY, POLICY, AND RESEARCH

ENGAGEMENT OF MULTIPLE SETTINGS

Community dissemination of evidence-based parenting programs for obesity should be augmented by engagement in multiple settings. Schools, early childhood centers, medical and health centers, sport/recreation clubs, and religious organizations are all potential targets for intervention, promotion, and implementation.

The general practitioner is generally considered the coordinator of primary care for families; however, most report that they are quite uncomfortable about discussing child weight issues with a parent (Wethington, Sherry, & Polhamus, 2011) and are not confident with subsequent management of childhood obesity (Gerards et al., 2012). General practice may be an environment for case ascertainment and to encourage parents to participate in interventions. A recent report in the American Academy of Pediatrics (2016) suggested that pediatricians and other pediatric health practitioners in a family-centered health context have the propensity to assess risk, link families to resources, and coordinate care with community partners. The role of the medical practitioner as a referral agent for the obese child can be greatly augmented by their support for a universal health education program for all families.

It would seem that the best strategy for implementation of a universal program would be to target schools and child care centers, rather than general medical practice alone. Nguyen and colleagues (2012) recommended schools as one of the most successful recruitment tools for obesity programs. A short program such as the seminar series could easily be offered to all parents and potentially be delivered to substantial numbers within an educational setting.

A TRAINED LOCAL WORKFORCE

One potential obstacle to the delivery of an evidence-based parenting program for childhood obesity can be a lack of an adequately trained workforce. Lifestyle Triple P, for example, does not require highly specialized training and accreditation. Professionals from multiple disciplines are able to receive training to deliver the intervention with fidelity. Increasing the capacity of the public health workforce to manage the obesity epidemic is key to population-level change.

A MONITORING AND FEEDBACK SYSTEM

Few countries have established systems for regular monitoring of child height and weight. In Australia, there have only been two national surveys in the last decade, and they have not provided detailed data in relation to ethnicity, socioeconomic status, or parenting behavior. More regular monitoring of prevalence and trend data is required. Indicators should include not only body measurements but also individual risk factors, such as parenting practices and child lifestyle behaviors. A brief, reliable measure that is sensitive to population-level changes can be performed as part of national health surveys and could offer a means of assessing parental feed-back regarding challenges faced with raising their children, the type of support needed, and the motivating factors for program participation.

A COST-EFFECTIVE OBESITY INITIATIVE

Cost-effectiveness of interventions in obesity initiatives is a central consideration for poli-cymakers and service providers. This is particularly relevant in relation to population-level interventions. The assessment of cost-effectiveness is difficult to perform given the mul-tifactorial nature of the societal cost of childhood obesity. Most of the costs manifest in adult life, such as disease comorbidities and work productivity, which makes it difficult to estimate the impact of childhood interventions. Few evaluation trials have conducted cost assessments, other than to investigate the costs of delivering the intervention (Lobstein et al., 2015). Conducting in-depth cost analysis research on obesity interventions may strengthen the argument for policymakers.

FATHER INVOLVEMENT IN OBESITY PROGRAMS

There is emerging evidence for a relationship between the father's parenting practices and child feeding styles with the child's eating behavior and weight status (Fraser et al., 2011). The extent to which fathers show warmth and support also predicts better weight outcomes and mainte-nance of weight loss over time (Stein, Epstein, Raynor, Kilanowski, & Paluch, 2005). Father-only interventions targeting lifestyle habits demonstrate significant decreases in father BMI and improvements in child lifestyle behavior (e.g., Morgan et al., 2011). However, father data remain underrepresented in the obesity literature. Future research should aim to identify the differences between mother and father attendance motivators to allow formulation of appropriate recruit-ment and engagement strategies. Future studies should also assess father outcome data to evalu-ate intervention effectiveness and tailor interventions (if required).

REACHING AT-RISK GROUPS

Given that obesity is associated with lower socioeconomic status and some ethnic minori-ties (Vereecken, Keukelier, & Maes, 2004), it is important from a public health perspective to engage these at-risk groups. Parent-centered interventions for childhood obesity should assess their effectiveness in relation to socioeconomic status and ethnicity. Disadvantaged families may require additional interventions beyond lifestyle-specific support (e.g., strengthening mother–child attachment or psychosocial support to vulnerable caregivers), and from a policy perspective, lifestyle programs, such as Lifestyle Triple P, may be delivered as part of a package alongside these other inputs. Cross-cultural delivery of programs may be challenging given the diversity in food items and nutritional guidelines in different countries. This may require tailoring the program through close consultation with the local workforce followed by inde-pendent evaluation.

CONCLUSIONS

Health authorities worldwide are calling for effective interventions to address childhood obesity. Parent-centered interventions have proven effective. The Lifestyle Triple P multilevel system applies a population health framework to childhood obesity prevention and management. The efficacy of Group Lifestyle Triple P (Level 5) and the Lifestyle Triple P Seminar Series (Level 2) has been validated in the literature. Future research should be conducted to establish the population-level effects of the entire Lifestyle Triple P system delivered at a community level. It is anticipated that the obesity epidemic will worsen into the future without appropriate preventive and treatment measures, and a population approach is likely to be a major part of the ultimate solution.

KEY MESSAGES

- Evidence-based parenting programs are a recommended pathway to prevent and treat childhood obesity.
- Despite their proven success, significant problems exist with parental recruitment and retention.
- A population health approach to parenting support for childhood obesity must be adopted to support parents and families.
- The Lifestyle Triple P multilevel system incorporates a suite of interventions, including (a) a media and communications campaign; (b) a light-touch, brief seminar series for all parents; and (c) an intensive intervention for parents of children who are overweight or obese.
- Taken together, these interventions provide a framework for policymakers and government representatives in the prevention and treatment of childhood obesity.

REFERENCES

American Academy of Pediatrics Council on Community Pediatrics. (2016). Poverty and child health in the United States. *Pediatrics, 137,* 1–14. doi:10.1542/peds.2016-0339

Arredondo, E. M., Elder, J. P., Ayala, G. X., Campbell, N., Baquero, B., & Duerksen, S. (2006). Is parenting style related to children's healthy eating and physical activity in Latino families? *Health Education Research, 21,* 862–871. doi:10.1093/her/cyl110

Bartlett, J. A., Desha, L. N., Poulsen, A. A., Macdonald, D., Abbott, R., . . . & Leong, G. M. (2017). *Kinder Overweight Activity Lifestyle Actions (KOALA) Healthy Lifestyle Program for children with obesity: A randomised controlled trial.* Manuscript in preparation.

Bartlett, J. A., Sanders, M. R., & Leong, G. M. (2017). *A randomised controlled trial of a parenting program for the prevention of childhood obesity: The Lifestyle Triple P Seminar Series.* Manuscript in preparation.

Bauman, A. E. (2004). Updating the evidence that physical activity is good for health: An epidemiological review 2000–2003. *Journal of Science and Medicine in Sport, 7,* 6–19. doi:10.1016/S1440-2440(04)80273-1

Benton, D. (2004). Role of parents in the determination of the food preferences of children and the development of obesity. *International Journal of Obesity, 28*, 858–869. doi:10.1038/sj.ijo.0802532

Carnell, S., Edwards, C., Croker, H., Boniface, D., & Wardle, J. (2005). Parental perceptions of overweight in 3–5 year olds. *International Journal of Obesity, 29*, 353–355. doi:10.1038/sj.ijo.0802889

Child and Adolescent Community Health Service. (2011a). *Lifestyle Triple P: Full report of the 2009 Western Australian community health pilot.* Unpublished report. Perth, Australia: Department of Health Western Australia.

Child and Adolescent Community Health Service. (2011b). *Lifestyle Triple P: Key findings of the 2010 Western Australia community health pilot.* Unpublished report. Perth, Australia: Department of Health Western Australia.

Clark, H. R., Goyder, E., Bissell, P., Blank, L., & Peters, J. (2007). How do parents' child feeding behaviors influence child weight? Implications for childhood obesity policy. *Journal of Public Health, 29*, 132–141. doi:10.1093/pubmed/fdm012

Crowle, J. & Turner, E. (2010). *Childhood obesity: An economic perspective.* Melbourne, Australia: Productivity Commission Staff Working Paper. Retrieved from http://www.pc.gov.au/research/supporting/childhood-obesity/childhood-obesity.pdf

Cruz, M. L., Shaibi, G. Q., Weigensberg, M. J., Spruijt-Metz, D., Ball, G. D. C., & Goran, M. I. (2005). Pediatric obesity and insulin resistance: Chronic disease risk and implications for treatment and prevention beyond body weight modification. *Annual Review of Nutrition, 25*, 435–469. doi:10.1146/annurev.nutr.25.050304.092625

Cullen, K. W., Baranowski, T., Owens, E., Marsh, T., Rittenberry, L., & de Moor, C. (2003). Availability, accessibility, and preferences for fruit, 100% fruit juice, and vegetables influence children's dietary behavior. *Health Education & Behaviour, 30*, 615–626. doi:10.1177/1090198103257254

Davison, K. K., & Birch, L. L. (2001). Weight status, parent reaction, and self-concept in five-year-old girls. *Pediatrics, 107*, 146–153. doi:10.1542/peds.107.1.46

De Bourdeaudhuij, I., Yngve, A., te Velde, S. J., Klepp, K. I., Rasmussen, M., Thorsdottir, I., . . . Brug, J. (2006). Personal, social and environmental correlates of vegetable intake in normal weight and overweight 9 to 13-year old boys. *International Journal of Behavioral Nutrition and Physical Activity, 3*, 37–46. doi:10.1186/1479-5868-3-37

Faith, M. S., Scanlon, K. S., Birch, L. L., Francis, L. A., & Sherry, B. (2004). Parent-child feeding strategies and their relationship to child eating and weight status. *Obesity Research, 12*, 1711–1722. doi:10.1038/oby.2004.212

Fraser, J., Skouteris, H., McCabe, M., Ricciardelli, L. A., Milgrom, J., & Baur, L. A. (2011). Paternal influences on children's weight gain: A systematic review. *Fathering, 9*, 252–267. doi:10.3149/fth.0903.252

Gardner, D. S. L., Hosking, J., Metcalf, B. S., Jeffery, A. N., Voss, L. D., & Wilkin, T. J. (2009). Contribution of early weight gain to childhood overweight and metabolic health: A longitudinal study (EarlyBird 36). *Pediatrics, 123*, e67–e73. doi:10.1542/peds.2008-1292

Garnett, S. P., Baur, L. A., Jones, A. M., & Hardy, L. L. (2016). Trends in the prevalence of morbid and severe obesity in Australian children aged 7-15 years, 1985–2012. *PlosOne, 11*, 1–7. doi:10.1371/journal.pone.0154879

Gentile, D. A., & Walsh, D. S. (2002). A normative study of family media habits. *Applied Developmental Psychology, 23*, 157–178. doi:10.1016/S0193-3973(02)00102-8

Gerards, S. M. P. L., Dagnelie, P. C., Gubbels, J. S., Van Buuren, S., Hamers, F. J. M., Jansen, M. W. J., . . . Kremers, S. P. J. (2015). The effectiveness of Lifestyle Triple P in the Netherlands: A randomized controlled trial. *PloS One, 10*, 1–18. doi:10.137/journal.pone.0122240

Gerards, S. M. P. L., Dagnelie, P. C., Jansen, M. W. J., De Vries, N. K., & Kremers, S. P. J. (2012). Barriers to successful recruitment of parents of overweight children for an obesity prevention intervention: A qualitative study among health care professionals. *BMC Family Practice, 13*, 37. doi:10.1186/1471-2296-13-37

Gerards, S. M., Sleddens, E. F. C., Dagnelie, P. C., De Vries, N. K., & Kremers, S. P. J. (2011). Interventions addressing general parenting to prevent or treat childhood obesity. *International Journal of Pediatric Obesity, 6*, e28–e45. doi:10.3109/17477166.2011.575147

Golan, M. (2006). Parents as agents of change in childhood obesity—From research to practice. *International Journal of Pediatric Obesity, 1*, 66–76. doi: 10.1080/17477160600644272

Golan, M., & Crow, S. (2004). Targeting parents exclusively in the treatment of childhood obesity: Long-term results. *Obesity Research, 12*, 357–361. doi:10.1038/oby.2004.45

Griffiths, L. J., Wolke, D., Page, A. S., Horwood, J. P., & ALSPAC Study Team. (2006). Obesity and bullying: Different effects for boys and girls. *Archives of Disease in Childhood, 91*, 121–125. doi:10.1136/adc.2005.072314

Guh, D. P., Zhang, W., Bansback, N., Amarsi, Z., Birmingham, C. L., & Anis, A. H. (2009). The incidence of co-morbidities related to obesity and overweight: A systematic review and meta-analysis. *BMC Public Health, 9*, 88. doi:10.1186/1471-2458-9-88

Gustafson, S. L., & Rhodes, R. E. (2006). Parental correlates of physical activity in children and early adolescents. *Sports Medicine, 36*, 79–97. doi: 10.2165/00007256-200636010-00006

Halliday, J. A., Palma, C. L., Mellor, D., Green, J., & Renzaho, A. M. N. (2014). The relationship between family functioning and child and adolescent overweight and obesity: a systematic review. *International Journal of Obesity, 38*, 480–493. doi:10.1038/ijo.2013.213

Hardy, L. L., King, L., Espinel, P., Cosgrove, C., & Bauman, A. (2011). *NSW Schools Physical Activity and Nutrition Survey (SPANS) 2010: Full report*. Canberra, Australia: Ministry of Health.

Haynos, A. F., & O'Donohue, W. T. (2012). Universal childhood and adolescent obesity prevention programs: Review and critical analysis. *Clinical Psychology Review, 32*, 383–399. doi:10.1016/j.cpr.2011.09.006

James, P. T. (2004). Obesity: The worldwide epidemic. *Clinics in Dermatology, 22*, 276–280. doi: 10.1016/j.clindermatol.2004.01.010

Jones, A. R., Parkinson, K. N., Drewett, R. F., Hyland, R. M., Pearce, M. S., & Adamson, A. J. (2011). Parental perceptions of weight status in children: The Gateshead Millennium Study. *International Journal of Obesity, 35*, 953–962. doi:10.1038/ijo.2011.106

Kelishadi, R. (2007). Childhood overweight, obesity, and the metabolic syndrome in developing countries. *Epidemiology Reviews, 29*, 62–76. doi:10.1093/epirev/mxm003

Kelly, A. S., Barlow, S. E., Rao, G., Inge, T. H., Hayman, L. L., . . . Daniels, S. R. (2013). Severe obesity in children and adolescents: Identification, associated health risks, and treatment approaches: A scientific statement from the American Heart Association. *Circulation, 128*, 1689–1712. doi: 10.1161/CIR.0b013e3182a5cfb3

Kim, D. D. & Basu, A. (2016). Estimating the medical care costs of obesity in the United States: Systematic review, meta-analysis, and empirical analysis. *Value Health, 19*, 602–613. doi:10.1016/j.jval.2016.02.008

Kuczmarski, R. J., Ogden, C. L., Grummer-Strawn, L. M., Flegal, K. M., Guo, S. S., . . . Johnson, C. L. (2000). *CDC growth charts: United States*. Hyattsville, MD: National Center for Health Statistics.

Lindsay, A. C., Sussner, K. M., Kim, J., & Gortmaker, S. L. (2006). The role of parents in preventing childhood obesity. *The Future of Children, 16*, 169–186.

Lobstein, T., Jackson-Leach, R., Moodie, M. L., Hall, K. D., Gortmaker, S. L., . . . McPherson, K. (2015). Child and adolescent obesity: Part of a bigger picture. *Lancet, 385*, 2510–2520. doi:10.1016/S0140-6736(14)61746-3

Loveman, E., Al-Khudairy, L., Johnson, R. E., Robertson, W., Colquitt, J. L., . . . Rees, K. (2015). Parent-only interventions for childhood overweight and obesity in children aged 5 to 11 years. *Cochrane Database of Systematic Reviews*, (12), 1–205. doi:10.1002/14651858.CD012008

Mamun, A. A., Lawlor, D. A., O'Callaghan, M. J., Williams, G. M., & Najman, J. M. (2005). Family and early life factors associated with changes in overweight status between ages 5 and 14 years: Findings from the Mater University study of pregnancy and its outcomes. *International Journal of Obesity, 29*, 475–482. doi:10.1038/sj.ijo.0802922

Moore, L. L., Lombardi, D. A., White, M. J., Campbell, J. L., Oliveria, S. A., & Ellison, R. C. (1991). Influence of parents' physical activity levels on activity levels of young children. *Journal of Pediatrics, 118*, 215–219. doi:10.1016/S0022-3476(05)80485-8

Morgan, P. J., Lubans, D. R., Callister, R. C., Okely, A. D., Burrows, T. L., Fletcher, R., & Collins, C. E. (2011). The "Healthy Dads, Healthy Kids" randomized controlled trial: Efficacy of a healthy lifestyle program for overweight fathers and their children. *International Journal of Obesity, 35*, 436–447. doi:10.1038/ijo.2010.151

Napolitano, C., Walsh, S., Mahoney, L., & McCrea, J. (2000). Risk factors that may adversely modify the natural history of the pediatric pronated foot. *Clinics in Pediatric Medicine and Surgery, 17*, 397–417.

Narang, I. & Mathew, J. L. (2012). Childhood obesity and obstructive sleep apnea. *Journal of Nutrition & Metabolism, 2012*, 1–8. doi:10.1155/2012/134202

Ng, M., Fleming, T., Robinson, M., Thomson, B., Graetz, N., . . . Gakidou, E. (2014). Global, regional, and national prevalence of overweight and obesity in children and adults during 1980–2013: A systematic analysis for the Global Burden of Disease Study 2013. *Lancet, 384*, 766–781. doi:10.1016/S0140-6736(14)60460-8

Nguyen, B., McGregor, K. A., O'Connor, J., Shrewsbury, V. A., Lee, A., Steinbeck, K. S., . . . Baur, L. A. (2012). Recruitment challenges and recommendations for adolescent obesity trials. *Journal of Pediatrics and Child Health, 48*, 38–43. doi:10.1111/j.1440-1754.2011.02183.x

Olds, T., Maher, C., Shumin, S., Peneau, S., Lioret, S., Castetbon, K., . . . Summerbell, C. (2011). Evidence that the prevalence of childhood overweight is plateauing: data from nine countries. *International Journal of Pediatric Obesity, 6*, 342–360. doi:10.3109/17477166.2011.605895

Park, M. H., Falconer, C., Viner, R. M., & Kinra, S. (2012). The impact of childhood obesity on morbidity and mortality in adulthood: A systematic review. *Obesity Reviews, 13*, 985–1000. doi:10.1111/j.1467-789X.2012.01015.x

Prospective Studies Collaboration. (2007). Blood cholesterol and vascular mortality by age, sex, and blood pressure: a meta-analysis of individual data from 61 prospective studies with 55,000 vascular deaths. *Lancet, 370*, 1829–1839. doi:10.1016/S0140-6736(07)61778-4

Puhl, R. M., & Heuer, C. A. (2010). Obesity stigma: Important considerations for public health. *American Journal of Public Health, 100*, 1019–1128. doi:10.2105/2FAJPH.2009.159491

Rampersaud, G. C., Pereira, M. A., Girard, B. L., Adams, J., & Metzi, J. D. (2005). Breakfast habits, nutritional status, body weight, and academic performance in children and adolescents. *Journal of the American Dietetic Association, 105*, 743–760. doi:10.1016/j.jada.2005.02.007

Rasmussen, M., Krolner, R., Klepp, K-I., Lytle, L., Brug, J., Bere, E., & Due, P. (2006). Determinants of fruit and vegetable consumption among children and adolescents: A review of the literature. Part I: Quantitative studies. *International Journal of Behavioural Nutrition and Physical Activity, 3*, 22–41. doi:10.1186/1479-5868-3-22

Reinehr, T. (2013). Lifestyle intervention in childhood obesity: Changes and challenges. *Nature Reviews Endocrinology, 9*, 607–614. doi:10.1038/nrendo.20213.149

Sallis, J. F., Alcaraz, J. E., McKenzie, T. L., & Hovell, M. F. (1999). Predictors of change in children's physical activity over 20 months: Variations by gender and level of adiposity. *American Journal of Preventive Medicine, 16*, 222–229. doi:10.1016/S0749-3797(98)00154-8

Sallis, J. F., Alcaraz, J. E., McKenzie, T. L., Hovell, M. F., Kolody, B., & Nader, P. R. (1992). Parental behavior in relation to physical activity and fitness in 9-year-old children. *American Journal of Diseases of Children, 146*, 1383–1388. doi:10.1001/archpedi.1992.02160230141035

Sanders, M. R., Kirby, J. N., Tellegen, C. L., & Day, J. J. (2014). The Triple P—Positive Parenting Program: A systematic review and meta-analysis of a multi-level system of parenting support. *Clinical Psychology Review, 34*, 337–357. doi:10.1016/j.cpr.2014.04.003

Sleddens, E. F. C., Gerards, S. M. P. L., Thijs, C., De Vries, N. K., & Kremers, S. P. J. (2011). General parenting, childhood overweight and obesity-inducing behaviours, a review. *International Journal of Pediatric Obesity, 6*, e12–e227. doi:10.3109/17477166.2011.566339

Stein, R., Epstein, L., Raynor, H., Kilanowski, C., & Paluch, R. (2005). The influence of parenting change on pediatric weight control. *Obesity, 13*, 1749–1755. doi:10.1038/oby.2005.213

van der Horst, K., Oenema, A., Ferreira, I., Wendel-Vos, Q., Giskes, K., van Lenthe, F., & Brug, J. (2007). A systematic review of environmental correlates of obesity-related dietary behaviors in youth. *Health Education Research, 22*, 203–226. doi:10.1093/her/cyl069

Vereecken, C. A., Keukelier, E., & Maes, L. (2004). Influence of mother's educational level on food parenting practices and food habits of young children. *Appetite, 43*, 93–103. doi:10.1016/j.appet.2004.04.002

Waters, E., de Silva-Sanigorski, A., Burford, B. J., Brown, T., Campbell, K. J., Gao, Y., . . . Summerbell, C. D. (2011). Interventions for preventing obesity in children. *Cochrane Database of Systematic Reviews*, (12), 1–224. doi:10.1002/14651858.CD001871.pub3

West, F., Sanders, M. R., Cleghorn, G. J., & Davies, P. S. W. (2010). Randomised clinical trial of a family-based lifestyle intervention for childhood obesity involving parents as the exclusive agents of change. *Behaviour Research and Therapy, 48*, 1170–1179. doi:10.1016/j.brat.2010.08.008

Wethington, H. R., Sherry, B., & Polhamus, B. (2011). Physician practices related to use of BMI-for-age and counseling for childhood obesity prevention: A cross-sectional study. *BMC Family Practice, 12*, 80. doi:10.1186/1471-2296-12-80

World Health Organization. (2006). *WHO child growth standards: Length/height-for-age, weight-for-age, weight-for-length, weight-for-height, and body mass index-for-age: Methods and development.* Geneva, Switzerland: World Health Organisation. Retrieved from http://www.who.int/childgrowth/standards/Technical_report.pdf

World Health Organization. (2012). *Population-based approaches to childhood obesity prevention.* Geneva, Switzerland: World Health Organisation. Retrieved from http://www.who.int/dietphysicalactivity/childhood/WHO_new_childhoodobesity_PREVENTION_27nov_HR_PRINT_OK.pdf

CHAPTER 13

ADOLESCENTS AND YOUNG ADULTS WITH PSYCHOSOCIAL DIFFICULTIES

ALAN RALPH

S ignificant numbers of teenagers globally are reported to have significant health and mental health problems (World Health Organization [WHO], 2014). Behaviors that begin in adolescence can affect health then and into the future. Some of these behaviors, such as suicide attempts, injuries, and unprotected sexual behavior, are associated with major causes of mortality and morbidity among adolescents. Other behaviors begun in adolescence are associated with tobacco or alcohol use and becoming overweight or obese. Many of the health-related behaviors that emerge during adolescence appear to be linked. Adolescents who use tobacco are more likely to drink alcohol as well, to be involved in bullying or fighting, and to be injured. This is particularly likely when the onset of tobacco use or drinking or sexual behavior occurs in early adolescence (WHO, 2014).

THE ROLE OF PARENTS AND FAMILY FACTORS

Parenting factors have been shown to be related to adolescent health and mental health problems as well as other social determinants (Robinson, Power, & Allan, 2010). The authors identified research highlighting the link between family environment and adolescent depression and other negative psychosocial markers. They also pointed to research showing that close relationships with parents can be a protective factor against such outcomes (e.g., Luthar, 2006).

THE ROLE OF PARENTING INTERVENTIONS FOR THESE ISSUES

Parenting interventions have been shown to be effective at improving parenting behaviors that are linked to a decrease in child and adolescent problem behaviors (e.g., Biglan, Brennan, Foster, & Holder, 2004; Fossum, Handegard, Adolfsen, Vis, & Wynn, 2016). They have also been shown to have a protective effect (De Vore & Ginsburg, 2005). Recent research on the Triple P—Positive Parenting Program in particular has also reported positive effects on young adolescents (Lindsay, Strand, & Davis, 2011). However, making such programs accessible to parents has proven to be challenging (Chu, Farrugia, Sanders, & Ralph, 2012).

HOW TRIPLE P HAS BEEN APPLIED TO THE PROBLEM

Teen Triple P was developed as an upward extension of the Triple P—Positive Parenting Program for parents of young children aged from birth to 12 years. It was developed as an early intervention/prevention program aimed at children making the transition from elementary/primary school into high/secondary school. It recognized four particular aspects of child and adolescent development that were observed to occur around this transition period: an increased exposure to different people, ideas, and beliefs; increased demands for access to adult opportunities and activities; hormonal changes during puberty; and significant neural pruning and rewiring continuing into their early 20s.

The Teen Triple P suite of programs provides support for parents with children nominally aged from 12 to 16 years, although there will be some children in the 10- to 11-year age range for whom the teen version may also be suitable. All five levels of the Triple P system contain elements suitable for parents of teenagers, although the dedicated teen programs are primarily organized in Levels 2, 3, and 4.

Teen Triple P differs from the program for parents of younger children in several ways. Generally speaking, there is an increased emphasis on parents changing how they interact with teenagers in ways that acknowledge their impending transition into adulthood. This is characterized by a trend toward more negotiation, compromise, and shared decision-making. While parents are still expected to take a major role in setting limits and consequences, it is recommended that teenagers should actively participate in discussions around these topics. Also, the focus on preparing parents for specific events that they find stressful shifts to an emphasis on preparing teenagers for events or activities that pose a potential risk to their health or well-being. More specifically, the 17 strategies that form the foundation for Triple P are adapted and in some cases replaced by more age-appropriate ones. As with the program for parents of younger children, a dedicated audiovisual presentation, *Every Parent's Guide to Teenagers* (Sanders & Ralph, 2011) has been developed that provides an introduction to the key principles, parent traps, and strategies that form the basis of Teen Triple P. This resource is provided to practitioners to assist them in delivering the Teen Triple P program variants to parents.

The four main areas of development identified for younger children are just as relevant for teenagers: social and language skills, emotional self-regulation skills, independence skills, and problem-solving skills. Parents are encouraged to reflect on specific skill subsets in determining the goals they wish to work toward. This assists in the selection of relevant strategies.

The three strategies that are designed to promote a positive relationship between parents and children are retained, but with a different emphasis. Thus, spending time, talking with, and showing affection to children are equally important with teenagers, but the topics, timing, and methods will change to reflect a more adult-like relationship. The three strategies designed to encourage positive behavior are also retained. Praise and attention also need to take on more adult-like characteristics, and having interesting activities becomes more focused on encouraging teenagers to explore and try out different activities, preferably under appropriate supervision. Changes start to appear in relation to the strategies designed to teach new skills and behaviors. While setting a good example is still critically important, strategies such as incidental teaching and ask-say-do morph into coaching problem-solving that teaches an important life skill that teenagers need to acquire. Behavior charts are simply upgraded to behavior contracts that require more negotiation and problem-solving, although the underlying principles are fundamentally similar.

In the realm of managing problem behavior, the use of rule-setting and directed discussion remains central to ensuring teenagers are aware of parents' expectations and the consequences of meeting or not meeting them. Again, parents are encouraged to involve their teenagers in agreeing on family rules and appropriate consequences. Planned ignoring has been omitted as the focus on using attention as a means of decreasing inappropriate attention seeking seemed less relevant for teenagers. However, there will inevitably be times when parents might do well to ignore certain behavior to concentrate and remain focused on the issue they wish to discuss. Giving clear calm instructions becomes making clear, calm requests to acknowledge the changing nature of the parent–teenager relationship, but there is still an emphasis on making it clear that cooperation is expected, even though some negotiation may be permitted around timing in some circumstances. Logical consequences still play an important part in teaching teenagers that failure to comply with reasonable adult requests will result in the loss of privileges or desired activities for a brief period. As in the program for parents of younger children, the emphasis here is on providing parents with an alternative to harsh, punitive responses, with a focus on teaching appropriate behavior rather than simply punishing misbehavior.

The strategies of quiet time and time-out have been modified under the heading acknowledging teenagers' emotions. However, the underlying principles remain. The strategy recognizes that there will be occasions when teenagers will become upset when things do not turn out the way they might wish. The aim is to provide teenagers with an opportunity to acquire self-control so that they can better manage their emotions. This can be achieved most easily when parents do not provide additional, unnecessary verbal stimulation and model calmness themselves. Teaching parents to focus primarily on acknowledging and validating the emotion the teenager may be experiencing avoids the difficult task of engaging the cortex of the teenager brain in rational debate while the evolutionarily older part of the brain that responds to threat perception is still in control.

LEVEL 2 SELECTED SEMINAR TEEN TRIPLE P

The Level 2 Selected Seminar Teen Triple P program comprises three seminars that each address the primary environmental domains of home, school, and the wider community. Each is designed to be delivered over a 90-minute period, with the first hour dedicated to providing relevant goals, examples, and strategies, with the remaining 30 minutes available to respond to questions from the audience. A PowerPoint presentation with annotations is provided to the practitioner, and tip sheets summarizing the material covered are provided to those attending. A study by Chand, Farruggia, Dittman, Chu, and Sanders (2013) included reports by teenagers whose parents attended, with the results showing favorable outcomes, including the promotion of important aspects of positive youth development. Seminars have been shown to act as a useful light-touch intervention for some parents, whereas others with more serious difficulties can use them as an entry point, subsequently seeing a practitioner for a somewhat more intensive individual or group program.

LEVEL 3 PRIMARY CARE TEEN TRIPLE P

Designed as a four-session program usually conducted face to face with a practitioner, the structure and format of Level 3 Primary Care Teen Triple P is identical to Level 3 Primary Care Triple P. However, the content varies to address adolescent issues. There are currently 12 tip sheets that address the following issues: truancy, anxiety, depression, friends and peer relationships, smoking, sex and dating, drinking alcohol, taking drugs, rudeness and disrespect, fads and fashion, eating habits, and money and work. An additional seminar and accompanying tip sheet on being cybersmart has yet to be disseminated. All tip sheets have a similar structure: (a) an explanation about possible causes and the identification of parent traps that may contribute to the problem behavior; (b) the introduction of strategies to prevent the problem from occurring; and (c) additional strategies to manage and reduce the problem behavior if it is already established. Implementation of the primary care model was shown to be associated with significant improvement in practitioners' consultation skills, greater satisfaction with their consultations, and high levels of participant satisfaction with the training provided (Sanders, Murphy-Brennan, & McAuliffe, 2003).

LEVEL 3 DISCUSSION GROUP TEEN TRIPLE P

Discussion groups are designed as single-session events, each 2 hours long; a small group of parents with a common concern can develop a parenting plan with the aid of a practitioner. Again, the format and structure are similar to those for parents of younger children. There are currently four discussion group topics available for parents of teenagers: reducing family conflict, coping with teenagers' emotions, getting teenagers to cooperate, and building teenagers' survival skills. Parents are each provided with a booklet that they complete as they construct their plan. These booklets evolved along similar lines to the tip sheets referred to in Level 3 Primary Care and follow a similar structure.

Some preliminary evaluations of these discussion groups reported promising findings (Jacobs, 2011; Ng, 2011; O'Connor, 2012; Sweeney, 2011). More recent research was conducted by Dittman, Burke, and Barton (2016) of the family conflict and coping with emotions discussion groups. Parents who participated in the discussion group aimed at reducing family conflict reported significant reductions in oppositional behavior and improvements in interpersonal relations. Parents who participated in the discussion group aimed at coping with teenagers' emotions reported reductions in emotional difficulties and improved connectedness. Although these conclusions are limited by the relatively small number of participants, they nonetheless signal the potential of this level of intervention to assist parents who have specific concerns in common.

LEVEL 4 GROUP TEEN TRIPLE P

As with Level 4 Group Triple P, Level 4 Group Teen Triple P is designed to be optimally conducted with groups of parents over eight successive weeks, with sessions one to four and eight delivered face to face and sessions five to seven conducted individually, often by telephone or some other similar medium (e.g., Skype). The audiovisual presentation *Every Parent's Guide to Teenagers* (Sanders & Ralph, 2011) is used to guide parents through the various discussions and exercises, together with dedicated PowerPoint presentations for each session and a parent workbook for the parents to record their progress. Several trials of Group Teen Triple P have reported positive outcomes across a range of salient variables (Arcan & Guvenir, 2016; Chu, Bullen, Farruggia, Dittman, & Sanders, 2015; Kliem, Aurin, & Kröger, 2014; Ralph & Sanders, 2003, 2004, 2006; Ralph, Stallman, & Sanders, 2016; Sutherland, 2015). A case example is provided in Box 13.1.

LEVEL 4 STANDARD TEEN TRIPLE P

The Level 4 Standard Teen Triple P program guides parents through the same material as that covered in the group program but is delivered individually, typically over 10 weekly sessions. Wherever possible, the teenager is encouraged to attend some of the sessions to provide the practitioner with opportunities to undertake direct observations of the parents as they attempt to implement the strategies and bring about change in the family relationships and interactions. This differs from family therapy as the focus of the program is primarily on changing the parents' behaviors on the premise that this will bring about concomitant change in the teenager's behavior. Salari, Ralph, and Sanders (2014) reported decreased levels of teen disruptive behaviors and parent–adolescent conflict, as well as a reduction in the use of ineffective parenting strategies and conflict over childrearing issues. These positive changes were maintained at the 3-month follow-up.

LEVEL 4 SELF-DIRECTED TEEN TRIPLE P

It is recognized that parents prefer to have options when deciding how to access support. Not every parent wishes or is able to meet with a practitioner over several sessions. A self-directed workbook was therefore developed, based on the workbook used in the Standard Teen program, for Level 4 Self-Directed Teen Triple T. A study by Stallman and Ralph (2007) compared parents

---

**BOX 13.1: Case Example of a Teenager
With Behavioral Difficulties**

Lily, aged 15 years, was refusing to attend school, showed behavioral difficulties and aggression at home, and engaged in significant risk-taking behavior, including staying out late, drinking, smoking, engaging in unsafe sexual behaviors, and antisocial behaviors with peers. She had changed school five times and found it difficult to adjust to high school, where she made few friends and was bullied by other girls. Lily's mother was 16 years old when Lily was born and was involved in a domestically violent relationship with Lily's father. Lily had been witness to most of the violence within the relationship, including sexual violence toward her mother. Lily's mother acknowledged that she was aggressive toward Lily, with Lily then reacting aggressively herself and often "smashing up" the house. Her mother had previously been on antidepressants for 6 years but had recently stopped taking them. She described feelings of depression at the time of initial assessment, which revealed that Lily was in the clinical range on almost all the subscales of a measure of child adjustment (including emotionality, conduct problems, and hyperactivity), and that Lily and her mother were both in the clinical range on a measure of conflict. Lily's mother scored in the clinical range in relation to her parenting style, alternately being both lax and overreactive. In addition, she scored in the borderline/clinical range on measures of stress, anxiety, and depression.

Lily's mother was initially referred for Group Teen Triple P but did not engage well. She then completed Standard Teen Triple P, with follow-up assessments revealing that Lily and her mother subsequently scored within the normal range on all preassessment measures. Lily had taken up full-time education, by her own choice, and her mother commenced retraining, working toward gaining entry-level English and mathematics with a view to attending a college course. The quality of the relationship between Lily and her mother was greatly improved; they reported spending regular time together doing mutually enjoyable activities. Lily was no longer staying out and was not engaging in risky or antisocial activities. She also gained casual employment, doing an early morning paper round with a friend. There was now little conflict in the house, and Lily and her mother reported being able to deal with problems in a calm and nonaggressive way.

---

who received the workbook and the *Every Parent's Guide to Teenagers* DVD with those who were randomly assigned to receive additional telephone support. A wait-list control group provided a third arm of the study. Results indicated that parents in the telephone support condition reported significantly fewer adolescent behavioral problems and less use of overreactive parenting strategies than parents in either the standard or the wait-list conditions. Improvements were maintained at 3-month follow-up.

Doherty, Calam, and Sanders (2013) conducted an RCT using the Self-Directed Teen Triple P workbook and a specially designed chronic illness tip sheet with parents of adolescents with type 1 diabetes. Results showed significantly improved diabetes-related conflict, suggesting that this type of intervention could be tailored for other diverse adolescent health problems.

TEEN TRIPLE P ONLINE

Following the success of the eight-module Triple P Online program, an adapted version for parents of teenagers has just been released. Modeled on the Level 4 Self-Directed Teen Triple P format, the Teen Triple P Online program was reduced to six modules based on data from Triple P Online users indicating only a small proportion of parents completed all eight modules. Research trials are planned to seek evidence to support the effectiveness of this new online version.

OTHER TEEN TRIPLE P VARIANTS

Connections Teen Triple P was developed for carers working in residential hostels where teenagers are placed for various reasons. The aim of the program is to provide the care team with an evidence-based, consistent approach to interacting with the teenagers under their care. The challenge of providing a predictable, safe, and supportive environment for teenagers in these settings can be significant, particularly if some carers are inexperienced and poorly trained. Creating a coherent, consistent, and caring environment was seen as a primary goal.

The program has been trialed in the Netherlands, with promising outcomes (De Graaf, Jonge, & Okma, 2016). The program was implemented over a 10-month period in four residential care groups within de Rading, a Dutch institute for youth care. In the evaluation study, 18 staff members and 15 teenagers participated in the pretest–posttest design. Despite the low number of participants in the study, some significant results were reported by the staff members and teenagers. Staff members reported a decrease of conflict behavior and improvements of social support, climate, discipline style, self-efficacy, and competences. Furthermore, the staff members reported a reduction in problem behavior of the teenagers (e.g., conduct problems, peer problems, and total problems).

An adaptation of this program was also trialed in boarding schools in Queensland, Australia, with some success (Hodges, 2013; Hodges, Sheffield, & Ralph, 2016), and another variation has been developed for parents of teenagers who have a disability. The Stepping Stones Triple P program has been successful in assisting parents of young children who have a disability, but until recently there has been no upward extension for parents of teenagers. This omission has typically resulted in parents being offered a combination of Stepping Stones Triple P and Teen Triple P, but without an appropriate framework or evidence base to support this approach. A recent trial of Building Bridges Triple P involving the parents of adolescents with autism spectrum disorder was conducted to attempt to remedy this gap. This trial found promising outcomes in terms of parenting practices and adolescents' emotional and behavioral adjustment (Jenkins, 2016).

The current state of knowledge relating to adolescent brain development, coupled with trends in many countries for teenagers to remain in the family home into their 20s, indicates that parents may benefit from support well beyond their children's age of 16 years currently addressed by Teen Triple P. Tarrant (2012) examined the impact of coresidency on parental adjustment with 113 Australian parents with a child over the age of 18 living at home. Results indicated that parenting style, in particular those parents who were disapproving, had an impact on levels of parental depression, anxiety, and stress. Perceived adulthood status of the adult child living at home and parenting style were also found to significantly predict levels of parent-child conflict. In addition, the relationship between perceived adulthood status of child and parent–child conflict was partially mediated by disapproving parenting, suggesting that if parents and young adults disagreed about adulthood status, parents disapproved as a consequence, leading to increased levels of parent–child conflict.

IMPLICATIONS FOR PRACTICE, POLICY, AND RESEARCH

Although the research base for Teen Triple P is not yet as comprehensive as it is for Triple P overall, it is nevertheless positive and diverse. While there is clear demand from parents for support in parenting teenagers, there are two main challenges that need to be addressed to increase access to trained practitioners. The first is the tendency among workers in the adolescent mental health field to be oriented to working directly with the teenager. This is premised predominantly on adherence to a medical model that assumes the problem is within the individual rather than a function of the environment in which the individual is living. Even when the family environment is deemed to be of importance, there is often a preference for a family therapeutically oriented approach where all family members are required to participate, which limits access to those who can satisfy this criterion. Both of these approaches are limited by the need for highly qualified practitioners, who work individually over lengthy periods of time, and thus have limited reach and are expensive to operate. Creating a recognition that working through the parents can be as or more effective and efficient than these other models is a slow process and not without resistance at many levels.

The second challenge is to identify and train a workforce with the capacity and opportunity to work with parents of teenagers. There is broad diversity in the workforce available to parents of young children, primarily as these parents are in direct contact with them, sometimes on a daily basis. The same cannot be said of parents of teenagers. While there are community settings where parents of teenagers might feel comfortable, they often do not have dedicated staff who would see parenting as part of their duty statement. These might include libraries, community centers, school halls, churches, youth clubs, and sporting venues. Practitioners who are external to these venues are therefore required to offer their services. However, practitioners who might fill this role often have full-time positions elsewhere that constrain their availability for extracurricular activity such as this.

One potential solution requires policy change at a government level to recognize the value and importance of providing support to parents of teenagers as a continuum of prevention from the early years through to early adulthood. As discussed previously, many of the same risk factors or adverse childhood experiences are implicated in school dropout, unemployment, criminality, substance abuse, relationship breakdown, and mental and physical health. Making parenting support available more broadly into early adulthood has the capacity to repay such an investment many times over by reducing or eliminating these factors.

The provision of proven online services that bypass regular practitioner support models also has potential to massively increase parental access to support. However, research suggests that some parents completing an online program do better when they also have access to a support-ive, trained practitioner.

While parents have been the main focus of this chapter, it is also the case that many teen-agers live in settings without their parents. From time to time, these settings are thrust into the media spotlight by some crisis or other, and for a while there is a discussion about how to improve the standards of care. Unfortunately, there is little motivation for agencies run-ning residential care centers to invest in evidence-based staff training. The demand for places from the government agencies responsible for placing children in care usually far exceeds the number of places available, and the costs to government of placing these children are often already high. Any government attempts to improve standards by requiring the adoption of evidence-based programs, which typically require extensive staff training, are likely to be met with care organizations shifting their intake to other less demanding government agen-cies or substantially increasing their charges. However, the population-wide introduction of parenting support can be expected to result in a decreased requirement for children to be taken into care, thus freeing up the system to accommodate improved standards of care in the longer term.

KEY MESSAGES

- Parenting support for parents of teenagers should not be seen as an optional extra but should be part of a seamless population-wide framework to promote the health and men-tal health of children and adolescents on their journey toward adulthood.
- The challenge of identifying a workforce of practitioners who can assist parents of teenag-ers across a broad range of community settings must be taken up with more vigor if effec-tive programs such as Teen Triple P are to provide the kind of support these parents need.
- There is clearly scope for the core of Teen Triple P to be further adapted to help promote the development of adolescents and young adults worldwide. Some examples have been briefly described in this chapter, but there is still much work to be done to strengthen the existing evidence base and to conduct research in new domains.

REFERENCES

Arcan, B., & Guvenir, T. (2016). *The efficacy and acceptability of the Triple P Positive Parenting Program with Turkish parents.* Manuscript submitted for publication.

Biglan, A., Brennan, P. A., Foster, S. L., & Holder, H. D. (2004). *Helping adolescents at risk: Prevention of multiple problem behaviors.* New York, NY: Guilford.

Chand, N. L., Farruggia, S. P., Dittman, C. K., Chu, J. T. W., & Sanders, M. R. (2013). Promoting positive youth development through a brief parenting intervention programme. *Youth Studies Australia, 32,* 29–36.

Chu, J. T. W., Bullen, P., Farruggia, S. P., Dittman, C. K., & Sanders, M. R. (2014). Parent and adolescent effects of a universal group program for the parenting of adolescents. *Prevention Science, 16,* 609–620. doi:10.1007/s11121-014-0516-9

Chu, J. T. W., Farrugia, S. P., Sanders, M. R., & Ralph, A. (2012). Towards a public health approach to parenting programmes for parents of adolescents. *Journal of Public Health, 34*, S1, i41–i47. doi:10.1093/pubmed/fdr123

De Graaf, I. M., de Jonge, M. C., & Okma, K. (2016). *Effects of the implementation of an evidence-based parenting program for use in residential youth care.* Unpublished manuscript.

de Vore, E. R., & Ginsburg, K. R. (2005). The protective effects of good parenting on adolescents. *Current Opinion in Pediatrics, 17*, 460–465. doi:10.1097/01.mop.0000170514.27649.c9

Dittman, C. K., Burke, K., & Barton, K. (2016, June). *A mixed methods evaluation of the efficacy of brief, targeted parenting groups for parents of teenagers.* Paper presented at the 8th World Congress of Behavioural and Cognitive Therapies, Melbourne, Australia.

Doherty, F., Calam, R., & Sanders, M. R. (2013). Positive Parenting Program (Triple P) for families of adolescents with type 1 diabetes: A randomised controlled trial of self-directed Teen Triple P. *Journal of Pediatric Psychology, 38*, 846–858. doi:10.1093/jpepsy/jst046

Fossum, S., Handegard, B. H., Adolfsen, F., Vis, S. A., & Wynn, R. (2016). A meta-analysis of long-term outpatient treatment effects for children and adolescents with conduct problems. *Journal of Child and Family Studies, 25*, 15–29. doi:10.1007/s10826-015-0221-8

Hodges, J. (2013). *Implementation and evaluation of connxionz for boarding school staff* (Unpublished doctoral thesis). University of Queensland, Brisbane, Australia.

Hodges, J., Sheffield, J., & Ralph, A. (2016). Staff and boarders perceptions of the boarding environment. *Journal of Child and Family Studies, 25*, 1045–1056. doi:10.1007/s10826-015-0287-3

Jacobs, E. (2011). *Getting teenagers to cooperate: An evaluation of a brief parenting discussion group for parents of young adolescents* (Unpublished master's thesis). University of Utrecht, Utrecht, Netherlands.

Jenkins, M. (2016). *Building Bridges Triple P: A pilot study of a behavioural family intervention for adolescents with autism spectrum disorder* (Unpublished master's thesis). Curtin University, Perth, Australia.

Kliem, S., Aurin, S. S., & Kröger, C. (2014). Zur Wirksamkeit des adoleszenzspezifischen Elterntrainings Group Teen Triple P. Eine Randomisiert-kontrollierte Studie. *Kindheit und Entwicklung.* doi:10.1026/0942-5403/a000129

Lindsay, G., Strand, S., & Davis, H. (2011). A comparison of the effectiveness of three parenting programmes in improving parenting skills, parent mental well-being and children's behavior when implemented on a large scale in community settings in 18 English local authorities: The Parenting Early Intervention Pathfinder (PEIP). *BMC Public Health, 11*: 962. doi:10.1186/1471-2458-11-962

Luthar, S. (2006). Resilience in development: A synthesis of research across five decades. In D. Cicchetti & S. Cohen (Eds.), *Developmental psychopathology: Risk disorder and adaptation* (Vol. 3, pp. 739–795). New York, NY: Wiley.

Ng, H. N. (2011). *An evaluation of a brief parenting discussion group for parents with difficulty in coping with a teenager's emotions.* Unpublished manuscript, University of Queensland, Brisbane, Australia.

O'Connor, B. (2012). *A preliminary evaluation of the Teen Triple P Discussion Group "Reducing Family Conflict."* Unpublished manuscript, University of Queensland, Brisbane, Australia.

Ralph, A., & Sanders, M. R. (2003). Preliminary evaluation of the Group Teen Triple P program for parents of teenagers making the transition to high school. *Australian e-Journal for the Advancement of Mental Health, 2.* Retrieved from http://auseinet.flinders.edu.au/journal/vol2iss3/inde x.php

Ralph, A., & Sanders, M. R. (2004). Community-based parenting program for the prevention of adolescent antisocial behaviour. *Trends and Issues in Crime and Criminal Justice, Australian Institute of Criminology, 282*, August, 281–300.

Ralph, A., & Sanders, M. R. (2006). The "Teen Triple P" Positive Parenting Program: A preliminary evaluation. *Youth Studies Australia, 25*, 2, 41–48.

Ralph, A., Stallman, H. M., & Sanders, M. R. (2016). *Towards a population-level approach to the school-based delivery of parenting and family support.* Unpublished manuscript.

Robinson, E., Power, L., & Allan, D. (2010). *What works with adolescents? Family connections and involvement in interventions for adolescent problem behaviours.* Melbourne, Australia: Australian Institute of Family Studies.

Salari, R. S., Ralph, A., & Sanders, M. R. (2014). An efficacy trial: Positive Parenting Program for parents of teenagers. *Behaviour Change, 31,* 34–52. doi:10.1017/bec2013.31

Sanders, M. R., Murphy-Brennan, M., & McAuliffe, C. (2003). The development, evaluation and dissemination of a training programme for general practitioners in evidence-based parent consultation skills. *International Journal of Mental Health Promotion, 5,* 13–20. doi:10.1080/14623730.2003.9721914

Sanders, M. R., & Ralph, A. (2011). *Every parent's guide to teenagers* (DVD and booklet). Brisbane, Australia: Families International.

Stallman, H. M., & Ralph, A. (2007). Reducing risk factors for adolescent behavioural and emotional problems: A pilot randomised controlled trial of a self-administered parenting intervention. *Australian e-Journal for the Advancement of Mental Health, 6,* 1–13. Retrieved from http://www.tandfonline.com/doi/abs/10.5172/jamh.6.2.125?journalCode=ramh19

Sutherland, F. (2015). *Group Teen Triple P: Promotion of self-regulation and effects on their adolescent children.* Unpublished manuscript, University of Canterbury, Christchurch, New Zealand.

Sweeney, G. (2011). *Getting teenagers to cooperate: An evaluation of a brief parenting discussion group for parents of young adolescents.* Unpublished manuscript, University of Queensland, Brisbane, Australia.

Tarrant, E. (2012). *The impact of co-resident adult children on Australian parents: A pilot study.* Unpublished manuscript, University of Queensland, Brisbane, Australia.

World Health Organization. (2014). *Health for the world's adolescents: A second change in the second decade.* Geneva, Switzerland: Author.

APPLICATIONS OF POSITIVE PARENTING WITH DIFFERENT TYPES OF FAMILIES AND FAMILY MEMBERS

APPLYING POSITIVE PARENTING PROGRAMS WITH DIFFERENT TYPES OF FAMILIES AND FAMILY MEMBERS

An Introduction

MATTHEW R. SANDERS

Children are raised by parents in many different contexts that can affect the course of human development (Bronfenbrenner, 1999). Different types of parents and families living in very different circumstances have to work out for themselves, often with little or no support or guidance, how best to look after children in their care and promote healthy development. While some parenting responsibilities are shared across all parents and caregivers (e.g., keeping children safe, providing basic care, food, shelter, medical assistance if needed), others are nonshared responsibilities and require adaptations by parents to the nuances of the parenting role. These differences in a broader ecological context for parenting arise at different stages of the life cycle, creating special challenges for all parents involved.

The return to paid employment after childbirth is an almost universal experience for families in modern times, where surviving economically on a single income is extremely difficult. Having paid employment means that while parents have greater financial resources at their disposal to support children, new challenges arise for parents in balancing and managing sometimes incompatible or competing work and family responsibilities (Michel, Kotrba, Mitchelson, Clark, & Baltes, 2011).

Keown (Chapter 15, this volume) reviews evidence linking the quality of the paternal relationships between fathers and their children and children's development. Fathers have been relatively neglected compared to mothers in both the developmental and the parenting intervention literatures. They are less likely to know about available resources to support parenting, participate less frequently than mothers in parenting programs, and when they do participate, often do not achieve the same level of changes as reported by mothers. In Chapter 15, Keown documents how the combining of developmental research on fathering with consumer strategies to assess the identified needs of fathers led to adaptation of Group Triple P to couple families and was able to produce similar positive outcomes and high satisfaction for both mothers and fathers (Frank, Keown, & Sanders, 2015).

Similarly, when grandparents assume major parenting responsibilities with grandchildren, grandparents either by circumstance (such as a parent having a substance abuse or mental health problem or is incarcerated) or by cultural tradition (e.g., in many Asian cultures where multigenerational households are common), the grandparenting role can be stressful. Kirby's Chapter 16 in this volume highlights the need to adapt parenting programs to attend to the unique needs and challenges grandparents face in their role with their grandchildren. A grandparent's relationship with a child's biological parent and their grandchildren can be disrupted and become be a major source of stress affecting the grandparent's mental health and well-being. It is grandparents who are required to step in and assume primary parenting responsibilities of their grandchildren when the biological parent develops serious mental health problems, substance abuse issues, or is incarcerated.

Kirby's Chapter 16 provides insights into how Triple P can be applied to improve grandparents' relationships, communication, and capacity to amicably resolve conflict with parents to produce a three-generational mental health benefit for grandparents themselves, their adult children, and their grandchildren. The chapter illustrates the value of using consumer input to help design and then test an adaption of Group Triple P to address more specifically the needs of noncustodial grandparents who provide regular care for grandchildren (Kirby & Sanders, 2012). The program produced a three-generational benefit to grandparents, parents, and grandchildren, resulting in fewer behavior problems in grandchildren as reported by both grandparents and parents and less emotional distress in grandparents and improved relationship satisfaction with the parent.

Approximately one in five adults develops a serious mental illness over their lifetime. When parents develop serious mental health problems, such as chronic depression, anxiety, and psychosis and many other forms of mental health difficulties, children are often exposed to disrupted parenting that can increase children's risk of developing behavioral and emotional problems themselves. Calam and Wittowski (Chapter 17, this volume) discuss the need for parenting programs for parents living with a mental illness. They indicate the important of attending to the parenting needs of parents with depression in the perinatal period, parents with bipolar disorder, and parents with schizophrenia. They identify a number of important future research opportunities to further strengthen evidence relating to the application of Triple P with parents who have a mental illness, including the benefits for children and parents of using technology-supported intervention via the combination of Triple P Online and an online program for parents with bipolar disorder (Jones et al., 2014).

Another important context for parenting is when family life is disrupted due to the breakdown of the parent's relationship. Relationship breakdown is a highly distressing experience for many parents and is considered one of the most stressful life events for parents and children. Millions of children each year experience the disruption to their family lives due to their parent's relationship breakdown. The experience of separation and divorce affects not only parents and children but also grandparents, extended family members, and friends. The chapter by Stallman and Ohan (Chapter 18, this volume) discusses evidence linking relationship breakdown to both parents' and children's adjustment. They introduce Family Transitions Triple P, a group or individually administered adjunctive intervention designed specifically to meet the need of parents who have experienced relationship breakdown.

This section shows how a comprehensive, population approach to parenting support that aspires to be truly inclusive of all families must be flexibly adapted to ensure the unique circumstances of families are taken into account. These adaptations to Triple P are based on gaining an understanding of unique parenting contexts and parenting situations families confront; the adaptations draw on relevant research and consumer input. Adapted intervention protocols have then been trialed to determine their effectiveness before being introduced as part of the Triple P system of parenting support.

REFERENCES

Bronfenbrenner, U. (1999). *Environments in developmental perspective: Theoretical and operational models* (pp. 3–28). Washington, DC: American Psychological Association.

Frank, T. J., Keown, L., & Sanders, M. R. (2015). Enhancing father engagement and intraparental teamwork in an evidence-based parenting intervention: A randomized controlled trial of outcomes and processes. *Behaviour Therapy, 46,* 749–763. doi:10.1016/j.beth.2015.05.008

Jones, S., Calam, R., Sanders, M., Diggle, P. J., Dempsey, R., & Sadhnani, V. (2014). A pilot web based positive parenting intervention to help bipolar parents to improve perceived parenting skills and child outcomes. *Behavioural and Cognitive Psychotherapy, 42,* 283–296.

Kirby, J. N., & Sanders, M. R. (2012). Using consumer input to tailor evidence-based parenting interventions to the needs of grandparents. *Journal of Child and Family Studies, 21,* 626–363. doi:10.1007/s10826-011-9514-8

Michel, J., Kotrba, L., Mitchelson, J., Clark, M., & Baltes, B. (2011). Antecedents of work-family conflict: A meta-analytic review. *Journal of Organizational Behavior, 32,* 689–725. doi:10.1002/job.695

CHAPTER 15

WORKING WITH FATHERS

LOUISE J. KEOWN

NATURE OF THE ISSUE

There is extensive evidence that behavioral family interventions reduce child behavior problems and associated family risk factors (Dretzke et al., 2009; Sanders, Kirby, Tellegen, & Day, 2014). However, the majority of program participants are mothers with fathers underrepresented in parenting interventions (Panter-Brick et al., 2014). The importance of engaging fathers in parenting programs is increasingly recognized due to the mounting body of research linking fathers' behaviors with children's well-being. In addition, researchers have identified a range of barriers to father inclusion and retention in parenting programs and made recommendations for what needs to be done to better engage fathers and co-parents (Fabiano, 2007; Panter-Brick et al., 2014). This chapter begins by summarizing key evidence about the paternal parenting and co-parenting factors that relate to positive and negative child behavior outcomes. The importance of father-inclusive parenting programs for reducing child behavior problems and increasing positive child and parenting behavior and parental well-being is next discussed. Key barriers to father engagement are subsequently identified. This is followed by several illustrations of how Triple P has engaged fathers to support the success of Triple P interventions, and key findings from these studies are presented. The chapter concludes with recommendations for practice based on these study findings and recommendations for future research on father engagement in parenting programs.

THE ROLE OF FATHERS
IN CHILDREN'S DEVELOPMENT

In general, the literature shows that father involvement has positive effects on children. This is illustrated by evidence from a systematic review of 24 longitudinal studies involving 22,300 children, which found that paternal involvement (such as talking and interacting with their child and having a significant role in child care) reduced the frequency of behavior problems in boys and psychological problems in young women (Sarkadi, Kristiansson, Oberklaid, & Bremberg, 2008). A growing body of research examining the father–child relationship and its impact on child outcomes has also highlighted unique contributions of father involvement over and above the effects explained by maternal involvement.

Specifically in early childhood, positive links have been found between fathers' sensitivity (NICHD Early Child Care Research Network [ECCN], 2004) and authoritative parenting style (Mattanah, 2005) and children's subsequent behavioral adjustment. For example, longitudinal data from the NICHD Study of Early Child Care and Youth Development indicated that observed paternal sensitivity (including emotional support, lack of hostility, and respect for the child's autonomy) in early childhood contributed uniquely to lower levels of children's externalizing scores in middle childhood (NICHD ECCN, 2004).

Studies of high-risk samples have identified the role of early fathering in the subsequent trajectories of behavioral functioning in children with preschool behavior problems. For instance, a prospective 3-year longitudinal study, which investigated preschool parenting predictors of attention deficit hyperactivity disorder (ADHD), found that lower levels of paternal sensitivity were uniquely predictive of higher levels of inattentiveness in middle childhood, and that intrusive paternal behaviors were predictive of hyperactive–impulsive behaviors at school (Keown, 2012). In another 3-year follow-up study by Herbert, Harvey, Lugo-Candelas, and Breaux (2013), findings suggested that fathers' depressive symptoms, use of lax parenting, and frequent commands may play a role in the prognosis of preschool children with behavior problems.

New research examining independent effects of father and mother behaviors on child executive function is relevant to understanding the role of paternal parenting in the development of early self-control. For example, in a study of 607 families, Lucassen et al. (2015) found that harsher parenting of the father was related to lower scores of emergent metacognition (the child's ability to initiate, plan, organize, implement, and sustain future-oriented problem-solving) and inhibitory self-control (the child's ability to modulate actions, responses, emotions, and behavior via appropriate inhibitory control) in early childhood.

Along with the growth of research on fathering has been an increased interest in co-parenting. A meta-analysis of 59 studies found that children's positive adjustment has been associated with high-quality co-parenting behaviors, such as teamwork and support for the other parent, lack of conflict over childrearing, and agreement on child-related topics (Teubert & Pinquart, 2010). Furthermore, the quality of co-parenting may moderate prospective associations between father involvement and child adjustment. Support for this possibility was provided by Jia, Kotila, and Schoppe-Sullivan (2012), who found that father involvement in play predicted decreases in externalizing and internalizing behaviors and increases in social competence at school only when accompanied by supportive co-parenting.

Collectively, this body of research highlights the unique role of paternal parenting in children's early behavioral development and subsequent adjustment and the importance of high-quality co-parenting. The research underscores the importance of involving fathers in parenting interventions to foster positive child development.

THE NEED FOR FATHER-INCLUSIVE PARENTING PROGRAMS

Father-inclusive parenting programs are important for reducing child behavior problems and increasing positive parenting behavior and parental well-being. Involving both fathers and mothers in early parenting interventions is likely to reduce the negative parenting and parent–child interactions, which are associated with child behavior problems, from becoming entrenched. In addition, it may be one way to increase early and ongoing positive father–child interactions and paternal involvement in children's lives (Ramchandani & Iles, 2014). Other potential benefits of father involvement in parenting interventions are reductions in parenting stress and coercive parenting strategies and improvements in authoritative parenting practices, parenting satisfaction, and sense of competence. Less optimal levels of these parenting behaviors and parental well-being have been reported by fathers of children with behavioral difficulties (Keown, 2011; Sanders, Dittman, Keown, Farruggia, & Rose, 2010). Furthermore, some evidence suggests that postintervention improvements in child outcomes are more likely to be maintained over time when both parents take part in the program (Bagner & Eyberg, 2003).

Including both parents in a parenting intervention is likely to strengthen the partner relationship, enhance co-parenting support, and reduce the extent to which parents undermine each other's parenting efforts. When parents get the same message about child management strategies, the result may be fewer interparental disagreements and more consistency in implementing parenting strategies (Bagner, & Eyberg, 2003; Cowan, Cowan, Pruett, Pruett, & Wong, 2009).

The potential impact of parenting programs is diminished because of nonparticipation or inconsistent father participation (inconsistent attendance, lack of homework completion, dropout), and a range of barriers to father engagement need to be addressed. Numerous reasons have been suggested for low father participation, including the way programs are advertised and promoted to families and aspects of program content and delivery (Fabiano, 2007). For example, fathers may be put off by advertisements that imply the parenting program addresses parenting shortcomings and may not seek help if it means admitting there is a problem (Fabiano, 2007; Frank, Keown, Dittman, & Sanders, 2015). Furthermore, the content of parenting programs may be viewed by fathers as less relevant to their needs compared to mothers' needs (Fabiano, 2007). Practical issues such as program scheduling and lack of child care are often-mentioned barriers to father participation. However, as Ramchandani and Iles (2014) pointed out, these barriers likely apply to mother participants as well given the numbers of mothers in paid work in many countries.

Researchers have made some key recommendations about what needs to be done in research and practice to obtain good-quality data on father and couple participation and impact (Panter-Brick et al., 2014). These include engaging with co-parents, using the same data collection procedures for both parents, and reporting intervention effects separately for fathers and mothers. The next section provides an example of how these recommendations can be implemented and how barriers to engagement have been addressed.

HOW TRIPLE P CAN BE APPLIED TO INCREASE FATHER ENGAGEMENT

This section examines how Triple P has engaged fathers to support the success of Triple P interventions. A recent randomized controlled study by Frank, Keown, and Sanders (2015) evaluated the Level 4 Group Triple P program that was completed by fathers and mothers, from 42 families, of children aged between 3 and 8 years with conduct problems. To engage fathers, the study used a range of strategies that were based on father preference data (Frank, Keown, Dittman, et al., 2015). Prior to participation, program advertisements were worded to include positive messages about father involvement, to alert fathers to program content of specific interest to them (e.g., build a positive relationship with your child, enhance your child's social development), and to mention that the evidence-based program was run by trained practitioners. The inclusion of this specific information was derived from findings of a community survey of fathers' parenting support needs and preferences, such as preferred program features and program delivery methods (Frank, Keown, Dittman, et al., 2015).

Both fathers and mothers were involved in screening interviews about their child's behavior and to explain to them what their participation in the program entailed. Group sessions were run in the evenings in community locations to enable both parents to attend together. Drawing on father preference data (Frank, Keown, Dittman, et al., 2015), new content was incorporated into the program to maximize fathers' engagement and teamwork between parents. Additional topics included explaining the benefits of both father and mother involvement for children's development and strategies to develop children's social skills (e.g., Lamb & Lewis, 2010). Other father-identified areas of interest included strategies for managing father-identified parenting challenges, such as balancing work and family, how to gain cooperation with their partner in parenting, the range of ways to show physical affection with children, and how fathers can contribute to enhancing their child's self-esteem. These adaptations were made with the full support of program developers and, to maintain the fidelity of Group Triple P, no content was omitted to allow room for the new material (Mazzucchelli & Sanders, 2010). In some instances, existing examples and exercises were replaced with new material to provide father-specific or co-parenting illustrations of parent techniques.

During the group sessions, each parent had their own workbook. Fathers were asked about their specific concerns, as opposed to just asking the mothers about their children. Fathers and mothers were encouraged to set their own homework tasks between sessions and to each report back their progress on implementing parenting strategies. Telephone consultations were conducted with fathers and mothers participating together, using a speakerphone or multiple handsets, and each parent was encouraged to contribute. Both parents were included in all aspects of the data collection process, and the data analysis was gender disaggregated.

After completing the intervention, both parents reported significantly fewer child behavior problems and increased use of positive parenting practices. There was also less conflict between parents about childrearing, and the mothers felt more confident and reported that their partners' parenting practices had improved (see Box 15.1). These effects were maintained at 6-month follow-up. Fathers and mothers recorded similar levels of completion of the program, which was high, as well as high levels of program satisfaction.

Findings from another Triple P trial by Palmer, Keown, Sanders, and Henderson (2017), which specifically invited father participation, suggest that low-intensity parenting groups may be another delivery format that is effective and acceptable with fathers and mothers. The study evaluated Level 3 Triple P Parenting Discussion Groups by comparing child and parent outcomes for mothers and fathers who attended a one-off 2-hour discussion group on dealing with disobedience (the single-exemplar condition) or a series of four topic-specific discussion groups (dealing with disobedience plus three other topic choices, 2 hours each; the multiple-exemplar condition). Participants were mothers and fathers from 78 families with a 5- to 8-year-old child displaying mild-to-moderate conduct problems. Both parents were encouraged to participate in the program and to complete the study assessments. Fathers and mothers in

> ## BOX 15.1: Group Triple P Case Study: Benefits for Fathers and Couples
>
> As fathers participated in Group Triple P and learned about the importance of a father's interactions and play with his children, they became more actively involved in parenting and spent more quality time with their kids. For example, fathers said the following:
>
> - "Originally, I went along to support my wife, but I have found that I learnt a lot, and I am pleased that I went because I am part of the situation, too."
> - "I play more with my children after completing the course, and this has helped with our relationship and has improved my children's behavior and mine."
>
> Couples who completed Group Triple P also discovered the benefits of greater cooperation with their partners:
>
> - "We have been talking a lot more. Good things come from talking."
> - "I recognize when [my wife] is at the end of her tether, and I jump in and help, whereas I used to see her explode and think, 'What is her problem?'"
> - "Thank you for putting my mind at ease and getting my wife and I on the same page."

the multiple-exemplar condition reported greater improvement in their child's disruptive behavior than parents in the single-exemplar condition. These findings extend current literature on low-intensity topic-specific parenting programs, based largely on mother participants, to fathers (Dittman, Farruggia, Keown, & Sanders, 2016; Joachim, Sanders, & Turner, 2010; Morawska, Haslam, Milne, & Sanders, 2010). Furthermore, parents in the multiple-exemplar group reported higher levels of program satisfaction than parents in the single-exemplar condition. The results suggest the possibility that offering several topic-specific parenting discussion groups, tailored to particular parenting challenges, may be an attractive program option for fathers as well as mothers.

IMPLICATIONS FOR PRACTICE, POLICY, AND RESEARCH

Findings from the Group Triple P study by Frank, Keown, and Sanders (2015) suggest a number of implications for researchers, providers, and agencies. When it comes to the relatively high retention rates, the study authors suggested this might have been due to the fact that because both parents attended together, each was accountable to the other and therefore completion was more likely. They also suggested that efforts taken to increase teamwork between mothers and fathers, such as joint telephone sessions and tailoring the content for fathers and mothers, may also have contributed to the high levels of program satisfaction. The study creates a compelling case for flexible delivery times, which could include offering evening sessions or full-day weekend workshops in easy-to-access settings, as well as making allowances for child care.

Father preference data (Frank, Keown, Dittman, et al., 2015) indicate that it is important to offer a range of program delivery options to cater for a range of father needs and reduce barriers to father involvement. Consistent with the approach adopted by Frank, Keown, and Sanders (2015), it is also recommended that ways are found to make the program design and content appealing to both fathers and mothers (Ramchandani & Iles, 2014). By adapting programs based on the preferences of both parents and offering support with varying levels of practitioner involvement in delivery methods, we are more likely to increase the number of fathers and mothers who are receiving parenting support at a level that meets their needs.

As the study by Frank, Keown, and Sanders (2015) did not compare a mothers-only intervention with a group involving both mothers and fathers, additional studies are needed to further understand the role of dual-parent involvement compared with one-parent involvement to clinically important changes in child behavior. Future research on engaging fathers in parenting interventions needs to be extended to fathers and mothers from diverse ethnic, cultural, and economic backgrounds and high risk or less traditional families, such as same-gender couples and blended families, and to families of children with other types of behavioral difficulties, such as ADHD. In relation to this last point, the findings from Keown (2012) offer suggestions for tailoring parenting interventions for both fathers and mothers of preschool children presenting with signs of ADHD.

New research is required to find effective strategies for engaging both parents in other variants of the Triple P program, such as online delivery. This view is supported by a recent study of Triple P Online (TPOL) for parents of preschool-aged children with ADHD symptoms (Franke, Keown, & Sanders, 2016). This study found intervention effects for reductions in child symptoms, maternal stress, and negative parenting practices; however, the study did not specifically target father involvement. Therefore, future research needs to include fathers as well as mothers. If both parents are included in all aspects of the intervention and data collection, a better understanding could be gained about the effectiveness of the TPOL, targeted at preschool ADHD, for fathers separately from mothers. Other potential benefits of engaging both parents in TPOL include increasing teamwork in the implementation of parenting strategies and enhancing the likelihood of long-term maintenance of improvements in child behavior. Father preference data collected by Frank, Keown, Dittman, et al. (2015) indicate that Internet program delivery may appeal to many fathers. A key task for future research is to investigate how to motivate and support teamwork between parents during participation in an online parenting program.

Finally, it is important to emphasize that multiple ways of engaging fathers are needed as their needs vary considerably. For example, more research is needed with couples with co-occurring marital and child problems, using Enhanced Triple P (Level 5), which includes a module on partner support. For fathers who have experienced separation and divorce, their parenting support needs could be met by Family Transitions Triple P (Chapter 18, this volume; Stallman & Sanders, 2007), with its specific focus on reducing the adverse impact of the relationship breakdown on parents' emotional well-being and their parenting practices. Last, some high-risk fathers who are offenders or have substance abuse and mental health problems will need concurrent interventions beyond those involving parenting.

KEY MESSAGES

- There is compelling evidence highlighting how fathers can contribute to children's well-being that strongly support father involvement in parenting interventions to foster optimal child development.
- Efforts should be made to effectively engage fathers and co-parenting couples to support the success of parenting interventions.
- Parenting program design and content should acknowledge and cater for concerns and interests of both fathers and mothers and encourage interparental teamwork.

REFERENCES

Bagner, D. M., & Eyberg, S. M. (2003). Father involvement in parent training: When does it matter? *Journal of Clinical Child and Adolescent Psychology, 32*, 599–605. doi:10.1207/S15374424JCCP3204_13

Cowan, P. A., Cowan, C. P., Pruett, M. K., Pruett, K., & Wong, J. J. (2009). Promoting fathers' engagement with children: Preventive interventions for low-income families. *Journal of Marriage and Family, 71*, 663–679. doi:10.1111/j.1741-3737.2009.00625.x

Dittman, C. K., Farruggia, S. P., Keown, L. J., & Sanders, M. R. (2016). Dealing with disobedience: An evaluation of a brief parenting intervention for young children showing noncompliant behavior problems. *Child Psychiatry & Human Development, 47*, 102–112. doi:10.1007/s10578-015-0548-9

Dretzke, J., Davenport, C., Frew, E., Barlow, J., Stewart-Brown, S., Bayliss, S., . . . Hyde, C. (2009). The clinical effectiveness of different parenting programs for children with conduct problems: A systematic review of randomised controlled trials. *Child and Adolescent Psychiatry and Mental Health, 3*, 7. doi:10.1186/1753-2000-3-7

Fabiano, G. A. (2007). Father participation in behavioral parent training for ADHD: Review and recommendations for increasing inclusion and engagement. *Journal of Family Psychology, 21*, 683–693. doi:10.1037/0893-3200.21.4.683

Frank, T. J., Keown, L., Dittman, C., & Sanders, M. (2015). Using father preference data to increase father engagement in evidence-based parenting programs. *Journal of Child and Family Studies, 24*, 937–947. doi:10.1007/s10826-014-9904-9

Frank, T. J., Keown, L. J., & Sanders, M. R. (2015). Enhancing father engagement and inter-parental teamwork in an evidence-based parenting intervention: A randomized-controlled trial of outcomes and processes. *Behavior Therapy, 46*, 749–763. doi:10.1016/j.beth.2015.05.008

Franke, N., Keown, L. J., & Sanders, M. R. (2016). An RCT of an online parenting program for parents of preschool-aged children with ADHD symptoms. *Journal of Attention Disorders*. doi:10.1177/1087054716667598

Herbert, S. D., Harvey, E. A., Lugo-Candelas, C. I., & Breaux, R. P. (2013). Early fathering as a predictor of later psychosocial functioning among preschool children with behavior problems. *Journal of Abnormal Child Psychology, 41*, 691–703. doi:10.1007/s10802-012-9706-8

Jia, R., Kotila, L. E., & Schoppe-Sullivan, S. (2012). Transactional relations between father involvement and preschoolers' socioemotional adjustment. *Journal of Family Psychology, 26*, 848–857. doi:10.1037/a0030245

Joachim, S., Sanders, M. R., & Turner, K. M. (2010). Reducing preschoolers' disruptive behavior in public with a brief parent discussion group. *Child Psychiatry and Human Development, 41*, 47–60. doi:10.1007/s10578-009-0151-z

Keown, L. J. (2011). Fathering and mothering of preschool boys with hyperactivity. *International Journal of Behavioral Development, 35*, 161–168. doi:10.1177/0165025410380982

Keown, L. J. (2012). Predictors of boys' ADHD symptoms from early to middle childhood: The role of father-child and mother-child interactions. *Journal of Abnormal Child Psychology, 40*, 569–581. doi:10.1007/s10802-011-9586-3

Lamb, M. E., & Lewis C. (2010). The development and significance of father-child relationships in two-parent families. In M. E. Lamb (Ed.), *The role of the father in child development* (5th ed., pp. 94–1531). Hoboken, NJ: Wiley.

Lucassen, N., Kok, R., Bakermans-Kranenburg, M. J., Van IJzendoorn, M. H., Jaddoe, V. V. W., Hofman, A., . . . Tiemeier, H. (2015). Executive functions in early childhood: The role of maternal and paternal parenting practices. *British Journal of Developmental Psychology, 33*, 489–505. doi:10.1111/bjdp.12112

Mattanah, J. F. (2005). Authoritative parenting and the encouragement of children's autonomy. In P. A. Cowan, C. P. Cowan, J. C. Ablow, V. K. Johnson, & J. R. Measelle (Eds.), *The family context of parenting in children's adaptation to elementary school* (pp. 119–138). Mahwah, NJ: Erlbaum.

Mazzucchelli, T. G., & Sanders, M. R. (2010). Facilitating practitioner flexibility within an empirically supported intervention: Lessons from a system of parenting support. *Clinical Psychology: Science and Practice, 17*, 238–252. doi:10.1111/j.1468-2850.2010.01215.x

Morawska, A., Haslam, D., Milne, D., & Sanders, M. R. (2010). Evaluation of a brief parenting discussion group for parents of young children. *Journal of Developmental and Behavioral Pediatrics, 31*, 136–145. doi:10.1097/DBP.0b013e3181f17a28

NICHD Early Child Care Research Network (ECCN). (2004). Fathers' and mothers' parenting behavior and beliefs as predictors of children's social adjustment in the transition to school. *Journal of Family Psychology, 18*, 628–638. doi:10.1037/0893-3200.18.4.628

Palmer, M. L., Keown, L. J., Sanders, M. R., & Henderson, M. (2017). *Enhancing outcomes of a low-intensity parenting group program through generalization promotion strategies: A randomized control trial.* Manuscript submitted for publication.

Panter-Brick, C., Burgess, A., Eggerman, M., McAllister, F., Pruett, K., & Leckman, J. F. (2014). Practitioner review: Engaging fathers—Recommendations for a game change in parenting interventions based on a systematic review of the global evidence. *Journal of Child Psychology and Psychiatry, 55*, 1187–1212. doi:10.1111/jcpp.12280

Ramchandani, P. & Iles, J. (2014). Commentary: Getting fathers into parenting programmes—a reflection on Panter-Brick et al. (2014). *Journal of Child Psychology and Psychiatry, 55*, 1213–1214. doi:10.1111/jcpp.12321

Sanders, M. R., Dittman, C. K., Keown, L. J., Farruggia, S., & Rose, D. (2010). What are the parenting experiences of fathers? The use of household survey data to inform decisions about the delivery of evidence-based parenting interventions to fathers. *Child Psychiatry and Human Development, 41*, 562–581. doi:10.1007/s10578-010-0188-z

Sanders, M. R., Kirby, J. N., Tellegen, C. L., & Day, J. J. (2014). The Triple P—Positive Parenting Program: A systematic review and meta-analysis of a multi-level system of parenting support. *Clinical Psychology Review, 34*, 337–357. doi:10.1016/j.cpr.2014.04.003

Sarkadi, A., Kristiansson, R., Oberklaid, F., & Bremberg, S. (2008). Fathers' involvement and children's developmental outcomes: A systematic review of longitudinal studies. *Acta Pædiatrica, 97*, 153–158. doi:10.1111/j.1651-2227.2007.00572.x

Stallman, H. M., & Sanders, M. R. (2007). "Family Transitions Triple P": The theoretical basis and development of a program for parents going through divorce. *Journal of Divorce & Remarriage, 47*, 133–153. doi:10.1300/J087v47n03_07.

Teubert, D., & Pinquart, M. (2010). The association between co-parenting and child adjustment: A meta-analysis. *Parenting: Science and Practice, 10*, 286–307. doi:10.1080/15295192.2010.492040

CHAPTER 16

WORKING WITH GRANDPARENTS AND EXTENDED FAMILY MEMBERS

JAMES N. KIRBY

B oth mothers and fathers have a significant positive influence on their child's developmental outcomes, including emotional, social, and behavioral developments (Scourfield, Cheung, & Macdonald, 2014). Although working with mothers and fathers is the most important avenue for assisting children (Sanders, 2012), it has been argued that the field of parenting adopt a broader social ecological perspective and consider the impact that outside influences—such as extended family members, including grandparents—have on the social, emotional, and behavioral development of children (Kirby, 2015). This notion supports Bronfenbrenner's (1979) social ecological framework, which postulates that an expansive view of possible influential factors needs to be considered in relation to child development. Consequently, it is important to move beyond the child's immediate home environment with their parents and evaluate the impact that other family members (e.g., grandparents), friends (e.g., neighbors), and environments (e.g., school) can have on child outcomes.

A growing number of researchers have identified that one clear example of extended family involvement is that of the grandparents (Kirby, 2015; Smith & Palmieri, 2007). Grandparent involvement in family life can influence children's adjustment either directly (e.g., providing support) or indirectly (e.g., supporting the parent; Attar-Schwartz, Tan, Buchanan, Flouri, & Griggs, 2009; Coall & Hertwig, 2010; Kirby, 2015). The focus of this chapter is to illustrate how the involvement of grandparents can enhance parenting and family outcomes, which can then be used as an example when considering the involvement of other extended family members. This chapter focuses on five key areas: (a) why the inclusion of grandparents is helpful; (b) which grandparent factors affect families; (c) the role parenting interventions can have with extended family members, specifically grandparents; (d) how Triple P has and can be applied to this population; and (e) clinical implications.

WHY THE INCLUSION OF GRANDPARENTS AND EXTENDED FAMILY MEMBERS IS HELPFUL

To best address the question of why the inclusion of grandparents and extended family members is helpful, it can be useful to adopt an evolutionary perspective to families. Humans are classified as cooperative breeders (Burkart, Hrdy, & van Schaik, 2009), meaning that we have evolved as a species to work in groups when raising offspring. Indeed, this is a defining aspect of the human species; whereas other species pass on very shortly after losing their ability to reproduce, adult humans have a long postreproductive period, up to 40–50 years in some cases (Coall & Hertwig, 2010). This has led to the suggestion that the maternal grandmother is the second most helpful adult family member behind the mother when raising children (Coall & Hertwig, 2010; although this point is arguable as fathers have a very important parental investment role). However, in support of this position, one of the strongest and most robust findings across the grandparent literature is that "maternal grandmothers invest the most in, have most contact with, and have the closest relationships with their grandchildren" (Coall & Hertwig, 2010, p. 5).

The grandmother hypothesis (Alvarez, 2000) postulates that grandmother involvement in family life helps increase her daughter's fertility and the chance of the grandchildren surviving. Indeed, research has found that if the grandmother is present in the family, it doubles the odds of more children being born (Hawkes & Coxworth, 2013). One of the primary interpretations of this finding is that, as a result of having the grandmother available, a mother has assistance with the child care of her other children while she is able to tend to the needs of her newborn (Alvarez, 2000; Coall & Hertwig, 2010; Hawkes & Coxworth, 2013). Thus, grandparent involvement is pragmatically helpful for the growth in family member size. However, with increasing independence, geographical movement, reductions in family size, and isolation in Western culture, it raises the question of whether the old adage, "It takes a village to raise a child," still applies in today's modern age.

When examining the current trends of extended family involvement in families, we can see that grandparent involvement is still relatively common. In the United States, for example, approximately 24% of all children under five receive child care from their grandparents (Laughlin, 2013). This trend of grandparent care is also echoed in Australia, where approximately 25% of children 12 years or younger receive regular child care from their grandparents (Australian Bureau of Statistics, 2012), and across Europe it is estimated that 40% of children receive regular child care from their grandparents (Glaser, Price, Di Gessa, Montserrat, & Tinker, 2013). In Australia, grandparents are the largest providers of informal care, with extended family members such as siblings, aunts, and uncles also assisting, but at much lower rates (Australian Bureau of Statistics, 2012).

When reflecting on these trends of grandparent care, it is important to note how the majority of grandparents are not providing regular child care to children; indeed, grandparent care and involvement occur along a continuum. At one end of the spectrum, there are some grandparents who are in custodial grandparenting roles; at the other end, there are grandparents who have little or no involvement in the lives of their grandchildren. As such, there is great heterogeneity among the grandparenting population.

Given the heterogeneity of the grandparent population, it can be difficult to categorize grandparents into different groups. However, there appears to be two distinct groups, custodial grandparents and informal grandparent caregivers (Kirby & Sanders, 2012). The major distinction between custodial versus informal grandparent caregivers is that the former are the primary caregivers of their grandchildren, and the latter are secondary caregivers. As a result, both groups face different challenges, and intervention goals that aim to assist these two populations of grandparents need to reflect these differences.

GRANDPARENT FACTORS THAT AFFECT FAMILIES

IMPACTS ON GRANDPARENTS OF THE GRANDPARENT ROLE

There are many positive and negative impacts on grandparents who provide care to their grandchildren. For both custodial grandparents and grandparents providing informal care, many of the positives and negatives relate to aspects of the parenting role. Grandparents report specific positives as being given a second chance at successful parenting (Smith, Strieder, Greenberg, Hayslip, & Montoro-Rodriguez, 2016); feeling more useful and productive as individuals (Hayslip & Kaminski, 2005); and gaining a higher sense of satisfaction from life (Ochiltree, 2006). Grandparents reported some of the negatives as losing friendships (Smith et al., 2016); finding it difficult to manage more than one grandchild at a time (Ochiltree, 2006); and feeling as though they were being taken for granted by the grandchild's parents (Goodfellow & Laverty, 2003).

IMPACTS OF GRANDPARENTS ON GRANDCHILDREN

The impact grandparents have on childhood well-being varies depending on the type of care the child is receiving. Children in custodial grandparent care are likely to originate from family units where there have been parental difficulties (e.g., drug problems, child abuse/neglect, incarceration, death), and as a result have higher reported levels of emotional and behavioral problems compared to the general population (Smith & Palmieri, 2007). Smith and Palmieri (2007) compared children in custodial grandparent arrangements ($n = 733$, average child age 9.8 years) to children in normal parental living arrangements ($n = 9,878$) on the Strengths and Difficulties Questionnaire (SDQ). Custodial grandchildren fared significantly worse than children from typical parenting arrangements across all domains measured by the SDQ subscales, regardless of the child's gender. This result is not surprising, as for many grandparents becoming a custodial grandparent is unplanned, ambiguous, and undertaken with considerable ambivalence (Smith & Palmieri, 2007). As a result, custodial grandparents typically show elevated rates of anxiety, irritability, anger, and guilt (Szinovacz, DeViney, & Atkinson, 1999). Importantly, though, children in custodial grandparent care have lower rates of emotional and behavioral problems compared to children in out-of-home foster care arrangements (Tarren-Sweeney & Hazell, 2006).

Unlike custodial grandparenting, there is limited research investigating the impact that grandparents providing regular child care has on children's emotional and behavioral problems. Fergusson, Maughan, and Golding (2008) investigated both the extent of grandparent care in the United Kingdom and the psychological impact that grandparents can have on grandchildren.

Data were collected from 8,752 mothers, who completed a range of measures, one of which was the SDQ, at four time points: 8, 15, and 24 months and 4 years. Based on their large sample, the investigators found that 45% of children were regularly cared for by their grandparents at each time point. Fergusson et al. (2008) found that grandchildren who received child care from their grandparents, compared to children who received no grandparent care, were associated with elevated rates of hyperactivity and peer difficulties at age four. Although the study was not able to determine why this association existed, the authors suggested this was likely due to the family-of-origin characteristics (e.g., younger mothers, less educated backgrounds), as opposed to grandparent influence.

Attar-Schwartz et al. (2009) investigated the association between degree of grandparent involvement and adolescents' behavioral and emotional adjustment in the United Kingdom as a function of three family structures: two-parent biological families, lone-parent families, and families with one stepparent. Data were collected from 1,515 secondary school students (aged 11–16) who completed the SDQ. Attar-Schwartz and colleagues found that greater grandparent involvement with families was associated with significantly fewer emotional problems and with significantly more prosocial behavior. However, these results were not found in two-parent biological families. The results obtained by Attar-Schwartz et al. (2009) led Coall and Hertwig (2010) to postulate that, in situations of possible duress, grandparent involvement could offer a potential "buffering" effect for grandchildren against developing emotional and behavioral problems.

IMPACT ON GRANDPARENT–PARENT RELATIONSHIP

Mason, May, and Clarke (2007) suggested that grandparents do not stop being parents simply because their children have had children; indeed, parenting is a lifelong journey. However, being a parent to an adult who themselves is a parent requires a different skill set than being a parent to a child. There are significant differences in the challenges that custodial grandparents face compared to informal grandparent caregivers. In custodial arrangements, there can be deleterious effects in the grandparent–parent relationship when grandparents take on the custody of their grandchild. Indeed, the circumstances that lead to custodial grandparent care can often be a result of the substance abuse problems in the birth parents, child abuse/neglect, or incarceration; as a result, there are preexisting conflicts between parents and grandparents, and the custodial role may exacerbate these conflicts further (Kiraly & Humphreys, 2011). Moreover, custodial grandparents face boundary ambiguity of family roles, norms, and resources; this can lead to anger toward the parents (Bartram, 1996; Smith et al., 2008). Indeed, Hayslip and Kaminski (2005) found that the relationship with the parent is the most negatively affected relationship when grandparents assume custodial arrangements.

The relationship between grandparents providing informal care and parents can also experience conflict over a multitude of different scenarios, such as what parenting strategies are used by each party, what expectations people have, how people communicate with each other, and what ground rules to set. The underlying premise behind these challenges has been referred to as the double-bind effect (Thomas, 1990). The double-bind effect occurs when grandparents attempt to meet the parents' expectations, and parents' expectations are such that they expect the grandparents to be simultaneously supportive without interfering (Thomas, 1990). Indeed, one of the more consistent findings in the research on grandparent involvement in child care is that parents report that the grandparents' unsolicited advice on childrearing and their interference in childrearing were the worst aspects of having grandparents in the family (Kirby, 2012; Mason et al., 2007; Thomas, 1990). Thus, these are key factors to address in interventions aimed to help grandparent involvement in families.

THE ROLE OF PARENTING INTERVENTIONS TO HELP WITH THE INCLUSION OF GRANDPARENTS

I have argued previously that for a parenting intervention to be relevant for both custodial and informal grandparent caregivers, it needs to address three key components: (a) provide a refresher course in parenting strategies, (b) provide strategies to help manage the grandparent–parent relationship, and (c) provide coping strategies to manage stress and tension that can arise from the grandparenting role (Kirby, 2015; Kirby & Sanders, 2012). Yet, there remains a paucity of such interventions available (Kirby, 2015; McLaughlin, Ryder, & Taylor, 2016).

In an attempt to understand what interventions are available for grandparents, McLaughlin et al. (2016) conducted a systematic review, examining the type of intervention and its content. The systematic review identified 21 studies, which included a variety of different intervention approaches, including interdisciplinary case management programs, support groups, psycho-educational groups, and cognitive-behavioral or skills-based interventions. The conclusions of their systematic review were that cognitive-behavioral or skills-based interventions were the most effective. Specifically, the review highlighted how the intervention Grandparent Triple P (GTP; Kirby & Sanders, 2014) had the highest level of evidence showing beneficial outcomes for promoting grandparents' mental health and strengthening parenting skills. McLaughlin and colleagues (2016) also indicated that the field of grandparent intervention research needed improvements in methodology and suggested more randomized controlled trials (RCTs) with comparison groups would be helpful.

In terms of evaluating whether parenting interventions are effective for grandparents, I have suggested that measurement should focus on four key areas: (a) grandparent parenting behavior (i.e., parenting style, parenting confidence); (b) grandparent distress levels (i.e., depression, anxiety, and stress); (c) grandparent–parent relationship satisfaction (i.e., communication, perceived support); and (d) grandchild social, emotional, and behavioral outcomes. Indeed, this is the approach we took in evaluating GTP (Kirby & Sanders, 2014; Leung, Sanders, Fung, & Kirby, 2014).

HOW TRIPLE P CAN BE APPLIED TO GRANDPARENTS AND EXTENDED FAMILY MEMBERS

Grandparent Triple P (Kirby & Sanders, 2014) is a variant of the Level 4 Triple P—Positive Parenting Program that has been tailored to the concerns and needs of grandparents who provide care to their grandchildren (Kirby & Sanders, 2014). The aims of GTP are to provide a refresher course in parenting strategies (parenting strategies), to help improve the relationship between grandparents and parents (team strategies), and to provide coping strategies to manage stress and tension that can arise from the grandparenting role (coping strategies). GTP is a 9-week intervention that consists of six group sessions lasting 120 minutes and three telephone consultations lasting between 20 and 30 minutes. Table 16.1 describes the session content of the program.

Table 16.1: Description of Grandparent Triple P Session Content

Session	GTP Session Content
Session 1: *Parenting strategies*	Positive Grandparenting • The principles of positive grandparenting are introduced; grandparents are asked to set goals for change and taught how to keep track of grandparent/grandchild behavior.
Session 2: *Parenting strategies*	Helping Grandchildren Develop • A refresher course in positive parenting strategies is introduced to the grandparents. The strategies are aimed to build positive relationships, encourage desirable behavior, and teach new skills and behaviors to grandchildren. • Grandparents are taught how to apply the strategies of descriptive praise, talk, affection, and setting a good example to the parents.
Session 3: *Parenting strategies*	Managing Misbehavior • A refresher course in managing misbehavior strategies is taught to the grandparents.
Session 4: *Team strategies*	Building a Positive Parenting Team • Grandparents are introduced to possible grandparenting traps that can negatively influence the grandparent–parent relationship. • Grandparents are introduced to positive/negative communication skills, problem-solving strategies, and how to manage the emotional distress of parents.
Session 5: *Coping strategies*	Grandparent Survival Skills • Grandparents are introduced to the unhelpful emotions of stress, anxiety, depression, and anger, and how these emotions can affect the relationship with the parents, your partner, and grandchildren. • Grandparents are taught coping strategies to manage unhelpful emotions (e.g., controlled breathing, pleasant activity scheduling).
Session 6	Planning Ahead • Grandparents are taught how to assess for high-risk situations and develop routines on how to manage them (e.g., situations with the parents, going shopping).
Sessions 7–8	Telephone Consultation • Grandparents are given the opportunity to set an agenda and discuss positive and challenging situations they are having. The practitioner provides support utilizing a self-regulatory framework.
Session 9	Program Close • Grandparents are introduced to how to maintain change and identify future obstacles, and final family survival tips are discussed.

Grandparent Triple P was evaluated in a foundation trial with 54 grandparents who provided between 12 and 20 hours of care per week to a grandchild aged between 2 and 9 years (Kirby & Sanders, 2014). No custodial grandparents were involved in this trial. Families were randomly allocated to conditions of receiving either GTP or care as usual. Grandparents were assessed on a range of outcomes, including child behavior, parenting style, parenting confidence, psychological adjustment, and relationship satisfaction with the parent. Despite the parents not participating in the program, they were also assessed on child behavior and relationship satisfaction with the grandparent. Grandparents and parents were assessed at preintervention, postintervention, and 6-month follow-up. Relative to the care-as-usual group, grandparents in the intervention condition reported short-term improvements, including a reduction in child behavior problems; improved grandparenting confidence; reduction in depression, anxiety, and stress; and improved relationship satisfaction with the parent. Parents also reported significant child behavior problem reductions. These obtained short-term intervention effects were maintained at 6-month follow-up. A typical example of the benefits experienced from participating in GTP is provided in Box 16.1.

The results from this foundation RCT provided support for the initial efficacy of the GTP program. GTP has since been evaluated in another RCT with Hong Chinese families; in this trial, 56 grandparents who provided regular child care to their grandchildren participated in the program (Leung et al., 2014). The results from this replication trial in Hong Kong provided further evidence for the impact of the GTP program on producing significant decreases in child behavior problems and grandparents reporting increased parenting self-efficacy. The strengths

---

BOX 16.1: An Example Application of Grandparent Triple P

Dell is a single grandmother who attended GTP primarily to help manage the difficulties in her relationship with Melissa (her daughter) about parenting Cassie (her granddaughter). Dell reported not having great difficulty managing Cassie; however, she had great difficulty discussing aspects of parenting with Melissa. Dell reported that she could not speak to Melissa about parenting issues, as any form of communication they had about parenting would often result in yelling and disagreement. This would make Dell depressed, and she reported always feeling stressed when with Melissa, as she worried they would start to fight about parenting. Dell was seeking assistance for two key areas: improving her relationship with Melissa and helping manage her feelings of depression and stress.

Dell completed the GTP program. To specifically address Dell's primary concerns, this meant focusing on strategies to help her relationship with Melissa. A key strategy for Dell was the routine for dealing with parent emotional distress. This focuses on the grandparent remaining calm when the parent is emotional. The routine emphasizes that the grandparent "stop and listen" to the parent and try to acknowledge, name, and validate the emotion the parent is experiencing. The most important component of this routine is when the grandparent asks the parent what they would like them to do. In this way, the grandparent is avoiding the grandparent trap of providing unsolicited parenting advice to the parent. After completion of the intervention, Dell reported improvements in relationship satisfaction with Melissa, as well as reduced conflict. In addition, Dell felt less emotionally stressed.

of GTP are that it has been evaluated in two RCTs; it has obtained corroborating evidence from the parents of the grandchildren; it has produced three-generational effects from a single parenting intervention; and that the program was a modification of a current evidence-based parenting program built on social learning principles (i.e., Triple P). The limitations of GTP are the duration of the program (it is a 9-week course, with six sessions lasting 120 minutes), and that it has not been trialed with custodial grandparents.

CLINICAL IMPLICATIONS

There are a number of clinical and ethical implications researchers and clinicians need to be aware of when working with extended family members, specifically grandparents. First, it is important for clinicians and practitioners to carefully define the custody arrangements with grandparents and obtain appropriate consents for all involved in the intervention (e.g., parents, grandparents). Second, clinicians who are attempting to assist families with child behavioral difficulties should consider the involvement of grandparents who are providing regular child care, as they could be a useful intervention option. For example, the clinician could provide grandparents with the techniques and strategies that might be used for high-risk situations with the target child or provide grandparents with specific techniques that can support the parent. However, in doing so it is important to inform parents and grandparents of the limits of confidentiality at the outset of the intervention. Specifically, if grandparents are invited to participate as part of the treatment process, the clinician needs to inform both parents and grandparents that previous individual history might not be able to be discussed with the grandparent unless parents permit, despite some grandparents wanting to know. Third, given how parenting interventions have been successfully adapted to grandparents, examining its impacts with other extended family members involved in regular child care, such as aunts/uncles, would also be useful. Finally, if grandparents are in a position of providing consistent regular child care or custodial care, support through parenting interventions has been found to be an effective way to help both grandparents and grandchildren (Kirby & Sanders, 2014; Smith et al., 2016).

CONCLUSION

The ultimate aim of grandparent-based interventions and interventions for other extended family members should not be to replace parents from attending parenting programs, but to be implemented jointly to increase the exposure of children to the benefits of positive parenting practices. Adopting such an inclusive approach would be in alignment with creating nurturing environments for children (Biglan, Flay, Embry, & Sandler, 2012).

KEY MESSAGES

- Grandparents can provide a positive influence on grandchild outcomes.
- The inclusion of grandparent involvement in parenting interventions offers a novel approach to help with family functioning.

- The intervention focus can be not only to help grandparents with child-focused parenting strategies but also to help manage the relationship between parent and grandparent.

REFERENCES

Alvarez, H. P. (2000). Grandmother hypothesis and primate life histories. *American Journal of Physical Anthropology, 113,* 435–450. doi:10.1002/1096-8644(200011)113:3<435::AID-AJPA11>3.0.CO;2-O

Attar-Schwartz, S., Tan, J., Buchanan, A., Flouri, E., & Griggs, J. (2009). Grandparenting and adolescent adjustment in two-parent biological, lone-parent, and step-families. *Journal of Family Psychology, 23,* 67–75. doi:10.1037/a0014383

Australian Bureau of Statistics. (2012). *Childhood education and care, Australia, June 2011* (Catalogue No. 4402.0). Canberra, Australia: Australian Bureau of Statistics.

Bartram, M. H. (1996). Clarifying subsystem boundaries in grand families. *Contemporary Family Therapy, 18,* 267–277.

Biglan, A., Flay, B. R., Embry, D. D., & Sandler, I. N. (2012). The critical role of nurturing environments for promoting human well-being. *American Psychologist, 67,* 257–271. doi:10.1037/a0026796

Bronfenbrenner, U. (1979). *The ecology of human development.* Boston, MA: Harvard University.

Burkart, J. M., Hrdy, S. B., & van Schaik, C. P. (2009). Cooperative breeding and human cognitive evolution. *Evolutionary Anthropology, 18,* 175–186. doi:10.1002/evan.20222

Coall, D. A., & Hertwig, R. (2010). Grandparental investment: Past, present, and future. *Behavioral and Brain Science, 33,* 1–59. doi:10.1017/S0140525X09991105

Fergusson, E., Maughan, B., & Golding, J. (2008). Which children receive grandparental care and what effect does it have? *Journal of Child Psychology and Psychiatry, 49,* 161–169. doi:10.1111/j.1469-7610.2007.01840.x

Glaser, K., Price, D., Di Gessa, G., Montserrat, E., & Tinker, A. (2013). *Grandparenting in Europe: Family policy and grand-parents' role in providing child care.* London, England: Grandparent Plus.

Goodfellow, J., & Laverty, J. (2003). Grandparents supporting working families: Satisfaction and choice in the provision of child care. *Family Matters, 66,* 14–19. Retrieved from https://aifs.gov.au/publications/family-matters/issue-66/grandparents-supporting-working-families

Hawkes, K., & Coxworth, J. E. (2013). Grandmothers and the evolution of human longevity: A review of findings and future directions. *Evolutionary Anthropology, 6,* 294–302. doi:10.1002/evan.21382

Hayslip, B., & Kaminski, P. L. (2005). Grandparents raising their grandchildren: A review of the literature and suggestions for practice. *The Gerontologist, 45,* 262–269. doi:10.1093/geront/45.2.262

Kiraly, M., & Humphreys, C. (2011). *It is the story of all of us: Learning from aboriginal communities about supporting family connection family links: Kinship Care and Family Contact Research Series Report 2.* Melbourne, Australia: Office of the Child Safety Commissioner and University of Melbourne.

Kirby, J. N., & Sanders, M. R. (2012). Using consumer input to tailor evidence-based parenting interventions to the needs of grandparents. *Journal of Child and Family Studies, 21,* 626–636. doi:10.1007/s10826-011-9514-8.

Kirby, J. N. (2015). The potential benefits of parenting programs for grandparents: Recommendations and clinical implications. *Journal of Child and Family Studies, 24,* 3200–3212. doi:10.1007/s10826-015-0123-9

Kirby, J. N., & Sanders, M. R. (2012). Using consumer input to tailor evidence-based parenting interventions to the needs of grandparents. *Journal of Child and Family Studies, 21,* 626–636. doi:10.1007/s10826-011-9514-8

Kirby, J. N., & Sanders, M. R. (2014). A randomized controlled trial evaluating a parenting program designed specifically for grandparents. *Behaviour Research and Therapy, 52*, 35–44. doi:10.1016/j.brat.2013.11.002

Laughlin, L. (2013). *Who's minding the kids? Child care arrangements: Spring 2011. Current Population Reports* (pp. 70–135). Washington, DC: US Census Bureau.

Leung, C., Sanders, M. R., Fung, B., & Kirby, J. N. (2014). The effectiveness of the Grandparent Triple P program with Hong Kong Chinese families: A randomised controlled trial. *Journal of Family Studies, 20*, 104–117. doi:10.1080/13229400.2014.11082000

Mason, J., May, V., & Clarke, L. (2007). Ambivalence and the paradoxes of grandparenting. *The Sociological Review, 55*, 687–706.

McLaughlin, B., Ryder, D., & Taylor, M. F. (2016): The effectiveness of interventions for grandparent caregivers: A systematic review. *Marriage and Family Review, 53*, 509–531. doi:10.1080/01494929.2016.1177631

Ochiltree, G. (2006). The changing role of grandparents. *Australian Family Relationships Clearing House, 2*, 1–9. Retrieved from https://aifs.gov.au/cfca/publications/changing-role-grandparents

Sanders, M. R. (2012). Development, evaluation, and multinational dissemination of the Triple P—Positive Parenting Program. *Annual Review of Clinical Psychology, 8*, 1–35. doi:10.1146/annurev-clinpsy-032511-143104

Scourfield, J., Cheung, S. Y., & Macdonald, G. (2014). Working with fathers to improve children's well-being: Results of a survey exploring service provision and intervention approach in the UK. *Children and Youth Services Review, 43*, 40–50. doi:10.1016/j.childyouth.2014.04.009

Smith, G. C., & Palmieri, P. A. (2007). Risk of psychological difficulties among children raised by custodial grandparents. *Psychiatric Services, 58*, 1303–1310. doi:10.1176/appi.ps.58.10.1303

Smith, G. C., Palmieri, P. A., Hancock, G. R., & Richardson, R. A. (2008). Custodial grandmothers' psychological distress, dysfunctional parenting, and grandchildren's adjustment. *International Journal of Aging and Human Development, 67*, 327–367.

Smith, G. C., Strieder, F., Greenberg, P., Hayslip, B., & Montoro-Rodriguez, J. (2016). Patterns of enrollment and engagement of custodial grandmothers in a randomized clinical trial of psychoeducational interventions. *Family Relations, 65*, 369–386. doi:10.1111/fare.12194

Szinovacz, M. E., DeViney, S., & Atkinson, M. P. (1999). Effects of surrogate parenting on grandparents' well-being. *Journal of Gerontology: Social Sciences, 54B*, S376–S388. doi:10.1093/geronb/54B.6.S376

Tarren-Sweeney, M., & Hazell, P. (2006). Mental health of children in foster and kinship care in New South Wales, Australia. *Journal of Paediatrics and Child Health, 42*, 89–97. doi:10.1111/j.1440-1754.2006.00804.x

Thomas, J. L. (1990). The grandparent role: A double bind. *The International Journal of Aging and Human Development, 31*, 169–177. doi:10.2190/80J9-FGK7-2966-QHCB

CHAPTER 17

PARENTS WITH SERIOUS MENTAL HEALTH PROBLEMS

RACHEL CALAM AND ANJA WITTKOWSKI

OVERVIEW

Children growing up in families with a parent with serious mental health problems are themselves at increased risk of behavioral and emotional problems. Parenting difficulties represent significant stressors that may further exacerbate parental mental health problems. This chapter considers the experience of families when a parent has serious mental health problems and how Triple P may be of benefit, focusing on (a) parents, particularly mothers, with mental health problems in the perinatal period; (b) families with a parent with bipolar disorder; and (c) families with a parent with symptoms of schizophrenia and psychosis.

BACKGROUND

The mental health and well-being of parents and their children are closely intertwined. The transition to parenthood can be more challenging when a parent experiences serious mental health problems. While parents with such difficulties can parent well, mental health problems can negatively affect family life and children. Warm, positive, predictable, and reliable interactions help to build close and cooperative relationships. When a family member is distressed or unresponsive, quality of interaction can suffer. A wealth of studies point to the negative impact of parental mental health problems on children's socioemotional and cognitive development and the interplay between quality of parenting and risk factors influencing the developing child (Beardslee, Gladstone, & O'Connor, 2011; Goodman et al., 2011; O'Connor, Monk, & Fitelson, 2014). Parental distress and mental health problems increase the risk of mental health problems in children and adolescents; intervening early to improve the well-being of parents with young children appears most cost-effective (Bauer, Parsonage, Knapp, Iemmi, & Adelaja, 2014).

Through their impact on the quality of the parent–child relationship, parental mental health problems can exert a significant influence on the child's developmental trajectory (Peris & Miklowitz, 2015). Mothers with postnatal depression show poorer processing of faces (Arteche et al., 2011) and responsiveness, with long-lasting effects (Murray et al., 2010). The child's behavioral and emotional adaptations can act as stressors for the parent, adding to pressures associated with their mental health problems, further impairing their capacity to parent effectively, resulting in a negative, downward spiral.

Critical expressed emotion (EE) in the family environment increases risk of relapse in mood disorders, schizophrenia, and psychosis (Alvarez-Jimenez et al., 2012). EE is relevant to quality of parenting (McCarty, Lau, Valeri, & Weisz, 2004), with expressed criticism associated with poorer relationship quality. Crandall, Deater-Deckard, and Riley (2015) examined emotion and cognitive control, noting the impact of stress and fatigue on the parent's executive functioning. Identifying interrelationships between child and parent mental health using a stress vulnerability model indicates the need for integrated approaches addressing the needs of the parent, child, and their relationships. Potential positive outcomes for children can also be seen; children and young people living alongside parents with serious mental illness identified enhanced self-esteem and feelings of positive growth (Bee, Berzins, Calam, Pryjmachuk, & Abel, 2013).

Data from Australia and the United States suggest that well over half of service users with psychosis or psychiatric disorder are also parents (Royal College of Psychiatrists, 2011). In a major review and synthesis of interventions addressing parental serious mental illness and quality of life of children and young people, Bee et al. (2014) found limited evidence and poor-quality research. Only three trials involving families with a parent with psychotic symptoms were identified, all in the United States and none recent. In contrast, 26 trials were identified in relation to parents with severe depression, with medium-to-large effects reported for parental depressive symptoms. These showed little evidence of change in children's emotional health or social functioning. An integrated family intervention combining cognitive-behavioral therapy (CBT) strategies to treat depression with parenting skills using Triple P showed significant improvements in both parental depression and child behavior, with gains sustained over a 6-month period (Sanders & McFarland, 2001).

The importance of addressing parenting issues as well as parental mental health needs has been recognized (Reupert & Maybery, 2011). Schrank, Moran, Borghi, and Priebe (2015) reviewed the effectiveness of interventions designed to support parents with serious mental illness in parenting, finding only two trials meeting quality criteria and only one rated strong, a study of parenting and bipolar disorder. The study used an integrated approach, including self-directed Triple P combined with online resources (Jones et al., 2013). Enhanced and integrative approaches, combining elements of the Triple P system with materials tailored for specific adult needs, have the potential to afford families significant benefits. Family interventions for adults with serious mental health problems have not yet systematically evaluated specific skills components needed for needs of families bringing up children and adolescents.

The studies described in the material that follows aimed to equip parents with the necessary tools to improve their parenting skills, while making explicit acknowledgment of, and links with, the mental health problems they are living with. This, in turn, has the the potential to reduce stress; increase warmth, predictability, and organization in family life; increase parental confidence and competence; and reduce child behavioral and emotional problems. We outline ongoing or recently completed trials and clinical evaluations using Triple P with parents experiencing serious mental health problems.

PERINATAL MENTAL HEALTH

Numerous reports call for parents to be supported in raising children equipped to reach their full potential (Allen, 2011; Munro, 2011). Perinatal contact with health services provides an ideal time to assess the mother's mental health needs. The UK National Institute for Clinical Excellence (NICE, 2014) recommends routine assessments of current and previous maternal mental health ante- and postnatally and that services should be accessible to mothers at risk of mental health problems. Compared to any other time in her life, a mother is more at risk of developing a serious mental health problem in the postpartum period (Joint Commissioning Panel for Mental Health [JCP-MH], 2012). Between 10% and 20% of women develop mental health problems of varying severity during pregnancy or within the first year of having a baby (Bauer et al., 2014). Not only do maternal mental health problems have profound effects on the woman, her family, and child, but also perinatal depression, anxiety, and psychosis carry an estimated total cost to society of £8.1 billion for each 1-year cohort of UK births (Bauer et al., 2014). The most common forms of perinatal mental health problems include severe postnatal depression, affecting 30 women in 1,000 live births (JCP-MH, 2012), and postpartum (or puerperal) psychosis, which 1 to 2 women in 1,000 live births develop (Heron, McGuinness, Blackmore, Craddock, & Jones, 2008). An estimated 1% of women who develop severe mental health problems require specialist psychiatric services (NICE, 2014).

Some mothers with existing or perinatal onset mental health problems require hospital admission jointly with their babies, with the mothers presenting with difficulties that include (puerperal) psychosis, bipolar disorder, schizophrenia, severe affective illness such as postnatal depression, and mother–infant relationship difficulties. Mothers report that the demands associated with parenting while coping with significant mental health problems are considerable. A metasynthesis of 23 studies (Dolman, Jones, & Howard, 2013) describing experiences of motherhood from preconception to parenting identified themes of guilt, coping, dual identities, stigma, and the importance of being a mother to women with severe mental illness.

THE IMPORTANCE OF PARENTING SUPPORT
IN RESOLVING THE PROBLEM

Interventions in the early years to promote optimal outcomes for children have been widely advocated (e.g., NICE, 2012) and their benefits outlined in the literature (Gillham & Wittkowski, 2015; Tsivos, Calam, Sanders, & Wittkowski, 2015). Most interventions in the perinatal period focus on maternal mood and include use of medication, CBT, and interpersonal psychotherapy (NICE, 2014). However, as improved maternal mood alone does not necessarily change mother–baby interactions (Murray et al., 2010), interest in video-feedback has grown. Interventions using video feedback appear useful in improving interaction in mothers with severe mental health problems (Kenny, Conroy, Pariante, Seneviratne, & Pawlby, 2013). Mothers admitted to a mother and baby unit (MBU) may require more skills to cope with their dual roles of "patient" and "mother." Parenting competence and confidence allow parents to balance parenting demands with their own needs (Van der Ende, Venderink, & Van Busschbach, 2010); thus, effective interventions focusing on the parenting needs of parents with severe mental health difficulties are needed.

TRIPLE P IN PERINATAL MENTAL HEALTH

The Baby Triple P—Positive Parenting Program (Spry, Morawska, & Sanders, 2013) is designed to facilitate the transition to parenthood. Baby Triple P targets three areas: (a) addressing positive parenting skills to promote secure attachment and reduce parental and infant distress; (b) improving partner and social support to increase parental and overall family well-being; and (c) increasing parental coping resources to reduce the risk of developing mental health problems. The program consists of four sessions delivered face to face and four subsequent telephone consultation sessions.

The initial Australian pilot randomized controlled trial (RCT) of Baby Triple P with expectant couples without mental health difficulties (Spry et al., 2013) indicated that client satisfaction ratings were positive, but no significant group differences were found. A subsequent small pilot study examined the feasibility and acceptability of Baby Triple P for mothers with postnatal depression (Tsivos, Calam, Sanders, & Wittkowski, 2014), with all sessions delivered face to face with mothers postpartum. Results, while nonsignificant, were in the predicted direction for happiness, self-regulation, subjective bonding, and depression at post-treatment. Mothers engaged with all sessions, engaged in all follow-up assessments, and rated the intervention as highly acceptable. Furthermore, mothers from diverse socioeconomic backgrounds and without partners found the program acceptable.

The perceived acceptability of Baby Triple P for mothers admitted to an inpatient psychiatric MBU in the north of England was assessed using Q methodology (Butler, Walker, Hare, Wieck, & Wittkowski., 2014). Irrespective of direct experience of Baby Triple P, all mothers viewed it as positive and nonstigmatizing and believed it would provide a sense of achievement alongside skills applicable to other family problems. MBU staff viewed it as a positive intervention for mothers, believing in the potential sense of achievement by engaging in the program during admission and that the MBU was an ideal setting for delivery (Butler-Coyne, Hare, Walker, Wieck, & Wittkowski, 2017). A feasibility RCT of Baby Triple P is now under way in two UK MBUs.

Finally, the Trial of Healthy Relationships Initiatives for the Very Early-years (THRIVE) is a large, three-arm RCT in Glasgow, United Kingdom, for mothers identified as vulnerable in pregnancy and babies at elevated risk of maltreatment. Vulnerability includes such risk factors as maternal intellectual disability, substance misuse, domestic violence, and mental health problems. This trial, led by Marion Henderson (http://thrive.sphsu.mrc.ac.uk/), compares outcomes for mothers receiving one of two group interventions, mainly antenatally (Baby Triple P enhanced with additional postnatal sessions) and Mellow Bumps (http://www.mellowparenting.org/our-programmes/mellow-bumps/) against treatment as usual. Findings will be known after 2018.

BIPOLAR DISORDER

It is estimated that the prevalence rate of bipolar disorder is approximately 1.0% to 1.5% (Merikangas et al., 2007). Bipolar disorder presents particular features that are relevant to parenting. It is characterized by recurrence of times of high mood, sometimes termed *mania*, and of low mood and depression. Studies indicated elevated vulnerability to emotional and behavioral problems in children of parents with bipolar disorder, including attention deficit hyperactivity disorder (ADHD), and increased risk of subsequent development of bipolar disorder (Duffy, Alda, Crawford, Milin, & Grof, 2007).

The inconsistency in mood characteristic of bipolar disorder may disrupt parenting, affecting children's development. In a qualitative study of young children living with a parent with bipolar disorder (Backer, Murphy, Fox, Ulph, & Calam, 2017), children as young as 4 years of age were able to describe changes in their household depending on their parent's state of mind. For example, they described their parents as "giddy," "angry," and "irritable" or "sad" and "depressed." They talked about how their parent might sleep all day or might not be available to comfort them.

Reinares et al. (2016) highlighted the value of family interventions in bipolar disorder; however, their review did not focus on parenting. A pilot web-based trial (Jones et al., 2013) used a combination of the *Every Parent's Self-Help Workbook* (Markie-Dadds, Sanders, & Turner, 1999) with Internet-based resources, reporting significant improvements in children's behavioral and emotional adjustment postintervention and reductions in dysfunctional parenting. A subsequent larger scale trial (Jones et al., 2015) used Triple P Online (Sanders, Baker, & Turner, 2012), combining this with online written and video material that was developed and coproduced in collaboration with people with lived experience of bipolar disorder. This was designed to explain and contextualize the use of a parenting intervention in improving quality of life for the family and reducing difficulties for both parent and child. Significant changes in parent ratings of children's emotional and behavioral problems were reported. These studies demonstrate clearly the capacity for Triple P to contribute positively to reductions in parent-rated behavioral and emotional problems in children. The findings show promise for protecting and promoting children's mental health, but the capacity for this to bring about change in parent mental health in the longer term remains an open question.

SCHIZOPHRENIA

Schizophrenia, which has an estimated median lifetime prevalence of 0.5% (Simeone, Ward, Rotella, Collins, & Windisch, 2015), is a distressing and serious mental health condition that impairs psychological and social functioning and is often associated with significant comorbid problems. Psychotic experiences (hallucinations and delusions) have a projected lifetime prevalence of 5.8% (McGrath, Saha, Chant, & Welham, 2008), and the lifestyle of people with a diagnosis of schizophrenia can include disorganized behavior; poor self-care; poor social functioning; cognitive impairment; low social and economic status; unemployment; homelessness; smoking, drug, and alcohol abuse; as well as increased risk of violence. The UK Schizophrenia Commission (2012) concluded improving and increasing access to psychological therapies for people with schizophrenia and their families should be research and clinical priorities (https://www.rethink.org/media/514093/TSC_main_report_14_nov.pdf).

WHY PARENTING SUPPORT IS IMPORTANT
IN RESOLVING THE PROBLEM

While models of recovery and stress vulnerability now inform psychosocial interventions for schizophrenia, parents with this diagnosis remain a neglected population. UK NICE guidelines (20014) currently recommend that family interventions should be offered to all families who live with, or are in close contact with, someone with a diagnosis of schizophrenia. Multiple studies have shown that family interventions reduce relapse rates and improve symptoms, adherence to medications, and functioning (Pharoah, Mari, Rathbone, & Wong, 2010). Family interventions focus on adult family members and have not been designed to meet the specific needs of families with children. Further, adult mental health providers often do not ask in detail about parental status or child care responsibility, leading to invisibility (Royal College of Psychiatrists, 2011), and parenting skills lie outside usual mental health practitioner training in adult services. A child's difficulties may not be identified or reach thresholds for children's services to intervene, and, when need is identified, integration between child and adult services can be poor. Perceived stigma is also an important factor for parents (Lacey et al., 2015) and can make it difficult to engage and maintain trust with families.

Studies are currently testing Triple P. Consultation with parents with lived experience made it plain that parents had fears about revealing concerns over parenting and risk of removal of their children by protective services. To accommodate both significant limitations on service resource availability and parents' concerns, one model identified was that parents might be able to work through a self-directed intervention with a trusted caseworker supporting them as necessary with both literacy needs and encouragement to engage as required. *Every Parent's Self-Help Workbook* (Markie-Dadds et al., 1999) was identified as potentially valuable because (a) the self-directed format is flexible, which is particularly helpful in accommodating to disruption in day-to-day living; (b) evidence from the field of bipolar disorder was positive (Jones et al., 2013); (c) parents with experience of schizophrenia and psychosis and their relatives saw it as potentially beneficial; and (d) the book is low cost yet can produce improvement equivalent to group intervention (Sanders, Markie-Dadds, Tully, & Bor, 2000). Furthermore, the level of detail means a care provider can comprehend the approach readily and integrate this with other cognitive behavioral and family-orientated approaches that they might be using.

A clinical case series is testing the *Triple P Self-Help Workbook*, reporting in 2017 (L. Stockton, personal communication, June 2017). Key observations include the high levels of support needed by parents in engaging with the intervention, including literacy as well as emotional support and encouragement. A slow pace is required due to competing demands; accommodation must be made for disruptions due to parental illness and difficulties in managing daily life that have a significant impact on family life, capacity to engage, and time required for the program. Notwithstanding these challenges, there are initial reports of improvements in child behavior, parenting skills and confidence, and symptoms of schizophrenia (see Box 17.1 for a typical example).

IMPLICATIONS FOR PRACTICE, POLICY, AND RESEARCH

These studies across the areas of perinatal mental health, bipolar disorder, and schizophrenia show promise, with significant findings to date from samples of parents with bipolar disorder. Further work should identify delivery formats that work optimally with different populations, and the outcomes of trials that are ongoing will be important in highlighting these. Determining the best ways of delivering within services is also important.

> **BOX 17.1: An Example of Delivering Triple P With a Parent With Schizophrenia**
>
> Cathy, a 35-year-old mother of two children aged 5 and 11, used *Every Parent's Self-Help Workbook,* with weekly home visits and encouragement provided by two psychology Master's students (C. Croft & L. Stockton). Cathy met criteria for diagnosis of schizophrenia, with persistent delusional symptoms and experiences of continuously high levels of anxiety and fear about others. Her fears meant she was housebound apart from taking and collecting her children from school. She chose to work on the older child's physical and verbal aggression toward the younger sibling and other children. Cathy worked through the book at her own pace and completed the program, reporting reductions in her child's violent behavior and improvements in her self-efficacy and self-confidence dealing with parenting problems and also in her symptoms. Cathy said that she and the children were calmer, and family interaction had improved. She found the workbook highly acceptable and valued the personal support provided by the weekly visits.

KEY MESSAGES

- Promising outcomes have been found for initial trials investigating the delivery of parenting support to parents with serious mental health conditions, particularly bipolar disorder.
- More studies are required to refine approaches to parenting support so that they best suit different mental health conditions and contexts.
- There is significant scope to test combinations of intervention approaches to support parents with serious mental health conditions (e.g., family intervention combined with individual CBT).

REFERENCES

Allen, G. (2011). *Early intervention: The next steps—An independent report to Her Majesty's government.* London, England: Crown.

Alvarez-Jimenez, M., Priede, A., Hetrick, S. E., Bendall, S., Killackey, E., Parker, A. G., . . . & Gleeson, J. F. (2012). Risk factors for relapse following treatment for first episode psychosis: A systematic review and meta-analysis of longitudinal studies. *Schizophrenia Research, 139,* 116–128. doi:10.1016/j.schres.2012.05.007

Arteche, A., Joorman, J., Harvey, A., Craske, M., Gotlib, L. H., Lehtonen, A., . . . Stein, A. (2011). The effects of postnatal maternal depression and anxiety on the processing of infant faces. *Journal of Affective Disorders, 133,* 197–203. doi:10.1016/j.jad.2011.04.015

Backer, C., Murphy, R., Fox, J. R., Ulph, F., & Calam, R. (2017). Young children's experiences of living with a parent with bipolar disorder: Understanding the child's perspective. *Psychology and Psychotherapy: Theory, Research and Practice, 90,* 212–228. doi:10.1111/papt.12099

Bauer, A., Parsonage, M., Knapp, M., Iemmi, V., & Adelaja, B. (2014). *The costs of perinatal mental health problems*. London, England: Centre for Mental Health.

Beardslee, W. R., Gladstone, T. R. G., & O'Connor, E. E. (2011). Transmission and prevention of mood disorders among children of affectively ill parents: A review. *Journal of the American Academy of Child and Adolescent Psychiatry, 50*, 1098–1109. doi:10.1016/j.jaac.2011.07.020

Bee, P., Berzins, K., Calam, R., Pryjmachuk, S., & Abel, K. M. (2013). Defining quality of life in the children of parents with severe mental illness: A preliminary stakeholder-led model. *PloS One, 8*, e73739. doi:10.1371/journal.pone.0073739

Bee, P., Bower, P., Byford, S., Churchill, R., Calam, R., Stallard, P., . . . Abel, K. (2014). The clinical effectiveness, cost-effectiveness and acceptability of community-based interventions aimed at improving or maintaining quality of life in children of parents with serious mental illness: A systematic review. *Health Technology Assessment, 18*(8), 1–125. doi:10.3310/hta18080

Butler, H., Walker, S., Hare, D. J., Wieck, A., & Wittkowski, A. (2014). The acceptability and feasibility of the Baby Triple P Positive Parenting Programme on a mother and baby unit: Q-methodology with mothers with severe mental illness. *Archives of Women's Mental Health, 17*, 455–463. doi:10.1007/s00737-014-0429-4

Butler-Coyne, H., Hare, D. J., Walker, S., Wieck, A., & Wittkowski, A. (2017). Acceptability of a positive parenting programme on a mother and baby unit: Q-methodology with staff. *Journal of Child and Family Studies, 26*, 623–632. doi:10.1007/s10826-016-0564-9

Crandall, A., Deater-Deckard, K., & Riley, A. W. (2015). Maternal emotion and cognitive control capacities and parenting: A conceptual framework. *Developmental Review, 36*, 105–126. doi:10.1016/j.dr.2015.01.004

Dolman, C., Jones, I. & Howard, L. M. (2013). Pre-conception to parenting: A systematic review and meta-synthesis of the qualitative literature on motherhood for women with severe mental illness. *Archives of Women's Mental Health, 16*, 173–196. doi:10.1007/s00737-013-0336-0

Duffy, A., Alda, M., Crawford, L., Milin, R., & Grof, P. (2007). The early manifestations of bipolar disorder: A longitudinal prospective study of the offspring of bipolar parents. *Bipolar Disorders, 9*, 828–838. doi:10.1111/j.1399-5618.2007.00421.x

Gillham, R., & Wittkowski, A. (2015). Outcomes for women admitted to an MBU: A systematic review. *International Journal of Women's Health, 7*, 459–478. doi:10.2147/IJWH.S69472

Goodman, S. H., Rouse, M. H., Connell, A. M., Broth, M. R., Hall, C. M., & Heyward, D. (2011). Maternal depression and child psychopathology: A meta-analytic review. *Clinical Child and Family Psychology Review, 14*, 1–27. doi:10.1007/s10567-010-0080-1

Heron, J., McGuinness, M., Blackmore, E. R., Craddock, N., & Jones, I. (2008). Early postpartum symptoms in puerperal psychosis. *British Journal of Obstetrics and Gynaecology, 115*, 348–353. doi:10.1111/j.1471-0528.2007.01563.x.

Joint Commissioning Panel for Mental Health (JCP-MH). (2012). *Guidance for commissioners of perinatal mental health services. Volume two: Practical mental health commissioning*. Retrieved from http://www.jcpmh.info/wp-content/uploads/jcpmh-perinatal-guide.pdf

Jones, S., Calam, R., Sanders, M. R., Diggle, P. J., Dempsey, R., & Sadhnani, V. (2013). A pilot web based positive parenting intervention to help bipolar patients to improve perceived parenting skills and child outcomes. *Behavioural and Cognitive Psychotherapy, 42*, 1–14. doi:10.1017/S135246581300009X

Jones, S., Wainwright, L. D., Jovanoska, J., Vincent, H., Diggle, P. J., Calam, R., . . . & Lobban, F. (2015). An exploratory randomised controlled trial of a web-based integrated bipolar parenting intervention (IBPI) for bipolar parents of young children (aged 3–10). *BMC Psychiatry, 15*, 1. doi:10.1186/s12888-015-0505-y

Kenny, M., Conroy, S., Pariante, C. M., Seneviratne, G., & Pawlby, S. (2013). Mother–infant interaction in mother and baby unit patients: Before and after treatment. *Journal of Psychiatric Research, 47*, 1192–1198. doi:10.1016/j.jpsychires.2013.05.012

Lacey, M., Paolini, S., Hanlon, M. C., Melville, J., Galletly, C., & Campbell, L. E. (2015). Parents with serious mental illness: Differences in internalised and externalised mental illness stigma and gender stigma between mothers and fathers. *Psychiatry Research, 225*, 723–733. doi:10.1016/j.psychres.2014.09.010

Markie-Dadds, C., Sanders, M., & Turner, K. M. T. (1999). *Every parent's self-help workbook*. Brisbane, Australia: Families International.

McCarty, C. A., Lau, A. S., Valeri, S. M., & Weisz, J. R. (2004). Parent-child interactions in relation to critical and emotionally overinvolved expressed emotion (EE): Is EE a proxy for behavior? *Journal of Abnormal Child Psychology, 32*, 83–93. doi:10.1023/B:JACP.0000007582.61879.6f

McGrath, J., Saha, S., Chant, D., & Welham, J. (2008). Schizophrenia: A concise overview of incidence, prevalence, and mortality. *Epidemiologic Reviews, 30*, 67–76. doi:10.1093/epirev/mxn001

Merikangas, K. R., Akiskal, H. S., Angst, J., Greenberg, P. E., Hirschfeld, R. M., Petukhova, M., & Kessler, R. C. (2007). Lifetime and 12-month prevalence of bipolar spectrum disorder in the National Comorbidity Survey replication. *Archives of General Psychiatry, 64*, 543–552. doi:10.1001/archpsyc.64.5.543

Munro, E. (2011). *The Munro review of child protection: Final report a child-centred system. National Institute for Health and Clinical Excellence. Social and emotional wellbeing: Early Years* (NICE Public Health Guidance 40). London, England: National Institute for Health and Clinical Excellence.

Murray, L., Arteche, A., Fearon, P., Halligan, S., Croudace, T., & Cooper, P. (2010). The effects of maternal postnatal depression and child sex on academic performance at age 16 years: A developmental approach. *Journal of Child Psychology and Psychiatry, 51*, 1150–1159. doi:10.1111/j.1469-7610.2010.02259.x

National Institute for Health and Clinical Excellence (NICE). (2012). *Social and emotional wellbeing: Early Years* (NICE Public Health Guidance 40). London, England: Author.

National Institute for Health and Clinical Excellence (NICE). (2014). *Antenatal and postnatal mental health: Clinical management and service guidance* (NICE Guideline CG192). London, England: Author. Retrieved from http://www.nice.org.uk/guidance/CG192.

O'Connor, T. G., Monk, C., & Fitelson, E. M. (2014). Practitioner review: Maternal mood in pregnancy and child development—implications for child psychology and psychiatry. *Journal of Child Psychology and Psychiatry, 55*, 99–111. doi:10.1111/jcpp.12153

Peris, T. S., & Miklowitz, D. J. (2015). Parental expressed emotion and youth psychopathology: New directions for an old construct. *Child Psychiatry and Human Development, 46*, 863–873. doi:10.1007/s10578-014-0526-7

Pharoah, F., Mari, J., Rathbone, J., & Wong, W. (2010). Family intervention for schizophrenia. *Cochrane Database Systematic Review*, (12), CD000088.

Reinares, M., Bonnín, C. M., Hidalgo-Mazzei, D., Sánchez-Moreno, J., Colom, F., & Vieta, E. (2016). The role of family interventions in bipolar disorder: A systematic review. *Clinical Psychology Review, 43*, 47–57. doi:10.1016/j.cpr.2015.11.010

Reupert, A., & Maybery, D. (2011). Programmes for parents with a mental illness. *Journal of Psychiatric and Mental Health Nursing, 18*, 257–264. doi:10.1111/j.1365-2850.2010.01660.x

Royal College of Psychiatrists. (2011). *Parents as patients: Supporting the needs of patients who are parents and their children CR164*. London, England. Retrieved from http://www.rcpsych.ac.uk/publications/collegereports/cr/cr164.aspx

Sanders, M. R., & McFarland, M. (2001). Treatment of depressed mothers with disruptive children: A controlled evaluation of cognitive behavioral family intervention. *Behavior Therapy, 31*, 89–112. doi:10.1016/S0005-7894(00)80006-4

Sanders, M. R., Baker, S., & Turner, K. M. (2012). A randomized controlled trial evaluating the efficacy of Triple P Online with parents of children with early-onset conduct problems. *Behaviour Research and Therapy, 50,* 675–684. doi:10.1016/j.brat.2012.07.004

Sanders, M. R., Markie-Dadds, C., Tully, L. A., & Bor, W. (2000). The Triple P-Positive Parenting Program: A comparison of enhanced, standard, and self-directed behavioral family intervention for parents of children with early onset conduct problems. *Journal of Consulting and Clinical Psychology, 68,* 624. doi:10.1037/0022-006X.68.4.624

Schizophrenia Commission. (2012). *The Abandoned Illness; A report by the Schizophrenia Commission.* London: Rethink Mental Illness https://www.rethink.org/media/514093/TSC_main_report_14_nov.pdf

Schrank, B., Moran, K., Borghi, C., & Priebe, S. (2015). How to support patients with severe mental illness in their parenting role with children aged over 1 year? A systematic review of interventions. *Social Psychiatry and Psychiatric Epidemiology, 50,* 1765–1783. doi:10.1007/s00127-015-1069-3

Simeone, J. C., Ward, A. J., Rotella, P., Collins, J., & Windisch, R. (2015). An evaluation of variation in published estimates of schizophrenia prevalence from 1990–2013: A systematic literature review. *BMC Psychiatry, 15,* 1. doi:10.1186/s12888-015-0578-7

Spry, C., Morawska, A., & Sanders, S. (2013). *Baby Triple P group workbook.* Brisbane, Australia: Triple P International.

Tsivos, Z. L., Calam, R., Sanders, M. R., & Wittkowski, A. (2014). A pilot randomised controlled trial to evaluate the feasibility of the Baby Triple P Positive Parenting Programme in mothers with postnatal depression. *Clinical Child Psychology and Psychiatry, 20,* 532–554. doi:10.1177/1359104514531589

Tsivos, Z. L., Calam, R., Sanders, M. R., & Wittkowski, A. (2015). Interventions for postnatal depression assessing the mother-infant relationship and child developmental outcomes: A systematic review. *International Journal of Women's Health, 7,* 429–447. doi:10.2147/IJWH.S75311

Van der Ende, P. C., Venderink, M. M., & Van Busschbach, J. T. (2010). Parenting with success and satisfaction among parents with severe mental illness. *Psychiatric Services, 61,* 416. doi:10.1176/ps.2010.61.4.416

CHAPTER 18

PARENTS WHO ARE SEPARATING OR DIVORCED

HELEN M. STALLMAN AND JENEVA L. OHAN

Separation and divorce are significant life stressors that are often accompanied by other stressors in families, such as changes in living arrangements and location, finances, time spent with children, social support, and employment status. For couples who are not parents, separation or divorce enables partners to completely dissociate themselves from their former partner, discuss their version of the breakup publicly, make their own attributions to make sense of what happened, and move on to future relationships without having to have further contact with their former partner, if desired (Rollie & Duck, 2006). In contrast, to ensure the best outcomes for their child, separating or divorcing parents are required to transform their previously romantic relationship to a co-parenting relationship that prioritizes the needs of their child to have an ongoing positive relationship with both parents (Stallman & Sanders, 2007). The challenge for co-parents is to develop a functional co-parenting relationship to ensure optimal outcomes for their child at a time when they may wish to have nothing further to do with their former partner. Throughout this chapter, we use the term *divorce* to refer to relationships where parents separate, whether they were previously married or cohabiting and whether they are separated or legally divorced.

THE NATURE OF THE PROBLEM

Approximately 40% of marriages in the United States, United Kingdom, Canada, and Australia end in divorce, and almost half of these involve children under the age of 16 (Amato, 2010; Australian Bureau of Statistics, 2015; Milan, 2016; Office for National Statistics, 2015). The process of divorce may take many years, usually beginning with a preseparation period marked by high conflict and distress that is followed by multiple, stressful changes to family life that can extend over the ensuing two to three years. In the postseparation period, parents need to nego-tiate living arrangements, establish new routines, transition to parenting as a single parent, and redefine their family unit and social support (Carr, 2012). In causing these multiple and stress-ful transitions to a child's life, divorce can be seen as a form of adversity. As such, divorce does not affect a child by acting on any one specific problem trajectory; rather, it has the poten-tial to engender long-standing changes to a child's psychophysiological stress system (Fabricius & Luecken, 2007; McEwen & Wingfield, 2003), thereby increasing the risk of maladjustment across a broad range of developmental outcomes.

Consistent with this view, over four decades of research have documented that children whose parents have divorced are at increased risk for such diverse problems as antisocial behav-ior, emotional disorders, early and problematic alcohol consumption, lower academic achieve-ment, and health problems (Amato, 2010; Coleman & Glenn, 2010; Jackson, Rogers, & Sartor, 2016). For many children, these problems will resolve during or after the divorce process; how-ever, for some, the impact of divorce will continue into their adult lives (Hartman, Magalhaes, & Mandich, 2011). For example, adults who experienced their parents' divorce as a child expe-rience greater emotional distress and relationship problems, especially with romantic partners (Amato, 2010). Having divorced parents may also take an economic toll, as children of divorced parents are more likely to attain less education and have lower incomes in adulthood (Amato, 2010; Tartari, 2015). These long-lasting and pervasive impacts may therefore extend beyond the affected individual and onto ensuing generations, as evidence shows that the grandchildren of divorced couples also have lower educational attainment, greater marital discord, and poorer parent–child relationships (Amato & Cheadle, 2005). In summary, while many children adjust to parental divorce without significant problems, many children suffer across a variety of health, wellness, and academic indicators during childhood, and that for some, this has the potential to continue into adulthood and affect the subsequent generation.

PARENTING AND FAMILY FACTORS AS DETERMINANTS OF DEVELOPMENTAL OUTCOMES

Like all forms of adversity, divorce places children at risk for maladjustment (Jackson et al., 2016), but maladjustment is not a universal outcome (Amato, 2010). Whether children develop poor outcomes is influenced by a number of key determinants, including conflict between the parents, the parent–child relationship, maternal mental health, financial circumstances, and repeated family transitions (Coleman & Glenn, 2010). Of these, parental mental health, conflict between parents, and the parent–child relationship are parent-specific factors that determine a child's developmental outcomes postdivorce and hence are the focus of our review here.

Given the strain on finances, time, and energy during a divorce, emotional upheaval is a com-mon experience. Managing the tasks of parenting while going through divorce takes an even greater toll on emotional regulation, and a plethora of research has documented that divorced parents have lower subjective well-being and higher distress than married parents (Afifi, Cox, & Enns, 2006; Lizardi, Thompson, Keyes, & Hasin, 2009). Importantly, parental distress (in the form of depression, anxiety, and stress) predicts children's behavioral and emotional maladjustment beyond the divorce itself, even many years postdivorce (Lizardi et al., 2009; Storksen, Roysamb, Holmen, & Tambs, 2006). These findings might not extend to parents' feelings of anger. A recent study, for example, found that parents' state and trait anger scores were not elevated relative to community norms and were unrelated to child or youth behavioral, emotional, or social adjustment (Stallman & Ohan, 2016). Rather, it is more likely that anger is expressed between parents, which could undermine a child's sense of a safe and predictable world that influences child outcomes.

Anger between parents has the potential to result in conflict. Almost all divorcing parents experience conflict as they disentangle their emotional, social, financial, and physical lives from their former partner (Stallman & Sanders, 2007); however, for some, this conflict may become an entrenched way of relating to each other and outlast the divorce process (King & Heard, 1999). Entrenched, enduring conflict can prevent parents from reaching parenting agreements; consequently, this minority of parents utilizes disproportionate court resources and time (Kelly, 2003). In addition, after becoming locked into the adversarial system, parents can find it difficult to transform themselves into cooperative participants of a, court-ordered, shared parenting contract (Turkat, 2002). Conflict also risks limiting contact between children and their noncustodial parent, usually the father, despite plentiful evidence that a father's continued involvement and support are protective factors for children (e.g., Elam, Sandler, Wolchik, & Tein, 2016). For these reasons, it is not surprising that conflict is a robust predictor of psychopathology in children who have divorced parents, in both the short and the long terms (Amato & Cheadle, 2008; Christophersen & Mortweet, 2003; Garber, 2004; O'Connor & Dvorak, 2002; Strohschein, 2012).

In addition to this direct effect on children, conflict may compromise parenting, as parents who engage in prolonged and high conflict with their ex-spouse may have less emotional energy and availability to calmly and appropriately respond to their child (Ruschena, Prior, Sanson, & Smart, 2005). More generally, divorce risks disrupting positive parenting practices, such as providing consistently enforced clear rules, through parents' decreased emotional regulation and available time that can be devoted to parenting tasks (Stallman & Ohan, 2016). There is some evidence that positive parenting practices, such as monitoring, positive attention, and emotional availability, decline during and following divorce, and that overreactivity may increase (e.g., Stallman & Ohan, 2016; Sutherland, Altenhofen, & Biringen, 2012; Vuchinich, Vuchinich, & Wood, 1993). These parenting practices are well-known risks for children's psychosocial well-being, including children with divorced parents (e.g., Sutherland et al., 2012), and therefore need to be considered.

In summary, distress and interparental conflict experienced during and after divorce reduce parents' abilities to separate their own needs from those of their children, establish immediate and ongoing healthy co-parenting arrangements, and encourage solid parent–child relationships with both parents (Stallman & Sanders, 2007). Divorce also has the potential to disrupt positive parenting practices through decreases in parents' emotional and physical responsiveness and availability. In all of these ways, divorce can result in wide-ranging and durable problems for children throughout their development. Together, these highlight the need for targeted, evidence-based interventions to promote positive transitions through divorce for parents and children.

THE ROLE OF PARENTING INTERVENTIONS FOR THIS PROBLEM

Parenting interventions, particularly early in the separation process, have the potential to address modifiable family risk factors and enhance protective factors to optimize positive child and family outcomes following divorce (Stallman & Sanders, 2007). Topics such as understanding the needs of children following divorce, helping parents manage their emotions and conflict, and addressing disruptions in positive parenting practices that contribute to child problems are modifiable targets of intervention; changing these is therefore integral to the solution (Stallman & Sanders, 2007). Thus, prevention and early interventions for families going through divorce need to focus on parents, support their cooperation to smoothly transition through the divorce process, and provide a safe, predictable, and engaging environment for their child.

At first glance, such aims seem to overlap with general, established parenting programs, which also support skill development in positive parenting practices and parents' emotional regulation. However, typical parenting programs fall short of meeting the needs of families experiencing divorce because they do not consider their specific needs and circumstances, such as managing emotions and considering the needs of parents who have limited contact with their children. General parenting programs do not emphasize specific skills or issues that need to be addressed for divorced parents, such as developing and maintaining a co-parenting relationship (Stallman & Sanders, 2007). Furthermore, parenting interventions need to be helpful and relevant to parents, irrespective of the behavior of their former partner.

This recognition that parents are central to children's adjustment during and following the divorce process, and that typical parenting programs need to be modified to achieve best outcomes for families, has resulted in the proliferation of intervention programs for divorced parents (Stallman & Sanders, 2007). However, this level of productivity in designing or modifying programs has not been matched by equal emphasis on program evaluation. Of the interventions that have been rigorously evaluated, benefits have been seen on children's emotional and behavioral problems, parents' mental health, and interparental conflict (e.g., Forgatch & DeGarmo, 1999; Hughes, Clark, Schaefer-Hernan, & Good, 1994; Keating, Sharry, Murphy, Rooney, & Carr, 2016; Stallman & Sanders, 2014; Whitehurst, O'Keefe, & Wilson, 2008). Thus, using parenting interventions designed specifically for families experiencing divorce holds promise for improving child, parent, and family outcomes.

APPLICATIONS OF TRIPLE P TO PARENTS WHO ARE SEPARATING OR DIVORCED

Family Transitions Triple P (Stallman & Sanders, 2010) was developed in response to demand from both consumers and the court system for support for parents going through divorce (Stallman & Sanders, 2007). In its development, it was assumed that not all families experiencing divorce need a broad-reaching intervention, as evidence showed that not all children have poor outcomes. Rather, it was developed as a selective or indicated prevention and intervention program targeted for divorced parents whose children are at high risk of maladjustment due to divorce, who themselves have minimal but detectable symptoms of mental health problems, or who have entrenched conflict with the former partner (Stallman & Sanders, 2007). Thus, Family Transitions Triple P is recommended as a Level 4 group intervention or Level 5 intensive individual intervention in the Triple P system (see Chapter 3 of this volume for a description of Triple P multilevel support). As a Level 5 individual intervention, Family Transitions Triple P can be tailored to suit individual families and can therefore be flexible in helping families with a range of differing needs during the divorce process.

The broad aim of Family Transitions Triple P is to provide parents with skills to understand the needs of children during divorce and develop skills to manage their own emotions, co-parent effectively, develop a new family identity, and implement positive parenting strategies. As such, Family Transitions Triple P targets the parent-related factors that place children at risk for poor outcomes after divorce by employing both risk-reducing and resilience-promoting strategies. Specifically, through enhancing parental coping, communication, and conflict management skills, Family Transitions Triple P aims to change factors that predict children's problems. By the same token, children's resilience is enhanced through encouraging parents to build child skills that will enable the child to successfully negotiate high-risk environments. The overarching objective of the program is to increase parents' skills and confidence in making a positive transition through divorce and beyond for themselves and their children.

To accomplish these broad aims, Family Transitions Triple P has a core set of empirically informed, targeted, goals and strategies. These are covered over nine group or individual sessions and three brief telephone consultations. The first five sessions address parent-related factors that predict child maladjustment postdivorce, including managing the divorce transition; managing emotions and coping; developing skills needed to develop and maintain a healthy co-parenting relationship, including assertive communication and problem-solving; and balancing work, family, and play (Stallman & Sanders, 2007).

The following seven sessions are devoted to increasing general parenting skills for encouraging appropriate behavior and managing problem behaviors (Sanders, Markie-Dadds, & Turner, 2001). These can be delivered in a variety of formats, including group or individual, in-person, telephone-assisted, or self-directed programs (or any combination). This flexibility encourages parents from a wide range of backgrounds and circumstances (e.g., families from remote and rural areas) to participate, minimizing the high dropout rates often observed in traditional parenting group programs (Stallman & Sanders, 2007). This also paves the way for families to meet the requirements of court-ordered attendance in appropriate programs.

In its group format, Family Transitions Triple P has been examined with a randomized controlled trial for parents of children aged 2 to 14 years within 4 years of ending their relationship with their former partner (Stallman & Sanders, 2014). Relative to a wait-list control, parents who participated in the Family Transitions program reported significant reductions in child behavior problems and coercive parenting practices and improvements in their own mental health (see Box 18.1 for a typical response to the program). Improvements in parent mood persisted at a 1-year follow-up, showing sustained benefits to parents' depression, anxiety, stress, and anger. Although there were no immediate differences in co-parent acrimony and conflict after completing the program, significant improvements were also seen at the 1-year follow-up, suggesting that parents built on skills after the program ended. In sum, these results support the use of Family Transitions Triple P in preventing the development of serious conduct problems in children and increasing long-term co-parenting cooperation.

IMPLICATIONS FOR PRACTICE, POLICY, AND RESEARCH

Current practice for divorcing parents who want or need intervention is to self-seek a program or, in the case of parents who show ingrained and high levels of co-parenting conflict, for courts to recommend or mandate parenting therapy. If the courts mandate therapy, the intervention

---

BOX 18.1: A Typical Response to Transitions Triple P

Rachel was a 36-year-old mother of two boys aged 7 and 5 years. She had been separated for 5 months prior to entering a Family Transitions Triple P group program and was feeling stressed and depressed. Interactions with her ex-husband frequently ended in screaming matches and name-calling. Between these interactions and her return to full-time employment, she felt drained and without the energy and patience to handle her younger child's increasing emotional outbursts and her older child's defiance. She felt increasingly short-tempered with her sons and did not know how to handle their new problem behaviors.

After the first few sessions of the Family Transitions Triple P group, Rachel noticed that hearing from both other mothers and fathers helped her to appreciate her ex-husband's perspective and start thinking about him as a co-parent rather than her ex-husband. Rachel was developing skills in conflict management to better manage interactions with her former partner and started to use assertive communication, remaining focused on the children's needs. She also started to implement the emotional coping strategies she learned in the program. These helped her stay calm and focused in discussions with her co-parent and able to maintain consistent rules and consequences when parenting her boys. She began to notice that her boys were beginning to calm during transitions between their homes. By the end of the program, Rachel had developed new skills to prevent and better manage her boys' problem behaviors and noticed that they had decreased in both frequency and intensity. She worked to redefine her concept of her new family with her boys and encouraged her boys to have a positive and hopeful view of their redefined family, enabling a greater focus on positive family time.

---

usually occurs many months after the initial application for divorce when conflict has become more entrenched and child problems have already emerged.

There are clear ways that policy changes can be introduced to improve on this current practice. In particular, the time of the divorce application represents a first opportunity to provide parents with support that is targeted to their needs, with a goal of preventing either the occurrence or the worsening of poor child outcomes throughout the divorce process. Research supports early prevention and intervention as cost-effective in promoting positive child outcomes (e.g., Valentine & Katz, 2007), although there have been no cost-effectiveness evaluations with children at high risk for negative sequelae following parental divorce. Still, these cost analyses are likely to support early intervention considering that multiple domains of functioning are affected for each child, and that the impact of divorce can span generations. Thus, while the need for economic analyses remains, changes to policy such that parenting interventions are offered to families at an earlier stage are a logical way to improve on current practice.

We can also improve on the types of therapy that we are providing parents undergoing divorce. Parents who show entrenched patterns of conflict throughout their divorce are often mandated or recommended for therapy by the courts; however, these therapies are often of varied content and not based on science. Programs need to target areas that are most affected by divorce, as these are most likely to result in improved outcomes for children (Stallman &

Sanders, 2007) and, whenever possible, should be empirically tested to ensure optimal use of resources. Family Transitions Triple P offers a way to provide families with a high standard of care in promoting positive outcomes for children. While group sessions provide parents the perspective of other parents, further research is needed to evaluate other modalities, such as self-directed or individual, for parents who are unable to attend group sessions.

As a final note, new opportunities to help parents experiencing divorce may be undertaken. Over the past 20 years, there has been a rise in the proportion of divorce applications launched jointly in Australia (Australian Bureau of Statistics, 2015). As the application may be an early indicator of how families are managing the divorce process, this suggests that, at least in the initial stages, there is a rise in the proportion of divorcing couples who are able to work more collaboratively. This may create new opportunities to provide prevention programs that foster ongoing cooperation between former partners with respect to parenting tasks and prevent derailment into co-parenting conflict. Investigation into minimally sufficient programs to support these parents as they transition into redefining their families and continuing to parent harmoniously is needed, as these would be helpful to many families at the time of their divorce application.

KEY MESSAGES

- Divorce is a stressful life experience for parents and children. Children of divorcing parents are at risk of short- and long-term adverse outcomes, including behavioral and emotional symptoms, as well as physical health, social, and academic problems.
- Parenting programs have the potential to modify the risk factors for poor outcomes for children.
- Family Transitions Triple P is one of the few parenting programs that have been empirically evaluated. The program has been demonstrated to improve the competence and confidence of parents to manage the transition through divorce, irrespective of the behavior of their former partner.
- As an early intervention, Family Transitions Triple P has the potential to assist parents at the time of separation, prior to mediation, and as part of court-mandated orders. With high rates of divorces that involve children, this may be the key to promoting positive child outcomes.

REFERENCES

Afifi, T. O., Cox, B. J., & Enns, M. W. (2006). Mental health profiles among married, never-married and separated/divorced mothers in a nationally representative sample. *Social Psychiatry and Psychiatric Epidemiology, 41,* 122–129. doi:10.1007/s00127-005-0005-3

Amato, P. R. (2010). Research on divorce: Continuing trends and new developments. *Journal of Marriage and Family, 72,* 650–666. doi:10.1111/j.1741-3737.2010.00723.x

Amato, P. R., & Cheadle, J. (2005). The long reach of divorce: Divorce and child well-being across three generations. *Journal of Marriage and Family, 67,* 191–206. doi:10.1111/j.0022-2445.2005.00014.x

Amato, P. R., & Cheadle, J. E. (2008). Parental divorce, marital conflict and children's behavior problems: A comparison of adopted and biological children. *Social Forces, 86*, 1139–1161. doi:10.1353/sof.0.0025

Australian Bureau of Statistics. (2015). *3310.0—Marriages and divorces, Australia, 2014*. Canberra, Australia: Author.

Carr, A. (2012). *Family therapy: Concepts, process and practice* (3rd ed.). Chichester, England: Wiley.

Christophersen, E. R., & Mortweet, S. L. (2003). Dealing with divorce. In E. R. Christophersen & S. L. Mortweet (Eds.), *Parenting that works: Building skills that last a lifetime* (pp. 163–175). Washington, DC: American Psychological Association.

Coleman, L., & Glenn, F. (2010). The varied impact of couple relationship breakdown on children: Implications for practice and policy. *Children & Society, 24*, 238–249. doi:10.1111/j.1099-0860.2009.00289.x

Elam, K. K., Sandler, I., Wolchik, S., & Tein, J. Y. (2016). Non-residential father-child involvement, interparental conflict and mental health of children following divorce: A person-focused approach. *Journal of Youth and Adolescence, 45*, 581–593. doi:10.1007/s10964-015-0399-5

Fabricius, W. V., & Luecken, L. J. (2007). Postdivorce living arrangements, parent conflict, and long-term physical health correlates for children of divorce. *Journal of Family Psychology, 21*, 195–205. doi:10.1037/0893-3200.21.2.195

Forgatch, M. S., & DeGarmo, D. S. (1999). Parenting through change: An effective prevention program for single mothers. *Journal of Consulting and Clinical Psychology, 67*, 711–724. doi:10.1037/0022-006X.67.5.711

Garber, B. D. (2004). Directed co-parenting intervention: Conducting child-centered interventions in parallel with highly conflicted co-parents. *Professional Psychology: Research and Practice, 35*, 55–64. doi:10.1037/0735-7028.35.1.55

Hartman, L. R., Magalhaes, L., & Mandich, A. (2011). What does parental divorce or marital separation mean for adolescents? A scoping review of North American literature. *Journal of Divorce and Remarriage, 52*, 490–518. doi:http://d10.1080/10502556.2011.609432

Hughes, R., Clark, C. D., Schaefer-Hernan, P., & Good, E. S. (1994). An evaluation of a newsletter intervention for divorced mothers. *Family Relations, 43*, 298–304. doi:10.2307/585421

Jackson, K. M., Rogers, M. L., & Sartor, C. E. (2016). Parental divorce and initiation of alcohol use in early adolescence. *Psychology of Addictive Behaviors, 30*, 450–461. doi:10.1037/adb0000164

Keating, A., Sharry, J., Murphy, M., Rooney, B., & Carr, A. (2016). An evaluation of the Parents Plus—Parenting When Separated programme. *Clinical Child Psychology and Psychiatry, 21*, 240–254. doi:10.1177/1359104515581717

Kelly, J. B. (2003). Parents with enduring child disputes: Multiple pathways to enduring disputes. *Journal of Family Studies, 9*, 37–50. doi:10.5172/jfs.9.1.37

King, V., & Heard, H. E. (1999). Nonresident father visitation, parental conflict, and mother's satisfaction: What's best for child well-being? *Journal of Marriage and Family, 61*, 385–396. doi:10.2307/353756

Lizardi, D., Thompson, R. G., Keyes, K., & Hasin, D. (2009). Parental divorce, parental depression, and gender differences in adult offspring suicide attempt. *The Journal of Nervous and Mental Disease, 197*, 899–901. doi:10.1097/NMD.0b013e3181c299ac

McEwen, B. S., & Wingfield, J. C. (2003). The concept of allostasis in biology and biomedicine. *Hormones and Behavior, 43*, 2–15. doi:10.1016/S0018-506X(02)00024-7

Milan, A. (2016). Families, living arrangements and unpaid work. In *Women in Canada: A gender-based statistical report* (7th ed.). Ottawa, Canada: Statistics Canada. Retrieved from http://www.statcan.gc.ca/access_acces/alternative_alternatif.action?l=eng&loc=http://www.statcan.gc.ca/pub/89-503-x/2015001/article/14235-eng.pdf

O'Connor, B. P., & Dvorak, T. (2002). Conditional associations between interparental conflict and adolescent problems: A search for personality-environment interactions. In S. P. Shohov (Ed.), *Advances in psychology research* (Vol. 14, pp. 213–237). Hauppauge, NY: Nova Science.

Office for National Statistics. (2015). *Divorces in England and Wales: 2013*. London, England: Author.

Rollie, S. S., & Duck, S. (2006). Divorce and dissolution of romantic relationships: Stage models and their limitations. In M. A. Fine & J. H. Harvey (Eds.), *Handbook of divorce and relationship dissolution* (pp. 223–240). New York, NY: Psychology Press.

Ruschena, E., Prior, M., Sanson, A., & Smart, D. (2005). A longitudinal study of adolescent adjustment following family transitions *Journal of Child Psychology and Psychiatry, 46*, 353–363. doi:10.1111/j.1469-7610.2004.00369.x

Sanders, M. R., Markie-Dadds, C., & Turner, K. M. T. (2001). *Practitioner's manual for Group Triple P.* Milton, Australia: Triple P International.

Stallman, H. M., & Ohan, J. L. (2016). Parenting style, parental adjustment, and co-parental conflict: Differential predictors of child psychosocial adjustment following divorce. *Behaviour Change, 33*, 112–126. doi:10.1017/bec.2016.7

Stallman, H. M., & Sanders, M. R. (2007). Family Transitions Triple P: The theoretical basis and development of a program for parents going through divorce. *Journal of Divorce and Remarriage, 47*, 133–153. doi:10.1300/J087v47n03_07

Stallman, H. M., & Sanders, M. R. (2010). *Facilitator's manual for Family Transitions Triple P.* Brisbane, Australia: Triple P International.

Stallman, H. M., & Sanders, M. R. (2014). A randomized controlled trial of Family Transitions Triple P: A group-administered parenting program to minimize the adverse effects of parental divorce on children. *Journal of Divorce and Remarriage, 55*, 33–48. doi:10.1080/10502556.2013.862091

Storksen, I., Roysamb, E., Holmen, T. L., & Tambs, K. (2006). Adolescent adjustment and wellbeing: Effects of parental divorce and distress. *Scandinavian Journal of Psychology, 47*, 75–84. doi:10.1111/j.1467-9450.2006.00494.x

Strohschein, L. (2012). Parental divorce and child mental health: Accounting for predisruption differences. *Journal of Divorce and Remarriage, 53*, 489–502. doi:10.1080/10502556.2012.682903

Sutherland, K. E., Altenhofen, S., & Biringen, Z. (2012). Emotional availability during mother–child interactions in divorcing and intact married families. *Journal of Divorce and Remarriage, 53*, 126–141. doi:10.1080/10502556.2011.651974

Tartari, M. (2015). Divorce and the cognitive achievement of children *International Economic Review, 56*, 597–645. doi:10.1111/iere.12116

Turkat, I. D. (2002). Shared parenting dysfunction. *The American Journal of Family Therapy, 30*, 385–393. doi:10.1080/01926180260296297

Valentine, K., & Katz, I. (2007). *Cost effectiveness of early intervention programs for Queensland.* South Brisbane, Australia: Queensland Council of Social Service.

Vuchinich, S., Vuchinich, R., & Wood, B. (1993). The interparental relationship and family problem solving with preadolescent males. *Child Development, 64*, 1389–1400. doi:10.1111/j.1467-8624.1993.tb02959.x

Whitehurst, D. H., O'Keefe, S. O., & Wilson, R. A. (2008). Divorced and separated parents in conflict. *Journal of Divorce and Remarriage, 48*, 127–144. doi:10.1300/J087v48n03_08

USING POSITIVE PARENTING PROGRAMS IN DIFFERENT DELIVERY SYSTEMS

CHAPTER 19

USING POSITIVE PARENTING PROGRAMS IN DIFFERENT DELIVERY SYSTEMS

An Introduction

MATTHEW R. SANDERS

INTRODUCTION

The parenting role involves coming into contact with a variety of people, settings, services, and agencies as a normal part of raising a child. The precise configuration and timing of contact with these services and agencies varies somewhat depending on the country where children are raised. However, it is highly likely that the vast majority of parents in most Western countries will take their children to their general practitioner or family doctor when the children are unwell or need to be immunized. In the early years they may have regular contact with a community primary health care nurse or health visitor. Most parents these days will have contact with some kind of child care or early childhood education center; they will enroll their child in a school and get to know their child's teacher; and they will spend a lot of time in their place of work when they return for either part-time or full-time employment. These are places where it is common and not considered exceptional in any way for parents to seek and receive advice about various aspects of raising children, from information about children's health to promoting their learning and peer relationships. These settings are largely free of stigma and judgment; for most families, they are just a normal everyday aspect of living in a community. Each of these settings has unique opportunities to deliver effective evidence-based prevention interventions, such as evidence-based parenting support (EBPS).

The Triple P system was designed to take advantage of these destigmatized, socially normative points of contact for parents by designing specific interventions that could be delivered in each of these settings. It is possible to substantially increase the reach of evidence-based parenting programs (Sanders, 2008) by having multiple agencies and disciplines across the health, education, and welfare sectors collaborate in a population strategy. As no one service delivery sector has a monopoly or can be viewed as the only natural or legitimate home for parenting support, the Triple P system has aimed to engage with human service sectors that deal with children and families on a regular basis. The strengths and opportunities that arise when different service sectors work together toward a shared vision of increasing parental access to and involvement in positive parenting far outstrip the capacity of any single sector to reach parents on its own. In this section, we begin by discussing the advantages and challenges involved in using the primary health care system (Chapter 20), the early childhood development and child care setting (Chapter 21), the school system (Chapter 22), and the workplace (Chapter 23) as delivery contexts.

Turner and Metzler (Chapter 20) begin by discussing parenting programs in primary health care services. Primary care providers such as family doctors, pediatricians, general practitioners, and community child health nurses are often a first port of call after family and friends for parents seeking professional advice on parenting issues. Turner and Metzler's Chapter 20 describes how Triple P can be applied in brief, in-person, and online interventions through the primary health care system to help prevent and manage social, emotional, and behavioral problems in children. The roles of different types of primary care providers are discussed, along with factors that can contribute to the successful use of Triple P in primary care settings. Key implementation challenges are identified and discussed along with a review of available evidence supporting the effectiveness of Triple P in primary health care settings.

Another important but underutilized context for delivering parenting programs is the child care and early childhood centers. Turner, Dittman, Rusby, and Lee in Chapter 21 remind readers that raising children in contemporary society typically involves shared parenting responsibilities between parent carers and organized child care or in-home carers. Consistency in the management of child behavior in different parenting settings becomes important in any community-based effort for early intervention and prevention of child behavioral and emotional problems. This chapter describes how the Triple P system can be applied in a child care context.

The quality of children's educational experience at school has a major impact on a child's life. Schools in general and teachers in particular are under considerable pressure from multiple sources (e.g., parents, education authorities, teachers themselves, and politicians) to achieve the best academic outcomes. Compilation of league tables that compare schools academic performance and repeated testing of children place enormous pressure on individual teachers and schools' leadership and administration. Chapter 22 by Hodges and Healy discusses the school environment and education system as a context for delivering population-based parenting programs. Positive parenting programs can help ensure that children entering school for the first time have the necessary social, emotional, and language competencies to benefit from the typically more structured learning that takes place in the school environment. Schools represent another destigmatized context for the provision of both universal and targeted brief parenting interventions for many, but not all, parents. This chapter describes how schools can organize the delivery of parenting services to ensure good home–school communication and a common approach to the promotion of children's academic success. The chapter begins with a consideration of why the school context is appropriate as a place to deliver parenting programs. Key implementation challenges are discussed along with a possible model for delivery through schools of various aspects of the multilevel Triple P system. Indeed, individual schools can adopt the multilevel approach either on their own or with other nearby schools in partnership.

The vast majority of parents return to some kind of paid employment relatively soon after the birth of their children. This developmentally normative transition back to work brings some special challenges in balancing work and family responsibilities. Many parents can find the transition stressful, and it can adversely affect functioning at work and at home. Chapter 23 by Haslam and Penman discusses the relationship between parenting, family relationships, and the workplace and describes how the Triple P system can be applied to a variety of workplace environments (e.g., government, private sector) as well as through employee assistance programs. Following a brief review of the effectiveness of workplace Triple P in different types of workplaces, the authors discuss important implications for practice and future research.

Completing a program should become an everyday normal occurrence as unremarkable as participating in any other activity, such as going to birthing classes, getting a well-child check from a family doctor, getting children immunized, seeking advice from teachers about helping children with their homework, or seeing a taxation consultant to complete income tax forms. To make an integrated system of parenting support really work and to avoid redundancy requires various community stakeholders to build good collaborative relationships and working alliances so that multiple sectors can form meaningful partnerships.

A lead agency is required to coordinate parenting support; however, parenting support should not be controlled by a single service sector. Primary health care services and providers (e.g., general practitioners, pediatricians, and community child health nurses), early childhood education and care providers, and schools that collectively and individually engage with a large percentage of families every year should be good candidates for partnering in delivering EBPS. However, each of these settings has challenges and obstacles that, if not overcome, will result in low utilization of evidence-based programs, low participation of parents, and high cost per family. Low-intensity programs with the greatest reach, such as Triple P seminars, discussion groups, and individual consultations using Primary Care Triple P, are preferred for delivering parenting programs through specialized services (e.g., child and adolescent mental health services) that can be associated with stigma.

This section also discusses the challenge of supporting parents in the context of a natural disaster (Chapter 24, this volume). Following a natural disaster (e.g., a flood, wildfire, hurricane, tsunami, tornado, or earthquake), family life and the operation of all service delivery systems can be markedly disrupted. In the immediate aftermath of a disaster, entire families can experience considerable distress, anxiety, loss, and disruption of regular household routines. When everyday parenting is disrupted by acts of either nature or humankind, positive parenting practices can help return family life to some semblance of normality as soon as possible. Chapter 24 by Cobham, McDermott, and Sanders charts an important new area of research and development for Triple P, focusing on the role of parents to prepare children either to cope with a natural disaster or to recover postdisaster. The authors discuss the complementary role of brief parenting interventions in the form of parenting seminars as part of a comprehensive response to natural disaster to prevent the development of trauma-related disorders.

All population-based approaches to parenting support require an effective media and communication strategy to engage parents. In addition to accessing parenting support directly by speaking to a professional, modern parents increasingly look to the Internet and mass media for information about parenting. Chapter 25 by Metzler and Rusby examines how Triple P has used broadcast television programming and other media interventions (e.g., radio, advertising, video and audio streaming services, podcasts, and social media) to increase access to positive parenting in a popular format on a larger scale. Surveys in the United States, Canada, Australia, and the United Kingdom have shown that two of the most preferred ways for parents to access parenting advice is watching television programs on parenting or using the Internet (Metzler, Sanders, Rusby, & Crowley, 2012). This chapter details evidence such as trials showing that watching other parents participate in a group parenting program (Group Triple P) on television can be effective in changing the parenting practices of the viewing audience (Calam, Sanders, Miller, Sadhnani, & Carmont, 2008) and discusses the important considerations for using media approaches and embedding media in a larger system of community supports for parents.

Finally, we turn to the use of the Internet as a vehicle for delivery of online versions of Triple P. Triple P has embraced advances in technology and the explosion of information about parenting that modern parents can now access globally. However, much of this general information available through the Internet is not evidence based, and the fields of child and adolescent mental health and family intervention services are still working out how best to work with parenting programs that provide technology-based solutions to parenting problems. Turner, Baker, and Day's Chapter 26 documents the development, evaluation, and subsequent dissemination of Triple P Online, an interactive online platform targeting parents of children aged 2 to 12 years. The authors explore some unique opportunities and challenges in using technology in an age of technology to help raise children. This chapter examines the role of technology-assisted delivery of parenting programs and seeks to identify the conditions that enhance program outcomes and program completions by parents, including the provision of professional support.

This section illustrates that a population approach to parenting support is more likely to be effective if multiple agencies in a community that parents come into contact with embrace and support a coordinated approach and utilize media and technology tools effectively to reach parents. This section covers multiple contexts and media from which parents can obtain support and highlights the importance of a comprehensive strategy for making a population approach to EBPS really work.

REFERENCES

Calam, R., Sanders, M. R., Miller, C., Sadhnani, V., & Carmont, S. A. (2008). Can technology and the media help reduce dysfunctional parenting and increase engagement with preventative parenting interventions? *Child Maltreatment, 13*, 347–361. doi:10.1177/1077559508321272

Metzler, C. W., Sanders, M. R., Rusby, J. C., & Crowley, R. N. (2012). Using consumer preference information to increase the reach and impact of media-based parenting interventions in a public health approach to parenting support. *Behavior Therapy, 43*, 257–270. doi:10.1016/j.beth.2011.05.004

Sanders, M. R. (2008). "Going to scale": Implementing a population-level parenting and family support intervention. *The Behavior Therapist, 31*, 11–14.

PARENTING SUPPORT IN THE CONTEXT OF PRIMARY HEALTH CARE

KAREN M. T. TURNER AND CAROL W. METZLER

INTRODUCTION

When parenting programs are delivered through mental health settings, parents are often wary of stigma and are hesitant to access services due to the potential identification of their children's behavior as "pathological" or their parenting as "problematic." These services are also detached from ongoing health care relationships or support (Perrin, Leslie, & Boat, 2016). Many pediatric primary care health services are recognizing their role beyond traditional care in promoting social, emotional, and behavioral health, including directly offering parenting support (Oppenheim et al., 2016). Primary care providers such as family doctors, pediatricians, and community child health nurses have multiple contacts with young children and are a trusted first port of call for parents seeking advice on parenting issues and are, for many families, the only point of contact with a professional (Earls & Hay, 2006). This makes primary care settings ideal for providing parenting support as part of universal preventive "well-child" services (Perrin et al., 2016). This chapter describes how Triple P can be applied in brief interventions through the primary health care system to prevent and reduce social, emotional, and behavioral problems in children.

WHY A PRIMARY HEALTH CARE CONTEXT?

With its wide reach and normalized approach to delivering health care to children and families, the pediatric primary care visit holds much promise as an avenue for reaching parents. Several features of the pediatric primary care setting make it ideal for the early detection of child behavior problems and parenting difficulties and for disseminating universal and targeted parenting interventions. First, in the context of well-child services, access to universal parenting supports does not depend on the child or parent being identified as having a deficit or problem; thus, parents are not subjected to implied criticism or stigma. Second, the primary care relationship involves frequent routine well-child visits, providing multiple opportunities for screening, support, and intervention. Third, parents frequently seek advice about their children's behavior during health care visits, providing an ideal opening for the provision of evidence-based parenting supports. Fourth, preventive intervention can occur within a long-term, trusted, and supportive relationship with the health care provider. Finally, programs can be made available to all parents who are experiencing difficulties with their parenting or with their children's behavior or development or on the basis of screening for specific child behavior or parenting challenges (Perrin et al., 2016).

Several evidence-based parenting programs have been successfully integrated into primary care settings, demonstrating feasibility and showing promising effects on child and family outcomes. Studies with Triple P (McCormick et al., 2014); the Incredible Years (Perrin, Sheldrick, McMenamy, Henson, & Carter, 2014); and Healthy Steps (Piotrowski, Talavera, & Mayer, 2009) have shown that a wide range of health care staff can be trained to successfully implement parenting programs, producing positive changes in parents' discipline practices and in children's behavior (Leslie et al., 2016). In a meta-analysis of 13 studies of parenting interventions delivered in primary health care settings, Shah, Kennedy, Clark, Bauer, and Schwartz (2016) found consistently positive effects on parent–child interactions and stimulating activities.

PARENTING SUPPORT IN PRIMARY CARE SETTINGS

A wide range of health care providers may be deployed in the delivery of parenting support services in primary care settings. Physicians (general practitioners [GPs], pediatricians); nursing staff; specialists (behavioral health, mental health, or developmental specialists); social workers; patient care coordinators; and community health workers may all be involved in delivering parenting support services. Health care systems differ across countries and regions, and the way in which providers are utilized in the delivery of parenting support services may vary as well. These variations have implications for which provider does what, for clinic workflow, and for funding models for program implementation and sustainability (Kolko & Perrin, 2014). For example, physicians or nurse practitioners may deliver brief parenting interventions in dedicated consultation sessions, or they may begin the discussion with parents in the context of a regular clinic visit and then do a "warm handoff" or coordinated referral to another specialist within or external to the clinic. Parenting supports may be provided in one-on-one sessions, discussion groups, seminars, or workshops hosted by the clinic or through online programs with or without auxiliary practitioner support.

In some regions, there is effort under way to integrate services such that primary care settings become a health care "home" across the spectrum of physical, behavioral, and mental health needs. This movement toward integration provides a useful opening for the integration of parenting interventions as well. Interestingly, Triple P began this effort toward integration 25 years ago as part of its multilevel system approach to parenting support.

KEY IMPLEMENTATION ISSUES IN MAKING TRIPLE P WORK IN A PRIMARY CARE CONTEXT

Key issues in training health care practitioners to deliver Triple P include developing their confidence to effectively deliver parent consultations and skill rehearsal with parents. Behavioral rehearsal and using a self-regulatory approach to help parents develop their own solutions are consultation processes that are not always familiar to health practitioners, who are often more accustomed to providing expert advice and referrals. A second issue is achieving a good fit between program delivery format and a clinic's capacity and workflow, including specification of the clinical model (e.g., who delivers the intervention to whom, how, and when) and carving out the time needed for program delivery. These issues are discussed in more detail in the material that follows. A survey of Primary Care Triple P (PCTP) practitioners showed that program supports (e.g., quality of format and materials) and barriers (e.g., management difficulties and lack of fit) affected practitioners' self-efficacy, and higher self-efficacy was positively associated with program implementation (Turner, Nicholson, & Sanders, 2011).

WHAT ARE PRIMARY CARE TRIPLE P AND SELECTED TRIPLE P?

In the late 1990s, the Triple P multilevel system first extended from tertiary individual or group family interventions (Level 4) to the three- to four-session PCTP program (Level 3) with skill rehearsal for parents of children with mild-to-moderate specific emotional, behavioral, or developmental concerns, and a brief one- to two-session intervention (Level 2) providing early anticipatory guidance for mild issues to be delivered in primary health care settings (Turner, Sanders, & Markie-Dadds, 2010). Since then, it has also evolved to include PCTP Discussion Groups on specific topics (Level 3; Sanders & Turner, 2011) and Selected Triple P Seminar Series (Level 2; Sanders & Turner, 2012).

Level 3 Primary Care Triple P

Primary Care Triple P (Level 3) involves three or four 30-minute sessions that incorporate active skills training and the use of parenting tip sheets for common developmental and behavioral problems. The first session is an intake interview and establishes baseline monitoring of problem behavior. In the second session, monitoring results are reviewed to clarify the cause of the problem, and a parenting plan is developed and rehearsed. The third session involves a progress review and additional skill rehearsal as needed. A fourth session may be scheduled to troubleshoot any difficulties, refine the parenting plan, and encourage generalization.

Level 3 Triple P Discussion Groups

The Triple P Discussion Group Series at Level 3 addresses common developmental and behavioral concerns, such as disobedience, fighting and aggression, bedtime, and going shopping. Discussion groups are limited in size to about 10 parents or fewer to allow for open discussion and peer support. The 2-hour sessions involve video modeling, problem-solving exercises, and a tailored implementation plan. Parents may attend a single discussion group or a series of groups.

Level 2 Brief Primary Care Triple P

As an individual program, Level 2 Selected Triple P is a brief one- or two-session intervention for parents with specific concerns about their child's behavior or development. Practical information on preventing or solving a target problem is provided within a brief (up to 20 minutes) consultation format that clarifies the presenting problem and uses a parenting tip sheet to develop a tailored parenting plan. A follow-up appointment or telephone call is recommended to check on the family's progress.

Level 2 Triple P Seminars

Selected Triple P as a group program comprises three seminars (Level 2) designed for all interested parents. These seminars involve 60 minutes of presentation and 30 minutes of question time. Seminars focus on general principles as well as specific strategies. Topics include *The Power of Positive Parenting; Raising Confident, Competent Children*; and *Raising Resilient Children*.

BRIEF REVIEW OF EFFICACY

PRIMARY CARE TRIPLE P

The first foundational trial of PCTP was a randomized controlled trial (RCT) evaluating the impact of training GPs on their parent consultation skills, satisfaction, and confidence in conducting consultations with parents (Sanders, Turner, Maher, Tully, & McAuliffe, 2003). Compared to a wait-list control, GPs who received the PCTP training had greater use of targeted parent consultation skills and reported greater confidence in their consultation skills related to child behavior and greater satisfaction with the outcomes of these consultations (see Box 20.1 for an example of the type of feedback received from physicians).

The second RCT assessed family outcomes of PCTP delivered in routine care by community health nurses (Turner & Sanders, 2006). Compared to controls, families receiving PCTP reported lower levels of child behavior problems, dysfunctional parenting, and parental anxiety and stress, with results largely maintained at 6-month follow-up. Boyle and colleagues (2010) examined the generalization of effects across settings and found reduced child disruptive behavior in the target setting and in generalization settings.

Independent trials of PCTP have now been conducted. For example, trials have shown equivalent improvements in parenting style and reduction in child emotional and behavior problems compared to existing Dutch services for primary care parenting support, with slightly greater improvement for PCTP in the longer term (De Graaf, Onrust, Haverman, & Janssens,

---

**BOX 20.1: Pediatricians' Feedback on
Primary Care Triple P**

- Every parent can use some help with positive discipline, and I think this program provides a great framework. I would definitely recommend it to parents that are struggling with strong-willed children or are concerned about other discipline challenges.
- I would love to recommend it to most families as a part of well-child care. I would actually love to have my families see a parenting coach as a part of well-child care, but I think this kind of information would be great not only as treatment but as prevention!
- There was nothing about the program that I did not like.
- It was a revelation to me as a parent that my behavior/tone of voice/timing, has a lot to do with my children's behavior . . . making this point explicitly might help those who are slower (like my husband and I) to figure it out.

—Pediatricians' comments, Seattle, Washington, USA

2009; Spijkers, Jansen, & Reijneveld, 2013) and, when added to another group-based parent education program in Canada, higher levels of parent-reported need satisfaction (McConnell, Breitkreuz, & Savage, 2012).

One Dutch trial evaluated the impact of PCTP for children born prematurely or with perinatal asphyxia, compared to a wait-list control (Schappin et al., 2013), and found that intervention effects on emotional and behavioral problems did not maintain at 6- or 12-month follow-up. These results would not support the use of the program with perinatal intensive care recipients. Stepping Stones PCTP (Sanders, Mazzucchelli, & Studman, 2009), designed for parents of children with developmental disabilities, may be more appropriate. Compared to usual care, an Australian RCT showed that Stepping Stones PCTP improved child behavior, dysfunctional parenting, and parents' confidence, stress, and relationship quality for parents of children with autism spectrum disorder (Tellegen & Sanders, 2014).

TRIPLE P DISCUSSION GROUPS

Two foundational RCTs of the Discussion Group format were conducted. The first was for parents of children showing disruptive behavior on shopping trips (Joachim, Sanders, & Turner, 2010). Compared to a wait-list control, intervention effects were found for child problem behavior, dysfunctional parenting, and parenting confidence 4 weeks after the group session, and these were maintained at 6-month follow-up. A second RCT evaluating the Disobedience Discussion Group plus two phone calls (Morawska, Haslam, Milne, & Sanders, 2011) also showed reductions in child behavior problems and dysfunctional parenting and improvements in parental self-efficacy and parenting experience at postassessment, maintained at 6-month follow-up.

Discussion groups have also been successfully trialed in diverse cultures such as Panama (Mejia, Calam, & Sanders, 2015) and Hong Kong (Chung, Leung, & Sanders, 2015). The latter study allocated parents of preschool-age children to Group Triple P, the Disobedience Discussion Group, or a wait-list control. Both interventions led to a decrease in child behavior problems compared to controls. Comparable outcomes of the discussion group and intensive group program show promise for brief early intervention.

BRIEF PRIMARY CARE TRIPLE P

Less research has been conducted on Brief PCTP as a stand-alone intervention rather than as part of a multilevel offering. Early service evaluation work found slightly less strong outcomes for the one- to two-session program compared to the three- to four-session primary care intervention (Matthews, Cann, Sultana, & Rogers, 2001). A further study found that outcomes for the briefer intervention fell in between PCTP (which showed decreased child problems and aversive parenting compared to wait list) and a wait-list comparison, although there were no significant differences from either (Sultana, Matthews, De Bortoli, & Cann, 2004). Effects of such a light-touch intervention may be better viewed in terms of prevention of problems intensifying than in reducing elevated existing problems.

TRIPLE P SEMINARS

The first evaluation of Selected Triple P (Sanders, Prior, & Ralph, 2009) compared attendance at a single introductory seminar, attendance at all three seminars, and a wait-list control. The introductory seminar alone showed a reduction in parental reports of child problem behavior and dysfunctional parenting; however, exposure to all three seminars was associated with improvements in dysfunctional parenting and interparental conflict. Although there were no condition effects on parental adjustment, confidence, or relationship quality, the findings support the notion that positive outcomes for parents and children can be achieved through brief preventive interventions that require minimal time commitment from parents.

This was supported by an Indonesian RCT (Sumargi, Sofronoff, & Morawska, 2015), which found the Triple P Seminar Series led to a greater decrease in child behavior problems, dysfunctional parenting, and parental stress and a greater increase in parenting confidence compared to wait-list parents at postintervention, which were maintained at 6-month follow-up. In addition, a New Zealand single-group study (Chand, Farruggia, Dittman, Chu, & Sanders, 2013) showed the Teen Triple P Seminar Series was associated with increases in positive parenting and decreases in ineffective parenting; improvements were also observed in family relationships and reduced adolescent–parent conflict and interparental conflict.

BROADER IMPLEMENTATION ISSUES

Although primary health care settings have unique features that make them an ideal venue for delivering evidence-based parenting interventions, such as existing infrastructure, non-stigmatizing location, regular contact, trusted professionals, and broad reach, they also have features that create implementation challenges. Primary care settings have multidisciplinary staff, and visits are episodic, with a fast-paced, choreographed workflow and severe time constraints (Crawford & Briggs, 2016). Clinic visits are not divided into weekly sessions scheduled in advance, as in a mental health clinic. These features create the need to carefully plan for implementation issues in delivering parenting interventions.

THE CLINICAL MODEL

Issues concerning the clinical model center on how the parenting program will be integrated into clinic workflow. There are a number of factors to be considered:

- *Target population*: the target age groups and to what extent the program will be universally delivered to all families at a given age versus targeted at families with specific difficulties
- *Integration with current services*: the extent to which behavioral and mental health services are already integrated into clinic services and how the new parenting program can build on that integration
- *Screening and identification*: the inclusion criteria and screening process for identifying the families who might benefit from the program
- *Program delivery*: determining the format (consultation, self-administered, multisession groups, stand-alone discussion groups) that provides the best fit for clinic resources, time constraints, and patient population and whether the program will be delivered within the clinic and by whom and when or whether referral will be made to an off-site provider and how the referral will be handled to ensure follow-through
- *Family engagement and support*: how families will be invited to engage in the program and how their engagement will be supported

WORKFORCE DEVELOPMENT, CLINIC SUPPORT, AND FUNDING MODELS

Workforce development, clinic management support, and funding models are additional implementation factors that require careful planning. Training and supervision requirements must be considered, not only for those directly providing the program but also for those in support roles. Adjustments to physical space utilization and to scheduling, billing, and workflow systems may be needed to support effective and sustained implementation. Finally, sustainable funding models must be developed to ensure that primary care providers can be paid for providing these programs. The nature of funding models may differ dramatically across countries and regions, depending on the degree to which health care is funded by public versus private dollars and the specific regulations in place relevant to payment for parenting-related services (Leslie et al., 2016).

No doubt, the format of interventions adopted in primary care settings will continue to evolve. We are currently evaluating a triaged multilevel system of Triple P Online when recommended to parents by their pediatrician. Should such a self-directed format prove successful and desirable in this setting, funding models would again need to be explored.

IMPLICATIONS AND FUTURE DIRECTIONS

There are increasing calls for the application of science-based knowledge to improve the social, emotional, and behavioral health of children, including increased support for the widespread dissemination of evidence-based parenting interventions, and pediatric primary care is receiving increased attention as an important setting for delivery of these parenting supports. At the time of writing, a US national collaborative had been organized to advocate for evidence-based parenting programs in primary care, housed within the National Academies of Science, Engineering, and Medicine's Forum on Promoting Children's Cognitive, Affective, and Behavioral Health (Leslie et al., 2016). This collaborative is advocating advancement of policy to support integration and sustainable funding models, more research on parenting interventions delivered through primary care, and learning collaboratives to create effective implementation models. These goals represent important future directions for moving this effort forward around the world.

CONCLUSION

There is increasing interest in behavioral health integration that promotes healthy development at a population level. With greater awareness of the family protective factors that promote children's social and emotional as well as physical development, primary care providers can build on family strengths during health care visits. Delivery of evidence-based parenting interventions through pediatric primary care settings holds great promise for widespread reach and could benefit many more families than are currently being reached. As behavioral and mental health care are increasingly integrated into physical health care, the opportunity arises to build models that effectively and sustainably incorporate parenting support programs into primary care services. It is a critical time to design models for integrated care in pediatric practices and family-centered health settings and to build the policies, workforce, evidence base, and cost structures that will enable widespread uptake of evidence-based parenting support programs (Oppenheim et al., 2016).

KEY MESSAGES

- Primary care providers such as family physicians, pediatricians, and community health nurses are a trusted, nonstigmatized resource for parents seeking advice on parenting issues, making primary care an ideal setting for early detection of child behavior problems and parenting difficulties and for disseminating parenting interventions.
- Evidence-based interventions such as Triple P have proven acceptable to primary care practitioners, shown significant improvements in professionals' consultation skills regarding child behavior, and led to positive outcomes for parents and children.
- There are many considerations for pediatric practices in implementing evidence-based parenting programs, such as workforce training and supervision, clinic management support, physical space and appointment scheduling, and sustainable funding models.

- Integrating behavioral and mental health care with physical health care has the potential to dramatically increase the reach of quality parenting support.

REFERENCES

Boyle, C. L., Sanders, M. R., Lutzker, J. R., Prinz, R. J., Shapiro, C., & Whitaker, D. J. (2010). An analysis of training, generalization, and maintenance effects of Primary Care Triple P for parents of pre-school-aged children with disruptive behavior. *Child Psychiatry and Human Development, 41,* 114–131. doi:10.1007/s10578-009-0156-7

Chand, N. L., Farruggia, S. P., Dittman, C. K., Chu, J. T. W., & Sanders, M. R. (2013). Promoting positive youth development through a brief parenting intervention program. *Youth Studies Australia, 32,* 29–36.

Chung, S., Leung, C., & Sanders, M. (2015). The Triple P—Positive Parenting Programme: The effectiveness of Group Triple P and brief parent discussion group in school settings in Hong Kong. *Journal of Children's Services, 10,* 339–352. doi:10.1108/JCS-08-2014-0039

Crawford, D. E., & Briggs, R. D. (2016). The goodness of fit between evidence-based early childhood mental health programs and the primary care setting. In R. D. Briggs (Ed.), *Integrated early childhood behavioral health in primary care: A guide to implementation and evaluation* (pp. 35–70). Cham, Switzerland: Springer.

de Graaf, I., Onrust, S., Haverman, M., & Janssens, J. (2009). Helping families improve: An evaluation of two primary care approaches to parenting support in the Netherlands. *Infant and Child Development, 18,* 481–501. doi:10.1002/icd.634

Earls, M. F., & Hay, S. S. (2006). Setting the stage for success: Implementation of developmental and behavioral screening and surveillance in primary care practice—The North Carolina Assuring Better Child Health and Development (ABCD) Project. *Pediatrics, 118,* e183–e188. doi:10.1542/peds.2006-0475

Joachim, S., Sanders, M. R., & Turner, K. M. T. (2010). Reducing preschoolers' disruptive behavior in public with a brief parent discussion group. *Child Psychiatry and Human Development, 41,* 47–60. doi:10.1007/s10578-009-0151-z

Kolko, D. J., & Perrin, E. (2014). The integration of behavioral health interventions in children's health care: Services, science, and suggestions. *Journal of Clinical Child and Adolescent Psychology, 43,* 216–228. doi:10.1080/15374416.2013.862804

Leslie, L. K., Mehus, C., J., Hawkins, J. D., Boat, T., McCabe, M. A., Barkin, S., . . . Beardslee, W. (2016). Primary health care: Potential home for family-focused preventive interventions. *American Journal of Preventive Medicine, 51,* S106–S118. doi:10.1016/j.amepre.2016.05.014

Matthews, J., Cann, W., Sultana, C., & Rogers, H. (2001). *Brief behavioural family intervention incorporating written advice: Two studies with differing degrees of therapist input.* Paper presented at the World Congress of Cognitive Behavioural Therapy, Vancouver, Canada.

McConnell, D., Breitkreuz, R., & Savage, A. (2012). Independent evaluation of the Triple P Positive Parenting Program in family support service settings. *Child and Family Social Work, 17,* 43–54. doi:10.1111/j.1365-2206.2011.00771.x

McCormick, E., Kerns, S. E., McPhillips, H., Wright, J., Christakis, D. A., & Rivara, F. P. (2014). Training pediatric residents to provide parent education: A randomized controlled trial. *Academic Pediatrics, 14,* 353–360. doi:10.1016/j.acap.2014.03.009

Mejia, A., Calam, R., & Sanders, M. R. (2015). A pilot randomized controlled trial of a brief parenting intervention in low-resource settings in Panama. *Prevention Science, 16,* 707–717. doi:10.1007/s11121-015-0551-1

Morawska, A., Haslam, D., Milne, D., & Sanders, M. R. (2011). Evaluation of a brief parenting discussion group for parents of young children. *Journal of Developmental and Behavioral Pediatrics, 32,* 136–145. doi:10.1097/DBP.0b013e3181f17a28

Oppenheim, J., Stewart, W., Zoubak, E., Donato, I., Huang, L., & Hudock, W. (2016). Launching forward: The integration of behavioral health in primary care as a key strategy for promoting young child wellness. *American Journal of Orthopsychiatry, 86,* 124–131. doi:10.1037/ort0000149

Perrin, E. C., Leslie, L. K., & Boat, T. (2016). Parenting as primary prevention. *JAMA Pediatrics, 170,* 637–638. doi:10.1001/jamapediatrics.2016.0225

Perrin, E. C., Sheldrick, R. C., McMenamy, J. M., Henson, B. S., & Carter, A. S. (2014). Improving parenting skills for families of young children in pediatric settings: A randomized clinical trial. *JAMA Pediatrics, 168,* 16–24. doi:10.1001/jamapediatrics.2013.2919

Piotrowski, C. C., Talavera, G. A., & Mayer, J. A. (2009). Healthy Steps: A systematic review of a preventive practice-based model of pediatric care. *Journal of Developmental and Behavioral Pediatrics, 30,* 91–103. doi:10.1097/DBP.0b013e3181976a95

Sanders, M. R., Mazzucchelli, T. G., & Studman, L. J. (2009). *Practitioner's manual for Primary Care Stepping Stones Triple P: For families with a child who has a disability.* Brisbane, Australia: Triple P International.

Sanders, M. R., Prior, J., & Ralph, A. (2009). An evaluation of a brief universal seminar series on positive parenting: A feasibility study. *Journal of Children's Services, 4,* 4–20. doi:10.1108/17466660200900002

Sanders, M. R., & Turner, K. M. T. (2011). *Facilitator's manual for Selected Triple P* (2nd ed.). Brisbane, Australia: Triple P International.

Sanders, M. R., & Turner, K. M. T. (2012). *Facilitator's manual for Triple P discussion groups.* Brisbane, Australia: Triple P International.

Sanders, M. R., Turner, K. M. T., Maher, C., Tully, L. A., & McAuliffe, C. (2003). Training GPs in parent consultation skills: An evaluation of training for Triple P—Positive Parenting Program. *Australian Family Physician, 32,* 763–768.

Schappin, R., Wijnroks, L., Venema, M. U., Wijnberg-Williams, B., Ravian Veenstra, R., Corine Koopman-Esseboom, C., . . . Jongmans, M. (2013). Brief parenting intervention for parents of NICU graduates: A randomized, clinical trial of Primary Care Triple P. *BMC Pediatrics, 13,* 69. doi:10.1186/1471-2431-13-69

Shah, R., Kennedy, S., Clark, M. D., Bauer, S. C., & Schwartz, A. (2016). Primary care-based interventions to promote positive parenting behaviors: A meta-analysis. *Pediatrics, 137,* e20153393. doi:10.1542/peds.2015-3393

Spijkers, W., Jansen, D. E. M. C., & Reijneveld, S. A. (2013). Effectiveness of Primary Care Triple P on child psychosocial problems in preventive child healthcare: A randomized controlled trial. *BMC Medicine, 11,* 240. doi:10.1186/1741-7015-11-240

Sultana, C. R., Matthews, J., De Bortoli, D., & Cann, W. (2004). *An evaluation of two levels of the Positive Parenting Program (Triple P) delivered by primary care practitioners.* Unpublished manuscript, RMIT University, Melbourne, Australia.

Sumargi, A., Sofronoff, K., & Morawska, A. (2015). A randomized-controlled trial of the Triple P–Positive Parenting Program Seminar Series with Indonesian parents. *Child Psychiatry and Human Development, 46,* 749–761. doi:10.1007/s10578-014-0517-8

Tellegen, C. L., & Sanders, M. R. (2014). A randomized controlled trial evaluating a brief parenting program with children with Autism Spectrum Disorders. *Journal of Consulting and Clinical Psychology, 82,* 1193–1200. doi:10.1037/a0037246

Turner, K. M. T., Nicholson, J. M., & Sanders, M. R. (2011). The role of practitioner self-efficacy, training, program and workplace factors on the implementation of an evidence-based parenting intervention in primary care. *Journal of Primary Prevention, 32,* 95–112. doi:10.1007/s10935-011-0240-1

Turner, K. M. T., & Sanders, M. R. (2006). Help when it's needed first: A controlled evaluation of brief, preventive behavioral family intervention in a primary care setting. *Behavior Therapy, 37*, 131–142. doi:10.1016/j.beth.2005.05.004

Turner, K. M. T., Sanders, M. R., & Markie-Dadds, C. (2010). *Practitioner's manual for Primary Care Triple P* (2nd ed.). Brisbane, Australia: Triple P International.

CHAPTER 21

PARENTING SUPPORT IN AN EARLY CHILDHOOD LEARNING CONTEXT

KAREN M. T. TURNER, CASSANDRA K. DITTMAN,
JULIE C. RUSBY, AND SHAWNA LEE

INTRODUCTION

In contemporary society, raising children involves shared childrearing responsibilities between parents and early childhood educators. Given the high rate of social-emotional and cognitive development during the first 5 years of children's lives (Shonkoff & Phillips, 2000), it is advantageous for parents and early childhood educators to partner in facilitating optimal healthy development of young children. The early education setting has the potential to promote young children's executive functioning and social-emotional competencies, with likely long-term positive impacts. Critical to this endeavor is increasing the availability of research-based professional development programs for early childhood educators.

Consistency in the management of child behavior across settings becomes important in community-based efforts for early intervention and prevention of child behavioral and emotional problems. With this in mind, we recently developed the Positive Early Childhood Education Program (PECE), a variant of Triple P for early childhood learning contexts, to enhance consistency and teamwork between parents and educators. It is an active skills-training program designed to enhance the capacity of educators to promote prosocial behavior and reduce disruptive behavior in young children. Like Triple P, the program is based on social learning and cognitive-behavioral principles integrated with self-regulation concepts. This chapter describes the development and early pilot testing of the program, including the key considerations in applying a behavioral program to the early education setting.

Throughout this chapter, we use terms such as early childhood education and early childhood learning contexts to encompass the breadth of possible group settings that provide care and learning opportunities to young children. This includes formal kindergarten and preschool settings that follow a particular pedagogical philosophy or curriculum, as well as center-based child care and family child care or home-based child care, in which care is provided in the caregiver's home to a group of children who are not part of the caregiver's family. Including all types of community-based early childhood learning and care settings allows for a broad reach to diverse families and children.

WHY AN EARLY CHILDHOOD LEARNING CONTEXT?

Researchers from the behavioral, social, medical, and biological sciences have converged on the notion that nurturing environments play a critical role in promoting well-being (e.g., Biglan, Flay, Embry, & Sandler, 2012). Nurturing environments promote reciprocal language interaction (Hart & Risley, 1995); teach, promote, and reinforce prosocial behavior; and monitor and limit opportunities for problem behavior (Shonkoff, Committee on Psychosocial Aspects of Child and Family Health, Committee on Early Childhood, Adoption, and Dependent Care, and Section on Developmental and Behavioral Pediatrics, 2012). Such environments are argued to provide children with the cognitive, linguistic, social, self-regulatory, and physical skills needed to become successful learners, healthy and productive workers, and contributing members of the community. Research testing the effects of enriching the early environments of young children has, understandably, focused on enhancing the skills and competence of parents via parenting programs. Effective universal implementation of parenting programs has produced significant improvements in population-level indicators of child well-being, including reductions in child maltreatment and child behavioral and emotional problems (Poole, Seal, & Taylor, 2014). However, the impact of parenting programs can be vastly amplified if consideration is given to enhancing the capacity of other adults in a young child's life.

For many young children around the world, the other main caregivers in their lives are their early childhood educators. Participation in early education is increasing. For example, in the 35 Organization for Economic Cooperation and Development (OECD) countries, around a third of children aged under 3 years attend formal child care, and over 80% of 3- to 5-year-olds attend formal child care or early childhood education (OECD, 2014). Participation in high-quality early childhood education, that is, child care characterized by responsive and attentive educators and stimulating play and learning experiences, has been found to be linked to long-term social and academic gains in children during primary school, even after controlling for family background and parenting quality (e.g., Gialamas, Sawyer, Mittinty, & Lynch, 2014). Thus, educators are uniquely placed to provide nurturing environments for young children that support and bolster the effects of quality parenting and potentially buffer the effects of disadvantage and detrimental early family experiences (Goelman, Zdaniuk, Boyce, Armstrong, & Essex, 2014).

The challenge, however, is that the quality of early education and care within and across countries is varied. In addition, the delivery of high-quality early education and care is threatened by low job satisfaction and high staff turnover in the sector, which has been linked to the stress associated with managing significant disruptive child behavior (Rusby, Jones, Crowley, & Smolkowski, 2012). Thus, there is an urgent need for the development of evidence-based professional development and learning programs to better equip services and educators to promote prosocial behavior and manage children's challenging behavior in effective ways.

PARENTING SUPPORT IN EARLY CHILDHOOD EDUCATION SETTINGS

Early childhood educators have a significant caregiving role in children's lives and strive to facilitate children's cognitive and social development. Early childhood settings are an ideal vehicle to provide support to parents, such as with universal parent support campaigns. Parents can also support early childhood educators by providing information about their child that will help identify goals and useful strategies. It is valuable for parents and early educators to have conversations about ways of working with children and goals for their development. For example, low-income minority parents have reported that their children's social-emotional development was critical in preparing their children for entering the school environment (McAllister, Wilson, Green, & Baldwin, 2005).

Communication about the child's interests, strengths, and areas in which skills are developing helps provide information about what the child is likely to find engaging and areas that need support for skill building and growth. Parents bring the long-term perspective on their child's development, as well as knowledge regarding day-to-day experiences that may affect the child's mood and behavior. On the other hand, the early childhood educator brings knowledge about expected typical skills for different developmental levels. The educator also can provide parents with information about how their child interacts with adults and other children in a group setting away from home.

A collaborative approach allows parents and early childhood educators to work together on goal setting and to inform one another about strategies that may work well for the child. Collaborative partnerships between families and educators build trusting relationships and bring about a shared vision on goals and practices (Pianta, Kraft-Sayre, Rimm-Kaufman, Gercke, & Higgins, 2001). Consistency in the guidance of child behavior across home and early education settings is particularly important in community-based efforts for early intervention and prevention of child behavioral and emotional problems. Yet, it can be challenging to bring each individual child's goals in alignment with program priorities, to manage behavioral challenges, and to provide learning opportunities for children with varying developmental needs in a group setting.

KEY IMPLEMENTATION ISSUES IN AN EARLY CHILDHOOD LEARNING CONTEXT

The development and application of behavior management programs within an early learning context require careful consideration of the prevailing philosophies of early childhood education and care. This includes assessing differences in beliefs about child development and identifying any resistance or local regulations relating to particular terminology or behavioral strategies, such as rewards and exclusionary forms of time-out.

In an analysis of the fit of Triple P with the primary early learning philosophies in Canada—Montessori, Waldorf, Reggio Emilia, and High/Scope (Chi, Conliffe, Gatti, & Paul, 2012)—the five core positive parenting principles and 17 strategies were mapped onto each philosophical approach. Commonalities were found across all approaches for having a safe, interesting environment (e.g., quality time, talking to children), although none discusses affection. Similarly, there was universal agreement with having a positive learning environment (e.g., engaging activities, setting a good example); partial agreement on some strategies (e.g., only Montessori and High/Scope discuss praise or rewards, and High/Scope does not focus on providing attention); and none addresses teaching using ask-say-do and behavior charts. Although three approaches address having realistic expectations of children, none covers discipline strategies (with the exception of Montessori, which touches on rule setting and clear, concise instructions). None of the four approaches focuses on early childhood educators looking after their own needs.

The overall fit of Triple P with the common early childhood learning approaches is encouraging. However, the lack of coverage of how to manage difficult behavior indicates this is an area where many early childhood workers feel underskilled and lacking in confidence. Though an assortment of approaches and techniques have been developed for early childhood educators to manage behavior problems in young children while promoting social-emotional development (Brennan, Bradley, Allen, & Perry, 2008; Conners-Burrow, Whiteside-Mansell, McKelvey, Virmani, & Sockwell, 2012; Fox, Hemmeter, Snyder, Binder, & Clarke, 2011; Hemmeter, Ostrosky, & Corso, 2012), research indicates that early childhood educators do not customarily rely on research knowledge to solve practice dilemmas (Buysse & Wesley, 2006). Meeting the needs of children with social-emotional and behavioral challenges remains a key disparity in educators' knowledge and skills (Hemmeter et al., 2012), as is a focus on self-care and support networks for educators.

Over the years, there have been many requests to adapt the Triple P model for the early childhood learning context. The challenge was to do this in a way that allows flexibility to fit with different philosophical, pedagogical, and regulatory parameters. For example, praise and behavior charts do not fit with a philosophy focused on intrinsic motivation. Exclusionary time-out is not allowed under many regulatory and licensing frameworks, and alternatives needed to be explored. Certain language is preferred in many educational settings, such as "guidance" versus "consequences" and "teaching new ways to behave" versus "managing misbehavior." Therefore, as with parents, our aim was to develop a toolkit of strategies to present as options for consideration in developing a plan for each educator and setting.

Internationally, staff attrition in early childhood education environments is higher than that of most other occupations. For example, about half of US child care centers experience staff turnover in a 12-month period, with an average departure rate of 13% of staff (Whitebook, Phillips, & Howes, 2014). This poses another challenge for program implementation in early learning settings. The development and integration of a program for this sector need to allow for stability and sustainability beyond the staff as individuals and to expand to a culture of supported integration of the program and strategies throughout the center as a whole. Therefore, consideration of a variety of aspects, including how and when staff would access the program material, methods to promote equity among new and existing staff, and striking a balance between program philosophy and practice, is essential.

WHAT IS THE POSITIVE EARLY CHILDHOOD EDUCATION PROGRAM?

A parallel to Triple P, PECE is a skills-training program designed to enhance the capacity of early childhood educators to support the learning experiences and social and behavioral competencies of children in their care. The program is based on social learning and cognitive-behavioral principles integrated with concepts of self-regulation and attachment. The intervention has two components: a four-module online program (Turner, Sanders, Dittman, & Rusby, 2015) completed by educators, followed by two to four individual practice sessions that can be facilitated by a coach, such as a center director or lead teacher. The aim of the practice sessions is to support educators to implement the positive early childhood education strategies introduced in the online modules. A face-to-face, skills-based professional training program is available for coaches, covering the content of the online program as well as a model for supportive coaching, which involves practical training in the consultation skills necessary to facilitate coaching sessions using a self-regulatory approach.

Online Modules

The online program is designed to promote positive early childhood education practices, including the use of positive attention, responsivity and praise, strategies to promote children's early learning and independence skills, antecedent strategies to avoid problems and manage transitions, and effective practices for dealing with misbehavior. It comprises four modules: *What Is Positive Child Care? Building Children's Social and Emotional Skills; Developing a Positive Approach to Learning;* and *Helping Children Learn New Ways to Behave.* Each module takes around 60 minutes to complete, and users are given 8 weeks to complete the four modules during work time or at a time and place of their convenience.

The online program incorporates elements to engage participants and improve knowledge acquisition, self-efficacy, and behavior activation, including user-friendly navigation; video-based modeling of all skills and strategies; personalized content (e.g., goal setting, review); practical exercises to prompt problem-solving and self-regulation; and printable resources and e-mail prompting to increase the likelihood of program completion. The self-regulatory framework enables educators to set goals informed by their own values or education philosophy, personal goals, and workplace regulations.

Practice Sessions

The practice sessions are designed to assist educators with the practical implementation of the positive early childhood education skills introduced in the online program. Two to four sessions are conducted, depending on the educators' confidence and implementation skills. Contact is brief (35–50 minutes): 15–20 minutes for the practice task, 15–20 minutes' review and coaching, and 5–10 minutes to discuss other issues. These sessions encourage self-sufficiency in solving child behavior problems and promote generalization of skills across child behaviors and children. The sessions take an active skills-training approach in which educators set their own agenda and goals for session practice and then rehearse skills and self-reflect on their performance according to their goals. Feedback is provided using a self-regulatory approach that involves prompting educators to identify their own strengths, areas of difficulty, and goals for future practice and implementation.

BRIEF REVIEW OF EFFICACY

The online modules of the program (without practice sessions) were pilot tested with a convenience sample of six graduate degree–qualified kindergarten teachers in Australia (Turner,

Dittman, & Lee, 2016). Participants provided qualitative feedback and completed measures of educator discipline practices, confidence in behavior management, quality of educator–child relationships, and child behavior (for one target child) before and after completing the modules. While qualitative feedback on the interactivity and format of the modules was positive, participants reported that the content was better targeted at preservice undergraduate training or in-service professional learning for inexperienced or less qualified early childhood educators. Despite this, even in this small sample, there was a significant increase in the educators' confidence in managing children's behavior from pre- to postintervention, and educators reported a significant increase in children's prosocial behavior. Although no change was found for problem behavior, the pilot shows some promising results.

A randomized controlled trial of the program in its entirety was recently conducted in Alberta, Canada. Twelve child care centers were assigned to either PECE or a wait-list control condition. In total, 91 early childhood educators took part, each selecting a target child for whom they had some concerns about the child's social or emotional development or behavior. Program completion took longer than expected. At postintervention, after 10 weeks of program access, none of the participants in the intervention group had completed all online modules; therefore, none had participated in coaching sessions. Most had completed the online modules by 2-month follow-up, but less than 30% had participated in coaching sessions by that time. Most educators reported ease of accessing the program online, the flexibility that online delivery allowed in terms of demands on their own time, and the ability to watch and rewatch videos and explore exercises at their own pace as positive aspects of the program. Some indicated that they wished there was more support from their management team to complete the modules during their workday rather than being expected to do it on their own time. In centers where workday completion was made available, there was 100% completion of the modules. However, in centers where early childhood educators were asked to complete modules in their own time, participation was often delayed and occasionally incomplete due to competing demands. Those who participated in or facilitated coaching sessions reported improved communication among the child care team and between educators and parents.

Preliminary outcome findings were promising. Significant improvements were found in children's positive interactions with other children postintervention and with children and adults by follow-up. There was also a significant reduction in job stress at postintervention. Qualitative interviews indicated that educators found the program valuable in helping them teach children new skills and behaviors. Educators were also widely reflective about the role they play in supporting children's behavior (e.g., "What was good about the program for me is that it opened my eyes to little stuff that I take for granted over the years . . . let me see where I can do stuff different than I've been doing."). Developing insight into the role they play in the prevention of and response to challenging behavior has the potential to reduce educators' attributional bias and promote self-efficacy in initiating change (see Box 21.1).

IMPLICATIONS AND FUTURE DIRECTIONS

FLEXIBLE DELIVERY TO FIT CAPACITY

One of the greatest challenges for the provision of professional learning programs in busy early childhood education settings is time. Teacher professional development training is effective

> **BOX 21.1 A Child Care Center Director's Perspective on the PECE program**
>
> I found that at first it was a bit of a shift in the language that we were using, and that was a huge adjustment for everyone, because some things that we were referring to as something else, all of a sudden we were calling it an accidental reward, or were calling it all these other things. That took a little while to be able to be on the same page for what we were talking about with everyone; but then as that started becoming just a normal part of our discussion and our report with each other, it really started to blossom. Even in our staff meetings we talk about something that's been challenging the team, and then rather than having the leadership team offer suggestions to each other, they offer them to themselves to try to collaborate. And staff really came together and they were doing all of the problem-solving amongst each other and talking about some of the strategies that came out of the study. So, it's really, I think, bringing up not just reflective practitioners, but a reflective and supportive and solution-focused team, which has been phenomenal to see.
>
> —Child care center director, PECE Trial, Alberta, Canada

in improving classroom management strategies, such as with the Incredible Years (Webster-Stratton, Reid, & Stoolmiller, 2008), but typically has involved more than 1 week of face-to-face training and ongoing intensive support. Such professional development models for early childhood educators are costly and often unlikely in low-resourced child care settings. Online training has the benefit of being low cost, easily accessible, and flexible as it can be completed at times of convenience. However, completion of online modules requires commitment, and support from administrators/supervisors, and some form of external incentive may be required to enhance engagement.

To design an effective and sustainable implementation plan, it is important to gain an understanding of the unique workplace demands and capacity in each site. For example, it may be impractical for a center director to be the nominated coach as the time requirement could be substantial in a setting with large numbers of educators. Alternative methods of support for skill practice and development may need to be considered if establishing a center-based coach is not possible, such as external implementation consultants to conduct coaching; peer-supported practice and review (e.g., the Peer Assisted Supervision and Support model; Chapter 37, this volume); a guide for self-directed practice, self-evaluation, and goal setting; or a combination of these. Further, there may be no funding to relieve an educator from teaching and caretaking to allow time for group reflection and feedback on skills practice. In this case, other models of ongoing skills development must be explored, such as allowing time in regular team meetings for discussing individual educators' goals and skill development or developing strategies among co-educators to provide support for one another during the working day. Creativity is required to make an ongoing professional learning plan fit in the local context.

PRESERVICE AND IN-SERVICE PROFESSIONAL LEARNING

Early feedback about PECE has highlighted the variability in qualifications in the sector, from untrained, to diploma or certificate level training, to graduate and postgraduate qualifications. Specialized vocational training improves the competence, confidence, attitudes, and skills of educators in early childhood learning settings, and even with formal training, there are often differences in confidence, competence, attitudes, and skills, especially in relation to challenging behavior (Fukkink & Lont, 2007). This makes a one-size-fits-all approach to ongoing professional learning difficult and suggests that, as with Triple P, a multilevel program offering may be desirable (e.g., broad pre- or early vocational training and intensive specific professional development in targeted areas of concern). Consideration must be given to timing of training. Programs such as Incredible Years and PECE may sit well as preservice training components in communities where this is available or required. However, it remains most likely that building a culture of ongoing professional development expectations in the sector will provide the best opportunity for increasing warm and responsive teacher–child relationships and enhancing positive classroom strategies to facilitate social and cognitive development in young children.

CONCLUSION

There is increasing evidence of the power of parenting interventions to decrease risk and increase protective factors for children's development. However, not all families access parenting support, and often the next most significant adult in a child's life is the child's early childhood educator. Building the skills and capacities of educators to provide nurturing early childhood education and care environments will serve as a protective factor for all children, particularly those who are at risk due to economic disadvantage, developmental delays, or adverse family experiences.

Utilizing effective behavioral family intervention programs to inform early childhood learning settings is advantageous. Although much still needs to be done to bring together these two fields, there is increasing evidence of both need and impact. The question remains whether an online professional learning format is sufficient without practical implementation support. This is an area for future research inquiry. To build an evidence base, a focused program of research is required, including the testing of specific program formats and rigorous efficacy and effectiveness trials. By strengthening early childhood educators' capacity to improve child outcomes, programs such as PECE may vastly increase the population-level impact of current early childhood interventions.

KEY MESSAGES

- The early education setting has the potential to promote young children's executive functioning and social-emotional competencies, and to buffer the effects of disadvantage, through quality care and nurturing environments.
- PECE was developed as a variant of Triple P designed as a professional learning program for early childhood learning contexts to enhance the capacity of educators to promote

children's prosocial behavior and early learning and build consistency and teamwork between parents and educators.

- An effective and sustainable implementation plan should be tailored according to each unique workplace, including capacity for staff release time to complete training modules, the identification of skills practice opportunities, and potential coaching and peer support structures.
- Building a culture of ongoing professional development expectations in the sector will provide the best opportunity for increasing warm and responsive teacher–child relationships and enhancing positive classroom strategies to facilitate social and cognitive development in young children.

REFERENCES

Biglan, A., Flay, B. R., Embry, D., & Sandler, I. N. (2012). The critical role of nurturing environments for promoting human well-being. *American Psychologist, 67*, 257–271. doi:10.1037/a0026796

Brennan, E. M., Bradley, J. R., Allen, M. D., & Perry, D. F. (2008). The evidence base for mental health consultation in early childhood settings: Research synthesis addressing staff and program outcomes. *Early Education and Development, 19*, 982–1022. doi:10.1080/10409280801975834

Buysse, V., & Wesley, P. W. (Eds.). (2006). *Evidence-based practice in the early childhood field.* Washington, DC: Zero to Three.

Chi, J., Conliffe, A., Gatti, E., & Paul, N. (2012). *Triple P's five core principles in comparison with four early childhood education approaches* (Unpublished thesis). Seneca College, Ontario, Canada.

Conners-Burrow, N. A., Whiteside-Mansell, L., McKelvey, L., Virmani, E. A., & Sockwell, L. (2012). Improved classroom quality and child behavior in an Arkansas Early Childhood Mental Health Consultation Pilot Project. *Infant Mental Health Journal, 33*, 256–264. doi:10.1002/imhj.21335

Fox, L., Hemmeter, M. L., Snyder, P., Binder, D. P., & Clarke, S. (2011). Coaching early childhood special educators to implement a comprehensive model for promoting young children's social competence. *Topics in Early Childhood Special Education, 31*, 178–192. doi:10.1177/0271121411404440

Fukkink, R. G. & Lont, A. (2007). Does training matter? A meta-analysis and review of caregiver training studies. *Early Childhood Research Quarterly, 22*, 294–311. doi:10.1016/j.ecresq.2007.04.005

Gialamas, A., Sawyer, A. C. P., Mittinty, M., & Lynch, J. (2014). Quality of childcare influences children's attentiveness and emotional regulation at school entry. *Journal of Pediatrics, 165*, 813–819. doi:10.1016/j.jpeds.2014.06.011

Goelman, H., Zdaniuk, B., Boyce, W. T., Armstrong, J. M., & Essex, M. J. (2014). Maternal mental health, child care quality, and children's behavior. *Journal of Applied Developmental Psychology, 35*, 347–356. doi:10.1016/j.appdev.2014.05.003

Hart, B., & Risley, T. R. (1995). *Meaningful differences in the everyday experience of young American children.* Baltimore, MD: Brookes.

Hemmeter, M. L., Ostrosky, M. M., & Corso, R. M. (2012). Preventing and addressing challenging behavior: Common questions and practical strategies. *Young Exceptional Children, 15*, 32–46. doi:10.1177/1096250611427350

McAllister, C. L., Wilson, P. C., Green, B. L., & Baldwin, J. L. (2005). "Come and Take a Walk": Listening to Early Head Start parents on school-readiness as a matter of child, family, and community health. *American Journal of Public Health, 95*, 617–625. doi:10.2105/AJPH.2004.041616

Organization for Economic Cooperation and Development (OECD). (2014). *PF 3.2 Enrolment in child-care and pre-schools.* OECD Family database PF3.2. Retrieved October 9, 2016, from http://www.oecd.org/els/soc/PF3_2_Enrolment_childcare_preschool.pdf

Pianta, R. C., Kraft-Sayre, M., Rimm-Kaufman, S., Gercke, N., & Higgins, T. (2001). Collaboration in building partnerships between families and schools: The National Center for Early Development and Learning's Kindergarten Transition Intervention. *Early Education Research Quarterly, 16,* 117–132. doi:10.1016/S0885-2006(01)00089-8

Poole, M. K., Seal, D. W., & Taylor, C. A. (2014). A systematic review of universal campaigns targeting child physical abuse prevention. *Health Education Research, 29,* 388–432. doi:10.1093/her/cyu012

Rusby, J. C., Jones, L. B., Crowley, R., & Smolkowski, K. (2012). Associations of caregiver stress with working conditions, caregiving practices, and child behaviour in homebased child care. *Early Child Development and Care, 183,* 1589–1604. doi:10.1080/03004430.2012.742992

Shonkoff, J. P., Garner, A. S., and the Committee on Psychosocial Aspects of Child and Family Health, Committee on Early Childhood, Adoption, and Dependent Care, and Section on Developmental and Behavioral Pediatrics (2012). The lifelong effects of early childhood adversity and toxic stress. *Pediatrics, 129,* e232–e246. doi:10.1542/peds.2011-2663

Shonkoff, J. P., & Phillips, D. A. (Eds.). (2000). *From neurons to neighborhoods: The science of early childhood development.* Washington, DC: National Academy Press.

Turner, K. M. T., Dittman, C., & Lee, S. (2016, June). *Development and pilot evaluation of the Positive ChildCare Program for educators: Bringing a behavioural family intervention approach to early learning and childcare settings.* Paper presented at the 8th World Congress of Behavioural and Cognitive Therapies, Melbourne, Australia.

Turner, K. M. T., Sanders, M. R., Dittman, C., & Rusby, J. R. (2015). *Positive ChildCare Program* [4 module interactive Internet program]. Brisbane, QLD, Australia: Triple P International.

Webster-Stratton, C., Reid, M. J., & Stoolmiller, M. (2008). Preventing conduct problems and improving school readiness: Evaluation of the Incredible Years Teacher and Child Training Programs in high-risk schools. *Journal of Child Psychology and Psychiatry, 49,* 471–488. doi:10.1111/j.1469-7610.2007.01861.x

Whitebook, M., Phillips, D., & Howes, C. (2014). *Worthy work, STILL unlivable wages: The early childhood workforce 25 years after the National Child Care Staffing Study.* Berkeley, CA: Center for the Study of Child Care Employment, University of California, Berkeley.

CHAPTER 22

PARENTING SUPPORT AND THE SCHOOL SYSTEM

JULIE HODGES AND KARYN L. HEALY

For unless students feel that the two worlds of home and school understand, respect, and celebrate each other, they will be torn between the two.—Ada and Campoy, 2004, p. 32

The school is a natural home for parenting support. After all, most parents and schools share the common purpose of supporting children's development and in many ways are partners in raising the child. Parenting programs can help ensure that children entering school have the social, emotional, behavioral, and language competencies to benefit from the more structured learning environment of the classroom. Schools represent an accessible, destigmatized context for parents to access interventions to support children's learning. This chapter explores the partnership between a child's home and school and describes delivery of parenting services to optimize home–school partnerships, where parents and schools share a common approach to the promotion of children's well-being and academic success.

THE ROLE OF PARENTS IN EDUCATION

Much has been written about the benefits of parents' participation in their child's education. Wilder's (2014) metasynthesis found that, regardless of how parents' participation in their child's education was defined, there was a positive relationship between their investment and outcomes, such as academic achievement, self-efficacy for learning, attendance, peer relationships, behavior at school, school connectedness, and higher rates of graduation and tertiary education. These outcomes were consistent across socioeconomic status and ethnicity (Wilder, 2014). The terms *involvement* and *home–school partnership* are often used to describe parents' investment in their child's education; however, the term *parent engagement* best encapsulates the type of participation that is most likely to result in positive outcomes for children. Parent engagement is an intentional and collaborative strategy to leverage the knowledge, capacities, and social capital of families to improve learning and well-being of children and young people (Emerson, Fear, Fox, & Sanders, 2012, p. 34).

The benefits of parent engagement are supported by Bronfenbrenner's (1979, 2005) ecological model of development. This framework conceptualizes a child's development as directly influenced by the child's environments: their home, school, and immediate neighborhood. Bronfenbrenner also describes environments that exert a more distal influence on the child by affecting the proximal environments in which the child interacts. For example, aspects of a parent's employment, such as hours worked, location, and financial benefits, all indirectly influence the child via the home environment. Each of these environments not only influences a child's development, but also affects each other. Once a child begins formal education, interactions between a child's home and the child's school are particularly important.

Although parent engagement is multifaceted, researchers agree that good "at-home" parenting and participation in a child's learning at home are where parents can make the greatest contributions to their child's development (Desforges & Abouchaar, 2003; Harris & Goodall, 2008; Hattie, 2009; Perkins, 2014). Competent, positive parenting provides many advantages for children's success at school, including better school readiness, language development, physical health, academic achievement, peer acceptance, emotional regulation, and reduction in risk of antisocial behavior (Graziano, Reavis, Keane, & Calkins, 2007; Gutman & Feinstein, 2010; McDowell & Parke, 2009; Moffitt et al., 2011; Stack, Serbin, Enns, Ruttle, & Barrieau, 2010).

However, despite a clear desire of most parents and teachers for positive academic and well-being outcomes for children, there can be communication problems between home and school. Teachers are often positioned as experts in teaching and academic knowledge, and parents relegated to the role of helper, at best. The use of "edu-speak" with parents (e.g., in parent–teacher interviews and reporting) distances parents and perpetuates differences rather than identifying a shared interest in the child (2010, 2013). The availability of parenting programs in the school provides an ideal opportunity for the key players to get "on the same page," to develop shared language and goals for each child's development. The powerful, ongoing impact of parenting on children's development means that it is in schools' best interests to invest in improving parenting skills as part of their parent engagement strategy.

TRIPLE P—WHAT IS IN IT FOR SCHOOLS?

Several large meta-analyses, including the recent study by Sanders, Kirby, Tellegen, and Day (2014) demonstrated that Triple P has a well-established evidence base for improving children's social, emotional, and behavioral outcomes. The most compelling evidence directly linking parenting support and school-based outcomes comes from a 15-year follow-up of a 1996 population-level trial in Western Australian (Smith, 2015; Zubrick et al., 2005). An 8-week Group Triple P program was delivered to 804 parents/caregivers of 3- to 5-year-olds. Government administrative data showed improvements in attendance and long-term academic outcomes in reading and numeracy for children whose parents participated in the Group Triple P program. Smith (2015) argued that positive parenting improved academic outcomes via the child's capacity to regulate both emotions and behavior.

There is additional research demonstrating that parental participation in Triple P results in improved classroom behavior and academic achievement. McTaggart and Sanders (2003) demonstrated that participation of parents in Group Triple P resulted in greater reductions in the teacher-rated frequency and intensity of children's difficult classroom behavior. Havighurst et al. (2015) trialed a combination of a Triple P parenting program and a school socioemotional intervention for children with emerging conduct problems in lower primary school. Following the program, children in the intervention condition showed better emotional understanding and behavior compared to children in the control condition. Further, a recent study in mainland China (Guo, Morawska, & Sanders, 2016) found that, compared with a control group, parents who participated in Group Triple P reported greater satisfaction with children's academic achievement.

Triple P enables schools to engage with parents in developing students' emotional and behavioral regulation, social competence, and prerequisite skills for learning, such as regular attendance, organization, focusing, and completing homework. Triple P can help promote general development, as well as address specific problems. For instance, getting insufficient sleep is associated with poorer behavioral and social functioning for children (Becker, 2014). By establishing an effective evening routine, parents can improve the child's concentration, learning, and mood at school. So, working with parents to establish appropriate evening and morning routines to ensure students are rested and ready to learn is in the interests of schools as well as parents (see Box 22.1 for typical feedback from parents and teachers).

PARENTING SUPPORT—THE POTENTIAL OF THE SCHOOL CONTEXT

Schools are uniquely placed to offer parenting support. They are perhaps the only organizations that families are required to engage with regularly over the child's entire developmental period. Through ongoing relationships with families, schools can engage with parents to support children's development and overcome obstacles. Teachers have information that is different from, and complementary to, parents' knowledge of their child. This creates opportunities for valuable dialogue about effective strategies to provide a consistent approach to support students' learning and behavior.

BOX 22.1: Typical Feedback From Parents and Teachers on the Benefits of Triple P

[This course] has absolutely changed my life. I now have the tools and knowledge at my disposal to achieve daily success. This is a course all parents should do. . . . The support I received from the school was fantastic.

—Single mother of a 5-year-old girl

[Triple P] also enhances parents' conversation and cooperation with teachers knowing that they are able to speak the same language when discussing their child's behavior.

—Special needs teacher and facilitator

Another factor that makes schools a favorable context for parenting interventions is the flexibility offered by the nature of the school workforce. Schools employ a variety of professionals who have different relationships with and capacity to work with parents. This meshes well with the wide range of Triple P program variants and modes of delivery and gives schools multiple options to meet parents' needs. Table 22.1 summarizes opportunities for delivery of Triple P parenting programs in the school context.

Seminars and Discussion Groups enable parents to gain general information and strategies and to get to know and support each other and enable schools to identify parent needs. Seminars are perhaps best delivered by staff with responsibilities across the whole student body. For most parents, the classroom teacher is their main contact with the school and the person they would approach first to discuss a specific issue. The teacher's knowledge of the child places them in an excellent position to understand the child's needs (Randolph, Fincham, & Radey, 2009), so teachers are well placed to share quick tips with parents over a small number of meetings (using Level 2 or 3 individual programs and tip sheets). If a family needs more intensive support, it is helpful if the teacher can connect the family with other staff who have greater capacity to work with individual families (e.g., a guidance counselor).

GETTING TRIPLE P TO WORK IN A SCHOOL CONTEXT

To ensure a school gains maximum benefit from an investment in Triple P, it is important to plan how best to involve staff and parents. Sanders, Healy, Grice, and Del Vecchio (2017) suggested forming a steering committee to plan and coordinate ongoing delivery. In planning delivery of Triple P, it is important to take into account known enablers and obstacles for participation of staff as well as parents.

Shapiro, Prinz, and Sanders (2012) found that staff confidence in delivering a program enabled staff to participate. Triple P offers a variety of support mechanisms to develop staff confidence, including initial accreditation, regular updates on handling difficult issues, and access to clinical consultants. Practitioners are also encouraged to participate in ongoing peer supervision, which facilitates learning and problem-solving. When planning to offer Triple P, schools need to consider ongoing professional support of staff. If teachers are dedicating time to delivering Triple P outside school hours, school administration may consider ways to lighten their load, such as reducing their playground duties. As well as planning how to support staff, schools need to consider how best to engage parents.

Challenges of involving parents in parenting programs are well documented (e.g., Cunningham et al., 2000; Ohan, Seward, Stallman, Bayliss, & Sanders, 2015) but can be managed by addressing factors that enable or prevent participation. These factors include practical issues such as access and suitability of venue (Mytton, Ingram, Manns, & Thomas, 2014) and the timing of courses (Spoth & Redmond, 1995). Schools are already visited regularly by parents, so timing parenting courses to coincide with school drop-off or pick-up times can facilitate parent participation. However, to involve working parents, schools may need to consider evening programs (Mytton et al., 2014). Difficulty in accessing child care can prevent families from participating, so provision of child care can improve parent involvement (Saylor, Elksnin, Farah, &

Table 22.1: Delivery of Triple P Programs in the School

Triple P Level	Delivered by	Purpose	Optimal Timing
Level 2 Seminars	• Guidance counselors/school psychologist • Behavior support staff • Head of special education • School chaplain	• Developing shared language and connecting with families • Developing shared expectations • Developing skills, including self-regulation • Providing a nonstigmatizing gateway for parents who need more intensive support • Building parenting capacity	• On enrollment • Start of school year • Transition years • Available regularly to allow access by transitioning families (e.g., each term)
Level 3 Discussion groups	As above	All of the above purposes, plus • Developing targeted skills (e.g., bedtime routine), addressing concerns (e.g., disobedience)	• Start of school year • As need is identified
Level 2–3 Brief individual support	• Classroom teacher or any role listed above	• Addressing emergent specific needs or concerns • Developing skills applicable to other situations • Fostering parent–teacher relationships	• When individual parents identify a need
Level 4 Intensive (individual/group/online)	Same as for Level 2 seminars	All of the above, plus • Addressing a salient concern	• For individual sessions, when parent identifies a need • For groups, during school near drop-off and pick-up times
Level 5	• School psychologist, guidance counselor	• Providing additional support for parents needing support in emotion regulation or adjustment	• When a parent identifies a need

Pope, 1990). Provision of refreshments can also encourage participation (Saylor et al., 1990) and help parents socialize. As well as considering practical factors, schools also need to consider how parent attitudes may affect participation.

Decisions of individual families to participate in a parenting program are influenced by the attitudes of broader family, community, and cultural groups (Fontana, Fleischman, McCarton, Meltzer, & Ruff, 1989). In an Irish trial of the implementation of Triple P, Fives, Pursell, Heary, Nic Gabhainn, and Canavan (2014) found that parents were positively influenced by other parents discussing the program and sharing parenting tips. Schools can deliberately utilize this positive parental influence by inviting parents who have had a positive experience with the program to "spread the word" and provide testimonials. Parents are also more likely to participate in programs when they can recognize specific benefits for their family (McCurdy et al., 2006). Parents who live within a Triple P Stay Positive campaign area will learn about the program from billboards, radio, newspaper, and television (Sanders et al., 2008). Schools can inform parents about the program through newsletters, websites, social media, parents and citizen's associations, and specific school events and through parent–teacher meetings.

Despite the effectiveness of Triple P, it can be difficult to get some families involved. Research shows that although the most vulnerable families face the greatest barriers to participation (Harachi, Catalano, & Hawkins, 1997), they still benefit from participation in parenting programs (Heinrichs, Krueger, & Guse, 2006). Families dealing with high levels of conflict, hardships, trauma, and mental health issues face considerable personal hurdles in attending any program (Mytton et al., 2014). Yet, these families are often the ones that schools most want to involve because of concerns about child conduct problems (Hill & Tyson, 2004). Apart from the practical barriers to involvement listed previously, families with more complex needs can have concerns about privacy when invited to participate in a family-based program (Ohan et al., 2015; Spoth, Redmond, Hockaday, & Shin, 1996). There is a substantial stigma attached to being the parent of a child with a behavioral or emotional disorder, and feelings of blame and shame can discourage participation (Corrigan, Watson, & Miller, 2006). Recent availability of online Triple P provides another option to engage families who may be resistant to attending in person. Love et al. (2016) reported great success engaging and retaining highly vulnerable parents using online Triple P modified for use on mobile devices and reported sustained improvements in child behavior and parenting.

KEY IMPLEMENTATION ISSUES

When considering implementing Triple P in a school, it is important to first gain support of the principal. The principal's endorsement communicates that the program is a valued part of school business and will encourage both staff and parent participation. Forming a steering committee that either involves or consults with parents will help ensure parent needs are considered. Questions that the committee could consider include the following:

- How can the parenting programs be best normalized in the school context?
- What Triple P variants should be offered at the school?
- Which staff members are best placed to offer Triple P?
- What support will be provided to staff members who deliver the program?

- When and where should Triple P be delivered?
- What ongoing funding can support program delivery, including resources, refreshments, and, if possible, child care?
- What data will be collected to monitor the outcomes of programs?
- How will the availability of the program be promoted to parents?
- What is a simple way for parents to enroll?

IMPLICATIONS AND FUTURE DIRECTIONS

There is compelling evidence that both engaging parents in their child's education and involving them in parenting programs can enhance children's academic and well-being outcomes. What we do not know is the extent to which child outcomes can be enhanced when offering parenting programs in the school context as a vehicle for both parent engagement and building parents' self-regulatory capacity. Measures are currently available that will allow schools to monitor changes in the partnership between a child's home and the child's school (Australian Research Alliance for Children and Youth [ARACY], 2015; Kirby, 2014). This is important information that can be gathered by schools. From the school's perspective, parents and families are a virtually untapped resource; harnessing the knowledge, capacities, and social capital of parents as collaborators in children's education can surely be advantageous for all stakeholders, particularly the children!

CONCLUSION

Schools can enhance student outcomes by collaborating more closely with parents. Provision of parenting programs in the school setting can engage parents to enhance student outcomes and provide consistency of purpose and approach. Because parents need to visit and maintain connections with teachers over the course of the child's development, schools provide a natural setting for parenting programs. The variety of staff roles within a school enables delivery of different levels and modalities of Triple P, providing options for parents seeking general information as well as parents needing more intensive support. Schools could also consider options like online Triple P for parents who may be reluctant to visit the school. To get the most out of Triple P, a steering committee is recommended to plan how to best meet the needs of parents and staff and contribute to identified student priorities. Despite substantial effort involved in the initial engagement of some parents, the rewards are likely to make this worthwhile—for parents, young people, and teachers.

KEY MESSAGES

- Parents can make a positive impact on their child's academic, social, and emotional development via positive parenting and participation in their child's learning at home.
- Parenting programs delivered at school allow the key players to identify shared goals and to get "on the same page."

- Schools are uniquely placed to offer parenting support.
- Different types of Triple P can be delivered in schools by a variety of staff members.
- Steering committees can plan how best to deliver Triple P to meet parent needs and student priorities and to address any barriers to staff and parent involvement.

REFERENCES

Ada, A., & Campoy, F. I. (2004). *Authors in the classroom: A transformative education process.* White Plains, NY: Pearson Education.

Australian Research Alliance for Children and Youth (ARACY). (2015). *Progressing parental engagement in the ACT. Our evidence base. Measuring parental engagement.* Canberra, Australia.

Becker, S. P. (2014). External validity of children's self-reported sleep functioning: Associations with academic, social, and behavioral adjustment. *Sleep Medicine, 15,* 1094–1100. doi:10.1016/j.sleep.2014.06.001

Bronfenbrenner, U. (1979). *The ecology of human development: Experiments by nature and design.* Cambridge, MA: Harvard University Press.

Bronfenbrenner, U. Ed. (2005). *Making Human Beings Human: bioecological Perspectives on Human Development.* Thousand Oaks, CA: Sage Publications.

Corrigan, P., Watson, A., & Miller, F. (2006). Blame, shame, and contamination: The impact of mental illness and drug dependence stigma on family members. *Journal of Family Psychology, 20,* 239–246. doi:10.1037/0893-3200.20.2.239

Cunningham, C. E., Boyle, M., Offord, D., Racine, Y., Hundert, J., Secord, M., & McDonald, J. (2000). Tri-ministry study: Correlates of school-based parenting course utilization. *Journal of Consulting and Clinical Psychology, 68,* 928–933. doi:10.1037/0022-006X.68.5.928

Desforges, C., & Abouchaar, A. (2003). *The impact of parental involvement, parental support and family education on pupil achievement and adjustment: A literature review.* Retrieved from http://dera.ioe.ac.uk/id/eprint/6305

Emerson, L., Fear, J., Fox, S., & Sanders, E. (2012). *Parental engagement in learning and schooling: Lessons from research.* Canberra, Australia: Family-School and Community Partnerships Bureau.

Fives, A., Pursell, L., Heary, C., Nic Gabhainn, S., & Canavan, J. (2014). *Parenting support for every parent: A population-level evaluation of Triple P in Longford Westmeath. Final report.* Athlone, Ireland: Longford Westmeath Parenting Partnership.

Fontana, C. A., Fleischman, A. R., McCarton, C., Meltzer, A., & Ruff, H. (1989). A neonatal preventive intervention study: Issues of recruitment and retention. *Journal of Primary Prevention, 9,* 164–176. doi:10.1007/BF01325210

Graziano, P. A., Reavis, R. D., Keane, S. P., & Calkins, S. D. (2007). The role of emotion regulation in children's early academic success. *Journal of School Psychology, 45,* 5–14. doi:10.1016/j.jsp.2006.09.002

Guo, M., Morawska, A., & Sanders, M. R. (2016). A randomized controlled trial of group Triple P with Chinese parents in mainland China. *Behavior Modification, 40,* 825–851, doi:10.1177/0145445516644221

Gutman, L.M., & Feinstein, L. (2010). Parenting behviours and children's development from infancy to early childhood: changes, continuities and contribution. *Early Child Development and Care, 180,* 535-556, doi:10.1080/0300443080211042

Harachi, T. W., Catalano, R. F., & Hawkins, J. D. (1997). Effective recruitment for parenting programs within ethnic minority communities. *Child and Adolescent Social Work Journal, 14,* 23–39. doi:10.1023/A:1024540829739

Harris, A., & Goodall, J. (2008). Do parents know they matter? Engaging all parents in learning. *Educational Research, 50*, 277–289. doi:10.1080/00131880802309424

Hattie, J. (2009). *Visible learning: A synthesis of over 800 meta-analyses relating to achievement.* Oxford, England: Routledge.

Havighurst, S., Duncombe, M., Frankling, E., Holland, K., Kehoe, C., & Stargatt, R. (2015). An emotion-focused early intervention for children with emerging conduct problems. *Journal of Abnormal Child Psychology, 43*, 749–760. doi:10.1007/s10802-014-9944-z

Heinrichs, N., Krueger, S., & Guse, U. (2006). Der Einfluss von Anreizen auf die Rekrutierung von Elternund auf die Effektivitaet eines praeventiven Eltern-trainings [The effects of incentives on recruitment rates of parents and the effectiveness of a preventative parent training]. *Zeitschrift fuer KlinischePsychologie und Psychotherapie, 35*, 97–108. doi:10.1026/1616-3443.35.2.97

Hill, N. E., & Tyson, D. F. (2004). Parental school involvement and children's academic achievement: Pragmatics and issues. *Current Directions in Psychological Science, 13*, 161–164. doi:10.1111/j.0963-7214.2004.00298.x

Kirby, G. (2014). *Creation and evaluation of the Partners in Education Survey (PIES)* (Honours thesis). Retrieved from https://espace.library.uq.edu.au/view/UQ:362769

Love, S. M., Sanders, M. R., Turner, K. M., Maurange, M., Knott, T., Prinz, R., . . . Ainsworth, A. T. (2016). Social media and gamification: Engaging vulnerable parents in an online evidence-based parenting program. *Child Abuse and Neglect, 53*, 95–107. doi:10.1016/j.chiabu.2015.10.031

McCurdy, K., Daro, D., Anisfeld, E., Katzev, A., Keim, A., LeCroy, C., . . . Park, J. K. (2006). Understanding maternal intentions to engage in home visiting programs. *Children and Youth Services Review, 28*, 1195–1212. doi:10.1016/j.childyouth.2005.11.010

McDowell, D. J., & Parke, R. D. (2009). Parental correlates of children's peer relations: An empirical test of a tripartite model. *Developmental Psychology, 45*, 224–235. doi:10.1037/a0014305.

McTaggart, P., & Sander, M.R. (2003). The transition to school project: Results form the Classroom. *Australian e-Journal for the Advancement of Mental Health, 2*, 144-155. Doi:10.5172/jamh.2.3.144

Moffitt, T. E., Arseneault, L., Belsky, D., Dickson, N., Hancox, R. J., Harrington, H., . . . Caspi, A. (2011). A gradient of childhood self-control predicts health, wealth, and public safety. *Proceedings of the National Academy of Sciences of the United States of America, 108*, 2693–2698. doi:10.1073/pnas.1010076108

Mytton, J., Ingram, J., Manns, S., & Thomas, J. (2014). Facilitators and barriers to engagement in parenting programs: A qualitative systematic review. *Health Education and Behavior, 41*, 127–137. doi:10.1177/1090198113485755

Ohan, J. L., Seward, R. J., Stallman, H. M., Bayliss, D. M., & Sanders, M. R. (2015). Parents' barriers to using school psychology services for their child's mental health problems. *School Mental Health, 7*, 287–297.

Perkins, K. (2014). Parents and teachers: Working together to foster children's learning. *The Research Digest, QCT* (10). Retrieved from http://www.qct.edu.au/pdf/Research%20Periodicals/QCTResearchDigest2014-10.pdf

Pushor, D. (2010). Welcoming parents: Educators as guest hosts on school landscapes. *Education Canada, 47* (4). Canadian Education Association. Retrieved from https://www.edcan.ca/magazine/fall-2007/

Pushor, D., & Parent Engagement Collaborative. (2013). *Portals of promise: Transforming beliefs and practices through a curriculum of parents.* Rotterdam, Netherlands: Sense Publishers.

Randolph, K. A., Fincham, F., & Radey, M. (2009). A framework for engaging parents in prevention. *Journal of Family Social Work, 12*, 56–72. doi:10.1080/10522150802654278

Sanders, M. R., Healy, K. L., Grice, C., & Del Vecchio, T. (2017). Evidence-based parenting programs: Integrating science into school-based practice. In M. Thielking & M. D. Terjesen (Eds.) *Handbook of Australian school psychology: Bridging the gaps in international research, practice, and policy* (pp. 537–551). New York, NY: Springer.

Sanders, M. R., Kirby, J. N., Tellegen, C. L., & Day, J. J. (2014). The Triple P—Positive Parenting Program: A systematic review and meta-analysis of a multi-level system of parenting support. *Clinical Psychology Review, 34,* 337–357. doi:10.1016/j.cpr.2014.04.003

Sanders, M.R., Ralph, A., Sofronoff, K., Gardiner, P., Thompson, R., Dwyer, S., & Bidwell, K. (2008). Every family: A population approach to reducing behavioral and emotional problems in children making the transition to school. *Journal of Primary Prevention, 29,* 197–222. doi:10.1007s10935-008-0139-7

Saylor, C.F., Elksnin, N., Farah, B.A., & Pope, J.A (1990). Depends on who you ask: what maximizes participation of families in early intervention programs. *Journal of Pediatric Psychology, 20,* 557–569.

Shapiro, C. J., Prinz, R. J., & Sanders, M. R. (2012). Facilitators and barriers to implementation of an evidence-based parenting intervention to prevent child maltreatment: The Triple P—Positive Parenting Program. *Child Maltreatment, 17,* 86–95. doi:10.1177/1077559511424774

Smith, G. (2015). *A 15 year follow-up of WA Triple P trial.* Perth, Australia: Government of Western Australia Department of Health.

Spoth, R., & Redmond, C. (1995). Parent motivation to enroll in parenting skills programs: A model of family context and health belief predictors. *Journal of Family Psychology, 9,* 294–310. doi:10.1037/0893-3200.9.3.294

Spoth, R., Redmond, C., Hockaday, C., & Shin, C. Y. (1996). Barriers to participation in family skills preventive interventions and their evaluations: A replication and extension. *Family Relations,* 247–254. doi:10.2307/585496

Stack, D. M., Serbin, L. A., Enns, L. N., Ruttle, P. L., & Barrieau, L. (2010). Parental effects on children's emotional development over time and across generations. *Infants and Young Children, 23,* 52–69. doi:10.1097/IYC.0b013e3181c97606

Wilder, S. (2014). Effects of parental involvement on academic achievement: A meta-synthesis. *Educational Review, 66,* 377–397. doi:10.1080/00131911.2013.780009

Zubrick, S. R., Ward, K. A., Silburn, S. R., Lawrence, D., Williams, A. A., Blair, E., . . . Sanders, M. R. (2005). Prevention of child behavior problems through universal implementation of a group behavioral family intervention. *Prevention Science, 6,* 287–304. doi:10.1007/s11121-005-0013-2

C H A P T E R   2 3

PARENTING SUPPORT IN THE WORKPLACE

DIVNA M. HASLAM AND NICOLE PENMAN

INTRODUCTION

Over the past 40 years, societal and economic changes in developed nations have led to an increase in dual-earning families and the decline of stay-at-home parents (Australian Government, Australian Institute of Family Studies, 2010). In Australia, 65% of mothers and 90% of fathers with children under the age of 18 are employed in some capacity (Baxter, 2013). Similar rates are found in the United States, with 70% of mothers and 93% of fathers seeking work or working (United States Department of Labor, Bureau of Labor Statistics, 2016), and in Europe (Miani & Hoorens, 2014). Concomitant with these changes have been dramatic changes in working hours and technology that make the boundaries between work and family life more permeable.

The development of the smartphone and high-speed Internet has led, in part, to employees doing more work from home or outside traditional working hours. For example, 44% of employed persons in Australia use the Internet to work from home (Australian Bureau of Statistics, 2016), which can take time away from family interactions, increase work and family conflict, and decrease levels of well-being (Boswell & Olson-Buchanan, 2007; Chesley, 2005; Park, Fritz, & Jex, 2011). Changes in working hours mean that for many the workday is no longer limited from 9 a.m. to 5 p.m. or to the traditional workweek. Instead, employees are expected to work a range of hours, with as many as 35% working on weekends (United States Department of Labor, Bureau of Labor Statistics, 2016).

These changes mean that employees need to balance competing work and life commitments more than ever before (e.g., playing a sport, caring for parents, spending time with friends). For parents of dependent children, it can be extra difficult to juggle incompatible work and life commitments with parenting responsibilities (Michel, Kotrba, Mitchelson, Clark, & Baltes, 2011), and 90% of parents report trying to balance work and family is stressful (see Box 23.1; Sanders, Haslam, Calam, & Southwell, 2010).

CONSEQUENCES OF BALANCING WORK AND FAMILY COMMITMENTS

It is important to note that there are numerous positive effects for families having two parents in the workforce, including reduced financial pressure, career fulfillment, getting a break from children (Haslam, Patrick, & Kirby, 2015), setting a good example, and modeling a work ethic. Outcomes for children of working mothers include higher pay in later adulthood (Goldberg & Lucas-Thompson, 2014; Lucas-Thompson, Goldberg, & Prause, 2010) and, for children of low-income mothers who returned to work before the children were 8 months, enhanced socioemotional functioning compared to children with similar stay-at-home mothers, although this is not a causal relationship (Coley & Lombardi, 2013).

Researchers interested in improving the lives of working parents have paid particular attention to reducing negative effects of conflict between work and family responsibilities. One of the key variables with extensive research is work and family conflict (also known as work–family conflict), which can be conceptualized as conflict resulting from a mismatch in demands between work and family commitments (Greenhaus & Beutell, 1985). It is an overarching category that comprises two directional constructs: family-to-work conflict (FWC) and work-to-family conflict (WFC; Greenhaus & Beutell, 1985). FWC occurs when family life or responsibilities interfere with or negatively affect work functioning. For example, a mother who is late to work after dropping children to school would be experiencing FWC. In comparison, WFC occurs when work responsibilities affect family life or functioning. For example, a father who is distracted when talking with his children because he is thinking about work-related issues is experiencing WFC. A parent can experience either or both of these types of conflict at any given time. Extant

---

BOX 23.1: The Challenge of Balancing Work and Family Commitments: A Case Example

Simone is a 34-year-old married mother of one daughter (age 3). Simone and her husband, Anwar, have been married for 10 years. Simone works in finance 4 days per week. She would like to work fewer days, but the family needs her income. Although Simone enjoys her work and her career is progressing, she worries that it might be at the expense of her family. Her daughter often asks her why she has to work "all the time" and sometimes cries when they are saying goodbye in the morning. Simone often feels guilty about the fact that her daughter is in child care most days and wonders if her daughter misbehaves because she does not receive enough time with her mother. Simone's workplace offers some family-friendly policies, such as carer's leave and the option to work from home, but Simone does not use these because it might affect her chances for promotion. On a typical day, Anwar picks up their daughter from child care and feeds her dinner. Simone makes it a priority to be home in time to put her daughter to bed and read her stories, which is a special time for both mother and daughter. After their daughter is in bed, Simone and Anwar try to spend some time together, but often Simone is distracted by thinking about things at work or replying work e-mails.

research has demonstrated there are gender differences in the type of conflict commonly experienced, with fathers more likely to report high levels of WFC and mothers more likely to report higher levels of FWC (Byron, 2005). Conflict can be further subcategorized into (a) strain-based conflict, which results from the emotional strain of incompatible demands; (b) time-based strain, which results from time incompatibilities relating to functioning well at home and work (Frone, Russell, & Cooper, 1992; Greenhaus & Beutell, 1985); and (c) behavior-based strain, which results from difficulties in changing roles from work to family domain and vice versa.

High levels of work and family conflict are associated with a number of adverse consequences at an individual level (e.g., high stress, burnout, depression, substance use, health problems; Fiksenbaum, 2014; Grzywacz & Bass, 2003; Mian, Rodger, & David, 2012) and at an organization level, including increased absenteeism, sick leave, turnover, and displaced aggression toward colleagues or family members (Greenhaus, Parasuraman, & Collins, 2001; Kossek & Ozeki, 1998; Liu et al., 2015). In addition, high levels of work and family conflict affect home and family functioning, including decreased quality of the parent–child relationship and increased marital conflict (Hammer, Miccio, & Wagstaff, 2003; Marcello & Filomena, 2012; Väänänen et al., 2009).

WHY PROVIDE PARENTING SUPPORT IN THE WORKPLACE?

A key aspect of a population approach to parenting support is considering the broader ecological context in which parents live (Sanders, Prinz, & Shapiro, 2012). The workplace is one of the most significant contexts outside the family home, with the average parent, aged 24 to 56, spending 8.9 hours per day working (United States Department of Labor, Bureau of Labor Statistics, 2016). It is therefore important to consider the workplace and its influence when fully considering a family in context. There are two primary rationales for the provision of workplace parenting support. First, workplace parenting support may normalize help-seeking behaviors for parents; second, it may help improve employee and organizational outcomes through the reduction of work and family conflict.

First, parenting programs delivered in the workplace or via employee assistance services normalize help seeking for parents and may increase population-level access to parenting support and reduce stigma, resulting in population-level reductions in child emotional and behavioral problems (Prinz, Sanders, Shapiro, Whitaker, & Lutzker, 2009). As discussed elsewhere in this book, few parents access parenting support despite its known benefits. For example, some studies found as few as 10% of parents have accessed parenting support (Sanders, 1999), and fathers are particularly unlikely to attend clinical services (Scourfield, Cheung, & Macdonald, 2014). Workplace support may make it easier to engage hard-to-reach fathers. One survey of over 700 parents in the United Kingdom found 85% of parents believed workplace parenting support should be made available, and the overwhelming majority of both mothers (90%) and fathers (85%) reported they would attend a workplace parenting program (Sanders, Haslam, Calam, Southwell, & Stallman, 2011).

Second, given the numerous negative consequences of work and family conflict and occupational stress on individuals, their families, and their organizations, it is essential to reduce levels of conflict and improve parents' and employees' functioning. In attempts to reduce work and family conflict and the associated costs and to improve employee life balance, organizations have implemented "family-friendly" policies. Such policies are designed to improve the work–life balance of employees and improve family and community functioning. Family-friendly policies differ from organization to organization but may include such things as flexible working hours, telecommuting options, access to child care, access to part-time work options, job sharing, paid and unpaid parental or carer leave, and the provision of employee assistance services (Skinner & Chapman, 2013).

Literature suggests the benefits of family-friendly policies are mixed; in general, the provision of such policies, and employee satisfaction with policies provided, is associated with increased productivity and decreased turnover or turnover intentions (Belwal & Belwal, 2014; Butts, Casper, & Yang, 2013; Chen, Zhang, Sanders, & Xu, 2016; Chou & Cheung, 2013). However, a closer examination reveals a more complex picture. For example, some strategies, such as working from home or telecommuting, reduce WFC but actually serve to increase the extent to which family life interferes with work (Golden, Veiga, & Simsek, 2006).

We argue that family-friendly policies are positive, especially in addressing time-based aspects of conflict, but insufficient in effecting broad improvements for employees experiencing work and family conflict in isolation. Therefore, we argue that, in addition to supportive policies, skills-based programs that equip employees to manage competing demands and to reduce the known modifiable risk factors for strain-based and behavior-based conflict are needed. Parenting programs such as Triple P address the modifiable individual and family-related risk factors, such as externalizing child behavior and family stress, and as such they may be effective even when it is not possible to easily modify occupational risk factors such as shift work hours or work overload (Haslam, Sanders, & Sofronoff, 2013). Interventions can also focus on enhancing positive working experiences, such as how working benefits children, which qualitative research suggests may reduce parental guilt (Haslam et al., 2015).

DESCRIPTION OF THE WORKPLACE AS A CONTEXT FOR PARENTING SUPPORT

The workplace is different from many other settings given the power differential between employees and employers. It is important that line managers and senior management actively support workplace implementation and ensure employees feel comfortable attending any services provided. Strategies such as offering services during work hours or as a part of professional development can be effective. Managers sharing their own experiences in balancing work and family may also be helpful. Anecdotal evidence suggests that when school principals admit they struggle with balancing work and families, teachers were more likely to sign up for services. It would also be useful for management to track attendance rates to link these with any organizational improvements.

HOW TO MAKE TRIPLE P WORK IN AN ORGANIZATIONAL SETTING

As outlined, the workplace is a unique setting for the delivery of parenting support that could either increase or impede employees' willingness to attend programs delivered via the workplace. It is therefore important that implementation of services be carefully planned to maximize uptake. Perhaps the most important of these is that there should be a genuine desire from organizational management to offer employees support and a belief that assisting parents balance work and family is an important role of a caring organization. Companies that make token efforts to offer support but do not actively encourage or allow employees to access services or, even worse, actively discourage employees from accessing support or utilizing family-friendly policies will be unlikely to benefit from making services available. We recommend management indicate full support of programs offered and of the utilization of family-friendly policies, such as carer's leave, and that Triple P be offered as a part of a broader set of family-friendly policies. Some tips to enhance implementation in an organizational setting include the following:

- Offer a mix of online options alongside seminars and group sessions. Triple P Online (see Chapter 26, this volume) is a particularly useful program for large or diverse companies where it is difficult to get employees together for a group program.
- Provide seminars during lunchbox sessions rather than after hours to increase attendance. Delivering seminars at lunchtimes typically means only 30 minutes of work time are affected.
- Demonstrate active management support by ensuring management (not just human resources) encourages people to attend seminars or group programs. Highlight that the programs are relevant for both management and general staff. Staff will be more likely to attend if their managers are present.
- Ensure any employee assistance providers are trained in Triple P so families who need more assistance can access more personalized help.

BRIEF REVIEW OF EFFICACY

Data that support the efficacy of the application of Triple P in the workplace as a preventive measure and intervention come from both research trials and practical implementations that have not been published but that shed light on key aspects of successful implementation. In the previous section, the discussion regarding issues to consider in ensuring successful workplace delivery incorporated learning acquired from both types of evidence; however, in this section we limit our reporting to empirical research.

Trials examining Triple P in a workplace context fall into two primary categories. In the first category, there is evidence of the delivery of usual Group Triple P programs delivered in a workplace setting. These trials have primarily evaluated the impact of Group Triple P, with only minimal tailoring, when delivered to employees in the workplace. Randomized trials of this type typically show similar effects to those of Group Triple P delivered in other settings (e.g., improved child behavior, decreased dysfunctional parenting practices; Martin & Sanders, 2003; Sanders, Stallman, & McHale, 2011). These studies found that even when delivering Group Triple P with only minor tailoring, there were additional work-related benefits, such as increased workplace efficacy (Martin & Sanders, 2003; Sanders, Stallman, et al., 2011). For example, a study of 121 parents working as librarians found that Group Triple P delivered to librarian staff significantly increased occupational commitment, work satisfaction, and self-efficacy as well as the usual family-related improvements (Sanders, Stallman, et al., 2011). Some authors have also adapted primary care strategies for delivery of services in the workplace and found promising results, albeit without a control condition (Baugh, Ballard, Tyndall, Littlewood, & Nolan, 2015).

The second category of research in this area revolves around the development and evaluation of a specific version of Triple P for employed parents: Workplace Triple P (WPTP; this occurred simultaneously with publication of work in the first category as outlined). WPTP was developed as an intensive Level 4 intervention that is delivered in a group setting either over 2 days followed by three phone consultations or over 8 weeks (comprising five 2.5-hour group sessions) plus three personalized telephone consultations. WPTP not only encompasses the parenting content of Group Triple P but also equips parents with the coping skills to prevent and manage stress and guilt and teaches skills development to manage high-risk transition times (e.g., between work and home and from home to work).

Randomized trials of the intensive version of WPTP in Australia and Germany found significant improvements in work and family conflict (in both directions), occupational stress, depression, anxiety, work overload–related stress, and general stress (Hartung & Hahlweg, 2010; Haslam et al., 2013), with small-to-large effect sizes (Cohen's d = .35 to .85) and results maintained at 4- to 6-month follow-up. In addition, although no changes were observed for job satisfaction, the usual improvements in parenting and family functioning were observed.

Although the Level 4 WPTP program was effective, there has been concern about how readily it can be incorporated into workplaces given its length. A briefer Level 2 seminar version of WPTP was therefore developed. WPTP Seminars include a specific seminar on balancing work and family (90 minutes) and a slightly tailored version of the existing Level 2 seminar, the Power of Positive Parenting. The Balancing Work, Life, and Family seminar teaches parents the positive aspects of being a working parent and equips parents with coping skills to manage common emotions such as stress and guilt and provides practical strategies for managing high-risk transition times. Results of a randomized controlled trial indicated the brief seminars (a total of 3 hours of intervention time) resulted in significant reductions in both WFC and FWC conflict, stress, anxiety, and depression, as well has increases in work-related efficacy, efficacy in balancing work and family commitments, and work enrichment. This was in addition to the usual parenting and child behavior improvements. The effects of the WTP Seminars, although slightly smaller than the intensive program, demonstrate it is possible to improve work and family conflict even when organizational factors that contribute to conflict remain stable.

In conclusion, existing trials show promise for the delivery of parenting delivered in the workplace, particularly WTP at both improving family and occupational functioning. Consumer-focused research in the area suggested both mothers (Haslam et al., 2015) and fathers (Haslam & Gates, 2017) are welcoming of workplace support and see great value for both personal and professional lives.

IMPLICATIONS AND FUTURE RESEARCH DIRECTIONS

Research to date has highlighted that working parents and their organizations can benefit from workplace parenting support, and that parenting programs can reduce work and family conflict.

Future research should examine the cost-effectiveness of workplace program delivery, taking into account impact on work-related stress, absenteeism, turnover, and other costs associated with unhappy staff. Evidence of cost-effectiveness from an organizational perspective may increase organizational uptake of existing programs. Other research could examine the extent to which widespread workplace parenting support increases general access to parenting services and the impact of this on population indices of behavior issues.

CONCLUSION

This chapter examined the workplace as a context for the provision of parenting support. It outlined a rationale for integrating parenting programs into existing employee assistance services, including increasing access to parenting support, encouraging fathers to access support, reducing work and family conflict, and improving employee satisfaction. It discussed the importance of carefully planning implementation and ensuring programs are delivered in a context of management support where employees feel comfortable to access available services without fear of negative employment outcomes. A brief review of the efficacy of WTP and the delivery of existing Triple P programs within the workplace was conducted and showed that providing parenting support can enhance family and individual outcomes in employees. Addressing the needs of working parents is an important and ongoing priority for parenting researchers.

KEY MESSAGES

- Balancing work and family responsibilities can be stressful for families.
- Functioning in both family and work domains can be adversely affected. WFC is when work negatively affects family. FWC is when family negatively affects work.
- The provision of workplace parenting support may be beneficial for employees and their families as well as the organizations in which they work.
- Workplace parenting support may also reduce stigma associated with parents seeking support and increase population-level access to parenting services.
- Parenting support can be effectively implemented in the workplace and should form part of a broad-based family-friendly policy.
- Evidence is accumulating regarding the efficacy of Triple P delivered in the workplace at improving family and occupational outcomes.

REFERENCES

Australian Bureau of Statistics. (2016). *Household use of information technology, Australia, 2014–15* (8146.0). Retrieved from http://www.abs.gov.au/ausstats/abs@.nsf/mf/8146.0

Australian Government: Australian Institute of Family Studies. (2010). *Families then and now: 1980–2010*. Melbourne, Australia: Author. Retrieved from https://aifs.gov.au/publications/families-then-and-now-1980-2010.

Baugh, E., Ballard, S., Tyndall, L., Littlewood, K., & Nolan, M. (2015). Balancing work and family: A pilot evaluation of an evidence-based parenting education program. *Families in Society: The Journal of Contemporary Social Services, 96*, 195–202. doi:10.1606/1044-3894.2015.96.24

Baxter, J. (2013). *Australian mothers' participation in employment: Analyses of social, demographic and family characteristics using the Household, Income and Labour Dynamics in Australia (HILDA) survey* (Research Paper No. 52 ed.). Melbourne, Australia: Australian Government, Australian Institute of Family Studies.

Belwal, S., & Belwal, R. (2014). Work-life balance, family-friendly policies and quality of work life issues: Studying employers' perspectives of working women in Oman. *Journal of International Women's Studies, 15*, 96–117. Retrieved from http://vc.bridgew.edu/cgi/viewcontent.cgi?article=1737&context=jiws

Boswell, W., & Olson-Buchanan, J. B. (2007). The use of communication technologies after hours: The role of work attitudes and work-life conflict. *Journal of Management, 33*, 592–610. doi:10.1177/0149206307302552

Butts, M. M., Casper, W. J., & Yang, T. S. (2013). How important are work-family support policies? A meta-analytic investigation of their effects on employee outcomes. *Journal of Applied Psychology, 98*, 1–25. doi:10.1037/a0030389

Byron, K. (2005). A meta-analytic review of work-family conflict and its antecedents. *Journal of Vocational Behavior, 67*, 169–198. doi:10.1016/j.jvb.2004.08.009

Chen, W., Zhang, Y., Sanders, K., & Xu, S. (2016). Family-friendly work practices and their outcomes in China: The mediating role of work-to-family enrichment and the moderating role of gender. *The International Journal of Human Resource Management*, 1–23. doi:10.1080/09585192.2016.1195424

Chesley, N. (2005). Blurring boundaries? Linking technology use, spillover, individual distress, and family satisfaction. *Journal of Marriage and Family, 67*, 1237–1248. doi:10.1111/j.1741-3737.2005.00213.x

Chou, K. L., & Cheung, K. C. K. (2013). Family-friendly policies in the workplace and their effect on work–life conflicts in Hong Kong. *The International Journal of Human Resource Management, 24*, 3872–3885. doi:10.1080/09585192.2013.781529

Coley, R. L., & Lombardi, C. M. (2013). Does maternal employment following childbirth support or inhibit low-income children's long-term development? *Child Development, 84*, 178–197. doi:10.1111/j.1467-8624.2012.01840.x

Fiksenbaum, L. M. (2014). Supportive work–family environments: Implications for work–family conflict and well-being. *The International Journal of Human Resource Management, 25*, 653–672. doi:10.1080/09585192.2013.796314

Frone, M. R., Russell, M., & Cooper, M. L. (1992). Antecedents and outcomes of work-family conflict: Testing a model of the work-family interface. *Journal of Applied Psychology, 77*, 65–78. doi:10.1037/0021-9010.77.1.65

Goldberg, W. A., & Lucas-Thompson, R. G. (2014). College women miss the mark when estimating the impact of full-time maternal employment on children's achievement and behavior. *Psychology of Women Quarterly, 38*, 490–502. doi:10.1177/0361684314529738

Golden, T. D., Veiga, J. F., & Simsek, Z. (2006). Telecommuting's differential impact on work-family conflict: Is there no place like home? *Journal of Applied Psychology, 91*, 1340–1350. doi:10.1037/0021-9010.91.6.1340

Greenhaus, J. H., & Beutell, N. J. (1985). Sources of conflict between work and family roles. *The Academy of Management Review, 10*, 76–88. Retrieved from http://www.jstor.org/stable/258214

Greenhaus, J. H., Parasuraman, S., & Collins, K. M. (2001). Career involvement and family involvement as moderators of relationships between work-family conflict and withdrawal from a profession. *Journal of Occupational Health Psychology, 6*, 91–100. doi:10.1037/1076-8998.6.2.91

Grzywacz, J. G., & Bass, B. L. (2003). Work, family, and mental health: Testing different models of work-family fit. *Journal of Marriage and Family, 65,* 248–262. doi:10.1111/j.1741-3737.2003.00248.x

Hammer, C. S., Miccio, A. W., & Wagstaff, D. A. (2003). Home literacy experiences and their relationship to bilingual preschoolers' developing English literacy abilities: An initial investigation. *Language, Speech, and Hearing Services in Schools, 34,* 20–30. doi:10.1044/0161-1461(2003/003)

Hartung, D., & Hahlweg, K. (2010). Strengthening parent well-being at the work-family interface: A German trial on workplace Triple P. *Journal of Community and Applied Social Psychology, 20,* 404–418. doi:10.1002/casp.1046

Haslam, D., Patrick, P., & Kirby, J. (2015). Giving voice to working mothers: A consumer informed study to program design for working mothers. *Journal of Child and Family Studies, 24,* 2463–2473. doi:10.1007/s10826-014-0049-7

Haslam, D., Sanders, M. R., & Sofronoff, K. (2013). Reducing work and family conflict in teachers: A randomised controlled trial of Workplace Triple P. *School Mental Health, 5,* 70–82. doi:10.1007/s12310-012-9091-z

Haslam, D. M., & Gates, S. (2017). *Giving voice to working fathers: A consumer informed study to program design for working fathers.* Manuscript in preparation.

Kossek, E. E., & Ozeki, C. (1998). Work-family conflict, policies, and the job-life satisfaction relationship: A review and directions for organizational behavior-human resources research. *Journal of Applied Psychology, 83,* 139–149. doi:10.1037/0021-9010.83.2.139

Liu, Y., Wang, M., Chang, C.-H., Shi, J., Zhou, L., & Shao, R. (2015). Work–family conflict, emotional exhaustion, and displaced aggression toward others: The moderating roles of workplace interpersonal conflict and perceived managerial family support. *Journal of Applied Psychology, 100,* 793–808. doi:10.1037/a0038387

Lucas-Thompson, R. G., Goldberg, W. A., & Prause, J. (2010). Maternal work early in the lives of children and its distal associations with achievement and behavior problems: A meta-analysis. *Psychological Bulletin, 136,* 915–942. doi:10.1037/a0020875

Marcello, R., & Filomena, B. (2012). The relationship between work-family enrichment and nurse turnover. *Journal of Managerial Psychology, 27,* 216–236. doi:10.1108/02683941211205790

Martin, A. J., & Sanders, M. R. (2003). Balancing work and family: A controlled evaluation of the Triple P—Positive Parenting Program as a work-site intervention. *Child and Adolescent Mental Health, 8,* 161–169. doi:10.1111/1475-3588.00066

Mian, Z., Rodger, W. G., & David, D. F. (2012). Work-family conflict and individual consequences. *Journal of Managerial Psychology, 27,* 696–713. doi:10.1108/02683941211259520

Miani, C., & Hoorens, S. (2014). *Parents at work: Men and women participating in the labour force* (RAND Europe Short Statistical Report No. 2). Brussels, Belgium: European Union. Retrieved from http://www.rand.org/content/dam/rand/pubs/research_reports/RR300/RR348/RAND_RR348.pdf

Michel, J., Kotrba, L., Mitchelson, J., Clark, M. A., & Baltes, B. (2011). Antecedents of work-family conflict: A meta-analytic review. *Journal of Organizational Behaviour, 32,* 689–725. doi:10.1002/job.695

Park, Y., Fritz, C., & Jex, S. M. (2011). Relationships between work-home segmentation and psychological detachment from work: The role of communication technology use at home. *Journal of Occupational Health Psychology, 16,* 457–467. doi:10.1037/a0023594

Prinz, R. J., Sanders, M. R., Shapiro, C. J., Whitaker, D. J., & Lutzker, J. R. (2009). Population-based prevention of child maltreatment: The US triple P system population trial. *Prevention Science, 10,* 1–12. doi:10.1007/s11121-009-0123-3

Sanders, M. (1999). Triple P—Positive Parenting Program: Towards an empirically validated multilevel parenting and family support strategy for the prevention of behavior and emotional problems in children. *Clinical Child and Family Psychology Review, 2,* 71–90. doi:10.1023/A:1021843613840

Sanders, M. R., Haslam, D. M., Calam, R., Southwell, C., & Stallman, H. M. (2011). Designing effective interventions for working parents: A web-based survey of parents in the UK workforce. *Journal of Children's Services, 6,* 186–200. doi:10.1108/17466661111176042

Sanders, M. R., Prinz, R. J., & Shapiro, C. J. (2012). Parenting and child maltreatment as public health issues: Implications from the Triple P system of intervention. In A. Rubin (Ed.), *Programs and interventions for maltreated children and families at risk. Clinician's guide to evidence-based practice series* (pp. 297–312). Hoboken, NJ: Wiley.

Sanders, M. R., Stallman, H. M., & McHale, M. (2011). Workplace Triple P: A controlled evaluation of a parenting program for working parents. *Journal of Family Psychology, 25,* 581–590. doi:10.1037/a0024148

Scourfield, J., Cheung, S. Y., & Macdonald, G. (2014). Working with fathers to improve children's well-being: Results of a survey exploring service provision and intervention approach in the UK. *Children and Youth Services Review, 43,* 40–50. doi:10.1016/j.childyouth.2014.04.009

Skinner, N., & Chapman, J. (2013). Work-life balance and family friendly policies. *Evidence Base, 2,* 1–25. doi:10.4225/50/558217B4DE473

United States Department of Labor, Bureau of Labor Statistics. (2016). *Economic news release: employment characteristics of families summary.* Retrieved from http://www.bls.gov/news.release/famee.nr0.htm

Väänänen, A., Kouvonen, A., Kivimäki, M., Oksanen, T., Elovainio, M., Virtanen, M., . . . Vahtera, J. (2009). Workplace social capital and co-occurrence of lifestyle risk factors: The Finnish Public Sector Study. *Occupational and Environmental Medicine, 66,* 432–437. doi:10.1136/oem.2008.042044

CHAPTER 24

PARENTING SUPPORT IN THE CONTEXT OF NATURAL DISASTER

VANESSA E. COBHAM, BRETT MCDERMOTT, AND MATTHEW R. SANDERS

INTRODUCTION: THE SIGNIFICANCE OF NATURAL DISASTERS FOR CHILDREN

With climate change has come an increase in the frequency of extreme weather events and natural disasters worldwide (Pall et al., 2011). In 2015, EM-DAT, the international disasters database, recorded 346 natural disasters, with 22,773 people killed, over 98 million affected, and an economic impact of roughly US$66.5 billion (Guha-Sapir, 2016). Importantly, natural disasters do not affect isolated individuals. Rather, they cause significant losses to, and disrupt the functioning of, entire communities.

Although the literature on child outcomes following a natural disaster is limited compared to the research on adult outcomes, it is well recognized that, following a natural disaster, children can develop significant mental health problems. A review of natural disaster studies reported that 30%–50% of affected children and adolescents demonstrated moderate-to-severe symptoms of post-traumatic stress disorder (PTSD), while 5%–10% meet criteria for a full PTSD diagnosis (La Greca & Prinstein, 2002). More recent studies confirmed that a significant proportion of children develop PTSD symptoms following exposure to a natural disaster (Bokszczanin, 2007; Hoven et al., 2005).

In a review of studies examining the prevalence of depressive symptoms in children postdisaster (both natural and human-made), prevalence rates were reported to range from 2% to 69% (Lai, Auslander, Fitzpatrick, & Podkowirow, 2014). Studies examining the persistence of PTSD symptoms among children affected by a natural disaster indicated that approximately one third of youth with early-onset PTSD continue to display significant symptoms up to 2 years following the weather event (Yule, Perrin, & Smith, 2001).

It is critical to note that, although the mental health outcomes for children exposed to natural disasters can be significant, most children do not develop lasting difficulties (Bonanno, Brewin, Kaniasty, & La Greca, 2010). For this reason, a stepped care approach to intervention has been advocated (McDermott & Cobham, 2014), with universal interventions offered to all individuals in a disaster-affected area (regardless of degree of exposure or any other risk factors) and targeted, more intensive, interventions offered only to the minority of people who go on to develop a mental health problem.

Postdisaster, children and adolescents are indeed recognized as a particularly vulnerable group (McMichael, Neira, & Heymann, 2008). Children and adolescents are less likely than adults to have the cognitive and emotional capacity to effectively respond to the challenges involved in coping with a natural disaster and thus must often rely on support from the significant adults in their lives. This is in keeping with the idea that parents play a vital role in children's recovery from stressful life events (Scheeringa & Zeanah, 2001). From the child development literature in general, it is known that children look to important adults in their lives when assessing danger and attributing meaning to stressful events, as well as for protection (Feinman, Roberts, Hsieh, Sawyer, & Swanson, 1992; Pynoos, Goenjian, & Steinberg, 1995). However, in a postdisaster context, because the important adults (not only parents but also significant figures such as teachers and child care workers) in a child's life will typically have been affected by the same disaster, their capacity to support children and adolescents—or indeed, to even be aware of their needs—may be compromised (Silverman & La Greca, 2002).

In attempting to understand why some children and youth and not others develop post-traumatic mental health problems following a natural disaster, integrated psychosocial models (e.g., La Greca, Silverman, Vernberg, & Prinstein, 1996) have suggested that a combination of predisaster child characteristics, disaster exposure, and aspects of the postdisaster environment may be influential risk factors. Of these sources of potential risk, only the postdisaster environment can be modified once a disaster has occurred. A recent meta-analysis of risk factors for the development of PTSD in children and adolescents identified two environmental factors: parental psychopathology and poor family functioning (Trickey, Siddaway, Meiser-Stedman, Serpell, & Field, 2012).

Increasingly, models of understanding children's post-traumatic mental health problems have moved in the direction of focusing on not only risk but also resilience factors (Bonanno et al., 2010), where resilience is understood as a system's capacity to withstand or recover from significant challenges (Masten, 2011; Masten & Narayan, 2012). Operating from a risk and resilience framework, efforts are focused not only on mitigating risk but also on developing resilience in children who have been exposed to potentially traumatic events (PTEs).

In the absence of clear intervention guidelines for working with children and families in a postdisaster environment, it is useful to consider the broad intervention principles proposed by Hobfoll et al. (2007) in working with individuals exposed to community-wide trauma. These principles recommend the promotion of a sense of safety, calm, self- and collective efficacy, connectedness, and hope. This move toward a risk and resilience framework parallels the importance of moving beyond the field's traditional focus on the development of psychopathology in individual children to a more strengths-based, family-focused approach aimed at supporting adaptive coping in parents and children postdisaster (Cobham & McDermott, 2014).

THE IMPORTANCE OF PARENTING SUPPORT IN A NATURAL DISASTER CONTEXT

Parents have an important role to play in the way in which their children make sense of, and respond to, exposure to any kind of PTE. Because natural disasters almost always affect parents as well as children, they constitute PTEs in which parents may particularly benefit from support in taking on this role in their children's recovery. It has been proposed that one of the most important ways in which children are affected by a natural disaster is via the impact of these events on their parents, with the consequent implications for parenting and the parent–child relationship (Masten & Osofsky, 2010).

A well-researched pathway by which this may occur is parental distress postdisaster. The interdependence of parents' and children's distress postdisaster has been well established (Bonanno et al., 2010; Conway, McDonough, MacKenzie, Follett, & Sameroff, 2013; Masten & Narayan, 2012; Morris, Gabert-Quillen, & Delahanty, 2012). A large number of studies have found that, consistent with the conclusion of Trickey et al. (2012), parental distress (over and above shared exposure to the PTE) predicts children's post-traumatic stress symptoms (PTSSs; Kerns et al., 2014). A smaller body of work (focusing on terrorist attacks rather than natural disasters) has found that children's distress affects parental post-traumatic stress (Koplewicz et al., 2002; Levine, Whalen, Henker, & Jamner, 2005).

A pattern of reciprocal influence makes intuitive sense; however, a recent study specifically examined this question of direction in parent–child dyads' interdependent mental health following the 2006 Indonesian earthquake. These researchers found that, when trauma exposure was controlled for, parental post-traumatic stress predicted children's distress but not vice versa (Juth, Silver, Seyle, Widyatmoko, & Tan, 2015). In the context of a postdisaster environment, parental post-traumatic stress in its own right appears to constitute a highly significant risk factor for children's mental health outcomes.

It has been suggested that, in addition to parental PTSSs, changes in parenting behaviors (specifically, becoming more protective and less granting of autonomy and communicating a sense of current danger; Cobham & McDermott, 2014) and family environment factors may also put children at risk (Masten & Osofsky, 2010; McDermott & Cobham, 2012). Although many hypotheses have been advanced to explain how parent psychopathology and family functioning may be related to children's postdisaster outcomes, comparatively few empirical studies have examined these possible mechanisms. Even fewer studies have examined parent- and family-related factors that might be associated with resilience. In a recent review, Cobham, McDermott, Haslam, and Sanders (2016) concluded that empirical evidence exists to support several parent- and family-related pathways by which children's postdisaster vulnerability may be increased. These included "hostile" and "anxious" parenting styles, too much or too little conversation about the event, higher levels of conflict between parents and children or within the family, a perception by children and adolescents of lower family connectedness and greater worry about the family, family functioning that has become more dysfunctional in the wake of the disaster, and exposure to disaster-related media (see Box 24.1). In terms of factors associated with resilience, apart from an absence of the risk factors identified previously, there is some empirical support for parental encouragement of coping strategies that include acceptance, positive reframing, and emotional expression. In summary, the empirical research suggests that, in

---

BOX 24.1: Worrying About Mom and Dad

Rosie was a 15-year-old girl I interviewed in a community center following floods that devastated the state of Queensland, Australia, in January 2011. Rosie lived in a large rural community. Her parents were cotton farmers, and the floods had destroyed the first cotton crop they had expected to harvest after many years of drought. An only child, Rosie's home had also been inundated. Rosie reported a high level of flood-related distress during our conversations. However, no symptoms of post-traumatic stress were evident.

Instead, Rosie's distress centered on her parents' responses to the flooding. Rosie clearly described being "freaked out" by her mother's frequent tendency to check in with Rosie about her emotional well-being. From Rosie's perspective, her mother was "taking her emotional temperature" about the flood far too often—leading Rosie to believe that her mother was extremely distressed about the flood. Rosie also wondered whether she herself might be underreacting, to the extent that she asked me (as an external outsider) if there was something about the floods that she didn't know (and should be worrying about). Rosie explained that her father was taking the opposite approach—she felt as if he had barely had time to speak to her at all in the month since the crop and house were inundated. Finally, Rosie tearfully described a high level of "quiet" conflict between her parents ("when they think I'm not around") and talked about how worried she was about her parents—their individual well-being and their marriage. After talking to me about what was going on within her family, Rosie asked that I promise to say nothing about her concerns to her parents. We were able to talk this through and have a useful conversation with Rosie's mother about how Rosie was interpreting her parents' responses to the floods. Rosie's case, unfortunately, is quite typical.

—An account provided by the first author

---

a postdisaster context, a parenting intervention has the potential to be useful in addressing both risk and resilience factors, and that a useful parenting intervention would provide parents with information about the "parenting traps" identified here and tips for avoiding them, as well as about the value of encouraging certain coping strategies in their children.

DISASTER RECOVERY TRIPLE P

Disaster Recovery Triple P (DRTP; Cobham, McDermott, & Sanders, 2011) was developed following the January 2011 floods in Queensland, Australia. This disaster resulted in 78% of the state of Queensland (an area of over 1.85 million km² total) being declared a disaster zone. Thirty-three lives were lost; 2.5 million people were directly affected; 29,000 residences and businesses were destroyed or damaged; and $2.38 billion of damage was incurred (Queensland Floods Commission of Inquiry, 2012).

Disaster Recovery Triple P is a 2-hour universal parenting seminar that can be delivered to up to 100 people at a time. The seminar is psychoeducational in nature and involves a trained practitioner delivering a presentation, which combines didactic content, media footage relating to natural disasters, and video footage of interviews with parents and children who have been affected by a natural disaster. The presentation is followed by 30 minutes for questions from parents. Parents also receive a take-home tip sheet summarizing the content discussed.

The content covered includes common emotional and behavioral responses in children following a natural disaster; the natural course of these responses over time; predictable triggers for distress (e.g., media images, anniversaries); why some children are more affected than others; parent traps; managing children's emotional and behavioral responses; other things that can help (e.g., self-care and having a dangerous weather plan); answering children's questions; and referral pathways. The "parent traps" discussed include encouraging too much talk about the dangerous weather event, discouraging all talk about the event, being overly protective, and talking to children about your own fears and distress. Each of these parenting patterns is discussed in a nonjudgmental manner, with an emphasis on both the ease with which parents can fall into these traps and the potential importance of these traps in delaying children's natural recovery. Real parents and children talking about their experience of these parenting traps postdisaster make this content particularly powerful.

When talking about strategies for managing children's postdisaster emotional and behavioral responses, parents are encouraged to reassure their children that, in the short term, it is quite normal to be distressed; allow their children to be upset (while putting limits around this); make it clear that the danger is over now; show by example that they do not believe there to be any current danger; prompt children to use their existing coping skills; resume family routines to whatever extent is possible; give praise and attention for settled behaviors; stick to the facts of what happened; communicate confidence in their children's ability to cope; and remind children that the entire community is working hard to get back to normal.

Throughout the seminar, a recurrent theme is the need to communicate to children that while the world is a place where dangerous things can happen, the world is not always a dangerous place. All content selected for inclusion in the program was based on the literature relating to the role of parents, parenting, and family environment in the development and maintenance of postdisaster mental health problems in children. Finally, in the development of DRTP, the possibility that too much early intervention may inadvertently communicate a lack of confidence in families' and communities' resilience (Bonanno et al., 2010) was always kept in mind. DRTP is a program of parenting support designed to empower parents.

EFFICACY OF POSTDISASTER PARENTING SUPPORT PROGRAMS

Although the role of parent-related factors (including parental psychopathology, parenting, and the family environment) has increasingly come to attention in recent years, the literature on universal (or indeed, any type of) interventions for parents in the aftermath of a natural disaster is almost nonexistent. To the best of our knowledge, only one parent-focused intervention has published evaluation data (Powell & Leytham, 2014), with evaluation data for a second intervention—DRTP—reported here.

The Caregivers Journey of Hope (JoH) workshop is a 3-hour program that was delivered to 106 parents 3–8 months after an earthquake in Christchurch, New Zealand, in 2011 (Powell & Leytham, 2014). Developed by the Save the Children organization, this workshop had its origins in feedback from caregivers (parents, teachers, and child care workers) following Hurricane Katrina that they were concerned about the impact of their own distress on their ability to respond to children. The workshop consisted of five components: children's common responses to trauma, types and sources of stress, how stress affects the body, coping strategies, and building community assets and supports. Parents were surveyed before and after the workshop about their knowledge relating to stress as it pertained to themselves (e.g., how stress affects their body); current stress levels; understanding of coping strategies for handling their own stress; ability to identify strengths in managing their stress; knowledge of community and social supports available to them; and likelihood of considering a positive future for their community. Improvements were demonstrated from pre- to postworkshop on all items, with the largest changes seen on knowledge about breathing exercises to reduce stress and knowledge of the different types of stress. While the authors acknowledge the limitations of this evaluation (lack of a control group, one follow-up point only, measurement of knowledge gained rather than outcomes such as enhanced coping skills), this study represents the first step in evaluating one of the only parent-focused postdisaster interventions described in the literature.

Disaster Recovery Triple P (Cobham et al., 2011) was rolled out across the state of Queensland, Australia, between March and July 2011 as part of the Queensland Health Child and Adolescent Disaster Response (led by the first and second authors). The aim of the program was to assist parents in supporting their children following the disaster. As described previously, DRTP focuses on helping parents to understand and mitigate potential parent- and family-related risk factors (such as too much or too little conversation about the disaster), while promoting resilience-enhancing strategies (such as allowing the contained expression of distress).

Thirty-nine free seminars were delivered by trained practitioners around the state, reaching 196 parents. The seminars were widely advertised in all media—including local radio stations, major newspapers, and TV news stations. Flyers advertising the seminars were distributed to general practitioners' surgeries, pharmacies, local businesses, supermarkets, schools, and child care centers in disaster-affected areas (DAAs). A website was established and a Google advertisement link purchased. Google analytics indicated that 191,171 impressions were recorded throughout the campaign, with under a 6% Click Through Rate (the number of clicks an advertisement receives divided by the number of times it is shown).

ATTENDEES AND SATISFACTION

Of the parents who attended a DRTP seminar, 161 completed a demographic survey and a satisfaction survey. Most attendees were mothers (85%), 30% had a university education, 64% were employed in either full- or part-time work, 80% resided in an intact biological family, and 21% indicated that there had been a time in the past 12 months when their family had been unable to meet essential expenses. In terms of flood-related characteristics, 76% had their homes damaged, and 53% had been displaced by this damage. Attending parents expressed a high level of satisfaction with the seminar—with the seminar content and helpfulness receiving mean ratings of 6.10 and 6.01 of 7, respectively. Attendees reported a mean of 6.22 of 7 in terms of their intention to implement the parenting advice they had received.

Given the constraints of the situation, a quasiexperimental design was employed to evaluate the impact of DRTP on both parent and child outcomes. Participant parents ($N = 43$) completed questionnaires before the seminar (Time 1), 2 weeks after attending the seminar (post–Time 2), and 6 months after attending the seminar (Time 3). Data for both follow-up points were collected for 40 participants. Questionnaires included the Depression Anxiety and Stress Scale (DASS; Lovibond & Lovibond, 1995), which parents completed about themselves; the Strengths and Difficulties Questionnaire (SDQ; Goodman, 1997), which parents completed about their children's emotional and behavioral problems; and the specially developed Parenting After a Disaster Checklist (PADC; Cobham, Sanders, & McDermott, 2011).

The PADC consists of two subscales: (a) children's emotional and behavioral problems and (b) parental confidence in dealing with children's problems. Parents rated the frequency of each item over the past 4 weeks from 0 (Not true of my child at all) to 3 (True of my child very much or most of the time), as well as their confidence in dealing with each item from 0 (Certain I can't do it) to 10 (Certain I can do it). Sample items included "My child has nightmares about the flood" and "My child asks me lots of questions about the flood." Higher scores on the problems subscale indicate more problems, while higher scores on the confidence subscale indicate more confidence. Both subscales had excellent internal consistency within the evaluation ($\alpha = .88$ and .96, respectively).

OUTCOMES

Participant parents reported reductions from preseminar to each of the two follow-up assessments on the DASS total score, as well as on each of the DASS subscales. However, a one-way repeated measures analysis of variance (ANOVA) indicated that these differences were not significant. On the PADC, a one-way repeated measures ANOVA indicated that, over time, children's emotional and behavioral problems decreased significantly as rated by their parents over time. Although parents' mean scores on the confidence scale increased, these differences were not statistically significant. Finally, on the SDQ, a one-way repeated measures ANOVA indicated a significant reduction over time on the emotional symptoms subscale. Although means on the other subscales of the SDQ, as well as the total score, were reduced over time, these differences were not statistically significant.

This evaluation was limited by small sample size and the lack of a control group. The representativeness of the parents who attended DRTP seminars is also unclear. The challenges involved in conducting research in a postdisaster context have been well documented (Bonanno et al., 2010; Masten & Osofsky, 2010) and include many of the issues that limit the DRTP evaluation—for example, the lack of a wait-list control group, difficulties in recruiting research participants within the context of clinical service delivery, difficulties obtaining funding and training workers in a timely manner, and lack of predisaster data. However, to the best of our knowledge, this is the first evaluation of a parent-focused intervention that focused on parent and child postdisaster mental health symptoms, as well as parents' confidence in dealing with their children's postdisaster emotions and behaviors. Having follow-up data 6 months postintervention is a significant strength of the evaluation. DRTP appears to be highly acceptable to parents, and these preliminary data indicate that attendance at the seminar was associated with reductions in parents' perceptions of their children's general emotional problems (SDQ) and their children's disaster-specific emotional and behavioral problems (PADC).

MAKING TRIPLE P WORK IN A NATURAL DISASTER CONTEXT: IMPLEMENTATION ISSUES TO BE CONSIDERED

The existing literature suggests that offering an empirically based program of parenting support (such as DRTP) in a postdisaster environment is worthwhile. The DRTP evaluation data reported here are promising. However, there are a number of challenges inherent in working in a postdisaster environment that must be considered.

The first challenge is getting parents to attend a universal parenting intervention such as DRTP in a postdisaster environment. Following a natural disaster, people's time, energy, and thought tend to be directed toward practical tasks such as rebuilding. In line with Maslow's (1943) hierarchy of needs, concerns around physiological needs (e.g., food, clothing, and shelter) and safety (e.g., personal and financial security) will, as they must, take precedence over all other concerns. Related to this, most people in a postdisaster environment do not see themselves as requiring mental health support and are unlikely to seek assistance (Young Landesman et al., 2003). Particularly in areas where disasters are common—or indeed, seasonal—there is typically not the clear sense of being exposed to something that has the potential to be emotionally harmful. While most people will not develop ongoing mental health problems, this lack of awareness of the potential psychological threat means that some people who would benefit from mental health support will not receive it.

In the context of DRTP, it is suggested that many parents did not view the seminar as relevant to them—despite the fact that it was advertised as being useful for all parents in DAAs. When put together, parents' preoccupation with meeting their families' physical and safety needs, and their tendency not to expect disasters to pose an emotional threat, may have contributed significantly to the difficulty we experienced in getting parents to attend a universal parenting intervention. Another contributory factor to the difficulty in getting parents to attend may have been lack of knowledge about the seminars.

How to address this challenge of parent attendance? Certainly, an outreach approach using social marketing techniques is necessary. One thing that should help in the future is having a media strategy and campaign plan ready to implement in the short-term aftermath of a disaster. In the DRTP rollout, developing a website, making contacts, and running a media campaign took valuable time. Another strategy that may help is psychoeducation about the potential threat to children's psychological well-being for parents living in disaster-prone areas. In much the same way as Australian state governments launch public awareness-raising campaigns about keeping physically safe during storm/cyclone/bushfire seasons, a parallel campaign directed at parents and focused on helping children cope with natural disasters would be helpful in motivating parents to attend a universal program such as DRTP in a postdisaster environment.

Working with and through schools in the DAA (if they are intact and functioning) is another strategy that is likely to assist with attendance. Offering psychosocial support in schools has a number of advantages—including the capacity to reach a much larger number of parents in a normal and familiar context and the normalization of the support program being offered. Similarly, working with, and having the endorsement of, the local community support centers that spring up in a postdisaster environment is crucial. In a postdisaster context, many people and organizations (some with mandates and some without) are trying to help disaster-affected individuals and families. Sometimes, this can actually contribute to the sense of confusion and chaos that people experience after being affected by a disaster. The credibility that comes with being associated with the grassroots community support centers is crucial. When people move or change their phone number, it is their local community support center that they will inform. In line with this, it is certainly worth considering employing at least one local person to assume a leadership role in the rollout of a universal intervention such as DRTP. It should be noted that this is easier said than done.

A second important issue is timing. When is the right time to offer a universal parenting intervention such as DRTP? We would suggest that, for this particular program (with its preventive approach), delivery within 1–2 months postdisaster (when it is still early enough to help parents avoid parenting traps likely to increase their children's risk) is optimal. However, there will certainly be individual variation in terms of the "right time" for different parents to be receptive to a program such as DRTP. The key is likely to be a degree of flexibility.

Finally, making delivery of the program as flexible as possible is critical. DRTP was originally developed for group delivery by trained practitioners. However, we quickly learned that this model was unnecessarily prescriptive. Key community members to whom parents may turn (e.g., general practitioners) needed to have a store of the DRTP tip sheets that they could give to and discuss with individual parents during consultations. This in turn means that careful thought needs to be given regarding who is seen as "qualified" to talk with parents about the principles and strategies within a program such as DRTP.

IMPLICATIONS AND FUTURE DIRECTIONS

Although relatively sparse, the empirical literature does indicate that a postdisaster parenting intervention has value in terms of both mitigating parent- and family-related risk factors and helping parents to promote resiliency in their children. Although quite different in focus, both the JoH workshop and DRTP have obtained promising results, which require replication and extension. In the context of these programs, it is vital to provide parents with referral pathways through which they might receive additional parenting support (such as other variants of Triple P) around issues that either arise or persist in the months following a disaster.

Another important future direction for research focuses on disaster preparedness, which is of relevance in those countries (such as Australia) that have predictable disaster seasons. As an addition to DRTP, a preparedness tip sheet and video for parents (*Approaching Bad Weather: Helping Children Feel Prepared Rather Than Scared*; Cobham et al., 2011) were developed as a preparatory intervention resource. The tip sheet (with information about how to access the video) was freely distributed to all households in areas of Queensland at risk of dangerous weather during the 2011–2012 Australian disaster season (November to February). Undertaken as a public service initiative, no evaluation data were collected. However, anecdotally, parents reported the tip sheet was useful; funding to continue providing the preparedness tip sheet to parents in the lead up to the Australian disaster season is being sought.

CONCLUSION

Children represent a particularly vulnerable population in a postdisaster environment. Of the variables that contribute to children's risk of developing postdisaster mental health problems, the only one that is modifiable is the postdisaster environment. The importance of parents (and thus parenting support) in the postdisaster environment is clear. Although limited empirical research exists, there is preliminary evidence for both the JoH workshop and DRTP. While the many challenges in conducting rigorous research in a postdisaster setting must not deter us from attempting this, there probably also needs to be an acknowledgment that, when it comes to postdisaster interventions such as DRTP, it is very difficult for the evidence base to ever be as robust as it could be in a more controlled (nondisaster) setting. Thus, while it is important to continue to evaluate such programs, equally it is important that an evidence-based program such as DRTP should be made available to parents in the aftermath of a disaster. A program of parent support such as DRTP should be a key ingredient of any disaster plan.

KEY MESSAGES

- Children and adolescents represent a particularly vulnerable group, with a significant minority likely to develop persistent mental health problems postdisaster. However, the majority of children and adolescents will return to their predisaster level of functioning with the passage of time.
- The impact of disasters on parents (in terms of their own distress, altered parenting, and altered family environment factors) is critical in influencing children's outcomes. In a postdisaster environment, the limited existing research suggests that a parenting intervention that addresses both risk and resilience factors has the potential to be useful in supporting children and families.
- Despite the important role of parents in a postdisaster environment, to date only two postdisaster, parent-focused interventions (the Caregivers Journey of Hope workshop and Disaster Recovery Triple P) have been described and evaluated.
- Disaster Recovery Triple P (DRTP) is a 2-hour parenting seminar that was developed to specifically target empirically identified parent-/family-related risk and resilience factors (e.g., level of communication about the disaster, acceptance of children's negative emotional responses).
- Following the 2011 floods in Queensland, Australia, DRTP was rolled out across the state. The intervention was evaluated, with outcomes indicating that, following attendance at DRTP, children's emotional and behavioral problems (by their parents' report) had reduced significantly over time.
- Research indicates that a universal parent-focused intervention such as DRTP is indicated in a postdisaster environment. The DRTP data reported here are promising. However, there are a number of implementation issues that must be considered. These include the many factors that may act as obstacles to parents' attendance; the timing of such an intervention; and the need to be flexible in delivering a parent-focused intervention in a postdisaster environment.

REFERENCES

Bokszczanin, A. (2007). PSTD symptoms in children and adolescents 28 months after a floods: Age and gender differences. *Journal of Traumatic Stress, 20,* 347–351. doi:10.1002/jts.20220

Bonanno, G. A., Brewin, C. R., Kaniasty, K., & La Greca, A. M. (2010). Weighing the costs of disaster: Consequences, risks, and resilience in individuals, families, and communities. *Psychological Science in the Public Interest, 11*, 1–49. doi:10.1177/1529100610387086

Cobham, V. E., & McDermott, B. (2014). Perceived parenting change and child posttraumatic stress following a natural disaster. *Journal of Child and Adolescent Psychopharmacology, 24*, 18–23. doi:10.1089/cap.2013.0051

Cobham, V. E., McDermott, B., Haslam, D., & Sanders, M. R. (2016). The role of parents, parenting and the family environment in children's post-disaster mental health. *Current Psychiatry Reports, 18*, 53. doi:10.1007/s11920-016-0691-4

Cobham, V. E., McDermott, B., & Sanders, M. R. (2011). *Disaster Recovery Triple P: Parenting seminar.* Brisbane, Australia: Parenting and Family Support Centre, University of Queensland.

Cobham, V. E., McDermott, B., & Sanders, M. R. (2011). *Parenting After a Disaster Checklist.* Brisbane, Australia: School of Psychology, University of Queensland.

Conway, A., McDonough, S. C., MacKenzie, M. J., Follett, C., & Sameroff, A. (2013). Stress-related changes in toddlers and their mothers following the attack of September 11. *American Journal of Orthopsychiatry, 83*, 536–544. doi:10.1111/ajop.12055

Feinman, S., Roberts, D., Hsieh, K.-F., Sawyer, D., & Swanson, D. (1992). Social referencing and the social construction of reality in infancy. In S. Feinman (Ed.), *A critical review of social referencing in infancy* (pp. 15–54). New York, NY: Plenum Press.

Goodman, R. (1997). The strengths and difficulties questionnaire: A research note. *Journal of Child Psychology and Psychiatry and Allied Disciplines, 38*, 581–586. doi:10.1111/j.1469-7610.1997.tb01545.x

Guha-Sapir, D. (2016, February). Disaster data: A balanced perspective. *Cred Crunch, 41*. Retrieved from http://reliefweb.int/report/world/cred-crunch-newsletter-issue-no-41-february-2016-disaster-data-balanced-perspective

Hobfoll, S. E., Watson, P., Bell, C. C., Bryant, R. A., Brymer, M. J., Friedman, M. J., . . . Ursano, R. J. (2007). Five essential elements of immediate and mid-term mass trauma intervention: Empirical evidence. *Psychiatry: Interpersonal and Biological Processes, 70*, 283–315. doi:10.1521/psyc.2007.70.4.283

Hoven, C. W., Duarte, C. S., Lucas, C. P., Wu, P., Mandell, D. J., Goodwin, R. D., . . . Susser, E. (2005). Psychopathology among New York City public school children 6 months after September 11. *Archives of General Psychiatry, 62*, 545–552. doi:10.1001/archpsyc.62.5.545

Juth, V., Silver, R. C., Seyle, D. C., Widyatmoko, C. S., & Tan, E. T. (2015). Post-disaster mental health among parent–child dyads after a major earthquake in Indonesia. *Journal of Abnormal Child Psychology, 43*, 1309–1318. doi:10.1007/s10802-015-0009-8

Kerns, C. E., Elkins, R. M., Carpenter, A. L., Chou, T., Green, J. G., & Comer, J. S. (2014). Caregiver distress, shared traumatic exposure, and child adjustment among area youth following the 2013 Boston Marathon bombing. *Journal of Affective Disorders, 167*, 50–55. doi:10.1016/j.jad.2014.05.040

Koplewicz, H. S., Vogel, J. M., Solanto, M. V., Morrissey, R. F., Alonso, C. M., Abikoff, H., . . . Novick, R. M. (2002). Child and parent response to the 1993 World Trade Center bombing. *Journal of Traumatic Stress, 15*, 77–85. doi:10.1023/A:1014339513128

La Greca, A. M., & Prinstein, M. J. (2002). Hurricanes and earthquakes. In A. M. L. Greca, W. K. Silverman, E. M. Vernberg, & M. C. Roberts (Eds.), *Helping children cope with disasters and terrorism* (pp. 107–138). Washington, DC: American Psychological Association.

La Greca, A. M., Silverman, W. K., Vernberg, E. M., & Prinstein, M. J. (1996). Symptoms of posttraumatic stress in children after Hurricane Andrew: A prospective study. *Journal of Consulting and Clinical Psychology, 64*, 712–723. doi:10.1037/0022-006X.64.4.712

Lai, B., S., Auslander, B. A., Fitzpatrick, S., L., & Podkowirow, V. (2014). Disasters and depressive symptoms in children: A review. *Child Youth Care Forum, 43*, 489–504. doi:10.1007/s10566-014-9249-y

Levine, L. J., Whalen, C. K., Henker, B., & Jamner, L. D. (2005). Looking back on September 11, 2001: Appraised impact and memory for emotions in adolescents and adults. *Journal of Adolescent Research, 20*, 497–523. doi:10.1177/0743558405274893

Lovibond, S. H., & Lovibond, P. F. (1995). *Manual for the Depression Anxiety Stress Scales* (2nd ed.). Sydney, Australia: Psychology Foundation.

Maslow, A. H. (1943). A theory of human motivation. *Psychological Review, 50,* 430–437.

Masten, A. S. (2011). Resilience in children threatened by extreme adversity: Frameworks for research, practice, and translational synergy. *Development and Psychopathology, 23,* 493–506. doi:10.1017/S0954579411000198

Masten, A. S., & Narayan, A. J. (2012). Child development in the context of disaster, war, and terrorism: Pathways of risk and resilience. *Annual Review of Psychology, 63,* 227–257. doi:10.1146/annurev-psych-120710-100356

Masten, A. S., & Osofsky, J. D. (2010). Disasters and their impact on child development: Introduction to the special section. *Child Development, 81,* 1029–1039. doi:10.1111/j.1467-8624.2010.01452.x

McDermott, B. M., & Cobham, V. E. (2012). Family functioning in the aftermath of a natural disaster. *BMC Psychiatry, 12.* doi:10.1186/1471-244X-12-55

McDermott, B. M., & Cobham, V. E. (2014). A stepped-care model of post-disaster child and adolescent mental health service provision. *European Journal of Psychotraumatology, 5.* doi:10.3402/ejpt.v5.24294

McMichael, A. J., Neira, M., & Heymann, D. L. (2008). World Health Assembly 2008: Climate change and health. *The Lancet, 371,* 1895–1896. doi:10.1016/S0140-6736(08)60811-9

Morris, A., Gabert-Quillen, C., & Delahanty, D. (2012). The association between parent PTSD/depression symptoms and child PTSD symptoms: A meta-analysis. *Journal of Pediatric Psychology, 37,* 1076–1088. doi:10.1093/jpepsy/jss091

Pall, P., Aina, T., Stone, D. A., Stott, P. A., Nozawa, T., Hilberts, A. G. J., . . . Allen, M. R. (2011). Anthropogenic greenhouse gas contribution to flood risk in England and Wales in autumn 2000. *Nature, 470,* 382–385. doi:10.1038-nature09762

Powell, T., & Leytham, S. (2014). Building resilience after a natural disaster: An evaluation of a parental psycho-educational curriculum. *Australian Social Work, 67,* 285–296. doi:10.1080/0312407X.2014.902981

Pynoos, R. S., Goenjian, A., & Steinberg, A. M. (1995). Strategies of disaster intervention for children and adolescents. *Extreme Stress and Communities: Impact and Intervention, 80,* 445–471.

Queensland Floods Commission of Inquiry. (2012, March). *Final report.* Retrieved from http://www.floodcommission.qld.gov.au/__data/assets/pdf_file/0007/11698/QFCI-Final-Report-March-2012.pdf

Scheeringa, M. S., & Zeanah, C. H. (2001). A relational perspective on PTSD in early childhood. *Journal of Traumatic Stress, 14,* 799–815. doi:10.1023/A:1013002507972

Silverman, W. K., & La Greca, A. M. (2002). Children experiencing disasters: Definitions, reactions, and predictors of outcomes. In A. M. L. Greca, W. K. Silverman, E. M. Vernberg, & M. C. Roberts (Eds.), *Helping children cope with disasters and terrorism* (pp. 11–33). Washington, DC: American Psychological Association.

Trickey, D., Siddaway, A. P., Meiser-Stedman, R., Serpell, L., & Field, A. P. (2012). A meta-analysis of risk factors for post-traumatic stress disorder in children and adolescents. *Clinical Psychology Review, 32,* 122–138. doi:10.1016/j.cpr.2011.12.001

Young Landesman, L., Maililay, H., Bissell, R. A., Becker, S. M., Roberts, L., & Ascher, M. S. (2003). Roles and responsibilities of public health in disaster preparedness and response. In L. F. Novick & J. S. Marr (Eds.), *Public health issues disaster preparedness: Focus on bioterrorism* (pp. 1–63). Sudbury, MA: Jones and Bartlett.

Yule, W., Perrin, S., & Smith, P. (2001). Traumatic events and post-traumatic stress disorder. In W. K. S. P. D. A. Treffers (Ed.), *Anxiety disorders in children and adolescents: Research, assessment and intervention* (pp. 212–234). New York, NY: Cambridge University Press.

CHAPTER 25

BROADCAST MEDIA–BASED APPROACHES TO POSITIVE PARENTING

CAROL W. METZLER AND JULIE C. RUSBY

INTRODUCTION

A public health approach to parenting support requires an effective media and communication strategy to engage parents and increase the reach of evidence-based parenting programs. Efforts to apply a public health approach that enhances access to parenting supports have led to increased use of mass communication that aims to normalize and destigmatize participation in parenting programs and to impart positive parenting information directly to parents. Mass media communication strategies, such as television, radio, and streaming services, have considerable potential to increase the reach of parenting interventions, particularly for hard-to-reach, vulnerable, or disadvantaged parents. This chapter examines how Triple P has used television and other mass media formats as a means to promote positive parenting on a large scale. This chapter explores how mass media communication strategies can be used to reach and engage parents, promote acquisition of parenting knowledge and parenting skills, and complement a broader system of parenting supports.

WHY A MEDIA-BASED APPROACH?

A population-level mass media communication strategy has considerable potential to encourage parents to participate in parenting programs and to affect their parenting practices directly. The mass media exert a substantial influence over attitudes, beliefs, awareness, and behavior and potentially provide powerful teaching in today's society. The mass media have long been an important source of health information for the general public and have often been used to reduce health risk behaviors (e.g., substance abuse, HIV risk behaviors) and promote positive health behaviors (physical activity, nutrition; Abroms & Maibach, 2008; Wakefield, Loken, & Hornik, 2010). The application of a mass media approach to positive parenting is relatively new, however.

For the most part, broadcast media have generally been used to promote parents' awareness of, engagement in, and demand for parenting programs (e.g., Sanders, Calam, Durand, Liversidge, & Carmont, 2008). In addition, however, well-crafted mass media messages may also be an effective and attractive method for imparting positive parenting information that can complement clinic- or center-based programs, as they have good capacity for reaching a wide target audience, can potentially overcome barriers to attendance at parenting groups, can help to destigmatize and normalize parenting assistance, and can affect community norms regarding standards of care for children (Sanders & Prinz, 2008). In this way, mass media messages have potential for changing parents' parenting cognitions, affect, and practices.

THE PERVASIVENESS AND REACH OF MASS MEDIA

Broadcast media approaches potentially offer an efficient and affordable format for providing families with quality information about parenting. A primary advantage of a broadcast media approach is its capacity to dramatically increase the reach of evidence-based parenting supports, compared to traditional parent education methods, which rely on parents attending individual or group sessions on parenting. Of course, some families will require the more intensive support that a clinical intervention provides, but in a public health framework, mass media strategies are a critical part of a larger system of supports to families. Media approaches complement more intensive professional services and supports and enable parenting programs to reach families who might not otherwise be reached. Even modest effects of a wide-reaching program can translate into meaningful societal benefits when multiplied across all those affected.

Several studies have shown that television and online programming are parents' two most preferred methods for obtaining information about parenting (e.g., Metzler, Sanders, Rusby, & Crowley, 2012). This is not surprising, as watching television and accessing online resources are major leisure activities for most adults and the way that people most commonly acquire new knowledge and information (Brown, Steele, & Walsh-Childers, 2002). Virtually all US households have at least one television (96%); in 2014, the average adult aged 18-49 watched over 4 hours of content on the television screen per day and an additional 30 minutes (approximately) watching digital video on a computer or smartphone (Nielsen, 2014). The televised media and online networks are forums where parents are increasingly accessing both information and entertainment.

THE POWER OF VIDEO-BASED MESSAGES
FOR PROMOTING BEHAVIOR CHANGE

One important advantage of video-based broadcast media messages is that they can harness the power of video-based modeling and observational learning. There is extensive research on the value of observational learning and video-based modeling in promoting behavior change (e.g., Bandura, 1986; Flay & Burton, 1990; Harwood & Weissberg, 1987). Video examples that demonstrate to parents practical ways of handling common child behavior problems increase the likelihood that a parent can actually enact the demonstrated behaviors. Video modeling stimulates multiple sensory inputs, which increases attention to the message, recall of the message, and motivation to change behavior. In addition, witnessing a model successfully enact a behavior improves viewers' self-efficacy (Bandura, 1986; Maibach & Cotton, 1995). Furthermore, the social influence model (Cialdini, 2001) underscores the important social validation that modeling provides: Individuals are more likely to enact a behavior when they perceive that others like them are engaging in that behavior.

EXAMPLES OF MASS MEDIA APPROACHES: A CHANGING LANDSCAPE

Over the past 20 years, there has been a major transformation in the types of mass media communication opportunities available to promote behavior change. The increase in the number of television channels has reduced audience sizes for any given show, but the growth of subscription television, the Internet, streaming services, and social media has created many more opportunities for interventionists to directly reach a target audience (Lupis, 2017). The types of communication options available has expanded exponentially in a relatively short period of time.

The range of mass media communication options that could be deployed to support positive parenting include live and subscription television programming (infotainment, reality-based documentary-style coach shows, scripted fiction), radio programming, paid commercials, public service announcements, webcasts and webinars, podcasts, on-demand video and audio streaming, social media for video/audio streaming and sharing, embedding parenting tips into relevant news stories, and "hot topics" news interviews. Technology-assisted approaches, such as apps for mobile devices and parenting websites, can also provide video/audio content, downloadable information (e.g., tip sheets for parents), interactive programming, social networking connectivity with other users, and cell phone messaging (e.g., Triple P Online; Sanders, Baker, & Turner, 2012). It is clear that rapid changes in the media landscape and the growth of the Internet and social networking platforms has transformed our capacity to reach parents with different types of media messages in a variety of formats. It has also resulted in increased competition for parents' attention as they are bombarded with many more messages designed to influence them.

BRIEF REVIEW OF EFFICACY

Mass communications have long been an important source of health information to the general public and used to promote positive health behavior change (Abroms & Maibach, 2008; Wakefield et al., 2010). It is only within the past several years that these strategies have been applied to promoting effective parenting skills. Triple P provides some excellent examples of this broadcast media format.

TELEVISION PROGRAMS

Television is a popular vehicle for getting messages to large segments of the population. As noted, Metzler et al. (2012) found that television was parents' most preferred vehicle for accessing information about parenting. The capacity for reaching large segments of the population has to be balanced against the costs of production, limited control over program content, style of production, and scheduling. Nevertheless, several television productions on parenting have shown that television programming can be effective in improving parenting practices and child behavior outcomes.

Infotainment-Style Programming

As applied to parenting, this style of programming seeks to engage, entertain, and inform viewers about how to tackle common everyday parenting concerns using principles of positive parenting. Sanders, Montgomery, and Brechman-Toussaint (2000) evaluated the effects of an infotainment-style 12-episode television series, *Families*, which was broadcast in prime time on commercial television in New Zealand. This program provided parents with information and advice on a wide variety of parenting and family issues, and a 5- to 7-minute Triple P segment embedded in each 30-minute episode allowed parents to complete a 12-session Triple P intervention at home. Compared to wait-list controls who showed no change, mothers of children with conduct problems who viewed videotapes of the broadcast series and read accompanying informational tip sheets reported a greater reduction in disruptive child behavior, from 43% of children in the clinically elevated range prior to viewing the program to 14% following the program. Mothers who viewed the program also reported an increase in their own sense of parenting competence. These effects were maintained at a 6-month follow-up.

The Triple P Video Series is another example of an infotainment-style program. The Triple P Video Series consists of 10 episodes, with each episode lasting 12 to 15 minutes. The 10 episodes cover all content in Level 4 Triple P. Although designed for broadcast, the Video Series was evaluated in a randomized controlled trial (RCT) against a wait-list control, in which parents watched two episodes per week on DVD at home. Compared to controls, those who viewed the Video Series reported reductions in child problem behaviors and dysfunctional parenting practices and improvements in child positive behaviors, parents' use of positive parenting strategies, and observed parent—child interactions (Metzler, Rusby, Sanders, & Crowley, 2017). Examples of feedback from parents about the Video Series are provided in Box 25.1.

Reality-Based, Documentary-Style Coaching

Reality shows have been popular in television programming for some time. This genre includes "coached" shows, in which experts help individuals overcome challenges and improve their health, skills, and daily functioning. These shows typically have strong audience engagement; audiences appear interested in information and entertainment about how other people handle problems and challenges (McAlister & Fernandez, 2002). Parenting-related coaching shows such as *Supernanny*, and *Nanny 911*, in the United States and *House of Tiny Tearaways* and *Little Angels* in the United Kingdom had mixed reviews from professionals, but they attracted strong viewing audiences and were popular with parents because they seemed to capture the realities of

---

BOX 25.1: Parents' Feedback on the Triple P Video Series

- It has helped my family a lot. The "short-and-sweet" videos were great because I had time for them.
- I can't wait to review these videos again. They have helped me change my behavior as a parent, and I think that is the biggest difference in our home.
- The program provided a vehicle for my husband and I to build a customized plan that works for us and is specific to our kids and their behaviors. I love it that we have a specific plan and are on the same page with a process that was mutually attained. It has been exactly what we needed. I specifically love the "graduated" quiet time/time-out process—it works!

—Parents' comments, Oregon, USA

---

struggling to manage difficult children. In a survey of viewers of *Supernanny*, parents reported finding the program useful and being influenced to try the parenting techniques presented (Ganeshasundaram & Henley, 2009).

Triple P was evaluated as the subject of a six-episode documentary series on British television with additional online resources (Sanders, Calam, et al., 2008). *Driving Mum and Dad Mad* was broadcast on ITV (the largest commercial network in the United Kingdom), attracting a peak audience of 5.9 million viewers and an average weekly audience of over 4.2 million viewers. It covered the experiences of five families with children who had severe conduct problems; these families participated in eight-session Level 4 Group Triple P. The show displayed emotional and engaging footage, with highly distressed but relatable families. The families were shown trying the targeted positive parenting strategies and making substantial improvements in their families' and children's lives.

This series was tested in an RCT comparing two viewing conditions (standard vs. enhanced). Families in the standard condition watched the series and had access to online written informational tip sheets on the ITV website. Families in the enhanced condition watched the series and received additional individually tailored support through a 10-session self-paced workbook and access to a specially designed website. The website had downloadable tip sheets for each episode, e-mail reminders to watch the show, text message prompts to implement program tips, audio- and video-streamed positive parenting messages and demonstrations of the parenting techniques, and e-mail support from trained Triple P providers. Both conditions showed significant reductions in child conduct problems, coercive parenting, depression, anxiety, and stress and greater parental self-efficacy. The enhanced condition showed greater improvements in child behavior and parenting and parental adjustment, reduced marital conflict, and higher consumer satisfaction.

Calam, Sanders, Miller, Sadhnani, and Carmont (2008) showed that families with more severe child behavior problems were more likely to watch the entire series than families with fewer problems, and that problem severity at baseline did not predict outcomes.

These findings show that a mass media-based parenting intervention can have the power not only to increase awareness but also to change both parents' and children's behavior, even among high-risk families.

RADIO PROGRAMS

Radio programs are another source of broadcast media that can reach parents. The Australian Broadcasting Corporation (ABC), the national broadcaster in Australia, produced a regular 10-minute Triple P segment on positive parenting that was broadcast live to ABC listeners and then podcast. Between January 2008 and December 2011, there were 171 podcasts produced dealing with a diverse array of topics, ranging from issues concerning the development of babies to those involving adult children. Each segment dealt with a specific parenting issue or problem. The parenting expert was interviewed by the presenter about the topic and typically covered issues such as what the problem is, why it is a problem, and how the problem can be prevented or managed. An RCT evaluated the effects of listening to seven podcasted segments relevant to parenting toddlers and preschool-aged children with early onset conduct problems (Morawska, Tometzki, & Sanders, 2014). Postintervention, parents in the podcast condition reported significantly lower levels of child disruptive behavior and more positive parenting practices and self-efficacy than parents in the wait-list control condition.

SPECIAL CHALLENGES IN WORKING WITH THE MEDIA

CHANGING NATURE OF BROADCAST MEDIA

As stated previously, the media landscape is constantly changing and has shifted dramatically in just the past few years (Lupis, 2017; Nielson, 2014). This underscores the importance of those working with the media to stay abreast of new platforms and formats and the opportunities and challenges they represent. As consumption of live broadcasts, traditional TV and radio, and DVDs slowly and steadily declines, especially among young adults (Lupis, 2017), new opportunities are created through the steadily increasing consumption of streamed, web-delivered programming (e.g., digital video and podcasts) and social media sharing. It is important to remain nimble and flexible in the development of media assets, so that as technology advances and platforms, formats, and distribution channels shift, media assets created for an older platform or distribution channel can be repurposed for a new platform or distribution channel. This flexibility and adaptation to the "new media" are essential to staying relevant and reaching the target audience of parents.

NEED FOR INVOLVEMENT OF MEDIA EXPERTS AND MEDIA TRAINING FOR KEY PERSONNEL

Most parenting practitioners are not trained to work with the media, and many are wary of the prospect of being interviewed by the media. In addition, a successful media strategy requires parenting professionals to be informed about media outlets' different requirements, interests, priorities, and target audience demographics (Sanders & Prinz, 2008). Large-scale, population-level interventions benefit from having dedicated staff with media training to develop relationships with and work with media personnel. For example, a large-scale public health rollout of a parenting intervention will benefit from having one or more identified spokespersons to deal with media inquiries. The Every Family rollout (Sanders, Ralph, et al., 2008) and Triple P system trial (Prinz, Sanders, Shapiro, Whitaker, & Lutzker, 2009) had trained media consultants work with the implementation teams to achieve media coverage for the project. In addition, some media training for practitioners themselves can help practitioners be prepared and reduce their anxiety and therefore perform more effectively with the media. Developing clear, concise ways of conveying information makes it easier to get key messages accurately communicated.

RISKS AND CAUTIONS

Protecting Families' Privacy

Working with the media industry can be a rewarding experience, and stories can be produced that are positive, entertaining, and helpful to parents. Having a media liaison to negotiate the conditions under which visual footage is provided of real families is helpful. There are potential risks that professionals should be aware of, however. Steps must be taken to ensure that children are protected from any harm or exploitation that might arise from their appearance in a parenting program. Parents must be provided information about the potential risks and benefits of their involvement and give fully informed consent. It is recommended that the professional working with the family be available to provide support regarding any concerns that may arise as a consequence of the public viewing their footage. In addition, when parents consent to their family being filmed or interviewed, they are often unaware that their video footage will be cataloged and stored in the archives of the station or producer. Their footage will be classified and, in the case of problem behavior, may be cataloged as an "example of bad behavior in supermarket." Requesting that the footage be tagged by the journalist or producer as "not to be used with any other story" reduces but does not entirely eliminate the risk that the same footage will be used by another journalist or producer for a different story, removed from its original context. Parents and professionals who are asked to identify families who may be interested in participating in a story should be made aware of this risk. It is always advisable to discuss with the producer or journalist whether the station, network, or production company has procedures to protect or restrict further use of the footage.

Avoid Using Media Strategies in Isolation From Other Interventions

Mass communication coverage designed to promote parental awareness of parenting programs requires a trained workforce ready to deliver parenting interventions. Creating demand for programs without ensuring that there is capacity to meet the increased demand can lead to frustration on the part of parents and practitioners alike. The Every Family initiative (Sanders, Ralph, et al., 2008) provided workforce training for a wide variety of practitioners to deliver evidence-based parenting programs while the media strategy was being implemented.

IMPLICATIONS AND FUTURE DIRECTIONS

Mass communication programs can be a valuable element of a larger system of family supports, complementing more intensive supports for high-risk families, reaching those who might not otherwise be reached, and providing a sufficient level of intervention for many parents. Mass communication strategies can raise awareness, destigmatize and normalize parenting assistance, and encourage engagement in parenting programs. In addition, self-help media-based approaches to providing parenting supports can be effective in actually changing parenting practices by realistically showing parents implementing parenting skills and techniques to manage specific problem behaviors or parenting situations.

To effectively implement a large-scale, population-based parenting strategy requires a sustained media and communication effort that is dynamic, built around key relationships between professionals and the local media, and is responsive to media inquiries in a timely manner. Building a respectful and collaborative relationship with the media takes time. It is through the building of personal contacts and relationships with journalists that more opportunities can be created for positive media coverage for an intervention. For example, during the Every Family (Sanders, Ralph, et al., 2008) initiative, Channel 9's *Extra Program* in Australia produced a number of stories dealing with the prevention or management of a wide range of common behavioral issues. These editorial stories were filmed to discuss a common problem, to understand the causes, and then to depict a solution to the problem.

We contend that all parents can benefit from receiving information and guidance on effective parenting, and that media communication offers a useful mechanism for providing this information. As mass communication about parenting grows and the information explosion on parenting advice continues, parents who can learn effective parenting skills and handle their children's problem behaviors themselves with minimal assistance will do so, and as a result, practitioners in the future may be more likely to be working with more complex and change-resistant families who have already tried and failed with the self-help approach.

The changing media landscape will continue to offer new opportunities and challenges. There will continue to be a role for traditional broadcast media, where infotainment programming, reality-based documentary-style coaching, and scripted fiction (e.g., parent characters in a fictional series) remain popular. Web-based streaming services will likely provide an increasingly popular venue for distribution of programming. Growth in social media will provide new opportunities for professionals to share media messages with parents and for parents to share media messages with each other. Even virtual reality may one day allow parents to practice strategies for handling difficult situations (shopping or driving with misbehaving child) in a "safe" virtual environment. And, of course, future developments in technology and media platforms will create new opportunities for reaching parents in ways we cannot currently foresee.

CONCLUSION

Population-level communication strategies are a potentially powerful means of increasing the reach and impact of parenting programs to improve the well-being of children. A variety of broadcast communication strategies, including television programs, radio programs, streaming services, and social media, can be used to foster positive parenting. Studies to date have shown that parents are able to improve their parenting skills through mass communication approaches, and children have benefitted as a result. A carefully planned, theoretically informed, and evidence-based communication strategy that integrates messages about parenting with program supports available in the community holds great potential to strengthen population-based approaches to parenting support. The overall media approach can include specific strategies to increase parental awareness of and engagement in programs, promote public support for the parenting initiative, disseminate new research findings, and impart positive parenting guidance directly to parents.

KEY MESSAGES

- With their wide reach and powerful messaging, broadcast media–based approaches have considerable potential for encouraging parents to participate in parenting programs, as well as directly affecting parents' childrearing practices and community norms.
- Mass media options that can be deployed to support positive parenting include television programming and advertising, radio programming and advertising, video and audio streaming services, podcasts, social media, and embedding parenting into news stories.
- Media-based parenting programs, such as the Triple P examples described here, have shown both strong capacity to engage parents and positive effects on improving parents' parenting practices, children's behavior, and family functioning.
- There are many important considerations for media approaches, including providing protection for families' privacy, having media-trained individuals on staff, developing relationships with media outlets and being informed about their requirements and interests, and embedding the media strategy in a larger system of community supports for parents.
- The constantly evolving media landscape provides many new opportunities for reaching parents and challenges us to remain flexible and adapt to new media platforms and formats to stay relevant and continue reaching our target audience of parents.

REFERENCES

Abroms, L., & Maibach, E. (2008). The effectiveness of mass communication to change public behavior. *Annual Review of Public Health, 29*, 1–16. doi:10.1146/annurev.publhealth.29.020907.090824

Bandura, A. (1986). *Social foundations of thought and action: A social cognitive theory*. Englewood Cliffs, NJ: Prentice-Hall.

Brown, J. D., Steele, J. R., & Walsh-Childers, K. (2002). Introduction and overview. In J. D. Brown, J. R. Steele, & K. Walsh-Childers (Eds.), *Sexual teens, sexual media: Investigating media's influence on adolescent sexuality* (pp. 1–24). Mahwah, NJ: Erlbaum.

Calam, R., Sanders, M. R., Miller, C., Sadhnani, V., & Carmont, S. (2008). Can technology and the media help reduce dysfunctional parenting and increase engagement with preventative parenting interventions? *Child Maltreatment, 13*, 347–361. doi:10.1177/1077559508321272

Cialdini, R. B. (2001). *Influence: Science and practice* (4th ed.). Boston, MA: Allyn & Bacon.

Flay, B. R., & Burton, D. (1990). Effective mass communication strategies for health campaigns. In C. Atkin & L. Wallack (Eds.), *Mass communication and public health: Complexities and conflicts* (pp. 129–146). Newbury Park, CA: Sage.

Ganeshasundaram, R., & Henley, N. (2009). Reality television (*Supernanny*): A social marketing "place" strategy. *Journal of Consumer Marketing, 26*, 311–319. doi:10.1108/07363760910976565

Harwood, R. L., & Weissberg, R. P. (1987). The potential of video in the promotion of social competence in children and adolescents. *Journal of Early Adolescence, 7*, 345–363.

Lupis, J. C. (2017, January). *The state of traditional TV: Updated with Q3 2016 data.* Retrieved from http://www.marketingcharts.com/television/are-young-people-watching-less-tv-24817/

Maibach, E., & Cotton, D. (1995). Moving people to behavior change: A staged social cognitive approach to message design. In E. Maibach & R. Parrott (Eds.), *Designing health messages: Approaches from communication theory and public health practice* (pp. 41–64). Thousand Oaks, CA: Sage.

McAlister, A. L., & Fernandez, M. (2002). "Behavioral journalism" accelerates diffusion of healthy innovations. In R. C. Hornik (Ed.), *Public health communication: Evidence for behavior change* (pp. 315–326). Mahwah, NJ: Erlbaum.

Metzler, C. W., Rusby, J. C., Sanders, M. R., & Crowley, R. (2017). *Randomized controlled trial of a parenting video series: Effects on parenting practices and children's behavior.* Manuscript in preparation.

Metzler, C. W., Sanders, M. R., Rusby, J. C., & Crowley, R. (2012). Using Consumer preference information to increase the reach and impact of media-based parenting interventions in a public health approach to parenting support. *Behavior Therapy, 43*, 257–270. doi:10.1016/j.beth.2011.05.004

Morawska, A., Tometzki, H., & Sanders, M. R. (2014). An evaluation of the efficacy of a Triple P—Positive Parenting Program radio podcast series. *Journal of Behavioral Pediatrics, 35*, 128–137. doi:10.1097/DBP.0000000000000020

Nielsen. (2014, September). *Shifts in viewing: The cross platform report.* Retrieved from http://www.nielsen.com/content/dam/corporate/us/en/reports-downloads/2014%20Reports/q2-2014-cross-platform-report-shifts-in-viewing.pdf

Prinz, R. J., Sanders, M. R., Shapiro, C. J., Whitaker, D. J., & Lutzker, J. R. (2009). Population-based prevention of child maltreatment: The US Triple P system population trial. *Prevention Science, 10*, 1–12. doi:10.1007/s11121-009-0123-3

Sanders, M. R., Baker, S., & Turner, K. M. T. (2012). A randomised controlled trial evaluating the efficacy of Triple P Online with parents of children with early onset conduct problems. *Behaviour Research and Therapy, 50*, 675–684.

Sanders, M. R., Calam, R., Durand, M., Liversidge, T., & Carmont, S. (2008). Does self-directed and web-based support for parents enhance the effects of viewing a reality television series based on the Triple P-Positive Parenting Programme? *Journal of Child Psychology and Psychiatry, 49*, 924–932. doi:10.1016/j.brat.2012.07.004

Sanders, M. R., Montgomery, D., & Brechman-Toussaint, M. (2000). The mass media and the prevention of child behavior problems: The evaluation of a television series to promote positive outcomes for parents and their children. *Journal of Child Psychology and Psychiatry, 41*, 939–948. doi:10.1111/1469-7610.00681

Sanders, M. R., & Prinz, R. J. (2008). Using the mass media as a population level strategy to strengthen parenting skills. *Journal of Clinical Child & Adolescent Psychology, 37*, 609–621. doi:10.1080/15374410802148103

Sanders, M. R., Ralph, A., Sofronoff, K., Gardiner, P., Thompson, R., Dwyer, S., & Bidwell, K. (2008). Every Family: A population approach to reducing behavioral and emotional problems in children making the transition to school. *Journal of Primary Prevention, 29*, 197–222. doi:10.1007/s10935-008-0139-7

Wakefield, M. A., Loken, B., & Hornik, R. C. (2010). Review: Use of mass media campaigns to change health behavior. *The Lancet, 376*, 1261–1271. doi:10.1016/S0140-6736(10)60809-4

TECHNOLOGY-ASSISTED DELIVERY OF PARENTING PROGRAMS

KAREN M. T. TURNER, SABINE BAKER, AND JAMIN J. DAY

INTRODUCTION

Raising children in an age of technology has led to greater parental interest in accessing parenting information and support through the Internet. Using the Triple P Online (TPOL) family of web-based interventions as an example, this chapter examines the role of technology-assisted delivery of parenting programs, identifies some of the unique challenges to consider when providing parenting programs online, and highlights recent research exploring some of the implementation issues that influence engagement and program outcomes, including the provision of professional support.

The term *technology-assisted intervention* is broad in its scope. There have been more than two decades of research into the applications of technology to psychological interventions, covering many technologies, device types, and delivery formats (e.g., Barak, Klein, & Proudfoot, 2009). For this chapter, we focus on Internet-supported parenting interventions but recognize these build on a rich history of technology-assisted public health interventions incorporating "offline" technologies such as CD-ROM, television, video recordings, and telephony. Barak and colleagues (2009) defined Internet-supported or web-based interventions as those that deliver the majority of their treatment components through the Internet, utilizing interactive user experiences to increase knowledge and promote behavior change. With the proliferation of handheld technologies such as smartphones and tablets, Internet-connected devices present an opportunity to broaden the reach and availability of parenting information and support in an extremely cost-effective manner.

WHY PROVIDE PARENTING SUPPORT VIA THE INTERNET?

The widespread adoption of a comprehensive public health approach is an important step toward making parenting support universally accessible and improving child and family outcomes at a population level. With rising rates of preventable cases of child maltreatment and neglect and significant rates (10%–20%) of mental health issues in children and adolescents across low-, middle-, and high-income countries (Kieling et al., 2011), the lack of reach and uptake of current parenting support options remain a pervasive public health issue. Even when high-quality, evidence-based parenting support is available, relatively few parents (10%–34%) access face-to-face programs, and attendance and program completion rates vary across programs and delivery formats (Breitenstein, Gross, & Christophersen, 2014).

Web-based interventions provide a number of benefits compared to traditional forms of face-to-face delivery. The most apparent is the potential to reach many more users at low cost, including those in geographically isolated locations where Internet access is achievable but access to community-based resources is limited. There are ancillary benefits also, such as the relative ease of updating content compared to printed resources; potential to tailor content and feedback to the user; and the reduction of various barriers to participation through ease and immediacy of access, flexibility and self-paced delivery, and increased privacy.

It is not surprising that web-based access to support may be particularly appealing to time-poor parents. A consumer preference study with a diverse range of parents in the United States found that low-intensity, self-directed formats (television, the Internet, and written materials) were preferred over more intensive methods such as professional consultations, home visits, and parenting groups (Metzler, Sanders, Rusby, & Crowley, 2012), with Internet delivery the second-most preferred method for a parenting program after television. Similar findings have been reported in the United Kingdom, with online parenting support also the second-most preferred format, following individual sessions (Sanders, Haslam, Calam, Southwell, & Stallman, 2011). A recent systematic review found that roughly half of parents reported a preference for accessing advice through the Internet, although some studies reported that higher income parents were more receptive to Internet intervention delivery than lower income parents (Hall & Bierman, 2015).

Research has suggested that parents with significant adversity, such as low socioeconomic status, migration background, or high levels of stressful life events, are less likely to attend and complete a traditional parenting program (e.g., Cunningham et al., 2000), despite their children having increased vulnerability toward developing emotional or behavioral problems (Bradley & Corwyn, 2002). Web-based approaches may be important for reaching such families, as they have potential to overcome some of the logistical or perceived barriers to attending a service, such as organizing child care or concerns about being stigmatized.

A growing collection of empirical studies investigating the efficacy of web-based parenting interventions suggests that these approaches show promise. A number of meta-analyses and systematic reviews have identified studies of web-based or Internet-supported parenting programs targeting a variety of parent groups and conditions, including child disruptive behavior problems (Baumel, Pawar, Kane, & Correll, 2016; Breitenstein et al., 2014; Nieuwboer, Fukkink, & Hermanns, 2013). These consistently concluded that digital parent training results in positive improvements with small-to-medium effects for child behavior, parent behavior, and parental confidence.

The Internet is an ideal platform for delivering a comprehensive suite of parenting programs such as Triple P. Hallmarks of many psychological programs based on cognitive-behavioral and social learning principles include the use of key components such as psychoeducation; practical, skills-based learning; the introduction of concrete strategies in a structured, systematic, manner; and feedback mechanisms to monitor progress toward goals. Such techniques are well suited to the Internet and can easily be automated through intuitive and engaging user interfaces along with audio or visual guidance through the process.

SPECIAL CHALLENGES IN WORKING WITH TECHNOLOGY

There are several potential challenges to consider when working with web-based interventions. First, the initial design and development of online interventions is often costly and time consuming. Program design requires an interdisciplinary approach and ideally involves a team of professionals with diverse clinical knowledge and technical skills. For example, clinicians are involved as content experts; designers, web developers, videographers, and audio engineers create engaging content and user interfaces; computer programmers and database developers build program logic and data storage mechanisms. Even after the program has gone live, many programs require ongoing use of technical personnel for updates, server maintenance, and user support.

The second challenge concerns the rapid pace of advances in technology. Although this continual evolution provides exciting opportunities for novel approaches to behavior change interventions, it also presents a challenge to intervention developers. The timeline for developing web-based programs is often lengthy, disregarding the time then required for pilot testing and more robust randomized controlled trials (RCTs) to demonstrate intervention efficacy. In many cases, the technology may be outdated before it even reaches the end consumer.

The suitability of an online intervention can also depend on the setting or country in which it is to be implemented. While web-based delivery is among the preferred formats where Internet connectivity is widespread and reliable, preferences may be different when Internet availability is limited or computer literacy is poor. For example, recent studies have shown that 59% of parents from low-resourced communities in Panama reported having no computer literacy (Mejia, Calam, & Sanders, 2015). Women in shelters in South Africa considered lack of Internet access the most significant barrier to accessing a parenting program (Wessels & Ward, 2016), making online interventions the least preferred delivery format for parenting support. However, the "digital divide" seems to be reducing, with increasing numbers of vulnerable parents having access to the Internet and social media (Love, Sanders, Metzler, Prinz, & Kast, 2013).

KEY IMPLEMENTATION ISSUES IN MAKING TRIPLE P WORK IN A TECHNOLOGY-ASSISTED CONTEXT

Online programs can make use of video modeling and interactivity to deliver content in a way that engages the user; to structure, sequence, and personalize the content and dosage; to improve knowledge acquisition, positive self-efficacy, and behavior activation through practical exercises; and to use prompts and reminders to encourage ongoing participation. There is also an opportunity to tailor support, from completely self-directed through to a blended model with practitioner involvement. Our aim in translating Triple P to an online format was to draw on these benefits while mirroring as closely as possible the therapeutic and learning processes involved in face-to-face delivery, including the self-regulatory framework.

WHAT IS TRIPLE P ONLINE?

Triple P Online interventions are evolving in parallel with the multilevel system of face-to-face Triple P interventions, with varying levels of intensity and support. Each online program features video-based learning to introduce new skills and concepts; interviews with parents describing their parenting experiences; guided, interactive activities to prompt parental problem-solving, decision-making, and self-regulation; downloadable resources such as monitoring forms and worksheets; a dynamically generated workbook that allows users to review, track, and save their progress through the program; and optional user-initiated facilities for setting up technology-assisted program reminders (e.g., SMS, e-mail). Users receive personal login details and complete the program at their convenience. Through the program, users are encouraged to set and review goals for change, with prompts and reminders throughout to assess their progress, and are also encouraged to think about high-risk situations by combining strategies and principles learned into a cohesive personal parenting plan. Cultural sensitivity is achieved through the use of multicultural video models, and self-regulatory skills are encouraged by enabling parents to select goals informed by their own values, beliefs, and traditions. The programs include responsive design programming for smartphones, tablets, and desktops. Program variants are described next.

Triple P Online

Triple P Online (Turner & Sanders, 2011) is an eight-module parallel to Level 4 Triple P interventions such as Standard Triple P, with modules covering the following topics: What Is Positive Parenting? Encouraging Behavior You Like; Teaching New Skills; Managing Misbehavior; Dealing With Disobedience; Preventing Problems by Planning Ahead; Making Shopping Fun; and Raising Confident, Capable Kids. Modules are completed sequentially (i.e., module completion unlocks access to the next module). The first four modules cover core program content (positive parenting principles and 17 parenting strategies), and the remaining four modules focus on helping parents to integrate and generalize strategies through parenting plans. Modules can typically be completed in 40–60 minutes.

Triple P Online Brief

Triple P Online Brief (TPOLB; Turner & Sanders, 2013) is a five-module parallel to Level 3 Primary Care Triple P, which allows parents to focus on specific topics of interest. The modules include a compulsory introductory module, Getting Started With Positive Parenting, and four optional topic-specific exemplar modules: Disobedience; Fighting and Aggression; Going Shopping; and Self-Esteem. Users complete as many exemplar modules as they choose, in the order of their choice. The recommended dose is the introductory module and one or two exemplar modules. Modules each take 30–40 minutes to complete.

BRIEF REVIEW OF EFFICACY

To date, there have been seven efficacy trials investigating TPOL outcomes, program usage, and consumer satisfaction and one paper exploring outcome predictors. We briefly summarize the key findings from these trials in the material that follows.

TRIPLE P ONLINE

The foundational trial (Sanders, Baker, & Turner, 2012) included 116 parents of 2- to 9-year-old children with elevated levels of disruptive behavior, randomly allocated to TPOL or an "Internet-use-as-usual" (IUAU) control condition. At postintervention (after 12 weeks of access), the TPOL group demonstrated significant improvements on measures of child behavior problems, dysfunctional parenting styles, parenting confidence, and parental anger responses compared to the control group, with changes largely maintained at follow-up. A delayed effect was found for observed child behavior, parental stress, and partner conflict, with significant improvements seen at follow-up but not postassessment. Consumer satisfaction was rated highly, with 88% of participants at least "satisfied" with the program.

A second study (Sanders, Dittman, Farruggia, & Keown, 2014) employed a noninferiority design to compare TPOL with the *Every Parent's Self-Help Workbook*, a commensurate Level 4 self-directed Triple P intervention that has demonstrated efficacy (Sanders, Bor, & Morawska, 2007). Parents of 193 children aged 3–8 years with elevated levels of disruptive behavior problems were randomly allocated to receive TPOL or the workbook. Mothers in both conditions reported significant improvements across all measures of child behavior, dysfunctional parenting, parent confidence, quality of the parent–child relationship, risk of child maltreatment, parental anger, relationship quality, and parent adjustment at postassessment. Although response rate for fathers was lower, findings were largely similar with the exception of risk of child maltreatment and depression and anxiety (which were in the normal range at baseline). Relationship quality was in the nondistressed range at all time points. Intervention effects were largely maintained and some further improved at 6-month follow-up. In sum, TPOL was as effective as the more well-established self-directed workbook. Consumer satisfaction was equally high for both interventions.

A secondary study from this trial explored predictors of treatment outcomes (Dittman, Farruggia, Palmer, Sanders, & Keown, 2014). The findings suggest that program outcomes are not dependent on sociodemographic characteristics but may be influenced by preexisting levels of parenting difficulty, albeit through different mechanisms for mothers and fathers. The number of online modules completed significantly predicted disruptive child behaviors at postintervention (for both mother and father reports) and postintervention ineffective parenting (for mothers). In addition, baseline levels of disruptive child behaviors (for fathers) and ineffective parenting (for mothers) predicted their respective postintervention scores, while the initial quality of the parent–child relationship also predicted disruptive child behavior problems at postintervention for mothers. These data provide a helpful starting point for further investigation into the nuanced ways in which parents might respond differently to a web-based parenting program given their initial circumstances.

A recent independent RCT assessed the impact of TPOL on reducing dysfunctional parenting and stress in 52 young (<25 years), ethnically diverse New York public college students with children 2–6 years of age (Ehrensaft, Knous-Westfall, & Alonso, 2016). Mothers reporting elevated levels of stress were randomly allocated to TPOL or a wait-list control condition. The intervention period was 8 weeks, and at post-intervention, TPOL parents had lower scores on all measures of dysfunctional parenting. Effect sizes were higher for those who completed the minimum dose (at least the first four core modules of the online program). No differences were found on parenting stress.

TPOL PLUS AN ONLINE COMMUNITY AND GAMIFICATION

Love et al. (2016) published findings from an uncontrolled trial evaluating TPOL with added social media and gaming features designed to enhance engagement with the program and incentivize participation. The features included a closed online community discussion board where parents could post questions, share their experiences, and "like" other people's posts; incentives such as earning "badges" for practicing positive parenting strategies; a virtual identity (an avatar) to promote peer support while maintaining anonymity; and a Triple P accredited moderator to provide feedback, reward and feature parents' exceptional shared work, and monitor content. The trial included 155 highly vulnerable parents of 2- to 12-year-old children recruited through community agencies in Los Angeles. The majority experienced a number of risk factors associated with poorer parenting and risk of child maltreatment, for example, low income, incarceration, drug or alcohol abuse, and previous child maltreatment. Significant reductions were seen in disruptive child behaviors and child emotional problems, dysfunctional parenting, and parental stress at postassessment. No effects were found for parental confidence, attributions, depression, or anxiety (which were in the normal range at baseline). Positive effects were maintained or improved at 6-month follow-up. The participants engaged in the online community and valued its flexibility, anonymity, and shared learning. The cascade effect was that many also shared information with friends, family and other parents.

TRIPLE P ONLINE PLUS TELEPHONE SUPPORT

Day and Sanders (2017) reported a multisite RCT evaluating the additive benefit of regular, brief clinical telephone consultations provided as an adjunct to TPOL. A sample of 183 parents was randomly assigned to access TPOL on their own, with support from a practitioner who provided up to eight telephone consultations on a weekly basis, or to an IUAU control. Across the 16-week period of program access, participants in the clinically supported group engaged in four telephone consultations on average, with a mean duration of 20 minutes per call. Online module completion rates were significantly improved for parents receiving practitioner support. Relative to the control condition, at postassessment there were significant intervention effects on 9 of the 19 parent and child outcome measures for the TPOL condition and on 14 of the 19 measures for the TPOL-plus-support condition. Changes were largely maintained at 5-month follow-up for the TPOL condition (two moved into a borderline range), while all long-term effects were maintained for the supported condition.

A second RCT involving professional support assessed the impact of TPOL versus control on parenting and child outcomes for 53 families of 3- to 4-year-old children with high levels of hyperactivity and inattentiveness (Franke, Keown, & Sanders, 2016). The clinical support was two telephone consultations to help families tailor strategies to their situation. Significant postintervention improvements were found in mother-rated child hyperactivity/inattention, restlessness/impulsivity, defiance/aggression, social functioning, and teacher-rated prosocial behavior. There were also significant improvements in maternal dysfunctional and positive parenting, parenting satisfaction, self-efficacy, stress, and depression, with results largely maintained at 6-month follow-up. This is the first study to demonstrate that an online program can generate improvements for families of children with attention deficit hyperactivity disorder.

TRIPLE P ONLINE BRIEF

The foundational trial of TPOLB (Baker, Sanders, Turner, & Morawska, 2017) included 200 parents of 2- to 9-year-old children with elevated levels of disruptive behavior, randomly allocated TPOLB or a wait-list control (where parents accessed the Internet as usual). Parents completing TPOLB reported significantly decreased dysfunctional parenting and greater parental confidence in dealing with problem behavior immediately following 8 weeks of access to the intervention and at 9-month follow-up. In addition, parents reported significantly fewer child behavior problems at follow-up compared to controls. There were no significant changes in parental adjustment, conflict over parenting, or independently observed negative parent and child behavior, although these were possibly confounded by low baseline rates. Consumer satisfaction was high, with 77% of parents at least "satisfied" with the program. An example of typical feedback from consumers of this program is provided in Box 26.1.

IMPLICATIONS AND FUTURE DIRECTIONS

ENGAGEMENT

Online platforms allow for rich data collection relating to how users interact with programs. These analytics have shown moderate rates of engagement in the foundational trials (e.g., from 43% completing all eight TPOL modules, to 62% completing the recommended minimum TPOLB dose, including the introductory module plus one additional exemplar module). Do parents opt out of programs when they have achieved their goals? Or, are greater efforts needed to engage and retain participants through core program material? Improved outcomes associated with more exposure to content point to the latter, but further work is needed to determine what works for whom, and how much support is needed, so that we can best triage parents to appropriate levels of intervention. Such efforts are important for ensuring optimal intervention outcomes and benefit to families, while balancing cost-effectiveness and feasibility of large-scale dissemination.

BOX 26.1: Typical Feedback on Online Versions of Triple P

Casper was whining a lot; he would ignore us when we tried to give him instructions, quite defiant as well, and talking back to us, and we just felt like we weren't in any kind of control of disciplining him. The Online Triple P Program was really user friendly. It was easy to log on to, and it was easy to go through. It was good to see someone actually talking to you. You felt like you were doing it with someone, not doing it through a manual. Our family, now, is a lot more fun. We're enjoying each other's company, and the discipline process isn't difficult for us anymore.

—Fiona, mother of two children

KEEPING UP WITH EVOLVING TECHNOLOGY

We expect an increase in the availability of open, flexible, web-based frameworks designed for public health and psychological interventions, thus providing content experts with a mechanism to create web-based programs while bypassing costly infrastructure development. We developed such a content management system for TPOLB, which has since been used to develop modules for other training programs (e.g., the Positive Early Childhood Education Program; see Chapter 21, this volume). The advantage is that intervention developers can focus on content and harness an existing platform for the delivery mechanism without needing to invest resources into technical development. Alongside this, programming experts can focus on enhancing a platform's capabilities to keep up with rapid advances in modern devices. Separating the content and code domains allows both processes to be developed in parallel.

THE IMPORTANCE OF PROFESSIONAL SUPPORT

Entirely self-directed interventions may be viewed less positively than face-to-face approaches or when some support is provided (Rabbitt et al., 2016). In our experience, there is often resistance from agencies and practitioners to the provision of online programs without direct professional contact, yet families are keen to access programs directly online. There remains a lack of systematic evaluation of the added value of professional support in terms of program adherence, satisfaction, and outcomes. Unguided programs may increase parenting knowledge, while parenting attitudes and behavior change may benefit from supported programs; however, further empirical investigation of these putative mechanisms of change is needed (Nieuwboer et al., 2013). Direct-to-consumer and "place-based" delivery through service agencies are not mutually exclusive. Programs such as TPOL may have a place in a stepped care approach, with in-person support provided as needed, or as an active component of face-to-face interventions. They may also be offered at varying levels of intensity, triaged through online assessment, as in a current trial in pediatric practices in Seattle, Washington, USA (see Chapter 20, this volume, for more detail).

CONCLUSION

Web-based parenting interventions are well suited to broaden the portfolio of parenting interventions to increase reach and uptake of programs. Current evidence points to the efficacy of web-based programs, but more research is needed to determine who benefits most from online approaches, under what conditions self-help programs need to be augmented with professional support, and the minimum dose of content exposure needed to achieve durable change. It should also be noted that parent support preferences vary across cultures and reliability of the Internet varies across communities, meaning online programs are not a panacea. While they present some unique challenges, web-based programs do offer exceptional benefits and scope that can only further advance intervention delivery and community reach.

KEY MESSAGES

- Parents are increasingly looking to access quality parenting information and support through the Internet.
- Web-based interventions provide a number of benefits, including broad reach, low cost, individual tailoring of content and feedback, ease and immediacy of access, flexibility and self-paced delivery, and privacy.
- Triple P Online interventions are evolving in parallel with the multilevel system of face-to-face Triple P interventions, with varying levels of intensity and support.
- The challenge is to grow the evidence base for specific programs while keeping up with the rapid pace of advances in technology.
- Future research will determine who benefits most from online approaches, the minimum program dose needed to achieve durable change, and under what conditions professional support may be required.

REFERENCES

Baker, S., Sanders, M. R., Turner, K. M. T., & Morawska, A. (2017). A randomized controlled trial evaluating a low intensity interactive online parenting intervention, Triple P Online Brief, with parents of children with early onset conduct problems. *Behaviour Research and Therapy, 91,* 78–90. doi:10.1016/j.brat.2017.01.016

Baumel, A., Pawar, A., Kane, J. M., & Correll, C. U. (2016). Digital parent training for children with disruptive behaviors: Systematic review and meta-analysis of randomized trials. *Journal of Child and Adolescent Psychopharmacology, 26,* 740–749. doi:10.1089/cap.2016.0048

Barak, A., Klein, B., & Proudfoot, J. (2009). Defining Internet-supported therapeutic interventions. *Annals of Behavioral Medicine, 38,* 4–17. doi:10.1007/s12160-009-9130-7

Bradley, R. H., & Corwyn, R. F. (2002). Socioeconomic status and child development. *Annual Review of Psychology, 53,* 371–399. doi:10.1146/annurev.psych.53.100901.135233

Breitenstein, S. M., Gross, D., & Christophersen, R. (2014). Digital delivery methods of parenting training interventions: A systematic review. *Worldviews on Evidence-Based Nursing, 11,* 168–176. doi:10.1111/wvn.12040

Cunningham, C. E., Boyle, M., Offord, D., Racine, Y., Hundert, J., Secord, M., & McDonald, J. (2000). Tri-ministry study: Correlates of school-based parenting course utilization. *Journal of Consulting and Clinical Psychology, 68,* 928–933. doi:10.1037/0022-006X.68.5.928

Day, J. J., & Sanders, M. R. (2017). *A randomized controlled trial of Triple P Online with and without telephone support.* Manuscript submitted for publication.

Dittman, C. K., Farruggia, S. P., Palmer, M. L., Sanders, M. R., & Keown, L. J. (2014). Predicting success in an online parenting intervention: The role of child, parent, and family factors. *Journal of Family Psychology, 28,* 236–243. doi:10.1037/a0035991

Ehrensaft, M. K., Knous-Westfall, H. M., & Alonso, T. L. (2016). Web-based prevention of parenting difficulties in young, urban mothers enrolled in post-secondary education, *Journal of Primary Prevention, 35,* 527–542. doi:10.1007/s10935-016-0448-1

Franke, N., Keown, L. J., & Sanders, M. R. (2016). An RCT of an online parenting program for parents of preschool-aged children with ADHD symptoms. *Journal of Attention Disorders, 56,* 618–631. doi:10.1177/1087054716667598

Hall, C. M., & Bierman, K. L. (2015). Technology-assisted interventions for parents of young children: Emerging practices, current research, and future directions. *Early Childhood Research Quarterly, 33*, 21–32. doi:10.1016/j.ecresq.2015.05.003

Kieling, C., Baker-Henningham, H., Belfer, M., Conti, G., Ertem, I., Omigbodun, O., . . . Rahman, A. (2011). Child and adolescent mental health worldwide: Evidence for action. *The Lancet, 378*, 1515–1525. doi:10.1016/S0140-6736(11)60827-1

Love, S. M., Sanders, M. R., Metzler, C. W., Prinz, R. J., & Kast, E. Z. (2013). Enhancing accessibility and engagement in evidence-based parenting programs to reduce maltreatment: Conversations with vulnerable parents. *Journal of Public Child Welfare, 7*, 20–38. doi:10.1080/15548732.2012.701837

Love, S. M., Sanders, M. R., Turner, K. M. T., Maurange, M., Knott, T., Prinz, R., . . . Ainsworth, A. T. (2016). Social media and gamification: Engaging vulnerable parents in an online evidence-based parenting program. *Child Abuse and Neglect, 53*, 95–107. doi:10.1016/j.chiabu.2015.10.031

Mejia, A., Calam, R., & Sanders, M. R. (2015). Examining delivery preferences and cultural relevance of an evidence-based parenting program in a low-resource setting of Central America: Approaching parents as consumers. *Journal of Child and Family Studies, 24*, 1004–1015. doi:10.1007/s10826-014-9911-x

Metzler, C. W., Sanders, M. R., Rusby, J. C., & Crowley, R. (2012). Using consumer preference information to increase the reach and impact of media-based parenting interventions in a public health approach to parenting support. *Behavior Therapy, 43*, 257–270. doi:10.1016/j.beth.2011.05.004

Nieuwboer, C. C., Fukkink, R. G., & Hermanns, J. M. (2013). Online programs as tools to improve parenting: A meta-analytic review. *Children and Youth Services Review, 35*, 1823–1829. doi:10.1016/J.Childyouth.2013.08.008

Rabbitt, S. M., Carrubba, E., Lecza, B., McWhinney, E., Pope, J., & Kazdin, A. E. (2016). Reducing therapist contact in parenting programs: Evaluation of Internet-based treatments for child conduct problems. *Journal of Child and Family Studies, 25*, 2001–2020. doi:10.1007/s10826-016-0363-3

Sanders, M. R., Baker, S., & Turner, K. M. T. (2012). A randomized controlled trial evaluating the efficacy of Triple P Online with parents of children with early onset conduct problems. *Behaviour Research and Therapy, 50*, 675–684. doi:10.1016/j.brat.2012.07.004

Sanders, M. R., Bor, W., & Morawska, A. (2007). Maintenance of treatment gains: A comparison of Enhanced, Standard, and Self-Directed Triple P—Positive Parenting Program. *Journal of Abnormal Child Psychology, 35*, 983–998. doi:10.1007/s10802-007-9148-x

Sanders, M. R., Dittman, C. K., Farruggia, S. P., & Keown, L. J. (2014). A comparison of online versus workbook delivery of a self-help positive parenting program. *Journal of Primary Prevention, 35*, 125–133. doi:10.1007/s10935-014-0339-2

Sanders, M. R., Haslam, D. M., Calam, R., Southwell, C., & Stallman, H. M. (2011). Designing effective interventions for working parents: A web-based survey of parents in the UK workforce. *Journal of Children's Services, 6*, 186–200. doi:10.1108/17466661111176042

Turner, K. M. T., & Sanders, M. R. (2013). *Triple P Online Brief* [five-module interactive Internet program]. Brisbane, Australia: Triple P International.

Turner, K. M. T., & Sanders, M. R. (2011). *Triple P Online* [eight-module interactive Internet program]. Brisbane, Australia: Triple P International.

Wessels, I., & Ward, C. L. (2016). Battered women and parenting: Acceptability of an evidence-based parenting programme to women in shelters. *Journal of Child and Adolescent Mental Health, 28*, 21–31. doi:10.2989/17280583.2015.1132425

RESPONDING TO CULTURAL DIVERSITY IN FAMILIES

CHAPTER 27

RESPONDING TO CULTURAL DIVERSITY IN FAMILIES

An Introduction

TREVOR G. MAZZUCCHELLI

The tag line of Triple P—Positive Parenting Program is that it is "for *every* parent," reflecting the program's emphasis on the universal delivery of quality, evidence-based, parenting support. But, the adoption of a comprehensive population approach means that programs such as Triple P must truly be inclusive and relevant to all cultures. Parents of culturally diverse families in Western industrialized countries are less likely than other families to access evidence-based parenting (EBP) programs, despite the fact that these families are at greater risk of experiencing child emotional and behavioral problems (Alegria, Vallas, & Pumariega, 2010). Also, globally, families in many countries, particularly low- and middle-income countries, do not have the same level of access to high-quality parenting support as high-income countries, despite being at greater risk for developmental and health-related problems (Mejia, Calam, & Sanders, 2014). The present section explores how EBP support can best respond to barriers and challenges and embrace cultural diversity in families everywhere.

A population-based approach to parenting support requires effective parenting programs to be delivered to all families. Although studies have shown that empirically supported parenting programs are effective when delivered in different countries (Gardner, Montgomery, & Knerr, 2016) and that the core principles and strategies in Triple P are cross-culturally robust (e.g., Morawska et al., 2011), for some disadvantaged and marginalized communities, cultural fit may present as a barrier to program adoption. Turner, Sanders, Keown, and Shepherd in Chapter 28 suggest that in these cases there is a need for program adaptation. However, they argue that because developing and testing new programs is expensive and time consuming, the most efficient approach is to adapt an existing evidence-based program so that it meets the needs of the local context. But, how can this adaptation process be undertaken sensitively to have a successful outcome? They describe a collaborative participation adaptation model (CPAM) that can be used with communities to adapt evidence-based programs to take into account language, culture, and practical concerns. Drawing on examples from initiatives with Australian Aboriginal and New Zealand Māori communities, they illustrate how the CPAM process can be applied to develop culturally acceptable and effective parenting interventions.

The disparity in health and social outcomes for indigenous peoples and the challenges in addressing these problems are well known. In Chapter 29, Turner, Hodge, Forster, and McIlduff provide insight into these health and social disparities and the barriers to the uptake of evidence-based programs by exploring the social and political context of parenting in Indigenous cultures. They suggest that the adoption of evidence-based programs in Indigenous communities will be most effective when the assumption is made that Indigenous culture includes traditional knowledge about how to raise children well, resolve challenges, and heal intergenerational trauma. The challenge is to draw on both Indigenous and non-Indigenous knowledge to work toward the common goals of healing families and communities and creating nurturing environments for Indigenous children. They outline processes that have been employed in Triple P research and practice to successfully engage Indigenous families as they report on an evolving model of engaging communities collaboratively that extends on CPAM to enhance community adoption, ownership, effectiveness, and sustainability.

International bodies such as the World Health Organization (2009) recommend adapting an evidence-based program when it is delivered in different cultural context from that in which it was originally developed and tested. However, little guidance exists regarding how to adapt the content, format, and implementation to satisfy the needs of culturally diverse parents worldwide. In Chapter 30, Haslam and Mejia review the main theories addressing cultural differences across contexts and the implications for delivering EBP support in diverse cultural settings. Recognition that culture is something that is dynamic and changes over time and evidence of some "universal principles" of parenting provide a conceptual understanding for why EBP programs could be applicable across cultures. At the same time, they argue that successful delivery across cultures hinges on balancing program fidelity (i.e., adhering to the aspects of the program that effect change) with flexible tailoring of program content processes to fit the needs of participating families. They note that this is a core aspect of Triple P, making it ideally suited to applications with different ethnic and cultural groups. They make a number of practical suggestions and give examples regarding how Triple P has achieved this crucial fidelity/flexibility balance in a series of efficacious trials in a diverse range of countries, including those with collectivistic cultures.

In many cultures, religion has a major influence on how parents raise their children. Participation in organized religion may function as a protective factor, particularly for those families living in adverse circumstances, such as poverty and displacement due to war. In the final chapter of this section, El-Khani and Calam (Chapter 31) explore how religious beliefs can influence parenting beliefs, practices, and outcomes. They go on to report intriguing evidence concerning the ability of parents with strong religious beliefs, such as Muslim Arabs, to readily link the principles of positive parenting to their faith. They suggest that this has exciting implications for the delivery of EBP interventions to enhance engagement and promote positive parenting. El-Khani and Calam advocate for a tailored approach to the delivery of parenting interventions. They argue that to successfully deliver empirically supported parenting programs, it is important that practitioners understand a family's religious inclinations and how these interact with parenting practices. With this understanding, practitioners can tailor content and encourage parents to reflect and link program concepts with core beliefs and values and to self-evaluate their performance in relation to these. They go on to provide a number of practical examples and strategies for how this might be accomplished.

In summary, this series of four chapters provides encouraging support and future directions for applying EBP programs to diverse cultural groups and in a range of contexts. Themes that emerged across the chapters include the importance of understanding and respecting parents' beliefs and values, flexible and responsive delivery of EBP programs, and collaborative work toward shared goals. These chapters highlight the excellent conceptual and empirical work that is being undertaken in this area and provide optimism for the positive impact that EBP programs will have in the coming years for children, families, and communities globally. In the future, it is our hope that no family need miss out on accessing high-quality, effective, and acceptable parenting support.

REFERENCES

Alegria, M., Vallas, M., & Pumariega, A. J. (2010). Racial and ethnic disparities in pediatric mental health. *Child and Adolescent Psychiatric Clinics of North America, 19*, 759–774. doi:10.1016/j.chc.2010.07.001

Gardner, F., Montgomery, P., & Knerr, W. (2016). Transporting evidence-based parenting programs for child problem behavior (age 3–10) between countries: Systematic review and meta-analysis. *Journal of Clinical Child and Adolescent Psychology, 45*, 749–762. doi:10.1080/15374416.2015.1015134

Mejia, A., Calam, R., & Sanders, M. R. (2014). Examining delivery preferences and cultural relevance of an evidence-based parenting program in a low-resource setting of Central America: Approaching parents as consumers. *Journal of Child and Family Studies, 24*, 1004–1015. doi:10.1007=s10826-014-9911-x

Morawska, A., Sanders, M., Goadby, E., Headley, C., Hodge, L., McAuliffe, C., . . . Anderson, E. (2011). Is the Triple P—Positive Parenting Program acceptable to parents from culturally diverse backgrounds? *Journal of Child and Family Studies, 20*, 614–622. doi:10.1007/s10826-010-9436-x

World Health Organization. (2009). *Violence prevention the evidence: Preventing violence through the development of safe, stable and nurturing relationships between children and their parents and caregivers.* Retrieved from the World Health Organization website: http://apps.who.int/iris/bitstream/10665/44088/1/9789241597821_eng.pdf

C H A P T E R   2 8

A COLLABORATIVE PARTNERSHIP ADAPTATION MODEL

KAREN M. T. TURNER, MATTHEW R. SANDERS,
LOUISE J. KEOWN, AND MATTHEW SHEPHERD

INTRODUCTION

The implementation of a community-wide approach to parenting support requires parenting programs to be delivered to a range of parents from diverse cultural and language groups. If we consider a true population approach and the principle of proportionate universalism (Marmot, 2010), support should be universal and proportionate to the level of disadvantage. To achieve this, directing specific resources to increasing the reach of evidence-based programs (EBPs) in disadvantaged and marginalized communities is warranted. The development of an evidence base for a program takes time, requiring many randomized controlled trials (RCTs) by different researchers producing clinically meaningful effect sizes. Therefore, selecting an EBP and culturally adapting it as required to match local family and community needs is the most cost-effective route to achieving population reach, rather than creating a new unproven program, training system, and materials for each culturally diverse community (Kumpfer, Magalhães, & Xie, 2017). Contrary to traditional expectations that generalizability may be an issue in different settings, cross-country translation of EBPs has shown them to be at least as effective when transported to countries that are culturally quite different from the country in which they were developed (Gardner, Montgomery, & Kerr, 2016), particularly when tailored to a specific cultural group rather than a variety of cultural backgrounds, and are twice as effective when conducted in clients' native language (Griner & Smith, 2006).

However, where cultural fit is identified as a significant barrier to program adoption, the need for program adaptation cannot be ignored if programs are to be equally available for all families. Cultural adaptation of existing EBPs can be achieved through sensitivity and responsiveness to barriers such as language, cultural factors that influence receptivity to the program, and practical concerns in the local setting (Kumpfer et al., 2017). Such adaptation should take into consideration traditional worldviews, family structure and roles, and definitions of problem behavior and, based on this, use culturally relevant examples (Allen, Coombes, & Foxcroft, 2007). Surface-level adaptations have included changes in language, metaphors, images, program name, and format (e.g., session length and structure); deep-structure adaptations have included changes in content (e.g., inclusion of content about culture and biculturalism) and expansion of the concept of family to include other family members besides parents and children (Baumann et al., 2015; Mejia, Leijten, Lachman, & Parra-Cordona, 2016).

While culturally specific versions of a program do not necessarily lead to significantly greater outcomes than prior mainstream trials (Ortiz & Del Vecchio, 2013), they can result in better recruitment and engagement of families in the target community (Kumpfer, Alvarado, Smith, & Bellamy, 2002) and can increase the retention rate by 40% (United Nations Office on Drugs and Crime [UNODC], 2009). This chapter presents a model for cultural adaptation of the implementation of parenting programs. Included is consideration of variations relating to both content and process that may be required for different cultural groups.

WHAT IS COLLABORATIVE CULTURAL ADAPTATION?

Programs are likely to have a better ecological fit to the local context when program developers consult widely with consumers and end users of parenting programs during the program development stage. This consumer engagement approach has been used extensively in Triple P in recent years; the experiences and opinions are sought of parents as potential recipients of programs being developed and also of practitioners who will be trained to deliver programs to families (Sanders & Kirby, 2014). But, once a program is trialed and has an evidence base, the question is how transportable it is to populations other than the one for which it was developed. An innovative program design strategy is to develop hybrid programs that "build in" adaptation to enhance program fit and maximize fidelity of implementation, increase program effectiveness, and prompt community participation to enhance program outcomes (Castro, Barrera, & Martinez, 2004). Flexible delivery tailored to client needs while maintaining program fidelity is a key feature of any Triple P intervention (Mazzucchelli & Sanders, 2010), yet sometimes the development of a collaborative partnership to support adaptation to local circumstances is required.

Rather than the stance that existing EBPs should be delivered with strict fidelity to ensure effectiveness or the converse emphasis on the need for cultural adaptations of interventions when disseminated in diverse populations, it has been proposed that the process should be "both-and" rather than "either-or" (Mejia et al., 2016). Kumpfer and colleagues (2017) have detailed steps for culturally adapting EBPs that build on the UNODC (2009) recommendations, including (a) creating a cultural advisory group; (b) assessing specific needs; (c) translating language; (d) hiring implementers from the culture; (e) developing culturally adapted training; (f) making ongoing cultural adaptation during repeated delivery; (g) providing continuous fidelity and outcome evaluation; (h) developing dissemination partnerships; and (i) securing funding support for sustainability.

A COLLABORATIVE PARTNERSHIP ADAPTATION MODEL

To preserve program integrity but make it work for different communities, we focus here on a process of accommodating programs based on a collaborative partnership adaptation model (CPAM). The CPAM process (see Figure 28.1) involves extensive community consultation and partnership in program tailoring. It expands on Kumpfer and colleagues' steps a–c noted previously in extending beyond language translation to develop culturally sensitive program resources and delivery methods. This process was developed out of instances where a mainstream program presented too many barriers, in either resources or delivery, and minor delivery adaptation was deemed insufficient to create a cultural fit, thus preventing program adoption. As with the model of engaging communities collaboratively (see Chapter 29, this volume) for scaling up program implementation in community, CPAM is the first step in exploring cultural values and goals and evaluating the fit of program principles and strategies.

The consultation model we have developed involves a process of working collaboratively with community stakeholders or representatives to explore barriers to program acceptability and negotiate required delivery supports. The model involves developing partnerships with stakeholder organizations or community groups, consulting with elders and community leaders (often in a formal advisory group), and consulting with practitioners and parents as end users. This end-user consultation may be facilitated (e.g., structured meetings, focus groups) or independent, even anonymous (e.g., surveys, invited feedback). In any potential partnership adaptation, there must be a commitment to evaluation of acceptability and outcomes.

IMPLICATIONS FOR THE DELIVERY OF PARENTING SUPPORT

As Triple P is designed to be tailored to target identified risk factors for each family, it can readily accommodate culturally sensitive implementation in diverse communities. Studies examining the cultural acceptability of Triple P strategies in different countries (e.g., Mejia, Calam, & Sanders, 2015), and with different ethnic minority groups within Western countries (e.g., Morawska et al., 2012), have shown that the core principles and strategies of positive parenting

FIGURE 28.1: Collaborative participation adaptation model for cultural tailoring.

are cross-culturally robust. What may vary according to culture are the goals and target behaviors, practical implementation of strategies, and ways of sharing information. Triple P resources have to date had 22 language translations and been disseminated in 26 countries, with surprisingly little need for adaptation. Programs have been deployed effectively in many different cultural contexts (see meta-analysis by Sanders, Kirby, Tellegen, & Day, 2014), including ethnically diverse populations in Australasia (Australia, New Zealand); United Kingdom (England, Scotland); North America (Canada, United States); Western Europe (Ireland, Sweden, Germany, Belgium, Netherlands, Switzerland); Asia (Japan, China, Hong Kong, Singapore, Indonesia); Middle East (Iran, Turkey); Central and South America (Panama, Chile); and Africa (South Africa, Kenya).

Given the flexibility of Triple P in tailoring to parents' own values, priorities, and goals, often no significant program adaptation is required other than to find appropriate exemplars of strategies and work with families in a way that fits their learning style (e.g., storytelling or role play rather than relying on DVD or written resources) and cultural safety (e.g., including an elder or cultural advisor to create a safe place to learn and share). In some instances, variation of resources or the addition of resources has been beneficial. Following are examples of collaborative partnership adaptation initiatives.

INDIGENOUS TRIPLE P

The one major cultural adaptation of Triple P has been for Australian Indigenous families that commenced when the mainstream program was sought by Indigenous workers in Brisbane, Australia, in 1996, but potential barriers for families were identified. The CPAM process, funded by Queensland Health, involved establishment of an advisory group that steered statewide community consultation with community elders, professionals, and parents. This consultation invited feedback on the appropriateness of program content, resources, and delivery format, forming the basis for the development of a culturally sensitive adaptation of the mainstream Group Triple P that takes into consideration the cultural values, aspirations, traditions, and needs of Aboriginal and Torres Strait Islander communities. The aim was to reduce potential barriers for Indigenous families by developing parent resources that would convey evidence-based parenting support in an engaging and culturally appropriate way.

While program content was seen as appropriate, changes were made to the language and images used in program resources and the examples used to depict parenting strategies. A culturally tailored DVD (Turner & Sanders, 2007), workbook (Turner, Sanders, & Markie-Dadds, 2006a), and presentation aids (Turner, Sanders, & Markie-Dadds, 2006b) were developed. We began with Group Triple P and adapted the structure of group sessions: an introductory session to establish trust and discuss the historical, social, and political context for parenting in the community; longer sessions to slow the pace of presentation and allow more time for modeling and role playing, and for sharing personal stories about parents' experiences and attitudes relating to parenting; home-based consultations to support parents in their implementation of the positive parenting strategies through practice in a realistic context and enhance parents' ability to self-evaluate and to solve future parenting issues; and a final group session to share learnings from the program, set future goals and plan for these goals, celebrate program completion, and award certificates. This integrated home-group format offers parents two complementary learning experiences, where participants have control over the information they choose to share with the group and the issues they reserve for individual sessions.

Other learnings about program delivery included the importance of advertising the program using local images (e.g., photographs of local families), using word of mouth in developing trust and confidence in attending the program (e.g., knowing of someone else who had done the program), providing transport and child care, and incorporating sharing of food during the group.

TE WHĀNAU POU TORU

A second example, in New Zealand, is Te Whānau Pou Toru (TWPT), a collaborative partnership adaptation of the Primary Care Triple P Discussion Groups funded by the New Zealand Ministry of Health. The name *Te Whānau Pou Toru*, given by the Ngāti Hine Health Trust, the community partners, refers to three pillars of positive *whānau* ("parenting") practices. To determine the cultural relevance and acceptability of Triple P methods and resources to Māori whānau, a participatory action research process was conducted. The CPAM process began with forming a project team that decided on the scope and focus of the project, including which Triple P program to focus on, the target age group, and the region to conduct the work. A Māori reference group was established to advise the project team on cultural issues related to conducting the research.

The model involved reviewing relevant international literature on cultural adaptation theory and evidence of the efficacy of culturally adapted programs, particularly in New Zealand. Both parents and practitioners were asked to review and give their opinion about the relevance and cultural acceptability of the original program resources and materials and to make suggestions for how the program could be strengthened to meet the needs of Māori families. The project team reviewed suggestions for adaptation and prepared recommendations for the consideration of the program developers, including an estimate of costs that might be incurred by developers in making the proposed changes to the program.

The Māori reference group was also consulted about the recommendations. The purpose was to identify specific adaptations in both content and process of delivering Triple P that might enrich the program's Māori-centric qualities that display acceptability, relevance, and effectiveness with a broad range of Māori families. Following the consultation process, the integrity, session structure, and all core procedures and activities of the original Triple P Discussion Groups were preserved. No program content was removed, although ways of enriching the process through illustrating, explaining, and demonstrating it were modified to reflect Māori principles and values.

The project team, partner community organization, and community elders worked with the Triple P authors and the publisher to develop adjunct resources. These include a TWPT graphic connecting eight *tikanga* (Māori "values" and "ways of doing things") with the five Triple P positive parenting principles in the form of a Māori meeting house (*Whare nui*) image (Ngāti Hine Health Trust, The University of Auckland, & The University of Queensland, 2015a; see Figure 28.2). A worksheet was also developed that explained the eight tikanga in detail on one side and detailed the Triple P principles and strategies on the other (Ngāti Hine Health Trust, The University of Auckland, & The University of Queensland, 2015b).

The resources were used within the parenting discussions groups to illustrate how the Triple P principles and the tikanga of the local tribe (Ngāti Hine) can both work together to build parenting skills (see Box 28.1). This is considered a cultural adaption of the Triple P resource,

Te Whānau Pou Toru

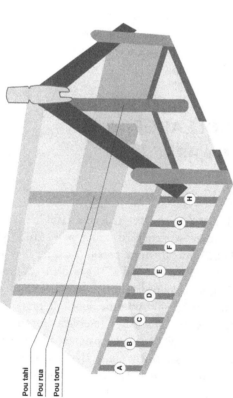

Pou tahi
Pou rua
Pou toru

A. **Whānau Motuhake** – Whānau are **autonomous** and self-managing.
Whānau use their strengths to achieve their goals and aspirations.

B. **Whānau Oranga** – Whānau are **healthy**.
Whānau work together to enjoy healthy lifestyles.

C. **Whānau Taki** – Whānau are **engaged** and participating in their environment.
Whānau are leaders within their communities.

D. **Whānau Manaaki** – Whānau are **nurturing**.
Whānau follow Māori values such as tika, pono, and aroha which includes caring and learning.

E. **Whānau Haumi** – Whānau are **secure** economically.
Whānau are able to plan for and work toward meeting their well-being economically.

F. **Whānau Marama** – Whānau are **confident** in Te Ao Māori.
The Mana of Whānau and Whakapapa is secure and Te Reo me Ona Tikanga is valued and practiced.

G. **Whānau Kaitiakitanga** – Whānau are **guardians** of the environment.
Whānau recognize the relationship between whenua and whakapapa.

H. **Whānau Matauranga** – Whānau are **knowledgeable**
Whānau are lifelong learners.

1. **Safe, interesting environment**
2. **Positive learning environment**
3. **Assertive discipline**
4. **Realistic expectations and boundaries**
5. **Taking care of yourself as a parent**

Note *The contributions of Ngati Hine Kaumatua and Kuia, Ngati Hine Health Trust, New Zealand Ministry of Health, Parenting Research Group at the University of Auckland, and the Parenting and Family Support Centre at the University of Queensland in compiling this resource are acknowledged.*
Copyright © 2015 The University of Queensland

FIGURE 28.2: Te Whānau Pou Toru diagram linking tikanga and positive parenting principles. Copyright 2015 by the University of Queensland. Reprinted with permission.

BOX 28.1: **Te Whānau Pou Toru, a Collaborative Partnership Adaptation of the Primary Care Triple P Discussion Groups**

Feedback from Māori parents attending Triple P with an additional cultural handout presented by a Ngāti Hine Kuia (local elder) showed the handout aligned extremely well with Māori values, and presentation by an Elder was an important process in terms of explaining the *tikanga* ("cultural principles and customs") and *kaupapa* ("topic") to participants. An example was when the elder discussed the concept of *Manaakitanga* ("support") and how this is important when caring for and being a role model to others, including children: "It fits in very well . . . the Ngāti Hine Kuia that came into our program, she was relating the program to kaupapa Māori. And then even listening to her way of putting the program was really helpful. 'Cause I can relate more to things Māori than things *Pakeha* [European]. So for me it was easier to relate to the Māori terms and put it into context" (parent attending a Te Whānau Pou Toru Triple P discussion group).

but it also highlights a partnership approach to parenting. In addition, practitioners used culturally appropriate examples to illustrate within-session exercises. Participants were welcomed into the group by a Māori facilitator and a Māori elder, through the use of *karakia* ("prayer"), *mihi whakatau* ("welcome"), and *whakawhānaungatanga* ("getting to know each other"). *Kai* ("food") was provided for participants during the discussion groups.

EVIDENCE SUPPORTING A COLLABORATIVE PARTNERSHIP ADAPTATION APPROACH

INDIGENOUS TRIPLE P

The first RCT exploring the acceptability and efficacy of Triple P for Indigenous families (Turner, Richards, & Sanders, 2007) involved 51 urban families with concerns about their 1- to 13-year-old child's behavior or their own parenting skills. While the term *parent* is used, carers were 67.3% mothers, 6.1% fathers, 16.3% grandmothers, 6.1% aunts, and 4.0% guardians. Compared to a wait-list control condition, parents attending Indigenous Group Triple P reported significant decreases in problem child behavior, with a mean shift into the nonclinic range and a significant decrease in dysfunctional parenting practices (verbosity). Intervention gains were primarily maintained at 6-month follow-up. There was no change for parental adjustment as, on average, parents were not clinically elevated at any assessment point. There were high rates of consumer satisfaction and positive comments about the cultural acceptability of the program content, resources, and format. Suggestions for change primarily pointed to improving engagement and allowing even more time in group sessions. An additional finding was that having a positive experience in this group program reduced obstacles to accessing mainstream services for individual assistance, such as personal coping skills and mood management.

A further effectiveness evaluation involved practitioners delivering Triple P with Indigenous families in 10 diverse urban, rural, and remote sites (Turner, Sanders, Richards, & Arthur, 2006). Results from 63 families were similar to those found in the efficacy trial, with significant decreases in problem child behavior, dysfunctional parenting practices (overreactivity), parental depression and stress (DASS); a significant increase in parenting confidence; and high rates of consumer satisfaction.

TE WHĀNAU POU TORU

A recent pilot RCT of an intervention comprising two Triple P Discussion Groups (Being a Positive Parent and Dealing With Disobedience) with complementary cultural handouts in comparison to a wait-list control followed 55 Māori parents and carers of 3- to 7-year-old children with behavior problems (Keown, Sanders, Shepherd, & Franke, 2017). The target community was in regional areas known to have higher rates of risk factors (unemployment, single parenthood, parents receiving various types of government assistance, large family sizes, and substance abuse). Preliminary results show promising short-term effects assessed 5 weeks after the intervention, with significantly lower levels of child behavior problems and functional impairment, significantly less interparental conflict, and significantly greater improvements in partner relationship quality. There were also significant time effects, showing improvement from preintervention to postintervention for dysfunctional parenting and parental anxiety in the intervention group. Semistructured interviews following the intervention highlighted a range of positive benefits from the program for parents and their children, the helpfulness of the strategies learned for managing their child's behavior, positive reports about improvements in children's behavior, and an appreciation of the culturally adapted content.

IMPLICATIONS AND FUTURE DIRECTIONS

COLLABORATIVE PARTNERSHIP ADAPTATION MODEL LOGISTICS

Assessing the Need for Adapted Resources

If the option of a uniquely tailored program and localized resources is mooted, most gatekeeper organizations and practitioners would opt for a completely locally based program; however, parents often find existing EBP content and processes culturally acceptable and relevant in their original form (Mejia et al., 2015; Morawska et al., 2012). To avoid unnecessary expenditure, cultural relevance checks with a variety of end users can help identify the minimum amount of tailoring required.

Funding Collaborative Partnership Adaptation Model Processes and Outputs

Program development (e.g., tailored versions of program resources such as workbooks and teaching aids) and development of adjunct resources (e.g., localized worksheets) require significant investment, in both time and development costs. For example, community partners incur costs associated with staffing for advisory group consultation and end-user focus groups. It should be noted that elders are often heavily committed, and respectful consideration should be given to ensuring the process is not overly burdensome or to including compensation for their expertise and time. Program developers incur costs in resource design and production and possibly development of adapted training programs, which may or may not be recouped through later commercial dissemination. Therefore, should the need for cultural adaptation of program supports be identified, a strategy for funding must be developed for both community partners and program developers.

Management of Intellectual Property

Where joint intellectual property in new resources is developed, this needs to be navigated with care, according to prior copyright in existing resources and also in cultural knowledge. Upfront negotiations about intellectual property licensing and potential future use of collaboration outputs can protect the interests of communities, publishers, and authors.

ESTABLISHING AN EVIDENCE BASE

Few studies have documented a rigorous cultural adaptation and effectiveness evaluation process (Baumann et al., 2015), and more needs to be done to explore the key ingredients of successful cross-cultural adaptation and implementation practices. There is a call to develop guidelines for consistent reporting of cultural adaptation procedures as a critical component of future investigations (Mejia et al., 2016). However, in doing so, appropriate research design and evaluation measures need to be considered for the constraints of low-resource communities (e.g., costs, literacy levels of carers, and local research capacity), as well as the cultural appropriateness of the assessment process itself. To address these concerns, research methods other than resource-intensive randomized designs need to be considered, and assessment measures are needed that are low cost, are easy to use and interpret, can be translated into different languages (Ward, Sanders, Gardner, Mikton, & Dawes, 2016), and potentially can rely on pictorial or action prompts rather than text.

CONCLUSION

The collaborative partnership adaptation initiatives described in this chapter provide examples of how the CPAM process could be applied in other communities and with other programs. If our aim is to increase access to evidence-based parenting interventions among underserved populations, we need to understand the best approaches in design, service delivery, and evaluation in each community context (Ward et al., 2016). Collaborative partnering to culturally adapt an existing EBP for specific cultural groups who would not access the mainstream program can result in high-quality, culturally acceptable, and effective parenting interventions. In each instance, evaluation of the necessity, cultural acceptability, and outcomes of such resources is important, as is the ability to take the intervention to scale given the resources and workforce available in each local context.

KEY MESSAGES

- Rather than creating a new unproven program, training system, and materials for each culturally diverse community, culturally adapting an existing EBP to match local family and community needs is the most cost-effective route to achieving population reach and can be at least as effective as for the population for which the program was developed.
- Flexible delivery tailored to client needs while maintaining program fidelity is a key feature of any Triple P intervention; however, where cultural fit is identified as a significant barrier to program adoption, the need for program adaptation cannot be ignored.
- Program developers can engage directly with communities to support adaptation of delivery and additional resources according to local circumstances as required.
- The collaborative partnership adapation model involves a process of consultation and working in partnership with stakeholder organizations, community groups, elders, community leaders, practitioners, and parents to explore barriers to program acceptability and negotiate required delivery supports.

REFERENCES

Allen, D., Coombes, L., & Foxcroft, D. R. (2007). Cultural accommodation of the Strengthening Families Programme 10–14: UK Phase I study. *Health Education Research, 22*, 547–560. doi:10.1093/her/cyl122

Baumann, A. A., Powell, B. J., Kohl, P. L., Tabak, R. G., Penalba, V., Proctor, E. K., . . . Cabassa, L. J. (2015). Cultural adaptation and implementation of evidence-based parent-training: A systematic review and critique of guiding evidence. *Children and Youth Services Review, 53*, 113–120. doi:10.1016/j.childyouth.2015.03.025

Castro, F. G., Barrera, M., & Martinez, C. R. (2004). The cultural adaptation of prevention interventions: Resolving tensions between fidelity and fit. *Prevention Science, 5*, 41–45. doi:10.1023/B:PREV.0000013980.12412.cd

Gardner, F., Montgomery, P., & Kerr, W. (2016). Transporting evidence-based parenting programs for child problem behavior (age 3–10) between countries: Systematic review and meta-analysis. *Journal of Clinical Child and Adolescent Psychology, 45*, 749–762. doi:10.1080/15374416.2015.1015134

Griner, D., & Smith, T. B. (2006). Culturally adapted mental health intervention: A meta-analytic review. *Psychotherapy: Theory, Research, Practice, Training, 43*, 531–548. doi:10.1037/0033-3204.43.4.531

Keown, L., Sanders, M. R., Shepherd, M., & Franke, N. (2017). *Preliminary findings from a randomised-controlled trial (RCT) of Te Whanau Pou Toru Whanau/Whanaungatanga Korero: Maori adaptation of the Triple P Discussion Groups.* Report to the Ministry of Health. Auckland, New Zealand: Whanau/Parenting Research Group, Faculty of Education and Social Work, The University of Auckland.

Kumpfer, K., Magalhães, C., & Xie, J. (2017). Cultural adaptation and implementation of family evidence-based interventions with diverse populations. *Prevention Science, 18*, 649–659. doi:10.1007/s11121-016-0719-3

Kumpfer, K. L., Alvarado, R., Smith, P., & Bellamy, N. (2002). Cultural sensitivity and adaptation in family-based prevention interventions. *Prevention Science, 3*, 241–244. doi:10.1023/A:1019902902119

Marmot, M. (2010). *Fair society, healthy lives: The Marmot Review. Strategic review of health inequalities in England post-2010.* London, England: Marmot Review.

Mazzucchelli, T. G., & Sanders, M. R. (2010). Facilitating practitioner flexibility within an empirically supported intervention: Lessons from a system of parenting support. *Clinical Psychology: Science and Practice, 17*, 238–252. doi:10.1111/j.1468-2850.2010.01215.x

Mejia, A., Calam, R., & Sanders, M. R. (2015). Examining delivery preferences and cultural relevance of an evidence-based parenting program in a low-resource setting of Central America: Approaching parents as consumers. *Journal of Child and Family Studies, 24*, 1004–1015. doi:10.1007/s10826-014-9911-x

Mejia, A., Leijten, P., Lachman, J. M., & Parra-Cardona, J. R. (2016). Different strokes for different folks? Contrasting approaches to cultural adaptation of parenting interventions. *Prevention Science, 18*, 630–639. doi:10.1007/s11121-016-0671-2

Morawska, A., Sanders, M. R., O'Brien, J., McAuliffe, C., Pope, S., & Anderson, E. (2012). Practitioner perceptions of the use of the Triple P—Positive Parenting Program with families from culturally diverse backgrounds. *Australian Journal of Primary Health, 18*, 313–320. doi:10.1071/PY11106

Ngāti Hine Health Trust, The University of Auckland, & The University of Queensland. (2015a). *Te Whanau Pou Toru* [Diagram]. Brisbane, QLD, Australia: Triple P International.

Ngāti Hine Health Trust, The University of Auckland, & The University of Queensland. (2015b). *Te Whanau Pou Toru: The three pillars of positive parenting practices* [Worksheet]. Brisbane, Australia: Triple P International.

Ortiz, C., & Del Vecchio, T. (2013). Cultural diversity: Do we need a new wake-up call for parent training? *Behavior Therapy, 44*, 443–458. doi:10.1016/j.beth.2013.03.009

Sanders, M. R., & Kirby, J. N. (2014). A public-health approach to improving parenting and promoting children's well-being. *Child Development Perspectives, 8*, 250–257. doi:10.1111/cdep.12086

Sanders, M. R., Kirby, J. N., Tellegen, C. L., & Day, J. J. (2014). Towards a public health approach to parenting support: A systematic review and meta-analysis of the Triple P-Positive Parenting Program. *Clinical Psychology Review, 34*, 337–357. doi:10.1016/j.cpr.2014.04.003

Turner, K. M. T., Richards, M., & Sanders, M. R. (2007). Randomised clinical trial of a group parent education programme for Australian Indigenous families. *Journal of Paediatrics and Child Health, 43*, 429–437. doi:10.1111/j.1440-1754.2007.01053.x

Turner, K. M. T., & Sanders, M. R. (2007). *Positive parenting: A survival guide for Indigenous families* [DVD]. Brisbane, Australia: Triple P International.

Turner, K. M. T., Sanders, M. R., & Markie-Dadds, C. (2006a). *Every parent's workbook for Indigenous Triple P.* Brisbane, Australia: Triple P International.

Turner, K. M. T., Sanders, M. R., & Markie-Dadds, C. (2006b). *PowerPoint presentation for Indigenous Group Triple P* [CD]. Brisbane, Australia: Triple P International.

Turner, K. M. T., Sanders, M. R., Richards, M., & Arthur, N. (2006). *Adapting and evaluating an evidence-based family intervention in Indigenous communities.* Paper presented at February the National Investment for the Early Years Conference, Sydney, Australia.

United Nations Office on Drugs and Crime (UNODC). (2009). *Guide to implementing family skills training programmes for drug abuse prevention.* New York, NY: Author.

Ward, C., Sanders, M. R., Gardner, F., Mikton, C., & Dawes, A. (2016). Preventing child maltreatment in low- and middle-income countries. *Child Abuse and Neglect, 54*, 97–107. doi:10.1016/j.chiabu.2015.11.002

CHAPTER 29

WORKING EFFECTIVELY WITH INDIGENOUS FAMILIES

KAREN M. T. TURNER, LAUREN M. HODGE, MICHELL FORSTER, AND CARI D. MCILDUFF

INTRODUCTION

Any comprehensive understanding of the health and adjustment of Indigenous children and youth has to take into account the broader sociopolitical factors that contribute to physical, emotional, and spiritual well-being. There is much existing research around evidence-based programs (EBPs) that can effectively address global health and social issues, but there is a large gap in empirical literature relating to successful delivery of programs in the real world, especially with disadvantaged communities. This chapter reviews program dissemination and implementation processes that can be employed to increase the likelihood of Indigenous communities successfully adopting EBPs, with local ownership of the implementation plan to ensure program fit and long-term sustainment.

SOCIOPOLITICAL FACTORS THAT CONTRIBUTE TO THE WELL-BEING OF INDIGENOUS CHILDREN

In colonized countries, most First Nations peoples have experienced some form of marginalization, dispossession, or discrimination due to colonial, postcolonial, and neocolonial processes, which have led to numerous physical and mental health issues (Spoon, 2014). Efforts to assimilate diverse cultures have affected cultural identity and subsequently the unity and stability of the Indigenous family unit or kinship structure (BigFoot & Funderburk, 2011; Healing Foundation, 2013). There are many sociopolitical factors that affect the well-being of Indigenous children and youth; these factors stem from past social policy and intergenerational trauma. The following, although not comprehensive, is a list of such factors: loss of traditional parenting roles and shared responsibilities, kinship structure, overcrowding, socioeconomic disadvantage, overpricing and shortage of healthy food, substance abuse, poor access to professional services, and lack of trust in available services. An awareness of the complex social and political context for parenting in Indigenous cultures is important to the success of parenting interventions (Benzies, 2014).

IMPLICATIONS FOR THE DELIVERY OF PARENTING SUPPORT

Many of these factors have a direct impact on the implementation of parenting support with Indigenous families and communities. Often, families' focus is on the foundational aspects of what many take for granted to be a healthy environment for the rearing of children. Securing suitable housing and budgeting to be able to provide their children with healthy food are among the top priorities. First, overcrowded housing often means inconsistent discipline or care of children when many adults in the home have differing approaches or older siblings take on much of the caring role. When one carer accesses a parenting program, there may be a lack of support and criticism for trying to implement new strategies and change the status quo. Involving as many of a child's carers and adults in the household as possible in any parenting support program can support consistency. In addition, excessive pricing and lack of availability of fresh, healthy, food are issues in many remote Indigenous communities, affecting health and development. Parent support programs can benefit communities by making the link between health issues and child behavior and identifying the importance of prioritizing healthy lifestyle choices.

The high rates of Indigenous children removed into out-of-home care, both historically and currently (e.g., seven times higher than for non-Indigenous children in Australia; Australian Institute of Health and Welfare, 2016) are alarming. Services are needed due to higher risk of emotional and behavioral problems (e.g., 26% vs. 16% of non-Indigenous children; De Maio et al., 2005) and to prevent families from entering the statutory child protection system or to support reunification of families where children had been in out-of-home placement. Yet, there is often suspicion of professional services for fear of being judged to be incompetent (in relation to parenting knowledge and skills or mental health), with catastrophic outcomes for the family. Due to the difficulties faced in day-to-day life and the epigenetic transfer of intergenerational experiences, mental health concerns contribute to the difficulty of raising children well. While these issues are slowly losing their stigma in contemporary society, the availability of psychological and family support services in many remote communities is sparse and often sporadic fly-in, fly-out services, and many are reluctant to access available services for fear of losing custody of their children.

Given the histories of First Nations peoples, it is no surprise that epigenetics play a large part in the current difficulties in Indigenous families and communities. Heritable epigenetics variations are adaptive and advantageous when people live in environments in which certain traumatic events occur regularly but unpredictably (Jablonca & Lamb, 1995), yet trauma affects one's ability for calm mindfulness, and thinking and learning abilities are hindered (Atkinson,

Nelson, & Atkinson, 2010). Learning ability is also hindered by the persistent tiredness that plagues many Indigenous families. This exhaustion results from issues like poor health, over-crowding, and loud chaotic environments. With this perpetual tiredness also comes the struggle to be calm, patient, and consistent with children.

Interventions to support parents of Indigenous heritage can focus on restoring cultural roles that have been disconnected (Benzies, 2014). This can be done through engagement with elders and community leaders who still hold the knowledge of traditional ways and culture. Strengthening Indigenous families and communities is as much about healing cultural trauma and attitudinal and behavioral change, as it is about the transfer of particular knowledge and skills (Lohoar, 2012). As in any culture that is different from the population for whom a program was developed, effort needs to be made to ensure that practitioners and families are made aware of the flexibility of using strategies within their own culture.

However, even with empirically supported, culturally tailored interventions available, there is no guarantee that practitioners will implement with fidelity and sustain an EBP over time (e.g., Fixsen, Naoom, Blase, Friedman, & Wallace, 2005). Many Indigenous services face obsta-cles such as competing community priorities, lack of availability of training, lack of supervision and skill rehearsal after training, difficulties in arranging workload to allow for delivery of par-enting groups or sessions, engagement issues, and reluctance for program evaluation (either for clinical use or to support further service funding; Turner & Sanders, 2007).

KEY IMPLEMENTATION ISSUES IN MAKING TRIPLE P WORK IN INDIGENOUS COMMUNITIES

The ideal implementation scenario is for Indigenous practitioners to deliver services to their communities; however, where this workforce does not yet exist, it is possible to support non-Indigenous practitioners to deliver programs in a culturally sensitive and safe way. In either case, community engagement, appropriate skills training, ongoing implementation support, and an organizational context with true commitment to self-determination and community control are important ingredients. Rather than trying to export unique cultural aspects into EBPs, program implementation strategies should involve importing EBPs into the local cultural environment, to be incorporated with local traditions and wisdom and ownership of program delivery.

ENGAGING WITH COMMUNITIES COLLABORATIVELY

In our experience, successful program adoption, implementation, and sustainment stem from working in partnership with an Indigenous organization, peak body, or ideally an entire community. The disadvantages faced by many Indigenous communities, and historically det-rimental experiences of service provision, demand a collaborative effort through which a bidirectional transfer of knowledge occurs to achieve understanding and change. Beginning with community engagement and partnership, for successful, sustained implementation to be possible, those involved need to acknowledge the historical and current community con-text, embrace culture, and empower communities to build the capacity to collaborate and to interpret and adopt new knowledge from an EBP. In addition, addressing program sustainability from the outset and developing systems to ensure access to ongoing support and supervision lead to better intervention sustainment and better outcomes for children (Novins, Green, Legha, & Aarons, 2013).

We are currently developing and evaluating a theoretical model of engaging communities collaboratively that encompasses the many aspects of engagement in an implementation initiative within a holistic partnership approach. As broad collaboration means many people are involved, this often equates to many potential implementation strategy ideas for local program delivery and support to bring them to fruition. The model includes recognition of community dynamics and capacity, establishing trust and relationship building, empowerment and mutual respect, as well as specific enablers and barriers to program implementation (McIlduff & Turner, 2017). Model development is being informed by the knowledge, experience, and guidance of First Nations practitioners internationally. The aim is to operationalize identified enablers and barriers to develop a protocol that will inform the dissemination of EBPs to Indigenous communities and the implementation of the program for practitioners and agencies on the ground.

CULTURALLY ACCOMMODATED PROFESSIONAL TRAINING AND SUPPORT

As part of a collaborative approach, planning for training can involve consultation with a local advisory group to help select the most appropriate program variants, timeline, location, potential practitioners, and delivery targets for the community. As practitioners often note a preference to have an Indigenous trainer or co-facilitator to support culturally-appropriate training and share stories of how a program can be used within culture, local cultural liaison should also be negotiated with community. Recognition of the different ways people learn is also important. Making professional training courses practical and engaging, with interactive activities, humor, and sharing of stories, allows for new and often reticent practitioners to be engaged and engender creative ideas of how a program can fit for the families they work with (Turner, Sanders, & Hodge, 2014).

The difficulty of moving from the training room to the practical setting can be eased by helping practitioners to understand the practicality of Triple P content and how to deliver flexibly, and supporting them to become confident in tailoring the program in ways that fit with each individual community or environment. Following training, programs operating in a supportive workplace are more likely to be sustained. An understanding of program requirements and implementation support from managers are vital to enable practitioners to rearrange their workload to allow for program delivery. In low-resource and remote settings, where many providers work alone or in small teams, there may also be little or no supervision in place, potentially leading to loss of skills, burn-out, and programs not being maintained (e.g., Stirman et al., 2012). Adequate supervision and peer support mechanisms are especially important in Indigenous communities where practitioners are faced with significant and ongoing trauma, and may be working with families they know personally.

CULTURALLY ACCOMMODATED PROGRAM DELIVERY

Cultural accommodation is an important part of the implementation process (Baumann et al., 2015) to bring a program to life in a local context and can be supported by program developers, trainers, and supervisors. It seems that once established in a community, some form of adaptation is a natural element of implementing EBPs (Carvalho et al., 2013). The key is to give permission for practitioners to use their clinical judgment and cultural strength to tailor programs appropriately, with the aim of promoting flexibility (e.g., using local examples and language) while maintaining program integrity (i.e., covering all core program content and processes; Mazzucchelli & Sanders, 2010). Allowing providers the flexibility to modify interventions, in this case culturally, can increase their sense of competence and ownership in program implementation because they believe they are providing the best practices to families (Self-Brown et al., 2011). The resources available to each family, each home, and each community will vary; therefore, flexibility again is important in determining what is needed to make the program relevant to each family's needs and community dynamics. Some ideas for flexible delivery are discussed briefly.

Dealing With Stigma or Shame

The first hurdle is for a practitioner to develop a reputation as a trustworthy parent support provider and to normalize program participation so that parents can attend without suspicion, stigma, or shame. Practitioners must also earn the respect of families so the information they present is taken seriously, despite potentially having personal issues known about the practitioner's own family in small communities.

Engaging Families

In many Indigenous cultures, sharing food is important, and this may be an incentive to attend a program regularly. Some organizations put in place additional measures, such as child care and transport, to overcome barriers that may prevent parents attending. Flexibility in inviting parents back to a service they have been unable to attend for extended periods for various reasons, or doing individual catch-up sessions between group sessions, can help maintain their involvement to program completion. Sometimes, parents want to know someone else who has done the program before they will attend, and group programs have been run, in the home, with one entire extended family. In addition, many parents are motivated by the certificate they receive for completing Triple P.

Working With Parents' Capacity

There are many things that influence a parent's ability to absorb new information in a session, including their learning style, literacy and first language, and health. Triple P sessions can be combined or broken into smaller segments. For example, Indigenous Triple P group sessions have been run as weekly 2.5-hour sessions or in short bursts like a full-weekend workshop or half days 2 to 4 days apart. In addition, creativity may be required to help parents consolidate key take-home learnings through homework that is visual, practical, and reflective so they can come back to the next session and discuss what is working for them.

Follow-up support is particularly important after these short bursts of learning to help parents put skills into practice and make changes in their home. Many families benefit from home visits to practice strategies and receive supportive feedback. This follow-up can also help support a parent living in an overcrowded house where other carers may be critical or obstructive. If a practitioner is not invited into the home, follow-up practice sessions may be arranged in another space where the family feels safe working with the practitioner.

Self-Care

It is imperative that practitioners are supported with clinical and cultural supervision as well as personal debriefing as they are supporting complex families and then often go home to similar issues in their own families. Capable, skilled Indigenous practitioners are often pulled in many directions within their community, with great demands on their knowledge, energy, and time. Access to supportive supervision and even external psychological services may be needed to best support these workers.

EVIDENCE SUPPORTING A CULTURAL ACCOMMODATION APPROACH

PROGRAM DELIVERY

As noted in Chapter 28 of this volume, Triple P resources and the group program format were adapted for Indigenous families soon after Triple P was first disseminated. The adaptation was in direct response to a request from local Indigenous Youth Health Services working with high-risk young Indigenous families. A process of community consultation, first with local Indigenous elders, professionals, and parents and then broader feedback from Triple P practitioners working with Indigenous communities, resulted in the development of a culturally tailored program. This program has shown positive child and family outcomes, as evidenced through randomized controlled evaluation (Turner, Richards, & Sanders, 2007) and effectiveness evaluation in diverse urban, rural, and remote sites (Turner, Sanders, Richards, & Arthur, 2006). The extensive process of engaging with community on cultural relevance and sensitivity has made this program variant appealing not only to Indigenous practitioners in Australia (see Box 29.1) but also to other First Nations groups (e.g., in Canada, New Zealand, and the United States).

TRAINING AND ONGOING TECHNICAL SUPPORT

Since the development of Indigenous Triple P, we have sought to continue to refine and tailor the corresponding training and support processes through national and international consultation. A survey of 777 Triple P practitioners from 15 countries showed that most training processes are rated equally helpful by Indigenous and non-Indigenous practitioners, although processes such as tailoring the pace of training (e.g., allowing time to share personal experiences) and simplifying the language in teaching resources were identified by Indigenous practitioners as important for the delivery of culturally competent training (Turner et al., 2014). The survey also showed

---

BOX 29.1: Feedback From an Indigenous Triple P Practitioner and Mother

I wish I could've had this type of training when I became a mum.
It would've given me a better understanding instead of parenting on the run.
I like the fact that these can be tools for life,
I will try to remember them when my kids get into strife.
The arguments fights and being disrespectful
always left me feeling sad, guilty and horrible.
I'm glad we've been taught the positive parenting way.
I can't wait to tell my countrymen and hear what they got to say.
I hope they feel like I do and practice almost every day.
'Cause it makes you feel real deadly when bringing up kids this way
and you can always be there to help the family understand the Triple P way.
—Donna Smith, Indigenous Triple P practitioner,
recited at accreditation day

---

that, although ratings of the helpfulness of training processes (e.g., group process, role play, and feedback) and posttraining support processes (e.g., self-directed learning, peer support) were significantly correlated with program uptake, the one key predictor of program use was post-training peer support. Results indicated that the stronger the sense of helpful peer support and mentoring, the more the practitioner had used Triple P in the previous month.

An international survey of 593 Triple P practitioners showed that those sustaining implementation at least 3 years posttraining were more likely to have supervision or peer support; reported higher levels of program benefit, workplace support, and positive leadership style; and lower program burden compared to practitioners who were no longer delivering the program (Hodge, Turner, Sanders, & Filus, 2016). This was mirrored in a longitudinal follow-up of 35 Indigenous family support workers implementing Triple P in the child protection sector. Partnership support (i.e., the degree to which providers felt their work benefited from the partnership between the researchers, training organization, child protection peak body, and child protection agency managers) predicted sustained implementation at 18 months posttraining, and the only significant predictor of sustained program implementation 36 months after training was supportive coaching (Hodge, Turner, Sanders, & Forster, 2017). These findings suggest the need to embed partnership support and supportive coaching in real-world implementation to improve the likelihood of EBP implementation and sustainment.

IMPLICATIONS AND FUTURE DIRECTIONS

PARTNERSHIP APPROACH

We know that providers are more likely to sustain a new program if they have open attitudes toward the program, it offers a better way of working, has observable benefits, is compatible with their values and needs, is adaptable for the local context, is not too complex, and offers adequate training and practice to maintain knowledge and skills (Hodge & Turner, 2016). We have seen Triple P adopted with great success by individual trailblazers, relying on their own intuition and community connections to bring Triple P to community. We have also seen extremely keen and excited practitioners leave training and never find the time or support to implement the program in their workplace. Supervision, peer support, and technical coaching after training in a new program can enhance program implementation and sustainment. Apart from this clinical support, what does a partnership approach look like?

We have now had several opportunities through research projects to work collaboratively with Indigenous organizations or communities to ensure the program is accepted and community led. This has involved steps such as developing a local advisory group to negotiate program variants, training format (e.g., realistic hours per training day, two-way knowledge sharing with a non-Indigenous trainer and Indigenous implementation consultant), assessment procedures, resources, and supervision structures. Such efforts have led to effective trust and relationship building, program tailoring, and practitioners having the support and supervision needed to enable them to complete accreditation and implement Triple P quickly and with confidence in their communities.

To scale up EBPs, partnerships involving program developers, program providers, agencies, communities, and policymakers working in unison can bring a program implementation effort to fruition. Such collaboration has significant time and financial cost, but money invested in training may be wasted if practitioners are not adequately supported to begin program delivery, develop their skills and confidence, and continue to offer programs with fidelity in the long term.

ONGOING EVALUATION

Assessment of program outcomes is a necessity, not only for clinical duty of care in designing program goals and evaluating whether families' needs have been met but also to allow agencies to demonstrate their impact and argue for continued funding. Many Indigenous communities have "assessment fatigue" as they have long histories of being surveyed and assessed, with no obvious benefit to the community. We often need to work with Indigenous practitioners to develop a shared understanding of the value and best methods of outcome measurement for their community, particularly where there are literacy issues or the language of program delivery is a parent's third or fourth language. Future work on the development of localized and less verbal assessment measures may be of benefit.

CONCLUSION

There are many challenges when working toward closing the gap in health and social disparity in Indigenous communities. To allow for a program to be acceptable and effective in each culture, in each community, and in each family, tailored, holistic supports need to be in place for practitioners delivering the program as well as for families. Cultural accommodation, which acknowledges the historical experiences and traditional strengths of the community in which the program is being delivered, is vital. Adoption of EBPs in Indigenous communities is most effective when guided by the assumption that Indigenous cultures possess traditional knowledge about how to teach healthy relationships, parenting, modeling, discipline, inclusion, and healing (BigFoot & Funderburk, 2011). Essentially, the approach to introducing an EBP, not just program delivery itself, is critical. The quest is to draw on both Indigenous and non-Indigenous knowledge to break the cycle of disadvantage and work toward a mutual goal of healing families and communities and creating safe, nurturing environments for Indigenous children (Atkinson et al., 2010).

KEY MESSAGES

- Community engagement, appropriate skills training, ongoing implementation support, and an organizational context with true commitment to self-determination and community control are important for the successful maintenance of evidence-based programs (EBPs) in Indigenous communities.
- Program implementation strategies should involve importing EBPs into the local cultural environment, to be incorporated with local traditions and wisdom, and ownership of program delivery.
- The model of engaging communities collaboratively extends on the program adaptation partnership to enhance community adoption, ownership, effectiveness, and sustainability.
- The model involves pretraining steps, such as developing a local advisory group to negotiate program variants to be adopted, desired training format, and appropriate assessment procedures, delivery parameters and resources, as well as posttraining supervision and support structures.

REFERENCES

Atkinson, J., Nelson, J., & Atkinson, C. (2010). Trauma, transgenerational transfer and effects on community wellbeing. In N. Purdie, P. Dudgeon, & R. Walker (Eds.), *Working together: Aboriginal and Torres Strait Islander mental health and wellbeing principles and practice* (pp. 135–144). Canberra, Australia: Australian Institute of Health and Welfare.

Australian Institute of Health and Welfare. (2016). *Child protection Australia 2014–2015* (Child Welfare Series No. 63). Canberra, Australia: Author.

Baumann, A. A., Powell, B. J., Kohl, P. L., Tabak, R. G., Penalba, V., Proctor, E. E., . . . Cabassa, L. J. (2015). Cultural adaptation and implementation of evidence-based parent training: A systematic review and critique of guiding evidence. *Children and Youth Services Review, 53*, 113–120. doi:10.1016/j.childyouth.2015.03.025

Benzies, K. (2014). Parenting in Canadian Aboriginal cultures. In H. Seline (Ed.), *Parenting across cultures: Childrearing, motherhood and fatherhood in non-Western cultures* (pp. 379–392). New York, NY: Springer.

BigFoot, D. S., & Funderburk, B. W. (2011). Honoring children, making relatives: The cultural translation of Parent–Child Interaction Therapy for American Indian and Alaska native families. *Journal of Psychoactive Drugs, 43*, 309–318. doi:10.1080/02791072.2011.628924

Carvalho, M. L., Honeycutt, S., Escoffery, C., Glanz, K., Sabbs, D., & Kegler, M. C. (2013). Balancing fidelity and adaptation: Implementing evidence-based chronic disease prevention programs. *Journal of Public Health Management and Practice, 19*, 348–356. doi:10.1097/PHH.0b013e31826d80eb

De Maio, J. A., Zubrick, S. R., Silburn, S. R., Lawrence, D. M., Mitrou, F. G., Dalby, R. B., . . . Cox, A. (2005). *The Western Australian Aboriginal Child Health Survey: Measuring the social and emotional wellbeing of aboriginal children and intergenerational effects of forced separation.* Perth, Australia: Curtin University of Technology and Telethon Institute for Child Health Research.

Fixsen, D. L., Naoom, S. F., Blase, K. A., Friedman, R. M., & Wallace, F. (2005). *Implementation research: A synthesis of the literature.* Tampa: University of South Florida, Louis de la Parte Florida Mental Health Institute, National Implementation Research Network.

Healing Foundation. (2013). *Growing our children up strong and deadly: Healing for children and young people.* Canberra, Australia: Healing Foundation. Retrieved from http://healingfoundation.org.au/wordpress/wp-content/files_mf/1369185755GrowingourChildrenupsinglesfeb2013.pdf

Hodge, L. M., & Turner, K. M. T. (2016). Sustained implementation of evidence-based programs in disadvantaged communities: A conceptual framework of supporting factors. *American Journal of Community Psychology, 58,* 192–210. doi:10.1002/ajcp.12082

Hodge, L. M., Turner, K. M. T., Sanders, M. R., & Filus, A. (2016). Sustained Implementation Support Scale: Validation of a measure of program characteristics and workplace functioning for sustained program implementation. *Journal of Behavioral Health Services and Research.* Epub ahead of print April 5, 2016. doi:10.1007/s11414-016-9505-z

Hodge, L. M., Turner, K. M. T., Sanders, M. R., & Forster, M. (2017). Factors that influence evidence-based program sustainment for family support providers in child protection services in disadvantaged communities. *Child Abuse and Neglect, 70,* 134–145. doi:10.1016/j.chiabu.2017.05.017.

Jablonca, E., & Lamb, M. J. (1995). *Epigenetic inheritance and evolution.* Oxford, England: Oxford University Press.

Lohoar, S. (2012). *Safe and supportive Indigenous families and communities for children: A synopsis and critique of Australian research* (Australian Institute of Family Studies Community Family Community Australia Paper No. 7). Retrieved from https://aifs.gov.au/cfca/publications/safe-and-supportive-indigenous-families-and-communities/introduction

Mazzucchelli, T. G., & Sanders, M. R. (2010). Facilitating practitioner flexibility within an empirically supported intervention: Lessons from a system of parenting support. *Clinical Psychology: Science and Practice, 17,* 238–252. doi:10.1111/j.1468-2850.2010.01215.x

McIlduff, C. D., & Turner, K. M. T. (2017). *The model of engaging communities collaboratively.* Manuscript in preparation.

Novins, D. K., Green, A. E., Legha, R. K., & Aarons, G. A. (2013). Dissemination and implementation of evidence-based practices for child and adolescent mental health: A systematic review. *Journal of the American Academy of Child and Adolescent Psychiatry, 52,* 1009–1025. doi:10.1016/j.jaac.2014.02.003

Self-Brown, S., Frederick, K., Binder, S., Whitaker, D., Lutzker, J., Edwards, A., & Blankenship, J. (2011). Examining the need for cultural adaptations to an evidence-based parent training program targeting the prevention of child maltreatment. *Children and Youth Services Review, 33,* 1166–1172. doi:10.1016/j.childyouth.2011.02.010

Spoon, J. (2014). Quantitative, qualitative and collaborative methods: Approaching indigenous ecological knowledge heterogeneity. *Ecology and Society, 19,* 33. doi:10.5751/ES-06549-190333

Stirman, S. W., Kimberly, J., Cook, N., Calloway, A., Castro, F., & Charns, M. (2012). The sustainability of new programs and innovations: a review of the empirical literature and recommendations for future research. *Implementation Science, 7,* 17–36. doi:10.1186/1748-5908-7-17

Turner, K. M. T., Richards, M., & Sanders, M. R. (2007). Randomised clinical trial of a group parent education programme for Australian Indigenous families. *Journal of Paediatrics and Child Health, 43,* 429–437. doi:10.1111/j.1440-1754.2007.01053.x

Turner, K. M. T., & Sanders, M. R. (2007). Family intervention in Indigenous communities: Emergent issues in conducting outcome research. *Australasian Psychiatry: Bulletin of Royal Australian and New Zealand College of Psychiatrists, 15*, S39–S43. doi:10.1080/10398560701701189

Turner, K. M. T., Sanders, M. R., & Hodge, L. (2014). Issues in professional training to implement evidence-based parenting programs: The preferences of Indigenous practitioners. *Australian Psychologist, 49*, 384–394. doi:10.1111/ap.12090

Turner, K. M. T., Sanders, M. R., Richards, M., & Arthur, N. (2006). *Adapting and evaluating an evidence-based family intervention in Indigenous communities.* Paper at February the National Investment for the Early Years Conference, Sydney, Australia.

CHAPTER 30

ACCOMMODATING RACE AND ETHNICITY IN PARENTING INTERVENTIONS

DIVNA M. HASLAM AND ANILENA MEJIA

INTRODUCTION

There are several parenting programs available, but few have considered the need for adapting content, format, and implementation frameworks to fit the needs of culturally diverse parents worldwide. A recent systematic review only identified eight studies (including Triple P) in which evidence-based parenting programs underwent refinement when delivered across different cultures (Baumann et al., 2015).

International organizations such as the World Health Organization (2009) and the United Nations Office on Drugs and Crime (2009) recommend the adaptation of parenting interventions and to tailor manuals to fit the needs of specific cultural and contextual settings to respect and not undermine the cultural values, aspirations, traditions, and needs of different ethnic groups. This chapter explores how Triple P achieves this objective when delivered in different host countries and contexts. We start by reviewing main theories addressing cultural differences across contexts, followed by discussing the implications of delivering parenting support in such diverse settings and the efficacy of Triple P across cultures.

DIMENSIONS OF CULTURAL DIFFERENCES ACROSS COUNTRIES

A central feature of human beings is that they are not the same everywhere. Their ideas, expressed motivations, behaviors, and social groups are different from place to place and changeable over time due to political and environmental transformations. In this section, we discuss the dimensions of cultural differences and how this diversity influences family functioning and parenting practices.

Richerson and Boyd (2005) defined culture as the patterns of behaviors, knowledge, and beliefs acquired through the socialization processes. It distinguishes one group of people from another group. These patterns are often acquired through teaching, imitation, and other forms of social transmission. Culture specifies designs for living that have proven effective in the past, ways of dealing with social situations, and ways to think about the self and social behavior that have been reinforced. Triandis (1989) suggested culture is to society what memory is to the person: a set of historical and social norms that allow survival. Many authors refer to culture as an evolutionary trait, given that human beings survive on culturally transmitted know-hows, abilities, and skills that cannot be acquired without socialization.

There are commonly used taxonomies to differentiate cultural groups and families, the most popular one being the cultural dimensions theory of Hofstede (1984). This theory proposes several dimensions in which worldwide cultures can be differentiated. One of these dimensions is the degree to which people in society are integrated into groups. On one hand, individualistic–autonomous cultures value individuals over the group; thus, personal goals and rights are promoted. In this type of culture, independence in children is highly promoted from early on. European countries such as the United Kingdom, Germany, and Norway are considered individualist–autonomous. On the other hand, in collectivistic cultures, the group is valued over individuals, and group membership is the norm. For example, in collectivistic cultures it is more common for young adults to live with their parents until later in life and for grandparents to take an active role in grandchildren's rearing. Most countries in Africa, Asia, and Latin America are considered collectivistic (Markus & Kitayama, 1991).

Although Hofstead's theory was developed based on studies mainly conducted in work and industrial settings, similar cultural dimensions shape parenting practices and can be observed in families. The field of cross-cultural family psychology focuses on cultural dimensions and how these affect family structure, family functioning, parenting practices, parenting goals, and consequently child development and functioning. It is possible to say that each family has a specific culture (i.e., their own norms and customs) that is influenced by the macroculture in which members were originally socialized (i.e., their national culture).

More research and theoretical frameworks are available on the disparities than on the similarities between cultures. However, in the field of parenting and family psychology, there are also some findings regarding "universal principles" or, in other words, those that seem to be consistent in parents across contexts. One of these universal principles is that parents are preadapted to help their children to overcome uncomfortable emotional states such as sadness, anger, and stress. This skill is known as contingent responsiveness (Papousek & Papousek, 1987) and refers to caregivers' intuitive supportive competence. However, there are context-specific ways in which parents react contingently to their child. While a parent from a collectivistic culture might employ proximal strategies such as hugging and kissing when their child is crying, a parent from an individualist culture might use more distal strategies, such as singing a song or giving a pat on the child's back.

Another parenting skill commonly referred to as "universal" and often present across cultures is caregiver sensitivity. This is defined as the caregiver's ability to perceive child signals, to interpret these signals correctly, and to respond to them appropriately (Ainsworth, 1989). Sensitive and responsive caregiving is a requirement for the healthy neurophysiological, physical, and psychological development of a child (World Health Organization, 2009). Any parenting intervention regardless of where it is going to be implemented should include activities for training parents in sensitivity and responsiveness to prevent later difficulties in children.

In summary, culture is an important evolutionary trait that is transmitted by parents primarily. Culture shapes children and families and influences how they behave. Main existing cultural distinctions refer to human relationships with others (i.e., individualistic vs. collectivistic). However, it is key to understand culture as dynamic and changeable throughout time given that it is related to societal changes. Currently, society, and thus local cultures, transforms rapidly due to economic, political, and demographical changes (i.e., war, immigration). When culture changes, families and parenting practices change.

IMPLICATIONS FOR THE DELIVERY OF PARENTING SUPPORT IN DIFFERENT HOST COUNTRIES

The considerations of cultural norms and values will have a significant impact on program delivery. The two most important areas to consider are the level of collectivism in a culture and the traditional parenting practices and values. In collectivist cultures, it is important to consider the impact of extended family, who may act as barriers or supports to parent implementation. In such cases, targeting the entire family system and identifying the family member with the most perceived power or influence are useful. This family member may be a grandparent or aunt, and not the biological parent. Similarly, in collectivist cultures, where family interdependence is valued, there is often less focus on teaching children independence early, and parents may not be motivated by this. Practitioners should work with parents to identify their own personal goals and values rather than impose their professional views on the parents with whom they work.

The traditional methods of parent and societal values about children will also affect parents' reactions to Triple P. For example, traditional methods of discipline are harsh in some cultures, and parents may not think assertive discipline strategies are sufficient to teach children. In addition, in some cultures it is not normative for parents to tell children they are loved or to show physical affection. Children show love to parents by deference and respect. In these cases, the practitioner will need to work with parents to discuss the value of showing some affection at a level where they can feel comfortable.

The values parents wish to instill in children will also differ across families and cultures. It is important that practitioners do not inadvertently give the impression there is a single way to parent correctly or that traditional practices are "wrong." Instead, strategies should be presented as an optional toolbox that empowers parents to achieve their own personal goals. The use of the self-regulatory approach is key even in hierarchical societies, where it will take more effort to implement (Sanders & Mazzucchelli, 2013).

HOW TO MAKE TRIPLE P CONTEXTUALLY APPROPRIATE IN DIFFERENT COUNTRIES

Meta-analytic reviews (e.g., van Mouriek, Crone, de Wolff & Reis, 2017) have found that making cultural adaptations to parenting programs (for delivery with different ethnicities) is associated with better outcomes. However, the key to successful delivery of interventions across cultures is to balance program fidelity (i.e., adhering to the vital aspects of the program that effect change) with flexibility in tailoring content and process.

In every new country or culture, changes may be required at two levels. First, formal program modifications may be required. However, only program authors or publishers can undertake formal program modifications, including both major modifications (e.g., the development of new materials or variants such as Indigenous Triple P) and minor modifications (e.g., language translations). Second, minor changes will nearly always be needed at the delivery level in terms of process and content. This is known as flexible delivery and is designed to ensure a good ecological fit between the program and the relevant client group. Flexibility is a key component of Triple P, and low-risk adaptations are recommended as a part of usual delivery (Mazzucchelli & Sanders, 2010). We strongly recommend that practitioners working across cultures are familiar with what kind of changes are considered low and high risk so that their implementation does not compromise family outcomes or the efficacy of the program.

Where possible, it is recommended programs be delivered by trained local practitioners who have detailed knowledge of local customs and practices, but if this is not possible, practitioners should consult with local parents and obtain as much information about local values and practices as possible. For example, in some tribes in Kenya it is conventional for women to refrain from speaking until any men present have voiced their opinions. Knowledge of these cultural norms can avoid the practitioner calling on women to respond at inopportune times. Similarly, it is important to be aware of prayer times or religious festivals like Ramandan when Islamic parents will fast. Practitioners delivering in cultures different from theirs cannot be expected to know all these norms but should seek the assistance or advice of locals, including asking the parents themselves. For example, in some African countries it is common to start group sessions with a song, and it is entirely appropriate to include these traditional norms into usual delivery (see Box 30.1 for an example). The following questions may be asked to assist in the understanding of local context (Table 30.1):

BOX 30.1: A Practitioner's Perspective on Delivering Triple P in Africa

We conducted Group Triple P with families living in informal settlements "slums" in Nairobi, Kenya. The group looked very different than a group in Australia. We started with one of the parents leading us in a traditional song and prayer, and since most parents weren't highly literate and storytelling is common, we shared a lot more stories than usual and did the group exercises by talking rather than writing. Most of the examples were different because these parents weren't having problems with children running through the house or fighting over computers. We also provided chicken for lunch, which in Kenya signifies important celebrations. We were honored that by the end of the group many of the parents asked us to call them by their African names, which was a sign of trust.

—Triple P practitioner

Table 30.1: Sample Cultural Differences and How to Adapt Triple P Delivery

Cultural Knowledge	Recommended Tailoring	Type of Change	What to Avoid
Families live in extended-family, collectivist communities or have family helpers to raise children.	Invite all interested caregivers to attend session. Tailor examples for working together as a team.	Low-risk process change Low-risk content change	Focus only on parents, ignoring the significant influence of others.
Specific religious beliefs have certain values/goals for children.	When having parents set their goals, prompt them to consider faith and values as well as behavior. Change training exemplars to fit local values (e.g., demonstrate how praise can be used to teach specific values; ask families how these strategies fit with their beliefs).	Low-risk content change	Tell parents Triple P works for every parent irrespective of religion. Fail to acknowledge the central role of religion in families' lives.
Families live in a single room and do not have bathroom for time-out.	Discuss how to deliver time-out in this setting. Tailor strategies as appropriate.	Low-risk content change	Deliver content as normal and tell parents not to use time-out if they do not have a room.
Families financially insecure and do not have issues with computers or money to purchase stickers for reward charts.	Identify common issue with children in this group and tailor examples to local need. Highlight that reward charts could be used with stones instead of stickers.	Low-risk content change	Keep same examples throughout when they are not relevant.
Culture has oral history of sharing information (no literacy).	Allow extra time for story sharing. Do workbook exercises orally rather than in book.	Low-risk process change	Deliver exercises exactly as usual even if parents do not write in the book. Skip all exercises.
Convention states groups typically meet outside.	Meet outside rather than in a room.	Low-risk process change	Deliver Triple P only in formal settings.
Cultural beliefs incompatible with Triple P (e.g., child is cursed).	Avoid belittling or discounting cultural belief but encourage parent to nevertheless experiment with strategies. Use resistance management strategies.	Low-risk process change	Tell parents that curses do not exist, and they should do this instead.

Table 30.1: Continued

Cultural Knowledge	Recommended Tailoring	Type of Change	What to Avoid
Harsh physical punishment is considered normative.	Discuss how they were raised and how this affected them. Include discussion of what parents are hoping to teach children and different ways of teaching this. Present strategies as options to try rather than prescriptions they must follow. Check back with parents about appropriate implementation.	Low-risk content change.	Avoiding telling parents they should not hit their children.

- Who is considered "family" and responsible for raising children? Who should be involved in the program?
- Who lives in the family home? Immediate family? Extended family? Family workers?
- What cultural or religious beliefs are held in the community?
- What is the status hierarchy for the community? And in the family?
- What are the traditional parenting practices, and how have these changed, if at all?
- What are the roles of men? Women? Children?
- What are traditional expectations of children regarding play, socialization, and independence?
- What are the typical occupations/work patterns/financial status of the community?

KEY IMPLEMENTATION ISSUES

Triple P is best implemented as a system of support so families can access services in a minimally sufficient way. However, it must take into account the host country's cultural values and resources. Parenting is a common pathway to improving multiple child and family outcomes. Governments may have different rationales for the implementation of support, including goals such as reducing child behavior problems, contributing to societal well-being, reducing violence, or providing economic health incentives. In high-income countries, governments can offer parenting support as a part of broader health or education initiatives. In collectivist cultures, this may extend beyond the immediate family to include grandparents and other key figures.

In low- and middle-income countries (LMICs), where resources are limited and families are often under extreme stress related to poverty and violence, many children still fail to reach their full developmental potential (Lu, Black, & Richter, 2016; Walker et al., 2007). Parenting support in LMICs is therefore often a part of a broader early child development and violence prevention focus. The provision of early child development services and "nurturing care" in the early stages of a child's life has the potential to improve lifelong outcomes in children, and researchers have called for parenting programs to be delivered alongside physical health, nutrition, and safety programs (Black et al., 2017).

Evidence suggests a life course approach is best where intervention targets change at different development points from pregnancy, birth, infancy, and childhood (Britto et al., 2017); thus, a range of parenting program options may be needed. Furthermore, it is recommended that programs must be scalable at a national level and should encompass a range of different sectors (e.g., health, child protection, education) (Richter et al., 2017). To deliver parenting support at a national level in LMICs, systems approaches that maximize resources are needed. From a parenting perspective, programs with strong evidence and clearly established training and dissemination models are needed; however, more research on how to best integrate these services with other child development programs is required.

Changing laws and an increase in the focus on children's rights also need to be considered. For example, in many LMICs, traditional parenting practices can include harsh physical punishment (World Health Organization, 2009). In this case, parenting services could be implemented alongside changing laws, increasing education about corporal punishment and the introduction of the United Nations Convention on the Rights of the Child (United Nations Office on Drugs and Crime, 2009).

BRIEF REVIEW OF EFFICACY OF TRIPLE P ACROSS CULTURES

Most studies of Triple P and other parenting interventions have been conducted in high-income countries mainly with an individualistic-autonomous culture (e.g., Australia, the United States, the United Kingdom, and Germany). Meta-analyses suggest their efficacy in these contexts (Sanders, Kirby, Tellegen, & Day, 2014). However, in recent years, several research groups have made efforts to evaluate the appropriateness and efficacy of Triple P interventions in collectivistic cultures different from where the program was originally developed and tested.

The first evaluation of Triple P in a vastly different collectivist cultural setting was conducted in Hong Kong (Leung, Sanders, Leung, Mak, & Lau, 2003). Group Triple P (Level 4) was implemented in two governmental health services: one that provided child and maternal health care to the general population and a different one for children referred because of developmental problems. Some superficial cultural adaptations took place, such as translating resources of the program into Chinese. However, content and format remained the same, although a local trained facilitator from Hong Kong delivered the intervention. A total of 91 parents of children 3 to 7 years old with disruptive behavior were randomized to receive the intervention or to a wait-list control group. Results suggested that Group Triple P, even without major cultural adaptations, was effective in Hong Kong. A later and larger study with a sample of 661 parents recruited from similar governmental services showed comparable results (Leung, Sanders, Ip, & Lau, 2006). Similar results were also found in Japan, another country of the region with a collectivistic culture (Matsumoto, Sofronoff, & Sanders, 2010).

Both Hong Kong and Japan are high-income, industrialized contexts. Although their culture is different from that where the program has been traditionally tested, most families in these contexts have their basic needs satisfied. There are now trials of Triple P in three LMICs: Panama,

Indonesia, and mainland China. In Panama, the Level 3 Discussion Group on Dealing With Disobedience was trialed with 108 parents (Mejia, Calam, & Sanders, 2015). Most parents were living with less than the minimum wage locally (i.e., US$300 per month). Results suggested that the program was effective, and effects were comparable to other trials of the same discussion group conducted in Australia (Morawska, Haslam, Milne, & Sanders, 2011). Qualitative interviews with 30 parents conducted after the trial suggested that most of them were highly satisfied with the intervention and agreed that the content of the program met their needs.

In Indonesia, a total of 143 parents of children 2 to 12 years old were randomly assigned to receive the Level 2 Triple P Seminars or to join a wait-list control group (Sumargi, Sofronoff, & Morawska, 2015). Comparable to other collectivistic settings, the intervention was found to be effective at decreasing behavioral problems, dysfunctional parenting practices, and parental stress.

Finally, a recent evaluation of Triple P was conducted in mainland China (Guo, Morawska, & Sanders, 2016). As in Hong Kong and Japan, in this study the efficacy of the eight-session Group Triple P was assessed. Again, significant improvements were reported in all outcomes. Interestingly, the intervention was also found to be effective at improving parents' satisfaction with children's academic achievement and at reducing children's academic problems at postintervention.

It seems there are more similarities than differences as parents in five collectivistic cultural settings seem to be satisfied with Triple P in its original form with only minimal adaptations undertaken (i.e., language translations). Recent studies also suggest that parents in Chile (Errázuriz, Cerfogli, Moreno, & Soto, 2016) and South Africa (Wessels, Lester, & Ward, 2016) considered Triple P met their needs and was culturally appropriate. However, it is important to say that cultural fit is not an all-or-nothing issue, and some levels of adaptation might be needed in specific settings, especially given how dynamic and changeable realities can be for families in a highly globalized world. Thus, it is key to evaluate consumers' acceptability and satisfaction with the intervention prior to implementation in order to increase reach, retention, and sustainability in the long term.

IMPLICATIONS AND FUTURE DIRECTIONS

It can be tempting to view evidence of Triple P across cultures presented in the previous section and say that "Triple P works everywhere irrespective of culture or of a country's resource status." However, it would be premature to say this. Certainly, there is likely more evidence of the efficacy and acceptability of Triple P across cultures and resource settings than perhaps any other Western-developed parenting program. Nevertheless, that is not to say Triple P works in every place. What we can state with confidence is that Triple P is highly likely to be effective when sensitive, highly trained practitioners take the local values, culture, and context into account and adapt their delivery (while maintaining fidelity). However, the establishment of a local evidence base and ongoing monitoring and evaluation of implementation are recommended.

One key area that requires substantially more research, particularly for low-resource countries, is the effectiveness of the training model for upskilling local practitioners. To date, Triple P in LMICs has been delivered by highly skilled practitioners, often those with advanced clinical training in high-income Western countries. This was an appropriate starting point for research in this area as it allowed researchers to confirm the program can be delivered effectively even in low-resource settings. However, these cases are atypical of usual services in a variety of resource and cultural contexts. Although Triple P is intentionally multidisciplinary in order to increase parental reach, in LMICs the number of available practitioners with advanced skills is low, and training of laypersons or local leaders may be needed to ensure sustainability of services (Petersen, Bhana, & Baillie, 2012).

Within the medical field, there has been a focus on "task shifting": Laypeople can be trained to conduct complex tasks to reduce the burden on health practitioners (Bhushan & Bhardwaj, 2015). There is some evidence that psychological therapies can also be successfully delivered by general health workers (Petersen et al., 2012). This suggests that task-shifting approaches may also work for the delivery of Triple P or other parenting programs. Future research is needed to examine the extent to which this is effective while maintaining good family outcomes and whether changes in training for lay practitioners are needed. A study comparing practitioner and parent outcomes following training of lay workers would strengthen the case for the suitability of Triple P delivered as part of usual services in LMICs. Such a study could also examine the mechanisms of training that are most important with enhanced family outcomes or if additional changes to the training model are needed.

A second challenge for broad-based dissemination in LMICs is associated with the costs of resources. Numerous studies have demonstrated that Triple P is cost-effective in high-income countries when implemented at a population level, but no research has examined cost-effectiveness in low-resource settings, where even printing materials are too expensive for many (Mihalopoulos, Vos, Pirkis, & Carter, 2011). In addition, literacy levels in many of these countries are low, and the number of languages per country is such that printed resources may not be appropriate (UNESCO Institute for Statistics, 2012). One way to approach this would be to determine the minimum level of materials required to obtain clinically meaningful effect sizes. If research were able to demonstrate that programs delivered with a low requirement for written resources are effective, the implications for sustainable delivery in LMICs would be substantial in terms of cost while increasing access to services for parents.

CONCLUSION

This chapter outlined how the Triple P program, developed in Australia, can be minimally adapted and implemented with fidelity and sensitivity across a variety of contexts and cultures. This is consistent with recommendations by the World Health Organization (2009) and the United Nations Office on Drugs and Crime (2009); they suggest adapting existing evidence-based programs rather than creating new ones.

We outlined the importance of being aware of culture and how it can affect family-related norms and, in turn, how and why this needs to be considered in implementing evidence-based programs. A brief review of an expanding body of research was provided, demonstrating that Triple P can be both efficacious and culturally acceptable when delivered across countries by culturally aware and sensitive practitioners who adapt to the needs of participating parents. We encourage practitioners not only to be aware of cultural issues but also to acknowledge the diversity of values, religious faiths, and worldviews that may be present within a single country or culture. Culturally aware practitioners must take steps to be informed, to constantly learn from the parents with whom they work, and to make flexible and sensitive adaptations as needed.

Finally, we highlighted that neither research nor culture is static and that ongoing adaptation, evaluation, and validation for cultural fit are needed. This reinforces the importance of establishing a local evidence base in new regions as part of any implementation process.

KEY MESSAGES

- What constitutes a "family" can differ across collectivist and individualistic cultures.
- Traditional values and parenting styles can differ across and within cultures. However, parents around the world have in common a desire to respond to and soothe children.
- Evidence-based parenting programs can equip parents and caregivers, across a range of cultures and contexts, with strategies to raise children in a safe, nurturing, nonviolent environment.
- Practitioners delivering parenting support in different cultures should be aware of the different cultural norms, beliefs, and values and tailor delivery in sensitive ways. Where necessary, it is appropriate to acknowledge lack of cultural knowledge and ask parents directly about their beliefs and values.
- In delivering parenting programs in different contexts, practitioners must balance program fidelity (i.e., retaining the key essential ingredients that make the program work) with program flexibility (i.e., adapting the program to ensure it adequately meets the needs of the parents).
- Research suggests Triple P, when delivered in culturally sensitive ways, improves a range of child and parent outcomes across a range of different cultures, including in low-resource environments.

REFERENCES

Ainsworth, M. S. (1989). Attachments beyond infancy. *American Psychologist, 44*, 709–716. doi:10.1037//0003-066x.44.4.709

Baumann, A. A., Powell, B. J., Kohl, P. L., Tabak, R. G., Penalba, V., Proctor, E. E., . . . Cabassa, L. J. (2015). Cultural adaptation and implementation of evidence-based parent-training: A systematic review and critique of guiding evidence. *Children and Youth Services Review, 53*, 113–120. doi:10.1016/j.childyouth.2015.03.025

Bhushan, H., & Bhardwaj, A. (2015). Task shifting: A key strategy in the multipronged approach to reduce maternal mortality in India. *International Journal of Gynecology and Obstetrics, 131*, S67–S70. doi:10.1016/j.ijgo.2015.03.016

Black, M. M., Walker, S. P., Fernald, L. C. H., Andersen, C. T., DiGirolamo, A. M., Lu, C., & Grantham-McGregor, S. (2017). Early childhood development coming of age: Science through the life course. *The Lancet, 389*, 77–90. doi:10.1016/S0140-6736(16)31389-7

Britto, P. R., Lye, S. J., Proulx, K., Yousafzai, A. K., Matthews, S. G., Vaivada, T., . . . Bhutta, Z. A. (2017). Nurturing care: Promoting early childhood development. *The Lancet, 389*, 91–102. doi:10.1016/S0140-6736(16)31390-3

Errázuriz, P., Cerfogli, C., Moreno, G., & Soto, G. (2016). Perception of Chilean parents on the Triple P Program for improving parenting practices. *Journal of Child and Family Studies, 25*, 3440–3449. doi:10.1007/s10826-016-0492-8

Guo, M., Morawska, A., & Sanders, M. R. (2016). A randomized-controlled trial of Group Triple P with Chinese parents in mainland China. *Behavior Modification, 40*, 825–851. doi:10.1177/0145445516644221

Hofstede, G. (1984). *Culture's consequences: International differences in work-related values.* Newbury Park, CA: Sage.

Leung, C., Sanders, M. R., Ip, F., & Lau, J. (2006). Implementation of Triple P-Positive Parenting Program in Hong Kong: Predictors of programme completion and clinical outcomes. *Journal of Children's Services, 1*, 4–17. doi:10.1108/17466660200600010

Leung, C., Sanders, M. R., Leung, S., Mak, R., & Lau, J. (2003). An outcome evaluation of the implementation of the Triple P-Positive Parenting Program in Hong Kong. *Family Process, 42*, 531–544. doi:10.1111/j.1545-5300.2003.00531.x

Lu, C., Black, M. M., & Richter, L. M. (2016). Risk of poor development in young children in low-income and middle-income countries: An estimation and analysis at the global, regional, and country level. *Lancet Global Health, 4*, e916–e922. doi:10.1016/S2214-109X(16)30266-2

Markus, H. R., & Kitayama, S. (1991). Culture and the Self: Implications for cognition, emotion, and motivation. *Psychological Review, 98*, 224–253. doi:10.1037/0033-295X.98.2.224

Matsumoto, Y., Sofronoff, K., & Sanders, M. R. (2010). Investigation of the effectiveness and social validity of the Triple P-Positive Parenting Program in Japanese society. *Journal of Family Psychology, 24*, 87–91. doi:10.1037/a0018181

Mazzucchelli, T. G., & Sanders, M. R. (2010). Facilitating practitioner flexibility within an empirically supported intervention: Lessons from a system of parenting support. *Clinical Psychology: Science and Practice, 17*, 238–252. doi:10.1111/j.1468-2850.2010.01215.x

Mejia, A., Calam, R., & Sanders, M. R. (2015). A pilot randomized controlled trial of a brief parenting intervention in low-resource settings in Panama. *Prevention Science, 16*, 707–717. doi:10.1007/s11121-015-0551-1

Mihalopoulos, C., Vos, T., Pirkis, J., & Carter, R. (2011). The economic analysis of prevention in mental health programs. *Annual Review of Clinical Psychology, 7*, 169–201. doi:10.1146/annurev-clinpsy-032210-104601

Morawska, A., Haslam, D., Milne, D., & Sanders, M. R. (2011). Evaluation of a brief parenting discussion group for parents of young children. *Journal of Developmental and Behavioral Pediatrics, 32*, 136–145. doi:10.1097/DBP.0b013e3181f17a28

Papousek, H., & Papousek, M. (1987). Intuitive parenting: A dialectic counterpart to the infant's integrative competence. In J. D. Osofsky (Ed.), *Handbook of infant development* (2nd ed., pp. 669–720). New York, NY: Wiley.

Petersen, I., Bhana, A., & Baillie, K. (2012). The feasibility of adapted group-based interpersonal therapy (IPT) for the treatment of depression by community health workers within the context of task shifting in South Africa. *Community Mental Health Journal, 48*, 336–341. doi:10.1007/s10597-011-9429-2

Richerson, P. J., & Boyd, R. (2005). *Not by genes alone: How culture transformed human evolution.* Chicago, IL: University of Chicago Press.

Richter, L. M., Daelmans, B., Lombardi, J., Heymann, J., Boo, F. L., Behrman, J. R., . . . Darmstadt, G. L. (2017). Investing in the foundation of sustainable development: Pathways to scale up for early childhood development. *The Lancet, 389*, 103–118. doi:10.1016/S0140-6736(16)31698-1

Sanders, M. R., Kirby, J. N., Tellegen, C. L., & Day, J. J. (2014). The Triple P-Positive Parenting Program: A systematic review and meta-analysis of a multi-level system of parenting support. *Clinical Psychology Review, 34*, 337–357. doi:10.1016/j.cpr.2014.04.003

Sanders, M. R., & Mazzucchelli, T. G. (2013). The promotion of self-regulation through parenting interventions. *Clinical Child and Family Psychology Review, 16*, 1–17. doi:10.1007/s10567-013-0129-z

Sumargi, A., Sofronoff, K., & Morawska, A. (2015). A randomized-controlled trial of the Triple P—
Positive Parenting Program Seminar Series with Indonesian parents. *Child Psychiatry and Human
Development, 46*, 794–761. doi:10.1007/s10578-014-0517-8

Triandis, H. C. (1989). The self and social behaviour in differing cultural contexts. *Psychological Review,
93*, 506–520. doi:10.1037/0033-295X.96.3.506

UNESCO Institute for Statistics. (2012). *Opportunities lost: The impact of grade repetition and early
school leaving*. Montreal, Canada: Author.

United Nations Office on Drugs and Crime. (2009). *Compilation of evidence-based family skills training programmes*. Retrieved from https://www.unodc.org/unodc/en/prevention/familyskillstraining.
html

van Mourik, K., Crone, M. R., de Wolff, M. S., & Reis, R. (2017). Parent training programs for ethnic
minorities: a meta-analysis of adaptations and effect. *Prevention Science, 18*, 95–105. doi:10.1007/
s11121-016-0733-5

Walker, S. P., Wachs, T. D., Gardner, J. M., Lozoff, B., Wasserman, G. A., Pollitt, E., . . . International
Child Development Steering Group. (2007). Child development: Risk factors for adverse outcomes
in developing countries. *Lancet, 369*, 145–157. doi:10.1016/S0140-6736(07)60076-2

Wessels, I., Lester, S., & Ward, C. L. (2016). *Engagement in parenting programmes: Policy brief*. Pretoria,
South Africa: University of Cape Town, Institute for Security Studies. Retrieved from https://issaf-
rica.s3.amazonaws.com/site/uploads/PolicyBrief82.pdf

World Health Organization. (2009). *Violence prevention the evidence: Preventing violence through the
development of safe, stable and nurturing relationships between children and their parents and caregivers*. Geneva, Switzerland: Author. Retrieved from http://apps.who.int/iris/bitstream/10665/
44088/1/9789241597821_eng.pdf

CHAPTER 31

THE ROLE OF VALUES
AND RELIGIOUS BELIEFS
IN POSITIVE PARENTING

AALA EL-KHANI AND RACHEL CALAM

INTRODUCTION

In many countries, there is a strong religious element to parenting, with religious beliefs fundamental to, and shaping, culture and family functioning. Participation in the context of organized religion may function as a protective factor for families living in adverse circumstances, including displacement and poverty. This chapter explores how, with an understanding of values and belief systems, parents' religious beliefs can be integrated into delivery of evidence-based parenting programs to better inform development and delivery.

HOW DO RELIGIOUS BELIEFS INFLUENCE PARENTING BELIEFS AND PRACTICES?

There is much interest in the influence of religion on different facets of people's lives, and its impact on family life, across diverse demographic contexts (Henderson, Uecker, & Stroope, 2016). While there can be significant conflict between religious theologies within and across religions, the core of most religious traditions promote positively framed virtues and values of parenting in which children are treasured and parents hold expectations of caring and facilitative parenting for themselves and their children. Religious institutions offer opportunities for family members to interact within frameworks that allow members to find greater meaning in their interactions (Volling, Mahoney, & Rauer, 2009). Research suggests that religious beliefs and associated practices are positively associated with relationship quality and stability

(Edgell, 2006; Petts, 2011). The religious beliefs caregivers hold are also associated with both the parenting practices they favor (Carothers, Borkowski, Lefever, & Whitman 2005) and their values and practices (Bartkowski, Xu, & Levin, 2008; Edgell, 2006). For example, one study with British Muslim families found that parents did not accept behaviors that they felt contradicted the teachings of their faith, such as lying or being disrespectful to elders (El-Khani, Knight, & Calam, 2017).

Providing a commonly accepted definition of religion is challenging; Paloutzian's (1996) description is one that is commonly referred to in theoretical and conceptual frameworks. He described religion as a "multidimensional variable that includes facets such as what people believe, feel, do, know, and how they respond to their beliefs" (p. 13). Sanctification is an important aspect of religion and describes a psychological process in which spiritual or religious significance is attributed to certain aspects of one's life, for example, life-changing experiences such as the birth of a child (Mahoney, Pargament, Murray-Swank, & Murray-Swank, 2003). Many religious people sanctify their role as parents as part of their larger religious commitments and view their parent–child relationship as holding great spiritual significance. Such parents may perceive hardships in a very different way than nonreligious parents, for example, expecting reward from God or another omnipotent being (see, for example, Box 31.1).

Religion is also highly associated with the promotion of self-regulation by increasing people's awareness of being monitored by God or a higher power. This is likely to make parents feel more conscious of their actions and the discrepancies between their actions and their own standards for their behaviors, which are informed by the religious framework (Baumeister, Bauer, & Lloyd, 2010). This may extend to motivating parents to try harder to better parent their children even in adverse circumstances, such as through war and displacement (El-Khani, Ulph, Peters, & Calam, 2016).

Research on the link between religiosity and family outcomes has flourished over the last few decades, highlighting religion as a potential resource for parents (Mahoney, 2010). Religion affects parents even before childbirth, with research indicating that women often view pregnancy as a spiritual period. Often, parents' time is spent in religious activities, such as turning to faith for ways of coping, for guidance on raising their unborn child well, and praying for the well-being of their child (Jesse, Schoneboom, & Blanchard, 2007). During childhood, parental religiosity (the degree and quality of being religious) is associated with various positive family outcomes for parents, such as higher parenting satisfaction, greater marital satisfaction, and lower parental stress (Abbott, Berry, & Meredith, 1990; Henderson et al., 2016; Mahoney, Pargament, Tarakeshwar, & Swank, 2008; Wolfinger & Wilcox, 2008). These positive "side effects" that religious parents

---

BOX 31.1: An Example of the Important Influence Faith Can Have on Parenting

Every aspect of my life, all decisions and actions I make, are influenced by my faith. I use it to motivate me to be the best parent I can be. Children are gifts from God, we must give them our best even when it's hard. I try to always keep that in mind when it's hard.

—British Muslim father

experience are highly likely to be due to the infusion of parenting activities with sacred meaning, making challenges feel more worthwhile and the parental role more fulfilling (Henderson et al., 2016). In a meta-analysis spanning 30 years, parents that sanctified their roles reported greater satisfaction and increased adaptive functioning (Mahoney et al., 2008).

Children also enjoy significant benefits, as parental religiosity in itself may promote warm and positive family relationships. In a study of Christian mothers, most mothers frequently engaged in bidirectional communication with their children with regard to issues of faith (Boyatzis & Janicki, 2003), a manner that has been retrospectively reported to be influential later in children's lives, although this study did not employ a comparison group (Wuthnow, 1999). Research with African Americans of low socioeconomic status indicated that religiosity and spirituality were robustly positively correlated with fewer dysfunctional parent–child interactions (Lamis, Wilson, Tarantino, Lansford, & Kaslow, 2014). This may be due to religious norms encouraging parents to spend more time and to engage in high-quality interactions with children (Bartkowski et al., 2008). Religious parenting is associated with parental responsiveness and higher levels of affection between children and parents (Abbott et al., 1990; Henderson et al., 2016; Mahoney et al., 2008; Wolfinger & Wilcox, 2008).

Regarding variation in the religiosity of parents and associated parenting styles, some strict religious beliefs may lead parents to be more likely to see conformity and autonomy as important values to instill in their children (Mahoney, 2010; Mahoney et al., 2008), placing high emphasis on obedience and thus teaching children to be submissive to authority; as well, these parents are more likely to use corporal punishment (Ellison, Bartkowski, & Segal, 1996). These values may prove to be disadvantageous to children, limiting their chances of developing self-control and decision-making capabilities, thus resulting in lower well-being (Unnever, Cullen, & Agnew, 2006). On the other hand, strict religious beliefs have also been associated with very positive parenting, such as being supportive, warm, encouraging, and responsive to children (Mahoney & Cano, 2014). However, recent reviews indicated that it is unlikely that religious beliefs alone determine parenting styles, and that other factors influence how parents behave and care for their children (Horwath & Lees, 2010).

Certain religious rituals may have a role in strengthening parent–child relationships through promoting the renewal of family relationships (Marks, 2006). For example, research with Jewish families indicated that rituals, such as the celebration of the Sabbath (lighting of candles, sacred prayers, and blessings), serve as family-strengthening practices (Kaufman, 1991). Other studies with Muslim, Christian, and Jewish families have also revealed that these faiths include practices that promote a sense of closeness with each other and with God (Dollahite & Marks, 2005; Marks, 2004). Prayer may help parents deal with challenges with their children, allowing them to interpret these as opportunities to learn or as part of a spiritual plan (Ano & Vasconcelles, 2005; El-Khani, Ulph, Peters, & Calam, 2017). Further, being part of a religious community provides a support network to aid coping with daily stressors, helping parents to support their children's well-being (Ellison, 1991).

Religious transmission is an important practical goal for many religious parents, with a child's religiosity often similar to that of their parents and religious community (Horwath & Lees, 2010), so that children are socialized and encouraged early to participate in religious activities. There are long-term benefits to parents' religiosity, such that it may moderate the parent–child relationship quality and well-being regardless of family structure in families where children attend religious services with their parents in late childhood (Holden & Williamson, 2014). Also, children who attend religious services with their parents are more likely to experience higher levels of psychological well-being throughout adolescence (Petts, 2014), with parents' religiosity related inversely to substance use and externalizing problems among adolescents (Brody & Flor, 1998; Kim-Spoon, Longo, & McCullough, 2012; Laird, Marks, & Marrero, 2011).

While parenting a child with a disability can be highly stressful and lead to lower parental satisfaction, parent religiosity has been associated with better functioning in parents of children with developmental disabilities (Poston & Turnbull, 2004) and chronic medical illness (Cardella & FriedLander, 2004). One study with parents of children with autism found parental religiosity positively correlated with parental well-being and acceptance of their children's disorder (White, 2009). Both religious beliefs and support from the local religious community aid parents in accepting and coping with the challenges of children with special needs (Dollahite, Marks, & Olson, 1998).

During war and conflict, parents experience highly significant changes to their family structure as well as emotional and behavioral changes in their children (El-Khani et al., 2016). Muslim Syrian refugee families residing in refugee camps revealed that, despite the extremely challenging circumstances they had experienced and were still going through, parents maintained a positive outlook for their families and were motivated to improve their parenting as well as meet the new parenting challenges they faced. They referred to their faith often, indicating their faith as a motivator and belief that God would reward their hardships (El-Khani, Ulph, et al., 2017).

IMPLICATIONS FOR THE DELIVERY OF PARENTING SUPPORT

Research indicates that interventions that have been adapted to be more sensitive and acceptable to a target population are more likely to be successful in recruitment (McCabe, Yeh, Garland, Lau, & Chavez, 2005). It is paramount to understand the specific religious needs of the parents targeted and what the parents perceive as acceptable in an intervention (Pemberton & Borrego, 2007). It is important to access parents directly rather than rely on the views of professionals serving families, who may act as "cultural gatekeepers," holding views on religious or cultural acceptability that may differ from the parents (Morawska et al., 2011).

Professionals working with families often lack the knowledge and skills needed for understanding those subscribing to strong religious beliefs (Godina, 2014). However, understanding a family's religious inclinations and how devout they are in practicing may be the first step in using a parenting intervention that is sensitive to their religion. Understanding that one person's definition of religion will be different from another's is also important and is highly significant for those assessing families for religiosity and faith practices (Horwath & Lees, 2010). In some cases, it may be possible that the religious beliefs and personal views of those working with families may influence practice and subsequently distort assessment findings (O'Hagan, 2001). Therefore, it is important for opportunities to be put in place for practitioners to regularly reflect on and analyze if, and how, parents' beliefs are affecting their decision-making process with regard to family support.

In addressing religious or cultural beliefs, practitioners can help parents to consider important aspects of their motivation regarding why they are taking part in a program. When parents are encouraged to make links between their religious beliefs and a parenting program, parents can reassure themselves that what they are doing fits in with their values. Parents may find the connection they make between the program and their beliefs valuable as they engage in and complete the program. If parents do not feel that the goals that the parenting program they are participating in support their religious principles, this may become a reason for parents not to engage with tasks or to drop out.

An example of using religious concepts in intervention can be found in the work of Yosef (2008) with Muslims. Yousef postulated the importance of identifying with the Islamic religion and using it as a tool to aid health belief promotion and provide competent care that is sensitive to the beliefs and practices of Muslims. He gave the example of the value of health in Islam, such that Muslims view their bodies as a gift from God. This gift was given to them by God with orders to take care of it and maintain its good health, advocating health promotion. Several prophetic sayings highlight the importance of looking after one's body, and practitioners are encouraged to use this knowledge when engaging with Muslims to make the health promotion more familiar for them and more likely to be carried out (Yosef, 2008). Similarly, using religious knowledge to aid interventions with religious beliefs provides exciting implications for parenting interventions to motivate positive parenting. For example, encouraging parents to reflect on how the positive parenting strategies they are learning may be harmonious with their religious principles may assist to engage parents in a program and encourage them to practice taught strategies with their children.

USING TRIPLE P IN DIFFERENT CONTEXTS

Differentiating between what is defined as "religion" and what is "culture" can be a real assessment challenge for those working with families. Research often views these two aspects as distinct parts of an individual's identity that interconnect (Dutt & Phillips, 2000; Healy, 2006; Stewart et al., 2000). For example, Jacobson (2006) explored the identities of young Muslims who were devout practitioners of Islam in comparison to those who no longer practiced their Muslim faith. He found a spectrum of similar identities, suggesting that cultural practices are often dictated by religious beliefs (O'Hagan, 2001).

In a study of Muslim Arabs in two regions, Saudi Arabia and the United Kingdom, El-Khani, Knight, et al. (2017) explored the cultural acceptability of Triple P to identify whether any cultural adaptations were needed to make it more acceptable to families. Results indicated that Muslim Arab parenting in both regions was influenced by both religious beliefs and culture, which were interlinked. Prior to viewing Triple P program content, parents said that they would only find a program beneficial and acceptable if it was sensitive to their religious beliefs. The program content was viewed as highly acceptable, and parents made links to how the concepts of positive parenting bridged well with their faith. In addition, they found the standard images of family members used in the Triple P program acceptable and did not feel the need for these images to be exchanged for those that they might identify with more. Further research would be useful to examine acceptability of program goals and content with our religious practicing cultures.

KEY IMPLEMENTATION ISSUES

It is valuable for practitioners to appreciate the significance of the beliefs of families that they are working with. In working with any individual or group of parents with strong religious or cultural beliefs, it is important to take time to find the fundamental core beliefs of the religion to which they adhere. Also, practitioners should specifically try to find how these beliefs express themselves in their everyday parenting practices. Practitioners can use resources such as the Internet or asking community leaders to obtain a good picture.

ADDRESSING THE NEEDS OF PARENTS WITH RELIGIOUS BELIEFS

The suggestions given next allow practitioners to build opportunities to explore family beliefs and to develop a better understanding of family motivations and needs. This increases practitioner sensitivity and may create opportunities for the practitioner to support parents to reflect on shared beliefs between program core values and their beliefs.

- Be aware of the importance of religion to the parents.
- Take time to try to understand the core religious beliefs of the parents.
- Look for incidental learning opportunities to produce links between a parenting strategy and an underlying belief that the parent may hold.
- Invite parents to comment on links they themselves may see.
- Invite other parents, even if they are not of the same religion, to comment and give their opinion.
- Create learning tasks and experiences that provide an opportunity for the parents to bridge gaps and make links.

Practitioners can demonstrate their sensitivity to parent's beliefs in a number of ways. For example, in the introduction to a program and during the establishment of parental goals, a practitioner could acknowledge to the parents how important it is for the parents to reassure themselves that what they are planning to do with their child fits with their religion and values. During the planning of tasks, practitioners can ask explicitly whether a particular approach fits well with the parents by asking them to rate, on a scale of 1 to 10, how confident they feel that the plan they have made is consistent with their beliefs and values. When a parent demonstrates satisfaction with the program, such as saying "I think it works," a practitioner could say in response "It sounds like this really makes sense to you and it is reassuring you," or "I'm noticing what you're doing is working for you."

Practitioners can also try to assist parents in providing a meaningful link between the program and their religion by saying: "Of all we have been through, pick two strategies that you think will be most useful for your family. For some of you, this might be informed by your religion or culture." If a parent expresses dissatisfaction with a program based on inconsistencies between a particular task and their values, practitioners could ask, "What would need to happen for this to fit more with your beliefs?" Practitioners should spend time working with families until the families feel comfortable that their values and beliefs are not contradicted with their engagement in the program tasks.

Before beginning a task, a practitioner could say, "Before doing this task ask yourself, 'Is this consistent with my religion or culture?'" Then, on completion of the task, allow the parent to self-reflect by saying something such as, "Now you have completed the task, do you feel you have done your best?" Questions of this kind enable the parent to reflect on how well the intervention fits with their values and provides important information for the practitioner. The aim here is not to advocate Triple P for Muslims or for Catholic parents or Jewish families, but rather for a tailored and sensitive approach to parenting interventions that takes into consideration parents' cultural and religious backgrounds. Ideally, this approach invites parents themselves to reflect in a self-regulatory way how they see the program being consistent with core values and beliefs. It is an approach consistent with the flexible delivery perspective emphasized in Triple P (Mazzucchelli & Sanders, 2010; Sanders & Mazzucchelli, 2013).

Practitioners may be faced with families expressing views that may be contentious and very different from their own personal views or of the majority of other participating members of a parenting group. For example, families may have varied beliefs on permissibility of their children dating and engaging in sexual behavior or experimenting with smoking, drugs, or gender roles. It is important that the practitioner keep in mind that the practitioner's role is not to change beliefs or opinions but rather to present opportunities for parents to learn ways of improving their family functioning with evidence-based strategies that have been successful with families such as their own. The practitioner must maintain respect for the family members and their values at all times and not allow others to disregard or mock the opinions and thoughts a member may not share with the practitioner.

BRIEF REVIEW OF EFFICACY

Various models of Triple P interventions have been successfully evaluated in a diverse range of cultural and religious contexts (see examples in Chapters 28–30, this volume).

IMPLICATIONS AND FUTURE DIRECTIONS

The findings and approaches discussed in this chapter indicate a range of important ways in which practitioners can help to reduce any perceived gaps between themselves and families they are working with and give families a sense that their religious beliefs, values, and priorities are understood.

CONCLUSION

Religion may often play a major role in the parenting goals, style, and practices of parents. Understanding a family's religious inclinations and how these interact with their parenting practices may be a crucial first step in bridging between religious motivations and positive parenting approaches, so that families engage with program content and optimize the benefit from tasks. By signifying the importance of understanding values and belief systems, parents' religious beliefs can be integrated into the delivery of evidence-based parenting programs to better inform the development and delivery of interventions.

KEY MESSAGES

- Religious beliefs have an important influence on how many parents raise their children. To be effective, it is important that parenting practitioners understand parents' core beliefs.
- When delivering a parenting intervention, practitioners should encourage parents to reflect and build links between their religion and program goals, offering support and encouragement.
- Practitioners should tailor parenting programs, creating learning tasks that allow parents to link program concepts with core beliefs and values and to self-evaluate their performance in relation to these.

REFERENCES

Abbott, D. A., Berry, M., & Meredith, W. H. (1990). Religious belief and practice: A potential asset in helping families. *Family Relations, 39,* 443–448. doi:10.2307/585226

Ano, G. G., & Vasconcelles, E. B. (2005). Religious coping and psychological adjustment to stress: A meta-analysis. *Journal of Clinical Psychology, 61,* 461–480. doi:10.1002/jclp.20049

Bartkowski, J. P., Xu, X., & Levin, M. L. (2008). Religion and child development: Evidence from the early childhood longitudinal study. *Social Science Research, 37,* 18–36. doi:10.1016/j.ssresearch.2007.02.001

Baumeister, R. F., Bauer, I. M., & Lloyd, S. A. (2010). Choice, free will, and religion. *Psychology of Religion and Spirituality, 2,* 67. doi:10.1037/a0018455

Boyatzis, C. J., & Janicki, D. L. (2003). Parent-child communication about religion: Survey and diary data on unilateral transmission and bi-directional reciprocity styles. *Review of Religious Research, 44,* 252–270. doi:10.2307/3512386

Brody, G. H., & Flor, D. L. (1998). Maternal resources, parenting practices, and child competence in rural, single parent African American families. *Child Development, 69,* 803–816. doi:10.1111/j.1467-8624.1998

Cardella, L. A., & Friedlander, M. L. (2004). The relationship between religious coping and psychological distress in parents of children with cancer. *Journal of Psychosocial Oncology, 22,* 19–37. doi:10.1300/J077v22n01_02

Carothers, S. S., Borkowski, J. G., Lefever, J. B., & Whitman, T. L. (2005). Religiosity and the socio-emotional adjustment of adolescent mothers and their children. *Journal of Family Psychology, 19,* 263–275. doi:10.1037/0893-3200.19.2.263

Dollahite, D. C., & Marks, L. D. (2005). How highly religious families strive to fulfill sacred purposes. In V. Bengtson, P. Dillworth-Anderson, D. Klein, A. Acock, & K. Allen (Eds.), *Sourcebook of family theory and research* (pp. 533–541). Thousand Oaks, CA: Sage.

Dollahite, D. C., Marks, L. D., & Olson, M. M. (1998). Faithful fathering in trying times: Religious beliefs and practices of Latter-Day Saint fathers of children with special needs. *The Journal of Men's Studies, 7,* 71–93. doi:10.3149/jms.0701.71

Dutt, R., & Phillips, M. (2000). Assessing black children in need and their families. In Department of Health, *Assessing children in need and their families: Practice guidance* (pp. 37–72). London, England: Stationary Office.

Edgell, P. (2006). *Religion and family in a changing society.* Princeton, NJ: Princeton University Press.

El-Khani, A., Knight, M., & Calam, R. (2017). *An exploration into Arab parenting: Assessing the cultural acceptability of Triple P as a possible parenting intervention for Arab parents*. Manuscript in preparation.

El-Khani, A., Ulph, F., Peters, S., & Calam, R. (2016). Syria: The challenges of parenting in refugee situations of immediate displacement. *Intervention, 14*, 99–113. doi:10.1097/WTF.0000000000000118

El-Khani, A., Ulph, F., Peters, S., & Calam, R. (2017). Syria: Coping mechanisms utilised by displaced refugee parents caring for their children in preresettlement contexts. *Intervention, 15*, 34–50. doi:10.1097/WTF.0000000000000136

Ellison, C. G. (1991). Religious involvement and subjective well-being. *Journal of Health and Social Behavior, 32*, 80–99.

Ellison, C. G., Bartkowski, J. P., & Segal, M. L. (1996). Conservative Protestantism and the parental use of corporal punishment. *Social Forces, 74*, 1003–1028. doi:10.1093/sf/74.3.1003

Godina, L. (2014). Religion and parenting: Ignored relationship? *Child and Family Social Work, 19*, 381–390. doi:10.1111/cfs.12054

Healy, J. (2006). Locality matters: Ethnic segregation and community conflict—The experience of Protestant girls in Belfast. *Children and Society, 20*, 105–115. doi:10.1111/j.1099-0860.2006.00018

Henderson, W. M., Uecker, J. E., & Stroope, S. (2016). The role of religion in parenting satisfaction and parenting stress among young parents. *The Sociological Quarterly, 57*, 675–710. doi:10.1111/tsq.12147

Holden, G. W., & Williamson, P. A. (2014). Religion and child well-being. In A. Ben-Arieh, F. Casas, I. Frønes, & J. E. Korbin (Eds.), *Handbook of child well-being* (pp. 1137–1169). Amsterdam, Netherlands: Springer. doi:10.1007/978-90-481-9063-8_158

Horwath, J., & Lees, J. (2010). Assessing the influence of religious beliefs and practices on parenting capacity: The challenges for social work practitioners. *British Journal of Social Work, 40*, 82–99. doi:10.1093/bjsw/bcn116

Jacobson, J. (2006). *Islam in transition: Religion and identity among British Pakistani youth*. London, England: Routledge. doi:10.1007/978-90-481-9063-8_158

Jesse, D. E., Schoneboom, C., & Blanchard, A. (2007). The effect of faith or spirituality in pregnancy a content analysis. *Journal of Holistic Nursing, 25*, 151–158. doi:10.1177/0898010106293593

Kaufman, D. R. (1991). *Rachel's daughters: Newly orthodox Jewish women*. New Brunswick, NJ: Rutgers University Press.

Kim-Spoon, J., Longo, G. S., & McCullough, M. E. (2012). Parent-adolescent relationship quality as a moderator for the influences of parents' religiousness on adolescents' religiousness and adjustment. *Journal of Youth and Adolescence, 41*, 1576–1587. doi:10.1007/s10964-012-9796-1

Laird, R. D., Marks, L. D., & Marrero, M. D. (2011). Religiosity, self-control, and antisocial behavior: Religiosity as a promotive and protective factor. *Journal of Applied Developmental Psychology, 32*, 78–85. doi:10.1016/j.appdev.2010.12.003

Lamis, D. A., Wilson, C. K., Tarantino, N., Lansford, J. E., & Kaslow, N. J. (2014). Neighborhood disorder, spiritual well-being, and parenting stress in African American women. *Journal of Family Psychology, 28*, 769. doi:10.1037/a0036373

Mahoney, A. (2010). Religion in families, 1999–2009: A relational spirituality framework. *Journal of Marriage and Family, 72*, 805–827. doi:10.1111/j.1741-3737.2010.00732.

Mahoney, A., & Cano, A. (2014). Introduction to the special section on religion and spirituality in family life: Pathways between relational spirituality, family relationships and personal well-being. *Journal of Family Psychology, 28*, 735–738. doi:10.1037/fam0000041

Mahoney, A., Pargament, K. I., Murray-Swank, A., & Murray-Swank, N. (2003). Religion and the Sanctification of Family Relationships. *Review of Religious Research, 44*, 220–236. doi:10.2307/3512384

Mahoney, A., Pargament, K. I., Tarakeshwar, N., & Swank, A. B. (2008). Religion in the home in the 1980s and 1990s: A meta-analytic review and conceptual analysis of links between religion, marriage, and parenting. *Psychology of Religion and Spirituality, 15,* 559–596. doi:10.1037/0893-3200.15.4.559

Marks, L. (2004). Sacred practices in highly religious families: Christian, Jewish, Mormon, and Muslim perspectives. *Family Process, 43,* 217–231. doi:10.1111/j.1545-5300.2004.04302007

Marks, L. (2006). Religion and family relational health: An overview and conceptual model. *Journal of Religion and Health, 45,* 603–618. doi:10.1007/s10943-006-9064-3

Mazzucchelli, T. G., & Sanders, M. R. (2010). Facilitating practitioner flexibility within an empirically supported intervention: Lessons from a system of parenting support. *Clinical Psychology: Science and Practice, 17,* 238–252. doi:10.1111/j.1468-2850.2010.01215.x

McCabe, K. M., Yeh, M., Garland, A. F., Lau, A. S., & Chavez, G. (2005). The GANA program: A tailoring approach to adapting parent child interaction therapy for Mexican Americans. *Education and Treatment of Children, 28,* 111–129.

Morawska, A., Sanders, M., Goadby, E., Headley, C., Hodge, L., McAuliffe, C., & Anderson, E. (2011). Is the Triple P—Positive Parenting Program acceptable to parents from culturally diverse backgrounds? *Journal of Child and Family Studies, 20,* 614–622. doi:10.1007/s10826-010-9436

O'Hagan, K. (2001). *Cultural competence in the caring professions.* London, England: Kingsley.

Paloutzian, R. F. (1996). *Understanding Religious Conversion* (Book). *The International Journal for the Psychology of Religion, 6,* 225–227. doi:10.1207/s15327582ijpr0603_9

Pemberton, J. R., & Borrego, J., Jr. (2007). Increasing acceptance of behavioural child management techniques: What do parents say? *Child and Family Behavior Therapy, 29,* 27–45. doi:10.1300/J019v29n02_03

Petts, R. J. (2011). Parental religiosity, religious homogamy, and young children's well-being. *Sociology of Religion, 72,* 389–414. doi:10.1093/socrel/srr021

Petts, R. J. (2014). Family, religious attendance, and trajectories of psychological well-being among youth. *Journal of Family Psychology, 28,* 759–768. doi:10.1037/a0036892

Poston, D. J., & Turnbull, A. P. (2004). Role of spirituality and religion in family quality of life for families of children with disabilities. *Education and Training in Developmental Disabilities, 39,* 95–108.

Sanders, M. R., & Mazzucchelli, T. G. (2013). The promotion of self-regulation through parenting interventions. *Clinical Child and Family Psychology Review, 16,* 1–17. doi:10.1007/s10567-013-0129-z

Stewart, S. M., Bond, M. H., Ho, L. M., Zaman, R. M., Dar, R., & Anwar, M. (2000). Perceptions of parents and adolescent outcomes in Pakistan. *British Journal of Developmental Psychology, 18,* 335–352. doi:10.1348/026151000165733

Unnever, J. D., Cullen, F. T., & Agnew, R. (2006). Why is "bad" parenting criminogenic? Implications from rival theories. *Youth Violence and Juvenile Justice, 4,* 3–33. doi:10.1177/1541204005282310

Volling, B. L., Mahoney, A., & Rauer, A. J. (2009). Sanctification of parenting, moral socialization, and young children's conscience development. *Psychology of Religion and Spirituality, 1,* 53–68. doi:10.1037/a0014958

White, S. E. (2009). The influence of religiosity on well-being and acceptance in parents of children with autism spectrum disorder. *Journal of Religion, Disability and Health, 13,* 104–113. doi:10.1080/15228960802581503

Wuthnow, R. (1999). *Growing up religious: Christians and Jews and their journeys of faith.* Boston, MA: Beacon.

Wolfinger, N. H., & Wilcox, W. B. (2008). Happily ever after? Religion, marital status, gender and relationship quality in urban families. *Social Forces, 86,* 1311–1337. doi:10.1353/sof.0.0023

Yosef, A. R. O. (2008). Health beliefs, practice, and priorities for health care of Arab Muslims in the United States: Implications for nursing care. *Journal of Transcultural Nursing, 19,* 284–291. doi:10.1177/1043659608317450

MAKING LARGE-SCALE, POPULATION-LEVEL IMPLEMENTATION WORK

MAKING LARGE-SCALE POPULATION-LEVEL IMPLEMENTATION WORK

An Introduction

MATTHEW R. SANDERS

We know that parenting programs are effective; however, this evidence is not enough to ensure programs are scalable and can be implemented successfully at a population level. Ensuring the Triple P system of interrelated programs can be scaled to a population level also requires a strong model for implementation that ensures fidelity, promotes program use, and supports practitioners. This section begins with Chapter 33 by McWilliam and Brown, which discusses a framework for successful implementation of the Triple P system from the perspective of a purveyor organization that provides assistance to agencies implementing Triple P. The implementation literature can be confusing as there are many different models, frameworks, and tools, making it difficult for organizations to determine how best to deploy evidence-based programs. The Triple P Implementation Framework provides a tailored approach to support organizations to adopt effective implementation practices based on implementation science principles. However, for sustained use of evidence-based programs, organizations need to become self-regulated with respect to implementation and take ultimate responsibility for determining how best to support their staff's use of Triple P in an ongoing way.

The initial selection and training of staff in an organization who will be trained in Triple P is an important consideration. Ralph and Dittman (Chapter 34) describe the training model developed to disseminate Triple P worldwide. This chapter outlines some of the challenges training organizations experience in delivering training in a way that ensures fidelity and highlights the need for ongoing research and evolution to quality delivery of programs with fidelity, while remaining responsive to the needs of parents.

A successful population approach to parenting support requires a strong communications strategy that will encourage parents (who all have competing demands for their time) to participate in programs. Low rates of participation can be the result of universal program offers, unless programs can be shared with parents in a way that makes it attractive to be involved. Wilkinson (Chapter 35) examines the role of social marketing in contributing to the success of population-based implementations of the Triple P system. The evidence showing that parenting programs work also needs to influence the social norms associated with public conceptions of "good" parenting. The Triple P "Stay Positive" social marketing strategy takes account of factors that deter or encourage parents to participate in parenting programs and offers a flexible range of multimedia components that can be customized to particular rollouts and local needs.

A hallmark of evidence-based approaches to parenting support is that routine evaluation of outcomes is integral to program delivery at an individual case level. It is also highly relevant to implementation at a population level. Morawska and Sanders (Chapter 36) explore a range of measurement issues associated with determining whether the population approach is achieving targeted outcomes. It is essential that brief, reliable, valid, and change-sensitive tools are available for deployment in implementing and evaluating Triple P. This chapter discusses some of the available tools.

Supervision of a workforce trained to deliver parenting programs is an important aspect of quality management and the promotion of fidelity of implementation. The final chapter in this section by McPherson and Schroeter (Chapter 37) documents the power of peer support in professional learning. The PASS (peer-assisted supervision and support) model blends a peer support/mentoring model with a self-regulation approach to promote high-quality implementation of programs by practitioners and the development of practitioner confidence in delivering the program with flexibility. The structure of PASS sessions is described, and the authors highlight the benefits of this form of supervision, including encouraging self-regulation, cost and time efficiency, and the normalization of evidence-based program delivery.

A FRAMEWORK FOR SUCCESSFUL IMPLEMENTATION OF THE TRIPLE P SYSTEM

JENNA MCWILLIAM AND JACQUIE BROWN

Evidence-based programs (EBPs) seek to answer the question: "What treatment, by whom, is most effective for this individual, with what specific program, and under which set of circumstances?" (Paul, 1967, p. 111). When EBPs are implemented in real-world settings, another set of questions becomes equally important: "What shall be implemented, how will the task be carried out, and who shall do the work of implementation?" (Ogden & Fixsen, 2014, p. 4). The *what* refers to the effective intervention (the EBP), the *how* is the process to establish what needs to be done in practice (the set of purposeful implementation activities), and the *who* refers to who will do the work to accomplish positive outcomes (the change agents, that is, the purveyors and implementation teams).

The successful application and sustainability of an EBP depends not only on the intervention's effectiveness, but also on how it is implemented and sustained (Fixsen, Naoom, Blase, Friedman, & Wallace, 2005). The importance of high-quality implementation is well established and evidenced across multiple sectors (Fixsen et al., 2005). Without high-quality implementation EBPs are unlikely to achieve their intended effects in practice, and core elements may be left out or used inconsistently (L. J. Damschroder & Hagedorn, 2011) leading to poorer clinical outcomes.

This chapter provides a summary of what we know about the implementation of Triple P from research, evaluation, and experience from the field. It provides a brief overview of the science of implementing EBPs, a summary of relevant research on the implementation of Triple P, and a description of the Triple P Implementation Framework.

THE SCIENCE OF IMPLEMENTING EVIDENCE BASED PROGRAMS

Implementation science is the scientific study of variables and conditions that affect changes at practice, organization, and systems levels—changes that are required to promote the systematic uptake, sustainability, and effectiveness of EBPs and practices in typical service and social settings (Blase & Fixsen, 2010, p. 5).

Implementation science has developed theories, strategies, and frameworks to describe and support effective implementation of evidence-based practices and programs (Nilsen, 2015). Over the last 20 years, a number of constructs and common elements have been identified for consideration when moving an EBP from the controlled environment of a randomized controlled trial to the infinitely variable environment of service delivery in social service or health systems. There are a burgeoning number of implementation frameworks and strategies; however, they display a general agreement about the constructs that should be considered. These are most clearly articulated in the Consolidated Framework for Implementation Research (CFIR). CFIR reflects and organizes all the constructs that have emerged through implementation science research to date (L. Damschroder et al., 2009).

"A critical yet unresolved issue in the field of implementation science is how to conceptualize and evaluate success" (Proctor et al., 2011, p. 65). Recent years have seen increased rigor in the science of implementation, with considerable attention on what to measure and how to measure it to identify critical components of implementation (C. C. Lewis et al., 2015). Proctor and colleagues (2011) have defined a taxonomy of implementation outcomes that are distinct from service system and clinical treatment outcomes. These outcomes provide an indicator of implementation success, a proximal indicator of implementation processes, and key intermediate outcomes to clinical outcomes.

Although implementation science provides good guidance on what to consider and has identified common elements that will contribute to effective implementation, it is limited in providing a definitive model for implementation. The context for implementation is critical and as such influences strongly the choice of framework and strategies that will support effective implementation for any given practice or organization. The application and adaptation of the various frameworks and strategies require a depth of knowledge of implementation science and frequently require facilitation from an external implementation agent (Katz & Wandersman, 2016) who can support implementers to apply the available implementation knowledge. Implementation science (theories, frameworks, and strategies), when adapted to context, increases the potential for effective implementation and sustained program delivery with fidelity.

FACTORS THAT INFLUENCE THE SUCCESSFUL IMPLEMENTATION OF EBPS

Frameworks such as CFIR and the taxonomy of implementation outcomes provide a useful frame to review and synthesize research on implementation factors, strategies, and processes. There is a growing literature that examines the implementation of Triple P, with research ranging from surveys of accredited Triple P practitioners to mixed-method studies conducted as part of large-scale rollouts. Research has been conducted in a number of countries (including Australia, the United States, and Canada), and surveys have included individuals' parents, practitioners from 15 countries, supervisors, and agency representatives.

Research related to the majority of outcomes identified by Proctor and colleagues (2011) has been undertaken; however, descriptions of strategies, processes, and outcomes are inconsistent and often not clearly described, which limits the ability to generalize findings. These outcomes are acceptability, appropriateness, feasibility, adoption, cost, fidelity, penetration, and sustainability. A number of studies have found Triple P to be acceptable, appropriate, and feasible with a range of different groups, including families involved in the child welfare system and culturally and linguistically diverse families (Fawley-King, Trask, Calderon, Aarons, & Garland, 2014; E. M. Lewis, Feely, Seay, Fedoravicis, & Kohl, 2016; Morawska et al., 2011).

Program adoption and factors associated with program uptake have been examined at both practitioner and organizational levels (Aldridge, Murray, Prinz, & Veazey, 2016; Breitkreuz, McConnell, Savage, & Hamilton, 2011; Seng, Prinz, & Sanders, 2006). Studies of large-scale Triple P rollouts have found the program is cost-effective (Foster, Prinz, Sanders, & Shapiro, 2008; Mihalopolous, Sanders, Turner, Murphy-Brennan, & Carter, 2007). The program has been found to be more cost-effective when agencies undertake a thorough readiness process prior to service delivery (Romney, Israel, & Zlatevski, 2014). Program fidelity has been explored in a Canadian study that found large variability in report program adherence (between 33% and 100%; Asgary-Eden & Lee, 2011).

Penetration was explored in the Longford Westmeath Parenting Partnership, which implemented Triple P in two communities in Ireland over a period of approximately 3 years. At the end of the initiative, 60% of respondents from the communities reported they had heard of Triple P, 36% knew someone who had taken part in Triple P, and 88% had reported receiving parenting tips from that person (Fives, Pursell, Heary, Gabhainn, & Canavan, 2014).

Sustainability has been explored recently in studies in Australia and the United States (Shapiro, Prinz, & Sanders, 2015; Turner, Sanders, & Forster, 2017), with a range of facilitators and barriers to program sustainability explored, such as usability of resources, confidence in program delivery, access to supportive coaching from an experienced facilitator, having enough time to use the program, and other workplace influences.

The majority of Triple P implementation studies have explored factors associated with program use, with a particular focus on practitioner and organizational factors. Practitioner-level variables associated with higher program use include completion of training (Seng et al., 2006); higher practitioner confidence and self-efficacy (Asgary-Eden & Lee, 2011; Sanders, Prinz, & Shapiro, 2009; Turner, Nicholson, & Sanders, 2011); and more favorable practitioner attitudes to EBPs (Shapiro et al., 2015). This focus on practitioner variables and perceptions in the implementation of Triple P is critical to understanding how to best support and enable program use, as practitioners are not passive recipients of innovations.

One of the biggest challenges to effective implementation is the organizational context in which the implementation takes place (Aarons, Hurlburt, & Horwitz, 2011). Some organizations have extensive experience in implementing EBPs and require minimal support, some may use an intermediary organization to provide support, and others may require significant support as they first attempt to implement an EBP (Aarons & Palinkas, 2007). Studies focusing on organizational-level variables and use of Triple P have focused on variables such as workplace support (Asgary-Eden & Lee, 2011; Sanders et al., 2009); partnership support (Hodge, Turner, Sanders, & Forster, 2017); implementation climate (McWilliam, Tucker, Sanders, & Jones, 2017); and supportive coaching (Hodge et al., 2017).

In a recent evaluation of the implementation of Triple P in a sample of 50 agencies in two counties in North Carolina, Aldridge and colleagues (2016) found a number of organizational variables associated with continued program use. Agencies with only one practitioner were almost 10 times more likely to become inactive, and there was a trend suggesting agencies continuing active implementation were more likely to have a positive implementation climate, more well developed agency leadership, and implementation teams in place. Agency implementation capacity was found to be significantly associated with continuation of implementation.

THE TRIPLE P IMPLEMENTATION FRAMEWORK

As the field of implementation science advances, focus has turned to strategies and processes that improve uptake and outcomes (Proctor, Powell, & McMillen, 2013) and the different roles of the various stakeholders involved in implementing EBPs. One influential stakeholder in this process is the purveyor organization (Oosthuizen & Louw, 2013). The purveyor organization for Triple P is Triple P International (TPI). TPI was established in 2001 and given the exclusive global license to disseminate Triple P by the University of Queensland's technology transfer company, Uniquest. In recent years, TPI has focused on a process of examining and exploring how purveyor organizations can influence and enhance the implementation of EBPs. The result of this work has been the development of an implementation framework and a new team responsible for working with implementing organizations to support the adoption, implementation, and sustainability of Triple P.

The Triple P Implementation Framework (the Framework; McWilliam, Brown, Sanders, & Jones, 2016) was developed by combining 15 years of dissemination and implementation experience at TPI and the knowledge available through implementation science frameworks and strategies. As with many implementation frameworks (Aarons et al., 2010), the Triple P Implementation Framework has multiple phases, encouraging a sequence of activities to increase effective Triple P service delivery and sustainability (Figure 33.1). The foundational

FIGURE 33.1: The Triple P Implementation Framework. Copyright 2014 by Triple P International Proprietary Limited. Reprinted with permission.

frameworks from which the Framework was developed are RE-AIM (Glasgow, Vogt, & Boles, 1999) and the National Implementation Research Network Active Implementation Frameworks (Fixsen et al., 2005).

Use of the Framework for implementation of Triple P is supported by an implementation consultant (IC) and multiple tools for use by either the IC or the implementing organizations. The IC works directly with leadership at the implementing organization and the local coordinator or those directly responsible for coordinating the adoption of Triple P (Box 33.1). The objectives of the Framework are to optimize use of the Triple P program by accredited practitioners, increase sustained service delivery, and increase the reach of Triple P in implementing communities. Application of the Framework is guided by two of the fundamental principles of Triple P: self-regulation and minimal sufficiency. These principles govern the approach taken by the ICs in supporting organizations through the implementation process.

The Framework identifies five phases: engagement, commitment and contracting, implementation planning, training and accreditation, and implementation and maintenance. The sequence and activities described in these phases are based on implementation science and adapted to the decision flow needed to adopt Triple P. Each phase includes a number of recommended activities and tools to support completing the activities. Although some activities are best completed in sequence, as is indicated in most implementation frameworks, there will be activities from different phases happening concurrently and an iterative process that repeats activities at different levels of the system and at different times.

BOX 33.1: Key Considerations in Preparing to Implement Triple P

Triple P implementation consultants (ICs) support implementing organizations to consider a range to topics throughout the implementation process. An IC works with the implementing organization to prompt the organization to consider the needs it is addressing through implementing Triple P and the outcomes the organization wants to achieve. Key questions during the early phases of a community rollout include the following:

- Which parents/caregivers do you want to reach and engage in service delivery?
- What outcomes do you want to achieve?
- How many parents do you want to reach?
- How do you typically deliver services? How do you want to deliver Triple P?
- What are the existing family support systems locally?
- How does Triple P fit with the existing family support systems? Does it meet community needs that are currently not being met?
- Does Triple P fit with local/regional government policies and initiatives?

This illustrates one of the processes used to establish the relationship between the IC and the implementing organization. The purpose of this is to lay the foundation for the organization to take ownership for its local implementation of Triple P.

ENGAGEMENT

Engagement is the phase in which information is shared between an organization interested in Triple P and TPI to establish if there is a "fit" between the organization's desired outcomes and the Triple P programs. This fundamental first step in the process of implementing Triple P involves the implementing organization moving from a point of initial contact to developing an understanding of the Triple P system and TPI gaining an understanding of the implementing organization, the scope and fit of the potential initiative, and the context in which the organization will be implementing Triple P. Exploring which Triple P programs might best address the needs and outcomes established, the manner in which service is delivered, and the nature of the workforce will all be given initial consideration and inform whether moving to the next phase is indicated.

At the conclusion of the engagement phase, the following objectives will have been achieved: The interested organization/initiative will have an increased understanding of the Triple P system; TPI will have an understanding of the organization/initiative, their workforce, their community, and their level of interest in Triple P; and both the interested organization/initiative and TPI will have developed clarity about the scope of interest and capacity.

COMMITMENT AND CONTRACTING

When the engagement phase has indicated that Triple P is a good fit and the Triple P system or parts thereof are likely to assist the implementing organization in achieving its desired outcomes, the next phase is to drill down and develop more specificity with respect to goals, programs, number of practitioners to be trained, level of service to be delivered, management, and funding/budgeting processes. A contract outlining the terms of the work together will be developed and signed. This will outline the scope of the implementation, identifying which training courses will be offered, the timelines within which the training will be accomplished, the implementation support that will be provided, and agreed-on responsibilities between the implementing organization and TPI. This phase provides for discussion of the implications and supporting activities needed to effectively implement and deliver Triple P. Within this phase, it is important to start developing a commitment to delivering Triple P that extends beyond the contract to train practitioners. Leadership and management will be involved in this process, and primary contacts will be established at both the implementing organization and TPI.

IMPLEMENTATION PLANNING

Planning to deliver Triple P effectively and sustain service delivery over years is dependent on a comprehensive implementation plan. Having developed the contract, *what* is to be implemented has been outlined, and the next phase is to determine *how* to implement and deliver Triple P. Training the practitioners is often considered the next step, but the "train-and-hope model" has been shown to be ineffective for sustained delivery of an evidence-based practice with fidelity. The implementing organization needs to establish an understanding of how "ready" it is to adopt an evidence-based practice and dedicate time and expertise to the planning process.

Through the implementation planning phase, the implementing organization addresses recruiting, preparing, and training practitioners; developing a peer support process; preparing supervisors to support trained practitioners; the development of data collection, analysis, and information feedback loops; the administrative and logistical support that practitioners will need; and planning and communication processes within the larger system in which the implementing organization is situated.

In addition to planning for training and service delivery, a monitoring and evaluation process is developed. All aspects of the implementation should be evaluated, including the practitioners' performance and the support functions and processes. The monitoring and evaluation process should be designed to support monitoring the fidelity of delivery. The implementation planning is supported by the IC using tools and activities that are available through the Framework. Primary responsibility for planning rests with the organization or initiative's leadership team and local coordinator.

TRAINING AND ACCREDITATION

Training, preaccreditation, and accreditation are provided by accredited Triple P trainers. Triple P provider training courses are interactive and participatory and use best practice for adult education. Prior to training, the implementing organization is supported to prepare each participant well in advance of the training sessions. Practitioners are asked to consider how the Triple P training they are to attend fits with their service delivery and their own style of practice. In addition, they are asked to commit to when they will begin to deliver the program in which they have been trained. The management of the implementing organization is encouraged to develop clear service delivery expectations, commit to time for Triple P trained practitioners to attend peer network sessions, ensure supervisors are confident in their ability to provide informed supervision, and confirm that everything that supports service delivery is in place and ready so the practitioners can start to deliver shortly after the training is completed. Training sessions are evaluated, and any implementation issues that arise are communicated to the local coordinator and the IC.

IMPLEMENTATION AND MAINTENANCE

The final phase of implementation is when the trained practitioners start to deliver the program. It is useful to determine an "initial" implementation period, typically 6 months, so that a thorough review of the service delivery, the support processes, and data collection can be conducted. This provides information about any revisions or changes that need to be made in the implementation process and confirms the effectiveness of supports and processes enabling good service delivery and client outcomes. Once the implementing organization has established and confirmed that the program is being effectively delivered consistently and repeatedly by the majority of practitioners, then it can institutionalize the processes, feedback loops, peer support mechanisms, and ongoing support that will enable the practice to become "business as usual."

THE ROLE OF THE IMPLEMENTATION CONSULTANT

Implementation science has informed essential activities to support an effective implementation process, and these activities are reflected in the Triple P Implementation Framework; however, context is the most important factor in how these activities and processes are applied. The role of the IC is to facilitate the application of the Framework and tools and provide guidance to assist the implementing organization in developing an effective implementation process tailored to its context. This guidance and support is provided through a facilitative leadership relationship encouraging ownership of the process by the organization and focused on increasing the implementation capacity and skill level of the organization.

The IC is available to all organizations engaging in adopting Triple P as part of its service delivery offering. As an interested organization engages with TPI, an IC is assigned and will be the primary contact for the organization throughout the implementation process and ongoing to support the maintenance of Triple P. Through discussion with the implementing organization, the IC establishes a relationship and partnership and introduces the Framework and the tools that have been developed to support effective implementation of Triple P. The IC tailors the type and level of support to each initiative; however, the IC is typically most active during the implementation planning phase. Support is provided through telephone consultation and face-to-face meetings. Specific workshops may also be provided if the implementing organization has particular requirements. The primary objective of the IC is to support the implementing organization to plan for Triple P in a way that is consistent with the learnings from implementation science.

As noted previously, the IC's support is provided through facilitative leadership. To ensure the principles of self-regulation and minimal sufficiency are honored, it is important for the IC not to assume a directive role but rather to adopt a process of inquiry and information sharing that promotes the implementing organization to assume primary responsibility for implementing activities. The Framework provides the IC with guidance on how to fulfill this role. Organizations are encouraged to adapt the tools made available to them so they reflect the language and processes of the organization while maintaining their intended purpose. The Framework and the role of the IC have been designed to reflect the processes and principles of the Triple P program. The congruency between what is being implemented and how it is being implemented increases the understanding of both the program and what is needed to deliver it effectively.

IMPLICATIONS FOR THE DELIVERY OF LARGE-SCALE ROLLOUTS OF PARENTING SUPPORT

The capacity to scale up an EBP is critical in a public health context. The design of the Framework allows it to be scaled up to facilitate effective implementation in large, complex, initiatives. The previous material described the implementation process as it is applied to a single implementing organization. In reality, due to the scope of the Triple P system, implementation frequently occurs through a multicommunity initiative that includes a number of communities, organizations, and sectors. In larger scale rollouts, the same stages, strategies, and principles described are applied through a cascading process that starts with the leadership level of the initiative and is moved down from the broadest coordination body through to local coordinating bodies and into the implementing organizations (Figure 33.2). When working at a community-wide level, it is critical to identify roles and responsibilities within the implementation structures. The role of the IC may also expand to working at the community coordination leadership level as well as local levels.

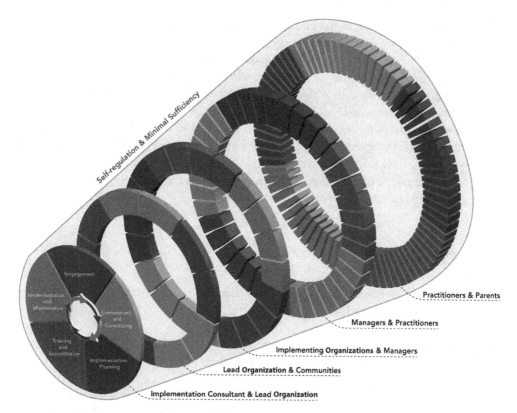

FIGURE 33.2: The Triple P Implementation Framework applied in larger-scale rollouts. Copyright 2014 by Triple P International Proprietary Limited. Reprinted with permission.

Broad place-based initiatives add a level of complexity to applying the Framework as there is often diversity in the participating communities. Diversity may include different types of communities (e.g., urban, periurban, and rural), diverse cultures, and diverse capacity and resources. Given context is a critical consideration in effective implementation. The process and strategies adopted must accommodate these differences. Using the Framework, the IC can tailor pacing and strategies to appropriately support the diversity that may exist in a broad, complex, initiative.

CONCLUSIONS AND FUTURE DIRECTIONS

When an effective practice is supported by effective implementation processes, there is increased potential for impact. With an EBP such as Triple P, the potential for this impact increases exponentially when the system is supported to scale up in a coordinated and integrated community implementation system. Given the number of implementation models, frameworks, and tools that now exist in the literature, there is a risk that organizations may struggle to determine which provides the best fit and how to tailor activities and tools to their context and to the EBP being adopted. The Triple P Implementation Framework enables efficiencies because it provides an already tailored application, and organizations are supported to adopt effective implementation practices as they are implementing Triple P.

While we are progressing in our understanding of how to support the implementation and scale-up of Triple P, there is the need for more rigorous research. There is also a need for further research and evaluation to move beyond an exploration of facilitators and barriers to determine the combinations of implementation strategies and processes that enable effective implementation of Triple P. It is critical to explore how these strategies and processes interact with the range of different contexts in which Triple P is implemented and develop an understanding of how to best match implementation strategies and processes to the context. There is the need for further research to determine if the Triple P Implementation Framework is achieving its desired outcomes, including high utilization rates for trained practitioners, long-term sustainability for implementing organizations, and expanded use of Triple P to support a population health approach within systems of care.

KEY MESSAGES

- Implementation science has developed a number of theories, frameworks, and strategies to guide what needs to be considered and what may contribute to implementation success.
- When implementing evidence based programs, including Triple P, it is important to consider a range of factors that influence effective implementation, particularly the implementing context.
- The Triple P Implementation Framework (the Framework) was developed to support the adoption, implementation, and sustainability of Triple P. The Framework is designed to optimize program use by accredited practitioners and increase service delivery and reach in the implementing community or organization.
- Application of the Framework is guided by two of the fundamental principles of Triple P: self-regulation and minimal sufficiency.
- The Framework consists of five phases: engagement, commitment and contracting, implementation planning, training and accreditation, and implementation and maintenance. Each phase corresponds with key decision-making and activity sequences that reflect the flow of effective implementation of Triple P.
- Triple P implementation consultants support organizations to adopt Triple P, apply the Framework, and guide the implementation process, tailored to the organization's context. This is a facilitative leadership process that focuses on encouraging ownership of the process by the implementing organization.
- In larger rollouts, Triple P can be supported to scale up using the Framework to apply a cascading process through multiple levels of the local systems to support implementation processes and create an enabling context for the implementation.

REFERENCES

Aarons, G. A., Hurlburt, M., & Horwitz, S. M. (2011). Advancing a conceptual model of evidence-based practice implementation in public service sectors. *Administration and Policy in Mental Health, 38,* 4–23. doi:10.1007/s10488-010-0327-7

Aarons, G. A., & Palinkas, L. A. (2007). Implementation of evidence-based practice in child welfare: Service provider perspectives. *Administration and Policy in Mental Health, 34*, 411–419. doi:10.1007/s10488-007-0121-3

Aldridge, W. A., II, Murray, D. W., Prinz, R. J., & Veazey, C. A. (2016). *Final report and recommendations: The Triple P implementation evaluation, Cabarrus and Mecklenburg Counties, NC.* Chapel Hill, NC: Frank Porter Graham Child Development Institute, University of North Carolina. Retrieved from http://fpg.unc.edu/node/8176

Asgary-Eden, V., & Lee, C. M. (2011). So now we've picked an evidence-based program, what's next? Perspectives of service providers and administrators. *Professional Psychology: Research and Practice, 42*, 169–175. doi:10.1037/a0022745

Blase, K. A., & Fixsen, D. L. (2013, February). *Implementation science: Building the bridge from good intentions to great outcomes.* Paper presented at Helping Families Change Conference, Los Angeles, CA.

Breitkreuz, R., McConnell, D., Savage, A., & Hamilton, A. (2011). Integrating Triple P into existing family support services: A case study on program implementation. *Prevention Science, 12*, 411–422. doi:10.1007/s11121-011-0233-6.

Damschroder, L., Aron, D., Keith, R., Kirsh, S., Alexander, J., & Lowery, J. (2009). Fostering implementation of health services research findings into practice: A consolidated framework for advancing implementation science. *Implementation Science, 4*, 50. doi:10.1186/1748-5908-4-50

Damschroder, L. J., & Hagedorn, H. J. (2011). A guiding framework and approach for implementation research in substance use disorders treatment. *Psychology of Addictive Behaviors, 25*, 194–205. doi:10.1037/a0022284

Fawley-King, K., Trask E., Calderon, N. E., Aarons, G. A., & Garland, A. F. (2014). Implementation of an evidence-based parenting programme with a Latina population: feasibility and preliminary outcomes. *Journal of Children's Services, 9*, 295–306, doi:10.1108/JCS-04-2014-0024

Fives, A., Pursell, L., Heary, C., Nic Gabhainn, S., & Canavan, J. (2014). *Parenting support for every parent: A population-level evaluation of Triple P in Longford Westmeath. Final report.* Athlone, Ireland: Longford Westmeath Parenting Partnership.

Fixsen, D. L., Naoom, S. F., Blase, K. A., Friedman, R. M., & Wallace, F. (2005). *Implementation research: A synthesis of the literature* (FMHI Publication No. 231). Tampa, FL: University of South Florida, Louis de la Parte Florida Mental Health Institute, National Implementation Research Network. Retrieved from http://ctndisseminationlibrary.org/PDF/nirnmonograph.pdf

Foster, E. M., Prinz, R. J., Sanders, M. R., & Shapiro, C. J. (2008). The costs of a public health infrastructure for delivering parenting and family support. *Children and Youth Services Review, 30*, 493–501. doi:10.1016/j.childyouth.2007.11.002

Glasgow, R. E., Vogt, T. M., & Boles, S. M. (1999). Evaluating the public health impact of health promotion interventions: The RE-AIM framework. *American Journal of Public Health, 89*, 1322–1327. doi:10.2105/AJPH.89.9.1322

Hodge, L., Turner, K. M. T., Sanders, M. R., & Forster, M. (2017). *Factors that influence evidence-based program implementation and sustainment for Indigenous family support providers in child protection services.* Manuscript submitted for publication.

Katz, J., & Wandersman, A. (2016). Technical assistance to enhance prevention capacity: A research synthesis of the evidence base. *Prevention Science, 17*, 417–428. doi:10.1007/s11121-016-0636-5

Lewis, C. C., Fischer, S., Weiner, B. J., Stanick, C., Kim, M., & Martinez, R. G. (2015). Outcomes for implementation science: An enhanced systematic review of instruments using evidence-based rating criteria. *Implementation Science, 10*, 155–172. doi:10.1186/s13012-015-0342-x

Lewis, E. M., Feely, M., Seay, K. D., Fedoravicis, N., & Kohl, P. L. (2016). Child welfare involved parents and Pathways Triple P: Perceptions of program acceptability and appropriateness. *Journal of Child and Family Studies, 25*, 1–11. doi:10.1007/s10826-016-0526

McWilliam, J., Brown, J., Sanders, M. R., & Jones, L. (2016). The Triple P implementation framework: The role of purveyors in the implementation and sustainability of evidence-based programs. *Prevention Science, 17*, 636–645. doi:10.1007/s11121-016-0661-4

McWilliam, J., Tucker, M. K., Sanders, M. R., & Jones, L. (2017). *Mechanisms of change in program implementation: organizational and practitioner factors predicting program use.* Manuscript in preparation.

Morawska, A., Sanders, M., Goadby, E., Headley, C., Hodge, L., McAuliffe, C., . . . Anderson, E. (2011). Is the Triple P—Positive Parenting Program acceptable to parents from culturally diverse backgrounds? *Journal of Child and Families Studies, 20*, 614–622. doi:10.1007/s10826-010-9436-x

Nilsen, Per (2015). Making sense of implementation theories, models and frameworks. *Implementation Science, 10*, 53–65. doi:10.1186/s13012-015-0242-0

Ogden, T., & Fixsen, D. L. (2014). Implementation science: A brief overview and a look ahead. *Zeitschrift für Psychologie, 222*, 4–11. doi:10.1027/2151-2604/a000160

Oosthuizen, C., & Louw, J. (2013). Developing program theory for purveyor programs. *Implementation Science, 8*, 23–32. doi:10.1186/1748-5908-8-23

Paul, G. L. (1967). Strategy of outcome research in psychotherapy. *Journal of Consulting Psychology, 31*, 109–118. doi:10.1037/h0024436

Proctor, E. K., Powell, B. J., & McMillen, J. C. (2013). Implementation strategies: recommendations for specifying and reporting. *Implementation Science, 8*, 139–149. doi:10.1186/1748-5908-8-139

Romney, S., Israel, N., & Zlatevski, D. (2014). Exploration-stage implementation variation: Its effect on the cost-effectiveness of an evidence-based parenting program. *Zeitschrift für Psychologie, 222*, 37–48. doi:10.1027/2151-2604/a000164

Sanders, M. R., Prinz, R. J., & Shapiro, C. J. (2009). Predicting utilization of evidence-based parenting interventions with organizational, service-provider and client variables. *Administration and Policy in Mental Health and Mental Health Services Research, 36*, 133–143. doi:10.1007/s10488-009-0205-3

Seng, A. C., Prinz, R. J., & Sanders, M. R. (2006). The role of training variables in effective dissemination of evidence-based parenting interventions. *The International Journal of Mental Health Promotion, 8*, 20–28. doi:10.1080/14623730.2006.9721748

Shapiro, C. J., Prinz, R., & Sanders, M. R. (2015). Sustaining use of an evidence-based parenting intervention: Practitioner perspectives. *Journal of Child and Family Studies, 24*, 1615–1624. doi:10.1007/s10826-014-9965-9

Turner, K. M. T., Nicholson, J., & Sanders, M. R. (2011). The role of practitioner self-efficacy, training, program and workplace factors on the implementation of an evidence-based parenting intervention in primary care. *Journal of Primary Prevention, 32*, 95–112. doi:10.1007/s10935-011-0240-1

TRAINING A WORKFORCE TO IMPLEMENT EVIDENCE-BASED PARENTING PROGRAMS

ALAN RALPH AND CASSANDRA K. DITTMAN

INTRODUCTION

This chapter describes the training model developed to disseminate the Triple P—Positive Parenting Program. The Triple P training model has been carefully developed to maintain the fidelity of the program, that is, to maximize the probability that the suite of programs delivered to parents globally closely matches those described and evaluated in the research literature. It examines three main areas: the recruitment, training, and support of Triple P trainers; the development, revision, and quality management of the training courses offered to practitioners; and the development, revision, and quality control of the resources provided to practitioners to support their delivery of the programs.

THREATS TO FIDELITY IN THE SCALING UP OF EVIDENCE-BASED PROGRAMS

A fundamental challenge in widespread dissemination of evidence-based programs (EBPs) is to meet local community needs and preferences without compromising effectiveness. The main threats to fidelity in taking EBPs to scale are (a) drift in the quality and consistency of the training of the potential workforce and (b) drift in the quality and consistency of program delivery by that workforce, both initially and over a prolonged period of time.

Many EBPs rely on a "train-the-trainer" model as a means of efficient and economical dissemination. However, the use of such a model can result in errors accumulating at each training so that the finished message deviates dramatically from the initial input, resulting in reduced adherence to the established treatment model. Where the material being transmitted is simple, brief, clear, and well documented, the train-the-trainer model may have some utility. However, the effectiveness of most EBPs depends on a delicate mix of clearly defined practices and appropriate tailoring to meet the diverse needs of different clients. For the individual practitioner, too much variation in the implementation of a program can be as risky as too little acknowledgment of the personal characteristics of the individual taking part in a program.

As the end user increases in distance from the program developer, a train-the-trainer model can also result in a diminishing level of investment in maintaining the program as it was designed and evaluated. Practitioners in such situations are more likely to add elements of their own choosing, perhaps omitting other elements to suit their own preferences. Such changes may or may not have an impact on the effectiveness of the program, but as they are untested, there can be no confidence in these disparate hybrid models.

The provision of comprehensive materials that guide the practitioner and parent through each program goes some way to reducing the likelihood that practitioners will depart significantly from the way the program was designed and evaluated. However, as funding and policy agendas increasingly emphasize the need for effective scaling up of EBPs, researchers have been challenged to identify strategies to maximize fidelity that go beyond manualized treatment design and delivery. A comprehensive strategy to maximize treatment fidelity must also incorporate optimal training models, methods for assessing practitioner knowledge and skill acquisition, and methods for sustaining effective delivery over time via effective supervision or consultation (Bellg et al., 2004; Garbacz, Brown, Spee, Polo, & Budd, 2014).

IMPLICATIONS FOR THE DELIVERY OF PARENTING SUPPORT

Parent training programs have among the most robust evidence of efficacy of all EBPs. Thus, effective dissemination of parenting support is critical to ensure that positive research outcomes for children and families translate to the real world. However, dissemination is complicated by the fact that parenting support comes in various packages, with each posing particular challenges when it comes to maintaining fidelity. Factors that affect fidelity include parent preferences for how, where, and when they wish to receive support; practitioner preferences for how, where, and when they wish to provide support; and service agency or organizational preferences for how they support varying practitioner and parent preferences.

The diverse ethnic, cultural, language, and belief systems that are present in many communities add other levels of challenge when it comes to maintaining fidelity. It is not uncommon for practitioners to react to program content or structure by raising doubts about their relevance or acceptability for "their" parents. This "gatekeeper" position is often the result of a level of protectiveness displayed by practitioners toward vulnerable families for whom they have been given some responsibility, but it can also include a closed mindset based on a position that the practitioner knows best what will work for these families. The danger for evidence-based parenting programs, then, is that practitioners "cherry-pick" those strategies that they believe are most relevant or acceptable to their parents, without fully considering or understanding the implications this could have on program effectiveness.

Interestingly, research in this area has shown that levels of acceptability of Triple P strategies reported by parents from culturally diverse backgrounds are high (Morawska et al., 2011) and are in fact higher than those of practitioners (Morawska et al., 2012). The key message here is that while the adoption of EBPs increases the likelihood that a practitioner will be effective in supporting parents, training programs need to equip practitioners with the skills and knowledge to gather data to determine whether a program is effective in supporting the parents with whom they work and to flexibly deliver and adapt EBPs to cater to the needs of different types of families (Mazzucchelli & Sanders, 2010).

There is also the question of whether interventions that derive their evidence-based status from one population can work as effectively in other settings. This is as true for the training of practitioners as it is for parents. A case example is provided in Box 34.1. Rather than assuming that adaptations will be required when engaging with populations from different cultural and ethnic groups, the recommended position (Mazzucchelli & Sanders, 2010) is to evaluate the existing program first to see if it retains its effectiveness before deciding whether changes are required. Indeed, practitioners can draw confidence from the abundance of evidence that Triple P is effective across a wide variety of cultural contexts and high-risk or clinical populations (Sanders, Kirby, Tellegen, & Day, 2014).

BOX 34.1: Overcoming Challenges of Engaging Indigenous Communities in Evidence-Based Parenting Interventions

The delivery of Triple P training to practitioners who work with Indigenous parents has presented unique challenges, particularly in Australia, but also in New Zealand, Canada, and the United States. Many of these families have experienced significant trauma or dislocation and often have a mistrust of interventions designed and promoted by those who are perceived as implicated in their colonization. While the basic tenets of Triple P have frequently been acknowledged as relevant and acceptable by many Indigenous people, their engagement and uptake of the programs has been less than optimal. Steps to improve the engagement process include extensive consultation with Indigenous practitioners and elders; additional education and training for trainers charged with training practitioners working with Indigenous communities; modification of training protocols to adjust to the pace and style of learning favored by Indigenous people; replacing video and written material to depict Indigenous families and relevant cultural activities; and providing additional support and opportunities to practice and complete the quizzes and competencies associated with accreditation.

A further strategy to engage Indigenous communities has been to attempt to recruit Indigenous trainers. However, this has been difficult, partly due to the small numbers of eligible practitioners and the high demand for them in many settings. In the interim, we have been fortunate to have recruited some Indigenous practitioners in a cofacilitation and engagement role, which has proven immensely rewarding in relation to both engagement and implementation of the Triple P programs in Indigenous communities.

THE TRIPLE P PROFESSIONAL TRAINING MODEL

The professional training curricula employed by Triple P was carefully developed with full awareness of the critical role of treatment fidelity in maximizing the success of the dissemination of the program, while being mindful of practitioners' and service agencies needs to implement Triple P across diverse communities, cultures, and contexts. Consistent with frameworks for enhancing fidelity of EBPs (Bellg et al., 2004), there are three key elements that form the foundation for all Triple P training courses. The first is a highly skilled, competent, and experienced team of trainers. The second is a set of well-designed and resourced practitioner training courses and accreditation processes. The third is the comprehensive library of program resources made available to practitioners to assist their program delivery.

TRIPLE P TRAINERS

Accredited Triple P trainers are the only people permitted to train practitioners to deliver Triple P programs with parents. Triple P trainers are recruited to meet specific geographic and language needs, and the intensive 6-day training courses are typically conducted every 12 or 18 months in various parts of the world. Although participant numbers in these courses vary, they typically range between 6 and 12. They are selected based on academic qualifications, training skills, and their knowledge of Triple P. A master's degree in clinical or developmental psychology, or its equivalent, is the minimum requirement, and many Triple P trainers have doctoral qualifications. A structured interview and reference checks complement the recruitment process.

Training is usually conducted by program developers, Drs. Matthew Sanders and Alan Ralph, and covers the core Triple P programs. Subsequent training in adjunctive Triple P courses is typically conducted by Dr. Ralph in his role as head of training at Triple P International. These courses may be held face to face or using online videoconferencing and mirror the practitioner training courses in their format and structure, methods for transmitting content, and the use of active skills training and self-regulatory learning and feedback (see next section). Successful completion of the training results in provisional accreditation as a Triple P trainer.

Following initial training, provisionally accredited trainers are required to complete a comprehensive written quiz that requires them to reflect on how to respond to practitioner questions during training. The primary focus of the quiz is to develop knowledge concerning key teaching points and deployment of the self-regulatory framework in a training context. In addition, provisionally accredited trainers will usually be provided with the opportunity to cofacilitate several training events with an experienced trainer.

Satisfactory completion of the quiz and at least two solo training events then leads to a trainer receiving full accreditation. Satisfactory completion is determined by ratings routinely collected from participants in all Triple P training events. Ratings are made on a series of 7-point scales measuring such constructs as the quality of the presentation, opportunities for active participation, and overall satisfaction. Mean ratings have been established that set benchmarks for trainer performance that must be met. Failure to achieve these benchmarks sets in motion a process whereby the trainer is interviewed to determine reasons for the low ratings and to determine whether any remedial action is required.

Full accreditation is held for the duration of each 2-year quality assurance period. These periods are specified in the license agreement between Triple P International and UniQuest, the technology transfer company of the University of Queensland. During each 2-year period, trainers are required to complete a minimum of 20 hours professional development that is directly related to maintaining and increasing their skills and knowledge as a Triple P trainer. Such activities include participation in structured peer support sessions, delivery of Triple P programs to parents, and attendance at authorized conference or training events.

Feedback regarding trainers' progress in fulfilling these requirements is provided every 6 months in the form of a detailed written report that includes their training performance for that period. Information for these reports is drawn from the electronic reports that each trainer is required to complete and submit immediately after every training or accreditation event. The report includes information about the suitability of the training venue and equipment provided, the availability of the relevant training materials, the engagement of the practitioners, and any issues that may need to be discussed with the organizers relating to implementation or practitioner support. These aspects are dealt with in greater detail in the chapter on implementation support.

In addition to the items mentioned, trainers are expected to conduct a self-evaluation of their performance, detailing things that went well and any goals they might have for improvement in the future. These reports are all read by the head of training and the relevant deputy head of training, who provide prompt feedback regarding any issues raised in the report. The Workshop Evaluation Survey (WES) ratings that participants complete are also scrutinized to ensure training events fall within the benchmark scores. Where a participant has recorded a low rating, a conversation is held with the trainer to investigate and to determine what action, if any, should be taken.

At the time of writing, there were 113 accredited Triple P trainers located in 14 countries. Languages spoken include Bahassar Indonesia, Cantonese, Dutch, Farsi, Flemish, French, German, Japanese, Mandarin, Spanish, Swedish, and Turkish. Trainers are required to meet regularly in peer support groups to evaluate their training experiences and review training materials and protocols. The head of training regularly monitors these activities with the support of several deputy heads of training who are located in several regional locations worldwide so that immediate support is available in the event of issues arising during a training event that may require prompt consultation.

PRACTITIONER TRAINING COURSES

All Triple P training is currently conducted live with the trainer and practitioners working together in the same location for a period of days. Typically, one trainer works with up to 20 practitioners at a time. Where a practitioner is attending a Triple P training course for the first time, the duration of the course is 2 or 3 days.

The training is a mix of didactic presentations, discussion of program content, small-group rehearsal of practical skills, and viewing audiovisual materials. The trainer presents the material using PowerPoint and video materials that have been extensively trialed and revised to ensure an optimum learning experience. Participants are provided with a set of participant notes that incorporate replications of all PowerPoint slides and other relevant training information.

Early in the training, practitioners are introduced to a segment addressing issues of flexibility and fidelity. They are encouraged to reflect on possible adaptations to the content or the process of the Triple P program they are learning about and to consider whether they pose a high or a low risk to the fidelity of the program. In this way, they learn where flexibility can occur to meet the specific needs of the parents they are working with and where changes might pose a risk to the effectiveness of the program.

The middle section of each training course introduces practitioners to the content and process of delivering a particular variant of Triple P. Specific sessions are explored, and participants practice and receive self-regulatory feedback on core elements that are considered to be essential to the efficient and competent delivery of the program (Sanders, Mazzucchelli, & Ralph, 2012). This includes a section on preventing and managing common process problems and how to address issues of both parent and practitioner resistance.

One of the final exercises of each training workshop is the introduction of the peer-assisted supervision and support (PASS) framework. This is designed to encourage and assist practitioners to form small peer support groups to enhance consolidation of the training experience and promote competent delivery of Triple P with parents. It is based on a self-evaluative approach where practitioners are prompted and supported by their peers to reflect on their knowledge and practice to identify elements they are confident about and to set goals for improvement in areas they are less confident about. Practitioners are encouraged to establish these groups as soon as possible to assist their preparation for accreditation, and then subsequently to enhance their skill development and adherence to program fidelity. See Chapter 37 of this volume for a more detailed discussion of the PASS model.

At the conclusion of the training, participants are scheduled into small groups for accreditation. Practitioners are required to have attended a minimum of 80% of a course to be eligible to attend accreditation. Practitioners who do not pass accreditation are not permitted to purchase additional Triple P resources. However, efforts are made to assist all practitioners to meet the accreditation requirements.

Accreditation events are usually scheduled approximately 6 to 8 weeks after training has taken place. More recently, a preaccreditation event has been introduced to assist practitioners to be better prepared when they attend accreditation. Practitioners usually attend accreditation in small groups of between 5 and 10. They are required to bring with them a completed quiz that tests their knowledge of the program they have been trained in, with the quiz then marked and feedback provided by the trainer conducting accreditation.

Practitioners are then required to demonstrate two or three designated key competencies that are deemed to be core to the successful delivery of the program with parents. There are some competencies that are compulsory and that everyone is required to successfully demonstrate and several others from which participants may choose. A detailed checklist of the steps required to complete each competence is provided, and the trainer records each participant's completion of these steps in real time. After a practitioner has completed each competency, he or she is asked to self-evaluate how well he or she satisfied the steps on the checklist and are given an opportunity to self-correct any areas that were insufficiently covered.

After all participants have demonstrated all the required competencies, they are provided with feedback about their success or otherwise. Most participants achieve accreditation, but some are required to recycle if their competency does not meet the required standards. This recycling can occur on the same or the following day or at another accreditation event to give the practitioner more time to practice.

Following successful completion of accreditation, the practitioner is sent an accreditation certificate. Practitioners are provided with access to the Triple P provider's website, where they can access a wide range of materials to assist in their delivery of Triple P. Accredited practitioners can also enroll in further courses, either for a different mode of delivery of the same materials or to extend their knowledge with new programs.

PROGRAM RESOURCES

Each Triple P program is supported by an extensive set of resources. At training, all participants receive a set of materials that enables them to deliver that specific Triple P program. This includes a comprehensive manual that describes the Triple P model, relevant evaluation tools, and session-by-session program details. They also receive other program-relevant materials, such as a parent workbook, PowerPoint presentations, tip sheets, or video materials.

All materials are developed jointly by the Parenting and Family Support Centre at the University of Queensland, which is responsible for the development and evaluation of Triple P interventions, and the publications department at Triple P International, which is responsible for publishing and disseminating them. Once there is sufficient research evidence to support a new program, a process of editing and proofing takes place to prepare the materials for publication.

In addition to the training and accreditation workshops, accredited practitioners are offered follow-up opportunities to assist them in maintaining or improving their skills. Clinical support workshops are offered at regular intervals either in person or by Skype or telephone. These provide an opportunity to revisit certain issues relating to Triple P delivery with a Triple P trainer using a supportive problem-solving approach. Additional workshops focus such topics as providing telephone support to parents, reviewing assessment measures, considering cultural diversity, engaging hard-to-reach parents, and further exploring the balance between fidelity and flexibility of program delivery.

BRIEF REVIEW OF EFFICACY

Since training to deliver Triple P courses started in 1996, data have been collected to assist in the evaluation of these courses. Over this period, it is estimated that 2,961 training courses have been conducted with 105,803 training places (the number of actual practitioners trained will be somewhat less as many practitioners train in multiple levels of Triple P).

Two measures are routinely collected during Triple P training and accreditation events to assess the effectiveness and quality of training, the Parent Consultation Skills Checklist (PCSC) and the WES. The PCSC is used to measure practitioners' self-efficacy and confidence in conducting behavioral family interventions. The PCSC is completed at the start and end of all Triple P training courses and after accreditation. The PCSC contains items assessing perceived proficiency in core skills, including assessment, active skills training, dealing with process issues, and clinical application of positive parenting strategies. Some of the specific skills assessed include establishing a conducive environment for parent consultations, selecting reliable assessment methods, discussing causes of children's behavior, setting appropriate goals, answering questions about parenting strategies, using behavioral rehearsal, shaping parent's skills, giving homework, and referring families. These items are rated on a 7-point Likert scale from 1, "not at all confident" (or "definitely not adequately trained"), to 7, "very confident" ("definitely adequately trained"), with higher values indicating a higher level of proficiency. This measure has high internal consistency, $\alpha = .96$ to $.97$ (Turner, Nicholson, & Sanders, 2011).

The WES assesses the quality of both the training and the accreditation workshops. This survey, completed by participants both at the end of training and on completion of the accreditation process, assesses (a) quality of the training course; (b) whether the amount of active participation within the course was appropriate; (c) quality of the content of the training; (d) whether respondents felt they have the skills to implement the program; and (e) overall satisfaction with the training course. Each of the items is rated on a 7-point Likert scale, with 1 indicating a negative and 7 indicating a positive evaluation. Reliability analysis using data from a study by Turner et al. (2011; $N = 1,013$) revealed high internal reliability ($\alpha = .85$). Practitioners are also asked to add any written comments about the perceived strengths or weaknesses of their training experience and to offer suggestions for improvement.

Analyses of data obtained from the PCSC and WES for 2961 training courses conducted between 2012 and 2016 are summarized in Figures 34.1 and 34.2. On the PCSC, mean ratings for adequacy, confidence, and skills all increased from pre- to posttraining and again at follow-up after accreditation.

These results support previous analyses of PCSC data collated from participants in Group Triple P training courses conducted between 2007 and 2012 ($N = 5,109$; Sethi, Kerns, Sanders, & Ralph, 2014), supporting the effectiveness of Triple P training in improving practitioners' confidence, knowledge, and skills in conducting behavioral family interventions with parents. Importantly, this previous analysis of Triple P training data found that there were no differences in practitioner efficacy between practitioners from diverse professions or with diverse educational qualifications, consistent with Triple P's multidisciplinary approach to workforce training. Furthermore, the

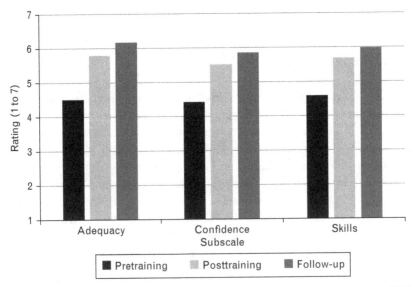

FIGURE 34.1: Mean pre- and posttraining and follow-up ratings on the Parent Consultation Skills Checklist.

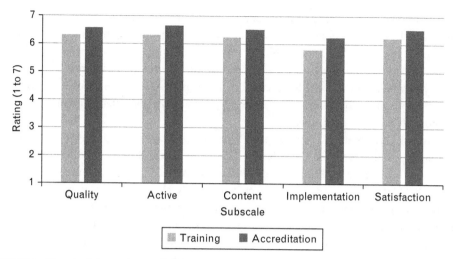

FIGURE 34.2: Mean training and accreditation ratings on the Workshop Evaluation Survey.

consistently high ratings across all aspects of the WES from 2012 to 2016 for both training and accreditation indicate that participants are highly satisfied with the Triple P training model.

CHALLENGES AND FUTURE DIRECTIONS

While these findings support the effectiveness of the standardized Triple P training curriculum, there are several challenges that require consideration as the Triple P model evolves over time to meet the needs of its consumers while ensuring fidelity in delivery. First, the designated number of 20 participants in each Triple P training course ensures a sustainable economy of scale together with a quality training experience. However, it is not always possible that an agency has exactly 20 suitable practitioners they wish to train. A related problem occurs where staff turnover occurs such that several Triple P trained practitioners leave an agency, and there is a need to train replacement staff. These have been partly addressed by the creation of Open Enrollment courses, which are scheduled by Triple P International or one of its international subsidiaries, with participants recruited from a range of different sources.

A second challenge occurs when practitioners who are trained in one course wish to be trained in another course that differs by level, content stream, or delivery mode. For instance, a practitioner accredited in Level 4 Group Triple P may wish to be trained in Level 3 Primary Care Triple P (level), or in Group Teen Triple P (content stream), or Standard Triple P (delivery mode). Extension courses that have been developed to address this situation are shorter (and cheaper) than the regular courses as the overlapping material can be omitted. However, there are often too few participants at any one time or location to justify running a particular extension course. The practitioner is then faced with the choice of waiting and hoping for an extension course to occur in the future or to enroll in the full, regular course that is more frequently available and accept some duplication of material. Many practitioners who take the second option find there is value in refreshing their knowledge, and some fee reduction is usually negotiated to recognize their prior investment. However, this does not suit everyone.

As additional Triple P programs are developed and accrue evidence for their effectiveness, there is also the challenge of fitting them around the existing training structure and format. The core Triple P programs currently offered for training comprise three content streams (children aged 0–12 years, teenagers aged 12–16 years, and children with a disability aged 2–12 years) and five delivery modalities (Level 2 Seminars, Level 3 Primary Care and Discussion Groups, and Level 4 Group and Standard). Adjunctive Level 5 programs are also offered to practitioners who have completed a Level 4 training.

However, there are now several additional programs designed to address specific parenting issues, such as bullying, work–life balance, disaster recovery, chronic childhood disease, and mealtime difficulties. In addition, there are newly developed programs that are designed for specific client populations, including foster carers, early childhood educators, and grandparents. The practitioners who are likely to be interested in being trained in these more specialized courses may be relatively few, spread sparsely across geographic regions, or unable to take time from their work practices to receive intensive training. Some of them may have already trained in several levels of Triple P, whereas others may be completely new to the model. One solution is a flexible approach in which practitioners train in a core Triple P program and then access a web-based training platform to add the extra knowledge required to be competent to deliver the more targeted or specialized program.

A challenge related to maintaining fidelity is that, currently, most practitioners receive open-ended accreditation for a specific Triple P program. There are currently no checks or balances on how well practitioners adhere to the delivery guidelines, although they are encouraged to participate regularly in peer support and supervision sessions in an attempt to address this issue posttraining. It is intended to introduce a reaccreditation protocol that would require practitioners to take some action to demonstrate a minimal level of professional competence. This could be achieved by either attending a Triple P workshop or adjunctive training or logging on to the Triple P provider website and completing an online reaccreditation course. The mechanisms for this procedure are currently being explored to ensure the creation of a cost-effective, valued activity that reduces threats to fidelity.

The proliferation of web-based learning platforms provides another potential area for evolution of the Triple P training model. However, online platforms are currently best placed to promote the transmission of knowledge. Triple P training makes extensive use of active skills training, involving modeling and behavior rehearsal, followed by self-evaluation and subsequent goal setting. Some of these elements can be integrated into web-based programs (e.g., modeling by video example, prompts to practice), but the opportunity for a practitioner to receive corrective feedback in real time currently eludes the technology. As technology advances, however, some more of the current face-to-face training (e.g., extension courses) could be transferred to this format.

One final challenge relates to occasions when it is not physically possible (illness, snowstorms, floods, airline strikes) or uneconomic for practitioners to attend accreditation sessions in person, despite the likely benefits of face-to-face accreditation for effective delivery. In such circumstances, practitioners are permitted to complete accreditation by Skype or videoconference or in extreme circumstances by recording and submitting their competency demonstrations electronically in a secure format. The feedback they receive is still valuable but lacks the level of detail and the vicarious learning from others that can be achieved when the trainer and the participants are in the same room.

From a scientific perspective, there is a plethora of opportunities for future research directions related to the Triple P training model specifically and more broadly as an example of a standardized training curricula used to train professionals in EBPs. For instance, evidence for the effectiveness of Triple P training relies primarily on self-report measures of self-efficacy and competence, and few evaluations have yet involved any objective measures of actual performance, fidelity in delivery, or subsequent implementation of Triple P (Sanders, Tully, Turner, Maher, & McAuliffe, 2003). The question of whether the improvements in practitioner self-efficacy associated with involvement in Triple P training predicts real-world implementation practices, such as involvement in peer support and supervision, and level of fidelity in delivery also merits further investigation. Furthermore, the Triple P training model has not been tested against alternative training approaches (e.g., that take a more didactic, information-giving approach, rather than emphasizing active skills training and self-regulation) or alternative delivery modalities (e.g., face to face vs. webinars or videoconferencing). Similarly, there is scope to evaluate the PASS model in comparison to other expert-oriented supervision models on delivery and implementation.

CONCLUSION

The Triple P training model has been explicitly designed to reduce the threats to fidelity that have been identified and discussed in this chapter. Analyses of the ratings made by participants in Triple P training courses suggest that the initial overall training experience is highly valued and contributes to increased practitioner knowledge, confidence, and competence. Ratings also indicate that training is seen as being of high quality, active, and well presented. It is clear that there are challenges ahead in making training available in more flexible ways that do not risk diminishing these attributes.

KEY MESSAGES

- Effective and efficient methods of ensuring ongoing adherence to program fidelity pose a major challenge to the scaling up of evidence-based parenting interventions.
- Triple P employs a comprehensive strategy for maximizing fidelity that incorporates manualized face-to-face training and methods for assessing practitioner knowledge and skill acquisition and for sustaining effective delivery over time.
- Care must be taken in embracing technological advances that offer online training to ensure the outcomes are comparable with current training models.
- Ongoing research is required to determine whether changes are required to established training and parent materials with special reference to low- and middle-income countries and culturally and linguistic diverse populations.

REFERENCES

Bellg, A. J., Borrelli, B., Resnick, B., Hecht, J., Minicucci, D. S., Ory, M., . . . Czajkowski, S. (2004). Enhancing treatment fidelity in health behavior change studies: Best practices and recommendations from the NIH behavior change consortium. *Health Psychology, 23*, 443–451. doi:10.1037/0278-6133.23.5.443

Garbacz, L. L., Brown, D. M., Spee, G. A., Polo, A. J., & Budd, K. S. (2014). Establishing treatment fidelity in evidence-based parent training programs for externalizing disorders in children and adolescents. *Clinical Child and Family Psychology Review, 17*, 230–247. doi:10.1007/s10567-014-0166-2

Mazzucchelli, T. G., & Sanders, M. R. (2010). Facilitating practitioner flexibility within an empirically supported intervention: Lessons from a system of parenting support. *Clinical Psychology: Science and Practice, 17*, 238–252. doi:10.1111/j.1468-2850.2010.01215.x

Morawska, A., Sanders, M. R., Goadby, E., Headley, C., Hodge, L., McAuliffe, C., . . . Anderson, E. (2011). Is the Triple P—Positive Parenting Program acceptable to parents from culturally diverse backgrounds? *Journal of Child and Family Studies, 20*, 614–622. doi:10.1007/s10826-010-9436-x

Morawska, A., Sanders, M. R., O'Brien, J., McAuliffe, C., Pope, S., & Anderson, E. (2012). Practitioner perceptions of the use of the Triple P—Positive Parenting Program with families from culturally diverse backgrounds. *Australian Journal of Primary Health, 18*, 313–320. doi:10.1071/PY11106

Sanders, M. R., Kirby, J. N., Tellegen, C. L., & Day, J. J. (2014). The Triple P—Positive Parenting Program: A systematic review and meta-analysis of a multi-level system of parenting support. *Clinical Psychology Review, 34*, 337–357. doi:10.1016/j.cpr.2014.04.003

Sanders, M. R., Mazzucchelli, T. G., & Ralph, A. (2012). Promoting parenting competence through a self-regulation approach to feedback. In R. M. Sutton, M. J. Hornsey, & K. M. Douglas (Eds.), *Feedback: The communication of praise criticism, and advice* (Vol. 11, pp. 305–321). New York, NY: Lang.

Sanders, M. R., Tully, L. A., Turner, K. M., Maher, C., & McAuliffe, C. (2003). Training GPs in parent consultation skills. An evaluation of training for the Triple P—Positive Parenting Program. *Australian Family Physician, 32*, 763–768.

Sethi, S., Kerns, S. E., Sanders, M. R., & Ralph, A. (2014). The international dissemination of evidence-based parenting interventions: Impact on practitioner content and process self-efficacy. *International Journal of Mental Health Promotion, 16*, 126–137. doi:10.1080/14623730.2014.917896

Turner, K. M. T, Nicholson, J. M., & Sanders, M. R. (2011). The role of practitioner self-efficacy, training, program and workplace factors on the implementation of an evidence-based parenting intervention in primary care. *Journal of Primary Prevention, 32*, 95–112. doi:10.1007/s10935-011-0240-1

CHAPTER 35

USING SOCIAL MARKETING STRATEGIES TO ENHANCE PROGRAM REACH

LEANNE WILKINSON

"If you build it, he will come" (Robinson, 1989). For those of you old enough to remember the 1980s, you might recognize this quotation from the Hollywood blockbuster, *Field of Dreams*. A young Kevin Costner, hearing a disembodied voice urging him to build a baseball pitch in the middle of an Iowa cornfield, does just that. Reluctantly plowing up his corn, Ray (Kevin Costner) builds a pitch and watches incredulously as a stream of blinking car headlights, stretching to the horizon and beyond, snakes its way to his gate. The fans have turned up in their thousands to watch a baseball game . . . a baseball game smack bang in the middle of a very big American nowhere. *Field of Dreams*, nominated for three academy awards, was truly the stuff of dreams for the Universal Pictures marketing machine.

But, the emotionally laden phrase, "If you build it, they will come," ranked 39 on the top 100 AFI movie quotations of all time, highlights the first stumbling block facing many marketers. For a large number of products and services, the reality is more the case of—if you build it, they most definitely and absolutely will not come. The disconnect between what creators or producers believe consumers want or need and what consumers actually want or need makes the desired action marketers seek difficult to accomplish. The interesting part of *Field of Dreams* is that Ray wasn't selling tickets to a baseball game in a remote Iowa cornfield. If he were, he would have failed. What Ray was actually selling was nostalgia and hope. He was fulfilling a longing in the heart and soul of a jaded America for a time when things were simpler, purer, clearer. In marketing jargon, the "exchange" was worth it in the mind of the consumer.

In a salutatory lesson for all marketers regarding the interconnectedness between a consumer's belief/value system and motivation to act, James Earl Jones's character, Terrance Mann, tells Kevin Costner the real reason people will "buy into" his baseball game: "This field, this game: it's a part of our past, Ray. It reminds us of all that once was good and it could be again. Oh . . . people will come Ray. People will most definitely come" (Robinson, 1989).

This chapter examines the social marketing principles underpinning a population approach to the communication planning, strategies, and learning associated with the promotion of the Triple P—Positive Parenting Program and seeks to understand the catalysts and barriers to both attitudinal and behavioral change surrounding participation in universal, evidence-based, parenting interventions.

WHAT IS SOCIAL MARKETING?

Although the term *social marketing* was first defined by Kotler and Zaltman in 1971 (Andreasen, 1994), thinking has evolved over the decades to incorporate more than just the concept of influencing the acceptability of social ideas. Andreasen offered a widely cited definition of social marketing as "the adaption of commercial marketing technologies to programs designed to influence the voluntary behavior of target audiences to improve their personal welfare and that of the society of which they are a part" (Andreasen, 1994, p. 110). Social marketing draws on the standard four *P*'s of marketing: Product, Price, Place, and Promotion. It then moves beyond to add a new series of "*P*'s"—Publics, Partnerships, Policy, and Purse strings—relevant to the arena of social change. Put simply, social marketing uses key marketing principles to influence target behaviors that will benefit society as well as the individual (Weinreich, 2006).

A key question every social marketer needs to ask is, Do the people whose behavior I am seeking to influence want, need, care about, or have an opinion on my product or service? Depending on the responses to this question, the social marketer may be faced with the complex and, in some instances, unrealistic task of creating that desire or need, changing entrenched opinions or cultural norms, and working with stakeholders upstream, midstream, and downstream to enable the desired behavior change. The social marketer also needs to understand barriers, obstacles, or associated factors positively or negatively affecting the uptake of the desired behavior.

WHY SHOULD WE CARE?

Governments, nongovernmental organizations (NGOs), academics, and professionals around the world know there are a handful of effective evidence-based parenting programs available. They know these programs work. They know they change lives for the long term and for the better. And, they know these programs benefit parents, kids, and society in general. So, we have to ask ourselves the question, why aren't parents beating down our doors and demanding evidence-based parenting programs in droves, right here, right now?

A literature search reveals a range of factors preventing large-scale uptake of evidence-based parenting programs, including perceived relevance, incompatibility with dominant cultural models of parenting, perceived benefit versus effort, cost, affordable access to child care, access to transport, suitability of session times offered, time-poor parents, distrust of services, stigma, and lack of widespread promotion. These are all valid problems, and solutions to a number of these issues are addressed through both the Triple P Implementation Framework (McWilliam, Brown, Sanders, & Jones, 2016) and Triple P International's social marketing strategy titled *Stay Positive*.

STAY POSITIVE—PUBLIC HEALTH SOCIAL MARKETING IN ACTION

Stay Positive began its life in 2006 when the Amsterdam City Council asked the Educational Support and Training Service Bureau (SO&T) to develop a mass media marketing campaign to support the rollout of the Triple P—Positive Parenting Program across the city of Amsterdam. SO&T worked with a local social marketing and advertising agency, Bureau Blanco, to develop a four-phase communications campaign designed to raise awareness of Triple P and normalize the notion of seeking parenting help. A tagline and positioning statement, Stay Positive, was created to support the Positief Opvenden (Positive Parenting) campaign. It was hoped that normalizing the notion of asking for parenting help would encourage more parents to use the free Triple P parenting services offered through child health centers social services in schools, parenting support centers, child protection services, and other institutions (De Jong, 2007, as cited in Goossens & de Graaf, 2010).

Understanding the importance of monitoring and measuring success, SO&T commissioned the Netherlands Institute of Mental Health and Addiction (Trimbos Institute) to undertake a 2-year independent research study of the Stay Positive rollout to measure campaign awareness, acceptance, and destigmatization. Phone, online, and face-to-face questionnaires were given one or more times to 1,922 parents in Amsterdam from 2008 to 2010. In total, 2,844 interviews were conducted with 1,922 parents. After Phase 1 (awareness/acceptance; June–October 2008), 50% of respondents remembered seeing the campaign, with 77% recognizing the campaign after being shown a poster.

Phase 1 results benchmarked favorably with other government civic/health campaigns. Phase 2 (destigmatization; November 2008–April 2010) aimed to destigmatize the idea of seeking parenting advice. Figure 35.1 shows a clear increase in the normalization of the concept of parents asking for information and assistance. Trimbos research also showed positive parent attitudes to the campaign, rating Stay Positive as more "striking" and "believable" than other government campaigns (Goossens & de Graaf, 2010).

The results of the study of the Stay Positive campaign indicated parents considered the campaign to be credible and relevant and believed it contributed to the normalization of raising questions about parenting. However, further research was needed to understand the role awareness and destigmatization played in encouraging actual attendance at evidence-based parenting interventions (Goossens & de Graaf, 2010).

STAY POSITIVE—THE NUTS AND BOLTS

Since the initial campaign in Amsterdam, Triple P social marketing tactics have been refined and enhanced to cater for Universal Triple P Level 1 rollouts in various populations worldwide. The

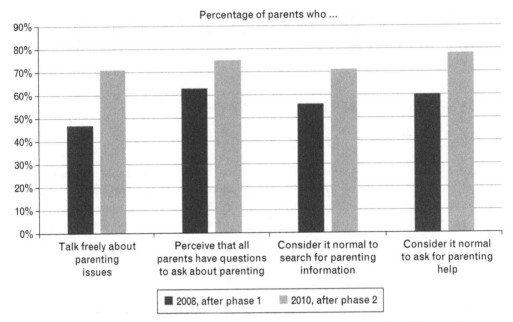

FIGURE 35.1: Results from a survey of parents before and after Stay Positive rollout in Amsterdam. Developed from data presented in "Positief Opvoeden. Campagne maakt stellen van opvoedvragen normal" ["Positive Parenting. Raising questions about parenting made normal through campaign"] by F. X. Goossens and I. M. De Graaf, 2010, *Jeugd en Co Kennis, 4*, 24–33. Copyright 2010 by Utrecht: Netherlands Youth Institute. Figure copyright 2014 by Triple P International Proprietary Limited. Reprinted with permission.

key to the design of the Stay Positive social marketing campaign is the phased, multistakeholder approach, ensuring timely targeted messages and calls to action delivered to particular stakeholders at particular points in time. Stakeholders range from commissioning bodies through to implementing organizations, supporting organizations, practitioners, communities, and parents.

The Stay Positive social marketing strategy works hand-in-hand with the Triple P Implementation Framework to facilitate organizational readiness and capacity. It is important to ensure implementing organizations understand, commit to, and are resourced to perform their respective roles in practical outreach and support. A range of communications materials has been developed for each strategy stage and each stakeholder group.

The "dangerous river" story, often cited in public health journals (French, 2012), is a useful analogy for the social marketer in terms of the staged planning necessary to uncover and address factors influencing, enhancing, or discouraging behavior change within key stakeholder groups. The dangerous river acknowledges the crucial role governments and organizations, operating upstream and midstream, play in minimizing parental struggles downstream. The analogy spotlights causal factors upstream and midstream that may be contributing to costly and time-intensive "rescue" operations downstream. Upstream and midstream factors may include government policy, organizational capacity, organizational commitment, and adequate resourcing.

The Triple P Implementation Framework and the Triple P Stay Positive social marketing campaign seek to facilitate and strengthen the role of all stakeholder groups in supporting the required social marketing phases. For instance, the rollout of Triple P across the population of Queensland required the creation of a range of communications materials to support stakeholders in their outreach to parents, such as a "Getting Started Guide" (Figure 35.2).

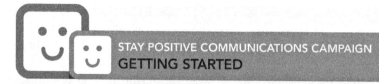

STAY POSITIVE COMMUNICATIONS CAMPAIGN
GETTING STARTED

Congratulations on completing your Queensland Government sponsored Triple P training! We know you'll be keen to start delivering straight away, so we've created some great tools and materials to make it easy for you to let parents and caregivers know about your services. It's simple:

Step 1:
Fill in your 'My Page' profile
on your secure provider site
Soon after you complete your training, you'll receive a welcome email. Click the 'Log on Now!' button. You'll be redirected to the provider website where you can create a new account by following the prompts.

Step 2:
Publish your location details so
parents can find you on our map
From the 'Promote your services' box, click 'Promote your location online'. Click on the 'Triple P Provider' link (under the grey box), then click on 'Add a location'. Fill in your details and your services will appear on the map on the parent website.

Step 3:
List your sessions so parents can RSVP
From the 'Promote your services' box, click 'Promote sessions online'. Choose the type of intervention you want to promote, then click 'Add a session' and fill in the details. The sessions will appear on the parent website. Parents are then able to RSVP and RSVPs will be sent to the email address you provided. When your session is full, mark the checkbox to indicate your session is full.

Step 4:
Re-ordering your program and
promotional resources
You will be sent your program and promotional resources straight after you have completed training (i.e. tip sheets, workbooks, brochures, posters). To re-order program resources or promotional materials, email qld@triplep.net

Step 5:
Promote your sessions - See over for more details

Finally
Remember to tell us your stories
We're looking for stories to share through the parent website, the Triple P – Positive Parenting Program Facebook page and in the media. Success stories, parent quotes, work blogs or videos and photos welcome. Please let us know if you or the families you help would like to participate.

For more information, contact qld@triplep.net

FIGURE 35.2: Example of one of the communication materials developed for the rollout of Triple P across the state of Queensland in Australia to support stakeholders in their outreach to parents. Copyright 2016 by Triple P International Proprietary Limited. Reprinted with permission.

The first component of Stay Positive addresses social marketing's foundational *P*'s of Publics and Partnerships through a series of meetings, information sharing, and development of supporting materials. Supporting materials have been produced for a variety of Publics, including government entities at various levels, NGOs, communities, media, and the private sector. Partnerships with media and social influencers known as key opinion leaders are also sought during this foundation phase. A planning questionnaire, PowerPoints, videos, PDFs, "how to" guides, media kits, promotional materials, and a website may be provided to commissioning bodies, implementing organizations, and practitioners to ensure each stakeholder group understands the campaign, is familiar with the materials, and is prepared for the role they will play in facilitating consumer action.

Smooth pathways into the implementing agencies are sought through commissioning entities, and communications channels are opened with various stakeholders. Senior management champions are sought from within the commissioning entities to help draw together and mobilize the many, potentially disparate, implementing bodies. For the implementing bodies themselves, champions are also needed to create practitioner motivation and commitment and to ensure marketing support through the implementing organization's various channels. Aligned organizations, with the potential to offer in-kind support (i.e., libraries, community groups), are identified. These aligned organizations are approached with messaging promoting the societal and community benefits of evidence-based parenting and are presented with proposals seeking clearly defined and realistic support actions. For practitioners, commitment to facilitate community outreach is sought, and tools are provided to enable practitioners to achieve this outreach, including web tools and encouragement of organizational peer support.

This first component of social marketing works to identify catalysts and barriers to stakeholder action and, where necessary, recalibrate expectations. It also works to acknowledge and agree upon actions and responsibilities and facilitate positive communication with commissioning entities, implementing agencies, supporting organizations, and on-the-ground practitioners. This phase is a crucial platform necessary to help build, extend, and sustain the next phase of the campaign—public awareness.

The public awareness phase involves the launch and distribution of campaign materials, including video, radio and outdoor creative, websites, social media sites, brochures, flyers, posters, and banners. A launch, aimed at attracting mainstream television, press, and radio and designed to raise the importance of parenting on the public agenda, is implemented. Digital and hard copy flyers, brochures, and posters are publically distributed through stakeholder and supporting organization channels, advertising is launched, and public relations mobilized. Depending on the size of the rollout, a Stay Positive public facing website may go live, acting as both a knowledge-sharing and conversion mechanism, with background information, tips, and blogs on common parenting issues, as well as an online booking system for parents and carers to sign up for interventions. These first two phases are interdependent, with the commitment of practitioners to upload session dates, times, and locations to the practitioner website crucial to the posting of local, conveniently available, help on the public facing website.

The next phase continues to build awareness, while focus shifts to destigmatization, primarily through a localized parent newspaper, referred to as the *Tippaper*. The *Tippaper* may be produced in both digital and hard copy and is designed as a "great read" for parents. It features inspiring and empowering parent stories, providing insights into the life changes, both big and small, experienced by a range of families who have undertaken Triple P. It also features family activities, offers tips for everyday parenting, and provides a sneak peak into what to expect if you attend a Triple P session. There are handy parenting facts and interesting "slice-of-life" snippets, as well as a page of contacts for any time you are ready to "do" Triple P. The *Tippaper* ticks the boxes for parental relevance and usefulness and is designed to compete with the best of the commercially available parent magazine format publications.

YOUR CONTENT STRATEGY IS THE NEW BLACK

Awareness and destigmatization are also addressed through a formalized and resourced content strategy. "Word of mouth" has proven to be a constant in terms of raising awareness of parenting programs (Sanders, Turner, & Markie-Dadds, 2002). In recognition of the value of word of mouth and also in recognition of the fact that word of mouth is now "world of mouth" (Qualman, 2013), a digital content strategy has been developed to support Stay Positive, tapping into social networks of parents and friends, building awareness and relationships through online conversations, and enabling the easy sharing of stories, blogs, and tips.

The content strategy has been developed to cater for a new way of "chatting." This virtual back fence has opened opportunities for the social marketer, facilitating sharing of valued, relevant, and timely content through trusted networks. The content strategy starts "conversations" and, if adequately resourced, supported, and monitored, is sustainable beyond flighted advertising campaigns. This ongoing visibility of parenting interventions is vital as, unlike short-purchase-cycle, fast moving, consumer goods like bread and milk, a parent may take time to move through various stages of readiness. A parenting program must be visible and accessible at any point in time a parent may have a need.

Ongoing promotion, public relations, editorial, and advertising are also needed to move parents, open to key messaging and behavior change, through the stages of readiness. When considering the choice of channels and strategies to facilitate behavior change, an understanding of the breadth of competitive alternatives informs social marketing tactics and adjusts expectations. In an environment where online searching for "parenting help" yields over 20 million results (not including China's version of Google, Baidu), and in an era where opinions, blogs, tweets, posts, and websites offering all manner of parenting advice vie for the eyeballs and attention of the parent, a complex set of challenges ensues.

For those actively seeking parenting help, the options are staggering, potentially conflicting, and aggressively competing with evidence-based parenting messages. Evidence-based parenting programs also face challenges through potential dissonance with cultural norms, which may place higher acceptability on help from family and friends in preference to formal services (Volmert, Kendall-Taylor, Cosh, & Lindland, 2016).

It is also useful to consider models predictive of behavior change, such as the transtheoretical model (stages of change; Prochaska & DiClemente, 2000); the health belief model (Hochbaum, Kegels, & Rosenstock, 2010); the theory of reasoned action model (Fishbein & Ajzen, 1992); and the theory of planned behavior (Ajzen, 1992) to understand the relationship between parent intent and action. Most theories of behavior change underline intention as dependent on perceived need or ability to perform the behavior, the equation of benefit versus effort, attitude toward the behavior, and an individual's subjective norm. This interplay of the range of catalysts and barriers, including practical, psychosocial, cultural, and competitive influences, affects the likelihood of a parent adopting the desired behavior.

A range of Stay Positive tactics, materials, and components has been implemented in various communities throughout the world, depending on local aims, capacity, and budget. The degree of outreach has been contingent on the number of phases and mix of tactics undertaken. The "perfect social marketing storm" is created when champions at both the upstream and the midstream stakeholder levels, as well as committed and inspired practitioners operating downstream, are strongest. Stay Positive also works optimally when partnerships with supporting publics are in place, purse strings have been loosened to support paid advertising, and the campaign is augmented with public relations and social media content.

SO, IF WE BUILD IT, WILL THEY COME?

Although applying social marketing principles to a population based approach to evidence-based parenting programs provides a framework for success, deep-seated parental and societal attitudes surrounding what it means to be a "good" parent and firmly held views on whose business the business of parenting is anyway are both emotive and divisive. Parenting—could there be anything more important or less important? At the heart of this paradoxical question is the Gordian knot facing the social marketer of population level, evidence-based, parenting programs. Although few would argue that parenting is vitally important, many also feel that parenting is innate, as well as something "learned" on the job (Volmert et al., 2016). At best, parent "training" is seen by many as good for "struggling" parents. At worst, parent training is seen as "big brother" interfering where he is not wanted.

Craig (2012, para. 11, 17) asked the question: "Can you teach someone who is not in need of urgent medical treatment to be a good parent, or is it more a matter of instinct, and willingness to learn on the job? . . . the question remains as to whether any government could, or should, attempt to improve the malfunctioning family." And then, this from Gentleman (2012, para. 15): "But can good parenting be taught, or is it a bit like trying to teach someone to be a good person?" These kinds of statements and questions are typical across public discourse, and it's important to note the loaded language: "good," "improve," "teach," and the automatic connection of parenting programs to the "malfunctioning family." The choice of language and the implied sentiment are indicative of mainstream cautionary comment surrounding "teaching people to be good parents.

Public comment also reinforces entrenched social beliefs that information on parenting is best provided by family and friends and raises questions around a government's role and responsibility in this arena. According to Craig (2012, para. 13): "What helped me survive wasn't minimal state provision of help, or even books such as Penelope Leach's *Baby and Child*, but the advice of friends . . . . Vouchers and lessons, however well-intentioned, are not likely to be received with enthusiasm."

Public wariness around whose business is the business of parenting is highlighted in research undertaken by the Queensland Children and Family Commission, which investigated a range of issues, including questions surrounding the impact of cultural norms in the uptake of parenting services. The Queensland Family and Child Commission (2016) found the majority of Queensland parents did not have a strong positive community norm for accessing support services and concluded that if parents do not believe in a strong positive community norm for support services, they are less likely to access support services when needed.

Recognizing this complexity surrounding uptake of early intervention and support services, the Queensland Children and Family Commission's study sought to understand the predictors, drivers, and barriers to parental "help seeking," "help offering," and "service usage" and whether there are different groups within the population that can be best influenced by social marketing. The study found that 72% of parents worried that others would see them unfavorably when they struggled with parenting. Seventy-six percent avoided telling others outside their immediate family when they were struggling. Eighty-three percent had heard others say unfavorable or offensive things about people when they struggled with parenting. Eighty-three percent had seen or read hurtful or offensive things about struggling parents in mainstream media, and 75% had seen this via social media. When asked to imagine they were struggling as a parent, 75% of parents believed they would be thought of in a less favorable way if they used support services. Parents also felt their community stigmatized people who needed support, and that most people felt seeking parenting support is a sign of personal failure. The research revealed that using services that parents think are linked to government and the child protective system are a barrier.

Despite government intention to adopt a population approach to the provision of parenting interventions, public rhetoric often reinforces that parenting programs are for the "most vulnerable," sending mixed messages through mass media and supporting the notion that parenting programs are for low-income, struggling parents most often living in deprived areas. Parent-blaming headlines in the United Kingdom following the 2011 riots were typical of this rhetoric. Governments are caught between a rock and a hard place as they struggle to normalize parenting programs, while simultaneously needing to be seen to address antisocial behavior.

The default public focus therefore continues to be on hard-to-reach populations and parents most in need of help. SO&T in Amsterdam opted to leave government logos off promotional and advertising material in response to indications of parental resistance to government operating in the area of parenting. Governments, in their public discourse, also refer to the "need" for parenting programs to "help" those parents who are "struggling" often in "deprived" areas. This public discourse is repeated worldwide, unintentionally reinforcing the notion that parenting programs are offered by governments as a last resort for failed parents.

Along with destigmatization and normalization, another piece of the social marketing puzzle is understanding the disconnect between the knowledge of NGOs, governments, academics, and professionals and the psychosocial openness of parents to receive this knowledge. A study by the Parenting Research Centre in Australia mapped the gaps between expert and public understanding of effective parenting in Australia, noting that "much of the public discourse about parents and parenting features commentary, view, and opinion built on the assumption that 'parenting comes naturally'" (Cann, 2016, para. 5). The report noted Australians' cultural models of parenting (the implicit, shared understanding, assumptions, and patterns of reasoning that the public draw on to think about parenting) make them resistant to thinking about parenting as a conscious, skill-based, practice that can be intentionally improved. Destigmatization and normalization alone are insufficient to trigger widespread behavior change. The cultural norm of parenting as innate needs to be reframed, and resistance to the notion of parenting as a set of skills that can be "intentionally improved" needs to be broken down.

Assumptions around the causes of family problems also need to be addressed. If a parent sees the child as the cause of the problem, that parent will not be looking for a parenting program, they'll look for something to fix the child. The following comment from a dad in the ITV prime-time television series *Driving Mum and Dad Mad* (Cecil, 2005) is typical of this sentiment: "I thought this bloke from Australia was going to fix my kid. What I didn't realize was it was me who needed to change."

IMPLICATIONS AND FUTURE DIRECTIONS

The language of public discourse also needs to be carefully considered. What does "good" mean, and what does "help" mean when it comes to parenting? Parenting help emphasizes the premise that parenting programs are primarily for those who either want or believe they need help.

For the majority of the population who believe they are already good parents, messages about parenting help through services may fall on deaf ears. The emphasis on "help" for problems takes precedence over "skills" to parent well. A shift in cultural norms is needed to transition beliefs about good parenting as innate, to beliefs about good parenting as also about intentionally acquiring skills.

Further research into which messages resonate with which specific parent segments is then needed to inform the creation of more targeted messages. Additional research is also needed to tease out nuances around that emotive and very ambiguous word *help*. We talk about "parenting help" as though everyone understands and agrees what this means. But, does help mean different things to different parents? Does a "struggling" parent have the same notion of help as a "nonstruggling" parent, and what kinds of problems are perceived as requiring help anyway? How do we then ensure a match between the kinds of help needed and the kinds of channels recommended, and how does perceived level of help (low/medium/high intensity) relate to perceptions around which channels are best placed to provide these different levels of help? Is there some kind of perceptual line in the sand that places informal help from family and friends on one side of the line and institutional help from parenting programs on the other side of the line?

Perhaps upstream action should be considered to embed and meld evidenced-based parenting "packages" into key transitional life stages when parents may be more open to receiving messages rather than help. Such points in time could include transition to child care, transition to preschool, transition to elementary school, and transition to high school. At the same time, reframing of cultural norms to position parenting as an intentionally acquired set of skills needs consideration within the context of cultural dissonance. Andreasen (2006) cautioned, however, against the notion that social marketers, alone, can bring about major societal value changes, arguing that social marketing should not be the technology of choice if dramatically large segments of the target population are ignorant of the behavior or opposed to the behavior on the basis of central community values.

CONCLUSIONS

The Stay Positive social marketing strategy takes account of the barriers and catalysts associated with parent uptake of a population-based parenting program, creating a range of mix-and-match components that can be implemented based on local circumstances and capability. Taking the lead from Ray in the *Field of Dreams* analogy, the social marketer of population-level parenting programs needs to offer something much more compelling than just "tickets" to a parenting program. The social marketer of population-level parenting programs needs to offer the possibility of transformation, empowerment, and happiness—the chance for parents to change family life for the long term and for the better. The social marketer needs to offer parents the opportunity to weave proven knowledge and tested skills into each parent's own innate capabilities, helping empower every parent to parent well.

Parenting programs can create magic. They can create hope, confidence, and happiness, transforming all those big and small moments of family life into the "stories" and patterns of behavior that will be passed down through each family, from generation to generation. We need to inspire parents to see parenting programs as more than just a "ticket" to a parenting class. In this hyperdigitally connected century, "if you build it," you will also need to build a comprehensive social marketing strategy, underpinned by an understanding of the catalysts and barriers to behavior change. Although gaining the attention of a fragmented, overstimulated, advertising-weary audience is challenging, and changing social and cultural norms around the notion of what it means to be a "good" parent is daunting, the societal rewards are unprecedented and the repercussions of not doing so simply too high.

KEY MESSAGES

- Understand the cultural model of parenting underpinning your target population. This model affects cultural norms and broad societal attitudes and determines the complexity of your task.
- Determine whether the target population, whose behavior you wish to influence, wants, needs, cares about, or has an opinion on the actions you wish them to take. This will influence segmentation and affect messaging.
- Determine whether there is a match or a disconnect between what you believe people want or need and what people actually want or need. This will ensure the right services reach the right people through the right channels.
- Consider theoretical models of behavior to identify readiness and intent to act.
- Work within an implementation framework to ensure stakeholders upstream and midstream understand their roles within the social marketing strategy.
- Ensure your social marketing plan is multi-layered, adequately resourced, measurable, and sustainable.

REFERENCES

Andreasen, A. (1994). Social marketing: Its definition and domain. *Journal of Public Policy and Marketing, 13*, 108–114.

Cecil, A. (Producer). (2005). *Driving mum and dad mad*. Manchester, England: ITV.

Cann, W. (2016). Forward. In A. Volmert, N. Kendall-Taylor, I. Cosh, & E. Lindland (Authors), *Cuing context: Mapping the gaps between expert and public understandings of effective parenting in Australia* (n. p.). Washington, DC: FrameWorks Institute. Retrieved from http://www.parentingrc.org.au/images/Publications/Perceptions_of_Parenting_FrameWorks_Report_2016_web-lr.pdf

Craig, A. (2012, May 15). Can good parenting classes ever work? *The Telegraph*. Retrieved from http://www.telegraph.co.uk/women/mother-tongue/9264712/Can-good-parenting-classes-ever-work.html

French, J. (2012). *Up-stream, mid-stream and down-stream social marketing. Defining the terms*. Retrieved from http://www.strategic-social-marketing.vpweb.co.uk/Free-Tool-Box.html

Gentleman, A. (2012, March 31). Do we need parenting classes? *The Guardian*. Retrieved from https://www.theguardian.com/lifeandstyle/2012/mar/31/do-we-need-parenting-classes

Glanz, K., & Bishop, D. (2010). The role of behavioural science theory in development and implementation of public health interventions. *Annual Review of Public Health, 31*, 399–418. doi:10.1146/annurev.publhealth.012809.103604

Goossens, F. X., & de Graaf, I. M. (2010). Positief Opvoeden. Campagne maakt stellen van opvoedvragen normaal. [Positive Parenting. Raising questions about parenting made normal through campaign.] *Jeugd en Co Kennis, 4*, 24–33.

Kline, N. (2006). *What is social marketing?* Retrieved from http://www.social-marketing.com/Whatis.html

Madden, T., Scholder Ellen, P., & Ajzen, I. (1992). A comparison of the theory of planned behaviour and the theory of reasoned action. *Personality and Social Psychology Bulletin, 18*, 3–9. doi:10.1177/0146167292181001

McWilliam, J., Brown, J., Sanders, M. R., & Jones, L. (2016). The Triple P Implementation Framework: The role of purveyors in the implementation and sustainability of evidence-based programs. *Prevention Science, 17*, 636–645. doi:10.1007/s11121-016-0661-4

Qualman, E. (2013). *Socialnomics. How social media transforms the way we live and do business.* Hoboken, NJ: Wiley.

Queensland Family and Child Commission. (2016). *Talking families campaign. Detailed findings and technical report* (Ipsos Project 15-036362-01). Brisbane, Australia: Queensland Government. Retrieved from https//www.qfcc.qld.gov.au

Robinson, P. A. (Director). (1989). *Field of dreams* [Motion picture]. Universal City, CA: Universal Pictures.

Sanders, M., Turner, K., & Markie-Dadds, C. (2002). The development and dissemination of the Triple P—Positive Parenting Program: A multilevel, evidence-based system of parenting and family support. *Prevention Science, 3*, 173–189. doi:10.1023/A:1019942516231

Volmert, A., Kendall-Taylor, N., Cosh I., & Lindland, E. (2016). *Cuing context: Mapping the gaps between expert and public understandings of effective parenting in Australia.* Washington, DC: FrameWorks Institute. Retrieved from http://www.parentingrc.org.au/images/Publications/Perceptions_of_Parenting_FrameWorks_Report_2016_web-lr.pdf

Whitelaw, S., Baldwin, S., Bunton, R., & Flynn, D. (2000). The status of evidence and outcomes in stages of change research. *Health Education Research, 15*, 707–718. doi:10.1093/her/15.6.707

CHAPTER 36

MEASURING CHILD, PARENT, AND FAMILY OUTCOMES AT INDIVIDUAL AND POPULATION LEVELS

ALINA MORAWSKA AND MATTHEW R. SANDERS

INTRODUCTION

Parent interventions based on social learning theory and cognitive-behavioral principles are well-established, evidence-based prevention and intervention approaches for child behavioral and emotional problems. We know that they produce positive changes in both parent and child. A multitude of programs, with a variety of delivery modalities, targeting a range of populations and problems have been evaluated and disseminated (Lundahl, Risser, & Lovejoy, 2006; Sanders, Kirby, Tellegen, & Day, 2014).

The hallmark of evidence-based approaches to parenting support is the systematic, comprehensive, and continuing measurement of outcomes, over time, across individuals and groups. Assessment is also a key phase of a behavioral epidemiological approach to behavior change at a population level (Sallis, Owen, & Fotheringham, 2000). For interventions that target change at the population level, validated approaches to assessment of a representative sample of parents in the population need to be implemented. It is also important that the consumers of the parenting intervention, the parents themselves, have a voice in relation to their preferences and needs for information and support services (Sanders & Kirby, 2012).

CHILD, PARENT, AND FAMILY OUTCOMES AFFECTED BY PARENTING INTERVENTIONS

The primary target of parenting intervention is change in child behavior. Typically, the target outcomes include reducing the presence of oppositional, noncompliant, and antisocial behavior, as well as reductions in internalizing problems and symptomatology (e.g., Morawska & Sanders, 2006; Tully & Hunt, 2015; Webster-Stratton & Reid, 2010; Westrupp, Northam, Lee, Scratch, & Cameron, 2015). Less frequently, the focus is on improving child prosocial behavior or enhancing behavioral competencies (e.g., Healy & Sanders, 2014). Furthermore, the majority of interventions focus on child behavior change within the home setting, although there is some evidence of generalization of outcomes to other settings (e.g., McTaggart & Sanders, 2003). Beyond behavior change, parenting interventions have also been noted to affect other broader aspects of functioning, including improved well-being, reduced physical health problems, and improved quality of life (e.g., Morawska, Mitchell, Burgess, & Fraser, 2016; West, Sanders, Cleghorn, & Davies, 2010).

All behavioral parenting interventions are based on a social interactional model, which describes how parents inadvertently shape their children's behaviors through reinforcement contingencies (Forehand, Jones, & Parent, 2013; Patterson, 1982; Schrepferman & Snyder, 2002), alongside associated cognitive and self-regulatory processes (Jones & Prinz, 2005; Karoly, 1993). Critical elements are coercion and the bidirectional cycles of escalating coercive and controlling behaviors in which children and parents engage. These interactions are viewed as the "the fundamental behavioral mechanisms" (Granic & Patterson, 2006, p. 101) by which child externalizing problems develop and are maintained. Most evidence-based parenting interventions assume that change in parenting is the key mechanism by which intervention leads to positive child behavior outcomes; thus, the goal of intervention is to decrease coercive interchanges. This is accomplished by teaching parents to use their attention and other positive behaviors, to provide structure, and to apply effective discipline when inappropriate behavior occurs.

Likewise, changes in parental self-regulation (Karoly, 1993) and self-efficacy (Jones & Prinz, 2005) may serve as key triggers for change in parenting behaviors. Parents may have adequate knowledge and information regarding suitable parenting strategies; however, they may lack the metaskills to appropriately guide and modulate their behaviors according to changing circumstances (Karoly, 1993), or they may lack confidence to implement this knowledge (Gross & Rocissano, 1988). Self-regulation is a process whereby individuals acquire the skills they need to change their own behavior and become independent problem-solvers and controllers of their own destiny (Karoly, 1993). The capacity for a parent to change his or her own behavior in a planned, self-initiated, and deliberate manner in response to cues and information regarding the current needs of his or her children is seen as a fundamental process supporting the maintenance of nurturing and noncoercive parenting practices (Sanders & Mazzucchelli, 2013). Parenting self-efficacy relates to the perception that one can effectively manage tasks related to parenting (Teti & Gelfand, 1991). Associations between parental self-efficacy and a range of parenting skills have been found (e.g., Morawska & Sanders, 2007). Parental self-regulation and self-efficacy are theorized to be important mechanisms in changing parenting behaviors and thus are central targets of parenting interventions. Many studies have demonstrated changes in parental self-regulation and self-efficacy following parenting intervention (e.g., Lundahl et al., 2006; Nowak & Heinrichs, 2008; Sanders, Kirby, et al., 2014; Tarver, Daley, Lockwood, & Sayal, 2014).

Beyond targeted parent behavioral and cognitive outcomes, parenting interventions can also affect other aspects of parent and family functioning. For example, as a result of parenting intervention, parents may experience lower levels of stress, anxiety, or depression (e.g., Sanders et al., 2014); improved well-being and life satisfaction (e.g., Nowak & Heinrichs, 2008); better couple and family relationships (e.g., Stallman & Sanders, 2014); and greater satisfaction in other domains of life, such as their functioning at work (e.g., Haslam, Sanders, & Sofronoff, 2013).

APPROACHES TO MEASURING INDIVIDUAL CHILD, PARENTING, AND FAMILY OUTCOMES

A wide range of approaches to assessment of child, parent, and family outcomes has been utilized in both research and practice. Multimethod assessments are generally cited as best practice in both research and clinical work (Snyder et al., 2006), with the aim of providing a comprehensive picture of existing behavior and adjustment, as well as to document change effectively. Ideally, assessment should be multimodal, with the aim of triangulating the sources of information. The assessment is aimed at the individual, child, parent, or family unit, and change is examined in relation to individual change.

A multimethod assessment may consist of (a) questionnaires completed by parents and children as well as other informants, such as teachers; (b) interviews with parents, children, or other informants, including structured diagnostic interviews; (c) monitoring of behavior or other outcome via self-monitoring or more recently via the use of technology (e.g., use of pedometers, medication adherence monitoring); (d) direct observation of behaviors and interactions; or (e) product measurement (e.g., school report cards).

Each approach has a variety of benefits and limitations, and while it is beyond the scope of this chapter to detail all of these, a brief overview summarizes the challenge of deciding on the most appropriate form of assessment. Questionnaires are generally quick and relatively easy to administer and can be particularly effective for capturing rare events (e.g., truancy) and cognitive and emotional constructs that may be difficult or impossible to access in other ways. However, questionnaires may be subject to social desirability bias, may not be culturally tailored or validated, and may be difficult or impossible to use with younger children.

Interviews can provide considerable richness of information and give insight into individual perspectives as well as mechanisms operating within a family; however, they can also be time consuming and difficult to replicate in a standardized manner. Like questionnaires, monitoring can be quick and easy for individuals to do and, particularly with the advent of various technologies, can be reliable and easy to collect. However, monitoring is also subject to social desirability and relies on the individual remembering to record all relevant events.

Direct observation has a long history in the field of parenting intervention and provides considerable advantages in terms of gaining access to actual behavior and interactions. Nevertheless, observational methods can induce reactivity effects and are expensive and time consuming to conduct.

As noted, each approach has inherent numerous advantages and disadvantages, and the choice of assessment approach depends on a range of factors, including the target of the intervention (e.g., parent vs. child), the aims of the assessment (e.g., narrow focus on mealtime behavior vs. broader change in family stress), as well as available resources (e.g., observational assessments require considerable time and expense vs. cheaper and easier-to-administer questionnaires). Although multimethod assessments are generally considered the gold standard, there is a paucity of data available on the correspondence between different measurement

approaches. For example, correlations between different types of assessment are often modest (e.g., Morawska, Basha, Adamson, & Winter, 2015; Morawska, Especkerman, & Adamson,
2015; Webster-Stratton, 1998). Thus, while the ideal is to use a multi-informant, multimethod
assessment to gain the most comprehensive picture of an individual or family, this needs to be
balanced with the burden of assessment on families, the practicalities of various assessment
approaches, and the resources available to conduct a thorough assessment.

APPROACHES TO MEASURING
POPULATION-LEVEL OUTCOMES

Assessing population-level outcomes presents a different level of challenge and aims to move
beyond individual indicators of adjustment to population-level gauges of child, parent, and family well-being. Understanding the epidemiology of a particular disorder or condition within a
population provides information that is vital to the provision and planning of health and social
services. Like in individual-level assessment, the choice of measurement approach depends on a
range of factors, including the target of the intervention (e.g., whole school community vs. entire
population); the aims of the assessment (e.g., child maltreatment outcomes vs. better attendance at child health visits, vaccination); as well as available resources (e.g., access to existing
population-level indicators or indices of relevant child outcomes). In addition to information
about the specific health or well-being outcome, intervention cost-effectiveness becomes a central question, as this helps to guide policy in terms of the costs and benefits of implementing
population-level interventions.

Various approaches to collecting population-level data have been utilized, including (a) surveys collected face to face, via telephone, or online (e.g., Fives, Pursell, Heary, Nic Gabhainn, &
Canavan, 2014; Sanders et al., 2005); (b) use of existing government archival databases on child
maltreatment (e.g., Prinz, Sanders, Shapiro, Whitaker, & Lutzker, 2009); and (c) use of existing hospital or school records (e.g., Smith, 2015). It is worthwhile noting, however, that there
are relatively few published population-level evaluations of parenting interventions, as most
have been evaluated in the context of a targeted or selected recruitment approach. This remains
an important gap in both the research literature and policy development and implementation,
although there is an increasing recognition of the need to ensure a nurturing environment for
all children and access to evidence-based parenting information for all parents (Biglan, Flay,
Embry, & Sandler, 2012).

One of the critical aspects of population assessment is to ensure that an accurate and gen-
eralizable sampling frame is selected and implemented. This means that methods to ensure that
the assessment collects a representative sample of the population are essential. Like methods of
individual assessment, each approach has its advantages and disadvantages. Conducting surveys at a population level has many of the same advantages and disadvantages as at the individual level, but the additional issues of ensuing an adequate sampling frame are critical. Unless
the sample is representative of the population, it can be difficult to extrapolate the information
to inform public health and social policy. Use of existing health or school records is relatively
unobtrusive and collects actual health or school outcome data. However, it is also reliant on the
accuracy and reliability of those records. Accessing existing government databases is generally relatively inexpensive (compared to conducting new, in-person household epidemiological

surveys) and is less reliant on parent self-report. However, they can be narrow in scope, and the classifications used within the database may not meet the needs of the assessment or be sufficiently related to the proximal targets of the intervention. Also, changes in policy can lead to retrospective changes in criteria for reporting episodes of child abuse and the recording of historically captured data (Prinz, 2017).

APPROACHES USED TO ASSESS THE EFFECTS OF TRIPLE P

Within the extant Triple P outcome literature, a variety of different types of measures, informants, data sources, and methodologies have been employed to assess outcomes at both the individual family and population levels. This variability is expected given the wide range of children, types of problems, age groups, and cultures and investigators that have participated in Triple P evaluations. Historically, much of the foundation single-subject research with Triple P in the 1980s favored the use of independent observational measures using trained blind independent observers (e.g., Sanders & Glynn, 1981).

Although such measures have a prized role in the parent training field, they also have significant logistical, methodological, and cost limitations. For example, they tend to be most useful in treatment studies where stable and relatively high base rates of problem behaviors can be captured in young children with disruptive behavior problems. They are less suitable for low-prevalence behaviors (e.g., fighting and aggression, stealing, lying) that are less likely to occur in home or clinic contexts involving independent observers. Suppression of base rates due to the demand characteristics of the observation setting can create "floor and ceiling effects" on assessment measures, thus limiting capacity to detect change over time.

Reliable and valid parent report measures of child behavior have been used extensively in the evaluation of parenting programs. These measures have included the Eyberg Child Behavior Inventory (ECBI; Eyberg & Pincus, 1999); Strengths and Difficulties Questionnaire (SDQ; Goodman, 1997); Child Behavior Checklist (CBCL; Achenbach, 2000); and more recently the Child Adjustment and Parent Efficacy Scale (CAPES; Morawska, Sanders, Haslam, Filus, & Fletcher, 2014). Additional measures have been used to assess child behavior in specific populations, such as the Child Adjustment and Parent Efficacy Scale—Developmental Disability (CAPES-DD; Emser, Mazzucchelli, Christiansen, & Sanders, 2016) and the Asthma Behavior Checklist (Morawska, Stelzer, & Burgess, 2008). Considerably more data are available from mothers than fathers. The use of other informants, such as teachers, is useful for school-aged children if there are problems at school; teachers are not the best informants relating to children's behavior at home or with parents.

Triple P studies have also used parent report measures of parenting practices, parental self-efficacy, and family adjustment extensively in evaluation studies. Commonly used measures include the Parenting Scale (Arnold, O'Leary, Wolff, & Acker, 1993); Parenting Tasks Checklist (PTC; Sanders & Woolley, 2005); and the Parent and Family Adjustment Scale (PAFAS; Sanders, Morawska, Haslam, Filus, & Fletcher, 2014). Measures that are reliable, valid, change sensitive, and in the public domain are recommended for routine use in service-based evaluation for every variant in the Triple P system.

An Automated Scoring and Reporting Application (ASRA) system has been developed by Triple P International to enable accredited practitioners and agencies to select assessment tools relevant to the specific program variant being implemented to assess outcomes achieved with Triple P. Many of the recommended instruments have been deployed in service-based evaluations to document the efficacy of Triple P when used in regular services.

IMPLICATIONS AND FUTURE DIRECTIONS

The adoption of an evidence-based program such as Triple P, whose efficacy has been extensively documented in randomized controlled trials, is no guarantee that the same program will be effective when implemented in a different context. Variations in implementation context and fidelity, participating populations of parents, and cultural differences all highlight the need for ongoing evaluation of effects achieved as a routine part of a quality improvement process. Hence, it is highly desirable that agencies and services using Triple P systematically collect, analyze, and report on their outcomes achieved with families using available evaluation tools. Although routine collecting of outcome data is not the norm in many service delivery settings, it should be mandatory and is an integral part of implementing any Triple P program with fidelity (Mazzucchelli & Sanders, 2010).

CONCLUSIONS

The hallmark of behavioral family intervention has been attention to the routine assessment of outcomes. Work is still required to develop better population-level measurement tools and indicators for assessing parenting practices and child well-being. A national parenting survey to complement or replace the existing International Parenting Survey (IPS; Morawska, Filus, Haslam, & Sanders, 2017) would be particularly valuable to complement

---

BOX 36.1: The International Parenting Survey

The *International Parenting Survey* (IPS) is a web-based survey of parental views on various aspects of family life and parenting; it was developed as an epidemiological assessment tool to assist policymakers, local authorities, and agencies conduct audits of community parenting practices. It aims to solicit parents' views on their children's behavior and adjustment, the parenting practices they use in raising their children, and the quality of parenting and family support services they access. The IPS can be utilized as a means of evaluating parenting programs over time by creating a repeated measures snapshot of community samples of parents periodically. The IPS provides a rich database of information about parents across the world, and it can be used to address a variety of theoretical and practical questions.

use of existing administrative databases in the health, welfare, and education sectors to assess population-level changes in parenting and family well-being. A nationally representative sample of parents of children of different ages would provide a useful population-level indicator that could be used to assess change at the population level and as such provide a tool to assess the impact of policy-based investments or reduction in funding for parenting and family support services (Box 36.1).

KEY MESSAGES

- Assessment is an integral component of the Triple P system of interventions.
- Parenting interventions have an impact on a wide range of child and parenting outcomes.
- Well-validated, psychometrically sound, assessment tools are available for a variety of outcomes and in various formats.
- Population-level assessments pose a challenge, and differing approaches are being developed to assess outcomes.

REFERENCES

Achenbach, T. M. (2000). *Child Behavior Checklist 1½–5*. Burlington: University of Vermont Department of Psychiatry.

Arnold, D. S., O'Leary, S. G., Wolff, L. S., & Acker, M. M. (1993). The Parenting Scale: A measure of dysfunctional parenting in discipline situations. *Psychological Assessment, 5*, 137–144. doi:10.1037/1040-3590.5.2.137

Biglan, A., Flay, B. R., Embry, D. D., & Sandler, I. N. (2012). The critical role of nurturing environments for promoting human well-being. *American Psychologist, 67*, 257–271. doi:10.1037/a0026796

Emser, T. S., Mazzucchelli, T. G., Christiansen, H., & Sanders, M. R. (2016). Child Adjustment and Parent Efficacy Scale—Developmental Disability (CAPES-DD): First psychometric evaluation of a new child and parenting assessment tool for children with a developmental disability. *Research in Developmental Disabilities, 53–54*, 158–177. doi:10.1016/j.ridd.2015.09.006

Eyberg, S. M., & Pincus, D. (1999). *Eyberg Child Behavior Inventory and Sutter-Eyberg Student Behavior Inventory—Revised: Professional manual*. Odessa, FL: Psychological Assessment Resources.

Fives, A., Pursell, L., Heary, C., Nic Gabhainn, S., & Canavan, J. (2014). *Parenting support for every parent: A population-level evaluation of Triple P in Longford Westmeath. Summary report*. Athlone, Ireland: Longford Westmeath Parenting Partnership.

Forehand, R., Jones, D. J., & Parent, J. (2013). Behavioral parenting interventions for child disruptive behaviors and anxiety: What's different and what's the same. *Clinical Psychology Review, 33*, 133–145. doi:10.1016/j.cpr.2012.10.010

Goodman, R. (1997). The Strengths and Difficulties Questionnaire: A research note. *Journal of Child Psychology and Psychiatry, 38*, 581–586. doi:10.1111/j.1469-7610.1997.tb01545.x

Granic, I., & Patterson, G. R. (2006). Toward a comprehensive model of antisocial development: A dynamic systems approach. *Psychological Review, 113*, 101–131. doi:10.1037/0033-295X.113.1.101

Gross, D., & Rocissano, L. (1988). Maternal confidence in toddlerhood: Its measurement for clinical practice and research. *Nurse Practitioner, 13*, 19–29.

Haslam, D. M., Sanders, M. R., & Sofronoff, K. (2013). Reducing work and family conflict in teachers: A randomised controlled trial of Workplace Triple P. *School Mental Health, 5*, 70–82. doi:10.1007/s12310-012-9091-z

Healy, K. L., & Sanders, M. R. (2014). Randomized controlled trial of a family intervention for children bullied by peers. *Behavior Therapy, 45*, 760–777. doi:10.1016/j.beth.2014.06.001

Jones, T. L., & Prinz, R. J. (2005). Potential roles of parental self-efficacy in parent and child adjustment: A review. *Clinical Psychology Review, 25*, 341–363 doi:10.1016/j.cpr.2004.12.004

Karoly, P. (1993). Mechanisms of self-regulation: A systems view. *Annual Review of Psychology, 44*, 23–52. doi:10.1146/annurev.ps.44.020193.000323

Lundahl, B., Risser, H. J., & Lovejoy, M. C. (2006). A meta-analysis of parent training: Moderators and follow-up effects. *Clinical Psychology Review, 26*, 86–104. doi:10.1016/j.cpr.2005.07.004

Mazzucchelli, T. G., & Sanders, M. R. (2010). Facilitating practitioner flexibility within an empirically supported intervention: Lessons from a system of parenting support. *Clinical Psychology: Science and Practice, 17*, 238–252. doi:10.1111/j.1468-2850.2010.01215.x

McTaggart, P., & Sanders, M. R. (2003). The Transition to School Project: Results from the classroom. *AeJAMH Australian e-Journal for the Advancement of Mental Health, 2*(3), 144–155. doi:10.5172/jamh.2.3.144

Morawska, A., Basha, A., Adamson, M., & Winter, L. (2015). Microanalytic coding versus global rating of maternal parenting behaviour. *Early Child Development and Care, 185*, 448–463. doi:10.1080/03004430.2014.932279

Morawska, A., Especkerman, J. F., & Adamson, M. (2015). Mealtime observations and parent-report: Correspondence across measurement approach and implications for intervention. *Behaviour Change, 32*, 175–189. doi:10.1017/bec.2015.9

Morawska, A., Filus, A., Haslam, D., & Sanders, M. R. (2017). *The International Parenting Survey: Rationale, development and potential applications.* Manuscript submitted for publication.

Morawska, A., Mitchell, A., Burgess, S., & Fraser, J. (2016). Effects of Triple P parenting intervention on child health outcomes for childhood asthma and eczema: Randomised controlled trial. *Behaviour Research and Therapy, 83*, 35–44. doi:10.1016/j.brat.2016.06.001

Morawska, A., & Sanders, M. R. (2006). Self-administered behavioural family intervention for parents of toddlers: Part I—Efficacy. *Journal of Consulting and Clinical Psychology, 74*, 10–19. doi:10.1037/0022-006X.74.1.10

Morawska, A., & Sanders, M. R. (2007). Concurrent predictors of dysfunctional parenting and parental confidence: Implications for parenting interventions. *Child: Care, Health & Development, 33*, 757–767. doi:10.1111/j.1365-2214.2007.00758.x

Morawska, A., Sanders, M. R., Haslam, D., Filus, A., & Fletcher, R. (2014). Child Adjustment and Parent Efficacy Scale (CAPES): Development and initial validation of a parent report measure. *Australian Psychologist, 49*, 241–252. doi:10.1111/ap.12057

Morawska, A., Stelzer, J., & Burgess, S. W. (2008). Parenting asthmatic children: Identification of parenting challenges. *Journal of Asthma, 45*, 465–472. doi:10.1080/02770900802040050

Nowak, C., & Heinrichs, N. (2008). A comprehensive meta-analysis of Triple P—Positive Parenting Program using hierarchical linear modeling: Effectiveness and moderating variables. *Clinical Child and Family Psychology Review, 11*, 114–144. doi:10.1007/s10567-008-0033-0

Patterson, G. R. (1982). *Coercive family process.* Eugene, OR: Castalia.

Prinz, R. J. (2017). Assessing child maltreatment prevention via administrative data systems: A case example of reproducibility. *Child Abuse & Neglect, 64*, 13–18. doi:http://dx.doi.org/10.1016/j.chiabu.2016.12.005

Prinz, R. J., Sanders, M. R., Shapiro, C. J., Whitaker, D. J., & Lutzker, J. R. (2009). Population-based prevention of child maltreatment: The US Triple P system population trial. *Prevention Science, 10,* 1–12. doi:10.1007/s11121-009-0123-3

Sallis, J., Owen, N., & Fotheringham, M. (2000). Behavioral epidemiology: A systematic framework to classify phases of research on health promotion and disease prevention. *Annals of Behavioral Medicine, 22,* 294–298. doi: 10.1007/bf02895665

Sanders, M. R., & Glynn, T. (1981). Training parents in behavioral self-management: An analysis of generalization and maintenance. *Journal of Applied Behavior Analysis, 14,* 223–237. doi:10.1901/jaba.1981.14-223

Sanders, M. R., & Kirby, J. N. (2012). Consumer engagement and the development, evaluation, and dissemination of evidence-based parenting programs. *Behavior Therapy, 43,* 236–250. doi:10.1016/j.beth.2011.01.005

Sanders, M. R., Kirby, J. N., Tellegen, C. L., & Day, J. J. (2014). The Triple P—Positive Parenting Program: A systematic review and meta-analysis of a multi-level system of parenting support. *Clinical Psychology Review, 34,* 337–357. doi:10.1016/j.cpr.2014.04.003

Sanders, M. R., & Mazzucchelli, T. G. (2013). The promotion of self-regulation through parenting interventions. *Clinical Child and Family Psychology Review, 16,* 1–17. doi:10.1007/s10567-013-0129-z

Sanders, M. R., Morawska, A., Haslam, D., Filus, A., & Fletcher, R. (2014). Parenting and Family Adjustment Scale (PAFAS): Validation of a brief parent-report measure for use in assessment of parenting skills and family relationships. *Child Psychiatry and Human Development, 45,* 255–272. doi:10.1007/s10578-013-0397-3

Sanders, M. R., Ralph, A., Thompson, R., Sofronoff, K., Gardiner, P., Bidwell, K., & Dwyer, S. (2005). *Every Family: A public health approach to promoting children's wellbeing* Brisbane, Australia: University of Queensland.

Sanders, M. R., & Woolley, M. L. (2005). The relationship between maternal self-efficacy and parenting practices: Implications for parent training. *Child: Care, Health and Development, 31,* 65–73. doi:10.1111/j.1365-2214.2005.00487.x

Schrepferman, L., & Snyder, J. (2002). Coercion: The link between treatment mechanisms in behavioral parent training and risk reduction in child antisocial behavior. *Behavior Therapy, 33,* 339–359. doi:10.1016/S0005-7894(02)80032-6

Smith, G. (2015). *15 year follow up of WA Triple P Trial.* Perth, Australia: Telethon Kids Institute.

Snyder, J., Reid, J., Stoolmiller, M., Howe, G., Brown, H., Dagne, G., & Cross, W. (2006). The role of behavior observation in measurement systems for randomized prevention trials. *Prevention Science, 7,* 43–56. doi:10.1007/s11121-005-0020-3

Stallman, H. M., & Sanders, M. R. (2014). A randomized controlled trial of Family Transitions Triple P: A group-administered parenting program to minimize the adverse effects of parental divorce on children. *Journal of Divorce & Remarriage, 55,* 33–48. doi:10.1080/10502556.2013.862091

Tarver, J., Daley, D., Lockwood, J., & Sayal, K. (2014). Are self-directed parenting interventions sufficient for externalising behaviour problems in childhood? A systematic review and meta-analysis. *European Child & Adolescent Psychiatry, 23,* 1123–1137. doi:10.1007/s00787-014-0556-5

Teti, D. M., & Gelfand, D. M. (1991). Behavioural competence among mothers of infants in the first year: The mediational role of maternal self-efficacy. *Child Development, 62,* 918–929. doi:1 0.2307/1131143

Tully, L. A., & Hunt, C. (2015). Brief parenting interventions for children at risk of externalizing behavior problems: A systematic review. *Journal of Child and Family Studies, 25,* 705–719. doi:10.1007/s10826-015-0284-6

Webster-Stratton, C. (1998). Preventing conduct problems in head start children: Strengthening parenting competencies. *Journal of Consulting and Clinical Psychology, 66,* 715–730. doi:10.1037/0022-006X.66.5.715

Webster-Stratton, C., & Reid, M. J. (2010). The Incredible Years parents, teachers and children training series: A multifaceted treatment approach for young children with conduct problems. In A. E. Kazdin & J. R. Weisz (Eds.), *Evidence-based psychotherapies for children and adolescents* (2nd ed., pp. 194–210). New York, NY: Guilford.

West, F., Sanders, M. R., Cleghorn, G. J., & Davies, P. S. W. (2010). Randomised clinical trial of a family-based lifestyle intervention for childhood obesity involving parents as the exclusive agents of change. *Behaviour Research and Therapy, 48,* 1170–1179. doi:10.1016/j.brat.2010.08.008

Westrupp, E. M., Northam, E., Lee, K. J., Scratch, S. E., & Cameron, F. (2015). Reducing and preventing internalizing and externalizing behavior problems in children with type 1 diabetes: A randomized controlled trial of the Triple P—Positive Parenting Program. *Pediatric Diabetes, 16,* 554–563. doi:10.1111/pedi.12205

CHAPTER 37

PROMOTING PROGRAM FIDELITY THROUGH PEER-ASSISTED SUPERVISION AND SUPPORT

KERRI E. MCPHERSON AND BIRGIT SCHROETER

INTRODUCTION

As noted in previous chapters, a range of interdependent factors can affect the successful transport of evidence-based programs (EBPs) from the controlled clinical trial environment to applied service delivery settings. In most instances, intervention programs earn their credentials as "evidence based" through assessment of efficacy or effectiveness, with little attention paid to the conditions under which optimal implementation in applied settings might occur. Localized data about barriers and facilitators to implementation of parenting and family EBPs have started to emerge (e.g., Casey, McPherson, & Kerr, 2016), but limited understanding of the pathways that connect implementation success/failure with program success/failure makes it difficult to ensure that EBPs are deployed with fidelity and efficiency across various applied settings (Proctor et al., 2011).

To address this, the deployment of Triple P is guided by an implementation framework (see Chapter 33, this volume) that defines organizational and administrative processes necessary to support successful and sustainable implementation. This includes initial training of the Triple P workforce to deliver the program with adherence (see Chapter 34, this volume). However, to ensure sustained practitioner adherence and the development of confidence and competence to deliver with flexibility, initial training must be supplemented with additional quality assurance mechanisms, such as clinical supervision.

In this chapter, we address the need for effective and efficient supervision and posttraining support for the EBP workforce to ensure the sustainability of delivery and the ongoing maintenance of program fidelity. We describe the Peer Assisted Supervision and Support (PASS) approach advocated for use in the deployment of Triple P, and embedded within the Triple P implementation framework, and present an overview of related research. Finally, we make recommendations to guide the development of a program of research to evidence the impact of PASS on program and stakeholder outcomes.

THREATS TO THE ONGOING DELIVERY OF EVIDENCE BASED PROGRAMS

A key threat to the ongoing delivery of EBPs in applied settings is an ill-prepared workforce. Predelivery training of EBP practitioners is typically managed by program developers or purveyor organizations and is designed to ensure consistency of experience, to promote consistency of output, across practitioners in different locales (Fixsen, Blasé, Duda, Naoom, & Van Dyke, 2010). Approaches to the training provided will necessarily be program dependent, and Triple P practitioner training is described in detail by Ralph and Dittman in Chapter 34. Acknowledging program-specific differences, initial training tends to include the provision of knowledge about the purpose and theoretical underpinnings of the program; an introduction to the key components and principles of the program; detailed understanding of the protocol/ manual; and opportunity for professionals to rehearse skills relevant to delivery and receive feedback and coaching from expert trainers (Fixsen, Blasé, Naoom, & Wallace, 2009; Fixsen, Naoom, Blasé, & Friedman, 2005). Initial training is, in effect, a vehicle for ensuring that the practitioner workforce understands the need for and purpose of the program, and that they have sufficient baseline knowledge and skills to deliver the program as prescribed in the manual. In addition to this, there will be early attempts to activate psychological processes known to support delivery with fidelity, for example, self-efficacy (Turner, Nicholson, & Sanders, 2011). However, initial training is, in itself, insufficient to guarantee the sustained implementation fidelity required if EBPs are to effect change in the population of families in need.

Practitioner adherence and competence are important dimensions of fidelity and are thought to affect implementation outcomes (Breitenstein et al., 2010; Fixsen et al., 2010). This includes the extent to which EBPs are appropriately used with families and the extent to which client outcomes are maximized through delivery that is both program adherent and tailored to meet the needs of recipient families (Fixsen et al., 2010). However, applied settings are unpredictable, clients are unknown, and practitioners require opportunity to review, rehearse, and hone their skills within ever-changing circumstances. In effect, practitioners need an opportunity for program-related professional development across the lifetime of delivery.

Linked to this, when a program has demonstrated it can effectively prevent or ameliorate problems faced by families, it is essential that affected families have access to it. However, practitioners do not always use programs they are trained to deliver, resulting in reduced cost-effectiveness for implementing agencies and poorer family outcomes (Asgary-Eden & Lee, 2012; Sanders, Prinz, & Shapiro, 2009). Key barriers to program use include organizational culture and support, such as adequacy of resources and opportunity for supervision, as well as practitioner motivation, confidence, and attitudes toward evidence-based practice (Asgary-Eden & Lee, 2012; Beidas & Kendall, 2010; Sanders et al., 2009).

IMPLICATIONS AND PROPOSED STRATEGIES
FOR THE DELIVERY OF PARENTING SUPPORT

If EBPs are to deliver expected outcomes in applied settings, quality assurance mechanisms to monitor, manage, and, where necessary, realign fidelity processes are critical, and a range of different approaches to this have been adopted (e.g., Breitenstein et al., 2010; Henggeler, 2011). To complement initial training, the Triple P Implementation Framework promotes quality assurance through regular clinical supervision for practitioners. Supervision is conceived as a mechanism to ensure optimal program fidelity at every stage of the implementation process, including the longer-term maintenance phase, where there is increased risk of program drift as purveyor/developer support is withdrawn (Fixsen et al., 2009; Mazzucchelli & Sanders, 2010).

Clinical supervision is used across a range of professions as a "formal process of professional support and learning which enables individual practitioners to develop knowledge and competence, assume responsibility for their own practice and enhance consumer protection and safety of care in complex situations" (Department of Health, National Health Service Management Executive, 1993, p. 15). While supervision during training is conceptualized as a connector of the "classroom and clinic" (Bernard & Goodyear, 2014), the provision of career-long supervision is an acknowledgment that professional development should not stop at the classroom door. Indeed, Proctor (1986) has previously argued that effective supervision has three core functions: normative functions, to monitor and evaluate practice; formative functions, to support practitioners to develop appropriate knowledge and skills; and restorative functions, to provide opportunity for practitioners to manage their own work-related well-being.

It is hypothesized that supervision acts to promote EBP fidelity in a number of different ways, including the development of practitioner knowledge and self-efficacy beyond that of initial training and the normalization of program use in an organizational context (Casey et al., 2016). However, while there is general agreement about its purpose, relatively few studies have been conducted to test the relationship between supervision and EBP outcomes. Studies that have been undertaken have been correlational in nature, and results have been mixed (Wheeler & Richards, 2007). Considerable disparity in the ways in which different professions and organizations operationalize the practice of supervision, including its relationship with line management and the format of delivery (e.g., face to face vs. at distance, individual vs. group), means there is also limited understanding of how these different practices might affect the acceptability, feasibility, and effectiveness of the supervision process.

In professions/organizations where supervision is part of the culture of support offered, there are differences in the amount of postqualification supervision that individual staff might expect. In many instances, supervision is prioritized during training, with less emphasis on in-service supervision (Davy, 2002). Where in-service supervision is provided, its relationship with line management also differs across organizational contexts. In some instances, professionals will receive separate management and supervision, and in others line managers will perform managerial and supervision functions.

Research investigating experiences of supervision has highlighted tensions that can arise when a dual role is held. For example, supervisees have reported concerns that dual supervision and management can focus on performance management, which might limit willingness of supervisees to discuss challenges in the workplace (Martin, Kumar, Lizarondo, & VanErp, 2015).

This, in turn, may promote fear of discussing program delivery challenges and limit opportunity for discussion of ways of overcoming these and learning for the future (Wilson, Davies, & Weatherhead, 2016).

Linked to this, the balance of power in supervisory relationships has previously been identified as having the potential to facilitate or impede optimal supervisory processes. Traditional models of supervision are often hierarchical in nature, and this creates an imbalance of power in favor of the supervisor (Bernard & Goodyear, 2014). This may be felt more acutely when the supervisor is an educator (when in training) or a line manager (when in practice). Indeed, in a recent meta-synthesis, power was identified as the most significant element of the supervisor–supervisee relationship, and it was linked with negative experiences among trainee therapists (Wilson et al., 2016).

Individual supervision is, by far, the most common, but it is not unusual for it to be complemented by group supervision, and in some instances, only group supervision is offered. Studies have reported that group and individual supervision have equal benefit on professional development and effectiveness; however, when compared, some supervisees report a preference for individual supervision (Bernard & Goodyear, 2014; Edwards et al., 2005; Ray & Altekruse, 2000). This perhaps reflects critiques that group supervision affords less individual time for each supervisee, that the group may exert pressure to create "groupthink," or that it requires time to manage group relations, thereby avoiding work-related issues (Bernard & Goodyear, 2014; Hawkins, Shohet, Ryde, & Wilmot, 2012).

These critiques notwithstanding, group supervision is an attractive option in the context of EBPs. Increasing the number of supervisees to each supervisor offers efficiency in terms of both cost and time (Bernard & Goodyear, 2014). In addition, the sharing of experiences offers supervisees the opportunity to learn from each other's practice in addition to their own (Jones, 2003). Group supervision has also been described as creating a safe and restorative environment in which practitioners are able to explore the emotional aspects of working with clients and to gain insight of self (Gonge & Buus, 2016; Taylor, 2014). The nature of group processes is such that group supervision may be more likely to promote the normalization of EBP delivery than individual supervision could (Taylor, 2014).

There is growing literature showing the potential that peers have in the context of professional support and development, and this suggests that changing the agent of supervision from a hierarchical supervisor to the supervisee themselves may be beneficial. For example, results of a recent systematic review demonstrated that peers can replicate similar mental health support outcomes as mental health professionals (Pitt et al., 2013). Moreover, in contrast to traditional supervision, peer group supervision for psychotherapists is considered to increase the number of solutions to problems that therapists face in practice; reduce feelings of professional isolation; help develop professional identity and esteem; and be more cost efficient. However, it must be acknowledged that peer supervision necessitates greater commitment from supervisees and risks the emergence of "group games" (Houston, 1985). This means that peer supervision needs clear structure to operate effectively and a shared understanding within the group of how supervision should operate (Bernard & Goodyear, 2014).

The challenges and benefits associated with clinical supervision have the potential to be more acute in the context of EBPs such as Triple P. Traditionally, supervision is managed within the context of a specific profession or organization, and practitioners from a homogeneous professional group or within a single organization are more likely to have shared expectations and experiences of supervision. The Triple P workforce is, by design, a heterogeneous group of practitioners that includes, but is not limited to, allied health professionals, nurses, social workers, education providers, and staff of the not-for-profit sector. While the practitioners will have received similar Triple P training, their retention within existing organizational structures means that their in-service experiences have the potential for considerable variation, and this includes their experience and expectations in relation to line management and supervision. Supervision to support the delivery of Triple P needs to be responsive to these variations, and it needs to complement, rather than circumvent, existing organizational processes.

Thus, implementation success and sustainability are dependent on cognitive and behavioral change at the level of the practitioner; this is a complex process that cannot be achieved through initial training alone (Beidas & Kendall, 2010; Fixsen et al., 2010; Turner et al., 2011). A model of supervision developed to exploit positive group processes, and using peers rather than hierarchical relationships, has the potential to be an effective and efficient quality assurance mechanism through which EBP practitioners can manage program adherence and delivery competence. In addition to this, the use of peers means the practitioner is both the agent and the recipient of supervision, allowing for a model of supervision that promotes the self-regulatory capacity of practitioners.

THE TRIPLE P SELF-REGULATORY, PEER-ASSISTED APPROACH

The model of supervision proposed in the Triple P Implementation Framework, peer-assisted supervision and support (PASS), was developed in response to experience gained during previous deployments of Triple P and feedback from trained practitioners (Sanders & Murphy-Brennan, 2010). In many instances, the practitioner workforce had limited access to appropriate supervision in their organization or available supervision had limited compatibility with the self-regulatory principles underpinning Triple P (Sanders, 2012). Moreover, as they began to deliver the program to families, Triple P practitioners sought reassurance around adherence and guidance about ways in which they could work responsively with families. In many of the implementing sites, practitioner peers rather than line managers or existing supervisors became the source of support.

Groups of peers are used by PASS to promote self-regulatory capabilities of practitioners (Sanders & Murphy-Brennan, 2010). PASS sessions are conducted in small groups of approximately four to six practitioners who meet regularly, normally every 2 weeks to ensure that supervision becomes normalized practice and the relationships within the group have continuity. With no supervisor, PASS sessions are structured through rotating roles and defined agendas. In PASS sessions, practitioners act as peer facilitators, peer mentors, and practitioners and use a prescribed agenda (Sanders & Murphy-Brennan, 2010).

Practitioners acting as peer facilitator take responsibility for setting up and facilitating the session. The individual in the practitioner role is responsible for bringing a short (5- to 10-minute) recorded segment of a Triple P session with parents that they want to receive feedback on. The peer mentors then act to encourage reflection through the use of question prompts and by offering constructive feedback. The roles are rotated every PASS session, ensuring that each practitioner has the opportunity to have his or her work reviewed, to learn from other's work, and to develop group facilitation skills.

The PASS sessions are designed to encourage discussion and constructive feedback and promote learning through each practitioner's own experience and the experiences of the practitioner's peers. The structured session agenda is designed to scaffold practitioners' self-regulatory processes, promoting goal-directed modification of one's own behavior (Karoly, 1993). It guides practitioners to select goals that are aligned with their developmental needs; choose appropriately tailored ways of working with families based on their individual needs; self-monitor and evaluate their own performance using checklists; and identify future goals for action (Sanders, 1999). In this way, PASS is used to foster confidence, optimize decision-making, and drive reflective and reflexive practice (Mazzucchelli & Sanders, 2010; Sanders, Mazzucchelli, & Ralph, 2012). In addition, the removal of the hierarchical supervisor means that the onus is placed on practitioners to make the changes they deem necessary to successfully implement the program, rather than waiting for "instruction" from others.

The PASS model was developed to be a systems contextual model of supervision that could be added to, replace, or complement existing organizational processes (Sanders & Murphy-Brennan, 2010). It is bound to a process model of learning and development rather than to a specific occupation and, as such, is accessible to practitioners irrespective of background, which is important for enabling cooperation in a multidisciplinary workforce. In addition, while PASS was conceived within the context of Triple P, the focus on development of self-regulatory skills rather than learning program content means this model of supervision has the potential to support EBP practitioners using a range of different interventions.

BRIEF REVIEW OF EFFICACY, ACCEPTABILITY, AND FEASIBILITY

As a fidelity mechanism, it is predicted that supervision should act to improve outcomes at the level of the practitioner (i.e., adherence and competence), which should, in turn, should effect better outcomes in families in receipt of EBPs. However, as noted, like the majority of fidelity/quality assurance mechanisms, the effect that supervision has across the range of EBP stakeholders is relatively untested (Henggeler, 2011; Schoenwald, Sheidow, & Chapman, 2009; Wheeler & Richards, 2007). Limited evidence in the context of family-focused EBPs suggests that practitioner adherence to protocols can be enhanced when they receive supervision from individuals perceived as competent in the program (Henggeler, Schoenwald, Liao, Letourneau, & Edwards, 2002; Schoenwald, Sheidow, & Letourneau, 2004). Results linking the focus of supervision and adherence are contradictory, with some studies reporting that fidelity-focused supervision was negatively associated with practitioner adherence (Henggeler et al., 2002) and others that it promoted adherence in program practitioners (Schoenwald et al., 2009). That said, Schoenwald and colleagues (2009) have been able to demonstrate that both the focus of supervision and practitioner adherence can affect client (child) outcomes, with fidelity-focused supervision, such as PASS, associated with better outcomes.

The PASS model was developed as a responsive blend of developer-led expectations in relation to quality assurance and feedback from the Triple P workforce; now manualized, it awaits effectiveness testing. At the time of writing, PASS had undergone acceptability and feasibility testing that will feed into the design of future randomized controlled trials to assess efficacy and effectiveness. For example, in a number of Triple P studies, trained practitioners have reported that lack of access to supervision acts as a barrier to program use, whereas opportunity to consult with other practitioners promoted program use in the short and long terms (Sanders et al., 2009; Shapiro, Prinz, & Sanders, 2012, 2015). The facilitative role of PASS mirrors research in other parts of the EBP showing practitioners welcome the support of regular supervision and talk about it as promoting enhanced delivery (e.g., Casey et al., 2016). Moreover, recent research with Triple P practitioners suggests that PASS supervision can attenuate the impact of other implementation barriers, such as seeing delivery as a burden, and it contributes to implementation sustainability (Hodge, Turner, Sanders, & Filus, 2016). Importantly, these results have been replicated in different implementation contexts, including different cultural contexts (e.g., Turner, Sanders, & Hodge, 2014).

Our own work has sought to extend the evidence available about the acceptability and feasibility of PASS to support Triple P practitioners (McPherson, Sanders, Schroeter, Troy, & Wiseman, 2016). Using a Q-methodological approach, we found that practitioners had a consensus view that PASS was an acceptable model of supervision. Participants presented PASS as creating a supportive environment and one where the difficulties noted with supervision relationships did not arise (for examples of typical feedback from practitioners, see Box 37.1). Importantly, some practitioners endorsed PASS as feasible; that is, they were able to incorporate PASS into their working lives and carry out the role and agenda demands with little difficulty. However, other practitioners reported some difficulties with finding time to engage with supervision or prioritizing it over other work-related demands, perhaps reflecting a lack of

---

BOX 37.1: Feedback From Practitioners on Peer-Assisted Supervision and Support

A great opportunity to work with professionals from different backgrounds and learn from their different skills and experiences.

—Male, social worker

Focussing on what is going well builds up skills in terms of what to do next time. It's nice to stop and reflect and see that you are doing a good job.

—Female, psychologist

I enjoy the support PASS provides. Everyone is doing the same group and experiencing similar achievements and difficulties and the group help each other work through this. We all have different jobs but the main aim is the same for Triple P delivery.

—Female, family support worker

I have been aware of how powerful the use of video reflection has been to other practitioners in the pass group. It focusses our discussions in PASS. There is genuine interest, honesty and commitment to the reflection it provides.

—Female, psychologist

organizational support. While there was not consensus on this, some practitioners reported that PASS resulted in enhanced delivery of Triple P.

IMPLICATIONS AND FUTURE DIRECTIONS

To summarize, evidence suggests that PASS has the potential to be an effective and efficient model of supervision to assist with achieving optimal implementation outcomes. The processes involved in PASS are acceptable, and participation is experienced as supportive and, with appropriate organizational backing, feasible. However, there remain three significant gaps in the literature about supervision that future research must address. First, it is particularly important that randomized controlled trials are designed to assess the impact that PASS has on practitioner adherence and delivery competence. Trials are also needed to evidence the hypothesized link between supervision and family outcomes. Without these data, it will be hard, in a time of increasing austerity, to argue for the retention of quality assurance mechanisms like supervision within implementation frameworks. Second, in addition to effectiveness and efficacy trials, there is little evidence in the literature to aid our understanding of the psychological processes that are activated by supervision. Understanding the psychological processes that lead to improved practice will enable developers to further refine available models of supervision. Finally, there must be consideration of practitioner variables that might affect the experience and effectiveness of supervision, such as ethnicity, practitioner experience, or self-perceived expertise (Turner et al., 2014).

CONCLUSIONS

In this chapter, we have highlighted the need for supervision to support the implementation of EBPs, such as Triple P, for parents and families. We have presented evidence that suggests that supervision is a necessary and desirable way of supporting practitioners to develop the capacity for fidelity with flexibility. By incorporating elements of supervision identified as beneficial in the supervision literature, the PASS model developed as part of the Triple P system has the potential to be an effective and efficient model of support for the Triple P workforce and other EBP practitioners. Indeed, PASS has already demonstrated that it is acceptable to, and relatively feasible for, Triple P practitioners working in applied settings. However, there is a pressing need for additional research to undertake systematic testing of the hypothesized relationship linking supervision to practitioner delivery and family-level outcomes. Without this, there is a risk that implementing organizations will view supervision as an expendable element of the implementation process, thus limiting the potential that EBPs have in effecting better outcomes for the families and children they serve.

KEY MESSAGES

- Supervision is a quality assurance mechanism to ensure sustained practitioner adherence and the development of confidence and competence to deliver with flexibility.

- Supervision should provide practitioners with opportunities to review, rehearse, and hone their intervention delivery skills.
- The PASS sessions are structured through rotating roles and defined agendas, with practitioners acting as peer facilitators, peer mentors, and practitioners seeking feedback.
- Structured PASS sessions are designed to scaffold practitioners' self-regulatory processes, promoting goal-directed modification of their own behavior.
- The group supervision structure of PASS offers efficiency in terms of cost and time. In sharing experiences, supervisees learn from each other's practice in addition to their own, and group supervision has the potential to promote the normalization of EBP delivery.
- In early testing, PASS has been described as an acceptable and feasible method of supervision for EBP practitioners.

REFERENCES

Asgary-Eden, V., & Lee, C. M. (2012). Implementing an evidence-based parenting program in community agencies: What helps and what gets in the way? *Administration and Policy in Mental Health and Mental Health Services Research, 39,* 478. doi:10.1007/s10488-011-0371-y

Beidas, R. S., & Kendall, P. C. (2010). Training therapists in evidence-based practice: A critical review of studies from a systems-contextual perspective. *Clinical Psychology: Science and Practice, 17,* 1–30. doi:10.1111/j.1468-2850.2009.01187.x

Bernard, J. M., & Goodyear, R. K. (2014). *Fundamentals of clinical supervision* (5th ed.). Harlow, England: Pearson Education.

Breitenstein, S. M., Gross, D., Garvey, C., Hill, C., Fogg, L., & Resnick, B. (2010). Implementation fidelity in community-based intervention. *Research in Nursing and Health, 33,* 164–173. doi:10.1002/nur.20373

Casey, B., McPherson, K. E., & Kerr, S. (2016). *Functional Family Therapy: Perceptions and experiences of key stakeholders in Glasgow.* Glasgow, Scotland: Glasgow Caledonian University.

Davy, J. (2002). Discursive reflections on a research agenda for clinical supervision. *Psychology and Psychotherapy: Theory, Research and Practice, 75,* 221–238. doi:10.1348/147608302169661

Department of Health, National Health Service Management Executive. (1993). *A vision for the future: The nursing, midwifery and health visiting contribution to health and health care.* London, England: Department of Health.

Edwards, D., Cooper, L., Burnard, P., Hanningan, B., Adams, J., Fothergill, A., & Coyle, D. (2005). Factors influencing the effectiveness of clinical supervision. *Journal of Psychiatric and Mental Health Nursing, 12,* 405–414. doi:10.1111/j.1365-2850.2005.00851.x

Fixsen, D. L., Blasé, K. A., Duda, M. A., Naoom, S. F., & Van Dyke, M. (2010). Implementation of evidence-based treatments for children and adolescents: Research findings and their implications for the future. In J. R. Weisz & A. E. Kazdin (Eds.), *Evidence-based psychotherapies for children and adolescents* (2nd ed., pp. 435–450). New York, NY: Guilford Press.

Fixsen, D. L., Blasé, K. A., Naoom, S. F., & Wallace, F. (2009). Core implementation components. *Research on Social Work Practice, 19,* 531–540. doi:10.1177/1049731509335549

Fixsen, D. L., Naoom, S. F., Blasé, K. A., & Friedman, R. M. (2005). *Implementation research: A synthesis of the literature.* Tampa, FL: University of South Florida. http://ctndisseminationlibrary.org/PDF/nirnmonograph.pdf

Gonge, H., & Buus, N. (2016). Exploring organizational barriers to strengthening clinical supervision of psychiatric nursing staff: A longitudinal controlled intervention study. *Issues In Mental Health Nursing, 37,* 332–343. doi:10.3109/01612840.2016.1154119

Hawkins, P., Shohet, R., Ryde, J., & Wilmot, J. (2012). *Supervision in the helping professions.* Maidenhead, England: McGraw-Hill Education (UK).

Henggeler, S. W. (2011). Efficacy studies to large-scale transport: The development and validation of multisystemic therapy programs. *Annual Review of Clinical Psychology, 7,* 351–381. doi:10.1146/annurev-clinpsy-032210-104615

Henggeler, S. W., Schoenwald, S. K., Liao, J. G., Letourneau, E. J., & Edwards, D. L. (2002). Transporting efficacious treatments to field settings: The link between supervisory practices and therapist fidelity in MST programs. *Journal of Clinical Child and Adolescent Psychology, 31,* 155–167. doi:10.1207/S15374424JCCP3102_02

Hodge, L. M., Turner, K. M., Sanders, M. R., & Filus, A. (2016). Sustained Implementation Support Scale: Validation of a measure of program characteristics and workplace functioning for sustained program implementation. *Journal of Behavioral Health Services and Research.* April 5. Epub before print. doi:10.1007/s11414-016-9505-z

Houston, G. (1985). Group supervision of groupwork. *Self and Society: European Journal of Humanistic Psychology, 13,* 64–66.

Jones, A. (2003). Some benefits experienced by hospice nurses from group clinical supervision. *European Journal of Cancer Care, 12,* 224–232. doi:10.1046/j.1365-2354.2003.00405.x

Karoly, P. (1993). Mechanisms of self-regulation: A systems view. *Annual Review of Psychology, 44,* 23–52. doi:10.1146/annurev.ps.44.020193.000323

Martin, P., Kumar, S., Lizarondo, L., & VanErp, A. (2015). Enablers of and barriers to high quality clinical supervision among occupational therapists across Queensland in Australia: Finding from a qualitative study. *BMC Health Services Research, 15,* 413. doi:10.1186/s12913-015-1085-8

Mazzucchelli, T., & Sanders, M. (2010). Facilitating practitioner flexibility within an empirically supported intervention: Lessons from a system of parenting support. *Clinical Psychology-Science and Practice, 17,* 238–252. doi:10.1111/j.1468-2850.2010.01215.x

McPherson, K. E., Sanders, M. R., Schroeter, B., Troy, V., & Wiseman, K. (2016). Acceptability and feasibility of peer assisted supervision and support for intervention practitioners: A Q-methodology evaluation. *Journal of Child and Family Studies, 25,* 720–732. doi:10.1007/s10826-015-0281-9

Pitt, V., Lowe, D., Hill, S., Prictor, M., Hetrick, S. E., Ryan, R., & Berends, L. (2013). Consumer-providers of care for adult clients of statutory mental health services. *Cochrane Database Systematic Reviews, 3,* CD004807.

Proctor, B. (1986). Supervision: A co-operative exercise in accountability. In M. Marken (Ed.), *Enabling and ensuring—Supervision in practice.* Leicester, England: National Youth Bureau for Education in Youth and Community Work.

Proctor, E., Silmere, H., Raghavan, R., Hovman, P., Aarons, G., Bunger, A., . . . Hensley, M. (2011). Outcomes for implementation research: Conceptual distinctions, measurement challenges, and research agenda. *Administration and Policy in Mental Health and Mental Health Services Research, 38,* 65–76. doi:10.1007/s10488-010-0319-7

Ray, D., & Altekruse, M. (2000). Effectiveness of group supervision versus combined group and individual supervision. *Counselor Education and Supervision, 40,* 19–40. doi:10.1002/j.1556-6978.2000.tb01796.x

Sanders, M. R. (1999). Triple P-Positive Parenting Program: Towards an empirically validated multilevel parenting and family support strategy for the prevention of behavior and emotional problems in children. *Clinical Child and Family Psychology Review, 2,* 71–90. doi:10.1023/A:1021843613840

Sanders, M. R. (2012). Development, evaluation, and multinational dissemination of the Triple P—Positive Parenting Program. *Annual Review of Clinical Psychology, 8,* 345–379. doi:10.1146/annurev-clinpsy-032511-143104

Sanders, M. R., Mazzucchelli, T. G., & Ralph, A. (2012). Promoting parenting competence through a self-regulation approach to feedback. In R. M. Sutton, M. J. Hornsey, & K. M. Douglas (Eds.), *Feedback: The communication of praise criticism, and advice* (Vol. 11, pp. 305–321). New York, NY: Lang.

Sanders, M. R., & Murphy-Brennan, M. (2010). Creating conditions for success beyond the professional training environment. *Clinical Psychology: Science and Practice, 17*, 31–35. doi:10.1111/j.1468-2850.2009.01189.x

Sanders, M. R., Prinz, R. J., & Shapiro, C. J. (2009). Predicting utilization of evidence-based parenting interventions with organizational, service-provider and client variables. *Administration and Policy in Mental Health and Mental Health Services Research, 36*, 133–143. doi:10.1007/s10488-009-0205-3

Schoenwald, S. K., Sheidow, A. J., & Chapman, J. E. (2009). Clinical supervision in treatment transport: Effects on adherence and outcomes. *Journal of Consulting and Clinical Psychology, 77*, 410. doi:10.1037/a0013788

Schoenwald, S. K., Sheidow, A. J., & Letourneau, E. J. (2004). Toward effective quality assurance in evidence-based practice: Links between expert consultation, therapist fidelity, and child outcomes. *Journal of Clinical Child and Adolescent Psychology, 33*, 94–104. doi:10.1207/S15374424JCCP3301_10

Shapiro, C. J., Prinz, R. J., & Sanders, M. R. (2012). Facilitators and barriers to implementation of an evidence-based parenting intervention to prevent child maltreatment: The Triple P—Positive Parenting Program. *Child Maltreatment, 17*, 86–95. doi:10.1177/1077559511424774

Shapiro, C. J., Prinz, R. J., & Sanders, M. R. (2015). Sustaining use of an evidence-based parenting intervention: Practitioner perspectives. *Journal of Child and Family Studies, 24*, 1615–1624. doi:10.1007/s10826-014-9965-9

Taylor, C. (2014). Boundaries in advanced nursing practice: The benefits of group supervision. *Mental Health Practice, 17*, 26–31. doi:10.7748/mhp.17.10.25.e866

Turner, K. M. T., Nicholson, J. M., & Sanders, M. R. (2011). The role of practitioner self-efficacy, training, program and workplace factors on the implementation of an evidence-based parenting intervention in primary care. *Journal of Primary Prevention, 32*, 95–112. doi:10.1007/s10935-011-0240-1

Turner, K. M. T., Sanders, M. R., & Hodge, L. (2014). Issues in professional training to implement evidence-based parenting programs: The preferences of Indigenous practitioners. *Australian Psychologist, 49*, 384–394. doi:10.1111/ap.12090

Wheeler, S., & Richards, K. (2007). The impact of clinical supervision on counsellors and therapists, their practice, and their clients. A systematic review of the literature. *Counselling and Psychotherapy Research, 7*, 54–65. doi:10.1080/14733140601185274

Wilson, H. M. N., Davies, J. S., & Weatherhead, S. (2016). Trainee therapists' experiences of supervision during training: A meta-synthesis. *Clinical Psychology and Psychotherapy, 23*, 340–351. doi:10.1002/cpp.1957

LEARNINGS FROM LARGE-SCALE, POPULATION-LEVEL IMPLEMENTATION OF PARENTING SUPPORT

LEARNINGS FROM LARGE-SCALE, POPULATION-LEVEL IMPLEMENTATION OF PARENTING SUPPORT

An Introduction

TREVOR G. MAZZUCCHELLI

There is now considerable evidence supporting the efficacy and effectiveness of parenting interventions based on social learning principles for a range of social, emotional, and health problems, involving a range of different types of families and family members and through a variety of different delivery systems (for a review of some of this research, see Sanders, Kirby, Tellegen, & Day, 2014). Implementation frameworks have been proposed, and technologies and methods developed to support and maximize the impact of large-scale, population-level implementation of parenting support. For instance, pedagogies for training a workforce (e.g., Chapter 34, this volume), methods for promoting the fidelity of implementation (e.g., Chapter 37, this volume), and strategies for enhancing the reach of a program have all been developed and evaluated (e.g., Chapter 35, this volume). But, translating research into practice is a complex process, and there are many lessons to be learned by studying real-world examples where efforts have been made to implement a full multilevel systems approach to parenting support and to assess outcomes at a population level. This section reviews three best practice exemplars that have taken place in the United States, Ireland, and Australia.

Child maltreatment occurs at high rates throughout the world, with devastating consequences for children, both in the short-term in the form of physical injury and emotional and behavioral problems and in the long-term in the form of chronic mental health conditions (Stoltenborgh, Bakermans-Kranenburg, Alink, & van Ijzendoorn, 2015). In Chapter 39, Prinz and Shapiro present a compelling rationale for why the universal delivery of parenting and family support should be a key component for the prevention of child maltreatment. Taking this further, they describe the groundbreaking place randomization study involving the Triple P system that they conducted in a southeastern state of the United States. This study involved the randomization of entire counties (as opposed to individual families) and focused on several routinely collected population indices of child maltreatment to assess the impact of the Triple P system. The results provided the first evidence that a population-wide approach to parenting and family support is a viable strategy for the prevention of child maltreatment. Important lessons for implementing parenting interventions at a population level are discussed as well as some of the key measurement and design considerations that are needed when evaluating such approaches.

One of the essential elements for the successful implementation of a population-level approach to parenting is for service-providing agencies to work together toward shared goals relating to parenting support and child and family outcomes. In Chapter 40, Owens, Doyle, Hegarty, Heavey, and Farrell describe the implementation of a population approach to parenting in the Republic of Ireland. The origin of this enterprise was the recognition by local service agencies that many families were experiencing preventable problems, but that no single agency was adequately placed to successfully address these issues on their own; a coordinated approach was needed. In this outstanding example of the application of the population approach, the authors describe key implementation lessons and particularly the partnership model they employed to optimize the alliances between agencies and their collaborative work for the benefit of all children and families.

Raising a child with a developmental disability, such as intellectual disability or autism spectrum disorder, is complex. In addition to experiencing difficulty learning a range of developmental skills, such as mobility, social, communication, and toileting skills, it is not uncommon for these children to also show significant behavior problems. These problems increase the burden of care and, if left unaddressed, can persist into adolescence and adulthood (Einfeld et al., 2006). Although evidence-based parenting programs have been shown to reduce caregiver stress, address behavior problems, and promote children's development, traditional models of service delivery have meant that relatively few families access such support (Einfeld et al., 2006). In Chapter 41, Sofronoff, Gray, Einfeld, and Tonge (2017) describe a unique application of Triple P as a multilevel system to address the significant unmet needs of children with disabilities and their families. The Stepping Stones Triple P System Project involved gradually rolling out all levels of Stepping Stones Triple P across three states of Australia. Sofronoff and her colleagues describe key lessons learned while addressing implementation challenges such as the engagement of providers in health, education, disability, and the nongovernmental sector as project partners; the evaluation of the project; and how the project catered for the heterogeneous needs posed by children with different syndromes and disabilities. Importantly, this project demonstrated that the delivery of an evidence-based parenting and family support program for parents of children with any developmental disability at a population level is feasible.

In conclusion, the three creative and rigorous real-world examples of the full multilevel systems approach to parenting support described in this section provide many important lessons regarding the barriers and facilitators that can influence an initiative's success and degree of impact. By illustrating how the approach can involve different populations, behavioral targets, evaluation designs, and means of assessing outcome, they also hint at the many possibilities that are available in future dissemination efforts. And, more dissemination efforts are needed if the goal is to have a positive impact on the well-being of all children, parents, and communities through access to parenting programs that have been demonstrated to work.

REFERENCES

Einfeld, S. L., Piccinin, A. M., Mackinnon, A., Hofer, S. M., Taffe, J., Gray, K. M., . . . Tonge, B. J. (2006). Psychopathology in young people with intellectual disability. *Journal of the American Medical Association, 296*, 1981–1989. doi:10.1001/jama.296.16.1981

Sanders, M. R., Kirby, J. N., Tellegen, C. L., & Day, J. J. (2014). The Triple P—Positive Parenting Program: A systematic review and meta-analysis of a multi-level system of parenting support. *Clinical Psychology Review, 34*, 337–357. doi:10.1016/j.cpr.2014.04.003

Stoltenborgh, M., Bakermans-Kranenburg, M. J., Alink, L., R. A., & van Ijzendoorn, M. H. (2015). The prevalence of child maltreatment across the globe: Review of a series of meta-analyses. *Child Abuse Review, 24*, 37–50. doi:10.1002/car.2353

CHAPTER 39

SHIFTING THE NEEDLE ON CHILD MALTREATMENT

RONALD J. PRINZ AND CHERI J. SHAPIRO

P revention of child maltreatment (CM) inarguably is an important societal priority in light of the human and economic costs associated with poor treatment of children (Fang, Brown, Florence, & Mercy, 2012). Parenting and family support can play a major role in the prevention of CM. This chapter provides a basis for the adoption and refinement of a population approach to CM prevention, with this approach built on a parenting intervention strategy such as Triple P.

CHILD MALTREATMENT AND PARENTING RISK

Child maltreatment is predominantly about the actions of parents and other caregivers in the family. We know that CM wreaks short- and long-term havoc on children in the form of injuries and fatalities, unhealthy home environments, social-emotional and behavioral problems, and markedly increased risk for medical disorders in adulthood (Bolger & Patterson, 2003; Fang et al., 2012; Felitti, 2009; Lansford et al., 2007; Mersky, Topitzes, & Reynolds, 2013). These well-documented consequences of CM provide strong rationales for prevention efforts, but there is an even broader justification for making parenting and family support intervention a key part of CM prevention. Troubled parenting, whether it rises to the level of "official" CM or not, has potentially detrimental effects on children based on everything we know about the importance of parenting.

Parenting is critical for children's health, development, and well-being in many different ways. The quality of parenting children receive and the relationships children have with parents and other adult caregivers, whether positive or negative, have a long-lasting impact on children's social, emotional, behavioral, cognitive, and physical functioning (Gilbert et al., 2015; Harper Browne & Shapiro, 2016; Shonkoff, 2010).

Children's interactions with parents and other adult caregivers affect a wide range of developmental outcomes. The development of self-regulatory skills in children, a cornerstone of effective cognitive and mental health functioning in adulthood, is strongly influenced by parent competencies and interactions (Sanders & Mazzucchelli, 2013). High-quality parenting interactions have a lasting impact on children's ability to thrive in academic environments. For example, emergent and acquired literacy, as well as general cognitive functioning, are significantly influenced by parental behaviors, such as talking and reading to children (Hart & Risley, 1995; Rindermann & Baumeister, 2015; Zuckerman, 2009). Similarly, parenting also influences children's dietary habits, which can have lasting influence on children's physical health (Peters, Sinn, Campbell, & Lynch, 2012).

In addition to influencing health and academic performance, parenting is one of the strongest influences on children's social, emotional, and behavioral functioning. Emotional availability has been identified as a key dimension of the parent–child relationship and has been linked with attachment (Easterbrooks & Biringen, 2009). Other lines of research have established that harsh, inconsistent, and low-warmth parenting is influential in the development of emotional and behavioral challenges in children and adolescents, including conduct disorder (Frick, 2012; Patterson, Dishion, & Bank, 1984).

Child maltreatment is integrally related to parenting and the many factors affecting parents and families. Those who engage in CM are typically parents or other adult caregivers (Finkelhor, Vanderminden, Turner, Hamby, & Shattuck, 2014). Invariably, parenting stress is a key influence within maltreating families (Holden & Banez, 1996). Mental health problems afflicting some parents and other family members exacerbate the conditions in which CM arises (Yampolskaya & Chuang, 2012).

Child maltreatment is a broad term, encompassing several types of maltreatment. The list and definition of specific CM categories can vary but typically include physical abuse, neglect, sexual abuse, and emotional abuse, and then other more technical variations pertaining to threat of harm, medical care, and the like. Among these categories, neglect is the largest category of CM in young children (e.g., Jud, Fegert, & Finkelhor, 2016), although it is recognized that the classification of neglect does not mean absence of other problematic parenting practices. CM is a global phenomenon (Appleton, 2013; World Health Organization, 2016). A major review of meta-analytic studies (Stoltenborgh, Bakermans-Kranenburg, Alink, & van IJzendoorn, 2015) found combined rates of 127/1,000 for sexual abuse, 226/1,000 for physical abuse, 363/1,000 for emotional abuse, 163/1,000 for physical neglect, and 184/1,000 for emotional neglect. A 2011 US national survey of children exposed to violence found that 12% of a sample of 4,503 children and youth had experienced at least one form of maltreatment (Finkelhor et al., 2014). Rates of physical abuse ranging from 3% to 9% have been identified in Nordic countries (Kloppen, Maehle, Kvello, Haugland, & Breivik, 2015). Self-reported rates of maltreatment are much higher than rates reported by other data sources, such as CM professionals, physicians, or teachers (Stoltenborgh et al., 2015). While child neglect is the largest category of CM in young children (Jud et al., 2016), it is common for several types of maltreatment to be occurring simultaneously (Jud et al., 2016; Kim, Mennen, & Trickett, 2017). Thus, given the high rates of direct reports of CM and data suggesting that perpetrators are typically parents or other adult caregivers, examination of interventions that can be applied broadly across the population are needed.

RATIONALE FOR POPULATION-WIDE APPROACH

The prevention of CM is a challenging endeavor for a number of reasons, such as the low base rate of official CM, heterogeneity of parenting problems associated with abuse and neglect, the many factors and conditions contributing to risk for CM, and the impracticality and inaccuracy of trying to identify which parents are going to engage in CM. The parenting intervention strategy needs to have a broad reach involving many segments of the parent population. Casting a broad net with parenting and family support increases the likelihood that parents at risk for CM might be engaged. Further, by normalizing participation, this strategy avoids the barrier of stigma that would be associated with identifying parents as at risk for CM.

It is reasonable to ask whether addressing the entire population of parents is a justifiable strategy if the solitary goal is the prevention of official CM cases. Two considerations bear on this question. First, reduction of official CM cases is important but does not capture all of the CM prevention charge. We know from anonymous surveys of parents (e.g., Theodore et al., 2005) that parenting practices that can reasonably be conceived as abusive are many times more prevalent than official CM records indicate. Reaching this broader segment of the population is important because abusive and otherwise problematic parenting practices are deleterious to children's well-being whether or not official action by child protective services is involved.

The second consideration justifying a population-level approach has to do with how other intervention goals can coalesce with the CM prevention goal. A population-wide approach such as the Triple P system has the potential to strengthen families and improve child and family well-being using the same set of interventions. Thus, combining CM prevention with other goals, such as increasing school readiness, preventing children's behavior problems, and reducing risk for adverse adolescent outcomes, has the potential to create overall intervention efficiency.

The issue of whether to adopt a population-wide versus a narrow approach to parenting/family support is sometimes couched as a choice between universal versus targeted prevention. This dichotomy obscures a more appropriate solution. It is quite possible and perhaps ideal to adopt a blended strategy, which combines universal and targeted interventions integrated within a coordinated arrangement. The Triple P system lends itself to this approach and makes use of a tiered structure that emphasizes less intensive options for universal intervention and more intensive ones as needed for targeted application.

EMERGING EVIDENCE

Evidence is emerging in support of a population-based approach to parenting and family support as a viable strategy for the prevention of CM. This proposition was tested in a place randomization study involving the Triple P system (Prinz, Sanders, Shapiro, Whitaker, & Lutzker, 2009, 2016). The thrust of this study was to randomize communities to intervention or control conditions, implement community-wide parenting and family support as a prevention strategy, and then examine the impact on population indicators related to CM. This study was a departure from the vast majority of CM prevention trials in two respects: (a) The focus of outcomes was on community-wide prevalence rates rather than on measurement of individual parents and children, and (b) the unit of randomization was place (in this case, county) as opposed to individual family.

In this study, 18 counties in South Carolina were randomized to either implementation of the Triple P system (intervention) or services as usual (control). Equivalence of the nine intervention and nine control counties at baseline was verified for county population size, poverty rate for the general population and for children, and racial composition, as well as for the three outcome variables (substantiated CM cases, out-of-home placements, hospital-treated CM injuries). To implement the intervention, over 600 service providers from the existing workforce were trained in various levels and formats of Triple P. Service sectors included a wide range of provider systems, such as education, school readiness, child care, mental health, social services, and health. Controlling for 5 years of baseline prevalence rates, the study found substantial preventive effects of the Triple P system on substantiated CM cases, child out-of-home placements, and hospital-treated CM injuries, compared with control communities (Prinz, 2017; Prinz et al., 2016). The outcomes were derived from three separate sources: child protective services, the foster care system, and the hospital system, respectively.

The Prinz et al. study provided initial evidence for the proposition that community-wide parenting and family support can contribute to the prevention of CM (Prinz, 2017; Prinz et al., 2009, 2016). This early investigation did not benefit from more recent developments in implementation science. Some of these implementation issues are discussed further in this chapter.

Other studies have utilized administrative records data to examine potential preventive effects. For example, Smith (2015) found in a quasiexperimental design using administrative data that implementation of Level 4 Group Triple P for parents of preschool children resulted in a reduced rate of hospital emergency department visits over childhood and adolescence based on a 15-year follow-up. Dodge et al. (2014) conducted a randomized test of a universal four- to seven-session postnatal nurse home-visiting program in the United States and found a positive impact with respect to CM cases and emergency room treatment. Recent initiatives have demonstrated the population-level impact of the Triple P system on parenting and child behavior outcomes, which indirectly makes a population-focused approach to CM prevention more viable because of multiple potential benefits from implementation of the same intervention (Fives, Purcell, Heary, Nic Gabhainn, & Canavan, 2014; Frantz, Stemmler, Hahlweg, Pluck, & Heinrichs, 2015).

Finally, Box 39.1 provides an example involving implementation of the Triple P system in a geographic area followed by an independent evaluation commissioned by the host community organization documenting the impact on CM.

MEASUREMENT AND DESIGN ISSUES

Whether in research or a program-evaluation context, a population-based approach to CM prevention has some inherent measurement and design challenges. Some of these are briefly discussed here. There are a number of measurement issues. The prevalence rates for CM-related indicators, including official CM substantiation, foster care placement, and CM injuries, reflect relatively low-frequency events in the population. Low base rates make it more difficult to detect changes over time as a function of intervention, especially for smaller geographic units and brief durations (e.g., monthly or quarterly). This problem can be addressed in part by focusing on larger geographic areas and capturing longer time durations, such as 6 or 12 months.

BOX 39.1: Field Implementation of the Triple P System

An implementation of the Triple P system took place in Santa Cruz, a diverse California county, to address the needs of families. Partnering with the county human services agency and others, the First 5 Santa Cruz County nongovernmental organization supported a program called *Families Together,* with Triple P as a critical component. Families Together is a differential response program, a strategy to intervene early with families in which there has been an allegation of CM. The five levels of Triple P were implemented and then sustained over a 5-year period. An evaluation conducted by First 5 Santa Cruz County, Applied Survey Research, and Optimal Solutions Consulting made these observations:

- The program reached 9,048 parents via Triple P, affecting 16,754 children in a 5-year span.
- The availability of the less intensive levels of Triple P increased parental engagement and led to greater opportunities for families to participate in other types of services.
- Improvement of parenting skills was documented in several domains.
- Parents with more serious parenting difficulties made the greatest improvements, including reductions in levels of risk for future child abuse.
- The county experienced reduced rates of substantiated CM over time.

Another measurement issue pertains to the assessment of intervention penetration. The success of a population approach to family-based intervention depends heavily on reaching many families to produce broad impact. It is not a simple task, however, to track family participation across agencies and organization throughout a community over time. Program implementers need multiprong strategies for monitoring and collating data on participation of parents over time.

Outcome research on population-based CM prevention necessitates methodologies that permit inferences at a population or aggregate level. Potential effects need to be evaluated at the level of place or cluster, but this requires many clusters to have sufficient statistical power to detect changes (Donner & Klar, 2000). One of the associated challenges is that the addition of each cluster (i.e., community, county, or other geographical unit) increases the extent of intervention implementation. A cluster-randomized design cannot succeed with only a few clusters. Similarly, program evaluation runs into the same obstacle, although it is less critical for such evaluations to be able to rule out as many threats to internal validity as is expected for outcome studies.

IMPLEMENTATION ISSUES

As is well documented, implementation of programs for prevention or intervention is a complex undertaking that requires attention to multiple levels of the social ecology: the intervention, providers, organizations, financial systems, and policy environment (Damschroder & Hagedorn, 2011; Greenhalgh, Robert, MacFarlane, Bate, & Kyriakidou, 2004; E. Proctor, 2012; E. Proctor et al., 2011; E. K. Proctor et al., 2009). Implementation of parenting supports at a population level is no exception. A number of implementation frameworks have been proposed, such as the Consolidated Framework for Implementation Research (CFIR; Damschroder & Hagedorn, 2011); the systems–contextual perspective (Beidas & Kendall, 2010); and other frameworks developed by program purveyors (e.g., McWilliam, Brown, Sanders, & Jones, 2016).

When approaching the challenge of implementation of strategies to address CM at a population level, the adoption of a systems–contextual perspective is particularly important. This perspective highlights factors operating at the level of the provider, organization, and client, each of which have been demonstrated to be important to implementation and sustained use of evidence-based parenting interventions (Shapiro, Prinz, & Sanders, 2012, 2015; Turner, Nicholson, & Sanders, 2011). Factors such as provider attitudes toward evidence-based interventions, provider confidence, support and supervision at the organizational level, and positive feedback from clients or obtaining favorable client outcomes are exemplified in this approach. CFIR expands on this perspective by offering five major cross-cutting domains that influence implementation: characteristics of the intervention itself (e.g., evidence, cost, and materials); outer setting (e.g., client needs, external policies); inner setting (primarily organization-level factors); individual provider characteristics; and process factors (Damschroder & Hagedorn, 2011). This last category of process includes the steps necessary to implement an intervention, such as planning, engaging, executing, and evaluation (Damschroder & Hagedorn, 2011). These frameworks provide the basis for understanding factors related to implementing intervention approaches but must be expanded when implementation of programs at a population level is being considered.

Prior research has documented some of the steps necessary to implement parenting interventions at a population level (Sanders et al., 2008; Shapiro, Prinz, & Sanders, 2010). Our focus here is to expand on these findings and to elucidate additional factors that must be considered when implementing at a population level.

Implementation of a parenting intervention at a population level requires a multilevel strategy as exemplified by Triple P, which was explicitly designed as a public health approach to parenting (Sanders, Prinz, & Shapiro, 2012; Sanders, Turner, & Markie-Dadds, 2002). Information to support positive parenting must be available for all families within a given population that promotes child and family well-being. Building on this are interventions of increasing intensity to meet the needs of parents who want and need more support. Thus, implementation at a population level requires engagement of existing media outlets (e.g., newspapers, radio, television) as well as enhancing what is available via electronic and social media. Engagement of multiple naturally occurring touchpoints for families with children, such as early care and education settings, schools, and primary care providers, are important. Further requirements include the ability to engage systems that serve children and families with higher levels of needs.

Within a population-level approach, supporting parents who need or want a more intensive level of support require interventions with significant collaboration across several diverse sectors serving children, youth, and their families throughout the community. Engaging of the key stakeholder groups and reaching consensus regarding implementation of specific interventions are lengthy and complicated processes. A number of barriers exist that can prevent organizations from supporting meaningful, cross-population adoption and implementation of evidence-based interventions (Garcia, Kim, Palinkas, Snowden, & Landsverk, 2016). One potential solution, at least in the United States, can be seen in the growth of federally funded systems of care that place children and families at the center of the process, support seamless service delivery, and emphasize the use of evidence-based interventions (US Department of Health and Human Services, 2015).

In addition to concerns related to service system fragmentation, the passage of time is not well represented in current models of implementation. Allowing for an adequate amount of time for implementation processes to unfold is important, especially when deploying an intervention at a population level. There are five primary considerations in this regard. First, the length of time it takes to engage diverse stakeholders serving pertinent segments of the community cannot be underestimated. While engagement can occur quickly in some jurisdictions, the time to reach all of the key decision-makers, stakeholder agencies, and organizations can sometimes stretch into months or years. Second, once stakeholders are engaged, the process of training a multidisciplinary workforce (necessary for population-level implementation of parenting supports) takes months or years to plan and execute. Third, the workforce that receives training requires sustained support over time, persistently and unconditionally, to become adept at program implementation. Maintenance of external supports over time might not be feasible, which makes the building of internal (i.e., within-organization) support critical, especially given high rates of staff turnover endemic to many service-sector agencies. (Building internal capacity for support is the goal of peer-assisted support and supervision, or PASS, a model incorporated into the Triple P dissemination process.)

Fourth, attrition over time in key organization leaders as well as among individuals designated to provide an intervention to families must be taken into account at the start of the implementation process. Understanding baseline rates of turnover across service sectors is necessary if implementation is to be sustained over time.

Last, it is important to consider changes in the fiscal infrastructure over time. Funding, both up front for training as well as over time for reimbursement of services, is required to fully establish a population approach to parenting. However, fiscal infrastructure is dynamic, not static. Funding mechanisms might be available at the start of implementation of a population-wide parenting support intervention, but the likelihood is high that this would change over time. For example, services might be reimbursable by third-party payers when implementation begins, but there is no guarantee that these reimbursement policies would exist 2 to 5 years, or even 1 year, into the future. The implication is that the types and stability of funding over time must be considered when planning for adoption and implementation of an intervention.

CONCLUSIONS

Community-wide implementation of parenting and family support, as exemplified by the Triple P system, can play a major role in the prevention of CM (Pickering & Sanders, 2016). A strategy such as Triple P, which involves blended prevention, has the potential not only to contribute to CM prevention but also to concurrently improve other child and family outcomes affected by parenting—strengthening the argument for a population approach. With respect to CM, parenting and family support interventions are critical but should not be seen as precluding the need for additional efforts related to substance abuse, poverty, access to health care, and early childhood education (Prinz, 2016). Finally, it is not sufficient to introduce a population approach. Such an approach can only succeed when it builds on the main tenets of implementation science.

KEY MESSAGES

- Parenting difficulties that can reasonably be considered as abusive, or at least detrimental to children's development and well-being, are many times more prevalent than official child protective services records capture.
- Population-based parenting and family support, although not the only thing needed, is a critical component of a broad public health strategy for the prevention of CM.
- Community-wide implementation of the Triple P system is a promising approach to the reduction or prevention of population indicators associated with CM.
- Diligent application of best practices emerging in the field of implementation science is likely to produce even greater impact in moving the needle on CM.

REFERENCES

Appleton, J. V. (2013). Child maltreatment: International and legal issues: Editorial. *Child Abuse Review*, *22*, 381–385. doi:10.1002/car.2309

Beidas, R. S., & Kendall, P. C. (2010). Training therapists in evidence-based practice: A critical review of studies from a systems-contextual perspective. *Clinical Psychology: Science and Practice*, *17*, 1–30. doi:10.1111/j.1468-2850.2009.01187.x

Bolger, K. E., & Patterson, C. J. (2003). Sequelae of child maltreatment: Vulnerability and resilience. In S. S. Luthar (Ed.), *Resilience and vulnerability: Adaptation in the context of childhood adversities* (pp. 156–181). Cambridge, England: Cambridge University Press. doi:10.1017/CBO9780511615788.009

Damschroder, L. J., & Hagedorn, H. J. (2011). A guiding framework and approach for implementation research in substance use disorders treatment. *Psychology of Addictive Behaviors*, *25*, 194–205. doi:10.1037/a0022284

Dodge, K. A., Goodman, W. B., Murphy, R. A., O'Donnell, K., Sato, J., & Guptill, S. (2014). Implementation and randomized controlled trial evaluation of universal postnatal nurse home visiting. *American Journal of Public Health*, *104*, s136–s143. doi:10.2105/ajph.2013.301361

Donner, A., & Klar, N. (2000). *Design and analysis of cluster randomization trials in health research*. New York, NY: Oxford University Press.

Easterbrooks, M. A., & Biringen, Z. (2009). Introduction to the special issue: Emotional availability across contexts. *Parenting: Science and Practice*, *9*, 179–182. doi:10.1080/15295190902844266

Fang, X., Brown, D. S., Florence, C. S., & Mercy, J. A. (2012). The economic burden of child maltreatment in the United States and implications for prevention. *Child Abuse & Neglect*, *36*, 156–165. doi. org/10.1016/j.chiabu.2011.10.006

Felitti, V. (2009). Adverse childhood experiences and adult health. *Academic Pediatrics*, *9*, 131–132. doi. org/10.1016/j.acap.2009.03.001

Finkelhor, D., Vanderminden, J., Turner, H., Hamby, S., & Shattuck, A. (2014). Child maltreatment rates assessed in a national household survey of caregivers and youth. *Child Abuse & Neglect*, *38*, 1421–1435. doi:10.1016/j.chiabu.2014.05.005

Fives, A., Purcell, L., Heary, C., Nic Gabhainn, S., & Canavan, J. (2014). *Parenting support for every parent: A population-level evaluation of Triple P in Longford Westmeath*. Final Report. Athlone, Ireland: Longford Westmeath Parenting Partnership.

Frantz, I., Stemmler, M., Hahlweg, K., Pluck, J., & Heinrichs, N. (2015). Experiences in disseminating evidence-based prevention programs in a real-world setting. *Prevention Science, 16*, 789–800. doi:10.1007/s11121-015-0554-y

Frick, P. J. (2012). Developmental pathways to conduct disorder: Implications for future directions in research, assessment, and treatment. *Journal of Clinical Child and Adolescent Psychology, 41*, 378–389. doi:10.1080/15374416.2012.664815

Garcia, A. R., Kim, M., Palinkas, L. A., Snowden, L., & Landsverk, J. (2016). Socio-contextual determinants of research evidence use in public-youth systems of care. *Administration and Policy in Mental Health and Mental Health Services Research, 43*, 569–578. doi:10.1007/s10488-015-0640-2

Gilbert, L. K., Breiding, M. J., Merrick, M. T., Thompson, W. W., Ford, D. C., Dhingra, S. S., & Parks, S. E. (2015). Childhood adversity and adult chronic disease: An update from ten states and the District of Columbia, 2010. *American Journal of Preventive Medicine, 48*, 345–349. doi:10.1016/j.amepre.2014.09.006

Greenhalgh, T., Robert, G., MacFarlane, F., Bate, P., & Kyriakidou, O. (2004). Diffusion of innovations in service organizations: Systematic review and recommendations. *Milbank Quarterly, 82*, 581–629. doi:10.1111/j.0887-378X.2004.00325.x

Harper Browne, C., & Shapiro, C. J. (2016). Building young children's social-emotional competence at home and in early care and education settings. In C. J. Shapiro & C. Harper Browne (Eds.), *Innovative approaches to supporting families of young children* (pp. 87–106). New York, NY: Springer.

Hart, B., & Risley, T. R. (1995). *Meaningful differences in the everyday experience of young American children*. Baltimore, MD: Brookes.

Holden, E. W., & Banez, G. A. (1996). Child abuse potential and parenting stress within maltreating families. *Journal of Family Violence, 11*, 1–12. doi:10.1007/BF02333337

Jud, A., Fegert, J. M., & Finkelhor, D. (2016). On the incidence and prevalence of child maltreatment: A research agenda. *Child and Adolescent Psychiatry and Mental Health, 10*, 17. doi:10.1186/s13034-016-0105-8

Kim, K., Mennen, F. E., & Trickett, P. K. (2017). Patterns and correlates of co-occurrence among multiple types of maltreatment. *Child & Family Social Work, 22*, 492–502. doi:10.1111/cfs.12268

Kloppen, K., Maehle, M., Kvello, O., Haugland, S., & Breivik, K. (2015). Prevalence of intrafamilial child maltreatment in the Nordic countries: A review. *Child Abuse Review, 24*, 51–66. doi:10.1002/car.2324

Lansford, J. E., Miller-Johnson, S., Berlin, L. J., Dodge, K. A., Bates, J. E., & Pettit, G. S. (2007). Early physical abuse and later violent delinquency: A prospective longitudinal study. *Child Maltreatment, 12*, 233–245. doi:10.1177/1077559507301841

McWilliam, J., Brown, J., Sanders, M. R., & Jones, L. (2016). The Triple P Implementation Framework: The role of purveyors in the implementation and sustainability of evidence-based programs. *Prevention Science, 17*, 636–645. doi:10.1007/s11121-016-0661-4

Mersky, J. P., Topitzes, J., & Reynolds, A. J. (2013). Impacts of adverse childhood experiences on health, mental health, and substance use in early adulthood: A cohort study of an urban, minority sample in the US. *Child Abuse & Neglect, 37*, 917–925. doi:10.1016/j.chiabu.2013.07.011

Patterson, G. R., Dishion, T. J., & Bank, L. (1984). Family interaction: A process model of deviancy training. *Aggressive Behavior, 10*, 253–267. doi:10.1002/1098-2337

Peters, J., Sinn, N., Campbell, K., & Lynch, J. (2012). Parental influences on the diets of 2–5-year-old children: Systematic review of interventions. *Early Child Development and Care, 182*, 837–857. doi:10.1080/03004430.2011.586698

Pickering, J. A., & Sanders, M. R. (2016). Reducing child maltreatment by making parenting programs available to all parents: A case example using the Triple P—Positive Parenting Program. *Trauma, Violence, & Abuse, 17*, 398–407. doi:10.1177/1524838016658876

Prinz, R. J. (2016). Parenting and family support within a broad child abuse prevention strategy. *Child Abuse & Neglect, 51*, 400–406. doi:10.1016/j.chiabu.2015.10.015

Prinz, R. J. (2017). Assessing child maltreatment prevention via administrative data systems: A case example of reproducibility. *Child Abuse & Neglect, 64*, 13–18. doi:10.1016/j.chiabu.2016.12.005

Prinz, R. J., Sanders, M. R., Shapiro, C. J., Whitaker, D. J., & Lutzker, J. R. (2009). Population-based prevention of child maltreatment: The US Triple P system population trial. *Prevention Science, 10*, 1–12. doi:10.1007/s11121-009-0123-3

Prinz, R. J., Sanders, M. R., Shapiro, C. J., Whitaker, D. J., & Lutzker, J. R. (2016). Addendum to "Population-Based Prevention of Child Maltreatment: The US Triple P System Population Trial." *Prevention Science, 17*, 410–416. doi:10.1007/s11121-016-0631-x

Proctor, E. (2012). Implementation science and child maltreatment: Methodological advances. *Child Maltreatment, 17*, 107–112. doi:10.1177/1077559512437034

Proctor, E., Silmere, H., Raghavan, R., Hovmand, P., Aarons, G., Bunger, A., . . . Hensley, M. (2011). Outcomes for implementation research: Conceptual distinctions, measurement challenges, and research agenda. *Administration and Policy in Mental Health and Mental Health Services Research, 38*, 65–76. doi:10.1007/s10488-010-0319-7

Proctor, E. K., Landsverk, J., Aarons, G., Chambers, D., Glisson, C., & Mittman, B. (2009). Implementation research in mental health services: An emerging science with conceptual, methodological, and training challenges. *Administration and Policy in Mental Health and Mental Health Services Research, 36*, 24–34. doi:10.1007/s10488-008-0197-4

Rindermann, H., & Baumeister, A. E. E. (2015). Parents' SES vs. parental educational behavior and children's development: A reanalysis of the Hart and Risley study. *Learning and Individual Differences, 37*, 133–138. doi:10.1016/j.lindif.2014.12.005

Sanders, M. R., & Mazzucchelli, T. G. (2013). The promotion of self-regulation through parenting interventions. *Clinical Child and Family Psychology Review, 16*, 1–17. doi:10.1007/s10567-013-0129-z

Sanders, M. R., Prinz, R. J., & Shapiro, C. (2012). Parenting and child maltreatment as public health issues: Implications from the Triple P system of intervention. In A. Rubin & A. Rubin (Eds.), *Programs and interventions for maltreated children and families at risk* (pp. 297–312). Hoboken, NJ: Wiley.

Sanders, M. R., Ralph, A., Sofronoff, K., Gardiner, P., Thompson, R., Dwyer, S., & Bidwell, K. (2008). Every family: A population approach to reducing behavioral and emotional problems in children making the transition to school. *The Journal of Primary Prevention, 29*, 197–222. doi:10.1007/s10935-008-0139-7

Sanders, M. R., Turner, K. M. T., & Markie-Dadds, C. (2002). The development and dissemination of the Triple P-Positive Parenting Program: A multilevel, evidence-based system of parenting and family support. *Prevention Science, 3*, 173–189. doi:10.1023/A:1019942516231

Shapiro, C. J., Prinz, R. J., & Sanders, M. R. (2010). Population based provider engagement in delivery of evidence-based parenting interventions: Challenges and solutions. *Journal of Primary Prevention, 31*, 223–234. doi:10.1007/s10935-010-02 10-z

Shapiro, C. J., Prinz, R. J., & Sanders, M. R. (2012). Facilitators and barriers to implementation of an evidence-based parenting intervention to prevent child maltreatment: The Triple P-Positive Parenting Program. *Child Maltreatment, 17*, 86–95. doi:10.1177/1077559511424774

Shapiro, C. J., Prinz, R. J., & Sanders, M. R. (2015). Sustaining use of an evidence-based parenting intervention: Practitioner perspectives. *Journal of Child and Family Studies, 24*, 1615–1624. doi:10.1007/s10826-014-9965-9

Shonkoff, J. P. (2010). Building a new biodevelopmental framework to guide the future of early child-hood policy. *Child Development, 81,* 357–367. doi:10.1111/j.1467-8624.2009.01399.x

Smith, G. (2015). *15-Year follow-up of WA Triple P trial, collaboration for applied research and evaluation.* Perth, Australia: Telethon Institute for Child Health Research under contract with the Department of Health.

Stoltenborgh, M., Bakermans-Kranenburg, M. J., Alink, L. R. A., & van IJzendoorn, M. H. (2015). The prevalence of child maltreatment across the globe: Review of a series of meta-analyses. *Child Abuse Review, 24,* 37–50. doi:10.1002/car.2353

Theodore, A. D., Chang, J. J., Runyan, D. K., Hunter, W. M., Bangdiwala, S. I., & Agans, R. (2005). Epidemiologic features of the physical and sexual maltreatment of children in the Carolinas. *Pediatrics, 115,* 331–337. doi:10.1542/peds.2004-1033

Turner, K. M. T., Nicholson, J. M., & Sanders, M. R. (2011). The role of practitioner self-efficacy, training, program and workplace factors on the implementation of an evidence-based parenting intervention in primary care. *The Journal of Primary Prevention, 32,* 95–112. doi:10.1007/s10935-011-0240-1

US Department of Health and Human Services. (2015). *The comprehensive community mental health services for children with serious emotional disturbances, report to Congress* (SAMHSA Publication No. PEP16-CMHI2015). Washington, DC: US Department of Health and Human Services.

World Health Organization. (2016). Child maltreatment. http://www.who.int/mediacentre/factsheets/fs150/en/

Yampolskaya, S., & Chuang, E. (2012). Effects of mental health disorders on the risk of juvenile justice system involvement and recidivism among children placed in out-of-home care. *American Journal of Orthopsychiatry, 82,* 585–593. doi:10.1111/j.1939-0025.2012.01184.x

Zuckerman, B. (2009). Promoting early literacy in pediatric practice: Twenty years of Reach Out and Read. *Pediatrics, 124,* 1660–1665. doi:10.1542/peds.2009-1207

CHAPTER 40

PARTNERSHIPS AND SCALING UP POPULATION-LEVEL INTERVENTIONS

CONOR OWENS, ORLA DOYLE, MARY HEGARTY, KAREN HEAVEY, AND EAMONN FARRELL

INTRODUCTION

The Triple P—Positive Parenting Program was implemented on a population basis in Ireland in 2010 by the Midland Area Parenting Partnership (MAPP) previously know as the Longford Westmeath Parenting Partnership. Six years later, in excess of 17,000 Triple P training places had been attended by local parents. The successful implementation of population-based parenting strategies required alliances and partnerships between service provision agencies, local government, and funders. This chapter describes the partnership approach that was used to implement population-level Triple P in the Republic of Ireland and provides lessons learned on the development of effective local partnerships to support effective parenting.

BACKGROUND

A common agenda of family support in Ireland is set by the national policy context and local need and is based on a number of policy documents, including Healthy Ireland, Investing in Families; Better Outcomes Brighter Futures National Policy Framework for Children and Young People, 2014–2020; and the Health Promotion Strategic Framework (Health Service Executive, 2011). A strong focus on effective strategies for supporting families is necessary given the high prevalence rates of child socioemotional and behavioral difficulties across most developed countries. In Ireland, 15% of 9-year-olds are classified as having "borderline" or "problematic" behavioral difficulties (Nixon, 2012). Social, emotional, and behavioral difficulties in child-hood can lead to a range of potential lifelong problems including poor health, unemployment, relationship difficulties, addictions, and child protection issues (Committee on Children and Young People, 2009), as well as social and financial implications for wider society (Department of Children and Youth Affairs, 2014).

Statutory, voluntary, and community organizations working with children and families in the Irish Midlands recognized that many families were experiencing preventable difficulties and that a coordinated approach was needed to tackle this issue. They recognized that no single organization was adequately placed to address this issue successfully on their own because of reach, access, and resource issues. Following an initial meeting, these organizations agreed to investigate evidence-based parenting programs that could be introduced across the whole com-munity. They wanted to adopt a universal approach to parenting rather than a targeted approach to address parental concerns across the socioeconomic spectrum. After reviewing the literature the Triple P—Positive Parenting Program was chosen as the program to implement in the Irish Midlands given its proven track record, as demonstrated by multiple studies and its universal approach to service provision (Sanders, Kirby, Tellegen, & Day, 2014). Triple P was also chosen as its principles (based on giving all parents the confidence and skills to be self-sufficient) fitted with the values and aspirations of the individual organizations. It was also the only parenting program to have been successfully trialed at a population level (Sanders et al., 2008).

The rollout of Triple P in the Midlands was the first implementation and evaluation of a population-based parenting program in Ireland. The Triple P population approach involves offering, access to different levels of the program to all families in the area based on the family's perceived need. This approach was adopted as it had the capacity to destigmatize and normal-ize participation in parenting programs, which in turn may help to increase program accept-ability and related help-seeking behavior (Prinz, Sanders, Shapiro, Whitaker, & Lutzker, 2016). A population approach has an impact on two general levels. At a societal level, it may reduce the prevalence rates of socioemotional problems for children and decrease parental psychological distress. At the family level, it may reduce the risk factors and increase protective factors associ-ated with socioemotional difficulties. The primary mechanism that MAPP used to deliver the intervention at a population level was by adopting a partnership approach.

WHY ARE PARTNERSHIPS ESSENTIAL IN THE DELIVERY OF POPULATION-LEVEL INTERVENTIONS?

The effectiveness of any preventive program in achieving outcomes for children is based on the evidence of effectiveness of the program, the implementation plan, and the enabling envi-ronment in which the program will operate (Fixsen, Naoom, Blase, Friedman, & Wallace, 2005). The enabling environment includes all the factors that support the Triple P population approach including the readiness of parents, practitioners, and managers of partner organiza-tions to embrace the program. Key to this is the need to have influence with, and access to, the whole population. This can be achieved through building alliances and partnerships. As individual organizations operating in the community have built trust and credibility with the populations they serve, coming together to form partnerships and alliances optimizes their credibility and authority both within the area of implementation and outside it. The enabling environment can be local, regional, and/or national. Thus, the effectiveness of one organization can be multiplied through the collaborations and cooperation offered by the partnership.

ESTABLISHING MAPP

Midland Area Parenting Partnership developed a common agenda to support and maintain an enabling environment that would lead to the effective implementation of Triple P. The partnership was a collaboration of committed organizations that pooled resources for the delivery of the program to achieve a collective impact and thereby increase reach, acceptability, local knowledge, and capacity to harness existing networks. This was fundamental in developing, nurturing, and sustaining the enabling environment.

Each of the partners was a voluntary and statutory organization encompassing health, education, community development and child, youth, parent, and family services. At the outset, the partner organizations agreed and adopted a memorandum of understanding (MoU) to provide an effective governance and operational framework. This framework expressed the vision, goals, values, and principles of the partnership, while delineating its scope and specifying accountability to partner members, partner organizations, funders, and the population it would serve. The process of developing the MoU was pivotal in building the foundations for the long-term work of the partnership, and it included an ongoing assessment of organization readiness by each partner organization. Organizational readiness is a consideration of key areas that are fundamental to commitment and starting the planning process (e.g., fit, feasibility, partnership commitment, implementation support and resources).

In MAPP's experience, partnership has many benefits, including the following:

- Giving both large and small organizations the opportunity to be part of an evidence-based initiative with potential for a large-scale and long-term impact, in line with national policy. Small organizations generally do not have the opportunity/resources to help drive large-scale interventions.
- Facilitating different organizations to work together on a common agenda to improve the lives of children and families.
- Supporting individual organizations to achieve their goals more efficiently by maximizing delivery, reducing duplication, and increasing access to families.
- Allowing organizations that are not in a position to commit financial resources to contribute other key resources (e.g., reconfiguring the use of staff time, providing facilities, etc.).
- Allowing large organizations to work with and have access to groups of parents in the community that it would be difficult for them to otherwise access.

THE IRELAND MIDLANDS AREA PARTNERSHIP TRIPLE P SYSTEM TRIAL

The MAPP timely access to Triple P, free of charge, to every family with children under the age of eight within counties Longford and Westmeath from September 2010. The aim was to reduce the prevalence rates of children showing socioemotional and behavioral problems, to alleviate parental anxiety and depression, and to help parents become more confident and competent.

The key principles of the MAPP population approach to Triple P were self-regulation, minimal sufficiency, and a focus on outcomes. By actively adopting these principles in its functioning, the partnership ensured that they were mirrored in program delivery, practitioner supports and partnership development. The principle of self-regulation was adopted to ensure that the community, practitioners and parents were able to self-manage, feel confident, accept responsibility for positive change, and sustain this without significant ongoing support. The principle of minimal sufficiency was adopted to ensure that the level of support provided was selected by the partners, practitioners or parents to match their current needs and available resources. The principle of an outcomes focus was adopted to ensure that a set of agreed-on, measurable outcomes for children and families was achieved. For partners, it also meant facilitating networking and building alliances among multiple agencies and services, as well as facilitating learning from and with other organizations.

The collaboration of the partner organizations gave the MAPP initiative credibility and authority with the families they wished to serve, which ultimately facilitated the implementation of the program. The partnership was also fundamental in creating program sustainability as the partner organizations committed resources, such as the reorientation of staff who were trained to deliver Triple P, commitment of free access to facilities and contact lists of families and use of partner communication systems. Most important, the partners allowed the Triple P initiative to be associated with their name, which helped to maximize program reach. Links were also established with other organizations and services in the community such as family resource centers, community development projects, child care facilities, primary schools and general practitioners.

The partnership was also effective in sourcing funding and other resources from the Atlantic Philanthropies, the Department of Children and Youth Affairs, the Health Service Executive and the Child and Family Agency. MAPP also reoriented some existing resources within the partner organizations. This meant that, after the initial research grant, the program was supported and implemented by the individual organizations from within their existing budgets and staff. MAPP contributed to the initiative support, management, communications and evaluation hub by committing administration and research resources and providing for the development of an implementation and outcome monitoring system.

A key action for the partnership was the devolution of the overall authority for the initiative to a core team who were responsible for developing and progressing the implementation plan. This strategy mirrored the process of self-regulation between practitioner and parent; that is, the core team practitioners took the appropriate amount of responsibility to help local practitioners become more independent, confident and competent practitioners. The core team consisted of a manager/coordinator, practitioners from the partner organizations who had dedicated a minimum of 3 days per week to the program, an administrator and access to research support. Essentially, the partnership fostered this enabling environment to develop and the core team became the key driver for the initiative. The latter also acted as an implementation support team for local practitioners and eventually for scaling up (see Box 40.1 for an example).

IMPLEMENTATION TEAM

Triple P was operating in the community on a small scale before this initiative was developed. It did not achieve the reach required and delivery became sporadic due to the lack of an implementation

---

BOX 40.1: Local Alliances Drive Delivery

School-based Triple P seminars were best promoted via personal contact involving a core team practitioner and the school principal. School principals need confidence in both the value of the message and the presenter. Initially, a core team member was allocated as a "driver" to develop these alliances and establish seminar delivery as a regular feature of the school year. This role was later subsumed by the area teams. Higher attendance at the seminars was achieved where the seminar was part of a parent induction or enrollment meeting. In the primary and secondary school seminars, examples were tailored to support this transition time. The main titles delivered were "The Power of Positive Parenting" and "Raising Competent Teenagers," and tips were provided on preparing children for each school type. In 2016, seminars were delivered to more than 3,800 parents. Currently, we work with in excess of 50% of schools in the region; this number is only limited by our present capacity. Seminars also provide an opportunity to explain other Triple P courses and to advertise the delivery calendar on the website and Facebook. Options are provided for parents at seminars to request further information or opportunities to discuss Triple P course options.

---

strategy. Building on the lessons learned from this process, the current initiative ensured that a clear implementation structure was developed and in place prior to population delivery. The administrative hub provided a source of information for parents, coordinated program bookings and delivery. It also dealt with the implementation database and all associated parent and practitioner paperwork. This was an essential support function for the practitioners and allowed them to focus on recruitment and program delivery. The core team developed significant levels of program confidence and competence which allowed them to offer quality mentoring support to the local practitioners who delivered the intervention less frequently. This resulted in enhancing of local practitioners' confidence and competence in the program and reduced the likelihood of nondelivery. This structure (Figure 40.1) addressed the lessons learned from early efforts. In the words of Fixsen, "It is not sufficient simply to introduce an evidence-based program," he warned: "It has to be put into practice with great care and effort" (Fixsen et al., 2005). The relationship between the evidence-based program, implementation plan and enabling environment was the active ingredient needed to achieve better outcomes. We believe that the implementation structure was a key determinant in achieving the positive results for partners, practitioners and families.

BRIEF REVIEW OF EFFICACY

As well as implementing the program, the partnership commissioned an evaluation of the impact of Triple P at a population level using a quasiexperimental approach. The evaluation covered a time span of September 2010 to December 2012 and involved a comparison of the two implementation counties to two comparison counties matched on sociodemographic characteristics using census data. The total eligible number of families with children in target age range was approximately 7,317. During that period, delivery consisted of Levels 1 through 4, namely:

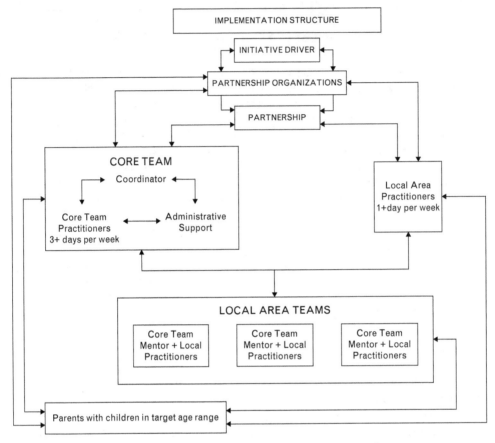

FIGURE 40.1: Implementation structure of the Midland Area Parenting Partnership.

- Level 1 Media Strategy: available to all of the population (with a specific focus on families with children aged 3–7 years);
- Level 2 seminars: uptake included 2,699 parents;
- Level 3 Discussion Groups: update included 1,047 parents; and
- Level 4 group: uptake included 803 parents.

Our implementation guide (Owens et al., 2016) details the evolution of the model of recruitment, delivery and fidelity-promoting practices. It also captures the lessons learned from the Stage 1 implementation and subsequent expansion through core team and local area practitioners and partnership.

PROGRAM EFFECTIVENESS

The population study was conducted to examine the impact of population Triple P within the intervention areas. Independent representative surveys with parents of 3- to 7-year-olds were conducted before and after the implementation of the program in both intervention and comparison counties. The study found that the program improved both parenting behavior and child outcomes. Specifically, parents in the MAPP counties reported better experiences of parenting and a more positive family climate, as well as improvements in parenting behavior/ attitudes, compared to parents in the comparison counties. The program also had a positive impact on appropriate disciplinary practices and parent–child relationships. Using the Strengths and Difficulties Questionnaire (Goodman, 1997), the study also found that the children in the MAPP counties reported better social and emotional outcomes and fewer behavioral problems. Specifically, the program reduced the incidence of children scoring within the borderline/abnormal range regarding emotional symptoms, conduct problems, and hyperactivity. Thus, overall the results from the population study supported the efficacy of Triple P in the Midlands, Ireland.

KEY IMPLEMENTATION ISSUES

The normalizing and destigmatizing of participation in a parenting program took longer than anticipated, which translated into slower-than-expected recruitment. However, this foundational work was essential, and the partnership needed to trust in the process. The MoU was essential in building the fit between partners' own values and ethos and that of the partnership. Organizational readiness was key in both the initial development of the partnership and the ongoing monitoring of the partnership. This process looked at fit, feasibility, commitments, implementation support, and resources. The partners appreciated that there was a structured process in place to develop practitioner confidence and competence, elements that included codelivery, mentoring, peer support and learning community.

The process for selecting staff to deliver the program was a motivating factor for the partner organizations. The latter commended the pretraining interviews to ensure that the right people were selected to deliver the program in terms of their commitment, motivation, support from their organization, and capacity to deliver on an ongoing basis. The provision of implementation support from the core team was another important element for partner organizations, the partners identified this support structure as a major factor in their initial and ongoing involvement. The high-quality support included training, core team meetings, mentoring, peer support meetings and quality assurance. This was a welcome divergence from the traditional "train-and-hope" approach. A number of the partners were initially concerned that Triple P was a universal program, whereas their previous focus was typically targeted on disadvantaged groups. Through the mix of the partnership members and the varying levels of Triple P provided, all groups of families from early intervention to targeted groups were accommodated, and partnership members were able to proactively target specific groups within the population approach.

IMPLICATIONS AND FUTURE DIRECTIONS

The relevance of the partnership and core team model has been evidenced by the expansion of delivery in both depth and breadth, that is, from two to four counties and expansion in age range from children younger than 8 to children younger than 15 years. The partnership contributes to normalizing and destigmatizing attendance at Triple P courses, and this maximizes the potential for social inclusion of parents across the population. Maintaining high-quality delivery requires ongoing review of implementation practices and outcomes by both MAPP and the core team.

The model needs to continually evolve in response to changes in the environment, policy initiatives, public sector priorities, changing needs of partner organizations and changing needs of parents and families. Parents have indicated that they value this service, they promote it among their peers, and they share the knowledge and skills gained thus illustrating the adoption of the key principles of Triple P. These principles have also proved essential to successful implementation by practitioners and their partner organizations.

KEY MESSAGES

- A partnership that focuses on the enabling environment and a core team that drives local implementation facilitates quality delivery, reach, scaling up and sustainability.
- The partnership and core team model benefit from routinely auditing decision-making practices and procedures against the principles of self-regulation, minimal sufficiency, and outcomes focus.
- The partnership and core team are continually evolving and need to respond to changes and lessons learned from ongoing review of implementation and outcomes.

ACKNOWLEDGMENTS

The MAPP partners are Tusla Child and Family Agency; HSE Health and Wellbeing and Primary Care Directorates; Athlone Community Services; Athlone Education Centre; Barnardos; Carrick on Shannon Education Centre; Longford Community Resources; Longford Vocational Education Committee; Westmeath County Childcare Committee; Westmeath Community Development; Laois Offaly Parents First; Arden View Family Resource Centre; Laois Offaly Education Training Board; Laois Partnership Company; Offaly Local Development Company; and Foroige. We also thank Professor Danny Perkins, Pennsylvania State University; Jacquie Brown, Triple P International; Dr. Phil Jennings, Expert Advisory Committee; National University of Ireland Galway; Centre for Effective Services; and Jane Clarke

REFERENCES

Bayer, J. K., Hiscock, H., Ukoumunne, O. C., Price, A., & Wake, M. (2008). Early childhood aetiology of mental health problems: A longitudinal population-based study. *Journal of Child Psychology and Psychiatry, 49,* 1166–1174. doi:10.1111/j.1469-7610.2008.01943.x

Committee on Children and Young People. (2009). *Children and young people aged 9–14 years in NSW: The missing middle* (Vol. 1). Sydney, Australia: New South Wales Parliament.

Department of Children and Youth Affairs. (2014). *Better outcomes brighter futures: The national policy framework for children and young people 2014—2020.* Dublin, Ireland: Stationery Office.

Department of Health. (2013). *Healthy Ireland: A framework for improved health and wellbeing 2013—2025.* Dublin, Ireland: Department of Health.

Fixsen, D. L., Naoom, S. F., Blase, K. A., Friedman, R. M., & Wallace, F. (2005). *Implementation research: A synthesis of the literature* (FMHI Publication 231). Tampa, FL: National Implementation Research Network.

Health Service Executive. (2011). *The health promotion strategic framework*. Dublin, Ireland: HSE National Health Promotion Office.

Kato, N., Yanagawa, T., Fujiwara, T., & Morawska, A. (2015). Prevalence of children's mental health problems and the effectiveness of population-level family interventions. *Journal of Epidemiology, 25*, 507–516. doi:10.2188/jea.JE20140198

Nixon, E. (2012). *Growing up in Ireland—How families matter for social and emotional outcomes of 9-year-old children*. Dublin, Ireland: Department of Children and Youth Affairs.

Owens, C., Heavey, K., Hegarty, M., Clarke, J., Burke, K., & Owens, S. (2016). *Triple-P-Implementation-Guide*. Athlone, Ireland: Midland Area Parenting Partnership. Retrieved from http://www.mapp.ie

Prinz, R. J., Sanders, M. R., Shapiro, C. J., Whitaker, D. J., & Lutzker, J. R. (2016). Addendum to "Population-Based Prevention of Child Maltreatment: The US Triple P System Population Trial." *Prevention Science, 17*, 410–416. doi:10.1007/s10935-008-0139-7

Sanders, M. R., Kirby, J. N., Tellegen, C. L., & Day, J. J. (2014). The Triple P—Positive Parenting Program: A systematic review and meta-analysis of a multi-level system of parenting support. *Clinical Psychology Review, 34*, 337–357. doi:10.1016/j.cpr.2014.04.003

Sanders, M. R., Ralph, A., Sofronoff, K., Gardiner, P., Thompson, R., Dwyer, S., & Bidwell, K. (2008). Every family: A population approach to reducing behavioral and emotional problems in children making the transition to school. *Journal of Primary Prevention, 29*, 197–222. doi:10.1007/s10935-008-0139-7

Shonkoff, J. P., & Garner, A. S. (2012). The lifelong effects of early childhood adversity and toxic stress. *Pediatrics, 129*, e232–e246. doi:10.1542/peds.2011-2663

CHAPTER 41

SUPPORTING FAMILIES OF CHILDREN WITH A DISABILITY

KATE SOFRONOFF, KYLIE M. GRAY, STEWART L. EINFELD, AND BRUCE J. TONGE

INTRODUCTION AND BACKGROUND

Developmental disabilities (DDs) refers to a range of enduring neurodevelopmental conditions that begin in early childhood (American Association on Intellectual and Developmental Disabilities, 2010). They include intellectual disability (ID), defined as deficits in adaptive behavior and more than two standard deviations below the mean IQ of the community (i.e., IQ below 70), and autism spectrum disorders (ASDs) that also demonstrate impairments in cognitive functioning and adaptive behavior.

THE MAJOR HEALTH PROBLEM OF DEVELOPMENTAL DISABILITY

In high-income countries, DDs adversely affect at least 3% of children (Maulik, Mascarenhas, Mathers, Dua, & Saxena, 2011). The prevalence is higher in poorer countries with higher rates of poor antenatal care and birth complications. Prevalence estimates do not include all of the approximately 1% of children with an ASD (Williams, MacDermot, Ridley, Glasson, & Wray, 2008). Internationally, there are marked inequalities in health care, education, welfare services, and community participation for people with ID. Approximately 7.3% of children under the age of 18 years are reported to have a disability as defined under the Disability Discrimination Act in the United Kingdom, with the implications for families described to include social isolation, financial hardship (Blackburn, Spencer, & Read, 2010), and more negative outcomes for siblings (Giallo & Gavidia-Payne, 2006). Using a comprehensive definition of DDs (including, e.g., attention deficit hyperactivity disorder, autism, learning disabilities), data from the US National Health Interview Surveys identified a rate of 14% of children aged 3–17 years (Boyle et al., 2011). Irrespective of definition, it is clear that a significant number of children and their families are affected by child DDs.

THE MAJOR MENTAL HEALTH PROBLEM OF DEVELOPMENTAL DISABILITY

Mental health problems refer to a clinically significant disturbance of emotions, mood, or thought, which can affect behavior and cause distress for the person or those around them. Young people with DDs have been found to have levels of mental health problems approximately three to four times higher than typically developing children (Einfeld, Ellis, & Emerson, 2011; Einfeld & Tonge, 1996). The Australian Child to Adult Development (ACAD) study, which commenced in 1990, is a longitudinal representative cohort study focusing on the mental health of over 800 young people with DDs (Einfeld et al., 2006; Einfeld & Tonge, 1996). It is representative, especially with respect to those with moderate, severe, and profound levels of ID, and has retained 80% of the original participants. The major findings of the ACAD study, which are likely to reflect the natural history of psychopathology in young people with a DD, are as follows:

- Rates of clinically significant mental health problems three to four times higher than in the general population are evident from early childhood. This finding was confirmed in other studies, for example, in the United Kingdom by Emerson, Einfeld, and Stancliffe (2010).
- These mental health problems persist if untreated through young adulthood, declining only slightly over this period.
- Parental mental ill health and stress correlate more closely with the severity of the child's behavioral and emotional disturbance than it does with the severity of the child's ID.
- Gender and severity of DD explain only a small part of the variance in psychopathology.
- Only 10% of the ACAD cohort received any specialist intervention for their mental health problems.

An understanding of the nature and symptoms of the mental health and emotional and behavioral problems in children and adolescents with a DD, which are common across all causes of DD, can be grouped according to factor analysis of the Developmental Behaviour Checklist (Einfeld & Tonge 1995). Examples are "disruptive" behaviors, such as hitting, biting, absconding, tantrums; "self-absorbed" behaviors, such as head banging, rocking, intolerance of change; "communication disturbances," such as talking aloud to self, preoccupations; "anxiety" symptoms, such as intolerance of being alone, phobias, nightmares; and "social 'relating' problems," such as not showing affection and resisting cuddling.

THE COSTS OF CARE

Mental ill health in association with DD is a major cause of failure of community residential placement (Bruininks, Hill, & Morreau, 1988) and reduced occupational opportunity in the postschool period (Anderson, Lakin, Hill, & Chen, 1992) and leads to major restrictions in participation in recreational and educational programs (Parmenter, Einfeld, Tonge, & Dempster, 1998). The family impact of a child with a disability is compounded by additional emotional and behavioral problems that frequently lead to high levels of parental stress, which impairs parents' capacity to interact optimally with the child. Parental mental health is more closely linked to the severity of the child's mental health problems than it is to the severity of the child's disability (Gray et al., 2011; Tonge & Einfeld, 2003). Distress among mothers has been linked to many adverse outcomes for children, including less-than-optimal parenting, failure to engage with services, decisions to seek out-of-home placement for the child, impeded child development, and higher rates of child psychopathology and antisocial behavior (Llewellyn, McConnell, Thompson, & Whybrow, 2005).

EARLY INTERVENTION THROUGH PARENTING PROGRAMS

Given the substantial evidence (e.g., from the ACAD study) that increased levels of behavioral problems in this population are evident from age 4, early intervention is vital. Parenting a child with a DD is complex because, apart from emerging behavior problems, the child often has delays and complications with developmental skills such as toileting, mobility, social, and language development. Early behavioral difficulties escalate and become increasingly complex, often leading to increasing burden of care. Therefore, it is crucial that parents of a child with DD have the understanding and skills necessary to introduce healthy and adaptive behavior patterns early in the life of their child.

A potential approach to intervening early is through provision of parenting programs (Prinz, Sanders, Shapiro, Whitaker, & Lutzker, 2009; Tonge et al., 2006), which have the potential to provide these skills and ameliorate some of the child and parent risk factors. Research findings from several studies demonstrated that there is a significant reduction in parent stress and an increase in self-efficacy gained through parents learning to manage behavioral and emotional problems in children with a DD (Sofronoff & Farbotko, 2002; Tonge et al., 2006; Whittingham, Sofronoff, Sheffield, & Sanders, 2009). However, traditional clinical models of service delivery reach relatively few families. The 6%–8% that do access parenting programs do not access evidence-based programs (Sanders et al., 1999). The percentage of parents with a child with a DD who receive an evidence-based parenting program has to date been largely confined to participants in efficacy trials (Tonge et al., 2006; Whittingham et al., 2009). A population approach is required to ensure that more parents can access parenting programs and to achieve a population-level reduction in the prevalence of social, emotional, and behavioral problems in children with DDs.

A POPULATION APPROACH

In a population approach, evidenced-based interventions are made available to all who choose to access them. This usually requires the intervention to be offered across multiple sites and by many different practitioners (e.g., in education, health, or disability sectors and nongovernment organizations [NGOs]). With respect to parenting programs, this also requires flexibility of delivery and flexibility of intensity. Most parents of children with a DD who have received a parenting intervention have done so in the context of an efficacy trial. In Australia and worldwide, this is a small number and is woefully inadequate. In the past decade, there have been a number of population-level trials, which have succeeded in delivering parenting programs on a large scale and have demonstrated significant changes in the rates of child maltreatment, reductions in negative parenting practices, and decreased child behavioral and emotional problems (Prinz et al., 2009; Sanders et al., 2008; Zubrick et al., 2005). These trials were all for families of typically developing children.

The benefits of a population approach rather than an approach targeted to families who are identified as experiencing difficulties are many. If programs are offered to every family enrolling a child in a kindergarten or school, for example, then participating is normalized, and any stigma that might occur is reduced or even eliminated. When programs can be accessed through multiple agencies, this will reduce the barriers to attendance for some families who might have competing demands if a program is only offered during school hours. The capacity to offer both light-touch brief interventions as well as longer, more intensive programs ensures that parents can access as much or as little as they require at a time.

THE STEPPING STONES TRIPLE P SYSTEM PROJECT

The Stepping Stones Triple P (SSTP) project was funded by a National Health and Medical Research Council (NHMRC) program grant and aimed to reach a greater proportion of the Australian population of families with children with disabilities in Queensland, Victoria, and New South Wales than any previous trial. The SSTP system of intervention was developed specifically for parents of children with a disability (Chapter 9, this volume; Sanders, Mazzucchelli, & Studman, 2004), has a strong evidence base (Tellegen & Sanders, 2013), has multiple levels of intensity from light touch to more intensive, and has the capacity to "go to scale"—that is, be rolled out across a large community (Mazzucchelli & Sanders, 2011).

The project began with a large survey for parent and practitioner (the *My Say* survey) that aimed to access information about the lived experience of raising a child with a disability and the capacity of practitioners to offer parenting support. Engagement with providers in health, education, disability, and the nongovernmental sector was essential, and many of these organizations became partners in the project. The engagement process began as a top-down approach to government representatives and senior advisors in health, education, and disability organizations and NGOs, with both local and national advisory groups being formed. This process was used to ensure the engagement of consumers by including an active consumer perspective into project design, delivery, and quality assurance (see Chapter 4, this volume). The advisory group assisted with access to the next levels of various organizations, who in turn directed us to schools, departments, and agencies that dealt directly with parents of children with disabilities.

The engagement process then became a bottom-up approach as we spoke directly with professionals who would potentially be interested in receiving training in SSTP and delivering the programs to parents. This approach is essential to ensure that the program meets the needs of the agencies, of the professionals, and of the parent communities. Relationships are forged that increase the likelihood of sustainability following the trial (Sanders & Kirby, 2015).

A website was created to support media outreach to both parents and professionals to provide information about the availability of parenting programs and to match parents with professionals. Many informational resources, such as posters, flyers, and booklets, were created (both electronic and hard copy) to allow professionals to engage with parents. Initially, this was aimed at engaging parents to participate in the survey and later to inform parents about Stepping Stones seminars and programs that they could attend. Professionals were selected to participate in training on the basis of their stated capacity to deliver programs to parents and to ensure a mix of urban and regional professionals. In all instances, the line managers within agencies were asked to sign a memorandum of understanding to indicate their support for the delivery of the program.

Taking a population approach also means that we needed to evaluate the success of the project in a different way from a typical trial. In the SSTPS project, we are using the RE-AIM (Reach, Efficacy, Adoption, Implementation, and Maintenance) framework (Glasgow, Vogt, & Boles, 1999). This framework evaluates the capacity to disseminate an evidence-based program to the population for which it has been developed. In using this framework, we are interested in the extent to which we can reach an adequate proportion of the population of target families; how successful the program is when implemented; the proportion of agencies and departments currently working with the families that adopt the program; the extent to which the program is implemented as intended; and the extent to which the outcomes from the program can be maintained both for individual families and for agencies after the trial is completed.

OUTCOMES FROM THE PARENT MY SAY SURVEY

Parents of children aged 2–10 years with a DD with or without ID in Victoria and Queensland (Australia) were invited to participate in a survey (My Say survey). The My Say survey was advertised through schools, early intervention centers, organizations that provided services and supports to children with disabilities, and parent support and advocacy groups. Parents completed a measure of behavioral and emotional problems, the Developmental Behaviour Checklist. Parents of children aged 4 and above completed the Developmental Behaviour Checklist–Parent/Carer version (DBC-P; Einfeld & Tonge, 1995), scored on a 0, 1, 2 scale, and parents of children aged under 4 years completed the Developmental Behaviour Checklist–Under 4 (DBC-U4; Gray, Keating, Sweeney, Einfeld, & Tonge, 2012), scored on a 0, 1, 2, 3 scale. Sample demographics for the two states are described in Table 41.1.

Across Victoria and Queensland, a total of 731 parents completed the survey and identified their child as having an ID or DD. Of the total sample, 109 children (14.9%) were under 4 years of age. Sixty-seven percent (n = 492, 67.3%) of parents reported their child had a diagnosis of an ASD, 6.2% (45) fetal alcohol syndrome, 4.8% (35) cerebral palsy, and 3.8% (28) Down syndrome. The Victorian and Queensland samples were comparable in terms of chronological age, gender, proportion of children with a diagnosis of an ASD, and rate of behavior and emotional problems. Overall, the mean age of the sample was 6.07 years (SD = 0.33), and 72.2% of the sample were male. The overall mean behavior problem score, or simply the DBC mean item score (MIS; Taffe, Tonge, Gray, & Einfeld, 2008) on the DBC-P was .66 (SD = 0.32), and 52.5% of the sample scored within the clinical/psychiatric caseness range (Einfeld & Tonge, 1996), indicating significantly high rates of behavior and emotional problems. For the younger children, the MIS was .93 (SD = 0.54), a rate significantly higher than a community sample of young children with developmental delay (Gray et al., 2012). Despite these high rates of parent-reported behavior

Table 41.1: Sample Demographics

	Victoria\n$n = 371$	Queensland\n$n = 360$
Male (%)	72	73
Mean age in years (*SD*)	6.2 (2.3)	5.9 (2.4)
Age range in years	2–10	2–10
ASD (%)	68.7	77.5
Behavior problems mean item score (*SD*)		
4 + years DBC-P	0.63 (0.32)	0.69 (0.32)
<4 years DBC-U4+[a]	0.97 (0.50)	0.89 (0.57)

Note: $N = 731$ with intellectual and developmental disability; $n < 4$ years = 109.

[a]Wider range of scores for less than 4 years group was due to different rating scale of DBC-U4 (0–3 compared to 0–2 of DBC-P).

and emotional problems, only 13.7% (100) of families reported having participated in a parenting program.

HOW TO ACHIEVE A POPULATION APPROACH THAT SERVES FAMILIES WITH A CHILD WITH A DEVELOPMENTAL DISORDER

The predominant models of service for people with a DD with emotional and behavioral problems include specialist services such as expert clinicians (e.g., psychiatrists and psychologists); syndrome-specific clinics; and disability-specific mental health services (e.g., behavior intervention support specialists). While such syndrome- and disability-specific service provisions have advantages, a significant limitation is the capacity to only service a small proportion of people with a DD and emotional and behavioral problems. High costs and reduced family income (Doran, Einfeld, Madden, & Emerson, 2012), long waiting periods, and travel to specialists (Hussain & Tait, 2015) are contributing factors that have an impact on a family's ability to access such services.

To address such limitations in accessing syndrome-specific services, the SSTPS project has developed supplemental materials that are tailored for some common causes of DD. To address issues of access, the project chose to train a broad range of professionals, to offer both light-touch and intensive intervention options, and to offer self-directed and online access to programs.

STEPPING STONES TRIPLE P SYNDROME-SPECIFIC MODULES

While it is evident that many of the behavioral and emotional difficulties seen by parents of children with a DD are common across different syndromes, it is important to acknowledge that some syndromes do bring specific issues that need to be addressed (Table 41.2). Syndrome-specific modules have been developed for seven syndromes: ASD, Down syndrome, fragile X, fetal alcohol spectrum disorder, Williams syndrome, Prader-Willi syndrome, velocardiofacial syndrome/22q deletion syndrome.

Table 41.2: Common Behavioral Phenotypes

Syndrome	Genetic Abnormality	Behavioral Phenotype
Autism spectrum disorder	• Multiple associated gene abnormalities • Increased risk with an affected twin, sibling, family history, complicated birth	• Wide range of IQ, from severe ID to above-average IQ • Core difficulties with social interaction and communication, restricted repetitive and stereotyped patterns of behaviors • Sleep disturbance, motor/gait abnormalities, fussy eating • Comorbid association with tuberous sclerosis, fragile X syndrome, attention deficit hyperactivity disorder, anxiety, depression and obsessive-compulsive disorder in adolescents, and epilepsy (with ID)
Down syndrome	• Trisomy 21 (approximately 1 in 800 births)	• Range of ID, usually moderate to severe • Relatively lower rates of emotional/behavioral problems (20%–30%) • Physical and sensory impairments (e.g., hearing loss or hypothyroidism can produce behavioral disturbance) • Can be stubborn, oppositional, inattentive, distractible, impulsive
Fetal alcohol spectrum disorder	• Maternal alcohol consumption during pregnancy (no safe level of consumption has been determined)	• Wide range of IQ to severe, but most have borderline-mild ID • Frontal lobe difficulties with information processing, response inhibition, language, visual-spatial abilities, learning, memory, processing speed, planning, set shifting, abstract concepts, decision-making, motor skills, adaptive behavior • Behavioral problems with emotion regulation, attention, aggression, hyperactivity, impulsivity, tantrums, anxiety
Fragile X	• Inactivation of *FMR1* gene on X chromosome • Females affected differently due to second active X chromosome	• Mild-to-moderate ID, lower in males, more variable in females • Learning difficulties but better visual and imitation skills • Delayed language development, speech disturbance (e.g., echolalia) • Social anxiety, gaze avoidance • Repetitive mannerisms (e.g., hand flapping)

Table 41.2: Continued

Syndrome	Genetic Abnormality	Behavioral Phenotype
Prader-Willi	• Paternal deletion long arm chromosome 15q13 (70%) or • Maternal disomy chromosome 15 (25%) or a mutation	• Mild-borderline ID • Language/speech problems (e.g., articulation), motor difficulties, specific learning problems • Hyperphagia, food obsession, temper, aggression, defiance, impulsivity • Adolescence/young adults: anxiety, depression, mood fluctuations, psychosis (with maternal disomy) > 60%
Smith Magenis syndrome	Chromosome deletion at 17p11.2	• Moderate ID • Severe behavior disturbance: hyperactivity; impulsiveness; aggression; stereotyped movements (e.g., self-hugging); self-injury (e.g., head banging, nail pulling); insomnia
Williams	• Microdeletion chromosome 7q11.23 (elastin gene)	• Moderate ID • Loquacious, stereotypic phrases but poor comprehension, inattention, visual-spatial, gross and fine motor skill deficits • Tend to be friendly, engaging, and irrepressible but suffer phobias or generalized anxiety • Hyperacusis and insomnia

Each module consists of the following:

- *Parent tip sheet*—provides a brief description of the syndrome, including common challenging behaviors, and gives brief tips or strategies for parents. This was distributed at all levels of SSTP, including seminars.
- *Professional resource sheet*—provides a brief description of the syndrome for professionals and provides details of resources that professionals can access for further information about the syndrome.
- *Strategies table*—outlines the application of the 25 SSTP strategies with families of a child with a specific syndrome. This was used by professionals when delivering Level 3–5 programs to families.

The development of these resources was based on previous successful parenting programs for autism (Tonge et al., 2006), autism-specific approaches to SSTP (Whittingham et al., 2009), and additional input from SSTP program developers. Each component of the module was prepared by research team members and refined by chief and associate investigators expert in each of the syndromes.

HOW SUCCESSFUL HAS THE TRIAL BEEN?

Over a 2-year period in each state at the time of writing, close to 2,500 families with a child with a DD had completed an SSTP program. Parents selected for themselves the type of program that they attended, and a significant majority opted for the lighter-touch 2-hour seminars. This raises an important question about dose; that is, how intensive does a program need to be for it to make a significant difference for a family? The questionnaires completed by parents before and after participating in a program indicated that there are strong effects for child behavioral problems. Parents reported significant reductions in problems, irrespective of whether the parents participated in a light-touch seminar or a more intensive group program and irrespective of whether the child presented with an intellectual impairment or was higher functioning. Parents also reported increased confidence in their ability to manage their child's behavior and increased parental well-being.

The measure used was the Parenting and Family Adjustment Scale (PAFAS; Sanders, Morawska, Haslam, Filus, & Fletcher, 2014), which measures both parenting style (e.g., I argue with my child about their behavior/attitude) and family adjustment (e.g., I cope with the emotional demands of being a parent). The 30-item scale is scored from 0 to 3, with some items reverse scored. Figure 41.1 provides a snapshot of changes reported by parents. These are outcome data from approximately 100 parents in Queensland showing significant improvements in reports of how coercive they were with their children from pre- to postintervention, with that change maintained at follow-up as well as a significant improvement in reports of maladaptive parent adjustment. While their reports of both positive encouragement of their children and consistency of management did not change at postintervention, they were significantly improved by follow-up.

THE ISSUE OF DOSE

As part of the project, we are trying to answer the question, How much extra benefit is gained at higher doses, compared to lower doses? In New South Wales, a defined area (Far North Coast)

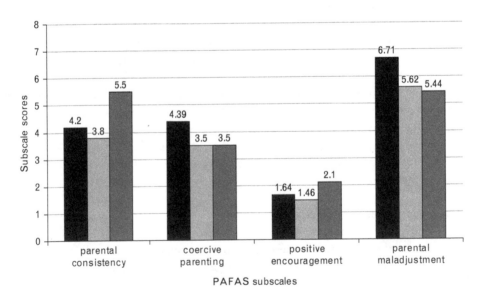

FIGURE 41.1: Outcomes reported by parents (*N* = 100) on the Parent and Family Adjustment Scale (PAFAS), showing darkest = preintervention; lightest = 3 months postintervention; middle grey = 12 months postintervention.

has been selected to receive higher levels of support during the rollout compared to the rest of New South Wales. As part of the standard training process, all professionals trained in SSTP programs receive support to implement Triple P within their organization; training in their selected Triple P course; and access to the Triple P Provider Network. Triple P International also offers a number of enhanced support options, including implementation training days for organizations, managers, and professionals; pre- and posttraining workshops; and clinical support with program delivery. A comparison between these levels of implementation support will be completed. Professionals in the Far North Coast of New South Wales will be allocated to receive all standard and enhanced support options. Professionals in the rest of the state will be allocated to receive only the standard support options.

LESSONS LEARNED

The process of engaging with key stakeholders is time consuming, and forming relationships takes time and patience. When we ask agencies and professionals to consider using a program with which they are not familiar, it is unreasonable to expect that this is a decision that will

---

BOX 41.1: Creating Change and Hope for the Future

Karen is a sole parent with a son Ben, who is 6 years old. Ben has a diagnosis of autism, and he has an intellectual impairment and limited speech. Ben attends a special school, and Karen has a major problem each day in encouraging Ben to enter the school. Ben experiences extreme anxiety and is overcome with terror when approaching the school, with its overwhelming noise and jostling students. The buildup of tension leads each day to Ben having a "meltdown." This looks a lot like a major tantrum, and Karen feels that other parents and children see her son as "naughty" and see her as an incompetent parent. Karen feels as though she is not a good mother. When Ben becomes excited or anxious, he will sometimes run away from Karen, and when she calls to him he will not stop. This has proven dangerous on several occasions when Ben has run in front of cars and into the street.

Karen decided to join a Stepping Stones Triple P parent group as a last resort to managing Ben's behaviors and keeping him safe. She did not really expect that she would learn anything very helpful, but she was prepared to give it a go. The first thing she did learn was that Ben responded extremely well to praise that was reinforced by visual praise cards and accompanied by a firm shoulder squeeze that Ben likes (other children might not like this and need something else). Karen added a visual "Going to School" schedule and backed up Ben's brave behavior with rewards—Pokémon cards are Ben's current fascination. Changes happened slowly, but both Karen and Ben built up their confidence. Karen also used verbal and visual praise and a visual schedule to teach Ben to stop when she asked him to stop. She found that many of the strategies in the Stepping Stones program made sense to her, including the additional parent tip sheet on autism, which was very helpful. In time, she said it was as if she had always known these strategies. Karen now feels that she has what she needs to move forward and teach Ben new skills.

be made quickly. Even when relationships and trust have been built and a program has been accepted, there can be changes in staff that will disrupt delivery, changes in government that have a serious impact on staff within government departments, and changes in policy with respect to funding for families with children with disabilities. These are just some of the difficulties to be faced when trying to introduce a program to a population. Perhaps the most important lesson, however, is that when families receive an evidence-based program, it can provide the basis for positive change and hope for the future (Box 41.1).

KEY MESSAGES

- The delivery of an evidence-based parent education and skills training program for parents of children with any developmental disability as a public health intervention is feasible, but there are barriers to reach and adoption that will be further investigated as the project continues.
- Stepping Stones Triple P (SSTP) is effective as a public health program, with improvements in parental mental health and well-being and improvements in child behavior and adaptation.
- Parents exercise an active choice in their level of involvement in the SSTPS, but any dose effects and benefits of level of therapist support are a focus of further research.
- The process of stakeholder engagement, critical to adoption and implementation, is a focus of ongoing inquiry as the project develops.

ACKNOWLEDGMENTS

We would like to acknowledge funding from the Australian NHMRC program grant (APP1016919) that has allowed this project to take place. Assistance with the chapter has also come from Louise Bezzina and Sian Horstead in New South Wales and Julie Hodges and Martha Schoch in Queensland. We acknowledge the Mental Health of Young People with Developmental Disabilities (MHYPEDD) team, who have worked alongside us for the past 4 years in New South Wales, Queensland, and Victoria.

REFERENCES

American Association on Intellectual and Developmental Disabilities. (2010). *Intellectual disability: Classification and systems of support* (11th ed.). Washington, DC: Author.

Anderson, D., Lakin, K., Hill, B., & Chen, T. (1992). Social integration of older persons with mental retardation in residential facilities. *American Journal on Mental Retardation, 96*, 488–501

Blackburn, C. M., Spencer, N. J., & Read, J. M. (2010). Prevalence of childhood disability and characteristics and circumstances of disabled children in the UK; secondary analysis of the Family Resources Survey. *BMC Pediatrics, 10*, 21. doi:10.1186/1471-2431-10-21

Boyle, C. A., Boulet, S., Schieve, L. A., Cohen, R. A., Blumberg, S. J., Yeargin-Allsopp, M., . . . Kogan, M. D. (2011). Trends in the prevalence of developmental disabilities in US children, 1997–2008. *Pediatrics, 127*, 1034–1041. doi:10.1542/peds.2010-2989

Bruininks, R., Hill, B. K., & Morreau, L. E. (1988). Prevalence and implications of maladaptive behaviours and dual diagnosis in residential and other service programs. In J. A. Stark, F. J. Menolascino, M. H. Albarelli, & V. C. Gray (Eds.), *Mental retardation and mental health* (pp. 3–29). New York, NY: Springer-Verlag.

Doran, C. M., Einfeld, S. L., Madden, R., & Emerson, E. (2012). How much does intellectual disability really cost? First estimates for Australia. *Journal of Intellectual and Developmental Disability, 37*, 42–49. doi:10.3109/13668250.2011.648609

Einfeld, S. L., Piccinin, A. M., Mackinnon, A., Hofer, S. M., Taffe, J., Gray, K. M., . . . Tonge, B. J. (2006). Psychopathology in young people with intellectual disability. *Journal of the American Medical Association, 296*, 1981–1989. doi:10.1001/jama.296.16.1981

Einfeld, S. L., & Tonge, B. J. (1995). The Developmental Behavior Checklist: The development and validation of an instrument to assess behavioral and emotional disturbance in children and adolescents with mental retardation. *Journal of Autism and Developmental Disorders, 25*, 81–104. doi:10.1007/BF02178498

Einfeld, S. L., & Tonge, B. J. (1996). Population prevalence of psychopathology in children and adolescents with intellectual disability: II. Epidemiological findings. *Journal of Intellectual Disability Research, 40*, 99–109. doi:10.1111.1365-2788.1996.tb00611.x

Emerson, E., Einfeld, S. L., & Stancliffe, R. J. (2010). The mental health of young children with intellectual disabilities or borderline intellectual functioning. *Social Psychiatry and Psychiatric Epidemiology, 45*, 579–587. doi:10.1007/s00127-009-0100-y

Giallo, R., & Gavidia-Payne, S. (2006). Child, parent and family factors as predictors of adjustment for siblings of children with a disability. *Journal of Intellectual Disability Research, 50*, 937–948. doi:10.1111/j.1365-2788.2006.00928.x

Glasgow, R. E., Vogt, T. M., & Boles, S. M. (1999). Evaluating the public health impact of health promotion interventions: The RE-AIM framework. *American Journal of Public Health, 89*, 1922–1927. doi:10.2105/AJPH.89.9.1322

Gray, K. M., Keating, C. M., Sweeney, D. J., Einfeld, S. L., & Tonge, B. J. (2012). Examining behaviour and emotional problems in preschool children with developmental delay. *Journal of Intellectual Disability Research, 56*, 695. doi:10.1111/j.1365-2788.2012.01583_5.x

Gray, K. M., Piccinin, A. M., Hofer, S. M., Mackinnon, A., Bontempo, D. E., Einfeld, S. L., & Tonge, B. J. (2011). The longitudinal relationship between behavior and emotional disturbance in young people with intellectual disability and maternal mental health. *Research in Developmental Disabilities, 32*, 1194–1204. doi:10.1016/j.ridd.2010.12.044

Hussain, R., & Tait, K. (2015). Parental perceptions of information needs and service provision for children with developmental disabilities in rural Australia. *Disability and Rehabilitation, 37*, 1609–1616. doi:10.3109/09638288.2014.972586

Llewellyn, G., McConnell, D., Thompson, K., & Whybrow, S. (2005). Out-of-home placement of school-age children with disabilities and high support needs. *Journal of Applied Research in Intellectual Disabilities, 18*, 1–6. doi:10.1111/j.1468-3148.2004.00201.x

Maulik, P. K., Mascarenhas, M. N., Mathers, C. D., Dua, T., & Saxena, S. (2011). Prevalence of intellectual disability: A meta-analysis of population-based studies. *Research in Developmental Disabilities, 32*, 419–436. doi:10.1016/j.ridd.2010.12.018

Mazzucchelli, T. G., & Sanders, M. R. (2011). Preventing behavioural and emotional problems in children who have a developmental disability: A public health approach. *Research in Developmental Disabilities, 32*, 2148–2156. doi:10.1016/j.ridd.2011.07.022

Parmenter, T. R., Einfeld, S. L., Tonge, B. J., & Dempster, J. A. (1998). Behavioural and emotional problems in the classroom of children and adolescents with intellectual disability. *Journal of Intellectual and Developmental* Disabilities, *23*, 71–77. doi:10.1080/13668259800033591

Prinz, R. J., Sanders, M. R., Shapiro, C. J., Whitaker, D. J., & Lutzker, J. R. (2009). Population-based prevention of child maltreatment. *Prevention Science, 10*, 1–12. doi:10.1007/s11121-009-0123-3

Sanders, M. R., & Kirby, J. N. (2015). Surviving or thriving: Quality assurance mechanisms to promote innovation in the development of evidence-based parenting interventions. *Prevention Science, 16*, 421–431. doi:10.1007/s11121-014-0475-1

Sanders, M. R., Mazzucchelli, T. G., & Studman, L. J. (2004). Stepping Stones Triple P: The theoretical basis and development of an evidence-based positive parenting program for families with a child who has a disability. *Journal of Intellectual and Developmental Disability, 29*, 265–283. doi:10.1080/13668250412331285127

Sanders, M. R., Morawska, A., Haslam, D. M., Filus, A., & Fletcher, R. (2014). Parenting and Family Adjustment Scales (PAFAS): Validation of a brief parent-report measure for use in assessment of parenting skills and family relationships. *Child Psychiatry and Human Development, 45*, 255–272. doi:10.1007/s10578-013-0397-3

Sanders, M. R., Ralph, A., Sofronoff, K., Gardiner, P., Thompson, R., Dwyer, S., & Bidwell, K. (2008). Every family: A population approach to reducing behavioral and emotional problems in children making the transition to school. *Journal of Primary Prevention, 29*, 197–222. doi:10.1007/s10935-008-0139-7

Sofronoff, K., & Farbotko, M. (2002). The effectiveness of parent management training to increase self-efficacy in parents of children with Asperger syndrome. *Autism, 6*, 271–286. doi:10.1177/1362361302006003005

Taffe, J. R., Tonge, B. J., Gray, K. M., & Einfeld, S. L. (2008). Extracting more information from behavior checklists by using components of mean based scores. *International Journal of Methods in Psychiatric Research, 17*, 232–240. doi:10.1002/mpr.260

Tellegen, C. L., & Sanders, M. R. (2013). Stepping Stones Triple—P Positive Parenting Program for children with disability: A systematic review and meta-analysis. *Research in Developmental Disabilities, 34*, 1556–1571. doi:10.1016/j.ridd.2013.01.022

Tonge, B., Brereton, A., Kiomall, M., Mackinnon, A., King, N., & Rinehart, N. (2006). Effects on parental mental health of an education and skills training program for parents of young children with autism: A randomized controlled trial. *Journal of the American Academy of Child and Adolescent Psychiatry, 45*, 561–569. doi:10.1097/01.chi.0000205701.48324.26

Tonge, B. J., & Einfeld, S. L. (2003). Psychopathology and intellectual disability. The Australian Child to Adult Longitudinal Study. *International Review of Research in Mental Retardation, 26*, 61–90.

Whittingham, K., Sofronoff, K., Sheffield, J. K., & Sanders, M. R. (2009). Stepping Stones Triple P: A randomized controlled trial with parents of a child diagnosed with an autism spectrum disorder. *Journal of Abnormal Child Psychology, 37*, 469–480. doi:10.1007/s10802-014-9927-0

Williams, K., MacDermot, S., Ridley, G., Glasson, E., & Wray, J. (2008). The prevalence of autism in Australia. Can it be established from existing data? *Journal of Paediatrics and Child Health, 44*, 504–510. doi:10.1111/j.1440-1754.2008.01331.x

Zubrick, S. R., Ward, K. A., Silburn, S. R., Lawrence, D., Williams, A. A., Blair, E., . . . Sanders, M. R. (2005). Prevention of child behaviour problems through universal implementation of a group behavioural family intervention. *Prevention Science, 6*, 287–304. doi:10.1007/s11121-005-0013-2

PROGRAM DEVELOPMENT, QUALITY ASSURANCE, AND INNOVATION

PROGRAM DEVELOPMENT, QUALITY ASSURANCE, AND INNOVATION

An Introduction

TREVOR G. MAZZUCCHELLI

E normous advances have been made in the field of parenting support since the 1980s, and many families are benefitting from evidence-based parenting support (EBPS) programs. However, to remain relevant to the needs of successive generations of families, it is essential that EBPS programs continue to evolve and adapt. Adaptive change will occur if we anticipate, as best we can, the challenges families may encounter in the future and are responsive to the changing ways in which parents would like to receive support. Consideration and planning are also needed to create the conditions that are likely to foster such responsiveness and innovation. This section considers future directions for Triple P and the parenting field more generally.

Ongoing change in the parenting landscape means that parenting programs must continue to evolve to remain relevant. In Chapter 43, Sanders and Kirby describe a quality assurance process that has gradually evolved over the development of the Triple P system to promote innovation and the dissemination of programs that work. They review this multistage program development cycle, from the program build phase through to effectiveness trials and large-scale implementations, highlighting potential pitfalls and how the developers of Triple P have managed them. A crucial phase in this cycle is the building of an evidence base. For a program to be recognized as efficacious and effective, it is essential that supporting research is regarded as trustworthy, reliable, and valid (Flay et al., 2005). Sanders and Kirby explore not only the complementary role that both developer-led and independently led evaluations have in the program development cycle to accomplish this, but also how both forms of evaluation are vulnerable to bias. They make a number of important suggestions for how bias, particularly conflict-of-interest risks, should be managed. The argument is that a clear and well-conceived quality assurance process will promote transparency in the research process and foster innovation and development.

Evidence-based parenting support is recognized as having an important role to play in future services aimed at the promotion of mental health and well-being at a societal level (e.g., Kazdin & Blase, 2011; Patel, Flisher, Hetrick, & McGorry, 2007). In Chapter 44, Sanders revisits the critical issues facing the field of parenting support as it embraces a population approach and seeks to make the model work in practice. Sanders begins by briefly reviewing the case for the adoption of a population approach before exploring a range of broader contextual and logistical issues about the science of parenting and child development that can better inform policy decisions, the professional community, and members of the wider public. He notes that while the tools and know-how required for a population approach to parenting currently exist, there is a need for effective policy support from government for this approach to be fully realized. To support the case, he addresses common misunderstandings and objections, for instance, that there is a need for more evidence for a population approach, that a population approach means inappropriately endorsing just one program, that it is too expensive, or that it could result in a number of negative societal outcomes, such as creating unnecessary stress in parents or widening social inequalities.

Innovation has characterized the field of behavioral family intervention since its inception. In Chapter 45, Sanders, Turner, and Mazzucchelli reflect on the significance of the various innovations that have occurred over the past three decades as the Triple P system and the field of EBPS have evolved. One of the most transformational of these has been the shift from a focus on developing and testing individual clinical treatments for high-risk or vulnerable children with disruptive behavior problems to a much more expansive focus on prevention, specifically the development of a population-based system of parenting support. Integral to this has been the development of a multilevel system of parenting support that is efficient, reduces the risk of dependency by parents, and ensures a good ecological fit with existing service systems. Despite these advances, Sanders and his colleagues note that there is still much that can be done to progress the field and yield greater benefit to families and communities. For instance, although many of the innovations over the past few decades have resulted in increased reach and enhanced engagement by parents, fathers and disadvantaged and vulnerable parents continue to be underrepresented. At present, most parenting programs focus on the preschool and school years, but there is the potential for parenting support to benefit families beyond this period. Parenting programs also have the potential to play an important role in addressing problems associated with sustainable development that are of global significance. Crucially, this chapter concludes by considering the optimal conditions for fostering the innovation and development that is needed if EBPS is going to realize its potential in further shaping society for the better.

In Chapter 46, Sanders turns to the future of EBPS, discussing challenges that need to be addressed to strengthen the impact of a population approach. These challenges include the need to increase the evidence base for a population approach while managing unavoidable conflicts of interest that arise from program developers being involved in evaluation trials, changing professional and public attitudes to parenting to increase receptivity to parenting support, undertaking research to further improve the quality of parenting techniques and interventions, and how best to support vulnerable and disadvantaged families who are less likely to benefit from EBPS. Sanders anticipates both challenges and opportunities for the provision of parenting support in the future as a result of demographic changes, consumers being better informed about the benefits of high-quality parenting programs, and the increased availability of universal parenting support. Sanders concludes by suggesting a range of future research directions, from expanding the theoretical basis of the Triple P system to incorporating the child's perspective on parenting.

Progress in the field of EBPS has been substantial; a great many families around the world have benefited, and developers, practitioners, and policymakers have much to be proud of, but we must not become complacent. Parenting interventions have the potential to make a major contribution to the long-term mental and physical health and well-being of children, adults, and communities. Further, because of the fundamental role parents have in shaping children's beliefs, values, and competencies, parenting programs could also play a role in the resolution of many other problems of global significance. The directions for future research and development are clear, and given Triple P and the field's history of innovation, there are good reasons to be optimistic that in the future the power of positive parenting will indeed transform the lives of all children, parents, and communities.

REFERENCES

Flay, B. R., Biglan, A., Boruch, R. F., Castro, F. G., Gottfredson, D., Kellam, S., . . . Ji, P. (2005). Standards of evidence: Criteria for efficacy, effectiveness and dissemination. *Prevention Science, 6*, 151–175. doi:10.1007/s11121-005-5553-y

Kazdin, A. E., & Blase, S. L. (2011). Rebooting psychotherapy research and practice to reduce the burden of mental illness. *Perspectives on Psychological Science, 6*, 21–37. doi:10.1177/1745691610393527

Patel, V., Flisher, A. J., Hetrick, S., & McGorry, P. (2007). Mental health of young people: A global public-health challenge. *Lancet, 369*, 1302–1313. doi:10.1016/S0140-6736(07)60368-7

CHAPTER 43

QUALITY ASSURANCE AND PROGRAM DEVELOPMENT

MATTHEW R. SANDERS AND JAMES N. KIRBY

To remain relevant to the needs of contemporary parents, parenting programs need to evolve and be "refreshed." A variety of innovations or adaptations in both the content and the process of delivering interventions have taken place within the Triple P system. These innovations and adaptations have evolved in the context of seeking better solutions to unmet needs faced by particular client groups or challenges practitioners face in implementing programs to service those needs.

This chapter focuses on the importance of having a continuous quality assurance (QA) process to ensure the continued success of programs. The ongoing search for better solutions to child problems continues to inspire Triple P program developers and researchers to develop and test new solutions for an increasingly wide range of problems, confirming the robustness of the intervention model and its core principles based on social learning theory, cognitive-behavioral principles, self-regulation, and behavior change techniques. We recently described a conceptual framework for program adaptation and innovation (Sanders & Kirby, 2014) to help guide the research and development process from initial theory building to scaling up of interventions for wide-scale sustained dissemination and implementation (Axford & Morpeth, 2013; Hodge & Turner, 2016). This chapter extends that earlier work by describing a QA process that can be used by program developers to facilitate program innovation. We describe a 10-stage research and development cycle that has informed the development of Triple P. Using the Triple P system as the exemplar, we illustrate how the model can be applied continuously from initial program development and program adaptation to global international dissemination to ensure the program is ready for dissemination and can benefit as many families as possible.

THE PROGRAM DEVELOPMENT PROCESS AND THE ROLE OF DEVELOPERS

Quality assurance refers to the process used to create and maintain reliable standards of deliverables. QA relates to activities before production work begins and is typically performed while the product is being developed (Crosby, 1984). In contrast, quality control (QC) procedures refer to quality-related activities used to verify that deliverables are of acceptable quality and that they are complete and correct (Stein & Heikkinen, 2009). QC activities are performed after the product is developed. In the context of developing an intervention program designed to solve a specific problem, an iterative process entailing both QA and QC steps is needed to ensure that the program meets the quality standards increasingly demanded by the field of prevention science.

PHASES IN THE DEVELOPMENT PROCESS

Recently, we developed a pragmatic model, depicted in Figure 43.1, to assist in the development, testing, and subsequent dissemination of our parenting work involving the Triple P system (Sanders & Kirby, 2014). This model guides both the QA and QC procedures used in the ongoing development of interventions. Iteration in the model is shown by the two double-headed arrows that guide program developers from theory building to eventual dissemination and implementation. The model is iterative in that each step builds on the previous step and incorporates the views of end users (practitioners and agencies) and consumers (parents and children) regarding the appropriateness, feasibility, cultural relevance, and usefulness of the intervention.

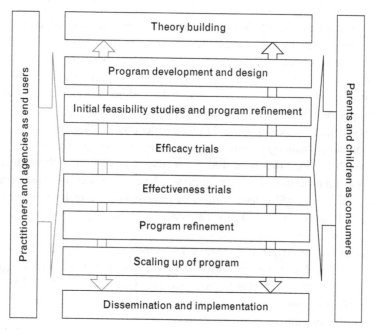

FIGURE 43.1: Iterative 10-step model for program design, evaluation, and dissemination.

As part of the iterative process program, developers need to be attuned to the changing ecological context within which the program would be deployed. The development process, which is outlined in Figure 43.1, may seem time consuming by service systems seeking to access programs rapidly. However, a balance is needed between meeting service system demands for programs that work with the need to develop a credible evidence base to justify the dissemination and scaling up of interventions (Winston & Jacobsohn, 2010). A clearly defined pragmatic framework facilitates program development, evaluation, and translation, enabling greater transparency and efficiency. The pressure to disseminate programs prematurely with insufficient evidence can do more harm than good and does a disservice to parents, children, and the community.

BUILDING A THEORETICAL BASIS FOR AN INTERVENTION

For interventions to work, they need to be built from solid theoretical foundations. These foundations include having a clear theoretical framework that informs the specific types of intervention procedures used and the development of component parts of the intervention. Although the most effective parenting interventions, including the Triple P system, evolved from a common social learning, cognitive-behavioral, and functional analysis framework, some programs also incorporate principles and procedures drawn from other theories, including attachment theory, developmental theory, and cognitive social learning and self-regulation theory and public health models of intervention (Sanders, 2012; Webster-Stratton, 1998).

PROGRAM DEVELOPMENT AND DESIGN

Impetus for considering an adaptation of an existing program or new program can stem from a variety of sources, including epidemiological studies (where available) that help define the extent of the problem in populations of interest. A systematic review that identifies current prevention and treatment programs for the problem is useful to identify potentially modifiable protective and risk factors. Research on cultural diversity and implications of cultural differences relevant to a program help to identify implementation challenges in working with target groups (Morawska, Haslam, Milne, & Sanders, 2011). Consumer preference surveys can be used to garner information about challenges, concerns, needs, and preferences of target groups (Sanders, Baker, & Turner, 2012). Finally, several studies have used focus groups with the intended population of interest and professionals to help improve "the ecological fit" of a new program to the target population. A further QA step is to develop intervention manuals for use in pilot studies (Chambless & Ollendick, 2001). At this early stage, it is critical to reach agreement regarding authorship and to avoid subsequent disputes.

In our center, as the Triple P system of interventions is owned by The University of Queensland, all staff and students working on Triple P projects are required to assign copyright of any new Triple P program materials to the University of Queensland. This policy ensures that a program can be disseminated under an existing licensing and publication agreement between the university and a dissemination organization.

INITIAL FEASIBILITY TESTING AND PROGRAM REFINEMENT

Pilot Studies

Once an intervention protocol has been developed, and before it is subjected to further evaluation through randomized clinical trials, it is useful to pilot test the actual protocols, including all materials, with individual cases or, more formally, using controlled single-case or intrasubject replication designs (Baer, Wolf, & Risley, 1968). Initial feasibility testing is the first opportunity to apply QC procedures to the developed intervention. The advantage of this early QC step is that the likely effects of the intervention can be determined, including the extent to which change occurs on primary outcome measures, the timing of observed changes (rapid or gradual), and whether changes across different outcome variables are synchronous or desynchronous (Kazdin & Nock, 2003).

Pilot studies also afford program developers the opportunity to learn how the program is received by the end users (e.g., practitioners and agencies), as well as consumers (parents and children). This can be achieved through including focus groups or questionnaires as part of the pilot trial aimed at examining whether the program is deemed acceptable, culturally appropriate, usable, and useful. Furthermore, during the initial feasibility testing the developer is alerted to any implementation difficulties, including process issues, timing of program activities, consumer acceptability and appropriateness of materials, and the sequencing of within-session tasks and exercises (Kazdin & Nock, 2003).

Program Refinement

After the initial feasibility testing, the first opportunity arises for program developers to refine the program in light of the obtained results from the quantitative and qualitative feedback. This might require modifications to specific program content and delivery to assist with successful implementation. For example, the steps outlined in protocol adherence checklists might need to be further detailed to best measure program fidelity.

EFFICACY TRIALS

Efficacy trials refer to the beneficial effects of a program under optimal conditions of delivery (Flay et al., 2005). After initial feasibility testing and program refinement, the developed program should then be evaluated in a randomized controlled trial, which is commonly implemented by the program developers—this is also referred to as the "proof-of-concept" phase (Valentine et al., 2011). The foundation trial should follow best practice guidelines such as those detailed by CONSORT (Consolidated Standards of Reporting Trials; Altman et al., 2001). Efficacy trials also permit the opportunity to examine the potential mediators, as well as the obtained behavioral outcomes of the intervention. In determining the impact that a certain variable (e.g., participation in a Triple P program) has on the outcome of interest (e.g., changes in parental behavior), it is important to examine not only the direct relationship between the two variables but also any mediation or moderation that occurs as a result of other variables, such as changes in parental stress, parental adjustment, or parental self-efficacy.

EFFECTIVENESS TRIALS

Programs that are disseminated need to be robust in terms of everyday service delivery circumstances (Hodge & Turner, 2016). Among prevention scientists, effectiveness trials refer to the effects a program achieves under real-world conditions (Flay et al., 2005). Effectiveness trials specifically permit the exploration of program outcomes when delivered as part of usual service delivery in community settings. Through effectiveness trials, programs can be assessed for their robustness, and implementation enablers and barriers can be identified (Flay et al., 2005). Effectiveness trials also provide an opportunity to conduct the first cost-effectiveness analysis on the program. Specific programs within the Triple P system of interventions have had numerous effectiveness, service-based, and cost-effectiveness–based evaluations, for example, the Level 4 Group Triple P program (e.g., Gallart & Matthey, 2005).

PROGRAM REFINEMENT

Each time an intervention is evaluated, an opportunity is created to revise, reflect, or refine intervention protocols. It is rare for trial prototypes of clinical procedures not to require further refinement before wider dissemination (Chambless & Ollendick, 2001). This process involves soliciting feedback from clients and practitioners concerning their experience of the program, including the readability of any written material, the relevance and usefulness of examples used, the types of activities involved, and the appropriateness and authenticity of video material (Winston & Jacobsohn, 2010).

SCALING UP INTERVENTIONS FOR DISSEMINATION

Dissemination refers to the process of taking evidence-based interventions from the research laboratory and delivering them to the community (Sanders, 2012). Dissemination requires a well-developed set of consumer materials or resources (such as manuals, workbooks, and DVDs), as well as professional training programs to train practitioners to deliver the intervention. A common problem faced by program developers when scaling up an intervention is that it can be difficult to do so in a university context that prioritizes research and teaching. Consulting with a university's technology transfer operation (TTO) to formalize an agreement concerning intellectual property rights and license arrangements with organizations (purveyors) with capacity to manage the dissemination process can overcome this obstacle. Depending on the agreement reached, the dissemination organization may then become responsible for the dissemination process, which includes publishing resources and materials, providing video production, delivering professional training, providing program consultation and technical support, and meeting QA standards and QC measures in the delivery of the intervention.

If a program developer does not have a dissemination partner, it can be helpful to contact the TTO. In many universities, the TTO can be a valuable business development resource in seeking potential partners and negotiating terms prior to agreements being put in place. The process can be time consuming, and a good TTO can provide business skills to compliment the academic scientific and clinical knowledge.

Universities differ widely in their level of coordination, resourcing, and focus on commercialization. Regardless, successful long-term relationships between program developers and purveyors requires a multidiscipline, commercial, strategic, and coordinated approach. From business development and due diligence activities, to tactical negotiation and drafting of complex legal agreements, as well as ongoing relationship and intellectual management, the pathway can be long and bumpy—and can lead to many dead ends before hitting on the desired destination.

Key characteristics of a suitable purveyor include the capability to undertake global business development, respect for adhering to and enforcing the fidelity requirements of developers, and adapting to changes in those requirements as required. A purveyor needs a commitment to a long-term relationship and access to additional investment to further the implementation and research agenda. The purveyor really needs an entrepreneurial approach. However, the relationship needs constant nurturing, not a "set-and-forget" approach. This involves continual maintenance, negotiation, and open communication. In most cases, a commercialization partner is embarking on a significant risk as it is likely that there is no existing well-established market for the intervention.

Determining the Costs and Benefits of Interventions

Cost-effectiveness analyses should be conducted before scaling up and translating evidence-based programs to systems (Little, 2010). Cost-effectiveness analyses can influence whether policymakers and other potential systems will adopt the program, as they need to know if investment in the program will have financial benefits for their constituency. Parenting interventions tend to fare well in cost–benefit analyses. For example, Aos et al. (2011) conducted a careful economic analysis of the costs and benefits of implementing the Triple P system using only indices of improvement on rates of child maltreatment (out-of-home placements and rates of abuse and neglect). Their findings showed that, for an estimated total intervention cost of $137 per family, if only 10% of parents received Triple P, there would be a positive benefit of $1,237 per participant, with a benefit-to-cost ratio of $9.22. The benefit-to-cost ratio would be even higher when higher rates of participation were modeled.

Cost–benefit considerations should also be incorporated at the program development stage. If the costs of developing and trialing a program are too high, the proceeds from the dissemination may never actually recover the initial investment costs.

DISSEMINATION AND IMPLEMENTATION

An implementation framework is needed to disseminate a program effectively. This includes engaging with systems and potential partners, developing contracts and commitments from partners to meet desired goals, developing the plan for implementation with the target system, and building training and accreditation days into the system. An implementation framework has been developed by purveyors for the Triple P system (McWilliam, Brown, Sanders, & Jones, 2016). The framework includes a range of specific tools for use by program consultants working with agencies to guide each stage of the implementation process (e.g., how to conduct line manager briefing, how to estimate population reach from different levels of investment in training).

In our efforts to disseminate Triple P internationally, we have always sought to encourage others to establish a local evidence base at the site where the program is being implemented. For example, we have collaborated with many institutions to identify interested and competent researchers to conduct local evaluations of specific programs of the Triple P system to help build a local evidence base. Sustainability is not only more likely with local evidence of impact but also strategic alliances can be built to increase the total pool of researchers around the world, contributing to the cumulative evidence base on parenting programs. Such an approach ensures that the program is responsive to local needs, fosters a spirit of openness and critical evaluation, and builds the local partnerships needed to sustain an intervention (Sanders, 2012). To maintain the local community of providers and researchers, it is useful to create links to the broader research community through international conferences (e.g., the Helping Families Change Conference— the biennial international conference for Triple P) and international networks (e.g., the Triple P Research Network, http://www.tprn.net) to further facilitate continued research collaborations and investments.

POTENTIAL RISKS AND MANAGEMENT OF RISKS

There are many potential risks that can occur across the program development cycle; however, two important areas that need attention are (a) managing developer-led and independently led evaluations and (b) managing conflicts of interest (COIs).

When building an evidence base for any field of research (e.g., parenting interventions) or specific programs within a field of research (e.g., Triple P), there is a complementary need for both developer-led and independently led evaluations. However, determining what constitutes a developer-led or independently led evaluation is more complicated than it appears. It is important to operationally define the two roles and then examine how the roles complement each other. Program developers are individuals who initiate the original idea and develop the program. Program developers may or may not own the program through a copyright agreement, a license agreement, or some form of intellectual property protection. It is common for employers to claim ownership of the copyright for a program. Developer-led research occurs when the program developers then evaluate the developed program (Sherman & Strang, 2009). Within the field of psychological intervention, program developers are most often involved in the early evaluation of interventions and provide the foundational evidence for the program (Sanders, 2015). In these early stages of evaluation, program developers must ensure that the evidence supporting the practice is reliable, robust, and transparent and is conducted in a manner that minimizes the potential for bias. Once proof-of-concept evidence is achieved (Valentine et al., 2011), program developers move toward replication research, and this is where the complementary process of independent evaluations is most valuable.

Independently led research is difficult to define. Independently led research occurs when the program developer is not involved in any stage of the research and is not an author on the subsequent publication. Typically, the research is conducted at an institution independent of the program developer. Many factors need to be considered when determining whether a study is independently led, including who conducted the study; where the study was conducted; who funded the study; who were the contributing authors and at which institution; who was responsible for the conceptual design of the study, measure selection, analysis, write-up, and interpretation of findings; and whether the developer or organization providing approved training of staff was consulted during the evaluation process.

Independent evaluations are important for several reasons, as they are a form of replication research. They help control for COI and some forms of bias and help identify issues or problems with program implementation. Commonly, independent evaluations may be conducted under more heterogeneous conditions, therefore providing a useful test of the robustness of the intervention effects (Sherman & Strang, 2009). One argument for independent evaluations pertains to the management of potential COIs, either financially or ideologically, that can occur when program developers are the leads on evaluation trials (Eisner, 2009). Therefore, it is important for evaluations that are developer led to include mechanisms designed to avoid or minimize bias. Such safeguards comprise, but are not limited to, including COI statements in publications, registering trials on clinical databases prospectively (e.g., ClinicalTrials.gov, https://clinicaltrials.gov/), publishing the prospective trial's protocol in peer-reviewed journals, and having an open data repository where independent evaluators for systematic reviews or meta-analyses can have open access to original data.

Independent evaluations also have limitations. As with any study, erroneous conclusions occur when interventions are implemented with poor fidelity, when findings are selectively reported, when there is a failure to accurately report on the actual level of developer involvement, and when independent findings are themselves not replicated and at variance to other available studies. Furthermore, independent evaluations are not free from potential bias. Sherman and Strang (2009) outlined a variety of factors that could bias an independent evaluation, such as skepticism, financial or organization pressures to show that programs do or do not work, the evaluation predicting null findings or negative results of a program, whether the independent evaluation has an affiliation with a competing program, or the independent evaluation being corrupted by a desire to disprove the value of a respected or popular program. While one form of evaluation is not considered "better" than the other, both need to safeguard against bias.

THE MANAGEMENT
OF CONFLICT-OF-INTEREST RISKS

In an attempt to manage the differing types of potential COI risks that can occur during the QA process of program development, Sanders (2015) developed a potential COI checklist for program developers, which is outlined in Table 43.1. A COI might exist when an author, or institution employing an author, has a financial relationship or otherwise with individuals or organizations that could influence the author's work inappropriately. Examples of potential COIs include, but are not limited to, academic, personal, or political relationships; employment, consultancies, or honoraria; and financial connections such as stock, royalties, or funding of research. COIs might occur in situations where an investigator has a significant financial or other interest (e.g., employment) that might compromise, or have the appearance of compromising, professional judgment in the design, conduct, or reporting of research. There are several forms of COI for individuals involved with research and dissemination (Table 43.1).

Table 43.1: Types of Potential Conflicts of Interest

Potential Conflict	Reasons for Potential Conflict
Authorial contribution to program resources	Authors of program resources that are disseminated by a purveyor company may benefit financially through receipt of royalties from sales of published program resources. This benefit could be current or anticipated if the program is deemed worthy of dissemination. Contributory authors may be university staff members, students, or collaborators from another university or research center working with a researcher or research team member. Another potential COI for authors is the avoidance of reputation damage if an intervention study fails.
Nonauthorial staff member or student	When an academic institution owns the copyright of a program, there could be a perception that staff and students affiliated with the institution may benefit indirectly from published research relating to the program. These benefits could include reduced resource costs due to discounts on the purchase of program materials, reduced training cost for research personnel, or increased opportunities to present at conferences or conduct workshops on an aspect of the program.
Consultant, trainer, or staff member of the training organization or one of its subsidiaries	A purveyor dissemination company may be licensed by the university to disseminate the program. A COI might exist if a consultant, trainer, or staff member employed by the training organization or one of its subsidiaries contributes to a research paper evaluating the program.
Member of a dedicated research network or interest group	Some programs have established international research networks or coalitions to promote quality research concerning the intervention. A perception may exist that membership in the network creates a COI even if no funds are provided by the network to support the individual's work.
Other authors contributing to research papers on the intervention	An independent researcher with no affiliation to the university or the training organization may also have a conflict of interest related to a bias or theoretical allegiance to an alternative program or intervention paradigm.

The Parenting and Family Support Centre (PFSC) at The University of Queensland has developed a COI management plan that aims to manage COIs and make potential COIs as transparent as possible at each stage of the program development process. Moreover, a collaboration between program developers from the Australian psychosocial science field to develop clear guidelines to manage COIs is currently under way. We encourage other program developers in the field of psychosocial research to reflect on their QA and QC processes, liaise with their university integrity research units, and develop tailored COI management plans.

THE ROLE OF CRITICAL APPRAISAL AND ONGOING INNOVATION

Ongoing research and evaluation means that no programs can rest on their laurels (Winston & Jacobsohn, 2010). The impetus for changing a program comes with evidence showing inadequate outcomes with a specific client group, feedback from practitioners or parents as consumers, and cross-fertilization from one area of research to another. This critical analytic approach is a dynamic process that should constantly strive for self-improvement. A single or indeed several well-conducted studies will never be the final word on the effects of a program.

IMPLICATIONS AND CONCLUSION

A major implication of QA issues is that developers working in research settings need to become more focused on the end user throughout program development and evaluation. If programs are to survive and flourish over time, there needs to be constant evolution and investment in research and development. Without such investment, programs become stale, are seen to be irrelevant to the modern generation of parents, or are seen to apply concepts and procedures that fail to reflect advances in knowledge relevant to understanding specific problems or client populations. On the other hand, a vibrant, thriving research and development group, working in collaboration with others, can create outstanding programs that have great potential to benefit

---

BOX 43.1: Example of a Quality Assurance Process in Triple P

Level 4 Group Triple P was initially delivered either individually or in a group setting. However, using a consumer perspective to program design, multiple parent surveys showed that many parents preferred receiving parenting information online, compared to the more traditional clinic-based delivery with a practitioner. This consumer feedback was responded to, and it led to the development of an online version of Triple P. Before dissemination, a web-delivered version was tested in a randomized controlled trial in Australia for parents of children with early conduct problems. These findings were then replicated in New Zealand and the United States.

Through this type of innovation in program delivery, Triple P has tried to remain relevant to parents and illustrates the iterative program development process that has fostered the continuing evolution of Triple P. Future innovation of the Triple P system will involve the continued evaluation of specific programs in low-income countries and with underrepresented populations in high-income countries (such as Indigenous populations).

children, families, and society for years ahead. In the case of Triple P, QA processes have gradually evolved and now inform all current and future research and development of its system in a continuous ongoing process that is designed to enable new generations of developers, researchers, students, and consumers to contribute to the program (Box 43.1 for an example of the Triple P QA process in action).

KEY MESSAGES

- Programs need to continually innovate to stay relevant to consumers in terms of both content and delivery.
- Constant intervention evaluation of outcomes and acceptability is needed to inform program refinements.
- Intervention developers can benefit from a QA framework to assist with innovation development.

REFERENCES

Altman, D. G., Schulz, K. F., Moher, D., Egger, M., Davidoff, F., Elbourne, D., . . . CONSORT Group. (2001). The revised CONSORT statement for reporting randomized trials: Explanation and elaboration. *Annals of Internal Medicine, 134*, 663–694. doi:10.7326/0003-4819-134-8-200104170-00012

Aos, S., Lee, S., Drake, E., Pennuci, A., Klima, T., Miller, M., . . . Burley, M. (2011). *Return on investment: Evidence-based options to improves statewide outcomes* (Document No. 11-07-1201). Olympia: Washington State Institute of Public Policy.

Axford, N., & Morpeth, L. (2013). Evidence-based programs in children's services: A critical appraisal. *Children and Youth Services Review, 35*, 268–277. doi:10.1016/j.childyouth.2012.10.017

Baer, D. M., Wolf, M. M., & Risley, T. R. (1968). Some current dimensions of applied behavior analysis. *Journal of Applied Behavior Annals, 1*, 91–97. doi:10.1901/jaba.1968.1-91

Chambless, D. L., & Ollendick, T. H. (2001). Empirically supported psychological interventions: Controversies and evidence. *Annual Review of Psychology, 52*, 685–716. doi:10.1146/annurev. psych.52.1.685

Crosby, P. B. (1984). *Quality without tears.* New York, NY: McGraw-Hill.

Eisner M. (2009). No effects in independent prevention trials: can we reject the cynical view? *Journal of Experimental Criminology, 5*, 163–183.

Flay, B. R., Biglan, A., Boruch, R. F., González Castro, F., Gottfredson, D., Kellam, S., . . . Ji, P. (2005). Standards of evidence: Criteria for efficacy, effectiveness and dissemination. *Prevention Science, 6*, 151–175. doi:10.1007/s11121-005-5553-y

Gallart, S. C., & Matthey, S. (2005). The effectiveness of Group Triple P and the impact of the four telephone contacts. *Behaviour Change, 22*, 71–80. doi:10.1375/bech.2005.22.2.71

Hodge, L., & Turner, K. M. T. (2016). Sustained implementation of evidence-based programs in disadvantaged communities: A conceptual framework of supporting factors. *American Journal of Community Psychology, 58*, 192–210. doi:10.1002/ajcp.12082

Kazdin, A. E., & Nock, M. K. (2003). Delineating mechanisms of change in child and adolescent therapy: Methodological issues and research recommendations. *Journal of Child Psychology and Psychiatry, 44*, 1116–1129. doi:10.1111/1469-7610.00195/

Little, M. (2010). Looked after children: Can existing services ever succeed? *Adoption and Fostering Journal, 34,* 3–7.

McWilliam, J., Brown, J., Sanders, M. R., & Jones, L. (2016). The Triple P Implementation Framework: the Role of Purveyors in the Implementation and Sustainability of Evidence-Based Programs. *Prevention Science, 17,* 636-645. doi: 10.1007/s11121-016-0661-4

Morawska, A., Haslam, D., Milne, D., & Sanders, M. R. (2011). Evaluation of a brief parenting discussion group for parents of young children. *Journal of Developmental and Behavioral Pediatrics, 32,* 136–145. doi:10.1097/DBP.0b013e3181f17a28

Sanders, M. R. (2012). Development, evaluation, and multinational dissemination of the Triple P—Positive Parenting Program. *Annual Review of Clinical Psychology, 8,* 1–35. doi:10.1146/annurev-clinpsy-032511-143104

Sanders, M. R. (2015). Management of conflict of interest in psychosocial research on parenting and family interventions. *Journal of Child and Family Studies, 24,* 832–841.doi 10.1007/s10826-015-0127-5

Sanders, M. R., Baker, S., & Turner, K. M. T. (2012). A randomized controlled trial evaluating the efficacy of Triple P Online with parents of children with early-onset conduct problems. *Behaviour Research and Therapy, 50,* 675–684. doi:10.1016/j.brat.2012.07.004

Sanders, M. R., & Kirby, J. N. (2014). Surviving or thriving: Quality assurance mechanisms to promote innovation in the development of evidence-based parenting interventions. *Prevention Science, 16,* 421–431. doi:10.1007/s11121-014-0475-1

Sherman, L. W., & Strang, H. (2009). Testing for analysts' bias in crime prevention experiments: Can we accept Eisner's one-tailed test? *Journal of Experimental Criminology, 5,* 185–200. doi:10.1007/s11292-009-9073-9

Stein, Z., & Heikkinen, K. (2009). Models, metrics, and measurements in developmental psychology. *Integral Review, 5,* 4–24. doi:10.1.1.533.3316

Valentine, J. C., Biglan, A., Boruch, R. F., Castro, F. G., Collins, L. M., Flay, B. R., & Schinke, S. P. (2011). Replication in prevention science. *Prevention Science, 12,* 103–117. doi:10.1007/s11121-011-0217-6

Webster-Stratton, C. (1998). Preventing conduct problems in Head Start children: Strengthening parenting competencies. *Journal of Consulting and Clinical Psychology, 66,* 715–730. doi:10.1037/0022-006X.66.5.715

Winston, F. K., & Jacobsohn, L. (2010). A practical approach for applying best practices in behavioural interventions to injury prevention. *Injury Prevention, 16,* 107–112. doi:10.1136/ip. 2009.021972a

CHAPTER 44

THE CURRENT STATE OF EVIDENCE-BASED PARENTING SUPPORT PROGRAMS

MATTHEW R. SANDERS

INTRODUCTION

Intervention efforts to improve the well-being of children at a population level are more likely to succeed if evidence-based parenting support (EBPS) is a central feature. This conclusion is based on evidence from numerous meta-analyses showing that parenting affects many different aspects of a child's development and the quality and stability of family life (see Chapter 2, this volume). Of all the potentially modifiable environmental risk and protective factors related to children's development, increasing the capacity (i.e., knowledge, skills, and confidence) of parents to raise their children well can lead to the greatest long-term benefit to children, parents, families, and entire communities.

This volume has provided an in-depth overview of how EBPS can be applied as an integrated, theoretically consistent, multilevel system to entire communities. This chapter revisits the critical issues facing the field of parenting support as it embraces a population approach and seeks to make the model work in practice. We begin by reviewing briefly the case for adoption of a population approach and then explore what must be done to strengthen the science and practice of the approach and some possible future directions.

THE CASE FOR ADOPTING EVIDENCE-BASED PARENTING PROGRAMS

ADVANCES IN NEUROSCIENCE

Advances in cognitive neuroscience and developmental research documenting the critical importance of the early years on human development and the impact of the environment on children's lives has helped promote greater public and political awareness of the importance of the early years and early intervention. Shonkoff, Radner, and Foote (2016, p. 15) summarized that "research in neuroscience . . . is generating insights about plasticity and sensitive periods in brain development that could inform more effective timing of specific interventions [and] advances in epigenetics are producing a deeper understanding of differences in vulnerability and resilience in the face of stress, as well as variability in response to interventions that could inform more efficient resource allocation."

Emphasis on the importance of environmental influences in the early years is not new to the fields of child development, prevention science, or mental health. However, the evidence showing developmental plasticity of the child brain and the long-term adverse effects on a child's life course stemming from prolonged exposure to adverse or "toxic" environments (including poverty, child maltreatment, and family violence) has made many policymakers pay much closer attention to the call to invest in the early years (Moffitt, 2013).

POLICY ENVIRONMENT

Government policies determine which services and programs are funded from the public purse. The volatile nature of politics can render policy commitments to fund parenting programs by one government fragile and easily defunded should there be a change in government. Nevertheless, many governments around the world have now recognized that increasing funding support for the delivery of EBPS programs is an important and worthwhile investment.

In the United Kingdom, major policy commitments led to support for the establishment of the National Academy of Parenting Practitioners in England to increase access to free professional training in evidence-based interventions (Scott, 2010). However, this program was not sustained with subsequent changes of administration. The National Institute of Clinical Excellence and Social Care (NICE) has produced clinical guidance for the commissioner of services advising that group parenting programs should be offered to parents of children with conduct disorders, with developmental disabilities, or with attention deficit hyperactivity disorder (Department of Children and Youth Affairs, 2015; National Institute for Health and Care Excellence, 2013, 2015).

The US federal government has supported parenting programs through a variety of initiatives (National Academies of Science Engineering and Medicine, 2016), including increased provision for targeted home visiting programs for young disadvantaged parents. In Canada, sustained policy advocacy from multiple groups has led to national recognition of the importance of parenting programs in influencing life course outcomes for all children (e.g., Truth and Reconciliation Commission of Canada, 2015). The Council of Europe developed a policy on positive parenting calling on all 47 member states to introduce positive parenting programs (Rodrigo, 2010).

There are advanced and evolving parenting support initiatives in many individual European countries, including Belgium, Ireland, the Netherlands, Germany, Norway, Sweden, and Switzerland. Some Latin American countries' governments have increasingly recognized the importance of supporting parents and families (e.g., Chile). Policy-led investments in parenting programs have also occurred in Australia at both federal and state levels (Australian Health Ministers' Advisory Council, 2015) and New Zealand (Advisory Group on Conduct Problems, 2009; New Zealand Government, 2012). As pointed out by Long (2016), there is increasing pressure on governments, agencies, and practitioners to only fund programs that have an evidence base and defund programs that do not.

Major international organizations, such as the World Health Organization (through its Global Violence Prevention Initiative; World Health Organization, 2009), the United Nations Office on Drugs and Crime (2009), and the United Nations Children's Fund (2012), have all advocated for some time that EBPS programs be made available in low- and middle-income countries and that building local capacity to implement culturally adapted evidence-based parenting programs is required to reduce the level of family violence, particularly harsh corporal punishment of children.

In many jurisdictions, government policies have prioritized vulnerable children living in poverty and the prevention of mental health problems (e.g., conduct disorders) or child maltreatment. Major government investments in parenting programs to date have focused on delivery of relatively high-intensity home visiting and group and individual programs (8 to 14 sessions) targeting vulnerable children. However, much more needs to be done to reduce the prevalence rates of child maltreatment and social, emotional, and behavioral problems.

COSTS OF NOT INTERVENING

Economists, such as Heckman (2011), have argued convincingly that effective early intervention, particularly with vulnerable children living in poverty, has major economic benefits to society if children at risk of serious problems can be helped early (Doyle, Harmon, Heckman, & Tremblay, 2009). Longitudinal studies have bolstered the strength of advocacy for early intervention. A major internationally renowned longitudinal study in New Zealand showed that the life course trajectories of children by at age three predicted costs to society 35 years later. Children were identified via a 45-minute examination that included an assessment of neurological soft signs, intelligence, receptive language, and motor skills and a rating of the child's frustration tolerance, resistance, restlessness, impulsivity, and lack of persistence in reaching goals (Caspi et al., 2016). Children who had a combination of four risk factors (childhood economic deprivation, maltreatment, low IQ, and poor self-control) caused a substantial burden on service delivery costs in adulthood. Although they comprised only 22% of the birth cohort, by age 38 they accounted for 66% of the birth cohort's welfare benefits, 77% of fatherless childhood years in the next generation, 54% of the cohort's tobacco consumption, 40% of the cohort's excess weight, 57% of the cohort's hospital bed nights, 78% of filled prescriptions, 81% of crimes charged, and 36% of injury claims.

EVIDENCE OF EFFECTIVENESS OF PARENTING PROGRAMS

After decades of research, there is general consensus that EBPS programs are among the most efficacious and cost-effective interventions available to promote the mental health and well-being of children (Dretzke et al., 2009; Kazdin & Blase, 2011). These interventions are particularly effective for children with conduct problems and children at risk of maltreatment and developing social and emotional problems (Collins, Maccoby, Steinberg, Hetherington, & Bornstein, 2000; Foster, Prinz, Sanders, & Shapiro, 2008; Mercy & Saul, 2009; Mihalopoulos, Vos, Pirkis, & Carter, 2011; O'Connell, Boat, & Warner, 2009) and have been shown to work in real-world clinical settings (Michelson, Davenport, Dretzke, Barlow, & Day, 2013). Increasing evidence demonstrates their effectiveness in developing countries (Gardner, Montgomery, &

Kerr, 2015), with culturally diverse parent groups (Chapter 30, this volume), and with ethnic minorities (van Mourik, Crone, de Wolff, & Reis, 2017). The strength of this evidence has built a compelling case to justify EBPS.

LIMITATIONS OF TARGETED INTERVENTIONS

While targeted EBPS programs in child and adolescent mental health services and family services are needed, the families seen by these services represent the "tip of the iceberg," and many practitioners have not been trained in and do not deliver evidence-based programs, as pointed out by Scott (2010) and many others. The vast majority of parents whose children are at risk and are likely to benefit from parenting programs do not participate, and of parents who do, as many as 51% fail to complete the full intervention (Chacko et al., 2016). Scott (2010) pointed out that many parents recruited to participate in randomized controlled trials (RCTs) do not enter trials, and those who do may represent a particularly motivated segment of parents of children with conduct problems. Many factors converge to explain the relatively low parent participation and completion rates, and as outlined in previous chapters, there is a lot that can be done to improve program engagement and completion rates; however, a different approach is needed to have an effect on prevalence rates at a population level.

REVISITING THE POPULATION APPROACH

EVIDENCE-BASED PARENTING AND FAMILY SUPPORT

Sanders and Prinz (Chapter 3, this volume) provided a basic rationale for adopting a population health approach to EBPS and argued that an integrated, multilevel population-based system is needed. Such a position is consistent with advocacy for the adoption of population health approaches to the delivery of child and adolescent mental health support services (Patel, Flisher, Hetrick, & McGorry, 2007); the reduction of family violence, including child maltreatment prevention (Prinz & Sanders, 2007); and calls to apply prevention science knowledge to the development of nurturing environments focused on the promotion of prosociality in children and young people (Biglan, 2015).

Figure 44.1 summarizes the possibilities of such an approach. In a hypothetical population of 100,000 families, we might expect a base rate of around 17,000 children (17%) in the abnormal or clinical range on the Strengths and Difficulties Questionnaire (SDQ) total (a measure of social and emotional problems in children). Using estimates from Fives, Purcell, Heary, NicGabhainn, and Canavan (2014), a population rollout of the Triple P system that reached around 35% of these families could see a 33% overall reduction in the number of cases of elevated or clinical levels of child problems, or about 5,700 fewer children. This shift is equivalent to moving the population mean by about *one fifth* of a standard deviation (0.2 SD). What if we could move the population mean by *half* a standard deviation instead (0.5 SD)? Extrapolating from the previous data, shifting the population standard deviation by 0.5 SD could result in drastic reductions in the number of clinical or elevated cases. This approach would result in many more children and parents benefitting, at lower cost than through reactive approaches based on referrals to clinical services.

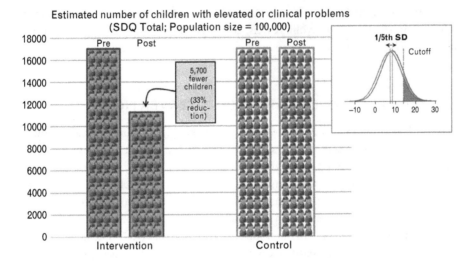

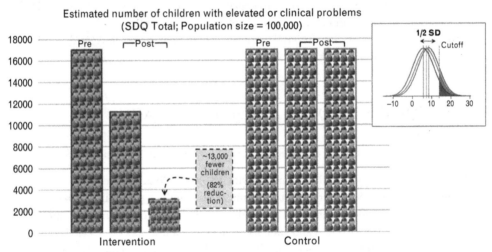

FIGURE 44.1: Shifting the population mean on psychological problems in children by 0.2 and 0.5 of a standard deviation.

CHANGING PUBLIC PERCEPTIONS ABOUT THE IMPORTANCE OF PARENTING

Even though experience with population rollouts of parenting programs shows that many parents are attracted to and seek to participate in programs, there are also major barriers that need to be overcome. According to a qualitative study by Volmert, Kendall-Taylor, Cosh, and Lindland (2016), many parents view parenting as a natural process and assume good parenting flows naturally and automatically from simply having a concern for one's children. Conversely, parenting experts emphasize that effective parenting requires a set of specific skills, knowledge, and practices. Viewing parenting as natural makes it difficult for many parents to recognize that parenting is skill based and that such skills can be learned and improved, and the belief may reinforce stigma against "bad parents" and help seeking. However, as outlined by Wilkinson

(Chapter 35, this volume), a well-developed social marketing and communications strategy supported by access to other program levels can change public perceptions of the importance of good-quality parenting programs.

THE NEED TO COORDINATE INVESTMENTS
IN PARENTING PROGRAMS

In many jurisdictions, funds have been allocated for preventively focused parenting support programs through to narrowly defined program areas targeting specific disorders or problems (e.g., conduct problems, antisocial behavior, substance abuse prevention, school readiness); however, these program areas are often uncoordinated. A more cost-effective alternative with much wider population reach involves pooling resources from multiple program areas across departments and collectively funding a comprehensive, multiagency, population-based EBPS system that would be relevant to all program areas and the entire community.

As an example, several provinces in Canada (e.g., Alberta, Manitoba, Prince Edward Island) have pooled funds from multiple departments to support parenting initiatives. For example, the Manitoba government's *Healthy Child Manitoba* initiative pooled resources from multiple ministries to fund a range of early childhood interventions, including the province-wide rollout of Triple P to promote better health and developmental outcomes for children. Ministries involved included Manitoba Education and Training; Manitoba Families; Manitoba Health, Seniors and Active Living; Manitoba Indigenous and Municipal Relations; Manitoba Justice; Manitoba Sport; and Culture and Heritage/Status of Women.

When funding decisions are made to prevent or treat a particular disorder or problem (e.g., child maltreatment, conduct disorders, crime, substance abuse, and youth suicide), an opportunity exists to simultaneously affect many other related developmental outcomes if different program areas are better coordinated with respect to parenting programs. Capable parenting has the potential to alter life course trajectories by altering common pathways to change for the better. This includes altering family risk and protective factors that are causally implicated in the origins or maintenance of many social, educational, mental, and physical health problems. The adoption of a population approach to EBPS from birth has the potential to concurrently improve multiple child and youth outcomes, but it requires strong multisector partnerships to "join the dots" in policy, research, and service delivery.

What differentiates Triple P from most other EBPS programs (while sharing many features in common) is the embrace of a population approach designed to reduce the prevalence rates of child and parent problems at a community level. We aimed to develop an integrated, multilevel system of parenting support that could be flexibly applied and sustained to address a wide spectrum of social, emotional, and health problems of children and adolescents, in diverse families, and at different stages of the life cycle from infancy to adolescence. Substantial progress has been made toward achieving this aim, but much work needs to be done.

Over the past four decades, EBPS has come a long way, with new programs emerging for a range of psychosocial problems. However, there is a long way to go before participation in a parenting program becomes something that parents look forward to as a socially normative rite of passage into a harmonious family life with children.

REPURPOSING EXISTING SERVICES
TO ENHANCE POPULATION REACH

The RE-AIM framework developed by Glasgow (see Gaglio, Shoup, & Glasgow, 2013) is a useful tool for conceptualizing the impact of population health interventions. The model involves developing metrics relating to the *Reach* of an intervention, the *Effectiveness* of a program, and the *Adoption, Implementation,* and *Maintenance* of programs. Many existing services respond to and are funded to provide help for families referred to their services. Many services need to reorient their mission to include a wider spectrum of preventive and early intervention services. This requires funders to be convinced that inclusion of outreach and prevention programs equals value for money. As illustrated in Box 44.1, organizations can markedly increase the number of families served (Reach) while maintaining costs incurred in delivering programs.

CRITICISMS OF THE POPULATION APPROACH

While there is growing support for tackling parenting support as a whole-of-population issue, there is by no means universal acceptance of the value of doing so, how it should be done, and methods of evaluation. In the next section, we examine some of these criticisms.

Criticism 1: Parenting Support for Everyone Is Unnecessary

Longitudinal studies show that certain children are much more likely than others to experience long-term adverse developmental outcomes (Caspi, Moffitt, Newman, & Silva, 1996; Moffitt &

**BOX 44.1: An Example of Increasing Reach
While Maintaining Costs**

If a single practitioner currently delivers five parenting groups per year with 10 participants per group over a 5-year period, 250 families will be assisted in roughly 400 hours of contact time. Assuming a family size of 1.6 children per family, 400 children will benefit. If the same practitioner reduced the number of small-group programs delivered with 10 participants to two per year and instead ran 10 seminars with 25 parents per seminar and 4 discussion groups with 15 parents and supported 20 parents to complete an online program (four calls at 15 minutes each per parent) for the allocation of roughly the same 400 hours of clinician time, the practitioner will have reached 1,750 families, benefitting 2,800 children. If we assume the practitioner adds preparation and setup time and attends a fortnightly peer-assisted supervision and support (PASS) supervision session, without any increase in overall staff time, the adoption of flexible delivery and outreach to the community can dramatically increase the number of families reached in a community from 250 to 1,750—a seven-fold increase. This hypothetical model assumes that the agency will have in place an active social marketing strategy to ensure there will be sufficient demand from parents to participate in the program.

the Klaus-Grawe 2012 Think Tank, 2013; Moffitt, Poulton, & Caspi, 2013). The combination of being raised in poverty, being exposed to child abuse and neglect, having low IQ, and having poor self-control in early childhood creates particular risk and is associated with a range of expensive long-term consequences in adulthood. However, to conclude that the solution lies in better targeting of families of the most vulnerable children is problematic for several reasons. If all of the parents of these children (which is highly unlikely) could be recruited and engaged and completed an EBPS early intervention, the vast majority of children who develop psychosocial problems would still be missed. Even though a much higher proportion of children who develop problems are from the lowest quintile of the income distribution, as well as the fact that this socioeconomic group accounts for more of the long-term service use costs, what is not accounted for are the majority of children who will develop behavioral and emotional problems—who are members of the 80% of families outside the bottom quintile.

Any parent can experience significant difficulties with their children from time to time and might benefit from being able to access high-quality parenting support. However, not all parents need the same level of support, such as face-to-face interventions. The Triple P model of parenting support uses a multilevel system that ensures universal access to all parents. Participation would be voluntary for the vast majority of parents, although it is recognized that some parents involved in the child protection system or in custody disputes may be required by courts to complete a parenting program. By enhancing opportunities for all parents to access parenting programs rather than only those parents who are considered at risk for future problems, participation does not become exceptional; it becomes the norm. It becomes the usual, expected, ordinary, and predictable activity that parents do to the *minimally sufficient* extent they and their children require to meet their needs for healthy development and family relationships. The principle of minimal sufficiency is essential to ensure parents get what they need and resources are used efficiently.

Criticism 2: A Population Approach Is Unable to Reach Highly Vulnerable Children

The parents of children who are considered most at risk for long-term adverse outcomes are a particularly important but hard-to-reach group unless the places and contexts that families connect with are involved in efforts to engage them (e.g., primary health care, child care, schools, and religious organizations). Sometimes, universal and more targeted approaches are seen as mutually exclusive rather than complementary. Large-scale rollouts of Triple P that blend universal and targeted elements can prioritize lower socioeconomic areas known to have higher concentrations of more vulnerable and disadvantaged families and also capture families already dealing with clinical-level problems. This flexibility allows implementing organizations some flexibility to prioritize vulnerable families and to provide matched services for their clientele.

Criticism 3: A Population Approach Is Too Expensive

The EBPS programs are not only among the most effective psychosocial interventions, but also they are relatively inexpensive and highly cost-effective, at least for indicated prevention and treatment. There have been fewer economic analyses of population approaches such as the Triple P system. However, a population approach can reach many more parents at much lower per family cost than targeted or indicated prevention programs or treatments. Population trials of the Triple P system to date showed that the majority of parents in a population rollout of a multilevel system are likely to participate in low-cost, low-intensity interventions (i.e., communication campaign, primary care consultations, seminars, discussion groups, or online programs), with more intensive programs (i.e., multisession group programs) being delivered to parents with children with more severe problems (Fives et al., 2014).

Several economic analyses have shown that the implementation of the Triple P system is considered to have good fiscal value, as reflected in the economic analyses reported by the independent Washington State Institute for Public Policy (2017). However, there needs to be further economic modeling based on more recent cost estimates for large-scale implementation in different countries where the cost base differs. It is inappropriate to generalize costs from one country to another across different service delivery systems, particularly to low- and middle-income countries where different models for implementation are required.

Criticism 4: There Is Not Enough Evidence to Justify Wide-Scale Use of the Population Approach

Stronger evidence from multiple RCTs exists to support the efficacy of parenting programs than was ever available before other large-scale implementations of population-based public health interventions. This includes interventions such as quit smoking campaigns to reduce cardiovascular risk, road safety and drink driving campaigns, health promotion campaigns to promote healthy eating and physical activity, and suicide prevention and alcohol prevention programs. The perceived importance of these issues led to action being taken well before any controlled research demonstrated the effects of these public health interventions. Some have argued that the lack of such intervention research helps explain why some public education campaigns have failed.

In contrast, focusing on Triple P studies at the time of writing (February 2017), a large number of evaluation studies have already been conducted, including 137 RCTs. The vast majority (95%) of these showed positive findings on child and parent outcomes. In addition, it has been demonstrated that implementing the Triple P system by targeting all parents on a large scale is both feasible and cost-effective when a robust implementation approach is taken (Fives et al., 2014; Prinz, 2016; Prinz, Sanders, Shapiro, Whitaker, & Lutzker, 2009). The cumulative evidence to date is clearly sufficient to justify wider scale deployment of the population approach, particularly in the context of robust independent evaluations of outcomes. Many of the most important learnings regarding what works in practice come from carefully studying the implementation process with action-oriented, solution-focused research, such as that done by Owens, Doyle, Hegarty, Heavey, and Farrell (Chapter 40, this volume) in Ireland and Aldridge, Murray, Prinz, and Veazey (2016) in the United States.

Criticism 5: Endorsing One Program Is a Mistake

Endorsing a single program is not a good idea as it restricts parental choice. However, it is inaccurate to characterize the Triple P system as a single program. It provides a wide range of program options at different levels of intensity, target populations, age groups, and delivery modalities to cater for individual differences in parental needs and preferences. One major advantage of the Triple P system is that it provides a common language in a community endeavoring to support families, and it facilitates interagency collaboration when different services are contributing to a same shared strategic goal (namely, reducing the prevalence rates of targeted child problems and child maltreatment by increasing parental access to EBPS programs). The multilevel approach can sit comfortably alongside other evidence-based programs (e.g., early child development programs, home visiting programs, school-based programs), and different types of early interventions in a community. Having an EBPS system that covers the spectrum of support from universal, selected, and indicated prevention interventions to early intervention and treatment options for some mental health problems is a major advantage.

Criticism 6: Universal Programs Only Reach People Who Do Not Need It

Reaching people who do not need intervention is sometimes referred to as targeting the "worried well." This criticism implies that Triple P is for middle-class families and parents with "real" or complex problems will not participate, and that resources needed to engage the most disadvantaged and vulnerable parent groups are wasted on helping people who do not need it or are resourceful enough to find solutions themselves. However, universally offered parenting programs can be successful in reaching many more low-income and vulnerable families as a low-threat, destigmatized entry point into appropriate care and services. An evaluation by Fives et al. (2014) found that families from low socioeconomic groups were in fact well represented in a population rollout of the Triple P system. Of the families who participated in Level 4 Group Triple P, 35% reported secondary school or less as their highest educational level, 27% reported working full time, and more than 25% reported difficulties meeting essential household expenses. Research suggests that parents from lower socioeconomic groups who complete a Triple P intervention do just as well as other parents (Sanders, Kirby, Tellegen, & Day, 2014). However, targeted outreach and engagement strategies that are recommended to improve participation and retention of low-income families (Morawska & Sanders, 2006) and fathers go hand in hand with building the local capacity of the workforce to deliver programs.

The somewhat pejorative term *worried well* unfairly implies that more socioeconomically advantaged parents needlessly worry about their children and do not really need help. However, parents from all socioeconomic strata can experience significant problems with children—including conduct problems, attention deficit hyperactivity disorder, learning difficulties, peer relationship problems, substance abuse, suicide, depression, anxiety disorders, and eating disorders—and can abuse their children. Parenting support should be based on need and the severity of the problem and not on the basis of social disadvantage alone. To ensure the neediest families are able to participate, Marmot's (2010) principle of proportionate universalism can be applied to ensure low socioeconomic areas are not neglected.

GAPS IN THE EVIDENCE

As the population approach to parenting support is relatively new, relatively few studies have been conducted testing the population-level outcomes from deployment of a full multilevel approach. The strongest tests of the efficacy of Triple P as a population approach are place-based randomized trials that link change in the prevalence rates of target problems to the implementation of the multilevel system in defined geographical catchment areas. More of these types of trials are needed. Available evidence relates to the application of the model to younger children, 3 to 9 years old. There are currently no population trials with other age groups, such as infants or adolescents. However, multilevel Triple P interventions have been developed for all age groups (including infants, toddlers, preschool-aged children, elementary school–aged children, adolescents). A large-scale trial targeting the entire range of families, including parents of children with a disability, would provide a more definitive test of the impact of the entire Triple P system and would ensure that families with children across multiple ages have the opportunity to participate.

It should also be noted that within the multilevel system, individual programs and variants have different strengths of evidence supporting them. Some newer programs, such as Resilience Triple P, to combat bullying by peers at school are supported by single RCTs (e.g., Healy & Sanders, 2014), while others, such as Group Triple P, which has been disseminated longer, have been replicated in multiple trials (Sanders et al., 2014).

CONCLUSION

Over the past 40 years, there has been an explosion in research on parenting interventions. There is ever-increasing scientific and theoretical support for providing universal access to EBPS not only to avert clinical cases in child and youth mental health but also to promote child, family, and community well-being.

KEY MESSAGES

- Evidence based parenting support (EBPS) programs offer tremendous potential to promote positive life course outcomes for children, families, and communities.
- Universal population health approaches to EBPS are gaining momentum, although much work is needed to explore appropriate evaluation methods and add to the evidence base.
- The increasing focus on population-level delivery, despite some common myths and criticisms, can only increase the reach of EBPS, providing cost-effective use of available public funds and maximum impact on population prevalence rates.

REFERENCES

Advisory Group on Conduct Problems. (2009). *Conduct problems: Effective programmes for 8–12 year olds.* Wellington, New Zealand: Ministry of Social Development.

Aldridge, W. A., Murray, D. W., Prinz, R. J., & Veazey, C. A. (2016). *Final report and recommendations: The Triple P implementation evaluation.* Chapel Hill, NC: Frank Porter Graham Child Development Institute, University of North Carolina.

Australian Health Ministers' Advisory Council. (2015). *Healthy, safe and thriving: National strategic framework for child and youth health: Commonwealth Government of Australia*. Retrieved from http://www.coaghealthcouncil.gov.au/Portals/0/Healthy%20Safe%20and%20Thriving%20-%20National%20Strategic%20Framework%20for%20Child%20and%20Youth%20Health.pdf

Biglan, A. (2015). *The nurture effect: How the science of human behavior can improve our lives and our world*. Oakland, CA: New Harbinger.

Caspi, A., Houts, R. M., Belsky, D. W., Harrington, H., Hogan, S., Ramrakha, S., . . . Moffitt, T. E. (2016). Childhood forecasting of a small segment of the population with large economic burden. *Nature Human Behaviour, 1*, 0005. doi:10.1038/s41562-016-0005

Caspi, A., Moffitt, T. E., Newman, D. L., & Silva, P. A. (1996). Behavioral observations at age 3 years predicted adult psychiatric disorders. *Archives of General Psychiatry, 53*, 1033–1039. doi:10.1001/archpsyc.1996.01830110071009

Chacko, A., Jensen, S. A., Lowry, L. S., Cornwell, M., Chimklis, A., Chan, E., . . . Pulgarin, B. (2016). Engagement in behavioral parent training: Review of the literature and implications for practice. *Clinical Child and Family Psychology Review, 19*, 204–215. doi:10.1007/s10567-016-0205-2

Collins, W. A., Maccoby, E. E., Steinberg, L., Hetherington, E. M., & Bornstein, M. H. (2000). Contemporary research on parenting: The case for nature and nurture. *American Psychologist, 55*, 218–232. doi:10.1037/0003-066X.55.2.218

Department of Children and Youth Affairs. (2015). *High level policy statement on supporting parents and families*. Dublin, Ireland. Retrieved from http://www.childandfamilyresearch.ie/media/ilascfrc/reports/20150413HighLevPolicyStatonFamilySupportParentsandFamENGLISH.pdf

Doyle, O., Harmon, C. P., Heckman, J. J., & Tremblay, R. E. (2009). Investing in early human development: Timing and economic efficiency. *Economics & Human Biology, 7*, 1–6. doi:10.1016/j.ehb.2009.01.002

Dretzke, J., Davenport, C., Frew, E., Barlow, J., Stewart-Brown, S., Bayliss, S., . . . & Hyde, C. (2009). The clinical effectiveness of different parenting programmes for children with conduct problems: A systematic review of randomised controlled trials. *Child & Adolescent Psychiatry and Mental Health, 3*, 7. doi:10.1186/1753-2000-3-7

Fives, A., Purcell, L., Heary, C., NicGabhainn, S., & Canavan, J. (2014). *Parenting support for every parent: A population-level evaluation of Triple P in Longford Westmeath*. Final Report. Galway, Ireland: Longford Westmeath Parenting Partnership. Retrieved from http://www.atlanticphilanthropies.org/app/uploads/2015/09/Report-Parenting-Support-for-Every-Parent.pdf

Foster, E. M., Prinz, R. J., Sanders, M. R., & Shapiro, C. J. (2008). The costs of a public health infrastructure for delivering parenting and family support. *Children & Youth Services Review, 30*, 493–501. doi:10.1016/j.childyouth.2007.11.002

Gaglio, B., Shoup, J. A., & Glasgow, R. E. (2013). The RE-AIM framework: A systematic review of use over time. *American Journal of Public Health, 103*, e38. doi:10.2105/AJPH.2013.301299

Gardner, F., Montgomery, P., & Kerr, W. (2015). Transporting evidence-based parenting programs for child problem behavior (age 3–10) between countries: Systematic review and meta-analysis. *Journal of Clinical Child & Adolescent Psychology, 45*, 749–762. doi:10.1080/15374416.2015.1015134

Healy, K. L., & Sanders, M. R. (2014). Randomized controlled trial of a family intervention for children bullied by peers. *Behavior Therapy, 45*, 760–777. doi:10.1016/j.beth.2014.06.001

Heckman, J. (2011). The economics of inequality: The value of early childhood education. *American Educator, 35*, 31–47. Retrieved from http://files.eric.ed.gov/fulltext/EJ920516.pdf

Kazdin, A. E., & Blase, S. L. (2011). Rebooting psychotherapy research and practice to reduce the burden of mental illness. *Perspectives on Psychological Science, 6*, 21–37. doi:10.1177/1745691610393527

Long, N. (2016). Future trends in parenting education. In J. J. Ponzetti (Eds.), *Evidence-based parenting education: A global perspective* (pp. 311–328). New York, NY: Routledge.

Marmot, M. (2010). *Fair society, healthy lives: The Mamort review; strategic review of health inequalities in England post-2010*. London, England: Marmot Review.

Mercy, J. A., & Saul, J. (2009). Creating a healthier future through early interventions for children. *JAMA, 301*, 2262–2264. doi:10.1001/jama.2009.803

Michelson, D., Davenport, C., Dretzke, J., Barlow, J., & Day, C. (2013). Do evidence-based interventions work when tested in the "real world?" A systematic review and meta-analysis of parent management training for the treatment of child disruptive behavior. *Clinical Child and Family Psychology Review, 16*, 18–34. doi:10.1007/s10567-013-0128-0

Mihalopoulos, C., Vos, T., Pirkis, J., & Carter, R. (2011). The economic analysis of prevention in mental health programs. *Annual Review of Clinical Psychology, 7*, 169–201. doi:10.1146/annurev-clinpsy-032210-104601

Moffitt, T. E. (2013). Childhood exposure to violence and lifelong health: Clinical intervention science and stress-biology research join forces. *Development & Psychopathology, 25*, 1619–1634. doi:10.1017/S0954579413000801

Moffitt, T. E., & the Klaus-Grawe 2012 Think Tank. (2013). Childhood exposure to violence and lifelong health: Clinical intervention science and stress-biology research join forces. *Development & Psychopathology, 25*, 1619–1634. doi:10.1017/S0954579413000801

Moffitt, T. E., Poulton, R., & Caspi, A. (2013). Lifelong impact of early self-control: Childhood self-discipline predicts adult quality of life. *American Scientist, 101*, 352–359. doi:10.1511/2013.104.352

Morawska, A., & Sanders, M. R. (2006). A review of parental engagement in parenting interventions and strategies to promote it. *Journal of Children's Services, 1*, 29–40. doi:10.1108/17466660200600004

National Academies of Science Engineering and Medicine. (2016). *Parenting matters: Supporting parents of children ages 0–8*. Washington, DC: National Academic Press. Retrieved from https://www.nap.edu/catalog/21868/parenting-matters-supporting-parents-of-children-ages-0-8

National Institute for Health and Care Excellence. (2013). *Antisocial behaviour and conduct disorders in children and young people: Recognition and management*. London, England: British Psychological Society and Royal College of Psychiatrists. Retrieved from https://www.nice.org.uk/guidance/cg158/evidence/conduct-disorders-in-children-and-young-people-full-guideline-189848413

National Institute for Health and Care Excellence. (2015). *Challenging behaviour and learning disabilities: Prevention and interventions for people with learning disabilities whose behaviour challenges*. London, England: National Institute for Health and Care Excellence. Retrieved from https://www.nice.org.uk/guidance/ng11/resources/challenging-behaviour-and-learning-disabilities-prevention-and-interventions-for-people-with-learning-disabilities-whose-behaviour-challenges-1837266392005

New Zealand government. (2012). *The White Paper for Vulnerable Children* (Vol. 2). Auckland, New Zealand: New Zealand government. Retrieved from http://childrensactionplan.govt.nz/assets/Uploads/whitepaper-volume-ii-web.pdf

O'Connell, M. E., Boat, T., & Warner, K. E. (2009). *Preventing mental, emotional, and behavioral disorders among young people: Progress and possibilities*. Washington, DC: National Academies Press.

Patel, V., Flisher, A. J., Hetrick, S., & McGorry, P. (2007). Mental health of young people: A global public-health challenge. *The Lancet, 369*, 1302–1313. doi:10.1016/S0140-6736(07)60368-7

Prinz, R. J. (2016). Parenting and family support within a broad child abuse prevention strategy: Child maltreatment prevention can benefit from public health strategies. *Child Abuse & Neglect, 51*, 400–406. doi:10.1016/j.chiabu.2015.10.015

Prinz, R. J., & Sanders, M. R. (2007). Adopting a population-level approach to parenting and family support interventions. *Clinical Psychology Review, 27*, 739–749. doi:10.1016/j.cpr.2007.01.005

Prinz, R. J., Sanders, M. R., Shapiro, C. J., Whitaker, D. J., & Lutzker, J. R. (2009). Population-based prevention of child maltreatment: The US Triple P system population trial. *Prevention Science, 10*, 1–12. doi:10.1007/s11121-009-0123-3

Rodrigo, M. J. (2010). Promoting positive parenting in Europe: New challenges for the European Society for Developmental Psychology. *European Journal of Developmental Psychology, 7*, 281–294. doi:10.1080/17405621003780200

Sanders, M. R., Kirby, J. N., Tellegen, C. L., & Day, J. J. (2014). The Triple P—Positive Parenting Program: A systematic review and meta-analysis of a multi-level system of parenting support. *Clinical Psychology Review, 34*, 337–357. doi:10.1016/j.cpr.2014.04.003

Scott, S. (2010). National dissemination of effective parenting programmes to improve child outcomes. *The British Journal of Psychiatry, 196*, 1–3. doi:10.1192/bjp.bp.109.067728

Shonkoff, J. P., Radner, J. M., & Foote, N. (2016). Expanding the evidence base to drive more productive early childhood investment. *The Lancet, 389*, 14–16. doi:10.1016/S0140-6736(16)31702-0

Truth and Reconciliation Commission of Canada. (2015). *Truth and Reconciliation Commission of Canada: Calls to action.* Manitoba, Canada: Truth and Reconciliation Commission of Canada. Retreived from http://www.trc.ca/websites/trcinstitution/File/2015/Findings/Calls_to_Action_English2.pdf

United Nations Children's Fund. (2012). *Inequities in early childhood development: What the data say: Evidence from the multiple indicator cluster surveys.* New York, NY: Early Childhood Development Unit, United Nations Children's Fund.

United Nations Office on Drugs and Crime. (2009). Guide to implementing family skills training programmes for drug abuse prevention. New York, NY: United Nations Office on Drugs and Crime.

van Mourik, K., Crone, M. R., de Wolff, M. S., & Reis, R. (2017). Parent training programs for ethnic minorities: A meta-analysis of adaptations and effect. *Prevention Science, 18*, 95–105. doi:10.1007/s11121-016-0733-5

Volmert, A., Kendall-Taylor, N., Cosh, I., & Lindland, E. (2016). *Perceptions of parenting: Mapping the gaps between expert and public understandings of effective parenting in Australia.* Washington, DC: FrameWorks Institute. Retrieved from http://www.frameworksinstitute.org/assets/files/Australia/PRC_MTG_Report_May_2016_final.pdf

Washington State Institute for Public Policy. (2017). *Benefit-cost results.* Retrieved January 27, 2017, from http://www.wsipp.wa.gov/BenefitCost

World Health Organization. (2009). *Preventing violence through the development of safe, stable and nurturing relationships between children and their parents and caregivers. Series of briefings on violence prevention: The evidence.* Geneva, Switzerland: Author. Retrieved from http://apps.who.int/iris/bitstream/10665/44088/1/9789241597821_eng.pdf

CHAPTER 45

INNOVATION IN PARENTING PROGRAMS

MATTHEW R. SANDERS, KAREN M. T. TURNER, AND TREVOR G. MAZZUCCHELLI

> Imagination is not only the uniquely human capacity to envision that which is not, and, therefore, the foundation of all invention and innovation. In its arguably most transformative and revelatory capacity, it is the power that enables us to empathize with humans whose experiences we have never shared.
>
> Very Good Lives–Copyright © J.K. Rowling 2008

INTRODUCTION

The basic principles and active skills training procedures used in the social learning approach to evidence-based parenting support (EBPS) have been studied for over four decades. Coercion theory as articulated by the late Patterson (1982) and the principles and techniques of behavior change stemming from applied behavior analysis (Baer, Wolf, & Risley, 1987; Wahler, 1969) provided a conceptual basis and procedural specificity relating to techniques of behavior change that have served the field well. Over this period, EBPS has become firmly established, mainstreamed, and fairly widely disseminated in many countries. The addition of population-based parenting programs such as Triple P has further extended the reach of parenting programs to a wider section of the community and has led to calls for universal adoption of EBPS (Mercy & Saul, 2009). The success of these efforts is undoubtedly a major contribution to the fields of prevention and treatment of child mental health problems and child maltreatment.

Despite these accomplishments, current approaches to parenting support cannot be viewed as a panacea, and there is little room for complacency. There is much work yet to be done to improve access to EBPS, even in Western countries where parenting programs are well established. Major problems relating to inequitable access to services, particularly for Indigenous and minority populations, remain. Scott and Dadds (2009) argued that between a quarter and a third of families do not respond to any available parenting interventions, and as such, there is much room for improving outcomes. Therefore, it is essential that any EBPS program, including Triple

P, not rest on its laurels but continue to evolve so even more families benefit from parenting support in the complex and demanding task of raising healthy and well-adjusted children.

This chapter reflects on the types of innovations that have occurred over the past four decades as the Triple P system and the field of EBPS have evolved and identifies possible avenues for future research and development needed for new innovations. We also discuss the types of research environments that might nurture a thriving culture of program innovation, and the type of organizational contexts that are needed to train the next generation of parenting researchers and program developers to tackle challenges with industry partners to deliver EBPS on a broader, global scale and thereby substantially enhance the well-being of all children, families, and communities everywhere.

THE TRIPLE P SYSTEM INNOVATION JOURNEY

INNOVATIONS TO DATE

In many ways, ongoing innovation has characterized the whole field of behavioral family intervention from its inception. Investigators and program developers in all major programs have generally been willing to redefine how their interventions can be deployed in response to cumulating evidence relating to effectiveness. Some of the most important changes that have influenced current directions in the parenting field are outlined next.

A shift From Treatment to a Broader Population-Based Prevention Model

Triple P was the first program to develop and test an explicit multilevel whole-of-population approach to parenting support (Sanders et al., 2008). The shift from a primary focus on developing and testing individual clinical treatments for high-risk or vulnerable children with conduct problems to a much more expansive focus on prevention and, specifically, the development of a population-based system of parenting support has been a transformational change. A whole new range of measurement, implementation, and logistical issues have come more sharply into focus as a result, ensuring that programs cater for a more diverse range of family risk factors and types of problems. This has led to the growth of a range of low-intensity self-help and technology-assisted interventions that have wider reach so more parents can participate at a lower cost. Triple P has become more inclusive, has been shown to be cross-culturally robust, and can be deployed in diverse settings, including low-resource environments, such as socially disadvantaged communities and low- and middle-income countries.

Development of a Multilevel System of Parenting Support

The evolution of Triple P has involved the development of a theoretically integrated, multilevel system of parenting support that moves beyond evidence-based group or individually administered interventions for high-risk populations (defined by characteristics of children or parents). The adoption of a systems-contextual approach required consideration of how a population of parents in a defined location might most usefully access parenting support based on a principle of sufficiency (Sanders, 2012). An important consideration was the concept of providing parents with "just enough" or the "minimally sufficient" level of support that enabled them to "get on with the job" of parenting their children with competence and confidence. We wanted to ensure that parents did not become unnecessarily reliant or dependent on others for parenting advice, and that programs were cost efficient. The system needed to be flexible and have a good ecological fit with existing service delivery systems and sources of funding. In the most successful examples of large-scale, population-wide implementations of the Triple P system, strong and coordinated local partnerships between organizations serving local communities has been a common thread (Fives, Purcell, Heary, NicGabhainn, & Canavan, 2014; Prinz, 2009). Families enter program variants according to self-assessed need and preference rather than population-based screening approaches, which can be expensive and rely on having a universal or near-to-universal primary health care system.

Development of an Effective System of Dissemination

Another major innovation has been the development of unique technology transfer arrangements for programs so that EBPS programs could effectively go to scale in a commercially viable way (see httpp://www.uniquest.com.au/triple-p). Our dissemination efforts with Triple P began in earnest in the mid-1990s from a development base in the School of Psychology at The University of Queensland, Australia. After developing a multidisciplinary training program in 1996 that evolved from a behavioral family intervention course and workshop taught to clinical psychologists from 1982 to 1995, it became apparent that a dedicated purveyor organization was needed for the delivery of an economically sustainable, high-quality, accreditation-based professional training and dissemination system.

At the time, we could find no existing example of a dissemination organization doing what we believed was needed to scale Triple P globally. A number of traditional academic publishers we approached had little interest in funding the complex "one-stop shop" that would publish books (practitioner kits) and necessary program materials (e.g., tip sheets, parent workbooks, audiovisual teaching aids) and be responsible for coordinating program dissemination, including running professional training courses and providing implementation support globally.

After beginning their association with the Parenting and Family Support Centre as a producer of the *Families TV* series in New Zealand and various Triple P video programs, such as the *Every Parent's Survival Guide* (Sanders, Markie-Dadds, & Turner, 2005), Triple P International Proprietary Limited (TPI) was formally licensed in 2001 to undertake publishing and global dissemination of the Triple P system on behalf of The University of Queensland. It has evolved from a small start-up company with a handful of staff to an organization with operations in several countries (Australia, Canada, Chile, Germany, Hong Kong, New Zealand, United Kingdom, and United States) and has formed alliances with third parties to disseminate Triple P in other countries (the Netherlands, Belgium, Costa Rica, Japan, and Turkey). TPI is a separate independent company. None of the program authors has shares in the company. The first author (Sanders) has been a consultant to TPI since 2001.

Development of a System of Multidisciplinary Training

In the early years, informal dissemination of parent training programs was through 1-day conference workshops, mainly at behavior therapy conferences, and university courses for graduate students (mainly in clinical psychology). Restricting the delivery of evidence-based parenting programs to a narrow range of practitioners (e.g., clinical psychologists and specialist mental health professionals) limited the program's accessibility to a small minority of parents, mainly of children with established conduct problems in large cities.

A different type of more widely accessible professional training was needed to provide on-the-job training for practitioners from diverse disciplines, including the health sector (nurses, general practitioners, pediatricians, psychologists); welfare sector (social workers, family support workers, parent educators); education sector (school counselors, guidance counselors, special education teachers, school chaplains); and, more recently, the voluntary sector (lay practitioners). The model of training developed (see Sanders & Murphy-Brennan, 2010) was designed to be an intensive, 2- to 5-day training (depending on level of intervention) delivered by an accredited trainer (master's or doctoral-level psychologist) employed by TPI. This was followed by a competency-based accreditation process approximately 2 months following initial training (Sethi, Kerns, Sanders, & Ralph, 2014). At the time of writing, over 7,170 training courses had been delivered to 76,500 practitioners across 28 countries.

Development of Different Delivery Modalities

Parenting programs were initially developed as individual or small-group programs, and these modalities are still widely used. However, Triple P now includes a much wider range of additional delivery modalities in an effort to enhance population reach and reduce logistical barriers for parents to attend programs. We have conducted trials evaluating mass media programs, such as multiepisode television programs; video series; radio programs; online programs delivered alone or in combination with an online social network, telephone, or e-mail support; large-group seminars; small-group topic- and age-specific discussion groups; self-help books; and, more recently, text messaging programs. Consumer preference studies showed that many parents are seeking the convenience of online support concerning parenting (Baker, Sanders, & Morawska, 2016; Metzler, Sanders, Rusby, & Crowley, 2012), and this is likely to lead to further web-based solutions as part of Triple P.

Use of More Diverse Delivery Contexts

In a further effort to increase the reach of interventions and to destigmatize participating in parenting programs, a diverse range of delivery contexts has been successfully employed. These include a television series on parenting; home visiting and home coaching; child care centers; preschools; schools; specialist medical clinics; pediatric practices; public and private inpatient and outpatient mental health services; prisons; religious organizations; local government services (e.g., public libraries); workplaces; government departments; universities and community colleges; community settings (e.g., movie theatres, shopping centers, bars); sports organizations; trains; and even outdoors under trees.

Development of a Media and Communications Strategy

As the managing director of TPI had a background in television, there was always a strong interest in developing a powerful communications strategy to promote program participation and to destigmatize parenting programs. The Stay Positive Level 1 intervention is an evidence-based, multimedia communications strategy (see Chapter 35, this volume). It combines a website (http://www.triplep-parenting.com/us-en/triple-p/?cdsid=rtsllprhlmfjnhkkolhujmujhjsnoslm) with print, radio, and television; promotional materials (e.g., billboards and posters); and social media.

Applications With Diverse Children and Families

Our approach to program development has been driven by principles of social justice and equity that seek to ensure equitable access to good-quality parenting support for all parents. In pursuit of this goal, Triple P has been applied by design to an increasingly diverse range of families. This has involved adapting existing programs and also developing entirely new programs with the inclusion of additional techniques derived from the literature pertaining to the treatment of particular conditions (e.g., Resilience Triple P for children experiencing bullying). Program variants have been tested with parents of children with disabilities (e.g., autism spectrum disorder, intellectual impairment, physical disabilities, traumatic brain injuries, fetal alcohol spectrum disorder); chronic health conditions (e.g., diabetes, asthma, eczema, obesity, recurrent pain syndromes); feeding disorders; anxiety disorders; and peer relationship difficulties and with parents of gifted and talented children. There are studies evaluating applications of Triple P with infants (e.g., Ferrari, Whittingham, Boyd, Sanders, & Colditz, 2011); toddlers (e.g., Tully & Hunt, 2015, 2017); preschoolers (e.g., Franke, Keown, & Sanders, 2016); school-aged children (e.g., McTaggart & Sanders, 2003); and adolescents (e.g., Salari, Ralph, & Sanders, 2014). As the program has become more widely disseminated, researchers and agencies have implemented Triple P with an increasingly heterogeneous sample of parents. These include parents with mental health problems (e.g., depression or bipolar disorder); parents at risk of harming their children; parents experiencing separation or divorce; parents who have been through natural disasters; parents experiencing difficulties managing work–life balance; and grandparents. The development of adaptations has been driven by a mixture of requests from parents and professionals for programs that directly relate to the parenting problems they are experiencing (e.g., going through divorce or having a child with a disability).

Embracing Cultural Diversity

Available evidence shows that the core principles of positive parenting appear to be cross-culturally robust around the world in both individualistic and collectivistic cultures (see Chapter 30, this volume). Studies have been conducted with parents from diverse cultural and racial backgrounds, including parents from Asian countries (Singapore, China, Hong Kong, Japan, Indonesia); North America (United States, Canada); Australia; New Zealand; Europe (United Kingdom and Ireland, Belgium, the Netherlands, Germany, Switzerland, Sweden, Turkey); and the Middle East (Iran).

Several studies have documented positive effects with Indigenous Māori families (whānau) in New Zealand; Aboriginal and Torres Strait Islander parents in Australia; First Nations parents in Canada and the United States; African American parents in the United States; and Spanish-speaking parents in the United States, Panama, and Chile. This is not to suggest that cultural differences are trivial or unimportant. On the contrary, many different aspects of culture have to be addressed (e.g., language, religious beliefs, traditions, priorities, learning styles) to ensure programs are delivered in a culturally appropriate manner (see Chapter 28, this volume).

Accommodating Advances in Implementation Science

There is now a much greater understanding of the important influence of the organizational context for implementation and what is needed to successfully engage practitioners, implement with fidelity, and sustain implementation of a program after initial staff training. In many ways, having the research and development base of Triple P in an academic institution (The University of Queensland), albeit in a relatively small research team in the Parenting and Family Support Centre, has attracted sustained investment from grants and strategic university funding to enhance the knowledge base underpinning development, delivery, and dissemination of Triple P, ensuring that the system continually evolves. Research into the program has contributed extensively to scholarship, and many honors, master's, and doctoral theses around the world have included Triple P studies. We continue to explore variables that will enhance community and practitioner engagement, program fidelity, and sustained program implementation.

AREAS WHERE FURTHER INNOVATION IS NEEDED

Each generation of parents faces new and different challenges in raising their children. Although some parenting issues are universal and remain the same in every generation (e.g., helping children get to sleep, dealing with discipline challenges, building skills, establishing daily routines, preparing children to start school), parenting programs must respond to contemporary issues faced by parents in each generation and anticipate, as best we can, the challenges families may encounter in the future. We also need to be "ahead of the game" in harnessing new technologies to ensure we are offering programs in the arenas where parents are looking for support. Mothers remain the most likely participants and beneficiaries of parenting programs, and unfortunately fathers are underrepresented as participants in parenting research, randomized controlled trials examining the efficacy of parenting programs, and service-based evaluations. In general, poor engagement and noncompletion of programs are also areas for continued program enhancement and delivery support.

Revisiting Widely Used Techniques to Enhance Their Effectiveness

Basic techniques of behavior change derived from learning theory have a well-established history. However, the principles and the techniques derived from them (e.g., praise and positive attention, instructions, backup consequences) should always be open to further investigation to enhance their effectiveness. For example, descriptive or labeled praise is widely used as a form of social reinforcement to encourage prosocial behavior and is considered a highly acceptable procedure by most parents in diverse cultures. Most evidence-based parenting programs advocate the liberal use of enthusiastic, contingent, descriptive praise to encourage prosocial behavior. However, a recent investigation showed that descriptive praise to encourage child compliance was no more beneficial than general, global praise, which was effective and actually preferred by parents (Leijten, Thomaes, de Castro, Dishion, & Matthys, 2016). Research on active ingredients in parenting programs and the study of mechanisms of change will further refine our understanding of the changes in parenting programs that are responsible for sustained child outcomes.

Changing Our Language

The language we use to describe positive parenting programs is important. The current terms used in the literature—parent training, behavioral parent training, parent management training, behavioral family intervention, or family therapy—all have significant limitations in a population approach that blends universal support and targeted programs and covers both prevention and treatment. We prefer to characterize our intervention as "evidence-based parenting and family support". Also, we believe the term *parent consultation* conveys a greater sense of collaboration between parent and service provider and has fewer connotations of "experts" telling parents how to raise their children. Parent consultation, in contrast to terms such as parent training or therapy, is more generically applicable and less linked to any particular delivery contexts or ways of working (e.g., health, education, welfare) and makes no assumptions that parents have skill deficits and need "training" to correct them.

Improving Father Participation and Outcomes

Increasing father involvement in both research and program participation remains a major challenge for the parenting field (Piotrowska et al., 2017). Many potential solutions have been suggested, including delivering programs at work, online, via fathers' interests (e.g., sporting activities), or as a couple enrichment activity. Current evidence suggests that existing programs, such as Group Triple P, are highly acceptable to fathers and, with relatively minor adaptations focusing on the current concerns and interests of fathers, can be made even more effective (Frank, Keown, & Sanders, 2015). It should be noted that relatively few men are involved in the delivery of parenting programs. Over 90% of practitioners trained in Triple P are women (Shapiro, Prinz, & Sanders, 2011). However, there is no evidence we are aware of to show that male or female practitioners differ in their effectiveness in delivering programs to either men or women. Strategies to increase the number of men involved in this important area of work would be valuable.

Improving Outcomes for Children in Poverty and Disadvantage

The social gradient associated with poverty and health outcomes is well known (Marmot, 2010), with people at the lowest end of the income distribution having high rates of a large number of adverse health and social outcomes (including higher rates of child mental health and learning problems). Parenting programs have an important role to play in reducing social inequities by enhancing educational, social, mental, and physical health outcomes for children. Preparation of children to make a successful transition to school is a particularly important target period of population-based approaches to parenting.

Recent work in Ireland with socioeconomically disadvantaged parents recruited in pregnancy highlights the value of integrating multiple levels of the Triple P system along with mentoring and baby massage into a home visiting program (PFL Evaluation Team, 2016). At school entry, children whose families received the combined intensive home visiting program had significantly higher levels of cognitive functioning, language development, social and emotional skills, and physical health compared to a group that received an enhanced care-as-usual condition. The program produced impressive effects compared to other home visiting programs, but intervention combinations like this are fairly intensive and expensive to deliver and are likely to reach a small proportion of children living in disadvantaged circumstances. Further work is needed to explore mechanisms for reaching the most disadvantaged and vulnerable in poorly resourced communities.

Changing the Focus to Children's Well-Being and Life Skills

A fundamental message to parents is that they should complete a parenting program to deal with current problems and avoid future ones. Parenting programs need to become more aspirational so that parents can view participation as enabling them to achieve valued long-term social outcomes for their children and themselves. This requires parents to articulate the kinds of values they have for their children, themselves, and their community.

Parenting programs need to be promoted as an effective and fun way for parents to help their children become capable, confident, caring, and resilient and to enhance children's success in school, relationships with others, and life opportunities. This requires programs to measure success differently and to focus on measuring prosociality and competence, not just reducing adverse outcomes (such as antisocial behavior, juvenile crime, and substance abuse). Absence of the negative is not the same as showing children developing prosocial skills. As long as parenting programs are promoted as primarily beneficial for parents with problem children, stigma associated with completing a parenting program is likely to remain. More evidence is needed focusing on the promotion of children's prosociality and the benefits for children's long-term development. When parents become attuned to their important role in promoting their children's lifetime success, rather than avoidance of failure, consumer "pull demand" is likely to grow for programs that really work and are made available to all parents. When a value is placed on these programs by parents, participation is more socially normative, nonexceptional, stigma free, and a predictable rite of passage for all parents.

Creating "Family-Friendly" Communities

Many opportunities exist for local governments, urban planners, designers, and engineers to work with parenting experts to design living environments that support positive parenting and quality family life (Riggio, 2002). The social infrastructure of new cities and urban renewal projects will need to ensure that the planned "built" environment caters for children and parents adequately by ensuring there are safe, interesting recreational environments for families of children of different ages. Coordinated planning of social infrastructure like roads, Internet access, and the built environment could also ensure that parenting programs are available through local child care centers, schools, and various community locations. Easy Internet access would enable parents to complete some programs online or use local workplaces as alternative locations for parents to access parenting advice. New residents to an area could receive a "starter pack" to encourage them to join a local positive parenting group or support network. The promotion of a city as a "great place to raise kids" and as a "family-friendly" environment could be a valuable social marketing tool along with parks, recreation, jobs, good schools, adequate child care, and convenient shopping to encourage families to move to an area. Table 45.1 summarizes the core values underpinning a family-friendly environment that could be promoted by local governments.

Strengthening Outcomes Across the Developmental Spectrum

Despite the importance of parenting in the first 1,000 days of a child's life, there is still surprisingly little convincing evidence from randomized trials that early parenting programs can alter infants' developmental outcomes. Programs showing the strongest effects are intensive home visiting programs, such as the Nurse–Family Partnership (Olds, 2006), which are typically offered to vulnerable, at-risk young women living in poor communities and delivered over a

Table 45.1: Essential Components of a Parent Friendly Environment

Principle	Brief Description	Example of Application
Values the parenting role	Values the parenting role and publicly acknowledges and celebrates parenting	Designs a social infrastructure to support parents and provides services
Recognizes parenting is a shared responsibility	Is inclusive of all types of parents and carers and fosters home–school partnerships	Enables grandparents and other carers to access parenting programs
Promotes self-determination of goals and autonomy in raising children	Recognizes parents' role in determining the values, skills, and behaviors they want to promote in their children and avoids being prescriptive, moralizing, or unfairly critical of families	Provides access to parenting programs that teach parents self-management skills, such as goal setting, self-monitoring, self-evaluation, problem-solving, and self-feedback
Promotes social and cultural connectedness of families	Creates events that bring families together using community resources and facilities	Arranges places families can visit and interact (e.g., cultural festivals)
Provides access for all to evidence-based parenting programs	Makes high-quality, culturally informed, evidence-based programs accessible for all families	Provides resources to train a workforce to deliver parenting programs
Ensures that parents participate in planning and decision-making that affects their families	Ensures parents are empowered and skilled to participate in planning and decision-making that affects children and families	Conducts regular surveys to capture parental viewpoints and has formal representation of parents on consumer groups to ensure parental opinion is represented concerning proposed plans and strategies

period of years. There is much less evidence concerning the effects of brief antenatal or postnatal programs (Evans, Boyd, Colditz, Sanders, & Whittingham, 2016).

In many regions, current care is of high quality, and positive program outcomes may yet be identified for brief programs where existing services and support are limited. At the other end of the developmental spectrum, in many countries, young people are dependent on their parents financially for longer than in past decades, and children with a disability may be dependent on their parents for support for much of their adult life. This dependency can create additional challenges for parents, and family conflict can occur. Research and program innovation is needed to develop programs to support families beyond children leaving school through to early adulthood.

Exploring the Role of Parenting Support in Addressing Global Issues

Every year, millions of people worldwide lose their lives or are displaced as a consequence of war or natural disasters such as hurricanes, wildfires, or earthquakes. The UNHCR (United Nations High Commissioner for Refugees) estimates there are currently 65 million displaced people worldwide (Martin, 2016). Parenting programs are needed in war and disaster zones and in areas of refugee resettlement to help parents manage the transition to normal life and to prevent secondary traumatization of children and parents in the resettlement and recovery process. Parenting programs also have a great deal to contribute to the 17 sustainable development goals listed in the United Nations Development Program (2016). These goals are listed in Table 45.2. Parenting programs have an untapped potential to influence broader behavior change, such as in relation to the environmental impact of development, commerce, and lifestyle. It is clear that a substantial amount of activity is needed to adapt existing parenting programs to low- and middle-income countries so they can be delivered in a sustainable manner. To do this, new dissemination models of training, resourcing practitioners, and providing technical support will need to ensure EBPS is affordable, scalable, and sustainable in these contexts.

Theory Development and Understanding Mechanisms of Change

Surprisingly little work has been done on understanding the mechanisms that explain change achieved through parenting programs (Fagan & Benedini, 2016). Behaviorally oriented programs seek to change the immediate antecedents and consequences of problem behavior by training parents to respond differently to episodes of problem behavior using clear, calm, consistent consequences and through positive attention for prosocial behavior. However, as these immediate contingencies of interaction change, there are multiple social, cognitive, and affective changes that might account for some of the change in child and parent outcomes. Socially, parents may report feeling more supported by a therapist, partner, or other parents or feeling less isolated and more connected to other people with similar concerns. Parents' knowledge of effective parenting practices may change, and they may develop more realistic expectations of themselves and their child. As parenting stress decreases due to less arguing or friction with children, parents' mood may improve, resulting in them feeling more confident and positive and less overwhelmed or pessimistic about their future. The quality of the parent–practitioner relationship may increase parents' motivation to carry out their parenting plan. Currently, it is not known which of these factors alone, or in interaction with other factors, explain changes in child

How Evidence-Based Parenting Programs (EBPS) Might Help Achieve:

GOAL 1: End poverty in all its forms everywhere. EBPS can work alongside other poverty-reduction strategies to help parents develop the skills they need to nurture their children and teach them the social and emotional skills they need to do well at school and in life.

GOAL 2: End hunger, achieve food security and improved nutrition, and promote sustainable agriculture. EBPS can be combined with other public health initiatives to improve parents' skills in ensuring good nutrition with available resources and can reduce child neglect.

GOAL 3: Ensure healthy lives and promote well-being for all at all ages. EBPS can encourage and teach parents how to model, prompt, and reinforce their children to take care of themselves through learning actions, lifestyles, and ways of coping with stress that promote good relationships, healthy living, and being physically active.

GOAL 4: Ensure inclusive and equitable quality education and promote lifelong learning opportunities for all. EBPS can prepare parents and early childhood educators to prepare young children to enter school with the language, social, and emotional skills that enable them to attend regularly, participate fully, and get the most out of their schooling; support parents of school-age children to communicate well with teachers and participate in their children's education; and support teachers to collaborate with parents of students in ways that promote positive parental engagement with schools.

GOAL 5: Achieve gender equality and empower all women and girls. Parenting programs should provide equal access for men and women. They provide an opportunity to discuss gender roles and teamwork in parenting and use of self-regulation model encourages self-determination of parenting goals. This empowers parents to make changes in their lives, not just in parenting. Parents can be encouraged to promote gender equity in their own and their children's lives.

GOAL 6: Ensure availability and sustainable management of water and sanitation for all. EBPS can teach children conservation and sanitary behaviors and to dispose of refuse in ways that do not contaminate valuable water sources.

GOAL 7: Ensure access to affordable, reliable, sustainable, and modern energy for all. Parenting specialists can work with those in other disciplines, such as engineers, to help families gain access to and prioritize use of modern, nonpolluting, sustainable energy when available to facilitate child development (e.g., for nonpolluting cooking equipment, supporting literacy with homework and bedtime stories).

GOAL 8: Promote sustained, inclusive, and sustainable economic growth, full and productive employment, and decent work for all. EBPS can help reduce social inequalities by helping parents and carers teach children the life skills they need to receive a good education, get a job, have healthy positive relationships with others, and contribute to the economy through productive work.

GOAL 9: Build resilient infrastructure, promote inclusive and sustainable industrialization, and foster innovation. Good parenting along with good schooling can help promote capable, resilient, self-determining children and young people. These are the future workforce, who can innovate and become socially and environmentally conscious adults who are motivated to change the world for the better.

GOAL 10: Reduce inequality within and among countries. Positive parenting is an investment in the future generation of parents and children that can promote values of equality, caring, compassion, and nonviolent ways of resolving conflict. Positive parenting everywhere may even help reduce violent conflict between nations.

GOAL 11: Make cities and human settlements inclusive, safe, resilient, and sustainable. Parenting experts can work with city planners to promote safe and engaging community spaces for children and families and to ensure parenting support is part of the planned social infrastructure of new cities and in urban renewal projects.

GOAL 12: Ensure sustainable consumption and production patterns. EBPS can include conservation behaviors as possible goals and targets for behavior change in families. Parental modeling and values-based discussions with children can help children recognize the role they and their peers can play as consumers.

GOAL 13: Take urgent action to combat climate change and its impacts. EBPS programs promote children having good relationships with parents, siblings, extended family, and peers. This concept should be extended to include children's relationship with the natural environment and the broader ecosystem that we live in (e.g., learning to take care of pets [companion animals] and other animals; learning to value our environment and to practice conservation behaviors related to climate change, such as reducing energy consumption, using nonpolluting sources of energy, avoiding polluting river systems and oceans). Taking care of the environment is a family issue as well as a political one. Collective action involves everyone playing their part.

GOAL 14: Conserve and sustainably use the oceans, seas, and marine resources for sustainable development. The depletion of fish stock and damage to coral reef systems through environmentally harmful fishing practices, such as the use of bomb fishing and cyanide, and disposal of refuse and chemicals into rivers and oceans are complex problems that require change in human behavior. For example, parenting programs supported by community leaders and schools in fishing villages involved in economically and environmentally nonsustainable practices may help teach children and parents alternative environmentally friendly values and behaviors so they can refrain from practices that damage valuable marine resources and develop new ways of generating sustainable income.

GOAL 15: Protect, restore, and promote sustainable use of terrestrial ecosystems, sustainably manage forests, combat desertification, and halt and reverse land degradation and halt biodiversity loss. Parenting programs can encourage parents to set values-informed goals for themselves and their children concurrently that relate to all family members taking care of and protecting the environment.

GOAL 16: Promote peaceful and inclusive societies for sustainable development, provide access to justice for all, and build effective, accountable, and inclusive institutions at all levels. EBPS programs can help reduce family violence and conflict by encouraging parents to use nonviolent ways of disciplining children and resolving family conflict and by teaching children nonviolent ways of resolving sibling and peer conflict.

GOAL 17: Strengthen the means of implementation and revitalize the Global Partnership for Sustainable Development. Parenting programs can be tailored to concurrently promote multiple sustainable development goals that would help to integrate currently disconnected efforts to produce a fairer, harmonious, and more environmentally conscious and just world.

or parent behavior. More research exploring potential mediators of intervention effects will help streamline intervention components that are associated with the greatest change in outcomes.

CREATING AN INNOVATION CULTURE IN PARENTING RESEARCH

Innovation is more likely to flourish in an environment that values, models, prompts, and reinforces people for innovation behaviors, and that provides training and experiences that further promote creativity and individual and collective capacity to innovate.

BUILDING AN ORGANIZATIONAL INFRASTRUCTURE THAT SUPPORTS INNOVATION

Within the Parenting and Family Support Centre, we have sought ways to enhance our staff and graduate students' capacity to innovate. This has included securing strategic funding from our university to review our center's operations and identify ways that innovation could be strengthened. Many of our research higher degree (RHD) students have been involved in developing and testing new program variants, including Pathways Triple P, Family Transitions Triple P, Lifestyle Triple P, Resilience Triple P, Grandparent Triple P, and Baby Triple P. The inclusion of program development experiences in RHD training will build a new workforce of scientist practitioners and innovators.

Addressing Systemic Obstacles to Innovation

Historically, academics interested in solving applied problems have been reinforced for grant success, scientific publications, and the quality of teaching, with much less emphasis on developing and disseminating programs or conducting research that makes a difference and achieves real social impact. Creating an innovation culture within a research center is much easier if indices of academic accomplishment, such as promotion or tenure, recognize the importance of solution-focused research that addresses major unresolved social or global problems. This requires universities to provide better training and support to staff and students in the areas of industry engagement, science communication, commercialization, and management of intellectual property and conflict of interest (Sanders, 2015).

Training a Future Generation of Parenting and Family Interventionists With Expertise in Population Approaches

Expertise in the fledgling field of population-based approaches to parenting and family support not only requires theoretical and clinical knowledge and experience in the fields of child development and EBPS, but also requires knowledge of epidemiology, measurement of parenting and child outcomes, research methods relevant to conducting and reporting on randomized controlled trials and place-based interventions, and understanding of the role of cultural diversity in parenting, economics, policy evaluation, science communication, social marketing, and community development. Involving students in projects that will give them experience in each of these areas relevant to their own projects is desirable but not always possible without careful planning.

Welcoming Null Findings

Innovation will inevitably lead to failures. Although disappointment is a natural reaction to experiments and intervention trials that produce null findings—outcomes inconsistent with the anticipated result or intervention effect—it is important to recognize the opportunities that such findings present. Many important learnings can arise from null findings, as long as the evaluation is of sufficiently high quality to provide informative results. Null findings have the potential to create momentum in innovation relating to evidence-based parenting programs and the process of implementation.

Jonas Salk argued that there is no such thing as a failed experiment because learning what does not work is a necessary step to learning what does (Kluger, 2004). Nonsignificant outcomes from an implementation trial provide an impetus to understand the null result and further enhance the program and the way in which it is implemented in the future. Was the intervention delivered with fidelity? Was practitioner training and supervision adequate? Was there sufficient organizational support? The Triple P quality assurance process (Chapter 43, this volume) ensures that the learnings from all trials are used to refine programs and implementation procedures, and that new programs are only disseminated once sufficient evidence has accrued that they work. Five percent of evaluations of Triple P interventions have had null findings; of those, two thirds were conducted by us as developers, leading to further program revisions and further trialing.

PARAMETERS FOR SERVICE DELIVERY, POLICY, AND PRACTICE

Who Should Be Able to Deliver Evidence-Based Programs?

When parents seek professional advice about parenting, they want well-trained and competent professionals who are empathic and knowledgeable to teach them about how to raise children. Parenting programs delivered with poor fidelity can lead to less significant and even adverse outcomes for children. However, what level of training and experience is needed to deliver evidence-based programs? Our starting position was to assume that programs based on cognitive-behavioral principles, such as Triple P, are likely to be most successful in the hands of a professional with advanced-level training in principles and techniques of behavior change, such as psychologists. Over time, it became apparent that a variety of different professionals could learn to effectively deliver Triple P and achieve excellent outcomes with families. No one discipline can or should own the knowledge about EBPS. This is particularly important in low- and middle-income countries, where there may be little access to the type of mental health services, family intervention specialists, or primary health care workforce that exists in wealthier Western countries (Ward, Sanders, Gardner, Mikton, & Dawes, 2016).

How Should Parenting Services Be Funded?

Much work is needed to make the economic case that population-based parenting programs are a sensible and economically justified investment in the well-being and future of children that will reap substantial economic benefits downstream (Mihalopolous, Sanders, Turner, Murphy-Brennan, & Carter, 2007). This case has been well argued by a number of influential economists (Doyle, Harmon, Heckman, & Tremblay, 2009; Heckman, 2006), but in most jurisdictions, funding of parenting programs is a relatively low priority. For example, the Australian National Disabilities Insurance Scheme, which provides funding for support services for people of all ages who have a disability, does not cover group-based parenting programs. Similarly, Medicare restricts funding for psychological intervention to children with a defined mental health disorder and only covers sessions where the child is physically present, which precludes most parenting programs. A lot of lip service is paid to the importance of parenting; however, in many countries it is a great challenge to ensure these programs are funded adequately. The most attractive funding mechanism is through a specific ring-fenced budget allocation to provide EBPS programs.

Faddism and Popular Culture

New ideas on raising children come and go, and the parenting field is full of self-appointed experts selling or giving away parenting advice, often generated by fads and popular culture. Because of increasing access to the Internet, there has likely never been a time when parents have had access to as much parenting advice. While unsolicited parenting advice is often ignored or seen as criticism, when parents are looking for practical advice to solve a problem, they generally want the advice to be clear, specific, based on good evidence, and presented by reliable and well-trained staff and to focus on programs that have been proven to work. As waves of different trends in parenting have obvious personal and societal impacts, there is an imperative to constantly protect the value placed on evidence of effectiveness and the need for scientific scrutiny before any large-scale dissemination effort.

CONCLUSION

The Triple P system has made a substantial contribution to the well-being of many children and families around the world. However, parenting programs must continue to evolve to remain relevant for successive generations of parents. This will occur by being aware of the broader socioeconomic conditions that affect the health and well-being of the population as a whole, and, as needed, by developing and testing adaptations, variants, and derivative programs with defined clinical population groups and different types of parenting communities as needed. It will also occur through the synergistic bringing together of knowledge from other disciplines interested in working with parenting experts and behavioral scientists to find solutions to major unresolved global problems. Parenting should be seen as central to the long-term mental and physical health and well-being of children, adolescents, adults, and communities. Policies on mental health promotion and community development should more explicitly identify the role of parenting programs in contributing to many indices of well-being, including the prevention of child maltreatment; the prevention and treatment of social, emotional, and behavioral problems; and encouragement of positive academic, social, and environmental outcomes.

KEY MESSAGES

- The Triple P system is built on a history that values program development innovation, rigorous evaluation, and sustainable dissemination.
- Innovation is a continual process with language, strategies, and professional training and support processes that must evolve with new evidence.
- New approaches are needed to improve outcomes in many areas of unmet need and to address contemporary issues for new generations of parents.
- Our focus must always be on balancing innovation with service delivery capacity and scientific evaluation to ensure the best access to quality parenting support globally.

REFERENCES

Baer, D., Wolf, M., & Risley, T. (1987). Some still-current dimensions of applied behavior analysis. *Journal of Applied Behavior Analysis, 20*, 313. doi:10.1901/jaba.1987.20-313

Baker, S., Sanders, M. R., & Morawska, A. J. (2016). Who uses online parenting support? A cross-sectional survey exploring Australian parents' Internet use for parenting. *Journal of Child & Family Studies, 26*, 1–12. doi:10.1007/s10826-016-0608-1

Doyle, O., Harmon, C. P., Heckman, J. J., & Tremblay, R. E. (2009). Investing in early human development: Timing and economic efficiency. *Economics & Human Biology, 7*, 1–6. doi:10.1016/j.ehb.2009.01.002

Evans, T., Boyd, R. N., Colditz, P., Sanders, M., & Whittingham, K. (2016). Mother–very preterm infant relationship quality: RCT of Baby Triple P. *Journal of Child & Family Studies, 26*, 284–295. doi:10.1007/s10826-016-0555-x

Fagan, A. A., & Benedini, K. M. (2016). How do family-focused prevention programs work? A review of mediating mechanisms associated with reductions in youth antisocial behaviors. *Clinical Child & Family Psychology Review, 19*, 285–309. doi:10.1007/s10567-016-0207-0

Ferrari, A., Whittingham, K., Boyd, R., Sanders, M. R., & Colditz, P. (2011). Prem Baby Triple P, a new parenting intervention for parents of infants born very preterm: Acceptability and barriers. *Infant Behavior & Development, 34*, 602–609. doi:10.1016/j.infbeh.2011.06.004

Fives, A., Purcell, L., Heary, C., NicGabhainn, S., & Canavan, J. (2014). *Parenting support for every parent: A population-level evaluation of Triple P in Longford Westmeath. Final Report.* Athlone, Ireland: Longford Westmeath Parenting Partnership. Retrieved from http://www.atlanticphilanthropies.org/app/uploads/2015/09/Report-Parenting-Support-for-Every-Parent.pdf

Frank, T. J., Keown, L., & Sanders, M. R. (2015). Enhancing father engagement and intraparental teamwork in an evidence-based parenting intervention: A randomized controlled trial of outcomes and processess. *Behavior Therapy, 46*, 749–763. doi:10.1016/j.beth.2015.05.008

Franke, N., Keown, L. J., & Sanders, M. R. (2016). An RCT of an online parenting program for parents of preschool-aged children with ADHD symptoms. *Journal of Attention Disorders.* Epub ahead of print. doi:10.1177/1087054716667598

Heckman, J. J. (2006). Skill formation and the economics of investing in disadvantaged children. *Science, 312*, 1900–1902. doi:10.1126/science.1128898

Kluger, J. (2004). *Splendid solution: Jonas Salk and the conquest of polio*. New York, NY: Penguin.

Leijten, P., Thomaes, S., de Castro, B. O., Dishion, T. J., & Matthys, W. (2016). What good is labeling what's good? A field of experimental investigation of parental labeled praise and child compliance. *Behavior Research & Therapy, 87*, 134–141. doi:10.1016/j.brat.2016.09.008

Marmot, M. (2010). *Fair society, healthy lives: The Mamort Review: Strategic review of health inequalities in England post-2010*. London, England: Marmot Review.

Martin, S. F. (2016). Rethinking protection of those displaced by humanitarian crises. *The American Economic Review, 106*, 446–450. doi:10.1257/aer.p20161063

McTaggart, P., & Sanders, M. R. (2003). The transition to school project: Results from the classroom. *Australian e-Journal for the Advancement of Mental Health, 2*, 144–155. doi:10.5172/jamh.2.3.144

Mercy, J. A., & Saul, J. (2009). Creating a healthier future through early interventions for children. *JAMA, 301*, 2262–2264. doi:10.1001/jama.2009.803

Metzler, C. W., Sanders, M. R., Rusby, J. C., & Crowley, R. N. (2012). Using consumer preference information to increase the reach and impact of media-based parenting interventions in a public health approach to parenting support. *Behavior Therapy, 43*, 257–270. doi:10.1016/j.beth.2011.05.004

Mihalopolous, C., Sanders, M. R., Turner, K. M. T., Murphy-Brennan, M., & Carter, R. (2007). Does the Triple P—Positive Parenting Program provide value for money? *Australian and New Zealand Journal of Psychiatry, 41*, 239–246. doi:10.1080/00048670601172723

Olds, D. L. (2006). The nurse–family partnership: An evidence-based preventive intervention. *Infant Mental Health Journal, 27*, 5–25. doi:10.1002/imhj.20077

Patterson, G. R. (1982). *Coercive family process*. Eugene, OR: Castalia.

PFL Evaluation Team. (2016). *Preparing for Life. Early childhood intervention final report: Did Preparing for Life improve children's school readiness?* Dublin, Ireland: UCD Geary Institute for Public Policy.

Piotrowska, P. J., Tully, L. A., Lenroot, R., Kimonis, E., Hawes, D., Moul, C., . . . Dadds, M. R. (2017). Mothers, fathers, and parental systems: A conceptual model of parental engagement in programmes for child mental health—Connect, attend, participate, enact (CAPE). *Clinical Child and Family Psychology Review, 20*, 146–161. doi:10.1007/s10567-016-0219-9

Prinz, R. J. (2009). Toward a population-based paradigm for parenting intervention, prevention of child maltreatment, and promotion of child well-being. In K. A. Dodge & D. L. Coleman (Eds.), *Preventing child maltreatment: Community approaches* (pp. 55–67). New York, NY: Guilford Press.

Riggio, E. (2002). Child friendly cities: Good governance in the best interests of the child. *Environment & Urbanization, 14*, 45–58. doi:10.1177/095624780201400204

Salari, R., Ralph, A., & Sanders, M. R. (2014). An efficacy trial: Positive Parenting Program for parents of teenagers. *Behaviour Change, 31*, 34–52. doi:10.1017/bec.2013.31

Sanders, M. R. (2012). Development, evaluation, and multinational dissemination of the Triple P—Positive Parenting Program. *Annual Review of Clinical Psychology, 8*, 1–35. doi:10.1146/annurev-clinpsy-032511-143104

Sanders, M. R. (2015). Management of conflict of interest in psychosocial research on parenting and family interventions. *Journal of Child and Family Studies, 24*, 832–841. doi:10.1007/s10826-015-0127-5

Sanders, M. R., Markie-Dadds, C., & Turner, K. M. T. (2005). *Every parent's survival guide*. Brisbane, Australia: Triple P International.

Sanders, M. R., & Murphy-Brennan, M. (2010). Achieving widespread dissemination of low intensity evidence-based practices: The experience of the Triple P—Positive Parenting Program. In J. Bennett-Levy, D. A. Richards, P. Farrand, H. Christensen, K. M. Griffiths, D. J. Kavanagh, . . . C. Williams

(Eds.), *Oxford guide to low intensity CBT interventions* (pp. 503–510). Oxford, England: Oxford University Press.

Sanders, M. R., Ralph, A., Sofronoff, K., Gardiner, P., Thompson, R., Dwyer, S. B., & Bidwell, K. (2008). Every Family: A population approach to reducing behavioral and emotional problems in children making the transition to school. *Journal of Primary Prevention, 29*, 197–222. doi:10.1007/s10935-008-0139-7

Scott, S., & Dadds, M. R. (2009). Practitioner review: When parent training doesn't work: Theory-driven clinical strategies. *Journal of Child Psychology and Psychiatry, 50*, 1441–1450. doi:10.1111/j.1469-7610.2009.02161.x

Sethi, S., Kerns, S. E. U., Sanders, M. R., & Ralph, A. (2014). The international dissemination of evidence-based parenting interventions: Impact on practitioner content and process self-efficacy. *International Journal of Mental Health Promotion, 16*, 126–137. doi:10.1080/14623730.2014.917896

Shapiro, C. J., Prinz, R. J., & Sanders, M. R. (2011). Facilitators and barriers to implementation of an evidence-based parenting intervention to prevent child maltreatment: The Triple P—Positive Parenting Program. *Child Maltreatment, 17*, 86–95. doi:1077559511424774

Tully, L. A., & Hunt, C. (2015). Brief parenting interventions for children at risk of externalizing behavior problems: A systematic review. *Journal of Child and Family Studies, 25*, 705–719. doi:10.1007/s10826-015-0284-6

Tully, L. A., & Hunt, C. (2017). A randomized controlled trial of a brief versus standard group parenting program for toddler aggression. *Aggressive Behavior, 43*, 291–303. doi:10.1002/ab.21689

United Nations Development Program. (2016). *UNDP support to the implementation of the 2030 agenda for sustainable development.* New York, NY: Author. Retrieved from http://www.undp.org/content/dam/undp/library/SDGs/SDG%20Implementation%20and%20UNDP_Policy_and_Programme_Brief.pdf

Wahler, R. G. (1969). Oppositional children: A quest for parental reinforcement control. *Journal of Applied Behavior Analysis, 2*, 159–170. doi:10.1901/jaba.1969.2-159

Ward, C., Sanders, M. R., Gardner, F., Mikton, C., & Dawes, A. (2016). Preventing child maltreatment in low- and middle-income countries: Parent support programs have the potential to buffer the effects of poverty. *Child Abuse & Neglect, 54*, 97–107. doi:10.1016/j.chiabu.2015.11.002

THE FUTURE OF EVIDENCE-BASED PARENTING SUPPORT PROGRAMS

MATTHEW R. SANDERS

INTRODUCTION

This volume has provided an in-depth overview of how evidence-based parenting support (EBPS) can be applied as an integrated, theoretically consistent, multilevel system for entire communities. This section brings together challenges that if addressed will further strengthen the impact of the population approach and thereby change the landscape of parenting support for the next generation of parents and children.

STRENGTHENING THE EVIDENCE BASE FOR A POPULATION APPROACH

The current evidence base supporting the Triple P system as a population approach to parenting support can be strengthened further by increasing the number of large-scale, place-based randomized controlled trials (RCTs). This evolving evidence base needs to ensure that contemporary standards of scientific reporting are observed, including the pretrial registration of all trials, and that trials are adequately statistically powered. Inevitable and unavoidable conflicts of interest (COIs) that stem from program developers being involved in trials need to be consistently declared in grants, scientific papers, reports, and conference presentations (see Sanders, 2015). Once declared, COIs need to be properly managed by individual academics, universities, and research institutions undertaking the research. Independent-of-developer evaluations (e.g., Fives, Purcell, Heary, NicGabhainn, & Canavan, 2014) are useful once programs have been disseminated, providing they are conducted competently.

There is a need to develop a series of brief, reliable, valid, and change-sensitive measures of parenting that can be used widely as a population indicator of parenting practices with different age groups. Such measures that can be linked to administrative data collected by health, education, and welfare authorities would allow for linkage of individual data with aggregate data at a population level. As population-level effects are likely to be influenced by parent-to-parent advocacy (a social contagion effect), geographical mapping of the spread of parent-to-parent sharing of advice and support across a geographical catchment area would be particularly useful to explore how program participation spreads through parent social networks across communities, including digital ones. Finally, trials of population-level intervention need to develop or use measures of the favorability of the policy environment and funding of services. For example, in Australia during a 3-year rollout of Stepping Stones Triple P as a population-level intervention in three states, the federal government introduced a National Disability Insurance Scheme that changed the funding of services for families of children with a disability, favorably affecting access to services.

CHANGING PROFESSIONAL AND PUBLIC ATTITUDES TOWARD PARENTS

Most parents do a good job in raising their children under, at times, extremely challenging circumstances. They love their children, try to protect them, and educate them; do not maltreat them; and seek to instill the values, skills, and behavior they believe their children need to succeed in their community and cultural context. The fundamental tasks of being a parent have not changed. No parent sets out to be an abusive or neglectful parent. For EBPS to be embraced by parents and within the broader community, public messages to the community at large should aim to convey respect and tolerance and acknowledge the challenges and joys that parents face, rather than shock campaigns that convey a subtext that says parents are failing or "You are at risk of harming your child, so get help now before it's too late." A well-designed population approach should seek to complement and build on the existing strengths and capabilities of people, not use shame, blame, humiliation, or guilt-inducing tactics to change parenting.

Evidence-based parenting support can provide flexible scaffolding to support families to the minimally sufficient extent that parents and children require to resolve a problem or issue or navigate a developmental phase. We should ask not only how much support parents require, but also "how little support do parents need to carry out their tasks and responsibilities with skills and confidence?" When parenting support is viewed from that perspective, the issue of "how little" support should not be interpreted as a call to cut already-scarce funding for parenting and family support programs or to deliver perfunctory, trivial, and ineffective support. On the contrary, it is a call to identify what kind of support different parents require, for which problems, at different stages of the life cycle, and to have a menu of practical, evidence-based options that parents can access readily.

Sometimes professionals from different disciplines can be critical and judgmental of parents. Parents under stress often feel scrutinized, judged, and disapproved of. Some professionals routinely use pejorative and disrespectful language in referring to parents in their absence, such as saying a particular child needs a "parentectomy" or "This child has a parent from hell." Engaging with parents in a respectful manner is an essential prerequisite for professionals seeking to provide guidance to parents and motivate them to change.

A good education for parenthood provides parents with the essential knowledge, skills, and confidence they need to effectively deal with common everyday challenges of raising children. As evidence continues to grow on the importance of parenting in influencing the course of human development, the need for high-quality, evidence-based, culturally informed, and affordable parenting programs is likely to accelerate. In most Western countries, there are still many parents who could benefit from parenting programs who do not participate, despite efforts to improve engagement methods. Furthermore, there remains a huge unmet need in the majority of low- and middle-income countries. Adoption of a population approach is an essential prerequisite to improved access.

IN SEARCH OF BETTER POSITIVE PARENTING TECHNIQUES

Observance of the principle "if it ain't broke don't fix it" can be dangerous. All parenting programs, including Triple P, can be improved. Triple P was originally designed as an intensive 10-session program that eventually became known as Level 4 Standard Triple P. Standard Triple P introduced parents to a range of principles and specific tools that they could use with their children both now and in the future and apply flexibly to whatever problems they encountered. These tools included using anticipatory and antecedent strategies to change the context for problems (such as arranging engaging activities at high-risk times, creating a safe play place, and increasing positive interactions between parents and children); teaching new skills and behaviors to children (such as through incidental teaching and "ask-say-do"); and providing parents with different options for managing children's problem behavior. This focus on teaching parents to become autonomous and independent was accomplished through teaching parents self-regulation skills, training them flexibly, and promoting generalization of parenting skills through training loosely, with sufficient exemplars (Stokes & Baer, 1977). This focus of self-regulation and generalization promotion has been embedded in all program levels and variants and influenced the design of the professional training, the supervision of staff, and the Triple P Implementation Framework.

Every positive parenting technique used in Triple P can be made to work well or to fail under certain circumstances. For example, valuable techniques such as descriptive praise are not a panacea. Praise can be overused, underused, or used inappropriately and therefore not motivate children to learn new skills or change their behavior or build their self-esteem. The same qualification applies to other parenting techniques, such as how we talk to and give attention to children, show affection, use incidental teaching, give instructions, introduce rules, respond to children's emotions, and use disciplinary consequences. No technique works for all children or all parents. Most parenting strategies (e.g., time-out) work best when appropriately combined with other strategies to promote alternative or competing behaviors (e.g., engaging activities, contingent positive attention for appropriate behavior).

The study of the conditions that might optimize or weaken the effectiveness of specific parenting techniques and their combinations for tackling different problems in different contexts and age groups is an area of research that is receiving less attention than it should. Parenting programs should embrace basic experimental studies that seek to vary and clarify conditions of optimum usage, including seeking the views of children regarding the type of parenting strategies they favor for different types of common child behaviors (e.g., fighting with siblings, disobedience).

IMPLICATIONS OF INDIVIDUAL DIFFERENCES IN PARENTAL CAPACITY FOR SELF-REGULATION

Parental capacity for self-regulation varies greatly and is influenced by multiple contextual and motivational factors in addition to the influence of genetic and biological factors affecting self-regulation. Parents differ in their capacity to self-manage their behavior and emotions and become truly independent of supportive professional guidance and support about parenting (Box 46.1).

These obvious entry-level differences in parents' self-regulatory capacity to address their parenting problems are among the key reasons for developing multiple levels of parenting support. However, regardless of severity or complexity of presenting problems, the goal should be to move the parent from his or her current level of self-regulatory capacity to the next highest level of proficiency (see Sanders & Mazzucchelli, 2013). Ideally, this movement from more to less "in person" support required to enable parents with very different starting points to enter, participate, and exit the program is enhanced when an intensity level and delivery variant are found that most closely approximate their needs. The challenge is to ensure that multiple levels of EBPS are actually available in a given community. When only one level is available (e.g., Group Triple P), capacity to tailor programs to a specific need is reduced.

IMPROVING THE TRIPLE P SYSTEM AS AN INTERVENTION MODEL

As with any program with many moving parts, there are certain program elements that can always be improved, ranging from the inclusion of additional helpful modules, refraining from adding new components because they do not improve outcomes, or removing components because they have minimal uptake or add little to program outcomes. Program resources can include examples that are not the "perfect" fit for a given family or the timing given for an activity can be completed in shorter or longer time than recommended in a practitioner manual. Practitioners need to tailor their delivery, based on clinical judgment and experience, to the needs of parents and children. Mazzucchelli and Sanders (2010) and Sanders and Burke (2014) have described specific ways that such tailoring and adaptation can occur while maintaining program fidelity.

Full revisions of programs are expensive. However, program resources, particularly video materials, need to be refreshed periodically to ensure that a program is as contemporary and relevant as possible. Using video resources, no matter how good they are, that were filmed 20 years ago or using written materials that look dated inadvertently encourages parental and practitioner perceptions of a program as being past its use-by date. To circumvent this problem, the Triple P system uses a "one-stop shop" publishing mechanism through Triple P International Proprietary Limited (TPI) that enables reprints, revisions, and translations to occur more frequently and quickly than would otherwise be the case.

BOX 46.1: Case Examples Illustrating Differences in Parental Self-Regulation Capability

Consider two very different parents (Martha and Shauna, both aged 31) with similar child problems but very different presentations. Martha presents to her general practitioner (GP) saying, "I have a 4-year-old and a 2-year-old, and they are driving me crazy, particularly Sven, the 4-year-old. Sven regularly hits his younger brother, Joshua, and throws tantrums when I try to stop him. I went to the Positive Parenting seminar at my local school last month hoping to get some answers on how to deal with Sven. I tried to follow a couple of the suggestions. I decided to keep track of his hitting and tantrums for a week. He hit or pushed his brother about 10 times in the week, which was less than I thought. I know I dealt with it differently each time. So, I've been pretty inconsistent. I then tried to be more positive by catching them playing nicely and praising them, and when the hitting happened, I tried to use quiet time. It worked well for a few days. Then it didn't work. So, I'm stuck. I've also looked at a million parenting websites and books. They gave different advice compared to what I was told at the school seminar. Any suggestions on what I should do now?" Many practitioners might think most of their families are not like this and have far more complex presentations like Shauna, described below.

Shauna is a lone parent who has a similar sibling conflict problem with her 5- and 3-year-old boys but has multiple other concerns as well. On presentation, she looked and sounded depressed and seemed overwhelmed by the task of being a parent. When asked by her GP how she was feeling, she said "Awful. Terrible. I've really had enough. My kids are driving me crazy again. They're fighting all the time, and I can't deal with it. I end up losing my temper and lashing out." Then, after a long pause she said, "The oldest one, Jack, has just got the devil in him. He's just like his father, and he's always been like that. I've tried absolutely everything. Nothing works. I want to quit this parenting business. It's their father's turn to look after them."

These two presentations reveal differences in levels of readiness to change their parenting behavior. Martha already has many problem-solving skills. She has defined the problem and wants to address it, as shown by the fact she kept a baseline record of her eldest son's behavior to help check her perceptions of the problems and to track change. She has also taken it on herself to attend a Triple P seminar to get some strategies and try them out. All of this was with no guidance or support. When she met a roadblock and could not go any further, she was motivated enough to do something about it. She recognized that her parenting needed to change to sort out the behavioral problems and asked for help from someone she knows and has a relationship with. In terms of self-regulatory capacity, she would be considered to have high-level entry skills and some insight into her problem. Shauna has much lower self-regulatory capacity. She is depressed, feels emotionally drained, cannot think about any specific goals for change, has not asked for help with her own parenting, and would like to withdraw from her parenting responsibilities altogether.

These case examples illustrate how parents with similar child problems on the surface differ greatly in their self-regulatory capacity. In Martha's case, a brief

Primary Care Triple P intervention by the GP using a tip sheet on dealing with fighting and aggression or referral to the Triple P Online website with follow-up support as needed could be an effective intervention. For Shauna, more is required to help her recognize the role that parenting might play in maintaining the problem and her role in resolving the problem. She could be referred to a Level 5 program (Enhanced Triple P and Pathways Triple P modules) to help address her depressed mood, attributional bias, and anger management problems. It would entail direct observation of the parent–child interaction, modeling of parenting skills, rehearsal or practice of skills, personal feedback from the practitioner using a self-regulatory approach, and assistance with the selection of attainable session goals.

IMPLICATIONS OF DIFFERENTIAL SUSCEPTIBILITY TO ENVIRONMENTAL INFLUENCES

Mapping of the human genome has rapidly changed our understanding of the role of genetic and neurobiological influences on child development and life trajectories. Epigenetic studies have shown that environments can influence the expression of genes. The notion of differential susceptibility suggests that rather than genes only conferring increased risk under adverse circumstances, some may also confer better outcomes under more favorable circumstances. Children with particular genes appear to be more responsive to both positive and negative environmental influences (Slagt, Dubas, Deković, & van Aken, 2016). Bakermans-Kranenburg and van Ijzendoorn (2011) have shown that the dopamine receptor gene DRD4 7-repeat allele confers worse outcomes with insensitive parenting, but better outcomes than average with more sensitive parenting. These kinds of studies suggest that several genes may confer more resilience or greater risk in adverse environments.

More intervention trials of parenting programs are being called for to examine how parenting programs might be used with genetically and biologically vulnerable children. Moffitt (2013) called on intervention scientists and stress biology researchers to collaborate in adding stress biology measures to randomized trials of interventions intended to reduce effects of violence exposure and other trauma in the lives of young people. Several groups have already taken up this call and have examined how family intervention programs influence biological processes related to progression of illnesses. How the immune system responds to changes in the family environment is a particularly interesting area of inquiry. Excessive inflammation is a chronic overreaction of the immune system linked to a variety of health problems in later life, including heart disease, depression, diabetes, and psychosis. Miller, Brody, Yu, and Chen (2014) conducted an RCT with children at age 11 from families with a low socioeconomic status families; the study was a family-focused intervention targeting parenting practices, parent–child communication, and helping children develop strategies for dealing with stressors. The intervention resulted in reducing inflammation assessed 8 years after the intervention, when the children were aged 19.

Although positive parenting has benefits for all children by reducing exposure to a "toxic" family environment, positive parenting may have greater positive effects on some children and parents than others based on genetic and biological differences. Long (2016) argued this type of research has important implications for parenting support in the future. If children or parents can be identified as being at greater genetic risk at birth for being a responder or nonresponder to positive parenting, some major ethical and practical dilemmas for funders of parenting programs, practitioners, and society at large can emerge regarding how to share such information with parents in a way that does not cause alarm, undue distress, or expense.

A useful population message to all might be that regardless of a child's genetic and biological makeup, parents, and families have a responsibility to do what they can to promote their child's development and well-being, to ensure they are not exposed to avoidable forms of toxic stress and adversity, and to create a safe, nurturing, and low-conflict home environment. Many children with conditions strongly influenced by genetics or syndromes linked with behavior problems respond well to positive parenting programs (see Chapter 41 of this volume). If the behavioral implications of specific syndromes or phenotypes are carefully factored into a parenting plan, then the parenting advice will be more relevant to the lived daily experience of parents in raising their children. The principles of tailoring and personalizing interventions that have been used to successfully address many unique contextual factors, such as separation and divorce, attention deficit hyperactivity disorder, developmental disabilities, being a parent of multiples, or having a preterm baby, can be applied to new findings regarding biological or genetic causation of children's problems. These influences will always interact with modifiable environmental factors to determine outcomes.

UNDERSTANDING NONRESPONDERS

A related issue comes from the study of nonresponders. Building on the argument of Sanders, Turner, and Mazzucchelli in Chapter 45 of this volume that null findings are an impetus to innovation, further improvements in parenting programs can stem from gaining a better understanding of individual cases, and indeed entire communities, where the Triple P system was implemented but did not work. A program may fail or only be partially successful for many reasons beyond genetic and biological factors, including poor or inadequate implementation of the program by the practitioner, failure of the parent to actually implement the techniques introduced in a clinical setting at home in their everyday interactions with children, or biased or selective reporting of results.

Other reasons include destructive couple conflict about parenting or other issues, interference or criticism by extended family members (such as grandparents), insufficient intervention dose because parents prematurely discontinued the program, irregular session attendance, failure to complete necessary between-session homework tasks, and adequate program implementation by both practitioners and parents but the child simply does not respond in the expected manner. Also, programs delivered might not meet parents' expectations or aspirations. However, nonresponse can also be related to child factors. Research on children with conduct disorders who have callous, unemotional traits, particularly nonresponse to EBPS, has led to research efforts to modify parent training to improve outcomes for these children (Dadds et al., 2014).

Although more vulnerable and socioeconomically disadvantaged families are more likely to drop out of all parenting programs, when these families remain and complete programs, they can do just as well as other less disadvantaged families. Further research is needed to clarify the extent to which inadequate or nonresponse to parenting programs is related to different causes. A study of the natural history of the factors associated with discontinuation during the course of an intervention would be particularly useful to help identify early indicators of poor response so practitioners can take preventive actions to forestall discontinuation. The reporting of research findings does not always differentiate clearly between different types of discontinuance, including failure to begin a program, attend all sessions, complete various assessments after completing a program, or complete assessments after not completing programs. Whole cases missing data following an intervention should not be confused with program participation, completion, or satisfaction. It is up to evaluators to allocate the resources needed to chase missing data, particularly at follow-up.

The quality of the practitioner–parent relationship and the practitioner's skill in managing parent resistance can be related to a poor response to an intervention. If parents do not get on well with or dislike the practitioner, they are more likely to be dissatisfied with their sessions and less likely to continue. On the other hand, parents can still drop out when the practitioner is removed entirely and the program is delivered as a web-based self-administered intervention (Sanders, Baker, & Turner, 2012). It is unlikely that practitioner factors are entirely responsible for high or low program completion rates.

Future studies are needed to more clearly distinguish between different types of noncontinuance in different delivery modalities. Parents may fail to enter a program, begin and then discontinue prior to achieving adequate exposure to the skills they need to solve a problem, complete enough of a program to solve a current problem and be satisfied enough to exit the program early, or complete a program successfully but fail to complete postintervention assessment requirements, giving a misleading impression that the program was not effective for that parent.

It would be useful to conduct brief assessments at the beginning of each session so that, regardless of the number of sessions parents complete, there is always a most recent outcome assessment available so that every parent completing Triple P has a known clinical outcome. This approach was successfully used in the IAPT (Increased Access to Psychological Therapies) program in the United Kingdom that substantially increased access to evidence-based treatments, mainly cognitive-behavioral therapy (CBT) for depression and anxiety, to enable outcome data (postintervention) to be collected from an impressive 94% of patients who started treatment (Clark et al., 2009). A session-by-session outcome monitoring system achieved unusually high levels of pre- to posttreatment data completeness. Large numbers of patients were treated, with low-intensity interventions (such as guided self-help) being particularly helpful for achieving high attendance throughout. Each Triple P practitioner manual has recommended outcome assessment tools that can be used for session-by-session monitoring.

IMPLEMENTATION ISSUES AND POPULATION EFFECTS

PLANNING FOR SUSTAINABILITY

This volume includes a number of chapters that clearly demonstrate that successful implementation of the Triple P system requires application of the important learnings from implementation science. Chapter 33 of this volume by McWilliam and Brown discusses the role of purveyor organizations in supporting agencies using the Triple P system to plan for sustainability. Ultimately, regardless of the level of purveyor implementation support, it is up to individual organizations to self-manage their implementation of evidence-based practices, including deciding how much or little of the system to invest in, having staff training, how trained staff are supported and supervised, "mainstreaming" the delivery of Triple P so it becomes core business, setting targets for parental participation, and how to use outcome evaluation as part of a quality improvement process. Fidelity "policing" using external purveyor organizations will always be seen as temporary and transitional at best (particularly by overseas organizations), difficult to maintain, and expensive to scale. Triple P uses a model that seeks to build the capacity of organizations and partnerships to be self-managing as far as possible.

MAKING USE OF AVAILABLE TOOLS, RESOURCES, AND IMPLEMENTATION SUPPORT

Specific web tools, outcome measures, and implementation tools can be used by agencies to support their implementation of Triple P. Table 46.1 describes some of the specific tools developed to assist agencies and practitioners to implement Triple P effectively and to evaluate outcomes.

PRACTICE IMPLICATIONS OF BETTER INFORMED CONSUMERS

As more parents develop an understanding of the benefits of high-quality parenting programs for their child's and their own well-being, parents are likely to become more actively involved as consumers. Pull demand refers to a demand for a service or product from one consumer group (e.g., retailers) that subsequently increases demand from another group (e.g., wholesalers). The pharmaceutical industry, for example, allocates considerable resources to direct-to-patient advertising of medications, encouraging people to "ask your doctor about this medication" (Santucci, McHugh, & Barlow, 2012). Social marketing that targets parents directly may lead to more parents requesting an evidence-based parenting program and potentially increase provider requests to access training so they can deliver the requested service.

Once completing a parenting course becomes more socially normative, consumer expectations are likely to change, with parents seeking the best available programs as they do for any other service or product. Program providers need to become more skilled at sharing accurate, up-to-date, and reliable information about the parenting programs they offer. An informed consumer would make a considered decision on the basis of checking out for themselves what programs are available. This includes being able to access information about the strength of evidence supporting programs offered by an organization; the type of commitment required (including costs such as fees, transportation, child care, taking time off work to attend, time commitments in and outside sessions); and what they can expect in terms of session activities.

When parents make a commitment to attend but the service is not delivered as expected, parents are likely to disengage or make a complaint to a practitioner, the agency employing the practitioner, registration authorities, and, in extreme cases, litigation, which could result if a

(continued)

Table 46.1: Dissemination Tools Developed to Support Evidence-Based Parenting Support

Type of Dissemination Activity	Program or Tools	Description	Evaluation Status
Training of practitioners to implement Triple P	Triple P Provider Training Program (TPPT)	A coordinated system of multidisciplinary professional training courses (1–5 days of initial training + 1-day accreditation).	Extensive ongoing evaluation of training outcomes as part of quality assurance process established by the PFSC and TPI
Training of trainers	Train the Trainer Program (TTP)	An intensive training course conducted by the PFSC for TPI, which delivers official Triple P courses to practitioners	Extensive evaluation of training outcomes as part of quality assurance process established by the PFSC and TPI
Implementation framework	Triple P Implementation Framework (TPIF)	Multistage implementation model to support organizations implementation of Triple P	Ongoing, multiple implementation studies
Supervision model	Peer-assisted supervision and support (PASS) model	A supervision model based on peer mentoring and guided self-regulation principles to promote competent delivery of various Triple P programs	Qualitative evaluation and extensive trialing in rollouts but no RCT conducted to date
Communication strategy	Stay Positive campaign	Part of a comprehensive communication strategy; includes both universal and targeted communications elements to destigmatize and encourage parental participation	Extensive service-based evaluations and one published evaluation
Process for cultural adaptation	Collaborative partnership adaptation model (CPAM)	A collaborative partnership model used to culturally adapt Triple P program delivery and resources for indigenous families	One RCT and a qualitative study
Estimating population reach needed	Triple P Capacity Calculator (CapCal)	A planning tool to help organizations plan population rollouts of the Triple P system	In progress
Client tracking and monitoring system	Automatic Client Scoring and Reporting Application (ASRA)	A web tool that scores pre-, post-, and follow up measures used in the implementation of Triple P	Ongoing use in rollouts of Triple P system
Fidelity promotion	Content and process fidelity measure (FPT)	A measure to assess content and process fidelity of practitioners' implementation of Triple P (self- and independent observer versions)	Being used in RCTs to promote protocol adherence

Table 46.1: Continued

Type of Dissemination Activity	Program or Tools	Description	Evaluation Status
Population-level outcome assessment tools	International Parenting Survey (IPS)	A brief parent report online survey of parenting practices, parents' concerns about children's behavior, preferences for way of participating in Triple P; used as a planning tool and as a consumer engagement strategy	Has been used in population surveys using convenience samples in Australia, Germany, Canada, United Kingdom, Hong Kong
Parent and practitioner preference surveys	My Say Survey and Your Say Survey	An online parent (My Say) or practitioner (Your Say) completed survey to assist planning rollouts of population model and consumer and end-user engagement	Used in population trial of Stepping Stones Triple P
Outcome measures	Outcome measures repository (OMR)	A repository of public domain assessment measures, such as the Parent and Family Adjustment Scale (PAFAS) and Child Adjustment and Parental Efficacy Scale (CAPES), that have been developed and validated and are available for use free of charge in research and clinical practice	Various publications on different measures
Knowledge transfer mechanisms	Helping Families Change Conference (HFCC)	A biennial international conference featuring the latest research on Triple P, evolving practice and implementation issues, and policy implications	Each conference evaluated through registrant feedback and an internal conference organizing committee review
	Triple P Update conferences	Locally organized research and practice updates for partner organizations and practitioners	
Science communications	Triple P Research Network (TPRN.net)	An invitational network for individuals and groups involved in research on various aspects of the Triple P model	Ongoing tracking of research outputs (grants, publications, and presentations)
Practitioner support and networking	Triple P Provider Network	A website that provides ongoing updates relating to new developments in Triple P	Ongoing
Triple P Trainers Network	Triple P Trainers Network (TPTN)	A web page to facilitate knowledge exchange between accredited Triple P trainers	Ongoing
PFSC International Research Training Program in parenting and family psychology	International Research Training Program (IRTP-P)	A new graduate-level training program focusing on population-based approaches to parenting and family support	Ongoing

poorly delivered service caused distress or other harm to the parent or child. I have received complaints from parents when practitioners stray too much from session content included in the parent workbook for Group Triple P. Greater consumer-driven demand for quality EBPS programs is an inevitable consequence of more parents realizing the impact good parenting can make on their children's lives. When public expectations and demand are higher, greater leverage can be achieved with governments and service providers to properly support parenting programs.

In some jurisdictions, nationally coordinated parenting websites have been developed. What is often missing from such sites is any comparative program-specific information in plain language that would better inform parents about program options available locally that might meet their needs and how parents can access such programs. Parents need to be able to compare all available programs in terms of their evidence, expected outcomes, commitments required of parents, and video examples of activities involved in undertaking a real-life program. This kind of information should be freely and publically accessible to consumers and referral agencies so that parents can make decisions that are more informed. These processes to empower consumers would drive accountability of agencies and build momentum for change.

PREPARING PRACTITIONERS TO DEAL WITH MORE DIFFICULT CASES

The increased availability of technology-assisted, self-directed, and universal parenting programs may mean that clinical psychologists and other mental health professionals who currently run parenting programs are likely to see the more complex and difficult cases that have not responded to lower intensity interventions. It is desirable and inevitable that the most highly trained practitioners deal with the most complex cases. However, there are specific consultation issues that arise when cases seen are nonresponders to previous parenting interventions. A critical challenge for practitioners is to understand why and how prior intervention was unsuccessful and to ensure that the new intervention plan does not simply replicate the same problems that led to prior nonresponse. These types of consultations require practitioners to be skilled at managing resistance from parents who may feel they have "been there and done that" and nothing works for their child. Rather than abandon Triple P, practitioners need to work with parents to understand what aspects of previous attempts failed and worked, and why, so that future intervention plans can take this history into account. Managing parental resistance is a critical skill for all parenting practitioners (Sanders & Burke, 2014; Sanders & Mazzucchelli, 2013).

GREATER PROFESSIONALIZING OF THE PARENTING PRACTITIONER WORKFORCE

A population approach has to contend with two opposing tensions in the workforce that delivers parenting programs. One view is that there should be greater professionalization of the workforce so that only well-trained, accredited, and highly skilled practitioners are able to deliver parenting programs. This would encourage the development of higher training standards, quality assurance mechanisms, accreditation and licensing, and a specific graduate-level qualification in parent education or parenting and family intervention. The alternative view involves moving in the opposite direction and seeks to deprofessionalize the workforce, making greater use of low-cost community volunteers or other parents who have completed the program as a parent and then receive additional training and supervision by an experienced practitioner. As no single discipline is responsible for the provision of guidance and support to parents, there is wide variability in the knowledge, skills, experiences, and opportunities of different professional groups to work with parents in different contexts. There is little agreement about the minimum qualifications a person needs to become a parenting practitioner.

A professional qualification is not an essential prerequisite for being able to effectively deliver an EBPS program. Patel et al. (2017) showed, in other areas of global mental health in low-resource settings in India, that laypeople who received specific training in CBT for depression and problem drinking successfully delivered the intervention. Different countries are likely to develop different standards based on prevailing economic conditions, professional standards, and the availability of a skilled workforce to deliver programs.

RESEARCH ON PROFESSIONAL TRAINING

Although training programs for EBPS have moved well beyond the "train-and-hope" model that characterized early dissemination efforts, there is still much to learn about how best to train a workforce in evidence-based programs in a cost-effective manner. One of the key issues confronting purveyor organizations is whether skills-based training as used in Triple P (see Chapter 34, this volume) can be successfully accomplished as an online process without a trainer. Sharing of basic information about program content and necessary knowledge can be readily done online. The more difficult part is to get a computer program to simulate adequately the important practical skills of "coaching" a parent to employ a parenting skill. This is a process whereby practitioners practice in small groups through a live behavioral rehearsal process, taking a parent through a series of steps as the parent introduces his or her child to quiet time or time-out routines. The practitioner self-evaluates his or her performance and receives personalized feedback from peers and the trainer about his or her performance. Furthermore, the practitioner skills of managing parental resistance (including parental distress) that emerge during live training of practitioners are more challenging to deal with online.

"BRANDED" VERSUS GENERIC PARENTING PROGRAMS

An emerging topic of debate in the field of evidence-based psychological practice more broadly has been the idea that the "branding" and commercialization of programs has not been good for the field. Chorpita and others (2017) have advocated for a model that involves encouraging child and adolescent mental health service providers not to use branded programs but instead have staff trained via a training program Modular Approach to Therapy for Children (MATCH) in what is referred to as a common elements approach. However, this program is disseminated through a privately owned fee-generating company that provides organizations with training and downloadable resources based on identifying from the literature core common components in successful treatments for different disorders and conditions.

Objections to named programs such as Triple P, Incredible Years, Nurse–Family Partnership, Parent–Child Interaction Therapy (PCIT), Helping the Noncompliant Child (HNCC), Family Check Up, and many others with developed dissemination mechanisms are that these programs share many elements in common with other programs and draw from a similar theoretical base in social learning theory. However, the dissemination mechanisms developed for programs such as Triple P and Incredible Years have enabled the most strongly supported EBPS programs to be widely used around the world. In a market economy, the branding of parenting programs is inevitable, unavoidable, and desirable. It matters little whether programs are proprietorial, government funded, or run by not-for-profit organizations simply because identities are needed for programs to create any public awareness or demand for the program.

Existing parenting programs are not all the same. On the surface, programs can appear similar on the basis of brief descriptions allowed in the literature because they have shared components. They also have important differences. To illustrate this point, many parenting programs based on the work of Constance Hanf (such as Incredible Years, PCIT, HNCC) and others, such as Triple P, use strategies such as labeled or descriptive praise, play, clear rules and instructions, and disciplinary consequences such as time-out to teach children new skills and behaviors. What is not always clear are the actual differences between programs in the procedures used, the expected outcomes, and the costs of program delivery.

Triple P emphasizes the importance of promoting self-regulation and a parent's capacity to generalize his or her skills across diverse siblings, settings, and time. It also has multiple delivery modalities, levels of intensity, and program variants for different populations across the spectrum of universal, indicated, and targeted prevention. The generic brand of the Triple P system is used to promote awareness of the commonalities across the entire range of related programs. Labeling (i.e., branding) these diverse interventions under another, less appealing generic, such as parent management training or behavioral family intervention, actually misrepresents what the program involves and aims to accomplish. Most parents participating in Triple P are not actually involved in a professionally administered "training" program at all. In accordance with the population approach, most parents participate in low-intensity experiences, such as exposure to Stay Positive media communications, seminars, or discussion groups, not training or treatments, although that level of intervention is available when required.

Another misconception is that branded, manualized programs are inherently rigid, inflexible, formulaic, and unresponsive to the clinical needs of families. Mazzucchelli and Sanders (2010) contended that manualized interventions used in Triple P do not fit that stereotype. In fact, we have argued that flexible tailoring of EBPS programs is essential for the practitioner to be considered to be applying the program with fidelity. Many chapters in this volume document how this tailoring process takes place (for an example of flexible tailoring with Indigenous families, see Chapter 28 of this volume).

THE "BUSINESS" OF DISSEMINATING EVIDENCE-BASED PARENTING SUPPORT

All successfully disseminated evidence-based parenting programs have established dedicated small-business entities to scale their programs, although it is not always as transparent as it should be who actually owns the programs (the developer, their employer [e.g., a university], or not-for-profit entities). This has been due to inadequate disclosure statements by authors in journals and inconsistent editorial policies relating to publishing disclosure statements. To avoid doubt, Triple P is owned by the University of Queensland, a major public university in Australia, and royalties from dissemination activities are split between the Faculty of Health and Behavioral Sciences, School of Psychology, and contributing authors. Where program resources are developed, such as DVDs, written materials, or online programs, they are typically copyrighted and use trademarks, have logos, and include program products (mainly professional training, resources, online programs, and technical support needed to implement programs).

Some programs use commercial publishers, and others such as Triple P have set up dedicated international publishing mechanisms. The approach taken with Triple P has been to work with a purveyor organization specifically created to disseminate Triple P. This initially was limited to publishing resources and over the years has expanded to cover the range of functions associated with disseminating Triple P globally. This partnership has been in place since 2001, through a licensing agreement established by the University of Queensland's main technology transfer company UniQuest.

Triple P International was established as a for-profit business by a social entrepreneur who continues to run the organization today. The commercial business structure has allowed the organization to develop and maintain a sustainable business model that has provided stability, managed risk, and led to a strong focus on driving innovation and being consumer focused. While there are many options available for managing the dissemination of EBPS, in the case of Triple P, this structure has worked effectively for more than 20 years. Being led by a social entrepreneur means that the organization values social impact as much as financial sustainability (now often referred to as a social business or social enterprise), and this social focus has allowed TPI to make decisions that may not always lead to the largest financial gain but supported the mission of helping families around the world access high-quality parenting support.

To maintain control over the quality of dissemination and to protect the University of Queensland's ongoing investment in research and development, all parenting programs developed as part of the Triple P system are identified as such. This is done to create "brand" awareness in the public and to enable research using Triple P to be synthesized and meta-analyzed. With a suite of evidence-based programs that share a common theoretical framework, the main advantage of using a privately owned purveyor company is that the necessary capital from multiple sources can be raised to scale, revise and update program resources (including translation where necessary), and cover all the costs associated with publishing training resources and materials, employing trainers or technical implementation consultants, and so on. Funding agencies that might fund aspects of program development from a grant rarely provide the funds necessary to disseminate and sustain programs following completion of initial demonstrations of efficacy by developers. Sustaining dissemination efforts at scale requires a self-funding, income-generating model. Many program developers at universities who put their programs in the public domain by writing a book or manual have little or no capacity to exert any quality control over dissemination. If the program is popular, they can incur considerable unanticipated costs in terms of time and resources simply trying to manage the logistics and administration of "giving away" the program (e.g., handling e-mail inquiries, answering requests for information about the program, requests for updates, and so on). Failure to develop an effective back-end operation to manage the business of dissemination will usually mean the program cannot be sustained. The main challenges for organizations trying to set up sustainable dissemination operations are that the whole sector delivering parenting and family services tends to be underresourced, the costs are relatively high, and margins are likely to be modest.

IMPLICATIONS OF DEMOGRAPHIC CHANGES

Planning and anticipating what kind of parenting support is going to be needed in the future is anyone's guess. However, over the next 30 years, program developers, agencies, and parenting practitioners will have to take into account expected demographic changes in the population (Organization for Economic Cooperation and Development [OECD], 2011). As population growth continues, children are likely to grow up in smaller homes in more densely populated cities. Parents will live longer, and more children will live in multigenerational households. The cost of entering the housing market is likely to increase, and more children will be economically dependent on parents for longer. The number of children raised in a traditional household with two biological parents will continue to decline. Due to increases in longevity, more children will have great-grandparents for longer periods of their life, and grandparent care is likely to increase. Parents and children are likely to experience rapid technological change throughout their lives, and the sophistication, speed, and capacity of this technology to be used in parenting programs are just beginning. Climate change, natural disasters, and global conflict could change the number of displaced and traumatized families needing support.

Rapid technological, social, and political change bring uncertainty and stress. The stability of the family unit becomes a major stabilizing influence in people's lives. The quality and harmoniousness of families to relate well to each other and support and care for each other and others in their social network (e.g., friends, relatives, neighbors, and work colleagues) have great potential to influence both individual and collective well-being, happiness, physical and mental health, productivity, and capacity to be a responsible global citizen. Parenting programs have a vital role to play in preparing parents, children, and young people to contribute toward these outcomes.

THE NEED FOR BETTER PRESERVICE TRAINING
IN PARENTING AND FAMILY PSYCHOLOGY

From our experience in training thousands of practicing clinicians from health, education, and welfare sectors to deliver evidence-based parenting programs, it is striking how few practitioners across all disciplines report feeling adequately trained and confident to deliver parenting programs effectively. Despite differences in the length of prior training, levels of experience, and discipline, most universities do not prepare students well to enter the workforce to work with children and families. Preservice training in the fields of evidence-based parenting programs is generally limited, with clinical psychologists fortunate enough to be trained in a program with a strong child stream and child placements or internships standing out. However, not all programs provide these opportunities.

Most professional training in the detailed knowledge of how to use specific programs is conducted as in-service training, workforce development, or continuing professional education required for licensing or accreditation in some disciplines. This lack of basic preparation of students through their university education to work with parents and children is a major omission from professional training of psychologists, social workers, pediatricians and general practitioners, educators, nurses, counselors, and family support workers. Advanced undergraduate and graduate courses in parenting studies and family psychology accessible across disciplines would ensure that training to deliver EBPS could be at a more advanced level, streamlined, and completed more efficiently.

SPECIALIZED TRAINING FOR PARENTING AND FAMILY INTERVENTION RESEARCHERS

Relatively few doctoral training programs provide specialized training for prevention science researchers in the field of EBPS and family psychology. As a consequence, relatively few new researchers are entering the field to study or develop new evidence-based programs.

DIVERSIFYING THE PARENTING SUPPORT WORKFORCE

An effective population-based parenting strategy requires a competently trained workforce to deliver different programs to parents. To deliver Group Triple P effectively (a Level 4 intervention), a master's or doctoral degree in psychology, social work, mental health, or counseling is not required before undertaking a training course. However, practitioners with no prior training in learning theory, CBT, or the application of behavior change procedures will need to learn the content and essential process skills to deliver programs effectively to parents, and practitioners must demonstrate basic competence in these skills.

The other side to this is that, as the parenting population becomes more aware of the vital role they play in shaping their children's development and future, more organizations and individuals promoting services as "parenting coaches" or "mentors" are likely to offer their services for a fee. The provision of parenting advice is a completely unregulated industry, and as a result parents are vulnerable to rogue players and self-appointed experts not bound by normal ethical principles or standards required of health professionals.

Individual evidence-based programs such as Triple P have defined who to train as well as clearly articulated the standards of competence required to begin successful delivery of programs. However, the introduction of greater regulation and minimum training standards needs to be applied to all parenting programs in the future. Virtually every other service industry has some quality standards, and the delivery of parenting programs should be no exception. At the moment, most parents do not have any clear understanding of who or what training is required to be able to deliver a parenting program. Parents as better informed consumers should be encouraged to select programs that have clearly defined training standards and accreditation mechanisms that are transparent and publicly verifiable by parents and referring agencies.

USING VOLUNTEERS IN SUPPORTING PARENTS

Some organizations have a long history of employing untrained volunteers to help parents cope with family life and parenting responsibilities. Volunteers have a potentially unique contribution to make in delivering Triple P. Some organizations have recruited volunteers to assist with the running of Triple P groups drawn from the pool of parents who have successfully completed a

Group Triple P program. Volunteers can work with professionals to engage and support vulnerable parents to participate in group sessions. If a parent has conquered a substance abuse problem by completing Triple P and has had his or her children returned to his or her care as a result, that parent might be a particularly valuable role model for other parents in a similar position.

In the field of global adult mental health seeking to bring effective treatments to people in low- and middle-income countries, there may be no options other than volunteers; a readily available workforce of psychologists, social workers, parent educator and counselors may not exist, particularly outside major cities (Singla et al., 2014). Patel and colleagues (2017) have recently shown that previously untrained community volunteers in India can be successfully trained to deliver CBT for depression and alcohol abuse. In an RCT, volunteers delivering CBT as therapists achieved comparable effect sizes to interventions using a CBT specialist. Volunteers in hospital outreach programs have been trained in Primary Care Triple P to be able to use tip sheets during home visits with vulnerable parents. However, no controlled trials have yet been conducted examining the effects of Triple P programs delivered by volunteers.

TOWARD A NEW SOLUTION-FOCUSED SCIENTIFIC AGENDA

EXPANDING THE THEORETICAL BASIS OF PARENTING PROGRAMS

Sanders and Prinz in Chapter 3 of this volume argued that the Triple P system has historically been characterized as a blending of social learning theory, applied behavior analysis, cognitive-behavioral principles, developmental theory, and public health principles. This theoretical mix made sense when it came to developing an intervention targeting the everyday interactions between parents and children with conduct problems. However, as Triple P began to be applied to a more diverse range of problems (internalizing, health problems) and gradually transformed into a multilevel system of intervention, other theoretical perspectives were essential to inform the intervention model.

In the 1980s, research and theories on marital interaction informed the early development of partner support procedures to build better teamwork in parenting and to reduce marital conflict in parents of children with conduct problems and co-occurring marital problems (Dadds, Schwartz, & Sanders, 1987). Models of population health seeking to prevent chronic health problems, such as coronary heart disease, inspired the development of a multilevel system of intervention, the embracing of the RE-AIM (Reach, Efficacy, Adoption, Implementation, and Maintenance) framework, and principles of "minimal sufficiency" and self-regulation. Organizational theories and implementation science theory informed the development of the Triple P Implementation Framework (McWilliam, Brown, Sanders, & Jones, 2016). Developmental theory and research relating to peer relationships informed the development of the concept of facilitative parenting used as the theoretical basis for Resilience Triple P for children who were bullied at school. Each of these additional elements have strengthened the model and allowed it to evolve.

Partly in response to evidence showing that between a quarter to a third of parents participating in parenting programs for young children with a conduct problem are nonresponders

(Scott & Dadds, 2009) and some studies showing that retention of parents through an intervention can be problematic, there have been calls to extend the theoretical base of parenting programs further. This extension would be to incorporate theoretical perspectives derived from relational frame theory (Whittingham, 2015), attachment theory (Scott & Dadds, 2009), mindfulness, and more recently, compassion theory (Kirby, 2016).

Using additional theoretical perspectives to enhance the effects of Triple P has met with limited success to date. The challenge in demonstrating the additive value of any additional components is to conduct an adequately powered trial with large enough sample sizes to detect whether the additional theoretically derived components (e.g., psychological flexibility, mindfulness or other procedure) actually improve outcomes over and above those achieved by the standard intervention once contact time is controlled between conditions. To date, when additional procedures have been combined with Triple P in two-arm trials with a care-as-usual control or wait-list control group, the existing standard programs tend to do just as well as the enhanced combined program.

In an effort to strengthen child outcomes from Group Triple P, Salmon, Dittman, Sanders, Burson, and Hammington (2014) were inspired by theory on children's emotional development to conduct a trial with children with conduct problems to enhance the children's capacity to identify and express their emotions (a capacity that has been shown to be more limited in these children). The trial compared a regular offering of the group-delivered Triple P—Positive Parenting Program with an enhanced version tailored to promote children's emotion competence. Families of children between the ages of 3 and 6 displaying early-onset conduct problems were randomly assigned to Group Triple P or Emotion-Enhanced Triple P (EETP), in which parents were encouraged to incorporate emotion labels and discussion of causes and to coach emotion competence during discussions of everyday emotional experiences with their child. Even though parents who received EETP increased their discussion of emotion labels and emotion causes in conversations with their child and used more emotion coaching (showing that the actual procedure was used) compared with parents who received regular Group Triple P, the addition of emotion coaching showed little advantage over regular Group Triple P. Parents were similarly satisfied with both interventions.

This study illustrates that trying to make Triple P more complex without an eye on the outcome data is a mistake. There are two ways to proceed: use insights from novel theoretical models to (a) investigate whether the addition of certain theoretically informed elements meaningfully improves desired outcomes (perhaps for particular populations) and (b) continue to try to "pare down," simplify, and find the minimally sufficient principles and strategies to achieve meaningful change. Both options are important and consistent with a proportionate universalism approach.

In contrast, in a two-arm trial that compared an enhanced variant of Triple P with a control group, the combined treatment did well. Brown, Whittingham, Boyd, McKinlay, and Sofronoff (2015) examined the effects of combining Stepping Stones Triple P with an Acceptance and Commitment Therapy workshop on parent, family, and couple outcomes of children who had an acquired brain injury. Postintervention, the treatment group showed significant, small-to-medium effect size improvements relative to the care-as-usual group on parent psychological distress, parent psychological flexibility, parenting confidence in managing behaviors, family adjustment, and number of disagreements between parents. Most improvements were maintained at 6-month follow-up.

Searching for ways of enhancing the effects of Triple P, the study of nonresponders for families showing early signs of being at risk for discontinuance is particularly welcome. Some exciting future enhancement possibilities include combining strategies such as mindfulness training and procedures derived from research on compassion with Triple P parenting strategies (see Kirby, 2016). Trials are needed to determine what effects such additions might achieve.

CREATING NEW SYNERGIES TO PROMOTE A CLEANER, ECOLOGICALLY SUSTAINABLE WORLD

A number of exciting evolving opportunities are bringing together parenting intervention researchers with other disciplines that study environmental and animal welfare issues, including the role of parents and families in taking care of the natural environment and the relationship of humans to the animal kingdom (McPhedran, 2009). These synergies, which involve working with currently relatively disconnected areas of inquiry, provide opportunities for program innovation and new lines of funding outside the field of mental health. Sanders et al., in Chapter 45 of this volume, outline some ways parenting programs can contribute to solving environmental and economic development problems.

INCORPORATING A CHILD'S PERSPECTIVE INTO RESEARCH ON PARENTING

Parenting intervention research has had a limited focus to date in capturing a child's perspective to assist with the development and evaluation of parenting programs. The focus has been largely restricted to ensuring that parenting programs change some important child-related outcomes (such as reducing conduct problems) and reducing children's exposure to child maltreatment. However, children themselves have a unique perspective to offer of the parenting they have received based on their lived daily experiences in families (Backer, Murphy, Fox, Ulph, & Calam, 2017; Fängström et al., 2016). Children are the primary beneficiaries and ultimate consumers of poor or positive parenting; however, little is known about how children perceive the specific parenting skills (e.g., quiet time, planned ignoring, or time-out) parents are taught in Triple P. Some parenting researchers have captured aspects of the child's experience using child report outcome measures in studies of peer victimization (Healy & Sanders, 2014); pain management (Sanders, Shepherd, Cleghorn, & Woolford, 1994); and parent–adolescent conflict (Chu, Bullen, Farruggia, Dittman, & Sanders, 2015). However, there is much that is unknown about children's views of how they are raised that could potentially inform the delivery of parenting programs.

Children could be asked in developmentally appropriate ways about their views on the specific skills parents are taught in Triple P (e.g., descriptive praise, discipline consequences, behavior charts, and contracts). Different dimensions could be asked about (e.g., usefulness, effectiveness, and fairness). They could be asked about how they would prefer their parents deal with particular situations (such as being bullied) and the changes, if any, they have observed in their parents' behavior since completing a program. Research could explore whether children's attitudes and preferences predict their own or their parent's response to Triple P. Children's views or reaction to changes in parenting may mediate or moderate changes in parenting and other child outcomes. The challenge is ensuring that measures are developmentally appropriate to children's level of language and comprehension and, in the case of written measures, reading capacity. Better information about a child's perspective as a consumer is likely to be of high interest value to parents and parent educators. Parents may be more receptive to parenting programs that children like and endorse.

MAKING MULTIDISCIPLINARY COLLABORATIONS WORK IN PRACTICE

Applying psychological theories and principles is not sufficient to develop a comprehensive population-based approach to promote healthy development. A broader multidisciplinary perspective is needed. The quality of parenting solutions developed for a particular problem (e.g., program for parents of children with a disability) have been enhanced greatly by input from a diverse range of disciplines. This multidisciplinary input provided specialist knowledge, relevant theories, measurement expertise, and experience relating to discipline-based and service sector implementation challenges that could be encountered in deploying programs in a particular domain (e.g., pediatric inpatient or outpatient settings, general medical practices, child and youth mental health services, child protection services, justice system, child care settings, and schools).

The specific disciplines involved varied depended on the problem being targeted and level of intervention. Teams have included medical and health professionals, general medical practitioners, pediatricians, child psychiatrists, oncologists, gastroenterologists, nutritionists, physiotherapists and nurses, epidemiologists, survey methodologists, statisticians, economists, sociologists, criminologists, state archivists, social workers, geographers, special educators, early childhood educators, climate scientists, engineers, and veterinarians.

Key learnings derived from these transdisciplinary collaborations have included the importance of being respectful of each other's disciplines and theories and logistic considerations that make a difference to the efficiency of meetings. Differences of opinion often require plenty of listening, clarifying, checking meanings, interpretations or conclusions, and willingness to read new relevant literature outside one's own discipline and area of expertise. Occasional misunderstandings regarding terminology or jargon can be avoided by speaking as much as possible in plain, jargon-free language. Interdisciplinary barriers are created when terms used have somewhat different meanings or referents and there is a tendency to resort to too many unnecessary acronyms that confuse participants from other disciplines or immediate sphere of work.

Being a good collaborator in a research team requires being able to both lead and follow colleagues at different stages of the research and development process. Having well-developed communication and interpersonal skills helps. Effective organizational skills also help. This includes respecting your own and others' time, not overcommitting to research tasks, and allocating the necessary time to complete tasks in a timely manner. Collaborators who consistently fail to complete tasks according to reasonable time frames can be a liability. This issue is a problem when the people concerned are senior investigators on a funded project whose behavior can threaten the achievement of key performance indicators required by funding agencies. Better training in effective and respectful interdisciplinary collaboration would be helpful for all disciplines.

Almost all Triple P research and development projects have required additional collaborations and partnerships with community agencies involved in delivering services to children and families. Critical issues involved in making such partnerships work in practice are addressed by Owens, Doyle, Hegarty, Heavey, and Farrell in Chapter 40 of this volume.

BUILDING RESEARCH NETWORKS TO ENHANCE INNOVATION

Many potentially useful innovations make no impact on major problems because they are never disseminated properly, or if they are disseminated, they flounder and are not supported by sustainable dissemination mechanisms. This is partly due to a lack of sustained commitment to ongoing research and development by developers to support the innovation. The Triple P model has benefited from knowledge exchange mechanisms that have attracted the interest of researchers from around the world who conduct research on various aspects of the Triple P system. To facilitate knowledge exchange between research groups and to disseminate research, the Parenting and Family Support Centre (PFSC) has provided consultative support to enable high-quality trials of Triple P to be conducted in different jurisdictions. The PFSC maintains a comprehensive evidence base of publications pertaining to Triple P and a research blog that disseminates findings to interested followers (http://www.triplepblog.net), and it runs a self-funded, high-quality international conference that brings together 200–500 practitioners, researchers, and policymakers (depending on location) every 2 years (Helping Families Change Conference [HFCC]; http://helpingfamilieschange.org). The HFCC provides a mix of keynote addresses, research updates, practice-focused workshops, and a dedicated preconference scientific retreat for researchers. Nineteen HFCC conferences will have been held by 2018. A major feature of the HFCC is that program content is informed by both a practitioner survey and a local parent online survey that helps to define current local hot topics for parents living in the local area and on occasions a public postconference seminar for local parents to address hot topics identified using conference delegates as presenters. Major research publications are disseminated quickly through the Triple P Provider Network (http://www.triplep.net), the Triple P Research Network (http://www.tprn.net/), the University of Queensland's media and communications office, and social media run by the PFSC (https://www.pfsc.uq.edu.au).

The development of a dedicated dissemination mechanism (Triple P International Pty Ltd) greatly accelerated research on Triple P, including international collaborations and independent studies. Figure 46.1 plots the growth of the Triple P evidence base across four decades. The formal commencement of a dedicated dissemination organization enabled the program to be studied by groups from around the world. Many researchers and academic institutions have conducted research on Triple P. This research is truly global with large- and small-scale projects being conducted across 30 different countries. As a consequence, more studies have been conducted on Triple P than any other single intervention, making it the most extensively evaluated parenting program in the world.

INTERNATIONAL PERSPECTIVES

A large amount of the extant literature on parenting interventions has been conducted in individualistic Western cultures in North America, Western Europe, and Australasia. The vast

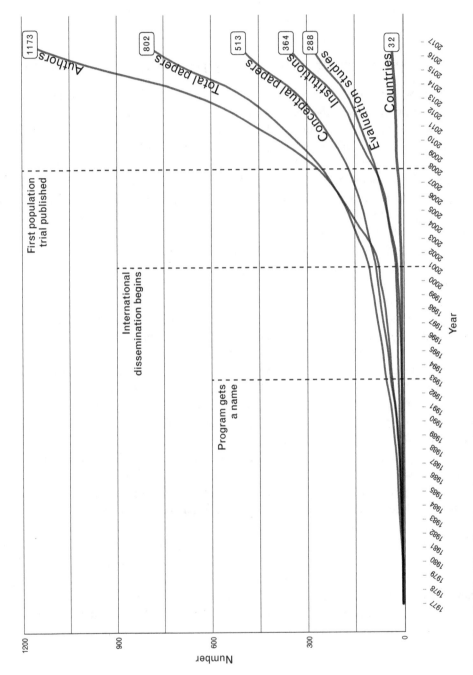

FIGURE 46.1: Growth of the Triple P evidence base over time.

majority of the world's children suffering from the adverse consequences of family violence or mental health problems live in other parts of the world in Asia, Middle East, Africa, and Latin America. There is a great need for more international collaborative projects to test adaptations of Triple P and other evidence-based programs, and if shown to be successful, effective mechanisms are required for successful implementation on a wide scale while preserving fidelity.

PARENTING AND POVERTY REDUCTION

Numerous groups (e.g., American Academy of Pediatrics [AAP] Council on Community Pediatrics, 2016) have advocated for evidence-based parenting programs, including Triple P, to be part of a comprehensive early intervention approach to reduce the number of children growing up in poverty. Research examining how parenting programs can be used to improve employment outcomes for families would be useful. For example, living with a very disruptive child can be a major barrier for an unemployed parent searching for work (e.g., difficulty with child care arrangements). Similarly, population-based parenting programs targeting low-income areas might help improve parental self-efficacy and could be combined with financial management skills training and job search training. Concurrently tracking rates of unemployment with other indicators in population-level evaluations of parenting programs would be valuable. To break the cycle of intergenerational poverty, it is important that low-income parents have the opportunity to develop positive parenting skills that enable children can acquire the social, emotional and cognitive competencies related to school achievement and the attainment of developmental milestones.

FUTURE DIRECTIONS

GREATER FOCUS ON RELATIONAL COMPETENCY

The Triple P system as described in this volume has evolved to accommodate the broader range of problems that have been shown to be affected by parenting and that parenting programs can address. The primary task of parents is not simply to control or manage their children's behavior; it is to help children learn the necessary social, emotional, language, and cognitive skills they need to be successful in life. Many behavior and emotional problems involve interactional difficulties with siblings and peers.

Facilitative parenting is an enabling approach that involves teaching parents skills to coach and support their children's efforts to learn social and emotional skills so they get on better with peers and better handle teasing and provocation. Healy and Sanders (2014) applied this approach in an RCT of Resilience Triple P in the context of assisting parents of children who were being bullied at school. The approach involved four sessions where children practiced social and coping skills with the assistance of a parent coach and practitioners. The study showed that children were less likely to be bullied and depressed and had greater liking for school than controls. However, the approach has much broader applicability than dealing with bullying, and future exploration of its usefulness is likely occur with children with conduct problems, depression, anxiety disorders, and autistic spectrum disorders.

A STRONGER VALUES ORIENTATION

One major advantage of a self-regulation framework (Sanders & Mazzucchelli, 2013) is that parents formulate their own goals. These goals can be informed by parents' own values, traditions, cultural beliefs, and priorities. Chapter 28 of this volume by Turner et al. illustrates how traditional Māori values can be successfully integrated with Triple P principles and techniques. Until now, Triple P has been relatively silent with respect to explicitly stating underlying values on which the program is based. This has been deliberate to avoid prescribing to parents how parents living in different cultures (individualistic and collectivistic) should raise their children. However, it has become increasingly apparent as Triple P has evolved that the program's core shared values should be more clearly enunciated.

The core values underpinning the Triple P approach to support parents include the following:

- *Being inclusive.* All parents should have the opportunity to participate in a high-quality, evidence-based parenting program to support their children's healthy development and well-being.
- *Creating equality of access.* Programs should enable equality of access for both genders and all family types, cultures, religions, and political beliefs.
- *Empowering parents.* Positive parenting programs should adopt an empowerment approach that is built strongly on a self-regulation framework. This self-regulation framework respects a parent's capacity to learn the necessary skills needed to raise his or her children and optimize their developmental potential. It respects a parent's right to make informed decisions about how the parent wishes to raise his or her children.
- *Raising confident, competent, resilient children is a shared responsibility.* Raising healthy well-adjusted children is a shared responsibility among all the carers in a child's life.
- *Demonstrating that capable parenting is influenced by the broader community.* Positive parenting programs should seek to create child-, parent-, and family-friendly communities.
- *Children are our greatest resource.* Children are our communities' most valued resource and ensuring their well-being requires a nurturing, caring environment with adults that care for, protect, educate, love, and empower children to lead healthy, happy, productive, and meaningful lives.

CONCLUSION

This volume has demonstrated that research into parenting is thriving. Triple P continues to evolve, with ongoing investment in research and development and program innovations. These ongoing developments in program content, format, and dissemination strategies seek to continually improve outcomes and are an integral regular feature of an evidence-based system of parenting support. The field will continue to evolve in line with the changing experience of parenting in each generation, the resources and service systems available, and the arenas where parents are looking for support.

As parenting is a lifelong commitment to offspring, additional research and development work is needed to address the parenting challenges adults experience throughout the life cycle, including the parenting of older adolescents, emerging adults, middle-age children who comprise the so-called sandwich generation (parents with aging parents and adult offspring with no children), or the "club sandwich generation" (parents with adult children, aging parents, and grandchildren). The development of positive parenting solutions for other phases of the life cycle awaits good epidemiological studies to define the types and severity of problems older parents experience and the specific parenting and family relationship issues that parents confront as their children mature, leave home, become financially independent, partner, find suitable housing, start their own families, and begin their own adult lives.

At present, it is unknown whether parents of older-age children living at home would view participation in a parenting program as a possible solution to improve their relationship and family functioning. However, there are emerging data showing that grandparents are willing to participate in parenting programs, such as Triple P, and report high levels of consumer satisfaction when they do participate (Kirby & Sanders, 2014). In an age of lifelong learning, such programs could prove popular if evidence shows that there are beneficial outcomes for multiple generations of older parents, their families, and grandchildren.

"ARE WE THERE YET?"

Parents might rightly ask, "How can we tell if we have succeeded as a parent?" It is important not to form conclusions too early about the life course experiences of children. Many people attend school reunions and are shocked to find that there are many children who were popular and did well at school but then floundered at university, with intimate relationships, in parenting, and in life. Others who did not do particularly well at school went on to flourish as an adult. How do parents gauge whether they have done a good job raising their children? It is certainly too early to tell when children are age 3. Parents should not base judgments of their success as a parent on children's accomplishments. These accomplishments are affected by factors outside the family and are beyond a parent's control. However, if parents have done what they can to create a safe, stable, loving environment in a low-conflict and harmonious home, they will have done well. If they have also taught their children to be self-regulated and resilient, have good communication and social skills, and have a strong sense of values and have provided sufficient practical and emotional support for children to independently address their own problems (big and small) in their school, social, work, and own family lives, parents will have done exceptionally well regardless of how children turn out as adults.

An expected increase in consumer-driven demand for high-quality parenting programs is desirable. Higher expectations of parents will put pressure on organizations and practitioners to upskill and support staff so that effective programs can be delivered. It will also put pressure on governments so that EBPS programs are properly funded.

A CALL TO ACTION

Deep-seated attitudes can be difficult, expensive, and potentially impossible to shift. This is particularly so when it comes to the emotionally laden arena of parenting. Accessing evidence-based parenting programs or advice is simply not the default position for the majority of parent populations worldwide. At best, parenting programs have a brand issue (i.e., they are just for parents with problems); at worst, they are invisible. As practitioners, researchers, politicians, government departments, funding bodies, nongovernmental organizations, and businesses, we need to ask ourselves the question: Is this good enough? Is just helping the small percentage of parents who are already knocking at our door, or mandated to attend, and are eventually willing and motivated to complete an intervention program, enough? Or, knowing what programs like Triple P can do to transform lives, save relationships, save public money, save stress across the judicial and educational systems, positively affect mental health, positively affect communities, and simply create happier families, is it our responsibility to do more? We know that the trajectory of a child at age 3 has lifelong consequences. Large longitudinal trials, such as the Dunedin Multidisciplinary Health and Development Study (Moffitt, 2013) following the lives of a complete birth cohort of children born in one city in a single year, have shown that the level of a child's self-control (measured at age 3) predicts their health, wealth, employment, and criminality at age 33.

There are EBPS programs in existence that give parents the tools, knowledge, and skills they need to change the way their families work. And, the change is lasting. We know extraordinary change can happen when whole populations of parents are empowered by evidence-based positive parenting. But, how do we unlock this potential? How do we help parents understand the power they hold to transform their family life? Is it really possible to shift population attitudes on something as deeply emotive as what it means to be a "good parent"? Yes, it is, but it will take the concerted will of stakeholders worldwide to make it happen. It needs lateral thinking, financial commitment, and collaboration.

How do we pool resources and expertise to create aspirational parenting media messages and services that touch the hearts of parents worldwide—because where the heart is convinced, the mind and the action will follow? We need to inspire parents to be the best they can be and help parents understand that, like all great craftspeople, honing your skills creates the most extraordinary results. It is possible, and it is the single most important thing governments, philanthropic organizations, community service organizations, and businesses can do together as a united body to transform our world. Let us get the best minds across the world in the fields of marketing, creative production, diplomatic liaison, philanthropic liaison, media, and business and let us make it happen. Simply put, parents need to believe in and feel fantastic about doing a parenting program. The stakes are just too high for anything less.

KEY MESSAGES

- The Triple P system continues to evolve on the basis of a thriving research culture and an explicit knowledge exchange process that brings together researchers, disseminators, practitioners, policymakers, and consumers.
- A prevention agenda to promote the well-being of all children and forestall the development of social, emotional, behavioral, learning, and health problems will have been truly advanced when accessible, high-quality, and culturally informed positive parenting programs that really work are embedded in the social fabric of communities.
- Without significant investment in evidence-based parenting programs to properly support families, many children will continue grow up without reaching their full potential. The cost burden to the rest of society will be substantial.

REFERENCES

American Academy of Pediatrics (AAP) Council on Community Pediatrics. (2016). Poverty and child health in the United States. *Pediatrics, 137*, e20160339. doi:10.1542/peds.2016-0339

Backer, C., Murphy, R., Fox, J. R., Ulph, F., & Calam, R. (2017). Young children's experiences of living with a parent with bipolar disorder: Understanding the child's perspective. *Psychology and Psychotherapy: Theory, Research and Practice, 90*, 212–228. doi:10.1111/papt.12099

Bakermans-Kranenburg, M. J., & van Ijzendoorn, M. H. (2011). Differential susceptibility to rearing environment depending on dopamine-related genes: New evidence and a meta-analysis. *Developmental Psychopathology, 23*, 39–52. doi:10.1017/S0954579410000635

Brown, F. L., Whittingham, K., Boyd, R. N., McKinlay, L., & Sofronoff, K. (2015). Does Stepping Stones Triple P plus Acceptance and Commitment Therapy improve parent, couple, and family adjustment following paediatric acquired brain injury? A randomised controlled trial. *Behaviour Research and Therapy, 73*, 58–66. doi:10.1016/j.brat.2015.07.001

Chorpita, B. F., Daleiden, E. L., Park, A. L., Ward, A. M., Levy, M. C., Cromley, T., . . . Krull, J. L. (2017). Child STEPs in California: A cluster randomized effectiveness trial comparing modular treatment with community implemented treatment for youth with anxiety, depression, conduct problems, or traumatic stress. *Journal of Consulting and Clinical Psychology, 85*, 13–25. doi:10.1037/ccp0000133

Chu, J. T. W., Bullen, P., Farruggia, S. P., Dittman, C. K., & Sanders, M. R. (2015). Parent and adolescent effects of a universal group program for the parenting of adolescents. *Prevention Science, 16*, 609–620. doi:10.1007/s11121-014-0516-9

Clark, D. M., Layard, R., Smithies, R., Richards, D. A., Suckling, R., & Wright, B. (2009). Improving access to psychological therapy: Initial evaluation of two UK demonstration sites. *Behavior Research Therapy, 47*, 910–920. doi:10.1016/j.brat.2009.07.010

Dadds, M. R., Allen, J. L., McGregor, K., Woolgar, M., Viding, E., & Scott, S. (2014). Callous-unemotional traits in children and mechanisms of impaired eye contact during expressions of love: A treatment target? *Journal of Child Psychology and Psychiatry, 55*, 771–780. doi:10.1111/jcpp.12155

Dadds, M. R., Schwartz, S., & Sanders, M. R. (1987). Marital discord and treatment outcome in behavioral treatment of child conduct disorders. *Journal of Consulting and Clinical Psychology, 55*, 396–403. doi:10.1037/0022-006x.55.3.396

Fängström, K., Bokström, P., Dahlberg, A., Calam, R., Lucas, S., & Sarkadi, A. (2016). In My Shoes—Validation of a computer assisted approach for interviewing children. *Child Abuse & Neglect, 58*, 160–172. doi:10.1016/j.chiabu.2016.06.022

Fives, A., Purcell, L., Heary, C., NicGabhainn, S., & Canavan, J. (2014). *Parenting support for every parent: A population-level evaluation of Triple P in Longford Westmeath. Final Report.* Athlone, Ireland: Longford Westmeath Parenting Partnership.

Healy, K. L., & Sanders, M. R. (2014). Randomized controlled trial of a family intervention for children bullied by peers. *Behavior Therapy, 45*, 760–777. doi:10.1016/j.beth.2014.06.001

Kirby, J. N. (2016). The role of mindfulness and compassion in enhancing nurturing family environments. *Clinical Psychology: Science and Practice, 23*, 142–157. doi:10.1111/cpsp.12149

Kirby, J. N., & Sanders, M. R. (2014). A randomized controlled trial evaluating a parenting program designed specifically for grandparents. *Behaviour Research and Therapy, 52*, 35–44. doi:10.1016/j.brat.2013.11.002

Long, N. (2016). Future trends in parenting education. In J. J. Ponzetti (Ed.), *Evidence-based parenting education: A global perspective* (pp. 311–328). New York, NY: Routledge.

Mazzucchelli, T. G., & Sanders, M. R. (2010). Facilitating practitioner flexibility within an empirically supported intervention: Lessons from a system of parenting support. *Clinical Psychology: Science and Practice, 17*, 238–252. doi:10.1111/j.1468-2850.2010.01215.x

McPhedran, S. (2009). Animal abuse, family violence and child wellbeing: A review. *Journal of Family Violence, 24,* 41–52. doi:10.1007/s10896-008-9206-3.

McWilliam, J., Brown, J., Sanders, M. R., & Jones, L. (2016). The Triple P implementation framework: The role of purveyors in the implementation and sustainability of evidence-based programs. *Prevention Science, 17,* 636–645. doi:10.1007/s11121-016-0661-4

Miller, G. E., Brody, G. H., Yu, T., & Chen, E. (2014). A family-oriented psychosocial intervention reduces inflammation in low-SES African American youth. *PNAS Proceedings of the National Academy of Sciences of the United States of America, 111,* 11287–11292. doi:10.1073/pnas.1406578111

Moffitt, T. E. (2013). Childhood exposure to violence and lifelong health: Clinical intervention science and stress-biology research join forces. *Development and Psychopathology, 25,* 1619–1634. doi:10.1017/S0954579413000801

Organization for Economic Cooperation and Development (OECD). (2011). *Society at a Glance 2011—OECD Social Indicators.* Paris, France: Author. Retrieved from http://www.oecd.org/social/society-ataglance2011.htm

Patel, V., Weobong, B., Weiss, H. A., Anand, A., Bhat, B., Katti, B., . . . Fairburn, C. G. (2017). The Healthy Activity Program (HAP), a lay counsellor-delivered brief psychological treatment for severe depression, in primary care in India: A randomised controlled trial. *The Lancet, 389,* 176–185. doi:10.1016/S0140-6736(16)31589-6

Salmon, K., Dittman, C., Sanders, M., Burson, R., & Hammington, J. (2014). Does adding an emotion component enhance the Triple P—Positive Parenting Program? *Journal of Family Psychology, 28,* 244. doi:10.1037/a0035997

Sanders, M. R. (2015). Management of conflict of interest in psychosocial research on parenting and family interventions. *Journal of Child & Family Studies, 24,* 832–841. doi:10.1007/s10826-015-0127-5

Sanders, M. R., Baker, S., & Turner, K. M. T. (2012). A randomized controlled trial evaluating the efficacy of Triple P Online with parents of children with early-onset conduct problems. *Behaviour Research & Therapy, 50,* 675–684. doi:10.1016/j.brat.2012.07.004

Sanders, M. R., & Burke, K. (2014). The "hidden" technology of effective parent consultation: A guided participation model for promoting change in families. *Journal of Child and Family Studies, 23,* 1289–1297. doi:10.1007/s10826-013-9827-x

Sanders, M. R., & Mazzucchelli, T. G. (2013). The promotion of self-regulation through parenting interventions. *Clinical Child and Family Psychology Review, 16,* 1–17. doi:10.1007/s10567-013-0129-z

Sanders, M. R., Shepherd, R. W., Cleghorn, G., & Woolford, H. (1994). The treatment of recurrent abdominal pain in children: A controlled comparison of cognitive-behavioral family intervention and standard pediatric care. *Journal of Consulting and Clinical Psychology, 62,* 306–314. doi:10.1037//0022-006X.62.2.306

Santucci, L. C., McHugh, R. K., & Barlow, D. H. (2012). Direct-to-consumer marketing of evidence-based psychological interventions. *Behavior Therapy, 43,* 231–235. doi:10.1016/j.beth.2011.07.003

Scott, S., & Dadds, M. R. (2009). Practitioner review: When parent training doesn't work: Theory-driven clinical strategies. *Journal of Child Psychology and Psychiatry, 50,* 1441–1450. doi:10.1111/j.1469-7610.2009.02161.x

Singla, D. R., Weobong, B., Nadkarni, A., Chowdhary, N., Shinde, S., Anand, A., . . . Patel, V. (2014). Improving the scalability of psychological treatments in developing countries: An evaluation of peer-led therapy quality assessment in Goa, India. *Behaviour Research & Therapy, 60,* 53–59. doi:10.1016/j.brat.2014.06.006

Slagt, M., Dubas, J. S., Deković, M., & van Aken, M. A. (2016). Differences in sensitivity to parenting depending on child temperament: A meta-analysis. *Psychological Bulletin, 142,* 1068–1110. doi:10.1037/bul0000061

Stokes, T. F., & Baer, D. M. (1977). An implicit technology of generalization. *Journal of Applied Behavior Analysis, 10,* 349–367. doi:10.1901/jaba.1977.10-349

Whittingham, K. (2015). Connect and shape: A parenting meta-strategy. *Journal of Contextual Behavioral Science, 4,* 103–106. doi:10.1016/j.jcbs.2015.03.002

GLOSSARY

Creating a positive learning environment. Second principle of positive parenting: This involves educating parents in their role as their child's first teacher. In particular, how to respond positively and constructively to child-initiated interactions in naturally occurring situations (e.g., requests for help, information, advice, attention).

Dissemination. The process of spreading evidence-based intervention knowledge and materials to practice settings.

EBP. The acronym for evidence-based program.

EBPS. The acronym for evidence-based parenting support.

Evidence-based parenting programs. Prevention or treatment interventions supported by a high level of empirical evidence documenting significant change of targeted parent or child outcome variables.

Evidence-based parenting support. The full breadth of empirically supported means of helping parents raise their children. These means of support include communication messaging as part of a social marketing campaign, the use of low- and higher intensity parenting interventions using the Internet, and group and individual face-to-face delivery of parenting interventions. *See also* System of parenting support.

Evidence-based program. An intervention that is supported by a high level of evidence of effectiveness. If implemented with adherence to the developer's protocol, such a program is likely to produce positive outcomes.

Facilitative parenting. The combination of warm relating, enabling of child independence, coaching, support of friendships, and effective communication with the school to support children's development of peer social skills and emotional regulation skills.

Flexibility vs. fidelity. This terminology is often used to refer to the important balance between flexible tailoring of program delivery while maintaining fidelity to core program content.

Flexible delivery. Several of the levels of intervention in Triple P can be delivered in a variety of formats, including individual face-to-face, group, telephone-assisted, or self-directed programs or a combination of modalities.

Flexible tailoring. Within each level of Triple P intervention, considerable tailoring of the program to parents' particular circumstances is possible to enable specific risk and protective factors to be addressed.

Guided participation model of information transfer. This model is used to discuss assessment information with parents and to develop a shared understanding of the problem and possible contributing factors. The model involves providing descriptive, factual information and providing opportunities for parents to process and react to the practitioner's inferences and reasoning. The sharing of this reasoning provides a model for parents to examine causal inferences they make about their child's behavior.

Having a safe interesting environment. First principle of positive parenting: An environment that is full of interesting things to do stimulates children's curiosity as well as their language and intellectual development. It also keeps children engaged and active and reduces the likelihood of misbehavior.

Having realistic expectations. Fourth principle of positive parenting: Holding reasonable expectations, assumptions and beliefs about the causes of children's behavior, and goals that are developmentally appropriate for the child and realistic for the parent.

Implementation framework. A structure to guide the successful implementation of evidence-based parenting support in large-scale rollouts.

Levels of intervention. Refers to the five levels of Triple P interventions on a tiered continuum of increasing strength. Within each level, there is a choice of delivery methods. This provides flexibility to meet the needs of individual families and specific communities. It is designed to give parents as much help as they need—but not too much—to prevent overservicing and encourage self-sufficiency.

Media and communication strategy. A coordinated information strategy using print and electronic media and other health promotion strategies to promote awareness of parenting issues and normalize participation in parenting programs such as Triple P. Includes social marketing to increase program awareness.

Minimally sufficient. The least amount of intervention required to achieve a meaningful outcome.

Multilevel system. Refers to the suite of Triple P programs of increasing intensity, each catering to a different level of family need or dysfunction. This allows organizations or governments to implement a true population rollout or simply select the specific Triple P interventions that will meet its community's or clients' needs, as well as its own service priorities and funding. The system ranges from "light-touch" parenting help to highly targeted intensive interventions.

Outreach. Media outreach includes use of local radio and community radio; community advertisements on TV; and advertisements and features in community newspapers.

PASS. The acronym for peer-assisted supervision and support.

Peer-assisted supervision and support. A structured system of peer supervision and support usually organized to follow practitioner accreditation to promote fidelity of program delivery by practitioners.

Personal agency. With personal agency, the parents increasingly attribute changes or improvements in their situation to their own or their child's efforts rather than to chance, age, maturational factors, or other uncontrollable events (e.g., genetic makeup). This outcome is achieved by prompting parents to identify causes or explanations for their child's or their own behavior.

Planned activities routine. A planned activities routine is a parenting plan developed through planned activities training. The steps include choosing a high-risk situation, planning and preparing ahead, deciding on rules, choosing interesting activities for the high-risk situation, listing rewards for good behavior and consequences for misbehavior, and having a follow-up discussion to review how the routine went and set goals for next time.

Planned activities training. Planned activities training is a strategy for promoting the generalization of parents' skills. It involves training with sufficient examples to promote a parent's ability to spontaneously generalize his or her positive parenting strategies to new situations, different problems, and children other than the target child. The main aim of planned activities training is to prevent problems from occurring in high-risk situations.

Planning ahead routine. This is a framework that parents of teenagers are prompted to use when discussing teen requests to participate in activities that parents consider risky. The main aim of planning ahead is to teach teenagers to recognize risky situations, to anticipate likely problems, and to develop coping plans to reduce or eliminate these risks. It is therefore a preventive approach to risky situations.

Planning ahead routine for dealing with risky behavior. Steps parents are encouraged to follow when discussing with a teenager a plan to allow them to participate in an event with a relative high level of safety and enjoyment.

Population-based approach. An approach to parenting support that emphasizes the need to target parents at a whole-of-population level to achieve meaningful change in population-level indices of parent and child outcomes.

Population-level change. The associated changes in parenting practice and child behavior and emotion resulting from the adoption and implementation of a public health approach to parenting support.

Positive learning environment. One of the principles of positive parenting. It involves parents being available when their child needs help, care, or attention. It also involves helping a child to learn by encouraging them to try things for themselves.

Positive Parenting Program. The system of intervention programs known as "Triple P."

Practitioner. The professional delivering the program.

Prevention effects. A prevention effect is distinguished from a treatment or intervention effect. It refers to a situation where an intervention forestalled or reduced the likelihood of a problem developing in a population who did not already have the problem, but who may be at risk of developing the problem.

Principles of positive parenting. There are five key aspects to positive parenting: (a) having a safe, engaging environment; (b) creating a positive learning environment; (c) using assertive discipline; (d) having realistic expectations; and (e) taking care of yourself as a parent.

Problem-solving. Problem-solving involves six main steps: (a) define the problem; (b) generate alternative solutions (or brainstorm); (c) evaluate alternatives; (d) develop a solution; (e) put the plan into action; and (f) review and revise the plan.

Program sufficiency. This concept refers to the notion that parents differ according to the strength of intervention they may require to enable them to independently manage a problem. Triple P aims to provide the minimally sufficient level of support parents require.

Reach of an intervention. An intervention's reach refers to its coverage in a target population or the extent of access or exposure to the intervention across the population. For example, a universal or population-level intervention has the greatest reach. Many factors may have an impact on an intervention's reach, such as community engagement, media exposure, and access to resources and services.

Resilience. Resilience refers to the ability to deal well with adverse life events.

Resistance. Resistance can be shown by parents in response to a process of change. Research has identified multiple sources of resistance contributing to parental perceptions of defeat and avoidance of treatment. These factors include parents' history of defeat, emotions, psychopathology, and social disadvantage.

Risky situations. Situations that have the potential to result in harm to a teenager's health or well-being if they are not recognized and appropriately responded to.

Role play. This refers to active behavioral rehearsal or practice of a skill in a simulated scenario (e.g., a practitioner models a strategy with a parent playing the role of child, and then the parent practices the strategy with the practitioner or another parent playing the role of the child). This provides an opportunity for self-evaluation and constructive feedback and future goal setting for skill development.

Self-efficacy. Self-efficacy refers to a parent's belief that he or she can overcome or solve a parenting or child management problem.

Self-management. Each parent is considered to be responsible for the way he or she chooses to raise his or her children, so parents select those aspects of their own and their child's behavior they wish to work on, set goals, choose specific parenting and child management techniques they wish to implement, and self-evaluate their success with their chosen goals against self-determined criteria.

Self-regulation. Self-regulation is a process whereby individuals are taught skills to modify their own behavior. Clinically, it involves helping parents develop problem ownership and personal responsibility for decision-making. The aim is to enable them to become independent, confident problem-solvers and continue to monitor their own progress and develop their skills.

Self-sufficiency. Self-sufficiency involves parents becoming independent problem-solvers so that they trust their own judgment and become less reliant on others in carrying out basic parenting responsibilities.

Seminar. A presentation to a group that is more didactic than an interactive discussion group or a group involving active skill rehearsal (i.e., information is presented by a facilitator and questions from the audience are answered at the end of the presentation).

Stay Positive. A media communication strategy aimed at engaging parents in positive parenting strategies in a nonstigmatized way.

System of parenting support. An organized set of interdependent and theoretically consistent intervention programs designed collectively to create a family-friendly environment that better supports parents in the task of raising their children. Programs that are part of the system may differ in intensity, mode of delivery, intervention target, and target population.

Taking care of oneself as a parent. Fifth principle of positive parenting: Viewing parenting within a broader context of personal self-care, resourcefulness and well-being.

Tip sheets. Individual two- to four-page parenting tip sheets that provide suggestions for preventing and managing common developmental issues and behavior difficulties. Tip sheets are available in series specifically written for common issues relating to parenting, infants, toddlers, preschoolers, primary schoolers, and teenagers.

Triple P system. A system of parenting support comprising Triple P interventions. *See* System of parenting support.

Using assertive discipline. Third principle of positive parenting: Specific child management strategies are presented as alternatives to coercive and ineffective discipline practices (such as shouting, threatening, or using physical punishment). When parents use assertive discipline, children learn to accept responsibility for their behavior, to become aware of the needs of others, and to develop self-control.

INDEX

Page numbers followed by *f, t,* and *b* refer to figures, tables, and boxes respectively.